POWER AND PLENTY

THE PRINCETON ECONOMIC HISTORY
OF THE WESTERN WORLD

Joel Mokyr, Editor

POWER AND PLENTY

TRADE, WAR, AND THE WORLD ECONOMY IN THE SECOND MILLENNIUM

RONALD FINDLAY
KEVIN H. O'ROURKE

PRINCETON UNIVERSITY PRESS
PRINCETON AND OXFORD

Published by Princeton University Press,
41 William Street, Princeton, New Jersey 08540

In the United Kingdom: Princeton University Press,
3 Market Place, Woodstock, Oxfordshire OX20 1SY

ISBN-13: 978-0-691-11854-3 (alk. paper)

Library of Congress Control Number: 2007931677

A catalogue record for this book is
available from the British Library

This book has been composed in Utopia

Typeset by T&T Productions Ltd, London

Printed on acid-free paper ∞

press.princeton.edu

Printed in the United States of America

10 9 8 7 6 5 4 3 2 1

For Jane and Roseann

POLY-OLBION

GREAT BRITAINE

By
Michaell Drayton.
Esq:

London printed for M. Lownes. J. Browne. J. Helme. J. Busbie.

Through a *Triumphant* Arch, see *Albion* plas't,
In *Happy* site, in *Neptunes* armes embras't,
In *Power* and *Plenty*, on her *Cleevy* Throne
Circled with *Natures Ghirlands*, being alone
Stil'd *th'Oceans Island*.

Cleevy: abounding in "cleves" or cliffs (Oxford English Dictionary).

Michael Drayton, *Poly-Olbion*.
London: M. Lownes, I. Brown, I. Helme, I. Busbie, 1612.

CONTENTS

ACKNOWLEDGMENTS

THIS BOOK HAS BEEN a long time in the making, and we have accumulated an embarrassingly long list of debts along the way. We started working together on the history of world trade in 2000, when preparing for an NBER conference on "Globalization in Historical Perspective." This took place in Santa Barbara, California, in May 2001, and resulted in an early joint publication (Findlay and O'Rourke 2003). We are extremely grateful to the organizers of that conference, Michael Bordo, Alan Taylor, and Jeffrey Williamson, as well as to the NBER for prompting us to embark on what has proved to be a seven-year journey.

During those seven years, a great many people have helped us with queries, provided us with data, and shared their knowledge and experience with us. The process has yet again reminded us of how fortunate we are to be working in this wonderful field. Among those who have provided us with help or encouragement are Olivier Accominotti, Lee Alston, Remo Becci, Steve Broadberry, Andre Burgstaller, Bruce Campbell, Rich Clarida, Greg Clark, Bill Collins, Brendan Conroy, Max Corden, Eric Delépine, Brendan Dempsey, Javier Cuenca Esteban, Guillaume Daudin, Mike Edelstein, Barry Eichengreen, David Eltis, Antoni Estevadeordal, Bouta Etemad, Zoé Fachan, Rob Feenstra, Niall Ferguson, Michael Finger, Marc Flandreau, Dennis Flynn, Oded Galor, Mike Gibney, Arturo Giráldez, Barry Goodwin, Ann Harrison, Marc Harrison, Tim Hatton, Masahiro Hayafuji, Bob Holton, John Hegarty, David Hummels, Joe Inikori, Dominick Jenkins, Ron Jones, Koichi Kimura, Herb Klein, Jan Tore Klovland, Deepak Lal, Philip Lane, A. J. H. Latham, Jim Livesey, Mats Lundahl, Angus Maddison, Connie Malone, Jacques Mollard, Bob Mundell, Antoin Murphy, Patrick O'Brien, Lawrence Officer, Cormac Ó Gráda, Marcelo Olarreaga, William O'Neill, Bernhardine E. Pejovic, David Richardson, Jim Robinson, Lennart Schön, Barbara Solow, Robert Solow, Yuji Tamura, Peter Temin, John TePaske, Joachim Voth, Jan de Vries, Stan Wellisz, and Martin Wolf. We thank all of them most sincerely, as well as participants at the aforementioned NBER event, and any colleagues whom we may have inadvertently omitted. In several sections of the book, we draw heavily upon joint research with other colleagues, particularly Mats Lundahl and Jeff Williamson, and we are most grateful to them for allowing us to do so.

We would also like to particularly thank those colleagues who took the time to read sections of the manuscript and provide us with detailed comments: Bob Allen, Rosemary Byrne, François Crouzet, Stan Engerman, Şevket Pamuk, Alan Taylor, and Jeff Williamson. Nick Crafts, Doug Irwin, and Eric Jones actually went so far as to read the entire first draft of this book, and their feedback has helped improve it considerably. We are extremely grateful to all three. Regina Grafe and Joel Mokyr forced us to considerably tighten our argument at key stages of this book, and have our unreserved thanks for their probing and incisive comments. Vanessa Schaefer was an early and alert proofreader, as well as being a forceful critic of an earlier version of the manuscript. A special debt of gratitude is owed to Andrew O'Rourke, who read the entire manuscript in something close to its final version, and whose eagle eye enabled us to improve it in innumerable ways.

Several research assistants helped us with our work and deserve our thanks. They are Silvi Berger, Mark Clements, Maria Coelho, William Hynes, Paula Labrecciosa, Patrick Leahy, Sibylle Lehmann, Ronan Lyons, Matthew Pham, Alan Reilly, and Theodore Talbot.

Kevin O'Rourke began working on this book while a Government of Ireland Senior Research Fellow, and he thanks the Irish Research Council for the Humanities and Social Sciences for their generous financial support. Further financial support was provided by the Institute for International Integration Studies at Trinity College Dublin, and by the European Union, under its Research Training Networks program (contract numbers MRTN-CT-2004-512439 and HPRN-CT-2002-00236), for which we are both grateful. The IIIS enabled us to work together at a critical stage in Dublin in the spring of 2006. Kevin O'Rourke also thanks Alan Matthews for allowing him to take a further year's unpaid leave to continue writing the book, Marc Flandreau and Sciences-Po, as well as Mike Bordo, for making this a financially viable option, and the people of Le Villard and the Entremonts valley for providing him with such a congenial environment within which to work on this project.

A special word of thanks has to go to Maura Pringle, who prepared the maps. She combined great technical expertise with a remarkable degree of patience when faced with academic dithering on the part of both of us. Many thanks also to Bruce Campbell and Gill Alexander for putting us in touch with an outstanding professional who has made such a valuable contribution to improving this book. Her cartographer's insistence on precision for the boundaries of states and empires, and for the exact locations of ancient sites, forced us frequently to go back to our sources in the search for better answers. In addition to the many historical works referred to in the text, these included McEvedy (1961), Schmidt (1999), and the magisterial *Philip's Atlas of World History* (O'Brien 2002), also published as the *Oxford Atlas of World History*. We are very grateful to Charles Benson, Keeper of Early Printed Books at Trinity College Dublin, for locating the frontispiece from Michael Drayton's *Poly-Olbion* for us, and we wish to thank the Board of Trinity College Dublin for allowing us to reproduce it.

Jon Wainwright of T&T Productions Ltd was an outstanding copy-editor and typesetter, meticulous in his attention to detail, and an imaginative problem-solver. We have greatly enjoyed working with him, as well as with James Lamb, who not only expertly compiled the index but also, like Jon, corrected several errors along the way. It has also been a great pleasure to work with Richard Baggaley on this project, as well as with Emma Green and Carolyn Hollis at Princeton University Press. Richard has been a wonderfully generous editor, tolerant and encouraging, and he has our sincere thanks, and apologies for how sorely we must have tried his patience. While on the subject of patient colleagues, we also want to apologize to our coauthors on a variety of other projects, who have had to take a back seat for what must have seemed to them like an eternity. While we won't mention any names, they know who they are, and they have our gratitude.

The most important words of thanks come last. Our wives, Jane and Roseann, have each had to share their husbands with a possessive and demanding rival that has refused to go away for the better part of the last four years. We know that the relief we feel, on our final emancipation from this none too coy mistress, cannot compare with theirs. We dedicate this book to them, as a very inadequate expression of our gratitude, appreciation, and love.

New York City
Saint Pierre d'Entremont

PREFACE

THIS BOOK WAS WRITTEN in the belief that you cannot make sense of today's world economy, or indeed of the world more generally, without understanding the history that produced it. Contemporary globalization, and its economic and political consequences, have not arisen out of a vacuum, but from a worldwide process of uneven economic development that has been centuries, if not millennia, in the making. In turn, this process has been critically shaped by the changing ways in which the various world regions have interacted with each other, not only through trade, migration, and investment, but also politically and culturally, over time. Understanding this two-way interaction between the pattern and evolution of interregional trade, on the one hand, and long-term global economic and political developments, on the other, is the main purpose of this volume.

As is the case with many books, this one has been written for the primary benefit of the authors. Countless economic histories of countries or regions have already been written, and there is now a rapidly growing literature on world history, and indeed on world economic history. There is also a more specialized, but still immense, literature on the history of international trade, with individual authors typically focusing on particular regions or time periods. What both of us found, however, when preparing lectures on the long-run history of world trade, or writing research papers on the subject, is that there was no one place that we could turn to for answers to the questions that we, as economists, would ask about the subject. Instead, we have had to become familiar—although no doubt we remain insufficiently so—with a vast and highly specialized scholarly literature, and we have found ourselves on numerous occasions plowing through the same sources looking for the odd nugget of information that was relevant for our purposes. In this manner, we gradually became independently convinced of the need for a single book that would provide as comprehensive and integrated an overview as possible of the history of world trade during the second millennium.

Even if we consider such an apparently specific and familiar a subject as the spice trade, for example, we find that there is no single authoritative account of it available in the existing literature. The reasons why this is so are quite obvious. The spices were produced in the islands of the Indonesian archipelago, transported across the Indian Ocean by Persians, Arabs, Gujaratis, Portuguese, Dutchmen, and sundry others to the Red Sea or the Persian Gulf, or around the Cape of Good Hope, taxed by Abbasids, Fatimids, Mamluks, Safavids, and other Middle Eastern regimes, distributed further west and north by Venetians or Genoese, before being purchased as far west as England and France, usually with silver that then had to wind its way back again to the Moluccas before the circuit was closed. And this is only to consider spice flows to Europe, when flows to China and other Asian markets were much more important during most of history. No single historian, not even a Fernand Braudel, could command all the specialized knowledge and skills necessary to cover the entire stretch of space and time involved; and this is only one of many topics that we would like our history of world trade to cover. Providing such a book thus requires breaking free of the twin tyrannies of temporal and spatial parochialism, which is undoubtedly a risky venture.

There have been other world economic histories written in the recent past, but while we have learned much from them, none of them quite provided what we were looking for. Rondo Cameron's (1989) *Concise Economic History of the World: From Paleolithic Times to the Present* covers an even longer time span than our mere millennium. However, neither he nor Greg Clark (2007a) provides the sharp focus on trade and other contacts between the various world regions that is the concern of the present work. Janet Abu-Lughod's (1989) highly influential *Before European Hegemony: The World System A.D. 1250–1350*, on the other hand, is concerned with exactly the sort of interactive relationships between the different segments of the world economy that we consider here, but is temporally confined to a single, albeit crucial, century: the period of the *Pax Mongolica.* David Landes (1998) tells us in his preface that his aim is to "trace and understand the main stream of economic advance and modernization," which he locates firmly in Europe. While we will also of necessity be concerned with the process of economic growth, our emphasis is more on the pattern and structure of trade, on geopolitical evolution over time, and on the shifting balances of world primacy over the past thousand years.

As evidenced by the very title of his stimulating contribution, Eric Jones's (2003) *The European Miracle* is also Eurocentric in its orientation. Jones starts at about the time of the Discoveries, taking as his units of comparison the European system of competing nation-states and the non-European empires of the Islamic Ottomans and Mughals, and the Manchu Qing dynasty. The rise of Europe is one of the major themes of this book, as it is of his, but we cover a longer time span, and our units are the seven regions defined in chapter 1, rather than the European states and three Asian empires he considers. Jones has been the target of what he calls the "California School" of Sinocentric historians, in particular Kenneth Pomeranz (2000) and R. Bin Wong (1997), as well as Andre Gunder Frank (1998). We hope to convince our readers that, like Ulysses bound to the mast, we manage to avoid both the Scylla of Eurocentrism and the Charybdis of Sinocentrism in our account of how all seven regions, and the rest of the world besides, have contributed to the interactive emergence of the modern world economy, even though not necessarily to the same degree.

Thus we ourselves have had to laboriously piece together what is still a very rudimentary and inadequate account of trade during the last millennium. There are of course many specialists on each aspect of this subject whose knowledge vastly exceeds ours on their specialty, but we hope that we can at least lighten the labor of the many who might desire, as we did, an overview of this subject as a whole. Furthermore, the history of world trade is only one aspect of the task that we have had to undertake. A feature of the book that may strike some economists as odd or surprising, but will seem entirely commonplace to historians, is its sustained emphasis on conflict, violence, and geopolitics. When economics students are first exposed to the study of international trade, they are asked to contemplate two countries, A and B, who have each been endowed with a certain amount of the various factors of production—land, labor, capital, and so on—as well as with a given technology which translates those endowments into consumption goods, together with a set of preferences over these goods. The two countries then trade with each other, or not as the case may be, and the consequences of trade are derived for consumers and producers alike. If time is brought into the theory at all, and usually it isn't, this typically takes the form of allowing countries to gradually accumulate capital, breed new workers, or become better educated as a result of the voluntary decisions of rational, free individuals. The summit of unpleasantness attainable in such models is the use of tariffs, quotas, and other trade policy instruments that will benefit some individuals or groups (and possibly nations) but lower the utility of other domestic or foreign residents.

If only life were like this. As we point out below, the greatest expansions of world trade have tended to come not from the bloodless *tâtonnement* of some fictional Walrasian auctioneer but from the barrel of a Maxim gun, the edge of a scimitar, or the ferocity of nomadic horsemen. When trade required more workers, parental choices regarding quality/quantity trade-offs could often safely be ignored, since workers could always be enslaved. When trade required more profits, these could be earned via plunder or violently imposed monopolies. For much of our period the pattern of trade can *only* be understood as being the outcome of some military or political equilibrium between contending powers. The dependence of trade on war and peace eventually became so obvious to us that it is reflected in the title of this volume.

Politics thus determined trade, but trade also helped to determine politics, by influencing the capacities and the incentives facing states. The mutual dependence of "Power" and "Plenty," so well evoked by Jacob Viner (1948), will thus be a key feature of this book. The phrase itself comes from the first lines of Michael Drayton's Poly-Olbion, first published in 1612. These serve as a commentary on the frontispiece to that volume, which we have reproduced as a frontispiece to our own. Corbett and Lightbown (1979, p. 156) remark that Albion, or Britannia, here appears to be "prosperous and triumphant and for the only time in her long career, notably young and beautiful." Bedecked in pearls, secure on her island stronghold, and holding both a cornucopia and a scepter, she appears to be serenely contemplating not just her enjoyment of Plenty, but her exercise of Power as well.

As we shall see, this nymph-like creature would soon become the battle-hardened ruler not just of the English Channel but of the oceans of the world, and no history of international trade can ignore the causes or the implications of military exploits such as these. While economists have traditionally stressed the advantages of peaceful voluntary exchange, we should not forget that the use of force involves the allocation of scarce resources as well, and imposes costs and benefits both on those who use it and on those against whom it is used, as well as on third parties. It is therefore as much subject to the application of economic analysis—"the study of the relationship between ends and scarce means that have alternative uses" in the famous definition of Lionel Robbins—as any other sphere of human activity.

If all this may appear to have been less true over the course of the last two centuries, this is because of the overwhelming influence of the Industrial Revolution on all subsequent economic history. The nineteenth-century globalization that followed this breakthrough was unprecedented in many ways, and as we will see perhaps its most clearly distinguishing feature was its largely technological underpinnings (although even in this period imperialism still had an important role to play, and was itself facilitated in many ways by the new technology). The new technologies not only brought markets closer together than ever before, but opened up enormous income gaps between regions that remain with us today, and produced a stark division of labor between a manufacturing core and a primary-producing periphery. The big questions ever since then have been: How can developing countries catch up with the core? Should they do so by exploiting their natural resource advantages, as was successfully tried in the nineteenth century, or does this leave them excessively vulnerable to fickle international markets, as the interwar experience might suggest? Should they decouple themselves from international markets, as many did after 1945, or reintegrate with them, as they have done over the past two decades? These questions, and related ones such as how the West should adapt to the rise of India and China, have only arisen because of the asymmetries created by the Industrial Revolution, and are thus fundamentally historical in nature.

The Industrial Revolution, in turn, can only be understood as the outcome of a historical process with multiple causes stretching well back into the medieval period, and in which international movements of commodities, warriors, microbes, and technologies all played a leading role. Purely domestic accounts of the "Rise of the West," emphasizing Western institutions, cultural attributes, or endowments, are hopelessly inadequate, since they ignore the vast web of inter-relationships between Western Europe and the rest of the world that had been spun over the course of many centuries, and was crucially important for the breakthrough to modern economic growth. We are of course not the first to have argued this, but while historians promoting such an international perspective have often been Marxists, we are not. Like most mainstream economists, we view inventiveness and incentives, rather than sheer accumulation, "primitive" or otherwise, as being at the heart of growth, but this does not imply that European overseas expansion should be written off as irrelevant. Plunder may not have directly fueled the Industrial Revolution, but mercantilism and imperialism were an important part of the global context within which it originated, expanding markets and ensuring the supply of raw materials. Violence thus undoubtedly mattered in shaping the environment within which the conventional economic forces of supply and demand operated.

In this manner, many of today's key interregional tensions can be traced back to earlier interactions between the world's main regions. In seeking to understand this history, economists need to think seriously about another subject they have too often neglected, namely geography. By "geography" we do not mean the highly stylized models that pass for "economic geography" today, in which *ex ante* indistinguishable regions symmetrically situated on a featureless plane, straight line, sphere, or hexagon interact with each other and become different *ex post*, with small random events having impacts that are amplified and made permanent through the operation of increasing returns to scale. When we say geography, we mean geography: mountains, rivers, and all. If Genghis Khan had been born in New Zealand, he would have left no traces on world history. The Irish might have enjoyed holding the rest of Europe to ransom by controlling access to Southeast Asian spices, but never had the opportunities which geography afforded the rulers of Egypt. A European seeking direct access to India might well head westward and stumble across the Americas, but no Chinese sailor would have been foolish enough to seek an eastern passage to Arabia. Many possible outcomes in world history were ruled out *ex ante*, not just *ex post*.

The three great world-historical events of the second millennium, in our account, are the Black Death of the fourteenth century and the differing responses to it, the "discovery" and incorporation of the New World into that of the Old at the turn of the sixteenth century, and the Industrial Revolution at the turn of the nineteenth. As we hope to demonstrate conclusively, no single region was solely responsible for any one of these three transformational episodes, let alone all three. The first resulted from the *Pax Mongolica*, established by the nomads of Central Asia but consolidated and actively participated in by *all* of the other six regions. Western Europeans were the first Eurasians to sail to the New World, but it was Africans, against their will, who produced many of the commodities that it exported to the Old. The Industrial Revolution occurred within Western Europe, and more specifically in Britain, but the essential raw material that its leading sector required was produced by Africans in the Americas, and the final products were sold in markets around the entire world. The world economy continues to evolve, with the lead of Western Europe and its various overseas offshoots clearly eroding, as East, South, and Southeast Asia all expand much faster after previous centuries of relative stagnation.

Before asking the reader to plunge into one thousand years of history, it behooves us to provide a brief guide to the terrain that lies ahead. We begin in the first chapter with a consideration of basic methodological issues, and the delineation of the seven "world regions" into which we divide the Eurasian landmass and the southern littoral of the Mediterranean at the beginning of the second millennium. These regions are Western Europe, Eastern Europe, the Islamic World of the Middle East and North Africa, Central Asia, South Asia, Southeast Asia, and East Asia. Since all seven are defined not just by geography, but by culture and political history as well, we provide a brief account of what we consider to have been the defining characteristics of each. Thus we choose the division between western Roman Catholicism and eastern Orthodoxy to demarcate Western from Eastern Europe, rather than some geographical feature. The fall of Constantinople to the Ottoman Turks, in our scheme, transferred the remnants of the former Byzantine Empire to the Islamic World. In the case of Indonesia and the Malay world, however, we retain the geographic designation of these societies as Southeast Asian, along with their Buddhist neighbors, rather than shifting them into the Islamic World following their conversion to Islam, since we believe that they still had more in common with these neighbors than with Egyptians or Syrians.

The second chapter analyzes the trading and other relationships between these seven regions and an eighth, sub-Saharan Africa, at the turn of the second millennium. The reader might be surprised to learn that the only region in sustained direct contact with all the others at this time was the Islamic World, then undergoing its "Golden Age" under the Abbasid, Fatimid, and Umayyad caliphates based in Baghdad, Cairo, and Cordoba, while the one with the least contact with the others was Western Europe. The third chapter is a broad analytical survey of the evolution of the world economy from 1000 to 1500. The key events on which we focus in this chapter are the forging of the *Pax Mongolica* that knitted together most of the Eurasian landmass under the aegis of the Mongol Empire, and stimulated long-distance trade from the Atlantic to the Sea of Japan; the devastating consequences of the Black Death, itself unleashed by the formation of what has been called a "microbian common market" as a result of the Mongol conquests; and the subsequent expansion of population, output, and prices across the world, particularly in Western Europe and Southeast Asia.

This sets the stage for the launching of the Iberian voyages of discovery and their momentous consequences for the New World, Europe, Africa, and Asia, dealt with in the fourth chapter, covering the period from ca. 1500 to 1650. A key economic consequence of Columbus that we will be exploring at length is the worldwide trade in silver that emerged during the sixteenth century. The fifth chapter focuses first on the long struggle for hegemony in the emerging world economy between the Dutch Republic, Great Britain, and France during the age of mercantilism, and then on the hardly less momentous overland expansions, from opposite ends of Central Asia, of the Czarist empire of the Romanovs and the Chinese empire of the Manchu Qing dynasty.

One major theme of this chapter is the extent to which Asians were not just passive actors during this period, but adopted new military technologies, with similar political effects to those experienced in Europe; another is the mercantilist economic policies pursued by the leading states of the day.

The sixth chapter interrupts the historical narrative to take a close look at the breakthrough to modern economic growth which occurred in northwestern Europe, and more particularly Great Britain, at the turn of the nineteenth century. The Industrial Revolution merits a separate chapter, since it is the fulcrum around which the rest of the book turns. On the one hand, it set in motion economic forces that determined the future course of international trade, down to our own day; on the other, it was itself an outcome of the political and economic trends that preceded it. Thus we do not see the Industrial Revolution as springing up suddenly, like "Athena fully armed from the brow of Zeus," purely as a result of the creative imaginations of a group of inventors in the north of England in the late eighteenth and early nineteenth centuries. As we hope to be able to convince the reader, we see it instead as the culmination of a long historical process involving the interaction of all the world's regions through trade and the transfer of technology, as well as the use of armed force. This is not to deny the vital contribution of Great Britain, and more broadly Western Europe, but to provide a consistent and coherent explanation of why this event was so transformational in nature, rather than evanescent, as had been all the earlier "efflorescences" (Goldstone 2002) in the history of the world economy that we describe.

On one level, the economic history of the past two centuries can, as already noted, be viewed as the working out of the consequences of the Industrial Revolution: a "Great Divergence" in income levels between regions, as the new technologies diffused only gradually across the globe; a "Great Specialization" between an industrial core and a primary-producing periphery; consequent pressures to protect agriculture in the core, and manufacturing in the periphery; and, finally, a gradual unwinding of these trends as the Industrial Revolution spread to encompass an ever-increasing proportion of the globe. Indeed, we are still experiencing these entirely predictable consequences of events which took place in northern England two centuries ago. However, the evolution of these trends was *not* smooth, but was profoundly marked by the political consequences of three major world wars: the French and Napoleonic Wars that ended the age of mercantilism, World War I, and World War II. Warfare thus continued to exert a profound and long-lasting effect on the evolution of the international economy, and this is reflected in the structure of the book, with chapters 7–9 each beginning with an account of the relevant conflict, and then proceeding to trace out its short- and long-run consequences.

Chapter 7 resumes our narrative, and focuses on the "nineteenth century" from 1815 to 1914. The era was marked politically by the *Pax Britannica* and European imperialism, and economically by the consequences of the new steam technology of the Industrial Revolution, embodied in the railroad and the steamship. It was early in this period that a new sort of globalization, manifested by a significant narrowing of intercontinental price gaps for bulk commodities between points of origin and destination, occurred pervasively around the world as a result of dramatic declines in transport costs. It is also the period when the "Great Specialization" emerged, as a result of which the industrialized countries of Western Europe, eventually to be joined by the United States and Japan, exported manufactured goods to Asia, Africa, Australasia, and Latin America in exchange for primary foodstuffs and raw materials, with Europe also exporting capital to all these regions, and people to the Americas and Australasia. The end of this period was marked by the beginnings of a "backlash" against globalization, with the rising industrial powers of Germany and the United States, the food-importing countries of Continental Europe, the Latin American republics, and the settler dominions of the British Empire all raising tariffs, while the New World started to display a reluctance to remain open to mass immigration. This first "golden age of globalization" was of course brought to a tragic and abrupt end by the outbreak of World War I.

The interwar years from 1918 to 1939, covered in chapter 8, were dominated politically and economically by the aftermath of this catastrophe. While the 1920s saw an attempt to reconstruct the prewar international economy, which enjoyed only partial success, the 1930s were marked by the devastating consequences of the Great Depression, and the resulting retreat from globalization. World War II and its aftermath are the subject of chapter 9, the key political events being the establishment of the *Pax Americana* and the associated framework of multilateral international institutions set up under its aegis, the political transformations wrought first by the spread of Communism and then by its collapse, and the sweeping decolonization of areas in the Third World that had become imperial possessions of the European powers. We stress that the combined effect of these trends was to further disintegrate the world economy, with OECD liberalization constituting a regional exception to this general rule, until some time in the 1970s or 1980s. It was only then that Latin America, Asia, and Africa, where the bulk of humanity reside, started to open up to trade and investment with the rest of the world. Economically, the late twentieth century was to a large extent dominated by the attempt of newly independent countries to industrialize through policies of "import substitution." However, the period also saw the unprecedented expansion of world output and trade as a result of trade liberalization and growth in the industrial countries, and technological diffusion to "newly industrializing countries." This eventually led to the rapid growth of manufactured exports from these countries, particularly China and India, and to the beginnings of a narrowing of the huge per capita income gaps that have separated these once prosperous regions from Western Europe since the Industrial Revolution, and probably even before. The tenth and final chapter draws together some of the lessons which our extended survey has taught us, and which we believe may still be relevant at the start of the twenty-first century.

The reader will have noticed that our successive eras in the evolution of the world economy, and not just those covered by chapters 7–9, have been demarcated mostly by the outbreaks of major wars or imperial expansions. Each era can be seen as one in which trade is conducted within a geopolitical framework established by the previous major war or conflict, that is in turn altered by the outbreak of the next war, setting the stage for the next trade epoch, and so on. It is natural to suspect that the accumulating economic and geopolitical tensions unleashed in the course of each period of peace, prosperity, and trade culminate in successive rounds of conflict, so that wars, rather than being exogenous or external shocks to the world system, have been inherent in its very nature as it has evolved over the past millennium. For the most part this process will, we hope, become clear from our narrative, although we confess that World War I still appears as somewhat of a *diabolus ex machina* in our account. There is of course no shortage of authorities who have argued that the way in which the late-nineteenth-century world economy operated helps explain the eruption of World War I, but the causes of this disaster remain controversial. "Had we but world enough, and time," we might have done better, but there are only so many cans of worms that one can open in the course of writing a book, and this is one can that we have decided to leave closed.

Economics is often accused of being an imperialistic discipline, and plunder was an essential feature of many of the empires that we will be considering below. We have enthusiastically followed the example of the conquistadores in this respect, unscrupulously plundering the knowledge that has been laboriously produced by generations of historians and economists before us. Unlike the conquistadores, however, we have done so in the hope of being civilized by the natives, rather than the reverse. There is a lot in this book, therefore, that will be entirely unremarkable to any moderately well trained historian, but which we hope will be of interest in its present form not just to economists, economic historians, political scientists, sociologists, and anthropologists, but to the broad community of all those with a serious interest in globalization, and who like us want to better understand the origins of the international economy of the early twenty-first century. If the way that we approach the evidence as economists adds some value to historical debates, then so much the better.

Though our discipline strictly informs and shapes our argument at every point, we have not felt it necessary to burden our text with sustained stretches of formal mathematical or quantitative analysis, though we frequently refer to works, including some of our own, that use such methods to reach and sustain conclusions of interest to the general reader. Both of us can truthfully say that we know vastly more about the historical evolution of the world economy after writing this book than we did when we began, despite having devoted much of our previous professional lives to the study of it. We hope that we can pass on to the reader at least some of the excitement and understanding that this perhaps all too ambitious project has given us.

NOTE ON DATES

Dates following the names of monarchs and other rulers, such as Galdan, refer to the beginning and end of their reigns. Dates following the names of commoners, such as Ziryab, refer to their birth and death.

POWER AND PLENTY

Chapter 1

INTRODUCTION: GEOGRAPHICAL AND HISTORICAL BACKGROUND

THE SUBJECT OF THIS BOOK is the evolution of the pattern and structure of world trade over the past millennium. If we used the expression "world trade" for the current year or any period in the recent past it would have a clear and unambiguous connotation. The component units would be individual sovereign nation-states and "world trade" would be the goods and services that flow between them, across national borders. The individual nation-states, or "countries," could be classified in various ways: geographically on the basis of continent or climate zone, "stage of development" in terms of level of per capita income, or by their relative endowments of factors of production. We would then relate some classification of the commodities that enter world trade, say "primary products" and "manufactured goods" or "capital-intensive" and "labor-intensive" goods, to the geographical or other characteristics of the countries and this would constitute what is meant by the "structure and pattern of world trade."

It is when we turn to the question of the long-run evolution of this "structure and pattern of world trade" that a host of problems arises. What are the beginning and end points over which this evolution is to be examined? What if political boundaries shift, as they undoubtedly do, so that "countries" which exist at the end point did not exist at the beginning, or which existed at the beginning did not at the end? The longer the time span chosen the more acute this problem becomes, and a millennium is a very long time. A bold solution to this difficulty was offered in an influential article by Mauro (1961), who proposed an "intercontinental model" for the study of world trade in the early modern period, in the form of an interregional input–output table or matrix that would record the flows of goods and precious metals between the continents over time. This would eliminate the problem of shifting political boundaries by replacing the evanescent nation-state with the presumably immutable geographic entity of the continent. Toward the end of his article, Mauro explicitly evoked the invaluable work of the interwar International Scientific Committee on Price History (Cole and Crandall 1964), which collected internationally comparable price data for several countries, and expressed the hope that such a collaborative endeavor would fill in his trade matrix for the early modern period, and presumably other periods as well. While this hope has not as yet been fulfilled, we will adopt Mauro's basic organizing framework throughout this book. While not ignoring flows of goods and services within regions, our main focus throughout will be on interregional and intercontinental flows.

As Lewis and Wigen (1997) have pointed out, however, in the very title of their stimulating work, the notion of continents as fixed and self-evident divisions of the Earth's surface is itself something of a myth. They coin the useful term "metageography" (p. ix), to mean "the set of spatial structures through which people order their knowledge of the world." Examples of metageography, in addition to the familiar example of the continents, would be the "North–South" division of the world between advanced and developing countries, or the First, Second, and Third World classification that was common during the Cold War. While Australasia, Africa, North and South America, and Antarctica are clearly distinct physical entities with well-defined physical boundaries, the separation of Europe from the rest of the contiguous Eurasian landmass is arbitrary and problematic. The frequently invoked Urals have never been an effective barrier, and it has long been debated whether Russia is in Europe, Asia, or both. Indeed, at the time of writing the question of Europe's eastern boundaries was one of the key political headaches confronting the leadership of that continent.

Some classification of the Earth's surface, however, is obviously essential for our purposes. Lewis and Wigen (p. 13) propose the concept of "world regions," namely "multi-country agglomerations, defined not by their supposed physical separation from one another (as are continents) but rather (in theory) on the basis of important historical and cultural bonds." In what follows we will demarcate seven "world regions" covering the Eurasian landmass and Africa north of the Sahara. These are

- (i)   Western Europe,
- (ii) Eastern Europe,
- (iii) North Africa and Southwest Asia,
- (iv) Central or Inner Asia,
- (v)   South Asia,
- (vi) Southeast Asia, and
- (vii) East Asia.

The regions are defined and separated not solely on geographical lines but more importantly on social, political, and cultural lines that give each of them at least a modicum of coherence and unity while distinguishing it from the others. Economic integration was more advanced within each region than between the regions, largely as a result of these political and cultural divisions: according to David Northrup (2005) the end of the first millennium marks a turning point when the forces of cultural and political divergence between world regions, as populations adapted to their local environments, began to be overtaken in importance by countervailing forces of convergence.[1]

We initially confine ourselves to this "Afro-Eurasian Ecumene" because our focus is on intercontinental and interregional trade, and prior to the European voyages of discovery in the 1490s the Americas or Australasia were not engaged in trade with other world regions. On the other hand, we will be considering trade flows between our seven regions and an eighth, sub-Saharan Africa, when appropriate, although without analyzing sub-Saharan Africa as a separate region. We acknowledge that the early chapters of our work are thus "Eurasia-centric," and that this is a shortcoming, although it is an inevitable shortcoming given the limits of our knowledge.

On the other hand, our seven regions accounted for the vast majority of the world's population in 1000, at least if the figures in the admittedly highly conjectural but nevertheless indispensable *Atlas of World Population History* by McEvedy and Jones (1978) are to be believed. The population figures we obtain on the basis of their work are 25 million for Western Europe, 15 million for Eastern Europe, 28 million for the Islamic World, 9 million for Central Asia, 79 million for South Asia, 9 million for Southeast Asia, and 67 million for East Asia (with China alone accounting for 60 million). This gives a population of 232 million for the essentially Eurasian world with which we begin our study, as compared with a world population for the year 1000 of 265 million. Our seven regions thus accounted for almost 90% of the world total at the beginning of our period. The list of "world regions" that we work with will later be augmented and adjusted in the light of the evolution of the world economy subsequent to the 1490s.

---

[1] According to Fernández-Armesto (2006), these forces of divergence and convergence have overlapped "for perhaps the last 10,000 years or so" (p. 2). Bentley (1996, p. 750) also proposes periodizing world history "by examining participation of the world's peoples in processes transcending individual societies and cultural regions." For him, "cross-cultural interactions proceeded according to [different] dynamics" in the centuries after 1000, which he characterizes as "an age of transregional nomadic empires" (p. 766) that eventually ushered in the modern era.

WESTERN EUROPE[2]

We use this term to designate the western extremity of the Eurasian landmass, starting roughly at the eastern borders of the contemporary nation-states of Poland, Hungary, and the former Czechoslovakia, including also all the offshore islands in the Atlantic and the Mediterranean (see figure 1.1). The eastern boundary is chosen to reflect the extent of the cultural influence associated with the Roman Catholic Church and the Latin script. Thus the western Slavic nations of the Poles and Czechs are included while the eastern Slavic Russians and the southern Slavic Serbs are not. The Hungarians are also included on the basis of their religious affiliation with the Roman Catholic Church, despite their ethnic and linguistic differences from the rest of Latin Christendom. Our division of Western and Eastern Europe therefore turns on the difference between the heritages of the western and eastern branches of Christianity in the shaping of the political and social institutions of the two regions. Linguistically, our definition of Western Europe includes all Romance languages, except Romanian, all Germanic and Celtic languages, Polish, Czech and Slovak, Latvian and Lithuanian, Basque, Finnish, and Hungarian.

Geographically, this region has many natural advantages that have often been remarked upon. Perhaps the most important is the high ratio of coastline to land area, greater than for any other continent according to Rhoads Murphey (1970, p. 87). Western Europe also has the lowest average elevation and the greatest proportional extent of plains (ibid., p. 90). It enjoys a relatively mild temperature in relation to latitude, due to the effect of the Gulf Stream. The Great European Plain that stretches unbroken from the Atlantic to the Urals has long been highly fertile and productive. The many rivers, draining into the Baltic, the North Sea, the Atlantic, and the Mediterranean, have kept transport costs low and market areas connected. The mountain ranges that form the central spine of the peninsula provide valuable woodland and pasture for livestock in the high valleys, and are traversed by accessible passes that connect the shores of the Mediterranean in the south to those of the Baltic and the Atlantic in the north. At the same time, Eric Jones (2003) has observed that there are a sufficient number of natural barriers within the region—the Alps, the Pyrenees, and the English Channel, to name but three—to make its political unification

[2]Sources for this section include Barraclough (1976), Bartlett (1993), Becher (2003), Boussard (1976), Collins (1991), McCormick (2001), McEvedy (1961), McKitterick (1995, parts I and II), Murphey (1970), O'Brien (2002), Reuter (1999, parts I and II), and Riche (1993).

FIGURE 1.1. Western Europe.

militarily difficult. Finally, Murphey (p. 90) notes that Western Europe is "the tip of the great triangle formed by Eurasia as a whole" and is the "point of the land funnel" along which influences of all kinds can flow from east to west.[3]

---

[3] On this last point, see Diamond (1997).

Historically, the region has been shaped by the inheritance of the cultural, legal, and administrative institutions of the Roman Empire and the doctrine and practice of the Roman Catholic Church, not only in the southern areas of direct Roman rule but also as they were absorbed by the northern Germanic tribes that overran the empire in the fourth and fifth centuries, as well as by regions that had never been part of the empire in the first place, notably Ireland, Scotland, and Scandinavia. This fusion of the "southern" legacy of late antiquity with the energy and warlike prowess of the northern invaders resulted eventually in the establishment of the Carolingian Empire that extended from the Atlantic and the Pyrenees to the Elbe and the Danube, in other words most of continental Western Europe as we have defined it, except for the Iberian and Scandinavian Peninsulas. This political unity, marked by the crowning of the Frankish ruler Charlemagne as Holy Roman Emperor by the pope in 800, did not last long, however, and the empire disintegrated into competing kingdoms and principalities.

Charlemagne's grandfather was Charles Martel, the Merovingian "mayor of the palace" who defeated an invading Arab force from Spain at the Battle of Poitiers in 732, marking the limit of their penetration into Europe. His father was Pepin the Short, who deposed the last Merovingian king in 751 and took the Frankish crown for himself. Charlemagne succeeded Pepin as king of the Franks in 768. The new ruler undertook a series of aggressive military campaigns against the Saxons, forcibly converting them to Christianity, and the Avars, nomadic invaders from Central Asia who had established a base in central Europe. The Avars were utterly destroyed and their enormous hoard of looted treasure distributed to the church and his followers by Charlemagne. An appeal from the pope for help against the Lombard king of northern Italy led Charlemagne to cross the Alps and depose the Lombard ruler, after which the grateful pontiff crowned Charlemagne as king of the Franks and Lombards and emperor of the Romans. After Charlemagne's death in 814 the empire was ruled somewhat precariously by his son Louis the Pious until his death in 840, at which time the empire passed to his eldest son Lothar, whose claim to the undivided territory was vigorously challenged by his brothers Charles the Bald in the west and Louis the German in the east. The younger brothers joined forces to defeat Lothar decisively at the Battle of Fontenoy in 841, compelling him to divide the empire between all three of them, while he retained the imperial title.

This division of Charlemagne's empire into three contiguous vertical north–south blocks by the Treaty of Verdun in 843 is often taken as marking the beginnings of the subsequent nation-states of France in the west and Germany in the east, providing the "birth certificate of modern Europe" as Riche (1993, p. 168) eloquently puts it. The central band, stretching from the North Sea to Italy, was the territory that went with the imperial title to Lothar. The Carolingian line eventually died out, to be replaced in France by the dynasty of the Capetians in 987, and in Germany by the Ottonians of Saxony.

At its height the dimensions of Charlemagne's empire were undeniably impressive. According to Becher (2003, p. 118) it encompassed 1 million square kilometers with 180 dioceses, 700 monasteries, 750 royal estates, 150 palaces, and nearly 700 administrative districts. Given the available technology and resources, however, it was impossible to impose any unified central administration over such a vast domain. The court could not remain permanently in the capital at Aachen and wandered peripatetically from place to place throughout the year. The administrative districts were under counts, with dukes sometimes overseeing groups of counties. Central control was attempted through the dispatch of royal emissaries, known as *missi*, while diplomatic correspondence and administrative records were in the hands of clerics in the royal chapel. After the breakup of the empire toward the close of the ninth century the various dukes and counts, and even lower-level local leaders, increasingly began to govern independently, tied together only by the looser bonds of feudal vassalage. This tendency was particularly marked in the western sections of the empire, what is now France.

In the eastern or German section of the empire, the unity of the state was preserved to a much greater extent. Here the last Carolingian died in 911, to be replaced from 918 as king by Henry, duke of Saxony, who founded the Ottonian dynasty that lasted until 1024. The German kingdom in this era was a sort of federation of a few great duchies, such as Saxony, Bavaria, Franconia, Thuringia, and Swabia. The ducal ruling houses, as Barraclough (1976, p. 111) noted, were mostly descended from the commanders of imperial frontier armies, with a tradition of loyalty to central authority. They were willing to elect or nominate one among them to be somewhat more than "first among equals" in their own collective interest against barbarian and other enemies. During the long reign of Otto the Great (936–73), the German kingdom was established as clearly the most powerful state in all of Europe, with military victories over the eastern Slavic tribes as well as (and in particular) the Hungarians, who had been ravaging all the settled lands around them for decades, at the Battle of Lechfeld in 955.

Like Charlemagne, Otto also invaded Italy to protect the pope and was crowned Holy Roman Emperor in Rome in 962, a title that survived until it was abolished by Napoleon in 1806. Despite its prestige, in practice this title did not imply much more than the addition of northern Italy to the territories that Otto and his successors ruled in their native land, and considerable influence over the other states and cities in both Germany and Italy. In addition it involved them in a lengthy and exhausting struggle with the papacy over the investiture of bishops and other issues involving the "separation of church and state."

Despite the glamor of these Italian incursions, the main thrust of the Ottonians was their relentless pressure and expansion on the open plains to the east against the pagan Slavic tribes. Just as the Franks had done to the Saxons themselves two centuries earlier, the Saxons followed a policy of conquest and forced conversion of the Slavic tribes in their way. The frontier was extended eastwards by the establishment of fortresses and garrisons along the "marches," and also by episcopal foundations, the most important of which was at Magdeburg. A great uprising of the Slavs in 983 halted the expansion temporarily, but it was resumed after a generation. Support of the church was a major political technique of the Ottonians, enhancing their power not only on the frontier but also within the duchies themselves. Otto the Great's grandson, Otto the Third, died in 1002 at the age of 21 before his grandiose plans for a reunification of the eastern and western empires and churches through marriage to a Byzantine princess could be realized. The power and prestige of the Ottonians was maintained and preserved by the succeeding Salian dynasty, starting in 1025.

A notable development of the tenth century, reflecting the success of the Ottonians, was the adoption of Roman Catholic Christianity by the western Slavic peoples of Bohemia and Poland and by the previously nomadic Hungarian invaders soon after their defeat at Lechfeld. The Czechs of Bohemia, inhabiting the valley of the Vltava, a tributary of the Elbe, converted under German pressure early in the tenth century, with a bishopric established later at their capital Prague. Bohemia functioned henceforth as a duchy of the German Empire, closely related to Bavaria. The Polish ruler Mieszko the First, of the Piast dynasty, converted in 966 and shrewdly placed his realm under the protection of the Holy See to prevent complete German domination. His successor, Boleslaw Chrobry, the "Brave," expanded the domain in all directions against other Slavic peoples, while maintaining generally good relations with the empire. Otto the Third assisted him in the establishment of the capital Gniezno as an archbishopric in 1000. The year 1000 also saw the crowning of the future Saint Stephen as king of Hungary, after his conversion together with his father Géza in 995, followed by the establishment of an archbishopric at Esztergom. Thus by the year 1000 the eastern limits of Roman Catholic Christianity had just about been reached, with only the Prussians, Balts, and Finns still awaiting conversion.

We now look northwest to the British Isles, separated from the mainland by the North Sea and the English Channel, and consequently undergoing a development somewhat different in character but nevertheless reflecting the same broad historical processes. England had been incorporated into the Roman Empire since the first century B.C., with Hadrian's Wall separating it from the Picts in Scotland. The country experienced intensive Roman influence marked by a network of roads and flourishing urban centers such as London and York. By the early fifth century, however, Rome had withdrawn its legions and the island was invaded and occupied by Angles and Saxons from German, and Jutes from Danish, homelands. The native Britons were driven into Wales and other western regions or across the Channel to Brittany. By the close of the sixth century England was effectively divided into about a half-dozen contending Anglo-Saxon kingdoms.

Although the invaders were pagans, a Christian presence remained in the western fringes of the British Isles, and particularly in Ireland, which had been converted by missionaries from Roman Britain such as Saint Patrick. The roles were reversed in 563, when the Irish Saint Columba arrived on the isle of Iona in Scotland. From this base Celtic missionaries evangelized in Scotland and northern England, establishing such centers as Lindisfarne in Northumbria in 635. This relatively prominent role for what was subsequently to become something of a backwater was reflected in the fact that Ireland was probably the leading European book producer, in per capita terms, during the eighth and ninth centuries (Buringh and van Zanden 2006). Crucial in reestablishing English links with continental Europe, however, was the decision by Pope Gregory the Great in 597 to send a mission, headed by a monk named Augustine, to bring England back to the Christian faith. An early success was the conversion of the pagan king of Kent, possibly influenced by the fact that he was married to a Frankish Christian princess. Augustine became the first archbishop of Canterbury, and all the Anglo-Saxon kingdoms were converted to Christianity by 686.

The eighth century saw these kingdoms prospering from the expansion of trade in the North Sea and Baltic regions. The extent of the wealth generated by trade, tribute, and plunder accruing to these Anglo-Saxon kings can be gauged by the sumptuous treasures excavated in 1939 at the famous ship burial of one of them at Sutton Hoo. The Christianity professed by all of these rulers did not prevent them from waging relentless war against each other, ending in the establishment of the "Mercian Supremacy," the hegemony of the central kingdom of Mercia over all the others, for much of the eighth and early ninth centuries. King Offa, who ruled from 757 to 796, was notable for the volume and quality of his coinage, the scale of his public works such as the famous Offa's Dyke that he erected as a barrier against the Welsh, and the trade treaty that he negotiated with his great contemporary Charlemagne, who treated him as an equal. The level of culture attained by Anglo-Saxon England in this period is indicated by the "Ecclesiastical History of the English People" written by the Venerable Bede around 730, and the career of Alcuin of York, another great scholarly cleric.

The ninth century saw England ravaged by the Danish Vikings, who began by raiding monasteries and coastal towns before occupying extensive territory in the northeastern part of the country, which came to be known as the "Danelaw," with the capital at York. They met stubborn resistance by the English led by King Alfred of Wessex (871–99). He eventually defeated the invaders and confined them by treaty to the Danelaw. His successors eventually recaptured all of the lost areas and by 1000 ruled over a unified England. The Danish king Harold Bluetooth had meanwhile converted to Christianity in 965, followed soon after by Olaf Tryggvason of Norway and Olof Skötkonung of Sweden. The Danes returned in force to England soon afterwards and Harold's grandson Canute ruled England from 1016 to 1035.

What this brief synopsis has attempted to demonstrate is the emergence of the entity that we are calling Western Europe from a fusion of the legacy of the Roman Empire and the Roman Catholic Church with that of the Celtic, Germanic, and Slavic tribes. This fusion is well illustrated by the career of the aforementioned Alcuin, educated at the cathedral school in York, who met Charlemagne in Parma in 781 while the latter was on his way to Rome. Alcuin became Charlemagne's most influential adviser, and while abbot of Saint-Martin of Tours worked to promote a standardized version of written Latin, the Carolingian minuscule. This provided a means for information to be communicated and stored across the Carolingian Empire, allowing for the more efficient diffusion of both religious and secular knowledge across Western Europe (Blum and Dudley 2003). The process that began with the conversion of the Frankish king Clovis around 500 was brought to a close with those of the Czechs, Poles, Hungarians, and Scandinavians in the last century of the first millennium.

Eastern Europe[4]

The western borders of this region, for our present purposes, will approximately coincide with those of the contemporary states of the Russian Federation, Belarus, and Ukraine, together with the Balkan Peninsula (see figure 1.2). The major formative cultural influences on the region were the Byzantine Empire and the Greek Orthodox Church, so we will also include the entire area of the present state of Turkey, which constituted the core area of the empire, with its capital at Constantinople (now Istanbul). The eastern borders, with the neighboring world region of Central or Inner Asia, will be shifting with the frontier between the settled agriculture of the Russians on the one hand and the forest zone of the northern hunter-gatherers and the steppe of the pastoral nomads on the other, altering with the balance of military power. As defined it is a very large continental area with wide extremes of temperature. It is marked by major, partly navigable rivers such as the Don, the Dnieper, and the Volga, which drain into the Black Sea and the Caspian Sea. The main mountain ranges other than in the Balkans are the Urals and the Caucasus, bridging the isthmus between these two inland seas.

The first Russian state was the so-called Kievan Rus, a loose federation with its capital at Kiev. The Rus were Scandinavian Vikings, drawn to the east by the prospects of booty, mercenary military service, and the trade in furs, amber, and slaves for luxury products and silver from Byzantium and the Islamic World. They formed a small warrior aristocracy ruling over a mass of Slav peasantry. Between Kiev and the northern principality of Novgorod the Rus maintained a profitable monopoly of the trade routes linking the Baltic to the Black Sea and the Caspian along the rivers and the portages between them. The Rus always had to contend, however, with powerful steppe nomadic peoples such as the Bulgars, Pechenegs, and Khazars for control over these trade routes, and they also had to protect their own sedentary agricultural populations from these predators.

The Russians and other Slavic peoples were initially barbarians on the northern fringes of the Byzantine Empire. By the familiar logic of acculturation they fell under the cultural sway of the more advanced civilization. The Serbs and the Bulgarians in the Balkans were converted in the eighth and ninth centuries and the Kievan Rus Prince Vladimir was baptized and married the sister of the Byzantine emperor

[4]Sources for this section include Christian (1998, chapters 13 and 14), Franklin and Shepard (1996), Hoetzsch (1966, chapter 1), McEvedy (1961), Obolensky (1957), O'Brien (2002), Reuter (1999, part III), and Vernadsky (1948).

FIGURE 1.2. Eastern Europe.

in 988, a date that is even more significant than 1917 in Russian history. Vladimir's dynasty was that of the Rurikovichi, descendants of the possibly mythical Viking Rurik of Novgorod, the earliest trading center of the Scandinavians in northern Russia. The first ruler of Kiev was a certain Oleg (882–912), who laid siege to Byzantium in 907 and 911. Although he did not take the city he did obtain notable trading concessions from the empire. The successor to Oleg as the ruler of Kiev was Prince Igor (912–45), a member of his retinue. Despite his operatic fame, Igor's reign did not produce any lasting accomplishments. His son Svyatoslav was an infant when Igor died in 945 at the hands of rebellious tribesmen and the state was ruled by the royal widow, Olga, until the young prince came of age in 962. Olga proved to be a sagacious and formidable ruler, suppressing the tribe responsible for Igor's death and reforming the tribute collection system on a more centralized basis. She personally converted to Christianity on a visit to Constantinople but insisted on independence for the Kievan church before adopting it as the national religion. The Byzantines balked, prompting her to negotiate unsuccessfully with Otto the Great for the adoption of Roman Catholicism instead. Svyatoslav (962–72) was a staunch pagan and his reign was a whirlwind of military activity in all directions. He destroyed the prosperous and influential empire of the Khazar steppe nomads and intervened actively in Bulgaria and the Balkans both in alliance with and against the Byzantines. He was ambushed and killed by the Pechenegs while returning laden with booty from his Balkan conquests to Kiev.

At the time of Svyatoslav's death his three sons were serving as his lieutenants in key cities and regions. Vladimir, based in Novgorod, prevailed over his brothers with the aid of Viking and Turkish mercenaries in the ensuing struggle for power. He continued his father's support of paganism even though Christianity was spreading among the people. He eventually realized that paganism had no future and apparently considered Islam and Roman Catholicism along with Orthodox Christianity as possible choices for the future state religion. The matter was finally settled when the new Byzantine emperor Basil II (976–1025) urgently requested military assistance from Vladimir against an internal revolt. The inducement was marriage to his sister Anna, provided of course that Vladimir agreed to be baptized. In the royal marriage market of the tenth century a Byzantine *porphyrogenita* such as Anna was a prize catch. She had even been denied to Otto the Great as a bride for his son, the future Otto II, who had to accept another princess not "born in the purple." Vladimir sent a detachment of his Vikings to Constantinople and they promptly suppressed the rebellion. Basil now attempted to renege on the agreement and had to be persuaded by Vladimir's seizure of the strategic port city of Kherson in the Crimea before he dispatched the royal bride for the conversion and marriage, after which Kherson was returned to him by Vladimir as a "bridegroom's gift." Vladimir's conversion, which amounted to that of the entire Rus nation, thus set the seal on the series of such events in Scandinavia, Bohemia, Poland, and Hungary that were one of the most remarkable features of European history in the late tenth century. Vladimir embarked on an extensive program of church building, charitable works, and promotion of education. He died in 1015 and was canonized in the thirteenth century.

Another powerful early state in Eastern Europe was the Bulgarian Empire that mounted a serious challenge to Byzantium itself, even though its church organization and literary culture were completely derivative from that source. The Bulgars were a Turkic people, a branch of which had settled in the lower Danube basin, dominating the local Slavic peasantry. Under the pagan Khan Krum in 811 they defeated a Byzantine army and killed the emperor, making a drinking cup out of his skull. Krum and his successors conquered much of the Balkans, though checked in the west by the Germans and the Serbs. The cultural attraction and the political and military influence of Byzantium proved too strong, however, and under Boris I (852–89, died 907) the Bulgarians converted to Christianity in 869. A major later consequence of this decision was the adoption by Bulgaria of the Cyrillic script and Slavonic liturgy devised by the monks Cyril and Methodius, originally for the Czech state of Moravia, which, however, rejected it in favor of the Latin liturgy. Moravia's loss was the gain not only of Bulgaria but also of all the Slavic Greek Orthodox Churches, since it gave them linguistic independence from the Greek of Byzantium itself, a political asset of considerable value. This Cyrillic script used by all the Orthodox Slavic peoples, in contrast to the Latin of their western cousins, is a cultural difference between them that has persisted to this day. Despite these conversions, conflict in the Balkans and southern Russia was intense, not only between Orthodox Christians themselves but also with Germans and Poles in the north and west, and with pagan and Muslim nomadic peoples in the east.

Boris I conquered Macedonia and secured an opening to the Aegean Sea in the west of the Balkan Peninsula. His son Simeon I ruled from 893 to 927 and his reign is regarded as the apex of the country's history. He declared himself tsar of the Bulgarians and the Romans, i.e., a rival to the Byzantine emperor. He besieged Constantinople several times but never succeeded in capturing the great city. The Byzantines kept Simeon and his successors in check by inciting incursions by the Hungarians, Pechenegs, and Russians into Bulgarian territory. Basil II, the emperor who converted Vladimir, inflicted a crushing defeat on them in 1018, earning himself the designation of the "Bulgar-Slayer."

We have thus seen that by the year 1000 the Byzantine Empire had firmly established its Eastern European successor states in Russia and Bulgaria. Serbia had already entered the fold in the ninth century while neighboring Croatia went into the orbit of Rome, a dividing line that has persisted to this day. We now turn to the emergence of what can also be thought of as another successor state, though of a wholly different kind, the Arab caliphate.

NORTH AFRICA AND SOUTHWEST ASIA: THE ISLAMIC WORLD[5]

This is the region generally known today as the Middle East (see figure 1.3). It is the classic core area of the Islamic World, which is a designation that we will also use when there is no danger of ambiguity. It comprises the southern littoral of the Mediterranean, the so-called Fertile Crescent of the Nile Valley, the Levant and Mesopotamia, the Arabian Peninsula, the Iranian plateau, and Afghanistan. A high proportion of the land area of the region is arid or semiarid, with a pronounced scarcity and irregularity of rainfall. The valleys of the Nile, Tigris, and Euphrates, on the other hand, have been fertile and productive agricultural areas for millennia. The pure deserts have been uninhabited but the semidesert zone has supported pastoral nomadism, also for millennia. The region's most valuable natural asset, however, was its location relative to the other world regions, particularly prior to the European voyages of discovery. Europe was just across the Mediterranean, only a very short distance at the Straits of Gibraltar; Iran and Afghanistan were in direct contact with Central Asia and hence with the overland trade routes to China; India was reachable by sea, as well as overland along the Makran and Baluchi coasts to the mouth of the Indus, and through the Khyber Pass; spices from the Indonesian archipelago and Chinese products could be brought to the Persian Gulf and the Red Sea and either consumed or passed on to Europe at a profit; gold from West Africa could be exchanged for salt in the trans-Saharan caravan trade to circulate within the Islamic World or be exported to Europe or Central Asia.

The rise of Islam in the Arabian Peninsula and the subsequent rapid Arab conquest of the entire region in the seventh century was clearly one of the most decisive events in world history. The Islamic religion and the Arabic language with which it is indissolubly linked served as a powerful unifying cultural force from the Atlantic coast to the Himalayas. The heritage of classical antiquity and Byzantine and Sassanian methods of administration and statecraft were adopted by the new Islamic dynasties. The fusion of Arabic and Persian culture formed a creative new synthesis that influenced all walks of life. New crops and ideas were introduced from India and Southeast Asia. Just as Christianity civilized Germanic and Slav tribes, so did Islam with the Turks of Central Asia, who increasingly took over the military function in the Islamic states.

[5]Sources for this section include Fletcher (1992), Hourani (1991, part 1), Kennedy (1986), Lewis (1993), McEvedy (1961), O'Brien (2002), de Planhol (1959), Robinson (1996), and Shaban (1976, 1978).

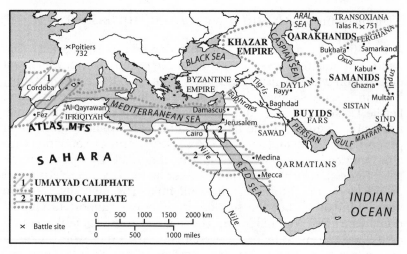

FIGURE 1.3. The Islamic World.

The early conquests were consolidated and extended by the Umayyad caliphate, which ruled from Damascus, the capital of the Islamic World from 661 to 750. It is possibly the oldest city in the world and was a provincial capital for most of the ancient empires up to the Byzantine. Situated east of the mountain of Jabal Qasiyun—from which descend streams that watered the lush oasis of al-Ghutah that served as a market garden of the city, with a rich variety of fruit trees, and close to a plain that could provide the crops to feed it—Damascus must also have appealed to the Umayyads on strategic and economic grounds as a crossroads of the caravan trade. They fortified the ancient citadel and constructed the architectural masterpiece of the Great Mosque on the site of the Christian cathedral. Ashtor (1976a, p. 13) cites an estimate that the Arab population of Syria in 720 was about 200,000 out of a total of about 4 million, or roughly 5%. The population of Damascus was said to have been 100,000 in 1350, when it "was well past its peak" (Watson 1983, p. 133). The peak must have occurred during the reigns of Abd al-Malik and his successors al-Walid (705–15) and Hisham (724–43), under whom the administration became more centralized along with the coinage, with Arabic becoming the language of the civil administration.

Despite intense internal conflicts, the Islamic World thrived economically, with a wide variety of new crops being introduced from the east, leading to the growth of large new towns, from Cordoba in Spain to Al-Qayrawan in Tunisia and Cairo in Egypt, while Damascus continued to expand. Arab armies advanced across the Oxus into Central Asia, occupying Bukhara and Samarkand in 710, defeating a Tang Chinese force at the Battle of the Talas River in 751, and entering the Ferghana Valley, the easternmost point of their advance. The Indian province of Sind was also conquered early in the eighth century, with Multan in the Punjab taken in 711. All of these areas were in addition to the initial acquisition of about two-thirds of the Byzantine Empire and the entire territory of the Persian Sassanian dynasty. The Arabs also controlled the southern half of the isthmus between the Black Sea and the Caspian Sea, including the towns of Tiflis and Derbent. The empire in 750 thus stretched from Agadir on the Atlantic coast to the Oxus in Central Asia and the Indus in India.

It was clearly impossible to establish any sort of unified administration over such an extensive terrain. But how was control to be exercised over the conquered lands? One possibility was to disperse the Arab rulers among the local populations, allowing them to extract taxes individually for their maintenance and support. Had such a course been followed it is likely that the Arab elite would eventually have been absorbed socially and culturally into the diverse communities over which they ruled, as happened to ruling-class Vikings in Normandy or Russia. The second caliph, Umar (634–44), made the far-reaching alternative decision of concentrating the Arabs in fortified garrison cities, maintaining themselves out of cash stipends or *ata*, paid out from the central treasury to which all taxes on the subject peoples were transmitted. Since Muslims were exempted from most taxes, this created an ambivalent attitude toward conversion on the part of the Arab conquerors. Local communities were thus relatively free to run their own affairs without bureaucratic interference, provided of course that they paid the *jizya* (poll tax), imposed only on non-Muslims, and the *kharaj* (land tax). The system could work well because the former Byzantine and Sassanian lands were already monetized under their previous rulers. Another major advantage was that by clustering together in their garrison cities the Arabs maintained their own language and culture, which were gradually acquired by the subject peoples instead. The disadvantage was that the new Arab ruling elite was in danger of becoming pure *rentiers*, except when they were called upon to fight against internal revolts or external invaders. Eventually, this crucial military function was increasingly turned over to specialized military slaves of Turkic or other foreign origin, with very adverse consequences for the caliphate.

In 750 the Umayyad caliphate was replaced after a violent overthrow by the Abbasids, who altered the Arabic tribal character of the regime in the direction of a more formal, bureaucratic, and centralized Persian model. They also gave more scope to the substantial population of converts, the *mawalim*, who were strongly represented in the urban mercantile and artisan classes. There was a notable acceleration of economic activity as a result and less emphasis on conquest and military operations. The second Abbasid caliph, al-Mansur (754–75), founded the city of Baghdad to serve as the capital of the new dynasty. Al-Mansur, his son al-Mahdi (775–85), and grandson Harun al-Rashid (786–809) were all able rulers, assisted by an efficient *kuttab* or secretariat, prominent among whom was the Iranian family of the Barmakids. The civil and military establishments were kept firmly apart. The Sawad, the fertile region around Baghdad, yielded substantial revenues on the basis of direct taxes on the value of agricultural output at rates of a third to a half, and Egypt was also a major contributor. These revenues enabled adequate military forces to be maintained to preserve internal order and to fight the Byzantines. The very success of the Barmakids in swelling the state coffers, however, and their own lavish lifestyle made them greatly resented by traditional interests and the family was sacrificed and its leader brutally executed by Harun in an effort to placate the opposition.

The horizon darkened with the succession crisis following the death of Harun in 809. He was succeeded by his son al-Amin, with the next in line supposed to be a slightly younger son al-Ma'mun, who was made the governor of the eastern region of Khurasan and other Iranian provinces. The brothers and their partisans soon fell out, however, and a bloody civil war ensued during which Baghdad itself was besieged for over a year by troops of the eastern faction of al-Ma'mun, after which al-Amin was executed by one of his brother's supporters in 813. Al-Ma'mun was obliged to reward the general Tahir, who commanded the contingents that brought him to power, with what amounted to independent and hereditary rule over Khurasan, though with the acknowledgement of Abbasid suzerainty.

The next caliph, al-Mu'tasim (833–42), abandoned Baghdad and built an extensive new capital at Samarra further up the Tigris, which held that position until Baghdad was restored in 889. Al-Mu'tasim was in part motivated by the desire to set up his "new model army" of Turkish and other *ghulams* in a location that permitted them to acquire land and other property, such as commercial concessions, in a setting free of the baggage of past associations in Baghdad. This professional standing army was intended to replace the original militia of Arab and Iranian part-time soldiers, the *Khurasaniyya*, upon which the regime had previously relied as its main military arm. The stipends that this group continued to draw as rewards for past service were abolished as part of a far-reaching military and fiscal reform. A new orthodoxy in religion was also imposed, holding that the Qur'an (Koran) was "created" and therefore subject to changing interpretation rather than being the unchanging and eternal word of God.

After the death of al-Mu'tasim in 842 the Abbasid regime had some brief periods of achievement and success, but the long-term trend was downward. The main reason seems to have been the difficulty of raising or even maintaining the revenue necessary to preserve the integrity of the state. Hugh Kennedy (1986, p. 189) states that the Sawad generated 100 million dirhems a year in revenue under the early Abbasids up to the reign of al-Ma'mun, but this fell to a mere 30 million a year under al-Muqtadir in 918. There were other prosperous regions such as Egypt and Fars but the center did not have access to these resources, which were largely under the control of local powers. The final blow to the prosperity of Iraq came when the great Nahrawan canal, the main source of water to the Sawad, was deliberately cut by a feuding warlord in 937 in an attempt to impede the march of a rival, thereby ruining the work of centuries (ibid., p. 199).

The tenth century also saw the caliphate fall under the "protectorate" of an Iranian warlord clan known as the Buyids (941–1055) because of their descent from a humble fisherman from the Caspian Sea area who went by the name of Buyeh. The three brothers who founded the fortunes of the clan came to power separately in Fars, Rayy, and Baghdad itself, but pooled their assets in a sort of family federation with each supporting the others. The basis of their power was the armies that they built up of infantry from their home area of Daylam, south of the Caspian, and mounted Turkish *ghulams*. This enabled them to control the Abbasid caliphs in conjunction with allies from the secretarial class, although the Abbasids continued to be maintained as spiritual figureheads. Despite being the "protectors" of a Sunni Arab caliphate, the Buyids had pro-Shia religious sensibilities and displayed an affinity to native Persian and Sassanian royal practices, thus enhancing the Persian cast that the Abbasids themselves gave to their own regime. Buyid officers were granted *iqtas*, lands from which they could enjoy the revenues in return for military service, thus creating a sort of feudalism, with their own role being like that of the Merovingian mayors of the palace or the later *shoguns* of Japan. On the whole their regime was quite an effective one, with the province of Fars in particular enjoying great prosperity. Thus the decline of Baghdad and its environs did not mean that the entire Islamic World or even the Abbasid lands as a whole were necessarily undergoing a similar experience. The fiscal imbalance between the claims of the army and the ability of the economy to generate the necessary revenue remained, however, and left the system vulnerable to external shocks and threats. Both the caliphs and their "protectors" finally fell victim to the rising new power of the eleventh century, the Seljuk Turks.

Not only was there constant conflict at the center of the Arab empire, the initial unity of the empire soon began to disintegrate as a consequence of internal dynastic quarrels, religious schism, and the natural tendency of the segments more distant from the center to go their separate ways. Thus by the ninth century there were independent dynasties in North Africa such as the Idrisids (789–906) of Morocco and the Aghlabids (800–909) of Tunisia. The founder of the Idrisids was from a family of *sharifs* (descendants of the prophet) who fled to North Africa from Medina after a failed revolt against the Abbasids. His lineage attracted a following of Berber tribes who helped him found the city of Fez as the capital of a new kingdom, attracting Arab immigrants from the east and Spain. The Aghlabid dynasty originated as a heredity fief granted to a military governor of Ifriqiyah (Tunisia and eastern Algeria) by the caliph Harun al-Rashid in return for payment of an annual sum of 40,000 dinars. The capital of this dynasty was at Al-Qayrawan, which was developed as both a religious and cultural center. The Aghlabids also invaded and eventually occupied Sicily and raided the vicinity of Rome.

In eastern Iran and Transoxiana the frontier states of the Tahirids (821–73), Saffarids (873–900), and Samanids (819–999) were independent in all but name of the Abbasid caliph in Baghdad. All of these dynasties were of Iranian extraction and founded by former Abbasid officials, except for the somewhat socially revolutionary Saffarids from the province of Sistan, founded by a coppersmith (*saffar*) who unseated the Tahirids by leading a band of religious dissidents and bandits against them. The Samanids, who ruled from Bukhara, were a particularly wealthy and well-administered state. The Turkic dynasty of the Ghaznavids (961–1186), based in Ghazna and Kabul in Afghanistan, extended their sway westwards to the borders of Iraq at the expense of the Abbasids and the Buyids that were the de facto rulers of their realm. Another Turkic dynasty, the Qarakhanids, displaced the Samanids in Bukhara, Samarkand, and Transoxiana in 999 and ruled until 1211. The pattern in the east was thus for the Arab Abbasids to lose much of their effective power, first to their Iranian subjects and eventually to Turks, whether as invading tribes or as their own military.

This process could be clearly seen in Egypt, where a Turkish military governor, Ahmad ibn Tulun, made himself into the virtually independent ruler in 868. Ibn Tulun built the magnificent mosque that still bears his name in Fustat or Old Cairo, which he extended with further encampments and commercial concessions for his army. He seems to have been one of the most enlightened rulers in the long history of Egypt, improving irrigation, reforming taxation in the interest of the peasant, and generally supporting economic development in his domain. Ibn Tulun is said to have had an annual revenue of 4 million dinars, and when he bequeathed Egypt to his descendants he left 10 million dinars in the treasury. However, his profligate son drove the state into virtual bankruptcy before the Tulunid dynasty fell in 905, with the Abbasids regaining control. This restoration proved to be brief, since another dynasty of Abbasid Turkish military governors, the Ikhshidids, seized power in 935. This dynasty essentially continued the policies of the Tulunids under the supervision of an extremely able *wazir*, a black slave eunuch of apparently Sudanese extraction named Kafur.

The most significant of all these rival dynasties was that of the Fatimids, who overthrew the Aghlabids in Tunisia at the head of dissident Berber tribes in 909. The Fatimid base was Ifriqiyah, roughly corresponding to the present Tunisia, where the former Aghlabid city of Al-Qayrawan was greatly expanded by them after its capture. They also established a major port and naval base at the new site of their first capital, al-Mahdiyah, where they constructed a massive fleet for use against their enemies, both Muslim and Christian. After building up their power base, the Fatimids then launched the conquest of Egypt in 969, seizing control from the Ikhshidids. The victorious Fatimid general Jawhar, also a slave but of Slavic origin, built the great capital of Al-Qahirah, or Cairo as we know it, north of Fustat as a worthy rival to Baghdad.

The Fatimids were followers of a dissident Shia sect, the Ismailis, claiming to be the true *imams* descended from Ali and Fatima, the daughter of the Prophet. They thus regarded the Abbasids as illegitimate usurpers and proclaimed their own caliphate after conquering Egypt. They not only carried on warfare and sectarian disputation with the Abbasids, but also made a successful attempt to divert the lucrative Indian Ocean trade from the Persian Gulf to the Red Sea. With the rich revenues of Egypt and vigorous promotion of foreign trade through the Red Sea, they had the resources to establish Cairo as an imposing new capital, as well as to maintain a powerful army of Berber tribal warriors and regiments of Sudanese and Turkish slave soldiers with which to challenge the Abbasids and the Byzantines in Syria and Palestine. Despite their fervent Ismaili Shia ideology, the Fatimids were very tolerant and open in the freedom they gave to other sects and faiths. They also relied to a considerable extent on Jewish and Christian advisers such as the *wazir* Yaqub ibn Killis, a Jewish convert of Iraqi origin who had served under Kafur with the Ikhshidids, and who wielded an enormous formative influence on the Fatimid administration of Egypt. Though in principle a theocratic state, the Fatimid Empire tended to be dominated by its military commanders and the various ethnic and regional factions into which they were divided.

In 1000 the Fatimid domains included most of North Africa, the western Arabian Peninsula including Mecca and Medina, and southern Syria and Palestine, including Damascus and Jerusalem. However, this would not last. When the Fatimids set off on the conquest of Egypt they left Ifriqiyah in the care of a dynasty of their Berber allies known as the Zirids. This dynasty, the first of many subsequent Berber dynasties in North Africa, initially served them loyally, transmitting revenues as required, but eventually by the middle of the eleventh century they broke with their masters and began to assert an independent policy. The Fatimid reaction was to unleash on the western regions a nomadic Bedouin tribe, the Banu Hilal, that, according to Ibn Khaldun, devastated the countryside like "a plague of locusts," a calamity from which these lands never seem to have fully recovered. The Arab nomads were unable to establish any lasting state structures and the way was opened to the emergence of the formidable Berber dynasty of the Almoravids. The consequences for the Fatimids were severe since their empire was now confined to Egypt and parts of Syria, where they also had to contend with a resurgent Byzantium and several assorted Islamic rivals as well. Furthermore, the mentally unstable Caliph al-Hakim (996–1021) may have unwittingly provoked the First Crusade nearly a century later by wantonly destroying the Church of the Holy Sepulcher in Jerusalem, to the outrage of all Christendom. The Fatimids, together with their enemies the Abbasids and the Byzantines, were all to suffer at the hands of two new actors on the west Eurasian political stage that were soon to make their appearance: the Seljuk Turks and the Frankish Crusaders.

At the western end of the Islamic World the turn of the millennium saw Muslim Spain at the height of its power. The initial Arab conquest was begun in 711 by a force consisting of seven thousand mostly Berber warriors, led by a governor of Tangier named Tariq, himself a recently converted Berber. They defeated the army of the Visigothic king Roderick, who was killed in the battle. A larger Arab force led by the Umayyad governor of Ifriqiyah reinforced the invaders, with the result that much of Spain was occupied by 714, when both leaders were recalled to Damascus never to return. The settlement of al-Andalus, as the areas of the Iberian Peninsula under Muslim rule were called in Arabic, seems to have been more a result of local initiative than central direction from the Umayyad capital. The Christian population was allowed to practice its religion under its own clerical establishment and left alone provided it paid taxes. Lands of towns that resisted were distributed among the Arabs and Berbers, with the Arabs generally living in towns on the rents of their estates and many of the Berbers engaged in sheep rearing as they did in their own homelands. The small Jewish population was concentrated in urban areas and seems to have fared much better than under the former Christian rulers. The Muslims themselves began to suffer from internal conflicts between Arabs and Berbers, as well as between tribal factions of the Arabs themselves. A Berber revolt in North Africa and Spain was only quelled by fresh Arab troops from Syria that strengthened the Arab element at the expense of the Berber in al-Andalus.

The violent overthrow of the Umayyads by the Abbasids in 750 led to a young prince of the fallen dynasty named Abd al-Rahman fleeing to North Africa. His distinguished ancestry won him a following of both Arabs and Berbers that enabled him to take power rapidly in Spain as a unifying influence above the existing factions. With his capital at Cordoba, Abd al-Rahman I established a rich and powerful state, symbolized by the palaces and the great mosque that he constructed during his reign (755–88). His court became a refuge for dissident Arabs and Persians wanting to escape his Abbasid enemies. The frontier with the Christians became stabilized along a northeast–southwest axis, with exchanges of raids and probes of each other's defenses (the defeat at Poitiers by Charles Martel in 732 having effectively ended attempts to invade French territory). Subsequent rulers generally maintained the position of the emirate, with the usual variations due to the abilities of the emirs themselves. The pinnacle of achievement was under Abd al-Rahman III (912–61), who felt strong enough to proclaim himself caliph in 929. The core of his regime was a professional army of largely Slavic slave soldiers, independent of the factions and loyal only to himself. He also maintained an efficient centralized bureaucracy.

The long and brilliant reign of Abd al-Rahman III finally ended after nearly fifty years in 961. His son al-Hakam II (961–76) and grandson Hisham II (976–1009) were weak and feeble rulers and the real power of the state, until his death in 1002, fell into the hands of the grand vizier and great statesman known to history by the honorific al-Mansur. He achieved a succession of spectacular victories over the neighboring Christian states, sacking Barcelona, Leon, and Burgos, burning the shrine of Santiago de Compostela, and bringing its great bronze bells to the mosque of Cordoba. He was similarly victorious against the Fatimids in North Africa. All of this success, however, and his extravagance and ruthlessness, led to a backlash against his son, who had the temerity to suggest himself as the legitimate heir to the puppet Caliph Hisham II. The outraged Arab court notables, who had long resented the Umayyads' reliance on their Berber troops, Slav mercenaries, and Jewish and Christian administrators, revolted and killed him in 1009. However, they were unable to maintain the integrity of the state, which soon broke into a collection of fragments ruled by provincial governors and warlords known as the *taifas* or "party kings," giving this name to the period from 1031, when the caliphate of Cordoba was formally abolished, to 1091. Needless to say, the descent of the mighty Umayyad regime into a handful of squabbling petty states was an unexpected boon to their Christian enemies, who lost no time in taking advantage of the situation. The Andalusi hold on North Africa was also fatally weakened and the Berber Almoravids would soon reverse the direction of hegemony across the Straits of Gibraltar.

The eleventh century can therefore be seen as a critical turning point in the destinies of all three great caliphates, the Abbasids in the east, the Umayyads of Cordoba in the west, and the Fatimids in the center. The Abbasids lost power to the Iranians and eventually to the Seljuk Turks; the Andalusians were squeezed by Berbers in the Maghrib and by Christians in the north of the Iberian Peninsula; and the Fatimids were confined to Egypt by their failures in Syria to the east and North Africa to the west, their millennial dreams of a universal Ismaili Shia state unrealized.

CENTRAL (OR INNER) ASIA[6]

This is the vast region in the interior of the Eurasian landmass, bounded to the south by towering mountain ranges and to the north by the Arctic tundra (see figure 1.4). The land can be divided into horizontal bands of forest (the so-called *taiga*), steppe, and desert. The primary ecological region is the steppe, the home of pastoral nomads since time immemorial. The eastern and western borders of

---

[6]Sources for this section include Barthold (1968), Christian (1998, chapters 10 and 11), Golden (1998), Hambly (1969), Lattimore (1973), McEvedy (1961), O'Brien (2002), and Sinor (1990).

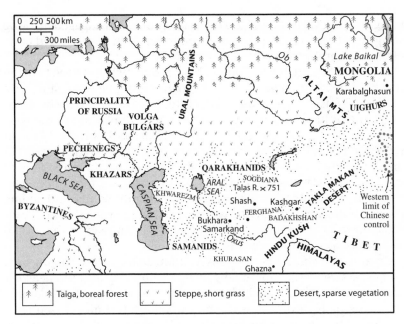

FIGURE 1.4. Central Asia.

Central Asia are shifting with the frontiers of the sedentary civilizations of China and Korea in the east and Russia and Iran in the west. The region as a whole is roughly six thousand miles from east to west and slightly less than half that distance from north to south (Sinor 1990, p. 19). It covers approximately the following areas: the modern post-Soviet states of Kyrgyzstan, Tajikistan, Turkmenistan, Kazakhstan, and Uzbekistan; Mongolia; and the parts of China known as Inner Mongolia and the Tibetan and Xinjiang Uighur Autonomous Regions (Hambly 1969, p. xi).

The interdependence between nomadic and sedentary peoples is one of the most persistent themes in history. The economic systems are complementary, with the possibility of mutual gain from the exchange of cereals and manufactures for animals, such as horses and camels, and animal products. The mobility of the mounted nomads, however, has also always left open the option of raiding and plundering the farms and cities of the settled populations. Outright conquest, on the other hand, has usually resulted in the acculturation and absorption of the much less numerous nomadic rulers by the subject populations. The Greeks and Romans had to contend with the Scythians and the Parthians, while the Huns, Avars, and Hungarians ravaged medieval Europe. The Han dynasty in China engaged in a long struggle with the Hsiung-nu, and various Turkic dynasties ruled parts of China after the fall of the Han in the third century A.D.

This is the region that Sir Halford Mackinder (1904) referred to in the title of his celebrated essay as "the geographical pivot of history." He saw this Eurasian "Heartland" as controlling, by its successive invasions, the outer crescent of the surrounding "Rimlands" to the east, west, and south. The ascendancy of the Heartland over the Rimland was halted but not ended, in his opinion, by the European voyages of discovery. The invention of the railway opened up the possibility of integrating the Heartland between China and Russia, thus once again imposing its domination over the surrounding Rimlands, and ending the era of Britannia ruling the world by ruling the waves.[7] In the year 1000, however, the greatest of all the nomadic invasions, that of the Mongols, was still in the future.

Central Asia should not be looked upon solely as the staging area for successive waves of nomadic invaders bursting into the peaceful sedentary civilizations on its borders. It has also served for millennia as a crossroads traversed by the flow of goods, technical inventions, art forms, and religions between the widely separated settled regions themselves. The fabled Silk Road, or rather Roads, have served for millennia not only to send silk, porcelain, and Chinese techniques westward but also to transmit Manichaeism, Nestorian Christianity, and Islam from the west and Buddhism from India to China, Korea, and Japan. Taxing the caravans that crossed the region was usually more profitable than simply plundering them. Even more profitable, however, was obtaining key commodities such as silk at the source in China and then trading it westwards, if this was possible by force of arms. This is precisely what a nomadic steppe empire attempted successfully in the middle of the sixth century.

This was what is known as the First Turk Empire, which was at its height in the second half of the sixth century. The steppe peoples linguistically form part of the Altaic group, subdivided into Turkic and Mongolian branches. The people who established this empire were known as the Gok, or Blue Turks, with blue the color of the sky having the connotation of "heavenly" or "divine." They were a confederation of tribes with one clan, the Ashina, recognized as dominant over all the others and providing the supreme ruler, known as the *kaghan,* and the

---

[7] As was presciently pointed out by Leopold Amery in his discussion of the essay at the Royal Geographical Society, however, it was control of the air, not land or water, that would determine the dominant hegemonic power of the new century, the last of the second millennium.

deputy, known as the *yabghu*. The tribe had a tradition of ironworking that may have been based on mines in their ancestral lands in the Altai mountain range. Their main striking force was armored cavalry that was possibly equipped by this industry.

At the time of their rise China was not unified and the single most powerful state, that of the Sinicized nomadic Northern Wei dynasty, was itself divided between a western branch with its capital at Chang'an and an eastern branch with its capital at Lo-yang. The Turks were able to extract enormous amounts of silk in exchange for horses at very favorable terms of trade in the light of the military pressure that they were able to apply. The silk was then sent westwards in the hands of Sogdian and other mercantile communities of the Silk Road, at great profit to the Turks themselves since they were successful in extending their control all the way to the frontiers of the Sassanian and Byzantine Empires in the west. They did not attempt any direct rule over other areas or peoples but exercised a loose form of suzerainty over the oasis cities and tribes along the Silk Road. Even so the realm was still so vast that it was divided between a senior eastern and a junior western branch. The empire fell when China became unified under the short-lived but powerful Sui dynasty (581–617), which had the military power to reassert Chinese command over the steppe. The vigorous emperors of the new Tang dynasty completed the work of the Sui in this respect, so that the suzerainty claimed by the Turk Empire over the entire length of the Silk Road passed to China itself.

The next contender for supremacy over the Silk Road was the Arab caliphate. The Arab forces overwhelmed the Sassanian Empire and occupied Iraq and western Iran very rapidly, but they took much longer to pacify the large eastern province of Khurasan and longer still to extend their authority across the Oxus to Bukhara, Samarkand, Shash (Tashkent), and other rich mercantile centers of Sogdiana. The merchant class seems to have been willing to reach an accommodation with the Arabs so long as they could continue to trade, but the landowners resisted more stubbornly along with their former Western Turk overlords. They also appealed for help to Tang China, their acknowledged suzerain, but not surprisingly in view of the distances got no effective assistance. The Arabs themselves sent diplomatic assurances to the Chinese that they would keep trade open. The Arabs and the Chinese were drawn into direct hostilities, however, when the ruler of Tashkent, an Arab client, attacked Ferghana, a Chinese client state. This led to the famous Battle of the Talas River in 751, where the Chinese were defeated when their Karluk Turkic allies switched sides. One notable consequence of the battle was that Chinese prisoners taken to Samarkand taught their captors the art of making paper. The two sides were never to confront each other directly again.

Transoxiana, and the associated provinces of Khwarezm and Khurasan, remained under Islamic influence and reached a peak of economic and cultural progress under the Iranian dynasty of the Samanids (819–999), who had their capital at Bukhara. As already noted, they acknowledged the spiritual authority of the Abbasid caliphate but were sovereign rulers in every other respect. They maintained the physical infrastructure of irrigation works for agriculture, water supply for the cities, and caravanserais for the great caravans that left in all directions toward Russia, China, and India, and supported religious and educational establishments to an unprecedented extent. Silver mines in the Badakhshan province in what is now Afghanistan were exploited and were the basis for a coinage of high quality. The military system was based on recruitment of military slaves from the steppes known as *ghulams* or cadets, who went through a lengthy period of training and promotion before becoming commanders and administrators in their thirties. The demand for military and other slaves stimulated a large trade in humans that was licensed and taxed by the state, with export taxes per slave of 30–70 dirhems as compared with an average price of 300 dirhems. Taxation covered costs of administration and a sumptuous court but was not so high as to discourage trade and industry. It is impressive that all military and civil officers were paid in cash, without the debilitating recourse to feudal land grants that most early states had to resort to.

The Turks of the steppes were becoming Islamicized themselves, however, thereby raising the level of their own social and political organization while maintaining their military prowess. A new dynasty, the Qarakhanids, a Turkic tribe converted to Islam by Sufi missionaries, arose in the vicinity of Kashgar and as we saw overthrew the Samanids just before the end of the millennium, when their state became wracked by internal dissension. Significantly, the *ulama*, the Muslim clergy of Bukhara, instructed the populace not to resist the invaders since they were also good Muslims. The cities of Transoxiana, now in post-Soviet Uzbekistan, have remained within the Turkic orbit to this day. While the Qarakhanids took Bukhara and the Samanid lands north of the Oxus, the area of Khurasan, south of the river, fell to another Turkic dynasty, the Ghaznavids (977–1186), whose leader, Mahmud, made devastating raids on India, returning each time with vast amounts of plunder.

In the east yet another powerful Turkic tribal confederation, the Uighurs, arose in 744 and held sway to 840. They were initially auxiliaries of the Tang who became increasingly dependent upon them for military assistance, particularly during the disruptive An Lu Shan rebellion of 755. In return they extracted a high price in terms of the familiar exchange of horses for silk, and also by frequently pillaging Chinese cities and provinces during the suppression of the rebellion. They were allied closely with the Sogdian merchant community and their ruler even adopted Manichaeism as a state religion under their influence. A Sogdian script, later adopted by the Mongols, was also introduced and literacy was apparently quite high. Their capital at Karabalghasun in Mongolia was a flourishing trading center for a very wide range of goods, including furs and other forest products from the north. It was surrounded by a considerable agricultural hinterland to feed the large population. Perhaps softened by their commercial success and peaceful religion, the Uighurs eventually fell victim to an invasion by their former vassals, the Kirghiz.

Two other Turkic empires in the western steppes were those of the Khazars in the area between the Black Sea and the Caspian, and the Volga Bulgars in the middle reaches of that river. Both were actively involved in the north–south and east–west flows of trade involving Slavic captives and northern furs, honey, wax, and amber, as well as silk and other luxury goods from the east, and silver from the Baghdad caliphate and the Samanid emirate of Bukhara. The Volga Bulgars converted to Islam while the Khazars adopted Judaism, presumably to avoid falling under the influence of either their Islamic or Orthodox Christian neighbors. Both states fell to the rising power of Kievan Rus before the end of the tenth century. Another Turkic tribe, the Pechenegs, never formed a state but their ferocity and martial prowess made them feared by all peoples who came in contact with them, whether sedentary or nomadic themselves.

South Asia[8]

Separated from Central Asia by the Himalayas and the Hindu Kush, India constitutes a subcontinental peninsula of the Eurasian landmass that is comparable with Western Europe in many ways (see figure 1.5). A distinctive culture arose out of a synthesis between the original Dravidian inhabitants and the Aryan pastoral nomads that entered from the north over three thousand years ago. An upper caste of

[8] Sources for this section include Arasaratnam (1964), Kosambi (1969), O'Brien (2002), Schmidt (1999), Stein (1998, chapters 1–3), and Thapar (2002).

Brahmins and warriors was supported by the harvests of the richly fertile Indo-Gangetic plain cultivated by the labor of the *shudra* caste. A number of kingdoms arose in the plain while the foothills of the Himalayas were the location of some tribal republics. The kingdom of Magadha on the lower Ganges eventually dominated the entire plain in the middle of the first millennium B.C. because of its favorable location for internal as well as overseas trade. Local deposits of iron ore gave it an edge in weaponry, while forests provided timber as well as a plentiful supply of war elephants. Northwestern India was subject to considerable Iranian influence and Taxila became a center for the fruitful exchange of ideas between the Indian and Persian traditions. The invasion of Alexander the Great in 330 B.C. extended Greek and Persian cultural influences in Gandhara, leaving their distinctive mark in Buddhist statuary. The southern Deccan plateau traversed by a succession of rivers also provided a variety of agricultural possibilities. A wide range of craft specialties and a distinctive cotton textile manufacture was developed from early times.

The Malabar and Coromandel Coasts in the west and east respectively had trading contacts with the Persian Gulf and the Red Sea and with both mainland and insular Southeast Asia. Roman coins have been found in considerable abundance, attesting to this trade. The Mediterranean traders also obtained Southeast Asian goods in the Indian ports, thus stimulating Indian relations with the source of those goods. Hindu and Buddhist religious and cultural influences, including fundamental political ideas about kingship and statecraft, were thereby transmitted to the emerging new states in Cambodia, Champa, Java, and Sumatra. The monuments of Angkor Wat, Borobudur, and Prambanan are the most visible evidence of the depth of this Indian influence.

Political unification of the Indo-Gangetic plain and much of southern India was achieved by the Mauryan Empire (321–185 B.C.) founded by Chandra Gupta Maurya that arose in the wake of the invasion of Alexander the Great. Chandra Gupta successfully challenged Alexander's Seleucid heir Nicator for areas in what is now eastern Afghanistan and the two states established peaceful diplomatic relations, with the Greek ambassador Megasthenes leaving a valuable account of India. The next Mauryan emperor made extensive conquests in the south and west. The third ruler of this dynasty was the famous Ashoka, remarkable for his piety and support of Buddhism to which he turned in remorse from his bloody conquest of Kalinga, the last component in the completion of the Mauryan Empire. The empire disintegrated soon after his death in 232 B.C. Seleucid rule in northwest India was followed

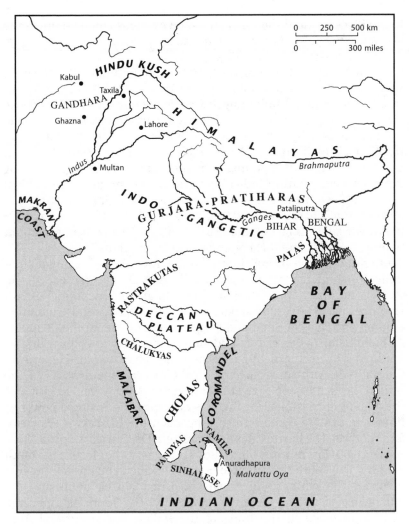

FIGURE 1.5. South Asia

by the emergence of the so-called Indo-Greek kings, of whom the most significant was Menander (155–130 B.C.). Two groups of Central Asian nomads, the Sakas and the Kushans, succeeded the Indo-Greeks and stimulated trade between India and the Silk Road in the first two centuries A.D. The Mauryan Royal Highway from Pataliputra to Taxila, which survives today as the Grand Trunk Road, was one segment of this trade route which then went on to Kabul and through Bactria to the Black Sea and the Caspian. Trade overseas could go down the Ganges to the Bay of Bengal and thence to Southeast Asia and Ceylon, or Sri Lanka as it is known today.

Another powerful empire, the Guptas, lasted from the fourth to the sixth century A.D. This is generally considered as the "classical age" of Indian civilization, culminating in the reign of Harsha (606–47), whose extensive conquests in northern India fell apart after his death. The age was marked both by material prosperity, at least for the ruling elite, and remarkable intellectual and cultural achievements. Both Hinduism and Buddhism were encouraged by the state and also supported by private donations from individuals and merchant guilds. Buddhism spread to Ceylon and Southeast Asia, as well as to Iran, Central Asia, and eventually to China along the Silk Road. Several Chinese Buddhist pilgrims visited India, such as Fa Hsien and Hsüan Tsang, and left notable records of their experiences and impressions.

After the decline of the Gupta Empire a number of regional kingdoms arose in the north as well as in the Deccan plateau. As in Western Europe, none of them could command the preponderance of resources necessary to dominate all the others and impose a unified empire. The Palas in Bihar and Bengal were notable for their support of Buddhism in the eighth and ninth centuries, and the Gurjara-Pratiharas in northern India resisted the incursions of Huns from Central Asia with some success. In the Deccan the division of the terrain into a number of river valleys running from west to east and the adjoining coastal strips made it difficult for any single power to dominate despite fierce struggles between the Chalukyas, Pallavas, and Pandyas. The Rastrakutas of the western Deccan were a prominent presence but lost power back to the Chalukyas by the close of the tenth century. The south saw notable cultural and religious developments involving the synthesis of Aryan and Dravidian elements and the emergence of a distinct Tamil personality. The south also became actively involved in the trade of the Indian Ocean. Several Arab merchants settled on the western Malabar coast, giving rise to the so-called Mapilla Muslim community that was later to play a significant role in both trade and the spread of Islam to Southeast Asia. By the turn of the first millennium the powerful dynasty of the Cholas rose to prominence, aggressively pursuing its interests not only on land but overseas in Ceylon and Southeast Asia as well.

Immigrants from northern India settled in the island of Ceylon some time around the fifth century B.C., probably sailing down the west coast. The original inhabitants were an Australoid people who do not seem to have put up any resistance. The location of the island made it a natural entrepôt for east–west traffic across the Indian Ocean. It was well-known to the Romans under the name of Taprobane and was also frequented by Persian, Arab, and Chinese vessels. Further immigration came from south India, specifically from the Pandya kingdom according to the traditional accounts. The first settlements were in the northwest along the Malvattu Oya River, with a capital established at Anuradhapura. Rice cultivation was the mainstay of the economy, supported by what eventually became a very elaborate system of irrigation.

Despite being devout Buddhists the immigrants brought the Indo-Aryan caste system along with them, though it operated in a looser and more flexible way with the main distinction being between agricultural and nonagricultural occupations. Relations with Buddhist centers in India and Southeast Asia were very close; Ceylon was the home of the more austere and pure Hinayana or Theravada school of Buddhism that was adopted in Burma, Cambodia, and Thailand. Ceylon was actively involved in the political conflicts of the southern Indian dynasties. The Cholas invaded Ceylon in 993, sacking the capital and annexing the island to their kingdom until 1070, at which time the Sinhalese recovered it. Ceylon was also involved in conflicts over trade with Burma and the Sumatran trading state of Srivijaya.

SOUTHEAST ASIA[9]

Southeast Asia can be defined as all of the Eurasian landmass east of India and south of China, together with the extensive chain of islands "flung like a girdle of jade around the Equator" (see figure 1.6). The natural division of the region is between the mainland and the islands of the archipelago. In terms of contemporary nation-states, the mainland comprises Burma, Thailand, Laos, Cambodia, Vietnam, and Malaysia while the islands comprise Singapore, Indonesia, the Philippines, Brunei, and East Timor. Malaysia, occupying the long narrow blade of the peninsula known to antiquity as the "Golden Khersonese" (Wheatley 1980), is best considered geographically and culturally as part of the island rather than the mainland world. The most prominent geographical feature of the mainland is the series of long river valleys, generally running north to south: the Irrawaddy, Salween, Maenam Chao Phraya, and Mekong, as well as the shorter

[9]Sources for this section include Coedes (1968), Hall (1968, part I), O'Brien (2002), Reid (1988), Tarling (1992, part I), Wang (1998), and Wolters (1999).

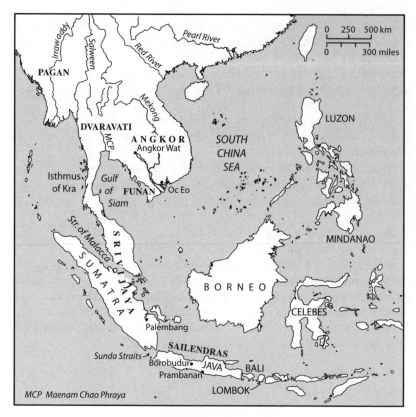

FIGURE 1.6. Southeast Asia.

Red River running west to east. The plains along these river valleys and those of parallel smaller rivers, and particularly the silt-rich deltas, are fertile areas for rice cultivation, the crop that has been the staple of the peoples in this area for millennia. Irrigation in areas of lower rainfall, such as the Dry Zone of central Burma, was, however, responsible for some of the highest yields and formed the economic base of early kingdoms and empires (Stargardt 1986). The river valleys are usually flanked by forested uplands that are more difficult to cultivate except on a slash and burn basis. The main islands of the archipelago are Sumatra, Java, Bali, Lombok, Borneo, Celebes, Mindanao, and Luzon but there are many other smaller islands of great economic and historical importance. The region is fully subject to the play of the seasonal monsoon winds, blowing from the southwest from May to September and the northeast from November to March. The average rainfall is high and on the mainland is concentrated during the period of the southwest monsoon.

The population of the islands and the peninsula is Malayo-Polynesian, descendants of a stock originally from southern China that migrated first to Taiwan and then to Southeast Asia and Polynesia as far east as Easter Island, and possibly even as far west as Madagascar. The mainland populations of Burma, Thailand, Cambodia, and Vietnam are a blend of Malayo-Polynesians and tribes originally from the area of western China and Tibet. The Khmer of Cambodia and the Mon of southern parts of Burma and Thailand have an Austronesian language, in contrast to the Sino-Tibetan languages of the Burmese and the Thai. The stress on the "Indianization" of Southeast Asia, by both Indian as well as European authors of an earlier era, such as George Coedes (1968), has been replaced in current research by an emphasis on the autonomy of the region, for example, in the authoritative work of O. W. Wolters (1999). The indigenous peoples of the region developed wet-rice cultivation, bronze and iron metallurgy, and distinctive cultural, social, and political traits well before historical times, and independently of India and China. Because of their intermediate location they did become subject in historical times to powerful influences from the great civilizations of their Indian and Chinese neighbors, but these have been blended into their own distinctive cultural patterns. The Hindu and Buddhist influences were also probably deliberately sought out by native peoples and rulers, rather than simply transplanted by Indian immigration or conquest.

The earliest political entity in the region to emerge in the historical record is known as Funan, and was located in the southern tip of the Gulf of Siam in an area that now straddles the borders of Cambodia and Vietnam. After the Han dynasty fell in A.D. 220. China entered the period known as that of the "Three Kingdoms" consisting of Wei in the north, Shu in the southwest, and Wu in the southeast (Hucker 1975, map 4). Access to Central Asia and the west through the Kansu Corridor was open only to Wei and the other possible overland route across the Burma–Yunnan border was open only to Shu. As Wang Gungwu (1998, chapter 3) points out, the only option left to the rulers of Wu if they wanted to trade with the west was overseas through ports in Southeast Asia.

The traditional overseas east–west trade route at that time involved transshipping goods and passenger traffic across the Isthmus of Kra, which at thirty-five miles is the narrowest crossing of the Malay Peninsula. The all-sea alternative of going through either the Straits of Malacca or the Sunda Straits would only be developed more than a century later. The nearest suitable port for Wu to consider was the site known to archaeologists as Oc Eo in the kingdom of Funan, because the fertile Mekong delta in which it was located could provide the necessary rice supplies for merchants and crews while they were waiting for the goods to be transshipped, and also because it was situated on the Gulf just opposite the points at which western and Indian ships unloaded passengers and freight on the Isthmus. The ruler of Wu sent embassies to open trade and diplomatic relations with the barbarian polity of Funan some time before the middle of the third century, and it is to the records of these Wu officials that we owe our knowledge of Funan. The "gains from trade" for the "small open economy" of Funan must have been great and provided the resources for territorial expansion around the rim of the Gulf of Siam to consolidate its control, and also for extensive irrigation works enhancing its agricultural productivity. After the Straits route was developed, however, shipping could bypass Funan, presumably causing its revenues to decline, and it ultimately fell to a Khmer state known as Chenla in the sixth century.

After the shift from the passage across the Isthmus of Kra to the Straits of Malacca and the associated Sunda Straits between Java and Sumatra it was inevitable that control over the new route would pass to a state in one of these islands. From the seventh to the eleventh century, this state was based at Palembang on the southeast coast of Sumatra and is known to history as Srivijaya. In order to fulfill its role as a trading empire, Srivijaya had to secure control over the supplies of the natural resource products of the region demanded by the Chinese, Persian, and Arab merchants, and also feed the merchants and crews during the long stopovers between the shifts in the direction of the winds. The first objective was met by a network of tributary relationships based on alliances backed ultimately by force, using mercenary troops and local levies as well as an informal but effective navy of Malay sea nomads. The rice supplies came across the straits from the allied Javanese kingdom of a dynasty known as the Sailendras. With these methods Srivijaya was able to exercise a degree of monopoly control over the seaborne trade between the west and China, now very lucrative during these centuries because of the prosperity of the Tang and Sung at one end and the Damascus, Baghdad, and Cairo caliphates at the other. Sustained by these revenues the rulers were able to maintain a court on elaborate Indianized lines and to support an extensive Buddhist religious establishment.

On the mainland also new states began to emerge around the turn of the millennium or soon thereafter, such as Pagan in Burma,

Dvaravati in Thailand, and Angkor in Cambodia, all of which were heavily influenced by Buddhism and other Indian cultural influences.

East Asia (China, Korea, and Japan)[10]

China, like India, can be considered as a subcontinent of Eurasia (see figure 1.7). It is bounded in the east by the Pacific Ocean, in the west by the steppe, deserts, and mountain ranges of Central Asia, in the south by the tropical jungles of Southeast Asia, and in the north by terrain unsuitable for the settled agriculture that has always been an abiding aspect of Chinese civilization. The fertile valleys of the Yellow River and the Yangtze have provided the agricultural foundation for all subsequent development. Characteristic of the North China Plain of the Yellow River area is the wind-blown loess dust that has built up the "yellow earth" that provided the ancestral home of the distinctive Chinese civilization. The earliest state was that of the Shang dynasty in the second half of the second millennium B.C., marked by its bronze weapons and ritual vessels, and the earliest Chinese ideographic script on the so-called "oracle bones." The bronze metallurgy and chariot warfare of the Shang are reminiscent of Indo-European parallels further west, but it is still an open question as to whether this is a case of cultural diffusion across the steppes of Central Asia or of independent development within China itself.

The fall of the Shang dynasty was followed by the nomadic Eastern Zhou dynasty, which introduced a more decentralized regime, sometimes characterized as "feudal." A long period of disunity eventually led to seven large regional kingdoms struggling fiercely for power during the "Warring States" period (403–221 B.C.). An increase in agricultural productivity, associated with the introduction of iron implements, generated larger revenues for the states and supported larger armies, supplemented by cavalry forces in imitation of nomadic methods of warfare. A new class of professional administrators and specialists arose, tending to replace kinship-based nobility with criteria based on merit and achievement. There was also an intellectual ferment, during which the three major Chinese philosophical systems of Confucianism, Taoism, and Legalism arose.

---

[10]Sources for this section include Blunden and Elvin (1983, parts 1 and 2), Ebrey (1996, chapters 1–6), FitzGerald (1966), Gernet (1982, parts 1–5), Hall (1970, chapters 1–6), Huang (1990), Hucker (1975), O'Brien (2002), Pulleyblank (1955), Reischauer and Fairbank (1962, chapters 1–6, 10–11), Ropp (1990), and Twitchett (1973).

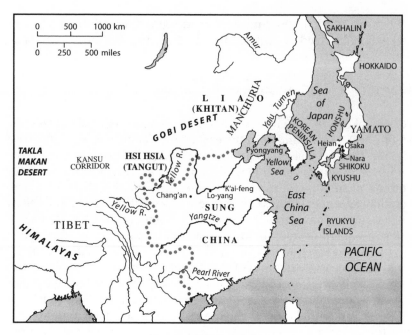

FIGURE 1.7. East Asia.

The protracted power struggles of the age of the Warring States ended with the victory of the western border state of Ch'in in 221 B.C., which Bodde (1981, p. 41) calls "the most important single date in Chinese history before the abolition of the monarchy in 1912." Its ruler took the name of Shi Huang Di, First August Emperor, and was the first sole ruler of the entire country. A centralized despotic regime was imposed, with standardized language, laws, weights, and measures administered by a civilian bureaucracy supported by a powerful army, terra cotta replicas of which are on display in his recently rediscovered tomb in Xian. The Great Wall was built and consolidated, and a number of other massive public works undertaken. The strain on society was so great that the empire fell shortly after Shi Huang Di's death in 210 B.C.

Imperial unity was soon restored, in 206 B.C., by the Han dynasty that took China to a level of achievement that challenged that of the contemporaneous Roman Empire in the west and the Mauryan Empire in India. Frontiers were extended into Korea in the north and Vietnam in the south, and deep penetration made into Central Asia in the west. A unified bureaucratic system, on more moderate Confucian lines rather than the harsh Legalism of the short-lived Ch'in

Empire, was established, modified originally by fiefdoms granted to allies and relatives. By the workings of the familiar dynastic cycle that has marked the pattern of Chinese history the Han eventually also lost the "Mandate of Heaven" after disruptive peasant rebellions and civil war in A.D. 220.

The fall of the Han led to several centuries of disunity. Generals and warlords, many of steppe nomad extraction, contended for power. One Turkic clan, the Toba, established the Northern Wei dynasty (386–534), based on the old Han capital of Lo-yang. It attempted to build a unified state by combining its Sinicized Turkic tribal aristocracy with ethnic Chinese institutions and landowning families, but without lasting success. Population shifted from the north to south of the Yangtze Valley, as the native Chinese tried to escape from the perils of civil strife and take advantage of the abundant availability of rice-growing land. People also increasingly turned to Buddhism as a spiritual refuge from temporal insecurity. Eventually, the dynastic cycle came full circle again when a family of generals established the short-lived but important Sui dynasty (581–618), whose main achievement was the construction of a canal system connecting the Yangtze Valley to the north. Just as the brief reign of the Ch'in led to the long and glorious period of the Han, the Sui was immediately followed by the Tang dynasty (618–907), which took China to a level beyond even that of the Han.

The nearly three centuries of the Tang were marked by the spread of Chinese culture and influence to Central Asia, Korea, and Japan. While the bureaucracy was based to a larger extent than before on an examination system, power was also decentralized to local aristocratic families. Economic expansion was considerable, with the spread of a money economy based on silver and the growth of merchant guilds. The center of economic growth continued to shift toward the rice-based economy of the south, with a greater reliance on markets and trade. Artistic styles were more open to Central Asian influences, and Buddhism flourished not only in religious terms but also with considerable amounts of landed and other forms of wealth passing into the hands of monastic institutions.

By the middle decade of the eighth century, however, the familiar signs of dynastic decline and difficulty began to appear. As we have seen, the Arabs defeated a Tang army at the Battle of the Talas River in 751, checking the dynasty's control over Central Asia, and there followed a devastating rebellion led by a general of Central Asian heritage, An Lu Shan, that was suppressed but only at great cost and loss of prestige by the ruling house. Fiscal crises led to the sequestration of monastic lands and the confiscation of their wealth. The dynasty lingered on until 907, after which it was succeeded by a period of contesting regimes known as the Five Dynasties, ended by the establishment of the Sung dynasty in 960, with its capital at K'ai-feng.

The Korean peninsula southeast of the Yalu and Tumen rivers that divide it from Manchuria has always had a distinct ethnic and linguistic identity that sets it apart from China, despite millennia of cultural and political influence from its giant neighbor. The Korean people apparently migrated into the peninsula from Manchuria in prehistoric times, speaking a Ural-Altaic language that has some affinities with the Tungusic tongue of some nomadic tribes of northern Manchuria. They developed a sedentary agricultural economy through the Paleolithic and Bronze ages, ruled by a hereditary tribal aristocracy sustained by a peasantry and a large servile class. The country was conquered by the Han dynasty in 108 B.C. and administered by four commanderies or military districts, the largest of which was based at a site close to Pyongyang, the capital of the present state of North Korea. Chinese political control waned after the fall of the Han and three independent Korean kingdoms emerged: Koguryo, ruling over what is now North Korea and southern Manchuria, Paekche in the southwest, and Silla in the southeast, the latter two divided by the mountain chain that forms the spine of the peninsula.

The three kingdoms all prospered on the basis of active trade with both China and the Japanese islands. Buddhism entered from China and was adopted as the popular religion, replacing the earlier shamanism, which still, however, continued to survive in vestigial form. Government and administration were based on Confucian models. Chinese ideographs were adapted, with some difficulty, to the writing of the entirely different Korean language. Ceramic and other arts developed under Chinese influence but with a distinctive local style. Early in the seventh century the second ruler of the Sui dynasty launched a great invasion of Koguryo in an attempt to gain back control that had been lost after the fall of the Han. The invasion was repelled by stubborn Korean resistance, which hastened the collapse of the short-lived Sui dynasty. The Tang also attempted another unsuccessful invasion, but eventually obtained the acknowledgement of Chinese sovereignty after yet another invasion in alliance with Silla. A unified Silla kingdom ruled the entire country within the Tang tributary orbit from 668 to 935, when it was overthrown by a new northern state, a successor to Koguryo known as Koryo, from which the present name of the country is derived. Koryo, and all subsequent Korean regimes, acknowledged Chinese sovereignty until 1895, which was the year of the defeat of the Manchu Qing dynasty in the Sino-Japanese Wars.

Japan, consisting of the four main islands of Hokkaido, Honshu, Shikoku, and Kyushu, from north to south, off the northeast coast of the Eurasian landmass, is a sort of bookend to the northwestern analogue of the British Isles. Unlike the latter, however, it has been much less subject to invasion and immigration in historical times and is unique in the degree of its long relative isolation from foreign influence, in comparison with other major modern nations. This has given its history and development a special cast, as has often been noted.

With the northern tip of Hokkaido at the same latitude as Montreal and the southern tip of Kyushu just above that of Jacksonville, Florida,[11] and washed by the warm Japan current, the climate is relatively mild without extremes of winter cold and summer heat. The land is mountainous, less than a fifth of it being arable. Compensating for this are timber from abundant forests and a rich variety of fish from the surrounding seas. The mountainous terrain has also led to the land being broken up into relatively small cultivable units, making political centralization difficult.

The ethnic composition of the early inhabitants is still a matter of controversy. The language, however, belongs to the same Ural-Altaic family as Korean, which would seem to indicate a northeast Asian origin. Archaeology has identified the Jomon culture, exemplified by "corded-ware" pottery, of a population of hunter-gatherers from about 10,000 B.C. Only very much later, around 300 B.C., appears what is known as the Yayoi culture, with irrigated wet-rice cultivation and bronze and iron metallurgy. The first signs of stratified political organization begin with the appearance of large burial mounds of a ruling elite of horse-riding warriors. Similarities with Korea are apparent, but it is not known for certain whether the horse-riders were invaders from the mainland or indigenous adaptations to external influences. Society was composed of hereditary classes, known as *uji*, each of which had a leader associated with an ancestral spirit or *kami*. The dominant class in the Yamato region of the Nara Plain, near Osaka, claimed descent from the sun goddess Amaterasu Omikami. The present imperial family of Japan is directly descended from this clan, which traces its undoubtedly mythical beginnings back to 660 B.C.

The Yamato rulers had extensive contacts with Chinese civilization, mostly through the intermediation of Korea. There even seems to

---

[11] See the interesting map on p. 453 of Reischauer and Fairbank (1962).

have been a Japanese enclave on the southern Korean coast. There is also evidence of considerable Korean immigration around this time. Access to more advanced technology conferred an advantage in the competitive struggle between the various *uji* for power in Japan. The gravitational attraction of Chinese culture was greatly enhanced after the Sui and Tang restored imperial unity early in the seventh century. The next three centuries saw a sustained and massive absorption of influences from China into the emerging Japanese state.

The founder and architect of the program of Sinification was Crown Prince Shotoku, related on his mother's side to the Soga, a great clan of Korean immigrant origin. He promulgated a seventeen-article constitution in 604, adopting the Buddhist Tripitaka and various Confucian principles of loyalty and service to the state and the emperor. Another major and lasting innovation was the adoption of the Chinese calendrical system. He also launched a series of embassies to the Sui, and later Tang, capital at Chang'an, each consisting of several ships and hundreds of men that brought back Buddhist Confucian texts and other artifacts of mainland civilization. The embassies continued long after his death in 622. Several Japanese also studied religion, statecraft, and other arts in China before returning with the benefits of the knowledge that they gained. All this is very reminiscent of Japanese involvement with the West after the Meiji Restoration in 1868. In 646 the so-called Taika Reforms were undertaken, involving a wholesale reform of the Japanese government, legal system, and administration on Chinese lines.

New capitals, on the lines of Chang'an, were set up at Nara from 710 to 754, and later at Heian (Kyoto) from 794, to be the centers from which the new imperial system was to radiate. It was not easy, however, to graft impersonal Confucian principles, based on merit and performance, on to the Japanese reality of personal and regional affiliations. Increasingly, the outward forms of bureaucratic and Chinese imperial logic and efficiency came to be supplemented by the substance of Japanese clan-based and local relationships. The sophisticated metropolitan Heian culture was eventually to give way to the cruder reality of provincial warlords and a Japanese variant of feudalism.

Chapter 2

THE WORLD ECONOMY AT THE TURN OF THE FIRST MILLENNIUM

THE FIRST CHAPTER DIVIDED the Afro-Eurasian Ecumene into seven world regions on the basis of a pragmatic mix of geographical, political, and cultural features and provided an outline of the historical and institutional evolution of each of them approximately up to the year 1000. The present chapter will examine the nature of the economic and other links *between* these regions, or at least some overlapping subsets of them. These links will not be limited purely to trade, or the exchange of goods, but will also consider the movement of people such as slaves, merchants, pilgrims, mercenaries, and others involved in cultural interaction and exchange in the broader sense, resulting in the diffusion of ideas and technical innovations as well as religious beliefs and practices.[1]

As the reader will already have noted from the first chapter, the only one of the seven regions that experienced regular and *direct* contacts with *all* of the others, as well as with sub-Saharan Africa, was the Islamic World of North Africa and Southwest Asia. Muslims and the Roman Catholic Christians of Western Europe fought and traded with each other in Spain and Italy as well as Sicily and other Mediterranean islands; Muslims wrested part of their empire from the Greek Orthodox Byzantines of Eastern Europe and spent almost every subsequent year in further military conflict at some point along their long borders, while at the same time often engaging in trade and diplomacy for mutual interest; Muslims exchanged salt and textiles for West African gold; Muslim armies invaded Central Asia and also had to fend off attacks by nomadic steppe raiders, while at the same time conducting extensive trade and missionary activity by Sufi mystics and others; Muslim armies invaded India, while there was extensive trade by both land and sea with India and by sea with Southeast Asia; finally, Muslim and Tang Chinese armies clashed in Central Asia at the Battle of the Talas River in 751, the caliphate sent several embassies to the

[1] The chapter draws on Findlay (1998) in several places.

Tang capitals, and Muslim merchants had sizable colonies in southern China and even got as far to the north and east as Korea. It is no surprise therefore that Arab and Persian geographers were the best-informed people about conditions all over the Afro-Eurasian Ecumene in those times (Kramers 1931).[2]

South Asia was also a fairly well-connected region, again by virtue of its relatively central geographical position, with Indian textiles being exported directly to East and Southeast Asia, Central Asia, sub-Saharan Africa, and the Muslim World. Central Asia bordered on and was in close touch with all the other regions except Western Europe, sub-Saharan Africa and Southeast Asia. Steppe nomads confronted Byzantium and Kievan Rus as well as trading extensively with each of them; Indian goods as well as Buddhism moved along the Silk Road, and China was a permanent source of cultural and economic influence on the Central Asian tribes. East Asia and Southeast Asia were clearly aware of Byzantium but did not have any sustained direct bilateral trade or other cultural exchanges with sub-Saharan Africa or Eastern Europe, and certainly not with Western Europe. In fact Western Europe was the most isolated of all the world regions at that time, along with sub-Saharan Africa, the former only being in direct touch with the Islamic World and Eastern Europe, and the latter only with the Islamic World and South Asia. To summarize, the Islamic World had contact with all seven other regions; South Asia with five; Central and East Asia with four; Southeast Asia and Eastern Europe with three; and sub-Saharan Africa and Western Europe with only two.

These interrelationships are summarized in table 2.1, which presents a stylized matrix showing the major direct interregional flows existing in ca. 1000. The remainder of the chapter will be concerned with outlining the nature of these flows. Before we begin, however, it makes sense to point out the overwhelming importance of geography for the narrative that is to follow. As figure 2.1 shows, Eurasia is an extremely long landmass, aligned on an east–west axis.[3] South and Southeast Asia had very different climatic and resource endowments than either China or Europe, while China had a highly evolved and ancient civilization, produced tea, and had well-developed industries producing luxury goods such as porcelain and silk. The land-abundant steppes of Central Asia were the source of horses, while the relatively

[2] See, in particular, his map (figure 12, p. 79) "showing the geographical extension of Islamic rule and its commercial influence in the tenth century A.D.," including the wide distribution of Muslim coins.

[3] This map draws on a variety of sources, including Abu-Lughod (1989) and Chaudhuri (1985).

TABLE 2.1. Interregional trade flows, ca. 1000.

From \ To	Western Europe	Eastern Europe	Islamic World	Central Asia	Sub-Saharan Africa	South Asia	Southeast Asia	East Asia
Western Europe	◻	Swords	Slaves, swords	—	—	—	—	—
Eastern Europe	Slaves, furs, silver	◻	Slaves, furs, silver	Furs, swords	—	—	—	—
Islamic World	Pepper, spices, textiles, silk, silver	Textiles, silver	◻	Textiles	Salt, textiles, manufactures, swords, horses	War horses	Gold	Spices
Central Asia	—	Silver	Paper, silver, slaves	◻	—	Silver, reexports from China and Muslim world	—	Horses
Sub-Saharan Africa	—	—	Gold, slaves, ivory, rice	—	◻	Timber, iron	—	—
South Asia	—	—	Pepper, spices, silk, teak, textiles	Pepper, textiles	Textiles	◻	Textiles, pepper	Textiles
Southeast Asia	—	—	Spices, perfumes	—	—	Silk, spices, teak, rice, rubies	◻	Perfumes, spices, sandalwood
East Asia	—	—	Silk, porcelain	Silk, tea	—	Silk, porcelain	Silk, copper, cash	◻

underdeveloped regions of Europe and Africa provided slaves and precious metals.

There was thus a natural basis for interregional trade, including trade between East and West. As the map makes clear, there were two routes which could in principle connect the two extremities of Eurasia, the first overland and the second by sea. There were specific problems associated with each route. The major problem that had to be solved if the overland route was to be made viable was that of

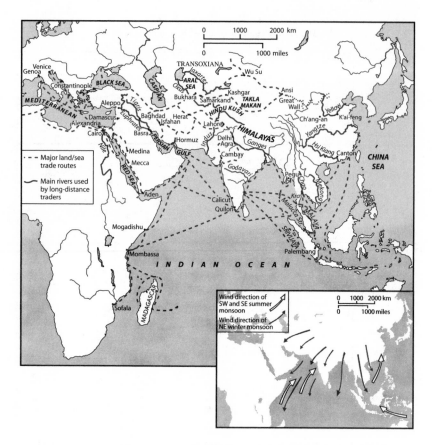

FIGURE 2.1. The land and sea routes.

providing security for merchants as they crossed the vast expanses of
Central Asia. Naturally, this was easier to do when centralized political
control existed over the region, or at least when Chinese, European, or
Middle Eastern empires extended as far as possible into the interior.
This dependence of trade on security was recognized more than two
centuries ago by the great Edward Gibbon, who when describing
Italian trade in Asia during the *Pax Mongolica* wrote that "the waters
of the Oxus, the Caspian, the Volga, and the Don opened a rare and
laborious passage for the gems and spices of India; and, after three
months' march, the caravans of Carizme met the Italian vessels in
the harbours of Crimea…. But this land or water carriage could only
be practicable when Tartary was united under a wise and powerful
monarch" (Gibbon 1907, pp. 122–23).

According to Philip Curtin (1984, p. 90), "with comparative suddenness, between about 200 B.C. and the beginning of the Christian era, regular overland trade came into existence across central Asia from China to the eastern Mediterranean," with trade between India and China being commonplace as well. The timing is explained by the emergence of a strong, unified China under the Han at one end of the route and of the Roman and Parthian Empires at the other. The key to the overland route, according to Curtin, was the Takla Makan desert in Xinjiang province, sufficiently arid so as to discourage steppe tribes from loitering with intent there, but endowed with a series of oases offering food and water for merchants (ibid., pp. 93–94). From there, caravans could travel westward to Transoxiana, from where they could continue west to the Roman Empire, or south to India.

There were two major problems concerning the sea route. The first was a technical one, having to do with the monsoon winds, which blew from the southwest during the summer (facilitating trips from Arabia or East Africa to India), and from the northeast during the winter across the Arabian Sea (facilitating the return journey). These winds also encouraged a seasonal pattern of sailing further east. The second leg of the sea journey was from India to Malaya, and the third from Malaya or Indonesia to China or Japan (ibid., p. 97). This seasonality encouraged specialization along each stretch of the journey, although some traders made the entire journey from Arabia to China, as we have already noted.

The second problem with the sea route was a political one. As can be seen from the map, there were two bottlenecks that had to be negotiated if goods were to pass between China and Europe. The first was the Malayan peninsula and Indonesian archipelago, and the second was the Arabian Peninsula. Clearly, control over either of these bottlenecks could give rise to substantial monopoly rents, and so a series of regimes arose in both regions that used military power to levy substantial taxes on trade. When the overland route was functioning well, their rents should have declined; when it broke down as a result of political instability, their rents should have increased. Western Europe's geographical peripherality, and in particular its encirclement by the Muslim World, meant that it was especially vulnerable to such monopolistic practices. The north–south orientation of Africa, located in just the wrong place from a European point of view, meant that European navigational techniques would have to be highly developed for them to find a way around the Arabian bottleneck.

We begin by discussing the state of both the overland and the sea routes at the turn of the millennium, and since it was the Islamic World that lay at the center of the world economy, it is convenient to first summarize the Islamic World's relationships with each of the other regions. We then proceed to describe some of the trade relationships that existed at the eastern end of Eurasia, through the prism of Sung China's interactions with other regions. The chapter next explores trade across the sea routes linking China with South and Southeast Asia, and ends with a more extended account of the interactions between the Muslim World and Western Europe, since this will allow us to introduce several of the themes that will crop up later in this book.

The Golden Age of Islam

The Arab conquests of the seventh and early eighth centuries united, for the first time in history, the Mediterranean world of Rome and the ancient empires on the one hand, and Mesopotamia and Iran on the other. Alexander's empire disintegrated into the competing domains of his generals at his death and the eastern frontier of the Roman Empire never reached the Euphrates. The Arabs unified the Byzantine possessions of Egypt, Syria, Palestine, and North Africa with the Sassanian territories of Mesopotamia and Iran. In addition they extended their eastern frontiers into Transoxiana, Afghanistan, and India. The way was thus opened for the movement of people, goods, techniques, and ideas flowing both east and west in one vast integrated space unified by Islam and the Arabic language. It is true that conversion took place only slowly and that Persian, Aramaic, Coptic, and Berber did not disappear overnight, but Arabic rapidly became the language of administration, law, and commerce as well as of the Islamic faith over most of the area.

The separation of the Byzantine and Sassanian worlds was aptly indicated by the difference in their monetary systems. The Byzantine coinage was effectively a monometallic standard based on the gold *solidus* or *nomisma*, of approximately 4.55 grammes of gold, while the Sassanian was also monometallic but based on silver, the *drachma* of approximately 4.15 grammes of silver. For the first few decades after the Arab conquests these coins continued to circulate and be minted as before, each within its own area of the caliphate. In the early 690s, however, the Umayyad caliph Abd al-Malik (685–705) undertook a fundamental monetary reform, replacing both the earlier systems with a bimetallic standard, a *dinar* of approximately 4.25 grammes of gold and a *dirhem* of approximately 2.97 grammes of silver, with an official exchange ratio of 20 dirhems to the dinar, implying a gold–silver ratio of fourteen to one for the same weight of metal. The new coins were also notable for the fact that they were purely epigraphic in character, i.e., they contained no representations of the monarch or deity as was customary but only an invocation to the Almighty, the name of the ruling monarch, and the date and place at which the coin was minted.

The fusion of the two empires was thus now symbolized by the new bimetallic standard replacing their older gold and silver monometallic regimes. As we shall see the caliphate could back up the monetary reform with enormous reserves of both the precious metals, and with continued access to fresh supplies. The entire royal treasury of the Sassanians, consisting of 9 billion drachmas according to one estimate, was seized intact and large amounts of gold and silver plate were obtained from the former Byzantine provinces of Egypt and Syria. The gold mines of Nubia and West Africa were also accessible through trade and the silver mines of Iran and Transoxiana contained an abundance of deposits. With these resources at their disposal the Islamic World was able to enjoy monetary stability without any significant resort to debasement for over three centuries, so that the description of this era as the "Golden Age of Islam" holds true not just figuratively but literally as well. Indeed, Arab coins were widely appreciated in the Christian world, as we will see.

This phrase, which we have used as the heading for this section, was the title of a classic book by Maurice Lombard (1975). In this brilliant work he said (p. 10) that "the Muslim World may be seen as a series of urban islands linked by trade routes" with the supply of precious metals lubricating the movement of goods and factors of production along these circuits. Each of these urban islands was a "center of purchasing power" or consumption, sustained both by local production and imports of consumer goods and raw materials, sometimes over great distances. Mecca and Medina were the cities in the Arabian Peninsula where the Islamic faith originated and they are to this day the two most revered holy sites. As we have seen, however, the political capital of the Islamic state was moved from Medina to the Syrian city of Damascus by the Umayyads and later to Baghdad by the Abbasids, and was never to return to the Arabian Peninsula. With both the Red Sea and the Persian Gulf in Muslim hands, the caravan trade across the peninsula lost its economic rationale. The holy cities were, however, the terminal points of the vast annual pilgrimages, the hajj, from all over the Islamic World and as such were of considerable economic importance as well. In addition, the peninsula served as a market for the trade in African slaves, and Medina became a center for training slaves in classical forms of music and dance that were then diffused all over the Muslim World. Another major economic activity was horse breeding, with the famous Arabian horses created by crossing Barbary and Iranian strains under the ideal climatic conditions of the high plateau of the Nejd in the northwest of the peninsula.

In Mesopotamia the Arabs established Kufa and Basra as fortified military settlements, with Wasit later set up between them. Basra grew rapidly as a consequence of land reclamation in the marshlands as well as trade through the Persian Gulf, with a population estimated at 200,000 in the ninth century, that of Kufa being about three-quarters of this (Ashtor 1976a, p. 89). The wealth generated in Basra and Kufa may have increased social tensions, since several dissident sects arose there with frequent outbreaks of violent revolts. The Umayyads settled several Arab tribes at various strategic locations in Syria and Mesopotamia to strengthen their hold in these regions. At the same time the cultivation of important new crops, originally from India, was introduced into Mesopotamia and Syria, notably rice, sugarcane and cotton. The area between the Tigris and Euphrates in Upper Mesopotamia was devoted to the cultivation of cotton that was spun and woven at the manufacturing center of Mosul, from which the word *muslin* is derived. The area around Tikrit, famous as the birthplace of both Saladin and Saddam Hussein, was devoted to wheat, barley, and the date palm. The southeastern part of Lower Mesopotamia, the region known as Khuzistan, was covered with extensive sugarcane plantations manned by the black slaves from East Africa known as Zanj, a conjunction eerily foreshadowing the more familiar pattern in the New World. These slaves staged a massive revolt in the ninth century, sacking Basra and threatening the very existence of the Abbasid caliphate for fourteen years, before being finally defeated in 883.

The importance of trade in the Muslim World is well symbolized by the design of the Abbasid capital, Baghdad. It was situated on the Tigris, but was linked to the Euphrates by a canal, so that cargoes from the Mediterranean and Syria could be readily transported downstream and imports from India and Southeast Asia upstream from the Persian Gulf through Basra. The city was constructed on a circular plan, with diagonally intersecting main roads leading to four gates. The northeast gate led to Iran and Transoxiana, the northwest to Syria, the southeast to Lower Mesopotamia and the southwest to Arabia and Egypt. The population came from all over the empire and grew rapidly with the

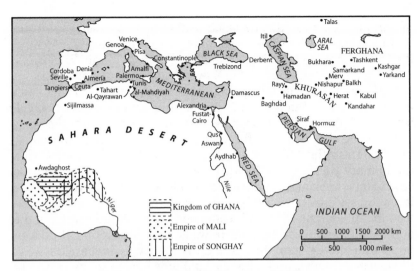

FIGURE 2.2. The Golden Age of Islam.

swelling wealth and revenues that flowed in from all directions. The
population of Baghdad was said to be almost 2 million at its peak,
which is certainly an exaggeration, but it may have been as high as
half a million, which would still be enormous for anywhere in the
world at that time. As for the protectors of the Abbasids, the Buyids,
the prosperity of Fars was not only due to a flourishing agriculture, but
to trade with the Far East through the port of Siraf on the Persian Gulf
that took over after the decline of Basra.

The cities of Iran and Transoxiana were usually stations on the great
caravan routes leading through Khurasan toward China and India to
the east (see figure 2.2). Lombard (1975, figure 3) shows the main
eastward route going from Baghdad to Hamadan, Rayy, and Nishapur,
before turning northeast to Merv, Bukhara, Samarkand, Tashkent,
and Talas before entering China. A branch between Samarkand and
Tashkent went to Ferghana, Kashgar, and Yarkand. From Nishapur
another route went due east to Balkh and from there to Kabul,
continuing either to India or looping westward to Kandahar and Herat.
There were also routes running southeast from Nishapur and Herat
to Siraf and Hormuz on the Persian Gulf. The main pack animal
for these caravans, which were often so large as to resemble small
towns on the move, was the Bactrian camel, a powerful and resilient
two-humped beast that was also bred in this area. The maintenance
and supervision of these routes was the responsibility of the *sahib*

al-barid or Postmaster-General, a position that was held in the late ninth century by the great geographer Ibn Khurradadhbih. Most of the trade seems to have been conducted by native Iranian peoples: the Sogdians with China and the Khwarezmians with Central Asia.

These cities had an interesting dualistic structure, with an Arab military *rabat* or cantonment, with mosque and markets attached, adjoined to the original four-gated Persian *shahristan* or walled city, symbolizing the fusion of the two cultures that was taking place. In addition to the Arabs and Iranians one must never lose sight of the military presence of the Turks, who would eventually gain the ascendancy. Most of these cities were situated at oases, with elaborate irrigation systems supporting market gardens and crop cultivation to feed the inhabitants. Since nomadic raids were all too common, the entire settlements were enclosed by walls and fortifications. The urban population consisted of the court, army, and civil service, along with the *ulema* or clerics, and absentee landlords in addition of course to the supporting artisans and service workers. Population estimates are scarce and unreliable but Barthold thinks that Samarkand could have had half a million and Watson (1983, p. 133) cites a guess of anywhere from one hundred to five hundred thousand for Nishapur.

In terms of manufacturing all the cities practiced a wide range of crafts, with the paper industry of Samarkand being perhaps the most significant, followed by silk and cotton textiles and of course carpets, with those of Armenia said to be the best. Barthold reports a most impressive list of both primary and manufactured exports and reexports by the various cities of the Samanid state, including paper from Samarkand that had entirely displaced parchment in the Islamic World by the end of the tenth century. Trade with the steppe nomads was very active, with local textile industries supplying the means of obtaining animals and animal products from them in return. Specific customs duties are given as 2 dirhems per camel load, not excessive in light of the fact that the monthly wage of an unskilled worker was 15 dirhems.

Turning now to Africa, Egypt with the "gift of the Nile" served as the breadbasket of the caliphate, just as it had for the heirs of Alexander and the Romans and Byzantines after them. After wheat the most important crop was flax, the basis of the flourishing linen industry. The reeds from the Nile were the raw material for another indispensable ancient industry, papyrus, and there was extensive sugarcane cultivation. According to Lombard another major resource that Egypt possessed for the benefit of its rulers was access to the gold supplies not only of the Nubian mines but more bizarrely from the tombs of the Pharaohs as well. In addition much of the gold from West Africa also found its way to Egypt along well-established caravan routes.

While still based in Ifriqiyah, the Fatimids' main port had been Tunis, which served as the hub of Mediterranean trade to both east and west because of its central location. Further west the Fatimids also captured Tahart, the wealthy capital of the Iranian Rustamids, which was at the intersection of both east–west and north–south trade routes. Their major objective here was control over the northern termini of the trans-Saharan trade routes, along which salt, textiles, and other manufactured goods were exchanged for gold and slaves in the *Bilad as-Sudan*, the "Land of the Blacks" in the Kingdom of Ghana in West Africa at the bend of the Niger.[4] The main route was between the oasis cities of Sijilmassa in Morocco and Awdaghost in what is now Mauritania. Devisse (1992) estimates the demand of the Fatimid mints for the fine gold dust of the Sudan at about a ton or so annually, or three tons at most allowing for additional demand, which is supposed to be from thirty to forty camel loads. Since many more camels apparently left Sijilmassa annually for Awdaghost, the question arises of what happened to the surplus camels on the way back or what cargo they might have carried, questions to which there are it seems as yet no clear answers. Devisse also says that thousands of shafts must have been dug annually to produce this amount of gold in the kingdom of Ghana, requiring a very considerable labor force, possibly of slaves.

This trade was extremely lucrative and seems to have attracted merchants from all over the Islamic World, even from as far away as Baghdad, Iran, and Transoxiana. An indication of the sums involved is provided by the account of the tenth-century geographer Ibn Hawqal, who reports that he saw a "*sakk*," translated by Lieber (1968, p. 233) as a "sight-draft," in Awdaghost for the staggering sum of 42,000 dinars, much greater than any comparable document that he had seen any-where else in the Islamic World.[5] Large profits are hardly surprising, given that, according to Arab writers, gold was so cheap at the source that it exchanged with salt at a price ratio of one to one by weight. This may be an exaggeration, but even still the terms of trade must have been highly favorable to those prepared to make the journey south.

---

[4] In our brief account of the economic links between the Islamic World and sub-Saharan Africa, given in this and subsequent paragraphs, we draw on Oliver and Fage (1970) and Hrbek (1992). See also the very helpful maps and discussion in O'Brien (2002, pp. 80–81).

[5] For further details on the trans-Saharan trade and Ibn Hawqal's description of it, see the useful article by Levtzion (1968).

These high profits did not come free of charge, however. The rulers of the sub-Saharan Ghana, Mali, and Songhai Empires taxed the trade, as did desert tribes such as the Tuareg, who controlled the routes across the Sahara. In turn, the Fatimids levied taxes on the gold before exporting it to Spain, Sicily, and the Christian cities of the Italian peninsula, as well as using it to mint dinars. These rents were supplemented by a range of manufactured exports such as textiles, ceramics, and glass, as well as the export of horses to the rest of the Islamic World as well as to sub-Saharan Africa.

The other major economic link between the Islamic World and sub-Saharan Africa was the slave trade. It is well-known that African slaves were prevalent in the lands of the Middle East since pre-Islamic times. Bilal, the first *muezzin*, was a manumitted black slave of the Prophet, and there were numerous followers including notable military commanders of the early Arab conquests. There were also many manumitted slaves that achieved distinction in poetry and music, including several females. Concubines of Fatimid caliphs are known to have exercised power and influence on behalf of their sons, such as the mother of al-Mustansir (1036–94). Like all Fatimid caliphs he employed black troops in his army, in his case as many as fifty thousand. African slaves were traded even further afield: Abyssinian mercenaries, known as *Habash*, were employed extensively in India, and young Africans of both sexes were household slaves in Southeast Asia and sometimes presented by local rulers as tribute to Chinese emperors. It is interesting that, despite the persistent inflow of African slaves into the Middle East for over one thousand years, there are no traces of their descendants anywhere constituting a separate community, which is perhaps a tribute to the social tolerance of the Islamic World in its ability to absorb "the other."

Gold from East Africa, as well as ivory and rock crystal, were exported from a series of trading ports along the east coast, such as Mogadishu, Mombasa, and Kilwa. The coastal stretch on which these and many other ports were situated was as much as 3,000 kilometers long, reaching as far south as Mozambique, and has been dubbed the "Swahili Corridor" by Mark Horton (1987). The Swahili were an African people who converted to Islam as a result of contact with Arab and Persian traders, and themselves engaged in extensive trade and navigation along the east coast of Africa. The Swahili language became a *lingua franca*, with Arabic vocabulary superimposed on a Bantu base. A widespread tradition traces their descent from early colonists known as "Shirazi," i.e., from the town of Shiraz in Iran, which was the seat of Buyid power in the tenth and eleventh centuries. According to

Horton and Middleton (2000, pp. 52–61), however, it is more likely that the association with a prestigious location such as Shiraz was adopted by the early African converts themselves, rather than indicating actual descent from inhabitants of that city. On the basis of archaeological research, Horton reports that the early settlements dating to the eighth century were completely African in character, but that by the ninth century there is clear evidence of an indigenous Muslim elite. Ivory and ambergris were exported to as far as China by merchants from Siraf on the Persian Gulf, while slaves and timber were exported to the Middle East. Iron ore mined near Mombasa was exported to India in the form of pig iron, and archaeological finds have revealed large amounts of Chinese as well as Middle Eastern ceramics on the African east coast.

This trade, oriented toward the Gulf, apparently went into a sharp decline by the early tenth century as a result of the fall of the Tang dynasty and the revolt of the Zanj. By the second half of the tenth century there was a strong revival of the East African trade, but it was now oriented toward the Red Sea and west to the Mediterranean, rather than to the Gulf and China. Horton finds stone buildings and mosques on his sites from 950 onwards, replacing the earlier earthen structures, indicating a substantial increase in prosperity. Most important, however, are the finds of coins, including one of over two thousand at a single eleventh-century site. The gold, estimated at an annual flow of 20,000 ounces, ivory, and rock crystal were obtained by the coastal Swahili through trade with the tribes of the interior, being exchanged for salt, cowrie shells, glass beads, and other trade goods. Horton and Middleton (2000, p. 101) cite an Arab geographer who says that the tribes of the interior would leave their chiefs and elders as hostages in exchange for the trade goods, redeeming them after delivery of the ivory obtained from as far west as the eastern fringes of the Kalahari Desert. Horton (1987) thinks that the ivory used to make an exquisite casket for the daughter of Abd al-Rahman III in Cordoba in about 960, as well as other notable Islamic, Byzantine, and Western European artistic treasures, must have come from the tusks of East African elephants.

After their conquest of Egypt, the Fatimids continued to take an active interest in trade, succeeding as we have seen in diverting the Indian Ocean spice trade from the Persian Gulf to the Red Sea. They thereby gained access to the most lucrative source of monopoly rent in the medieval world, sharing it with the newly emerging commercial city-states of Italy such as Amalfi, Genoa, Pisa, and Venice. The port of Aydhab on the western coast of the Red Sea was where the goods from the Indian Ocean were unloaded, then sent by camel caravans to the trading center of Qus at the head of the Nile near Aswan, before going downstream to Cairo and Alexandria, where they could be purchased for export by Italian as well as local merchants. Alexandria was a thriving city with two harbors, one for Christian and one for Muslim ships.

Fatimid Egypt enjoyed other economic advantages besides control over long-distance trade routes. The *anona*, the annual grain tribute, had in centuries past first gone to Rome and then to Constantinople. Under the caliphate it first went to the holy cities of Mecca and Medina, later to Damascus, and then to Baghdad under the Abbasids. It now, however, stayed in Egypt under the Fatimids, which clearly gave a boost to the local economy. Indeed, halting grain exports may have benefited the Egyptian economy by encouraging production of other goods, such as flax and sugar cane, which were not only major cash crops but also served as raw material inputs to the key industrial sectors of linen manufacture and sugar refining. Grain was also produced in Sicily, which was in Fatimid hands at this time, and Sicilian grain was exported to feed the cities of Ifriqiyah.

The production of high-quality linen, embroidered with gold and silver thread, for the court and as gifts for local dignitaries and foreign potentates, took place in state workshops called *tiraz*, as well as in private factories, and was a major export product all over the Mediterranean and even as far away as China. Frantz-Murphy (1981) considers the linen sector to have been the key one for the Egyptian economy from Tulunid to Fatimid times. She says that it even served as a store of value and a major asset in the portfolios of the elite, who produced flax on their own estates. Thus Ibn Killis himself was found to have been holding 500,000 dinars worth of luxury textiles at his death in 991, with a further 16,000 dinars invested in the industry. Ashtor says that sugar refining was a major capital-intensive industry, using very advanced technology, producing both for domestic consumption and export in Fatimid times, while papermaking was another important sector. In addition to manufactured exports and the transshipment of Eastern spices, the Fatimids also exported industrial raw materials such as cotton and alum to the emerging textile industries in Italy. These exports were paid for with some manufactured imports, such as woolen cloth, but for the most part with silver that was in turn reexported to the East to pay for the pepper and other spices.

With their control of access to the West African gold supplies and the Red Sea, the Fatimids were able to maintain a strong army of Berber, Turkish, and Nubian troops and a splendid court. They employed

Copts and Jews as administrators and financial advisors and followed what appears to have been a remarkably rational and consistent economic policy. Although they established large-scale royal factories for luxury textiles and some other items, and controlled trade in strategic materials such as iron, timber, and pitch, Ashtor (1976a) emphasizes the extent to which they permitted free enterprise in trade and industry. The administrative efficiency and economic policy of the Fatimids was apparently so successful that S. D. Goitein (1967, p. 33) speaks of the "miracle of the Fatimids," which he attributes to these factors as well as to trade with an increasingly prosperous Western Europe.

This economic policy, described by Goitein and others as being of an almost laissez-faire character, with very low customs duties and free movement of goods, people, and capital, needs to be interpreted more carefully. A. L. Udovitch (1988, p. 72), in a valuable case study of the mutually beneficial informal relationships between an anonymous emir, or military commander, of Alexandria and a Jewish merchant, concludes that while the merchants in Italian city-states might be in a position to say "l'état c'est moi," the merchants of Fatimid Egypt could say "l'état n'est pas contre moi." As Michael Brett (2001) points out, members of the court and the royal family, including the top civil and military leaders, were rewarded with a variety of privileges, such as the right of first purchase, and exemptions from taxation, that must have tilted the markets very much in their favor at the expense of less well-connected merchants and the general public. M. A. Shaban (1978, chapter 9) also contends that this laissez-faire approach may have involved the Fatimids neglecting maintenance of the agricultural infrastructure, which traditionally required from a third to a fourth of the annual revenue.

Granting all this, it still seems to have been the case that these generally enlightened policies brought significant wealth, as reflected in the immense luxury that all observers ascribed to Fustat-Cairo in the time of the Fatimids, from the Arab geographers Ibn Hawqal, al-Muqaddasi, and al-Idrisi, to the Persian traveler Nasir-i Khusraw and the French chronicler of the Crusades, William of Tyre. The magnificence of public building was not confined to palaces. They also built the great mosque and seminary of al-Azhar and a public library called the House of Knowledge, containing thousands of books on religious as well as secular subjects and open to all, with paper, pens, and ink provided for anyone who wished to make copies. Houses had six or seven and even up to fourteen stories, with two hundred or more people living in them (Wiet 1964, chapter 2).

The population of Fustat-Cairo was estimated at perhaps five to six hundred thousand in the middle of the fourteenth century (Watson 1983, p. 133), but could conceivably have been even larger under the Fatimids. The standing army of Ibn Tulun was supposed to have consisted of 24,000 Turkish *ghulams* and 42,000 black Nubian and Sudanese slave soldiers (Bianquis 1998, p. 98), and it would not be unreasonable to consider the population of Fustat to have been at least ten times that number early in the tenth century. The river traffic on the Nile was described as greater than that at Baghdad and Basra combined, which is certainly a testament to the prosperity of the Egyptian capital. No great city can escape complaints about pollution and Cairo was no exception, since Gaston Wiet (1964, p. 37) informs us of a physician named Ibn Radwan complaining about the blackish vapor hanging over the city especially in summer, the dust that always seemed to get into one's beard, and the bad habit of the Cairenes of throwing the carcasses of animals into the sources of their drinking water.

The economy of the western regions of North Africa was closely linked to that of al-Andalus. The economic basis of al-Andalus was a flourishing agriculture, probably the most diverse and technically sophisticated of any in the contemporary world. As Watson (1983) demonstrated in his pioneering study, the Arab conquests led to a veritable "green revolution" in the lands that they occupied as a result of the diffusion of crops and plants from India and Southeast Asia westwards into Iran, Iraq, and Syria, and then into those regions on both shores of the Mediterranean under their control. Since these eastern crops and plants were originally grown in a monsoon climate with plentiful rainfall, their cultivation in the more arid climate of the Islamic World required a complex irrigation technology to render it feasible. Here the legacy of ancient Persian and Mesopotamian devices, such as the underground irrigation canals or *qanat* and the water-lifting wheel or *noria*, proved indispensable. All of these developments came to fruition in al-Andalus, with the resulting agricultural system constituting a triumph of creative synthesis, according to Thomas Glick (1994, p. 977), "melding...Indian agriculture, Roman and Persian hydraulic techniques, and a legal regime of water distribution combining elements of Arab and Berber tribal norms, Islamic law and Roman provincial customary law." Reilly (1993, p. 62) states that cotton and the banana were introduced in the ninth century, followed by rice, hard wheat, sugar cane, eggplant, and watermelon in the tenth, and sorghum and spinach in the eleventh. Other important new additions included oranges, lemons, and other citrus fruits, as well as new varieties of figs and dates, often introduced by royal gardens and orchards maintained by the ruling house.

The sciences of botany, agronomy, and horticulture were highly developed in al-Andalus, building on the knowledge of classical antiquity as well as the transmission of Indian lore in these fields. The Arabs, originally a people of the desert, seem to have had a particular love of the greenery associated with oases, of trees and plants and flowers, as often reflected in their poetry. These new crops also had the effect of extending the area under cultivation by making more than one crop a year possible in many cases. The output of more traditional crops, like the olive and the grape vine, also expanded, the latter in spite of the well-known Islamic prohibition on the consumption of alcohol. The drinking of wine seems not to have been at all unusual in al-Andalus, at least among the social elite of the cities.

The social changes accompanying the Arab Conquest also seem to have been beneficial, replacing the slave plantations of the Roman and Visigothic eras with rent-paying tenant cultivators or sharecroppers, and with more flexible arrangements regarding land use and property rights being introduced. As Jaime Vicens Vives (1969, p. 107) says, "the farmers, those who tilled the fields, were much better off under the Arabs than under the Visigoths," even though they may have had to part with from a third to a fifth of their crops to the new ruling class. Most of these farmers were natives who had converted to Islam, the so-called *muwallads*. Those who did not convert, called *Mozarabs*, comprised much of the artisan class in the cities. The rearing of vast herds of sheep, moving seasonally in search of pasturage, was associated with the settlement of Berber tribal communities in al-Andalus, where they constituted the bulk of the immigrant Muslim population. The much less numerous easterners—the Arabs and Syrians—formed the elite of the ruling Umayyads and the landowning aristocracy. The small Jewish community played a role in commerce and administration out of all proportion to its size, because its education, literacy, and eastern origins enabled it to be a cultural mediator between the Muslims and Christians.

Industry and mining were also highly developed in al-Andalus. Major manufactured goods, such as silk, linen, woolen, and cotton textiles, that had originally been imported from the east, were eventually produced and exported to the Christian West, the Islamic east and North Africa. Paper became an important industry in Játiva, and Cordovan leather and Toledo steel acquired a fame that they have never lost. Copper, iron, and mercury were important industrial raw materials that had both domestic and foreign markets. Timber was particularly valuable in the relatively arid and deforested Islamic World, and Spanish oak and pine for furniture and ships met this pressing need.

The emirate of Cordoba was itself undergoing a golden age during the tenth century, marked as we have seen by the proclamation by Abd al-Rahman III of the Umayyad caliphate, rival to that of the Abbasids and Fatimids. The Umayyads captured Ceuta in 931, Tangier twenty years later as well as other segments of North Africa, and engaged in protracted hostilities with the Fatimids for control of the outlets of the trans-Saharan trade. Each side made use of various Berber tribes as proxies, the Fatimids of the Sanhaja confederation and the Umayyads of the more westerly Zanata. Access to southern gold supplies enabled Abd al-Rahman III to issue his own gold coinage after he declared himself caliph in 929. Both sides also used their considerable naval strength to raid each other's coasts. Despite these conflicts the natural complementarity of this "Hispano-Moorish" economic system asserted itself, with a flourishing trade across the western Mediterranean involving the exchange of southern agricultural products for northern manufactures, timber, and metals. Both sides also had an interest in suppressing the piracy and freebooting that plagued Mediterranean trade in earlier times but declined noticeably from the tenth century onwards.

In a rare quantitative contribution Pedro Chalmeta (1994) estimates a total population of 10.3 million for al-Andalus in this period, with 1 million being urban, of which Cordoba alone accounts for a half. Chalmeta also estimates what he calls the "gross revenue" of the country at between 36 and 54 million dinars, of which between a third and a half may have been taken in taxes, which certainly seems suspiciously high. Vicens Vives (1969, p. 118) gives a figure of 20 million dinars as the annual revenue of Abd al-Rahman III, which is consistent with these estimates of Chalmeta. Gross income per capita was thus roughly speaking between four and five dinars. While it would be difficult to compare this estimate to present levels, Chalmeta (p. 756) is clear that "for the Christian kingdoms in the north of the Iberian Peninsula, al-Andalus represented a kind of El Dorado or Promised Land" whose riches provided a powerful additional incentive to the religious zeal of the *Reconquista*. Reilly (1993, p. 66) says that the Spanish Christian kings were buried in rich Andalusian fabrics, while the relics of saints would often be placed in ivory caskets and altars covered with linen fabrics that were all products of al-Andalus. Muslim coins, or imitations of them, circulated in the Christian lands.

All of these cities and areas of the Islamic World, from Spain and North Africa in the west to Afghanistan and India in the east, were in constant touch with each other, with apparently no restrictions at all on the free flow of people, ideas, techniques, fashions, goods, and capital, as the lives and work of geographers like Ibn Hawqal himself attest, in spite of the frequent political conflicts and warfare between the individual Muslim states. The hajj of course was a major unifying factor in this regard but by no means the sole one. The prosperity and tolerance of the Fatimids and Umayyads in the west served as a magnet to ambitious soldiers, intellectuals, bureaucrats, poets, dancers, singers, and sundry others to "go west and grow up with the country" in a manner almost reminiscent of Horace Greeley and a much later western frontier situation. An interesting example in this regard is provided by the celebrated Ziryab (789–852), a black freedman who began his spectacular career as a musician, singer, and poet at the Abbasid court of Baghdad before moving to Qayrawan and then to Cordoba, where he was a major cultural influence not only in music but also as an arbiter of taste and fashion. He is credited with such surprising innovations for his time as the use of toothpaste and underarm deodorants as well as the practice of changing clothing with the seasons and dividing meals into separate courses. The material and cultural products of the east stimulated not only imitation, but also transformation and development in the west to the enrichment of the entire civilization. This would in turn imply a priceless legacy for Western Europe and the rest of the world.

China: The Sung Economic Miracle

At the turn of the first millennium, under the Sung dynasty, just as now at the turn of the second, China was undergoing an unprecedented economic expansion. As we have seen, the Sung came to power in 960 after a brief interregnum following the fall of the Tang dynasty in 907. During the Tang, the economic center of gravity, or "key economic area" as defined by Chao-Ting Chi (1936), shifted from the Yellow River basin in the north to the region of the Yangtze Valley and the area to the south. Political and military power continued to be located in the north. North and South China were linked together by an extensive network of canals and other waterways, notably the famous Grand Canal. Millet and wheat were the main grains grown in the north while rice was the staple crop in the south. The higher yields per acre obtainable from rice were enhanced by the introduction of a new strain, the so-called "early ripening rice" from Champa in what is now Vietnam (Ho 1956). This enabled double and even triple cropping to be introduced, so that production rose sharply as the new seeds and subsequent strains were diffused over the entire region of South China from Fujian province, which was the first to adopt the Champa variety.

As a result of this agricultural revolution, a massive increase in the population of China occurred, from the 50 million or so it had been at the height of the Tang in 750 (which was less than the 63 million estimated for the year 200), to well over 100 million by the twelfth century (McEvedy and Jones 1978, p. 167; Maddison 1998, p. 169). As Mark Elvin (1973) pointed out, this can be seen as the operation of a classical Malthusian-type model, with population growth eventually wiping out gains in productivity. In the eleventh and twelfth centuries under the Sung the lag between the productivity gain and population growth was long enough to have led to a remarkable burst of prosperity. This period saw a great extension of markets, trade, and specialization, accompanied by technological change in industry and transportation as well as agriculture, and a remarkable increase in urbanization. The enormous cities that so impressed Marco Polo were created by the Sung, the very dynasty that had been ousted by his Mongol patron.

China under the Sung had a thriving, bustling, and buoyant economy with highly diverse regions and cities (Elvin 1973; Shiba 1992). These centers each specialized in what they were best suited to produce and were linked together by a highly sophisticated network of merchants, brokers, and other commercial agents. Central to this network was what must certainly have been the most extensive and convenient system of water transport anywhere in the world. All Chinese dynasties traditionally relied on agriculture as the main source of revenue. The expansion of commercial and industrial activities under the Sung, however, meant that taxes on trade came to play an increasingly important role in the fiscal basis of the state. The Southern Sung, in particular, apparently drew the bulk of their revenues from trade taxes and the profits of state monopolies rather than land taxes. Among these state monopolies the most profitable were salt and the national drink, tea.

The economic performance of Sung China is all the more remarkable in light of the fact that the entire history of the dynasty was marked by incessant conflict on its northern borders with powerful nomadic states. The Sung army, used mostly for defense against the inroads of the nomads, was of the order of 1.25 million. This was a crushing burden for the economy to bear, despite its prosperity. The Sung were forced in 1126 to abandon China north of the Yangtze to the Jurchen nomads, who established the so-called Chin dynasty, and as we will see in the next chapter both the Jurchen and the Southern Sung eventually fell to the Mongols. The very threats that they faced on their land frontiers may paradoxically have made the Chinese of the Sung era turn in novel directions. During the earlier great ages of the Han and the Tang, China had interacted with the west across the caravan trails of Central Asia. It was by the Silk Road that China received the major impulses of Buddhism, Islam, and Nestorian Christianity, as well as a number of artistic and technological innovations. When access to the west was cut off by the presence of the powerful seminomadic states of the Hsi Hsia and the Khitans, it was only logical to turn to the alternative avenue of the sea. China has traditionally been seen in the West as an "inward-looking" land-based power, but Laurence J. C. Ma (1971, p. 30) points out that "the ocean in Sung times was the front door of China and it was wide open to all those who were interested in commercial interaction with China."

Even though the Tang had encouraged trade, Guangzhou (Canton) was the only port with an official customs post under that dynasty. Under the Sung, however, there were no fewer than nine port cities with imperial customs posts, each under a high official bearing the title of Superintendent of Maritime Shipping. Canton was for a long time the main one but it was eventually overtaken in the volume of trade handled by Quanzhou (Zaiton), located opposite the Taiwan Strait. Interestingly, one of these nine ports was Huating, later to rise to fame after it was renamed Shanghai (ibid., p. 39). These port cities attracted large communities of foreign merchants, mainly Arabs and Persians, who enjoyed substantial legal protection under a form of extraterritoriality for their activities. Many of them were absorbed into high positions in the Sung bureaucracy. The most famous and successful of them was an Arab with the Chinese name of Pu Shou-keng, who was the Superintendent of Maritime Shipping at Quanzhou, and who surrendered the city to the victorious Mongols in the thirteenth century (ibid., p. 42).

Trade with Korea and Japan increased under the Sung, but the main channel of contact was to the south, with Java, Sumatra, and other Indonesian isles, Annam and Champa in Vietnam, and ultimately with the lands around the Red Sea and the Persian Gulf. During the Tang it was the Arabs and Persians who came all the way to China in their own ships. Under the Sung, however, the Chinese built their own oceangoing vessels, great junks with several masts, watertight compartments for their hulls, stern-post rudders, movable sails, and other nautical innovations well in advance of the rest of the world. The art of navigation, based on the mariner's compass, star charts, and detailed knowledge of winds and currents, was also very far advanced at the time of the Sung.

Sung China exported porcelain, silk, and other Chinese manufactures to Southeast Asia in exchange for spices, medicinal herbs, and other natural-resource products. Lucrative as the Southeast Asian spice trade with the Middle East and Europe was, it must have been dwarfed by the volume of the trade with China. The much greater population and the higher incomes of at least the upper classes in China, as well as the greater proximity to the sources of supply, must have made it by far the greater market for these exotic products of world trade, as noted later by Marco Polo.

Associated with this trade was a class of very wealthy merchants and shipowners, many of whom, like Pu Shou-keng, were Muslims of Arab, Persian, or Turkic origin who settled in the port cities of China. The state itself seems to have both fostered and hindered the lucrative maritime trade of the era. It wanted to promote an increasingly important source of revenue, from customs duties as well as from the resale within China or reexport overland to Central Asia of selected imports reserved as state monopolies (such as tortoise shell, ivory, rhinoceros horn, coral, agate, frankincense, and high-quality or "weapons grade" steel) that it purchased at controlled prices from the merchants. On the other hand, it was also forced by the exigencies of war to frequently requisition merchant vessels to serve as warships or military transports. Eventually, a pragmatic compromise was worked out with ships rotated between civilian and military use.

Running against the obvious financial benefits of openness to trade was the strong Confucian preference for self-sufficiency, and an agrarian rather than a commercial economy. This led the emperor Kao-tsung to ban luxury imports in 1127 but in 1137 he was obliged by economic necessity to backtrack and issue a famous edict in which he declared that "the profit from maritime trade is very great and, if properly managed, would amount to millions of strings of cash. Would it not be preferable to promote this trade rather than to tax the people?" (Wheatley 1959, p. 30). The tariff schedule of the Sung was a very moderate one, at one-tenth ad valorem for goods of "fine" quality and one-fifteenth for goods of "coarse" quality (ibid., p. 22).

The government assisted the private sector by constructing an extensive infrastructure of harbors, warehouses, and other facilities, as well as beacons and lighthouses along the coasts. These activities are reminiscent of the close collaboration between government and business that many have seen as characterizing the East Asian economic miracle of our own times. They are far removed from the traditional picture of "oriental despotism" that many Western writers associated with China. In fact the Sung emperors, more than those of any other dynasty, seem to have been genuinely interested in the welfare of the common people over whom they ruled. They attempted to scrupulously preserve the independence of the bureaucracy and even seemed to think of themselves as "chief administrators" rather than as absolute monarchs.

Jung-Pang Lo (1955, 1969) pointed out that China's emergence as a sea power during this era was marked by a mutually reinforcing relationship between maritime commerce and naval warfare. After their expulsion from North China by the Jurchen, the Southern Sung dynasty (1127–1279) relied for their defense on clever strategic and tactical use of the complex network of rivers and canals. Their reliance on water for transport of troops was made all the more necessary because they lost access to the supply of horses from Central Asia for their cavalry. As a leading official said in 1113, "The seas and the Yangtze River are the new Great Wall of China, the warships are the watch-towers and the firearms are the new weapons of defense."

These firearms that the Sung developed out of necessity to resist the traditional cavalry attacks of their nomadic opponents were the clear antecedents of the artillery and musketry that transformed the art of war in the West a couple of centuries later. They were based on the use of gunpowder to provide an explosive charge and the use of guided projectiles launched from tubes of one kind or another. Chinese warships relied for their firepower on archers and crossbow-men, supplemented by the use of explosive grenades, rockets, and flamethrowers. By the familiar dynamics of armed conflicts, these very same weapons and tactics were also adopted by the Jurchen and the Mongols against the Sung, and the Mongols themselves later took to the sea in their unsuccessful invasions of Japan and Java.

The constant warfare led to the establishment of another major defense-related industry, iron and steel. Robert Hartwell (1962, 1966, 1967, 1982) has demonstrated the remarkable expansion in the pro-duction of iron and steel in China during the Northern Sung (960–1126). The scale of total production, and of the levels of output and employment in individual plants, was far in excess of anything attained before England in the eighteenth century, at the time of the Industrial Revolution. Hartwell estimated that iron production in China in 1078 was of the order of 150,000 tons annually. The entire production of iron and steel in Europe in 1700 was not much above this, if at all. The growth rate of Chinese iron and steel production was no less remarkable than the level, increasing twelvefold in the two centuries from 850 to 1050.

Iron coins, which supplemented the usual copper coins in some areas of western China, absorbed about 10,000 tons of this output.

Another major source of demand for iron was for ploughshares, sickles, and other agricultural implements. These implements obviously raised productivity per worker in the agricultural sector. The largest demand of all, however, probably came from the military, for the manufacture of weapons and armor. One consequence of the loss of the North to the Jurchens after 1126 was the loss of the metallurgical capacity concentrated near the Northern Sung capital of K'ai-feng, around which there were substantial deposits of iron ore and coal. The conjunction of natural resources with the huge market of the capital made it possible to take full advantage of economies of scale and to minimize transport costs for the heavy raw materials.

The population of K'ai-feng appears to have been around 750,000 in 1078, undoubtedly making it one of the largest cities in the world and probably the largest. The population could not have been sustained without the plentiful and regular supply of grain from the south through the Grand Canal. Cheap water transport was thus doubly important for the iron and steel industry around K'ai-feng, not only lowering the cost of moving inputs in and products out, but also supporting a heavy concentration of demand from both the public and private sectors. A full-time labor force was employed in the industry and there seems to have been signs of class conflict between the wage earners and the wealthy ironmasters for whom they worked. These entrepreneurs probably came from the landowning gentry class, many of whom, however, may have been newly rich entrants to this privileged group.

Sinologists are generally agreed that the Sung era represented the height of the achievements of Chinese civilization in the arts, literature, and philosophy as well as in the economy, technology, and public administration. Its fall to the Mongols therefore represented a tragic setback to what possibly could have been a breakthrough to modern industrial society and civilization well ahead of the West. Although the Mongols themselves became increasingly Sinicized during their rule, and their successors, the Ming, initially supported the "outward-looking" maritime orientation of the Sung and the Yüan, they eventually turned inward, as we will see, while in the intellectual sphere there was a revival of Confucian orthodoxy and the pragmatic, experimental spirit of the Sung was discarded. The Mongol onslaught thus put a lamentable end to a truly remarkable early "efflorescence" of economic growth (Goldstone 2002) that fully matched, and even surpassed, the Golden Age of Islam that was roughly contemporaneous with it.

The Indian Ocean and Southeast Asian Trade

The position of Southeast Asia athwart the sea-lanes connecting China to the Middle East meant that the concurrent prosperity at one end under the Tang and Sung, and at the other under the Abbasids and Fatimids, was bound to lead to a flourishing transit and export trade in both directions in this region (Wolters 1967). As we noted briefly in the first chapter it was this fact that first stimulated the rise of the Indo-Chinese kingdom of Funan and the trade across the Isthmus of Kra, which was later replaced by the Sumatran commercial empire of Srivijaya that controlled passage through the Straits of Malacca as well as the Sunda Straits. However, the trade was too lucrative not to induce competition from other rival states, not only from nearby Java but also from Cambodian, Thai, and Burmese rulers on the mainland as well as from Ceylon. The main threat came from the powerful and aggressive Chola dynasty (850–1279) of southern India. Chola trade was in the hands of large, well-organized Tamil merchant guilds that hired their own mercenary troops and enjoyed considerable autonomy, though apparently working in concert with royal authority.

Relations between Srivijaya and the Cholas were friendly at first, with the ruler of the former kingdom endowing a Buddhist monastery at the principal port city of the Cholas, Nagapattinam, presumably for the use of merchants from Southeast Asia. In 1025, however, the Chola ruler Rajendra I (1012–44) launched an apparently devastating naval raid on Srivijaya from which it never recovered its former prestige and authority (Wolters 1970). Hall and Whitmore (1976) maintain that the raid disrupted the hegemony of Srivijaya, leading to trade moving away from the route through the Straits toward the northern and western shores of Sumatra and eastern Java and reviving the trans-peninsular route across the Isthmus of Kra. The Khmer monarch Suryavarman I (1002–50) developed Tambralinga on the east coast of the Malay Peninsula as a base for trade across the Isthmus and opened diplomatic and trade relations with Ceylon and South India. However, the Khmer were eventually obliged to withdraw from these western-oriented activities to deal with internal disorders and threats to their eastern frontiers. The rising Pagan Empire in central Burma also moved south to take advantage of the vacuum that was opening up during what Hall and Whitmore call "The Isthmian Struggle" unleashed by the decline of Srivijaya. The Burmese actively engaged in trade across the Bay of Bengal with Ceylon and South Indian ports, and also participated in a number of religious exchanges of relics and monks with Buddhist centers in Ceylon and India. This did not prevent a later Ceylonese raid on Lower Burma in the 1160s, apparently prompted by trade disputes.

The trade of South India from the ninth to the thirteenth century and the role that the Tamil merchant guilds played in it have been the subject of a classic article by Burton Stein (1965) and a detailed pioneering study by Meera Abraham (1988). Abraham points out that, located midway between Southeast Asia and the Islamic World, both Ceylon and the kingdoms of South India were able to act as intermediaries as well as suppliers of their own products, in a chain stretching from the South China Sea to the Red Sea and the Persian Gulf. Stein (1965, p. 49) notes that the port of Conjeeveram on the eastern Coromandel Coast of the Indian peninsula had established trade relations dating back to the first century A.D. with both China and the Roman Empire. Jewish and Christian traders from the Middle East established small but durable communities in India, such as that of the "Syrian" Christians that still thrives today in the Indian state of Kerala. The legendary founder of this church, the apostle Thomas, is said to have made his way to India in the company of a merchant and Abraham (1988) cites documentary evidence of Christian merchants and clerics from Syria and Palestine, such as Bishop Thomas of Cana, settling at the port of Quilon in the late eighth and early ninth centuries.

Stein cites (p. 50) temple inscriptions from the tenth to the thirteenth century regarding the activities of two of the main guilds, the Ayyavole and the Manigramam, which "give the impression of energetic and confident merchants organized in large, mobile groups carrying on business in a wide assortment of commodities from horses to precious stones." An inscription states that "the commodities they trade are elephants and horses; sapphires, moonstones, pearls, diamonds, rubies, onyx, topaz, emeralds, and corals; cardamom and cloves; sandalwood, camphor and musk." They are also said through the payment of customs duties to "fill the ruler's treasury with gold and jewels and provide him with weapons." A trade mission dispatched to the Sung court by Rajaraja in 1015 sent "21,000 ounces of pearls, 60 elephant tusks and 60 catties (= 1.25 lb. each) of frankincense" as well as 3,300 catties of aromatic woods (Abraham 1988, p. 139). The frankincense was from the Middle East and the aromatic woods from Southeast Asia, indicating the ability of the Cholas to obtain such highly prestigious items and thereby impress the Chinese emperor with their own value as "first-class" trading partners of the Sung. The pearls were from the pearl fisheries of the Gulf of Mannar on the northwest coast of Ceylon, an area that the Cholas brought under their control and where archaeologists have discovered Chinese and Islamic ceramics dating to the tenth and eleventh centuries, the period of Chola occupation. Rajaraja's son Rajendra, who carried out the raid on Srivijaya in 1025, also sent a trade mission to the Sung in 1033. The Tamil merchant guilds seem to have been ubiquitous across Southeast Asia and even as far as the major Chinese port of Quanzhou, where a temple erected by them still stands, while inscriptions have been found in Sumatra, the Malay Peninsula, and Pagan.

Exposure to these trade currents seems to have made the rulers of South India and Ceylon anxious to acquire the revenues that encouraging trade and taxing it moderately could bring. As already noted the traders themselves hired mercenary troops that supplemented royal armies and navies, so trade and military expansion were often combined. The Cholas sent military expeditions to Southeast Asia and the Maldive Islands, and their invasions of Ceylon were also not unmotivated by trade considerations. In contrast to Spencer (1976, p. 409), who argues that the purpose of these incursions was "based upon more ruthless plunder and destruction of major political and religious centers," Abraham (1988, p. 130) believes that "trade was an important factor in framing Chola policy and that Chola rulers had links with the merchant community, and that some degree of mutual benefit was derived, both by the ruler and the merchant, from an external policy which supported the trader." In the case of the raid on Srivijaya, conquest could not have been the motive since there were apparently no attempts to occupy or garrison Southeast Asian territory. According to Abraham (1988, p. 142), "the raid was undertaken partly at least to establish rights for Tamil-speaking merchants in those areas, a trade from which the ruler, the merchant and the Chola bureaucracy could expect sizable profits." A commercial motive, possibly instigated by the merchant guilds, seems the likeliest explanation, and is furthermore not inconsistent with plunder as an added incentive for the royal army and the mercenaries of the merchant guilds that must have participated in the operation, at least as its naval arm. After the fall of the Cholas the role of these merchant guilds in the economy and society of South India diminished greatly, though they did linger on until as late as the seventeenth century (Stein 1965, p. 59).

In sum the evidence points toward an era in which trade expansion was combined with active cultural contact and political interaction across the eastern Indian Ocean and the South China Sea. Perhaps the most notable feature of the eleventh century in this region was the interaction between international trade, the emergence of major new states, and the establishment of Theravada Buddhism as the dominant cultural formation on the mainland of Southeast Asia and Ceylon that has remained unchanged to the present day.

Much of our knowledge about the places and products associated with the vast arc of trade from the South China Sea to the Persian

Gulf and the Red Sea comes from a work compiled in 1225 by a Sung official named Chau Ju-kua, who held the office of Superintendent of Maritime Trade at Quanzhou. This remarkable and indispensable work is entitled *Chu-fan-chi,* translated as "Description of Barbarian Peoples" or more politely as "Records of Foreign Nations," and is apparently based on a number of earlier Chinese texts but also on first-hand observation and enquiry by the scholar-official in the course of his duties.[6] From this work we see that the Chinese of the Sung dynasty were informed not only about insular and mainland Southeast Asia but also about Ceylon, India, the Middle East, and East Africa, and even about some parts of the Mediterranean such as Sicily.

In terms of the commodity composition of trade Chau Ju-kua lists a vast array of mainly exotic products, some 339 in all, which were imported into China from all these regions. As Wheatley points out, Chau Ju-kua was frequently confused about the original source of many of these imports, often ascribing the source of particular items to places from where they were reexported rather than actually produced. The most important commodities imported into China were aromatics and drugs, such as the biblical frankincense and myrrh from the Hadramaut, sandalwood from Southeast Asia, and ambergris from the East African coast. Spices from the Moluccas such as cloves and nutmeg were used for medicinal purposes, while elephant tusks and rhinoceros horns from Africa were highly prized. Young black slaves, both male and female, were also imported from Africa. While silk was a major Chinese export to Southeast Asia, the fine brocades and damasks of the Middle East, and cotton textiles from the Indian Malabar and Coromandel Coasts, were valuable imports. Steel and swords were imported from India and several minerals, mainly tin, from Southeast Asia. Porcelain along with silk was the main Chinese export and has been found in large quantities from Southeast Asia and Ceylon to the Arabian Peninsula, the Swahili coast of East Africa, and Zanzibar.

As Wheatley (1959) notes, it is surprising that the Sung Chinese seem to have been much better informed about the Middle East and even East Africa than about India. The explanation is undoubtedly that, with the exception of the Tamil merchant guild at Quanzhou, Indian merchants were much less well represented in Chinese port cities than the numerous Arab, Persian, and Turkic merchants whose presence was so noticeable in those places. Ma (1971, p. 14) states that there were no

---

[6]An English translation by Hirth and Rockhill (1964), with voluminous scholarly notes, is available, and the work is also the basis of a most valuable study by Paul Wheatley (1959).

fewer than twenty trade missions from the lands of the Islamic World during the Sung period, while there were only a few by the Cholas and other Indian kingdoms: further evidence of the economic centrality of the Islamic World during this period. We now turn to the western periphery of Eurasia, and to the impact of the Arab conquests there.

THE PIRENNE THESIS

"Without Mohammed Charlemagne would have been impossible," so the great Belgian historian Henri Pirenne (1939, p. 234) famously said, thereby launching one of the most fascinating and enduring of all academic controversies, one that has not been fully resolved to this day. Pirenne was attacking the received wisdom of his day, which was that the invasions of the Germanic tribes had overthrown the civilized framework of the Roman Empire in the province of Gaul, thus inaugurating the "Dark Ages" during which society reverted to a self-sufficient rural economy of a servile peasantry dominated by feudal lords. This was in place of the civilized bureaucratic empire of the urbanized Roman elite, financed by direct taxation of the land and tolls on the thriving overseas trade with the eastern Byzantine provinces. Pirenne argued that the new overlords of Gallo-Roman society, the Merovingian Frankish kings, in fact retained the essential features of Roman administration and even the gold coinage after their conversion to Roman Catholicism, thereby preserving continuity of the socioeconomic system with that of classical antiquity, the only change being in the composition of the leadership at the top. The real break, in his view, came not with the barbarian takeover of the late fifth and sixth centuries, but only after the Arab caliphate wrested control of the Mediterranean from the Byzantines, separating the eastern and western halves of the former Roman Empire from each other in the second half of the seventh century. According to Pirenne, it was the subsequent cessation of trade and other overseas links that caused Western Europe to revert to a more primitive self-sufficient economic basis under the rule of the Carolingian dynasty. Thus no Mohammed, no Charlemagne.

The empirical support for Pirenne's thesis was based on what Robert Lopez (1943) called "the four disappearances" from Western Europe, of papyrus, luxury fabrics, oriental spices, and gold coins, for all of which the West depended on Byzantium. Pirenne had of course to demonstrate not only that these items disappeared but also that the timing was consistent with the Arab conquests. Papyrus was used in the western empire for most record-keeping purposes by both church and state, and for major commercial transactions as well: according to Pirenne (1939, p. 92), "whole cargoes of this commodity must have been unloaded on the quays of the seaports." He claimed (pp. 169–76) that papyrus ceased to be used for royal documents by the Merovingians after 677, and that monks and merchants in Gaul also stopped using it beyond this date, though they perhaps continued to some extent in Italy. Silks and brocades were extensively used by the Merovingian court and church, to be replaced by plain Flemish woolen cloth under the Carolingians. Gold coins and oriental spices also seemed to pass out of use around this time.

Lopez disputed each of the four disappearances to at least some extent. Papyrus continued to be used in Italy, while in Gaul Lopez claimed that its decline was associated with that of the influence of Roman law, and that its fading out of use thus represented a fall in demand rather than a restriction in supply. As for luxury fabrics and oriental spices, he again maintained that a demand shift due to changing tastes rather than supply restrictions by the Arabs was responsible for their disappearance, though he offered no convincing arguments as to why such a shift might have occurred. On luxury fabrics such as the "royal purple" he thought that the Byzantines themselves might have restricted exports to deny the upstart Western rulers the symbols of imperial grandeur. On gold coins he argued that the Arabs in Spain were on a silver standard, obliging the Frankish rulers to follow suit, but again he did not give any strong arguments as to why this should be so.

A more compelling critique of the Pirenne thesis was by Daniel Dennett (1948), who raised the questions of why the Arabs would want to restrict trade with the West in the first place, and whether they had the power to restrict it should they have wanted to do so. After all, as we have seen, the Arabs traded with infidels of all stripes, pagan nomads in Central Asia, Hindus and Buddhists in India and Southeast Asia, and even with their great Christian rivals, the Byzantines. Why should they not have wanted to do so with the Franks of Western Europe, when they were already trading with their fellow Muslims but political rivals the Umayyads in Spain and the Christians in Italy? If trade did in fact decline with Gaul, might this not have been due to the disruptions caused by the barbarian invasions and the associated economic setback, just as the traditional view maintained, rather than to any deliberate embargo undertaken by the caliphate? In any case, Dennett argued that the Arabs could not have enforced an embargo without the capture of Sicily, which only happened after 827 when

the Aghlabid rulers of Tunisia invaded the island, capturing Palermo
in 831; it took them until 878 to take Syracuse and until 902 to take
Taormina, not gaining full control of the entire island until well into
the tenth century. One plausible defense of Pirenne, however, offered
by Eliyahu Ashtor (1976a), was that the almost perpetual warfare in the
Mediterranean after the Arab conquests disrupted and greatly reduced
trade, even though there may not have been any deliberate attempt to
do so by the Muslim side.

The Pirenne thesis thus maintains that the rise of Islam was a force
for deglobalization, at least insofar as Western Europe was concerned:
a paradox indeed, given the profound integrating impact that Islam
had more widely. Presumably, relative price data might help resolve the
issue. If Pirenne or Ashtor were right, then the relative price of luxury
imports into Western Europe should have risen, reflecting restricted
supply, while if Lopez is right, the relative price of papyrus and oriental
spices should have declined as a result of falling demand. Sadly, we are
not aware of any price data for so early a period, and so we have to make
do with more qualitative evidence on trade flows and trade routes. In
particular, recent scholarship has emphasized that the Mediterranean
was *not* the only avenue for trade between Western Europe and the
Islamic World. Another possibility was that Western goods could be
exchanged for the forest products of the far north such as furs, honey,
wax, and amber, and in turn be exported to the Islamic World in
exchange for whatever it could offer in return. In other words, the
Islamic and the Carolingian worlds could be connected through the
intermediation of those stalwart Scandinavian merchant-pirates, the
Varangians.

EASTERN EUROPE: THE VIKING CONNECTION

This was the bold hypothesis of the Swedish historian and numismatist
Sture Bolin (1953), who entitled his brilliant paper on this subject
"Mohammed, Charlemagne and Rurik." The basic argument put for-
ward by Bolin is clearly stated in the following quotation (p. 8):

> Firstly, whether or not trade ceased between Western Europe and the Arab
> world during the Carolingian period, it is quite certain that, within the
> Caliphate trade, industry and a town economy flourished as never before.
> Secondly, whether the trade of Western Europe increased or decreased
> during this epoch, the ancient connections between Western Europe and
> the northern and Baltic countries became very much more important,

especially in the first part of the Carolingian age. If these two accepted facts are set in juxtaposition, however, the main problem again thrusts itself forward. One is led to ask whether the communications between the Frankish empire and the North became more lively in consequence of reduced communications between the West and the Orient, or whether the same factors were responsible for the prosperity of trade both in the Caliphate and around the North Sea.

Bolin came down firmly for the second of these two alternatives, concluding that the prosperity of the Arab world indirectly stimulated trade and economic growth in the West through its initial impact on the Varangians and Kievan Rus. Thus Mohammed was in a sense the creator of the Carolingian state, as Pirenne argued, but by *promoting* economic growth and trade in Western Europe, *not* by retarding it. To begin with, Bolin argues that trade between Western Europe and the east did not dry up in the seventh and eighth centuries after the rise of Islam, but continued with the export of slaves, furs, and swords in exchange for silver and luxury products such as silks and spices. The slaves, however, were mostly eastern Slavs and the furs were also from the far north and east, so these commodities were reexports rather than exports, with only the swords being of Frankish manufacture. The Franks obtained the slaves and furs from the Baltic and North Sea regions in exchange for their own primary and manufactured products. The slaves were driven on foot along the roads from Prague to Kraków, collected at Verdun, and exported through Arles to Spain and other parts of the Islamic World, by the multilingual Rhadanite Jewish merchants whose contacts extended from Spain and North Africa to China.

By the early ninth century, however, Bolin believed that a fundamental shift occurred, with the Norsemen actively opening up a *direct* channel to the lucrative eastern markets by taking control of the Russian river systems, extracting the furs and slaves as tribute from the native Finnish and Slavic populations by brute force, and exchanging these for Islamic silver and Byzantine silks. The discovery of very rich silver mines in the areas of Tashkent and the Panjshir valley in what is now Afghanistan led to a massive flood of silver in the form of Abbasid and later Samanid coins passing into the hands of the Norsemen, and from them to the West (see figure 2.3).[7] Bolin compares this silver influx of the ninth and tenth centuries to that created by the New World conquistadores in the sixteenth century, with similar inflationary and expansionary effects.

[7]See the very helpful maps in O'Brien (2002, pp. 71, 78).

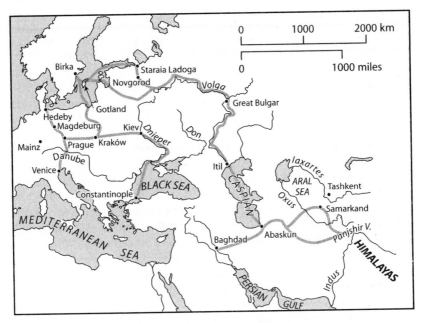

FIGURE 2.3. The Viking connection.

In order to establish this Bolin version, or rather *in*version, of the Pirenne thesis, three steps are involved. First, the economic expansion of the Islamic World from the seventh to the tenth century must be demonstrated, and this the preceding sections of this chapter have already done. Next, the exact nature and dimensions of the trade between the Swedes and Russians on the one hand and the Muslim economies on the other has to be specified. Finally, the link between the eastern trade and the West through the Baltic and the North Sea has to be established. The rest of this section will take up the crucial middle link in this chain of relations, what we refer to as the "Viking Connection." Fortunately, this subject has been greatly advanced since Bolin wrote, particularly by the penetrating research of the American historian and numismatist Thomas S. Noonan (1998), upon whose work we draw in what follows. The links between the Carolingian economy and the northern world of the Baltic and the North Sea will be the subject of the subsequent section.

Noonan (1998, chapter 1) begins by asking "why the Vikings first came to Russia." Certainly, they did not do it for booty or plunder, as in the West, where they were raiding the rich monasteries and towns on the coasts of England, Ireland, and France. Russia at that time was a thickly forested and sparsely populated land with no great treasures to extort. There was, however, a plentiful source of treasure available further south along the extensive Russian river systems and short portages that led along the Volga to the Caspian Sea and Baghdad, or along the Dnieper to the Black Sea and Constantinople. Particularly from the Islamic World, silver dirhems in abundance could be obtained in exchange for northern forest products such as furs, but also for Slavic slaves of both sexes obtained from the sedentary farming populations. The furs and slaves could be obtained partly in exchange for Baltic goods such as Frankish swords or glass beads, but mainly through tribute imposed by force on tribes of Finnish hunter-gatherers or Slavic farming communities. They did not even have to be taken all the way to Baghdad or Constantinople since the Khazars and the Volga Bulgars could serve as useful intermediaries, at whose camps the exchange of the northern goods and slaves for silver coins and luxury products such as silk could take place to the profit of all three parties, if not of the unfortunate captives.

The earliest Russian settlements and towns such as Staraia Ladoga, Novgorod, and Kiev itself mainly arose as collection points, trading posts and service stations for this long-distance commerce. Predation itself begets predation, however, and other nomadic steppe peoples such as the Pechenegs could profitably live off the proceeds of lying in wait for flotillas down the rivers at points where they were sufficiently narrow to attack from the shore, or where rapids made disembarkation and transshipment necessary. Trading and fighting were but two sides of the same coin, as we have already seen in the case of the Cholas and will see many times again in this book. The Kievan Rus state can be seen as arising from the necessity to organize both of these complementary activities efficiently.

Noonan (1998) reports on a number of hoards of Islamic silver dirhems found in various parts of Russian territory along the Volga and Dnieper rivers, dating mainly from between 800 and 840, and also similar finds in the eastern Baltic area over the same period. The total finds rise sharply from less than 300 in the 800–10 decade to over 1,750 in 830–40, over 4,720 coins in all, with the Baltic finds averaging 36% of the total. Thus at least one of every three Islamic coins that entered Russian lands ended up in the Baltic region, since there was no possibility of the coins getting to the Baltic without passing through Russia. Staraia Ladoga was the center at which the dirhems could be obtained in exchange for Western goods, and Polish and other western Slav merchants apparently did this, though only Swedes ventured beyond this point into the interior of Russia to obtain the dirhems more directly.

Noonan (1998, chapter 2) examines the question of why the trade in Islamic silver began only around the turn of the ninth century and not much sooner after the establishment of the caliphate. He argues that it was due to the "hundred years war" that was waged between the Arabs under the Umayyads and the Khazars for supremacy in the Caucasus, the mountainous region between the Black and Caspian Seas. In this struggle the Arabs had the power to defeat Khazar armies in the field but not the resources necessary to sustain occupation of their lands after subjugation. The Abbasids apparently realized this and made peace overtures that finally led to the cessation of hostilities by the close of the eighth century. This opened the door to mutually beneficial trade, with the Khazar capital at Itil at the mouth of the Volga on the Caspian Sea becoming a great entrepôt for merchants of all faiths.

The Khazars understood the need to give up their shamanism for a "religion of the book" but were reluctant to adopt either Islam or Orthodox Christianity for fear of domination by the corresponding great power, the caliphate or Byzantium, making the surprise choice of Judaism instead, as we saw in the previous chapter. The practice of Judaism, however, was apparently confined to the *khagan* and the ruling elite, with the people following a variety of other faiths. The Rus were at first subordinate to the Khazars, even taking service with them as mercenaries. Gradually, however, they began to wrest control over the Slavic tribes away from them, gaining more of the rents from the north–south trade and thus enhancing the flow of silver to the Baltic and the West. Another Turkic state of former steppe nomads engaged in collecting tribute in furs and slaves and exchanging these for silver was that of the Volga Bulgars. This state, with its capital at Great Bulgar in the middle Volga, adopted Islam and was another competitor to Kievan Rus and the Khazars. With its prime location in the middle stretches of the Volga, it was able to amass considerable wealth from tolls, in addition to the tribute that it was able to collect.

In 922 the caliph of Baghdad sent an embassy to the Bulgar capital in response to a request for what today would be called "technical assistance" in the setting up of an Islamic state. One of the members of this Abbasid diplomatic mission was a certain Ibn Fadlan, the account of whose *Rihla*, or journey to the remote land, has become a classic in the observation of one culture by another. Ibn Fadlan encountered what appears to have been a group of Vikings in the Bulgar capital who clearly both fascinated and repelled him. He was impressed by their gigantic stature, saying that they are "as tall as palm trees," and noted that every man was armed with weapons from which he was never separated. He described them as being obsessed by the drive to trade profitably, praying to wooden idols of their gods for commercial success. Their wealth was flaunted in truly Veblenesque fashion, adorning their wives with a necklace for every ten thousand dirhems that they earned, with many of the women displaying several of these symbols of commercial success around their necks at once. Their lack of hygiene shocked him, as did their consumption of vast amounts of alcohol and their fornication in public with the slave women that they owned in droves. Ibn Fadlan also gave a horrifying account, but with the clinical detachment of a modern anthropologist, of a chief's funeral, burnt in his ship with a favorite concubine gruesomely sacrificed to accompany him in the afterlife.

Other Arab writers, such as the geographers Ibn Khurradadhbih and Ibn Rustah, also left records of Rus characteristics, trade routes, and social practices. Kramers (1931, p. 101) gives a list of goods traded by the Rus (based on another Arab geographer, Al-Maqdisi) as "sables, miniver, ermines, the fur of foxes, beavers, spotted hares and goats; also wax, arrows, birch bark, high fur caps, fish glue, fish teeth (probably walrus tusks), castoreum, amber, prepared horse hides, honey, hazel nuts, falcons, swords, armor, maple wood, small and big cattle." Ibn Rustah in particular noted that they did not practice agriculture but lived solely by trading slaves and the products that they extracted from the Slavs and other native populations for silver from the Islamic lands through Bulgar and Khazar intermediaries, and also directly. It was even noted that they pretended to be Christians if this could reduce the duties or tolls that they had to pay on goods in transit.

The Swedes in Russia were always in close contact with their home base. The site of Birka, near modern Stockholm, is very rich in artifacts, particularly coins, from the Islamic World obtained during this period, as are the island of Gotland and the Danish site of Hedeby. Spufford (1988, p. 67) states that over 200,000 Islamic coins have been found in northern, central, and Eastern Europe, including 60,000 in Gotland, 45,000 in the rest of Scandinavia, and 20,000 on the Pomeranian coast of the Baltic in what is now Poland, with most of the rest in Russia itself. He also reports (p. 67) that 35 dirhems minted at Samarkand between 895 and 911 were found at sites dating from about 925–30 as far afield as Yorkshire. Birka and Hedeby were the points at which the dirhems obtained from the trade along Russian rivers could be exchanged for grain and wine, pottery, and iron manufactures such as the Frankish swords that were popular items of weaponry both among the Vikings and their eastern trading partners. According to Sawyer (1994, p. 130), Gotland was more of a pirate base than a trading center or commercial emporium, but this only affects the distribution of the coins between sites, not the fact that they came from the east by whatever combination of trade, tribute, or outright plunder by the Rus. The archaeologists Clarke and Ambrosiani (1995), in their meticulous survey of the evidence in the towns of the Viking Age, provide ample support to link the contemporaneous expansion and rich grave-goods of sites such as Birka, Hedeby, and Gotland with the influx of Islamic silver, even though they do not cite Bolin at all. They describe what must have been a flourishing industry using the plentiful local supplies of elk and reindeer antlers, as well as other animal horns and bones, to make a variety of personal items such as combs, pins, and brooches that can be found in sites from Russia to Ireland. Glass beads and pottery were also produced at Hedeby and other centers.

The Scandinavian countries and Poland had no separate coinage of any consequence in the ninth and tenth centuries and the dirhems probably circulated as the currency for everyday transactions as well as a store of value. The fact that many of the coins were cut into pieces, "hacksilver," is often taken as evidence of this. The Carolingians and Ottonians, who did issue silver coinage, would remint the dirhems for that purpose. The dirhems discovered in Russian and Western hoards rise very sharply for most of the tenth century before drying up completely after about 975. The reasons for this sudden cessation are not clear and various hypotheses have been put forward, such as the exhaustion of the Samanid mines in Central Asia and Afghanistan. The fact that the Rus themselves devastated both the Volga Bulgars and the Khazars around this time, and that the Samanid dynasty itself fell at the end of the tenth century, would seem to indicate that geopolitical shifts in the Central Asian world are the likelier explanation.

Hodges and Whitehouse (1983) enthusiastically adopt the Bolin hypothesis. They argue that the monetary reform undertaken by Charlemagne in 794, the introduction of the "heavy" silver denier or penny, would have required an amount of silver not available from Western sources alone and that it was these Islamic dirhems obtained through trade at centers like Hedeby and reminted that met the demand. The real money supply required to support the economic expansion of Carolingian Europe therefore came in their view as the indirect result of the eastern trade of the Vikings with the Muslim World. It should be noted, however, that Karl Morrison (1963) has questioned the possibility that Islamic silver from Scandinavia could have played such a crucial role without leaving more direct evidence of some kind. No hoards of these coins have been found west of the Rhine, nor are there any references to their being melted down and converted at Carolingian mints. Bolin (1953, p. 35) does, however, note the interesting fact that a "Jew from Spain" found Samanid dirhems struck at Samarkand in 913 in Mainz in 965. Spufford (1988) identifies him as Ibrahim ben Yaqub of Tortosa, sent on a diplomatic mission on behalf of the emir of Cordoba, and observes that most such coins would have been reminted in the Rhineland if not further east by Otto the Great of Saxony in his mint at Magdeburg.

The Spanish traveler also recorded his surprise at the abundance and variety of goods from India available at Mainz. There is certainly a strong case to be made that the northern European contacts with the Islamic states via the Dnieper, Don, and Volga were a positive influence on Western economic growth in the ninth and tenth centuries, with slave and other exports financing silver inflows, that then helped to monetize an expanding and commercializing European economy. In that sense Bolin was right to claim that it was "Rurik" who helped to bring Mohammed and Charlemagne together, thereby contributing to the beginnings of a decisive shift in the center of gravity of the European economy, away from the Mediterranean and toward the northern shores, that would be one of the outstanding features of European economic history during the subsequent millennium. We end this chapter with a brief account of trade and economic progress in Western Europe during this important period.

The Economy of Western Europe

The nature of the early medieval economy of Western Europe has long been a matter of controversy. One indisputable fact, however, is that the Carolingian world was much less urbanized than the Roman or early Merovingian. The Roman Empire can be succinctly described as "based on a network of two thousand cities supported by taxes on agricultural production" (Devroey 2001, p. 105). The cities were where the governing and religious elite lived, with the necessary physical infrastructure of forum, amphitheater, public baths, and cathedral (after Christianization in the fourth century), and all the working population necessary to provide them with the amenities of civilized life. The revenue necessary to sustain this vast superstructure, and a standing army of over 600,000 in imperial times, was provided by taxes on the agricultural sector, mainly consisting of large estates worked by slave labor, and on trade. As a result of the barbarian irruptions and warfare but mainly the destructive outbreak of bubonic plague in 542, during the reign of Justinian, there was a loss of population of 20–25% that must have made it impossible to maintain many of these cities at the necessary minimum scale, leading to the almost completely deurbanized society of Carolingian times.

The ruling class—civil, military, and ecclesiastical—now lived in the countryside in estates, abbeys, and monasteries accompanied by their retinue of followers, supporters, and servants and surrounded by peasant households, supporting themselves on their own plots and supplying their rents and labor dues to the demesne lands to which they were attached. Under these circumstances it is easy to imagine that this was a system of self-sufficient or "natural" as opposed to an exchange or "money" economy as many, including Pirenne, thought. Recent research, summarized by Verhulst (2002), has fairly conclusively demonstrated this supposition to be false. The estates all sold particular foodstuffs, raw materials, or manufactured products at various market places and regional centers, purchasing in return those goods that could not be produced, or only inadequately so, in their own fields and workshops. Indeed, one can think of each of these estates as a "country," as in the standard theory of international trade, with its own endowment of labor, land, and capital and set of consumer preferences, using market prices to maximize the value of its own production and consumption by "exporting" those goods in excess supply and "importing" those in excess demand at the given market prices. In strict economic logic cities by themselves are neither necessary nor sufficient for the existence of a market economy. The great staples of grain, wine, woolen and linen cloth, as well as a mass of manufactured items, could all be produced and allocated more or less efficiently in this way.

A key feature of the Carolingian system was the important role that the great abbeys and monasteries played in the economy. This reflected the strong concentration of land, capital, and labor in their hands as a result of the religious impulse of the age, which resulted in donations of these assets by rulers, magnates, and ordinary citizens. With the near monopoly of education and administrative capacity they enjoyed, they were also well-placed to exploit and manage these resources efficiently. The religious institutions played a prominent role not only in agricultural and industrial production for civilian use but also in the supply of troops from the ranks of the population assigned to them and in the manufacture of weapons on an extensive scale for their equipment. The armed forces of the regime were thus no longer the standing army of the Roman Empire or the war bands of the Frankish tribes, but the feudal levy imposed on all estate holders, lay and ecclesiastical alike. The smelting of iron and manufacture of weapons and agricultural implements would be done either in specialized workshops or by the attached workforce on their own premises as part of their feudal dues. Not surprisingly, the state imposed strict controls on the sale of weaponry, which also not surprisingly were often ineffective. Thus the high-quality Frankish sword blades, the best ones marked with the name of the maker "Ulfberht," were as we have seen a prized item in international trade from England to Russia and the Islamic World, despite the prohibition.

Manufacturing of different goods reflected strong regional specializations, such as the Frisian cloth woven and traded by those people and which was of such high quality that Charlemagne sent a consignment as a present to Harun al-Rashid. A special type of pottery known as Badorf ware, from a village of that name between Bonn and Cologne, was another famous item traded all over Europe and found in many archaeological sites, including Birka and Hedeby. High-quality glass was also produced and traded extensively.

Agricultural production was boosted by three famous technical innovations: the heavy iron plough drawn by teams of oxen or horses, the shoulder collar for horses, and the three-field rotation. The processing of grain was done with much greater efficiency in watermills, which came into general use by the eleventh century (Bloch 1969, chapter 5). The growth of population, recovering from the ravages of the Plague of Justinian, and the clearing of extensive forest land, together with these major innovations, led to substantial increases in cereal production, accompanied by growth in the cultivation of vines and olives.

Interregional trade in bulk staples such as grain, salt, and wine was conducted by specialized merchants as well as by the agents of the great estates. Salt was produced on the western Atlantic coast and distributed from Nantes by boats along the Loire. Salt was also produced at Metz in the northeast and at Reichenhall in Germany, from where it was shipped to Passau and sent eastwards along the Danube to the borders of the empire by Bavarian merchants, who were exempted from tolls on the foreign products they carried back on the return journey (Verhulst 2002, chapter 7). Mainz was an important center for collecting grain from eastern German territories as well as wine, sending these commodities north along the Rhine to the major emporium of Dorestad, from where they could be reexported to Scandinavia and England. The Frisians were the handlers of this trade, and also exported pottery and glass in very large amounts to Scandinavia. Quern-stones were another important item produced in Germany and sold by the Frisians around the North Sea and the Baltic.

Wine was produced on the estates of the abbey of Saint-Germain-des-Prés vastly in excess of its own requirements, the surplus being shipped along the Seine to Paris for sale at the fair of St Denis, which was the major wine market in Europe, frequented by Frisian and Anglo-Saxon merchants. Jellema (1955, p. 34) has described the role of the Frisians in the long-distance commerce of Northern Europe at this time as analogous on a smaller scale to that of the Hanseatic League almost five hundred years later. They were present at trade centers from York and London in England to Mainz and Cologne on the Rhine, Regensburg on the Danube, and Birka and Hedeby in Scandinavia. They were the preeminent sailors of Europe before the emergence of the Vikings, the indispensable cog that plied the medieval northern seas being a vessel of their invention (although its heyday was not until the thirteenth and fourteenth centuries, when it was adopted as their standard vessel by the Hansa) (see Jellema 1955, p. 32; Dollinger 1970, pp. 141–42).

Not far behind the Frisians in mercantile energy and drive were the Anglo-Saxons. The England of King Alfred and his successors was a compact and wealthy state that traded extensively with the Carolingian and Scandinavian worlds. In addition to York and London, there was the important trading center of Hamwic near the modern Southampton, directly opposite the Channel to the Carolingian port of Quentovic. The production and export of woolen cloth begins to appear as a distinctive feature of the English economy even from these early times. The coinage of the English kings, particularly Athelstan, was much sought after and appears in surviving hoards all over the northern lands.

It is no accident that our discussion of economic activity in Western Europe has so far been concerned largely with the Baltic, the North Sea, and both sides of the Rhine, which had become the main arteries of commerce. In Roman and Merovingian times it was Marseilles and the Rhone valley that had played this role. To that extent we have reflected the arguments of Pirenne and Bolin regarding the shift of the economic center of gravity away from the Mediterranean and toward the north. Nevertheless, the Mediterranean continued to be connected with central and northern Europe, but over the Alpine passes and up the Rhine to the north and along the Danube to the east. The toll stations at the passes seem to have collected considerable revenues, at the moderate rate of 10% on the value of the goods. Italy was thus an important avenue through which trade was conducted with both the Byzantine and Islamic east.

Bari was an important seaport, held from 840 to 870 by the Arabs but then recovered from them. Amalfi on the west coast and later Genoa and Pisa would see the volume of their trade grow increasingly. It was

Venice, however, in the lagoons at the head of the Adriatic, which used its Byzantine connections from the eighth century onwards and began to assert its historical destiny as the hinge between the east and the west. Among the inland cities Pavia, the former Lombard capital, was a major center, with a heavy volume of traffic along the Po with Venice. The great Hungarian raid into Italy in 924 is said to have burned forty-four churches in Pavia, which besides being a testimonial to the destructive capacities of the Hungarians is also a tribute to the size and wealth of the city itself. Ravenna slowly declined and Rome, which used to have 1 million people at the height of the Roman Empire, fell to between thirty and forty thousand. It was nevertheless still important as a financial center, in addition to its religious significance as the seat of the papacy and the main destination of heavy pilgrim traffic from all over Christendom. In the countryside the great estates, both lay and ecclesiastical, played the same role as in France of increasingly diverting handicrafts and small-scale industrial production from the cities to their own workshops.

In summary, the evidence clearly shows that trade and commercialization were key features of the increasingly monetized Western European economy during this period. Another important feature of the Carolingian economy that should not be lost sight of, however, is the continuing role that was played in it by the systematic plunder and expropriation of neighboring states and tribes, behavior that is normally associated only with the Vikings or the steppe nomads. Reuter (1985) argues that this was an essential element in the Frankish military system, necessary to reward the warrior retinues of the rulers and magnates. Vast sums were extracted from the Avars, Lombards, and Saxons and lesser amounts from the Basques, Bretons, and Frisians. The eastern parts of the empire offered more lucrative prospects in this regard, at the expense of Slavic tribes, than did the more settled west, which may explain why the latter area disintegrated into feudal disarray while the former was more successful in maintaining the unity of the ruling houses by providing their followers with more opportunities for loot. The capture and sale of slaves from the Saxon tribes before they were converted to Christianity, and of Slavs afterward, was an important aspect of this process.

The economic impact of the Viking raids on the coastal areas of the Low Countries, France, and Britain during the last two centuries of the first millennium is still rather obscure, but the traditional accounts of mass slaughter and wanton terror by the northern predators are no longer accepted uncritically by revisionist historians. The sacking of monasteries and port cities such as Dorestad itself doubtless disrupted economic activity severely, but there is also much evidence that it did not significantly alter the general upward trend. After the abandonment of Dorestad, vulnerable at the mouth of the Rhine, the Frisians shifted trade to such places as Tiel and Utrecht that were less accessible to the raiders. Population growth does not seem to have been checked discernibly. A. R. Lewis (1958a, chapter 5), in one of the fullest examinations of this issue, points out that mints in northern and western France continued their operations and that Atlantic commerce did not decline, while German trade east of the Rhine actually expanded. The account by Ibrahim ben Yaqub, cited earlier, of the abundance of eastern luxuries available in Mainz in 965 is a good indication of this. We also saw in the previous section that the influx of Islamic silver into the Baltic lands swelled during the course of the tenth century, which stimulated economic growth in the new expansive Polish state as a result of trade with both Russia and Scandinavia.

The Vikings were frequently bought off from their destructive raids by the payment of massive quantities of precious metal in either coin or bullion by the rulers of the Western European states. What did they do with the treasure that they received in this way? For an economist this is the familiar "transfer problem," of which perhaps the most famous example was German reparations after World War I leading to a great debate between Maynard Keynes and Bertil Ohlin. Some of the treasure would be hoarded but the rest would undoubtedly be spent on goods and services, within or outside the Viking lands. In either case eventually the original "financial transfer" would lead to a "real transfer" of the same magnitude in the form of an export surplus by the victim countries and a matching import surplus for the Viking territories, with the distribution of the precious metal stock ultimately returning to its initial state. A redistribution of real income would thus take place but there would not necessarily be any reduction of real income in the aggregate. In fact, to the extent that there was an underutilization of economic resources to begin with, the net outcome could well be an expansion of total real income.

This analysis of the Danegeld phenomenon could help to explain why the Viking depredations might not necessarily have been as damaging to the overall economy of Western Europe as might be imagined. Some amount of terror and destruction could have established the credibility of the Viking threat, after which a negotiated financial settlement would reduce the pure "deadweight loss" of further casualties and physical destruction. Simon Coupland (1995) has analyzed the issue of what impact the payments to the Vikings had on the West Frankish economy during the reign of Charles the

Bald from 840 to 877. His conclusion is that the payments were usually successful in preventing hostilities and destruction and that the taxation to raise the requisite sums from the magnates, the church, and the peasant population did not cause any significant economic damage or dislocation, contrary to many contentions in the previous literature.

Another factor which presumably led to lower costs eventually was the shift from "competitive" to "monopolistic" banditry, or from "roving" to "stationary" banditry in the language of Mancur Olson (1993). A Viking raid undertaken by a small independent group would not have an incentive to avoid killing the goose that lays the golden eggs by putting a vulnerable city or trading station out of business. Having such raids undertaken by the leader of a large state, such as the Danish king Svein Forkbeard or his son Knut, as happened in England early in the eleventh century, might solve this collective action problem. Lewis (1958a) indicates that the Viking attacks came in two waves: an earlier one that seemed to fit a pattern of independent small-scale raids and a later one of more systematic extortion and even administrative takeover, as in the case of the Danish conquest of England in the first half of the eleventh century.

An alternative way to buy off the Vikings, reminiscent of the ancient Chinese tactic of "using the barbarians to fight the barbarians," was to grant them land in strategic coastal areas and to let them defend it against their former compatriots. The most notable instance of course is the grant of the area in the vicinity of Rouen by Charles the Simple to a Viking chieftain, Rollo, as a fief. This was the origin of the Duchy of Normandy that was to play so significant a part in European and world history. The Norsemen seem to have rapidly become assimilated to the local language and culture, but their leaders displayed the bold ruthlessness and daring of their forebears, combined with an extraordinarily shrewd capacity for "statebuilding," as evidenced not only in the duchy itself but in England and Ireland after the Norman Conquest, and in Southern Italy and Sicily as well.

Thus in answer to the question of whether the Vikings were pirates, traders, or settlers, the answer is that they were undoubtedly all of the above, switching from one role to the other depending upon opportunity and circumstance. As colonizers and settlers their achievements were greatest in the northern Atlantic, with settlements established in the Orkneys, Faeroes, Iceland, and Greenland and a spectacular even if unsuccessful attempt on the mainland of North America. Of all the peoples, not only of Western Europe but of the entire Eurasian landmass, they undoubtedly did the most to widen the geographical horizons of their time.

Chapter 3

WORLD TRADE 1000–1500: THE ECONOMIC CONSEQUENCES OF GENGHIS KHAN

OUR FOCUS ON "WORLD TRADE" from 1000 to 1500 will mainly be on trade between the regional units defined in chapter 1, with attention where necessary being paid to intraregional developments as well. As we have already noted, trade in the Mediterranean and the Black Sea traditionally involved the Islamic World and both Western and Eastern Europe. The Indian Ocean linked the Islamic World, Eastern Africa, India, and Southeast Asia, while the South China Sea connected China directly to the Indonesian Archipelago and indirectly to India and the Islamic World. The Red Sea and the Persian Gulf were the crucial East–West overseas gateways in this period as they had been since Roman times and even earlier. The overland route was the alternative passage linking China to the Islamic World and both Eastern and Western Europe through Central Asia. It will thus be convenient to organize the discussion in terms of (i) the Mediterranean and the Black Sea, (ii) the Indian Ocean and the South China Sea, and (iii) overland trade from China to Europe across Central Asia. The lengthy period that we examine in this chapter saw decisive shifts in the control of these trade routes that had momentous historical consequences and it will be convenient to divide the period as a whole into two distinct eras, 1000–1350 and 1350–1500, demarcated by the initial onset of the Black Death.

Quantitative data for the early part of this period are scarce almost to the point of nonexistence, but a surprising amount of information does exist about the commodities exported and imported by each of the regions and the role that these played in their economic systems. Changes in trade routes and some qualitative assessments of the volume of trade along them will be noted. By the late medieval period, more data become available, particularly price data, and we will make use of these in the later sections of this chapter.

The economic history of Eurasia during this half millennium was marked decisively by the impact of two great (and interrelated) shocks, one geopolitical and the other biological. The first shock was the unification of most of the Eurasian landmass by the Mongols under the leadership of Genghis Khan. The second shock was the catastrophe of the Black Death, which struck around the same time as the Mongol Empire was disintegrating. This chapter will therefore dwell at length on the immediate and longer-run consequences of both these shocks. A third theme is the gradual emergence of Western Europe from the provincial and relatively isolated backwater of Eurasia that it had been at the beginning of the period to the powerful expansionist force all over the globe that it would become five hundred years later. In terms of Halford Mackinder's "geographical pivot of history," the half millennium covered in this chapter saw power begin to shift away from the "Heartland" of the Eurasian landmass, which had dominated it from the dawn of history, toward the "Rimland" of the western extremity of that landmass, culminating in the voyages of Christopher Columbus, Vasco da Gama, and Ferdinand Magellan as well as the combined military-nautical revolution of "guns and sails" (Cipolla 1965).

Trade and War in the Mediterranean and the Black Sea, 1000–1350

The Mediterranean, the "*Mare Nostrum*" of the Romans, even more than their celebrated roads, was the vital highway that created the economic unity of their empire. As we noted in the previous chapter, Henri Pirenne's famous claim that the Arab irruption of the seventh century made the sea a "Muslim Lake," cutting off commerce between Western Europe and Byzantium, and leading to an increasingly autarkic Western Europe, is no longer accepted by scholars. In fact, as Maurice Lombard argued, the Golden Age of Islam stimulated trade with Western Europe by providing her with an increasingly prosperous trade partner. Trade between the Islamic World and Europe can be analyzed within a "center–periphery" framework, with Europe specializing in resource-intensive and labor-intensive commodities and the Islamic World in more advanced manufactures. Slaves, the most labor-intensive of all labor-intensive commodities, were indeed the major export of Europe to the Islamic World for centuries, until the conversion to Christianity of the pagan Slavs dried up the supply. The decline of urban crafts and associated activities noted by Pirenne could then be attributed to the deindustrialization of a previously more balanced economic system by opportunities for lucrative exports of primary products to a more advanced and technologically sophisticated partner: an early example of what is now known as the "Dutch Disease," and the mirror image of the rising industrialization and declining grain exports of Fatimid Egypt which we noted in the previous chapter. Whatever the reason, there is no doubt that in 1000 both Western Europe and the Slavic part of Eastern Europe outside of the Byzantine Empire constituted an underdeveloped hinterland to the economically more advanced Byzantine Empire and Islamic World.

It is convenient to begin our examination of trade at "the market at the edge of the west" (Constable 1994), where the western edge of the Muslim Mediterranean world bordered on the southern edge of Christian Europe. As we saw in chapter 1, the original Umayyad dynasty in Iberia and the centralized state associated with it fragmented into a number of petty kingdoms early in the eleventh century, the so-called *taifas*. This disintegration of the Islamic state enabled the Christians to push their frontier southwards and to exact substantial tribute payments from the *taifa* states, and eventually to capture the major city of Toledo in 1085. This provoked an intervention by the Berber rulers of Marrakesh, who established a single unified state across the straits of Gibraltar, the dynasty of the Almoravids. The political cycle of disintegration followed by North African intervention was repeated in the twelfth century, with the new Berber dynasty of the Almohads establishing itself in 1147. With their control of access to the trans-Saharan gold supplies these unified Berber empires on both sides of the straits were economically dominant as well as militarily powerful. Their periods of glory, however, were eventually checked by the expansion of a resurgent Christian Europe. Cordoba and Seville fell to Castile by the middle of the thirteenth century, while Aragon reconquered Valencia and the island of Mallorca. Only the kingdom of Granada remained in Muslim hands by 1350.

As we saw in the previous chapter, the economic prosperity of al-Andalus was based on the transmission of crops, agricultural techniques, and manufacturing activities from east to west within the Islamic World. The conversion of the Slavs to Christianity and the success of the Norsemen in developing trade between Europe and the Islamic World, at the expense of competitors such as the Rhadanite Jews, meant that Arctic furs and Eastern European slaves no longer transited Iberia in significant numbers. The source for slaves was limited to captives from the Christian Iberian kingdoms, while the expensive sables and martens of the north were replaced by humbler rabbit skins. However, gold from West Africa continued to flow through al-Andalus, particularly after it had been minted by the Almoravids into the very popular *murabitun*, used and imitated by several of the Christian kingdoms.

As previously noted, timber was one of the main exports of Muslim Spain during this period, both in the form of wood itself and also embodied in ships. The timber was mostly from the extensive pine forests of the coastal regions and the Balearic Islands. The logs were floated downriver to the shipbuilding centers of Denia and Valencia, while the ships were sold to both Muslims and Christian buyers around the Mediterranean. Several minerals, particularly copper and mercury but also marble and tin, were exported. Two exotic but valuable exports were ambergris from the Atlantic coast and the crimson dye called *qirmiz*. A wide range of high-quality textiles, mainly silk, was exported around the Mediterranean. This must have been a high-value-added industry since the raw silk itself was produced in the country with the Sierra Nevada mountain range providing a favorable climate for the growth of mulberry trees. Geographers spoke of three thousand silkworm farms around Jaen and eight hundred workshops in Almería. The silk was both exported raw and worked up into expensive brocades and other fabrics. Linen, cotton, and woolen products were also exported, while silk and wool were exported in the form of carpets. Exports to the Christian states seemed to grow particularly rapidly after 1100 (ibid., p. 178).

Constable (1994, chapter 7) lists leather, paper, and ceramics as representing further important manufactured exports from al-Andalus. Paper was not only exported as such, but also combined with high-quality leather in the form of expensive books. She cites a commercial manual of the period advising merchants not to invest in "philosophical books since these are bought only by wise men and scholars, most of whom are poor, and whose numbers are few" (p. 195). Paper had an active market among bureaucrats and merchants who sought it for their records and correspondence.

The reconquest of much of the Iberian Peninsula by Castile and Aragon, starting in the first half of the thirteenth century, coincided with some momentous shifts in the pattern and direction of its trade. As Constable points out, the most significant alteration was the decline of silk and the rise of wool as the chief export from the region. The Muslim silk industry declined partly because of the disruption of its skilled workforce, but mainly because of competition from the rising Italian center of Lucca, and greater access to the supplies of the Far East because of the decline of Byzantium after the Fourth Crusade of 1204 and the establishment of the *Pax Mongolica*. The woolen industry created by the import of the merino sheep from North Africa to the plains of Castile, a truly momentous innovation, grew very rapidly, supplying the Flemish cities with the raw material that they needed for their flourishing manufactures. Iron also became an important new export while some traditional exports such as olive oil continued, despite the shift from Muslim to Christian rule. The slave trade continued, with the exception that, as a result of the progress of the *Reconquista*, it was now captured Muslims exported to Christian lands instead of pagan Slavs and captured Christians to the Islamic World (ibid., pp. 234–35).

As we have seen, the beginning of this period saw North Africa, Egypt, Syria, and Palestine under the rule of the powerful Fatimid dynasty (969–1171), which established an alternative Shiite caliphate in Cairo in rivalry with the Abbasid caliphate still surviving in Baghdad and Iraq. Despite its brilliant beginnings, the Fatimid state gradually disintegrated under the pressure of Bedouin revolts, warfare with Byzantines and Crusaders, and ethnic rivalries within the army. The Fatimid dynasty was overthrown by the Kurdish hero Saladin in 1171, who used the resources of Egypt to good effect against the Crusaders. He finally defeated them in the decisive Battle of Hattin in 1187, which led to the recovery of Jerusalem and most of the Holy Land for Islam. Saladin founded the Ayyubid dynasty that ruled Egypt, Syria, and Palestine until the middle of the next century. The Achilles heel of both these dynasties seems to have been the burdens imposed upon agriculture and the rest of the economy by the necessity to maintain their large armies. The officers were endowed with military fiefs that were short-term under the Fatimids but eventually became hereditary under the Ayyubids. Revenues from land taxes did not keep pace with rising expenditures, so increasingly heavy impositions were placed on industry and trade. Both the Fatimids and Ayyubids were thus weakened and finally brought down by the strain imposed on their revenue systems by the requirements of their large and increasingly unruly armies.

In 1250 the slave soldiers of the Ayyubids, the celebrated Mamluks, staged a coup d'état that amazingly kept them in power until Egypt was incorporated into the Ottoman Empire in 1517. Ethnically, these regiments were mainly Kipchak Turks and later Circassians, together with a sprinkling of Albanians, Hungarians, and other central and Eastern Europeans. Captured and purchased in their teens they were given a rigorous military training before being freed and "graduating" into the elite corps of the armies. Sons of Mamluks could not become genuine Mamluks themselves, since they would not have spent their early youth on the steppe and been purchased as slaves. Hence the Mamluks have been called a "one-generation military aristocracy." The sultanate itself was occupied by one of the officers, chosen by a competitive process involving intrigue and assassination between factions grouped around the contending emirs or military commanders.

Perhaps not surprisingly, the survivors of this Darwinian process were often very able rulers (Irwin 1986, chapter 8). The foundations of the Mamluk state were firmly laid by the immensely gifted and energetic general and administrator, Sultan al-Zahir Baybars (1260–77), and his contemporary and comrade in arms, Sultan al-Mansur Qalawun (1279–90). They successfully combined the Mamluk military system, involving the "men of the sword," with the civil bureaucracy of the largely Coptic "men of the pen," and the judicial system of the Islamic theologians and jurists, the "men of the turban," into a highly efficient, centralized state extending from the Nile to the Euphrates, that was able to resist all comers for over two hundred and fifty years.

The remuneration of the officers and soldiers was in the form of entitlements to rents from nonhereditary "fiefs" that were not contiguous and never evolved into feudalism of the western type. As we will see, this would have important consequences a century later. The rents from the spice trade continued to be an important source of revenue. The main historical achievement of the Mamluks was unquestionably their defeat of the Mongols at the Battle of Ain Jalut in Palestine in 1260, which marked the westward limit of their advance into the Islamic World. They also had the distinction of driving out the Crusaders from their remaining strongholds of Antioch, Tripoli, and Acre. After the fall of Baghdad to the Mongols in 1258 Cairo became the leading city of the Islamic World and the center of its art, architecture, and learning, as well as the residence of the Abbasid caliph, which gave legitimacy to the rule of the Mamluk sultan. There is no doubt therefore that the Mamluks deserved being called "the saviors of Islam" by Ibn Khaldun himself. By the logic of their peculiar social system, the maintenance of the Mamluks' ranks required continual replenishment by purchase of youthful slaves with the preferred ethnic backgrounds. Trade with the source of these slaves through the Dardanelles was thus essential to their system, even if only for its own reproduction, since the Mongol Il-Khans cut off the overland supply routes.

It is now time to turn to the powers that were eventually to dominate the trade of the Mediterranean, namely the maritime city-states of the Italian peninsula. Given its central location in the Mediterranean, and contact with the growing European economy through the Alpine passes, it is perhaps not surprising that Italy would come to play such a crucial role in this period. The growth of population, agricultural production, and urban centers in Europe meant a lucrative market for the Eastern luxuries that merchants from the peninsula were well situated to supply in exchange for wool, silver, and other primary products. North Italian towns such as Milan and Pavia became important manufacturing and banking centers nourished by this transalpine trade. It was the coastal cities of Amalfi, Bari, Pisa, Genoa, and preeminently Venice, however, that were the most spectacular success stories of this period.

An important feature of the Italian city-states was their self-governing status, enabling them to concentrate on trade and economic activity without being burdened by taxation and regulation under regimes devoted to other objectives, as was clearly the case in the Islamic World. Formal sovereignty over the region was divided between the Byzantine emperor, the Holy Roman Emperor, and the pope, enabling Venice and the other cities to exercise de facto autonomy by means of astute diplomacy and the occasional use of force. In this way the political disintegration of Western Europe from the fifth century onwards proved in the long run to be a source of competitive advantage (Jones 2003).

Another factor benefiting the city-states was the Crusades. Following Viking expansion in the North Atlantic and Christian expansion in Iberia, there was now a wholesale effort to repel Muslim advances against the Byzantine Empire, and recapture the Holy Land on behalf of Christendom. The first Crusade was proclaimed by Pope Urban II in Clermont in 1095, and initially met with considerable success, with Jerusalem being captured from the Fatimids in 1099 and several Crusader states being established in Palestine. While the shock troops of the Crusader forces were typically younger sons of the Norman or German nobility, eager to carve out territorial principalities for themselves in the east, the Italian city-states were active participants and profited greatly from the enterprise, providing transportation, financial services, and on some occasions direct naval support. In return, they were compensated with trading privileges in Syria and Palestine.

Venice began its glorious twelve centuries of existence as a separate political entity in a very humble way, eking out a living by boating and fishing in the lagoons. The main economic activity was originally the making of salt and its export to the cities of the hinterland. Increasingly, the Venetians turned to the sea, using easily available timber for galleys and sailing craft. Allegiance to Byzantium was rewarded with trading privileges, leading to its becoming a transit point for silks and spices from the East bound for inland towns and Europe beyond the passes. Gradually, by use of its fleet for both trade and warfare, the city-state extended its influence southwards in the Adriatic and to the Dalmatian coast, where slaves for export to the east were another source of profit. Support for the Byzantine emperor against the rising Norman power in southern Italy was rewarded with the Golden Bull of 1082, which gave Venetian merchants duty-free access to the empire. The republic was well on its way to becoming "Queen of the Adriatic."

Frederick C. Lane (1973) estimates the population in 1200 at about 80,000 for the lagoon area as a whole, rising to double that number a century later. The city itself had a population of nearly 120,000 in 1300, making it larger than Paris at the same time. (Milan, Florence, Naples, and Palermo were of comparable size to Venice, making the peninsula by far the most heavily urbanized region in Western Europe.) Even as early as 1000 it was noted that Venice was unique in that it was "the first city in the Middle Ages to live by trade alone" (Bautier 1971, p. 65). Supplies of wheat, wine, and olive oil were imported to provision the city and surrounding areas. The twelfth century saw Venice extend her power and influence in the eastern Mediterranean. On the one hand she acted to preserve the Byzantine Empire from threats by Normans and Muslims, and on the other to plunder and extract commercial advantage from the empire for herself. These activities culminated in the Fourth Crusade that sacked Constantinople in 1204. The reward obtained was three-eighths of the new Latin empire and the immense booty that was acquired. Venice took her share of the real estate in the form of the island of Crete and strategically located naval bases in the Aegean and the Ionian Sea. Another major advantage was open access to the Black Sea that Venice had previously been denied.

Venice was now well-placed to be the middleman between a growing and increasingly prosperous Western Europe on the one hand, and on the other not only the Islamic World but China across the overland route as well, as a result of its access to the Black Sea and the *Pax Mongolica* that was soon to be established. Pepper and other spices were in growing demand as well as supplies of raw cotton and silk for European industries. These imports were paid for not only in silver from new mines opened in central Europe, but also with the woolen cloth of Flanders and Florence and an increasing variety of other manufactured products as well. Despite sporadic warfare, commercial relations with the Ayyubids and later the Mamluks were maintained. In addition to this transit trade with the Levant, Venice also obtained extensive profit from controlling the trade in salt and wheat for most of northern Italy. She was able to use her naval power to enforce strict navigation laws requiring most imports to the northern Adriatic to pass through Venice itself. She also captured much of the local carrying trade in the Aegean and Ionian Seas. Venice obtained wheat not only from Sicily and Crete but also from as far away as the Black Sea, just as Athens had done in antiquity.

The great rival of Venice for this entire period and beyond was Genoa, on the northern edge of the western coast of the peninsula. Closed in by the Apennines, Genoa had an even more humble beginning than Venice, since she did not even have the salt of the lagoons as the basis for commercial success. Robert Lopez in a number of works has stressed the role of warfare and booty from the Arabs in the western Mediterranean as providing the "primitive accumulation" required to launch Genoa on her spectacular path of commercial and financial expansion. Pisa was an early rival for control over Sardinia and Corsica but the two cities collaborated in lucrative raids on the North African Muslim ports. Early collaboration with the Crusaders brought colonies and commercial privileges in the east as well. All the major Italian maritime cities participated in the trade of the Mediterranean, involving not only the spice and silks of the transit trade but also the export of industrial raw materials such as cotton and alum from Syria and Palestine and wool from North Africa for the flourishing Tuscan cloth industry.

The first half of the thirteenth century saw Venice dominant in the east and the Black Sea, the payoff from the Fourth Crusade of 1204. The Genoese, however, supported the Byzantine counterattack that reclaimed Constantinople for the dynasty of Michael Paleologus in 1261. In return they obtained extremely lucrative colonial and commercial rewards, at the expense of Venice. Genoa obtained trading stations in the Black Sea, the Sea of Marmara, and the shores of the Aegean. Luzzatto (1961, p. 90) says that "Genoese trade developed an enormous range, extending from the Crimea to the Straits of Gibraltar and eventually, after the late thirteenth century, to the ocean routes beyond." The peak of Genoese trade and revenue seems to have been reached in the last decade of the thirteenth century. Lopez (1987, p. 355) states that revenues from taxes on trade turnover rose more than fourfold from 1274 to 1293 and were seven times as high as the income of the contemporaneous French monarchy of Philip Augustus. Revenues from the overseas trading stations at Pera, Alexandria, and other strategically located sites grew to "a size approaching that of the motherland itself." Genoa also pioneered voyages through the Straits of Gibraltar to England and Flanders, exchanging Eastern and Mediterranean wares for English wool and Flemish cloth and adding a seaborne route integrating northern and southern Europe. In terms of population Genoa never seems to have exceeded 100,000 in the city itself, with perhaps four or five times as many living in surrounding areas. It was thus always smaller than its great rival Venice, but comparable with Paris, Milan, and other major European cities.

One interesting question raised by the prolonged and bitter conflict between Christians and Muslims during the Crusades is its effect on the willingness to trade with the enemy. The verdict is quite clear. Despite papal edicts prohibiting supplying the Muslims with war materials, the Italian maritime cities provided weapons, ship-building materials, and other goods, while the Genoese in particular maintained the supply of slave recruits from the Black Sea for the elite Mamluk troops, the very ones that were engaged in driving the remnants of the Crusader states out of the coastal regions of Syria and Palestine (Ehrenkreutz 1981). That task was completed in 1289, when Tripoli was taken, and 1291, with the capture of the last Christian stronghold in the Holy Land and the major port in the region at that time, Acre. To be fair, the Church's moral position was somewhat undermined by its sale of exemptions from the general ban, and while the cost of such exemptions represented an additional cost for European merchants the Mamluks were apparently willing to provide compensation for it. In this way, the Crusaders' coreligionists from the Italian maritime cities were gaining an almost complete commercial dominance on the Mediterranean and within Constantinople itself, accelerating the long decay of the "Eastern Rome" and threatening the economic supremacy of the Islamic World that had prevailed at the turn of the second millennium.

The Crusades also led to the transmission of ideas and technology between the Muslim and Christian worlds, to the long-run benefit of the latter. A famous example is the so-called Arabic numeral system, which in fact originated in India, as was well-known to both Muslims and their European interlocutors. The new numbers gradually displaced Roman numerals, eventually being used by European merchants for business purposes. More generally, as Alfred Lieber (1968, pp. 231–32) says, "the greatest contribution of the Muslim World to medieval economic life was the development of commercial methods based on writing and recording. This was made possible by the high degree of literacy of the Oriental merchants of that time, which, in its turn, was encouraged by the fact that relatively cheap writing materials had long been available in this part of the world.... This ability...played a still more important part in the development of superior methods of payment and of financing international trade." An additional advantage facilitating modern business practices, as both Lieber and Janet Abu-Lughod (1989, p. 216) emphasize, was that Islam had traditionally been well-disposed toward merchants, which may not be surprising given that Mecca had been an important commercial center at the time of Mohammed, who was himself a merchant.

We have already encountered the example of the bill of exchange which Ibn Hawqal came across in Awdaghost, and these instruments were used widely in the Islamic World, both by merchants and by imperial bureaucracies seeking to transfer revenues from the provinces to the capital, from at least the eighth century (ibid., pp. 233–34). Similarly, the *commenda* contract, which played such an important role in financing Mediterranean trade, has clear historical antecedents in the earlier Muslim *qirâd* contract.[1] As Lieber admits (p. 240), it is difficult to find proof of particular instruments being transmitted between cultures, and it is always theoretically possible, as John Pryor (1977, p. 6) points out, that similar contracts, such as the *commenda*, arose in different countries as "individual responses to similar economic needs in different places at different times." The fact that bills of exchange were in use in Tang China might be taken as evidence in favor of the latter view, although Lieber (pp. 234–35) points out that the Muslim merchants trading there may in fact have learned from the Chinese experience and transmitted the knowledge thus acquired to their homelands.

Udovitch (1962) regards the *qirâd* as being the clear precursor of the *commenda*, and argues that Western merchants learned such techniques from their Muslim colleagues from the eighth century onwards. Pryor (1977), on the other hand, finds antecedents for the *commenda* in the Roman *societas* and the Byzantine *chreokoinônia*, as well as the *qirâd* and the Jewish *'isqa*, and concludes that the *commenda* arose as a result of a creative European amalgamation of Roman, Byzantine, and Middle Eastern sources. Western merchants clearly had the opportunity to learn from their Muslim counterparts. A Muslim visitor to Acre in 1184 noted that the Christian clerks there were using Arabic to keep the customs records, while Pisan merchants were receiving letters, again in Arabic, from Tunisian correspondents in 1200 (Lieber 1968, p. 238). Finally, as Lieber (p. 230) points out, there is convincing linguistic evidence of the impact of Muslim commercial practice on medieval European business: European words such as *douane*, tariff, traffic, risk, and *fondaco* all have their origins in Eastern languages.

Another famous example of the Muslim World's influence on the West, which had monumental consequences for no fewer than three

[1] For a recent analytical account of the financing of Venetian trade, see González de Lara (2005). According to her definition, "the commenda or *collegantia*, as the Venetians called it, was a partnership agreement through which an investor supplied funds on which he both accepted the risk of loss and received a return depending on the trade conducted by a merchant" (p. 5).

continents a few centuries later, is sugar. As Barbara Solow (1987) has pointed out, once Christians had been introduced to the "sweet salt" they lost no time in cultivating it themselves, initially in their Crusader domains, but later in Crete, Cyprus, and Sicily. Ominously, sugar cultivation had been associated with slavery in the Muslim World, and now Christians used slaves to cultivate it as well, developing sugar plantations that were the direct precursors of the New World slave plantations of the future. By the early fifteenth century, the cultivation had spread as far west as Iberian possessions in the Atlantic, such as Madeira, and the slaves concerned were being imported from Africa. From now on, "European colonization was associated with sugar; sugar was associated with slavery; and slavery was associated with blacks" (ibid., p. 714).

THE INDIAN OCEAN AND THE SOUTH CHINA SEA, 1000–1350

The trade of the Mediterranean was linked to that of the Indian Ocean and the South China Sea through the Red Sea and the Persian Gulf, the historic channels for the flow of spices to Europe. The purveyors of these Eastern spices to western markets from about the ninth to the eleventh century were a community of Jewish merchants based in Fustat (Old Cairo) but with far-flung connections from Spain to India. The discarded commercial and other correspondence of this community accumulated in Fustat, the so-called "Geniza Papers," enabled S. D. Goitein (1967) to construct a richly detailed account of their economic and cultural activities. They not only obtained pepper and other spices from further east in India but also dealt extensively in silk, flax, and other commodities, especially with the North African ports. They flourished under the Abbasid governors and the Fatimids, but declined under competition from the Italians and the more strenuous atmosphere of the Crusades and the Islamic response to them.

Already during this period we can see signs of the Christians attempting to circumvent Muslim middlemen and gain direct access to Eastern spices. Particularly active in this regard was the notorious Crusader Reynaud de Châtillon, who repeatedly violated truces with the Muslims to raid their trade caravans. The Kurdish hero Saladin was particularly incensed by a raid that Reynaud launched on the Hijaz in Arabia in 1182, in the course of which he captured Eilat and attacked Muslim shipping in the Red Sea. This Saladin regarded as a threat not only to the hajj and the holy cities of Mecca and Medina, but also to the lucrative commerce of the Red Sea. Reynaud's fleet was eventually destroyed, and Reynaud himself had the honor of being personally beheaded by Saladin after being captured at the Battle of the Horns of Hattin in 1187 (Phillips 1998, p. 98).

Saladin seems to have turned to a group of exclusively Muslim merchants (except for some converted Jews and Christians) known as the "Karimi" for the supply of spices and other oriental wares. They were granted royal protection, fiscal privileges, and exclusive rights to import Eastern goods through the Red Sea. While these merchants may originally have proceeded themselves to India and even further east, they eventually concentrated on the Red Sea segment of the trade alone, purchasing their requirements at Aden at the mouth of the Red Sea, to which Gujarati and various other merchants brought the pepper and cotton textiles of India and spices and other products from further east. Aden was in the domain of the sultans of Yemen, who owed allegiance to the Ayyubid dynasty of Saladin and to his Mamluk successors. A long-run equilibrium of sorts seems to have been established, with the Yemenis getting a cut but never going so far as to provoke the more powerful Egyptians into full-scale warfare.

Aden was a flourishing commercial emporium at this time, with merchants from all over the Islamic World and beyond. Its cosmopolitan nature, as well as the vast profits which could be made there, is well illustrated by the career of one Arab merchant who had apparently spent forty years in China. He lost twelve ships at sea in a single storm but recouped his entire loss with the profits from the thirteenth, carrying porcelain and aloe wood. He also formed a "multinational corporation" of his own, with seven sons from seven wives in different parts of the world sending him goods in return for Levantine, Maghribi, and Frankish products (Labib 1970, p. 68).

Transport up the Red Sea was protected by the Egyptian sultans, who also provided facilities for the goods to be unloaded and transported by caravans and down the Nile to Cairo. The Italians and other European merchants were confined to their "funduks" or trading stations in Alexandria and Damietta. The main groups were from Venice, Genoa, Pisa, Marseilles, and Barcelona. Confining the westerners in this way obviously turned the "terms of trade" in favor of the Egyptian state and the Karimi agents. The foreigners were, however, given guarantees of personal safety and security of property and profits. Special incentives and tax exemptions were given for strategic goods, particularly slave recruits for the Mamluk armies. Muslim merchants seem to have paid import duties of around 25% while Christians frequently paid 20% or even as little as 10% for particular goods (ibid., p. 74).

Trade relations with the west coast of India and Ceylon were close and extensive. The main export from India was the famous black pepper from Malabar, the unique source of this product in world trade before it was introduced into Sumatra and other Indonesian islands, probably in the late fourteenth or early fifteenth centuries. Cotton textiles were the other great Indian export item, as in later centuries, with production concentrated in the three main areas of Gujarat, Bengal, and the Coromandel Coast. Iron and steel products, mainly weapons, and a wide variety of other goods detailed in Digby (1982) were also exported. This author disputes the widespread contention that the Red Sea displaced the Persian Gulf during this period. He points to the substantial export of an unusual but valuable commodity to India through the Persian Gulf, namely cavalry horses, for which there was a high demand due to the incessant warfare in the subcontinent and the inability to sustain horse-breeding domestically. The great traveler Ibn Battuta encountered Turkic tribes with thousands of horses that sold for as little as one dinar each, when the price in India could exceed two hundred dinars or even five hundred. He says that the animals were exported to India in droves of six thousand or so (Gibb 1986, p. 145). The anecdote is revealing in two ways, showing not just the widespread international trade of the time, but also the enormous price gaps that prevailed between markets. Racehorses were also imported from Yemen, Oman, and Fars at prices of up to four thousand dinars each. The Moroccan traveler gives interesting information on trade all over the Islamic World and the Indian Ocean at the time, and on shipping and ocean transport, including a fleet of junks on which he sailed to China from the west coast of India. One is struck by the extent of trade and specialization in the world of that time, with communities in the Horn of Africa entirely dependent on imports of rice and cloth from India, and Ethiopian slaves being used as marines on Chinese junks and as naval mercenaries in the service of Muslim rulers in India.

As is well-known, both Marco Polo and Ibn Battuta were tremendously impressed with the wealth of China during the Mongol Yüan dynasty, even though it probably fell short of the peak achieved under the Sung. A much-cited estimate by Polo of daily imports of pepper in the Fujian port of Zaiton (Quanzhou), of over 10,000 lb., gives some notion of the size of the "China market" of the times. Polo also claimed that, for every shipload of spices from Alexandria to Christian ports, one hundred arrived in Quanzhou. Ibn Battuta claimed to have seen "a hundred first-class junks together" and "smaller ones past counting" in Quanzhou and thirteen at one time in Calicut on the Malabar Coast in India. The crew of one of the ships that he saw was put at one thousand: six hundred sailors and four hundred highly specialized troops, including archers and "arbalists who throw naphtha" (ibid., p. 235).

Mongol policy in China with regard to the economy and trade was on the whole a continuation of that of the Sung, with occasional attempts at greater state intervention to obtain more revenue and profit. Overland trade with Central Asia and the West, as we will see in the next section, expanded greatly as a result of the imposition of the *Pax Mongolica* over the nomad kingdoms that had dominated the steppe under the Sung. Overseas trade with Southeast Asia and the Indian Ocean to as far as East Africa and the port of Kilwa revived, and there was substantial trade with Japan and Korea. Japan exported a variety of mineral products, including copper ore and silver, as well as steel swords, while Korea exported pottery, lacquer ware, copper ware, ginseng, and other medicinal items. In return, China exported porcelain, silk and other textiles, books, reexported southern spices and exotic products, as well as large amounts of copper cash that circulated as legal tender in Japan and provided the money supply for the growing Japanese economy. The flow of books to Japan and Korea is interesting, indicating cultural transmission to these Confucian countries from the source. The wreck of a vessel apparently bound for Japan and the Philippines contained over ten thousand pieces of porcelain (Shiba 1983, p. 106), providing some indication of a sizable volume of trade.

THE *PAX MONGOLICA* AND OVERLAND TRADE, 1000–1350

Having looked at the seaborne trade of Eurasia during the 1000–1350 era starting at its western end in Islamic Spain, it is appropriate to make the "return journey" overland at the eastern end, starting with Sung China. At the opening of the period Sung China confronted two powerful Sinicized nomadic states on her northern and western borders, the Khitans of the Liao dynasty and the Tanguts of the Hsi Hsia Empire. The "proto-Mongol" Khitans (who are responsible for the term "Cathay" that was used in the West from medieval times onward for China) held sway in the area of Manchuria and eastern Mongolia. Formidable mounted warriors, they were the elite of a multiethnic state that included other nomadic and forest peoples as well as a large sedentary population of Chinese farmers and craftsmen, comprising about 60% of the population, with the Khitans themselves and other non-Chinese 20% each (Lewis 1988, p. 11). They were Buddhists, used their own script as well as Chinese, and were very far from being "barbarians" despite their steppe nomad origins. The Hsi Hsia domain was in the regions of Kansu, Shensi, and western Mongolia. The population was ethnically diverse with the Tanguts forming the ruling stratum and the elite cavalry of the army, as with the Khitans. Their position athwart the east–west and north–south trade routes gave them substantial revenues from taxing the traffic.

Despite geopolitical competition and frequent conflict, both the border states had extensive trading relations with Sung China. The Liao exported horses and sheep, furs, slaves, woolen cloth and carpets, and, somewhat surprisingly, iron armor and weapons. China exported silk and brocade, tea, silver and gold ornaments, marine products, medicinal herbs and spices, and other products from Southeast Asia. In addition to trading their own products, Shiba (1983, p. 97) reports that the Liao controlled trade and received tribute from Korea and other nomadic tribes such as the Jurchen and the Uighurs, as well as from the oasis cities of Khotan and Kucha which provided jade, amber, agate, carpets, cotton cloth, ginseng, and gold and silver bullion. The main commodity that the Chinese desired from both the Liao and the Hsi Hsia was horses for their cavalry, the supply of which was naturally restricted by the border states at times of conflict. The Hsi Hsia were particularly well situated by their control of the Kansu Corridor, bounded by mountains on one side and the Gobi Desert on the other. Salt was a potentially major Hsi Hsia export that China wanted to restrict to protect its own monopoly of that essential item. Not surprisingly, smuggling of horses and salt seems to have thrived. When war cut off trade between one of the border states and China, the other was not slow to take advantage. Shiba (1983, p. 100) states that the price of silk was forty times higher in Hsi Hsia than in China during wars, leading to profitable exports from the Liao to them.

Unable to subdue either of the border states, the Sung attempted to "buy" peace by paying what amounted to de facto tribute to both of them. The Liao received 300,000 bolts of silk and 200,000 ounces of silver annually, while 70,000 ounces of silver, 150,000 bolts of silk, and 10,000 catties of tea went annually to the Hsi Hsia. Shiba states that most of the silver paid by the Sung returned to China to settle trade surpluses that prevailed with both of the border states. We learn that the terms of trade were 20 bolts of silk or 100 catties (or 125 lb.) of tea for one horse. Since the exchange of tea and silk for horses took place for over 2,000 years, a record of these two relative prices would provide an interesting index of nomad–sedentary relations at the eastern end of Eurasia, if the information could be recovered from the extensive dynastic records of the Han to the Qing Dynasties.

In the 1120s the Liao Empire was overthrown by the formerly subject Manchurian tribe of the Jurchen, although one of the empire's Khitan princes moved west with his followers and established the Qarakhitai (or "Black Khitai") Empire, which is also known as the Western Liao Empire in the Chinese annals. The Jurchen also drove the Sung out of North China and their capital at K'ai-feng, forcing them to retreat to the south. The Jurchen established a new dynasty, the Chin, which was overthrown along with the Southern Sung and the Hsi Hsia by the Mongols in the thirteenth century. They did maintain a flourishing economy for over one hundred years, continuing to trade extensively with the Southern Sung along the previous pattern of Khitan–Chinese relations.

While the Khitans, Tanguts, and Jurchen in the east had been Sinicized by their contact with China, and the western Turks Islamicized by their contacts with the Persians and the Arabs, the Mongol tribes of Inner Asia had continued with their pastoral nomadic life on the steppe. In the early thirteenth century they were forged into an effectively centralized union by the genius of one Temüjin, who was proclaimed as Genghis Khan, or "universal ruler," in 1206. Under his descendants the entire Eurasian landmass from Iraq, Iran, and Russia in the west to China in the east was conquered and the *Pax Mongolica* established. China was invaded in 1211, and Beijing captured in 1215, but the northern Chin Empire was only finally subdued in 1234, by which time the frustrated Mongols had "switched from a policy of massacre in punishment for rebellion to one of straight genocide," according to McEvedy and Jones (1978, p. 172). The same authors report that the total Chinese population loss during the Mongol conquest was a horrifying 35 million, compared with a population in 1200 of 115 million. In 1218 Genghis Khan destroyed the Qarakhitai Empire. While Phillips says that the Khitans "ceased to exist as a people" (Phillips 1998, p. 61), it should be noted that individual Khitans continued to play significant roles in Central Asian and even world history. For example, Yeliu Chu-tsai, the celebrated principal advisor of both Genghis and his son Ögödei, was himself a Khitan of the royal clan. Next was the turn of Khwarezm to the west, as well as the Hsi Hsia, during which campaign Genghis died in 1227. Ögödei established the Mongol capital of Karakorum, and attacked Iran, Iraq, and Russia, taking Kiev in 1240. In 1241 the Mongols conquered Hungary, reaching the Adriatic Sea, and a small group made it almost as far as Vienna. Fortunately for Europe, Ögödei died at this stage, and a planned invasion of the western half of the continent was postponed. After a brief reign by Ögödei's son Güyük, Möngke became the Great Khan,

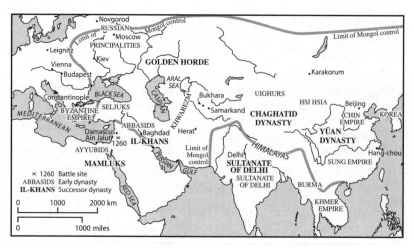

FIGURE 3.1. The Mongol Empire.

holding the position from 1251 to 1259. The Assassins in Iran were destroyed in 1256–57, Baghdad was taken the following year amid great slaughter, and Damascus shortly thereafter. Meanwhile the Mongols were advancing against the Sung Empire in Southern China, with its capital Hang-chou being taken in 1276 (ibid., chapter 4).

After the final conquest of the Southern Sung in 1279 gave the Mongols full control of all China, Khubilai Khan sought to consolidate the authority of the new Yüan dynasty (proclaimed in 1271) over what he regarded as China's vassal states and tributaries. Korea had already been subjugated after long and bitter resistance and its resources in manpower and shipping were pressed into service for the invasion of Japan, after the proud feudal ruling class had spurned Mongol demands for submission. An initial invasion in 1274 was a failure due to strong resistance and bad weather, but a massive invasion involving thousands of ships and about 140,000 troops was launched in 1281. Most of the ships, crews, and troops were either Korean or Chinese. As is well-known this invasion ended in disaster for the Mongols as a result of both the spirited defense of the feudal warrior class and the "divine wind" or *kamikaze* of a typhoon that sank most of the fleet. Another overseas invasion, this time of Java in 1292, also ended in failure. Land invasions of Burma led to the fall of the Pagan dynasty, without any discernible benefit to the Yüan, while land and sea invasions of Annam and Champa in what is now Vietnam also ended in failure. The death of Khubilai Khan in 1294 could be said to have ended the expansionary phase of the Mongol Empire in East Asia (see figure 3.1).

One important reason for the astonishing success of the Mongols, according to Adshead (1993, p. 61), was their ability to mobilize close to half of the horse population of the world, estimated at about 20 million at that time. While Mongol armies were not exceptionally large, at about 100,000 on major campaigns, each man had up to twenty remounts, so that a fresh animal was always available at decisive encounters. The availability of pasture was thus a major constraint on campaigns beyond the steppes, which may explain why they did not penetrate further into Europe, the Middle East, and Southeast Asia, despite the attempted invasions of Burma and Vietnam.

Central control by the "Great Khan" over the entire empire was loose and mainly symbolic after the death of Möngke (who was succeeded in the position by Khubilai). The enormous empire was divided among Genghis's grandsons, with Khubilai getting China and adjoining parts of Manchuria and Mongolia, while Hulagu obtained Iraq and Iran to be ruled as the empire of the Il-Khans or "viceroys" of the Great Khan. Domination over Russia and Ukraine was ceded to the so-called "Golden Horde" of Batu, and Central Asia between Iran and China passed to Chagatai.

Khubilai and his descendants ruled China as the Yüan dynasty, leaving Chinese civilization and administration largely intact even though they made extensive use of "outside experts" at the top levels of military, civil, and financial administration. These tended to be Muslim Central Asians, Tibetan Buddhists, and Nestorian Christians, out of distrust of the ethnic Chinese mandarin class. In a similar fashion the Il-Khans also preserved Persian and Arab traditions in their domains, again using Christians, Jews, and other outsiders as officials. The Golden Horde established a splendid capital at Sarai on the Volga but continued to maintain themselves physically apart from their Russian and other Slavic subjects. The heavy taxes of various kinds levied by the Mongols were collected on their behalf by the Russian princes themselves, with the cooperation of the Orthodox Church and under the supervision of Mongol inspectors. The "deal" was that the Russian church and princes were allowed to remain in office at the price of abject submission to the Mongols and effective performance of their duties as tax collectors for their overlords. This was the infamous "Tartar Yoke" under which the Russians were to suffer for centuries. The Central Asian steppes and oases of the Chaghatid dynasty were under loose central control, with the traditional mix of sedentary agriculture around the oases and pastoralism on the steppe.

Several of the major cities had been severely depopulated during the campaigns, but apparently recovered after a generation or two.

In China and Persia the Mongols directly ruled over large sedentary populations who formed the "tax base" of their empires. It was therefore rational for them to maintain and enhance the productive capacity of these lands. Khubilai Khan in particular made strenuous efforts on transport and irrigation projects, as did the more enlightened of the Il-Khans. Both regimes introduced paper currencies, with some success initially in China, though the Persian experiment was a disaster from the outset. Tabriz, the capital of the Il-Khans, was a flourishing commercial center at the hub of major caravan routes as well as being linked by sea with China and Southeast Asia, as evidenced by Polo's return voyage escorting a Yüan princess.

Despite competition and conflict between the components of the empire as a whole, particularly the Golden Horde and the Il-Khans of Persia, there was a reality to the *Pax Mongolica*. The Mongols always wanted to encourage trade and the routes across Central Asia were safer and busier than previously or subsequently. Thus despite the burden of the Tartar Yoke the Russian cities experienced considerable prosperity from participation in long-distance trade. Novgorod sent furs and other forest products to the west for silver and woolen cloth, as well as trading actively to the east. Trade with the Middle East and China continued to flourish. Even small towns and rural areas were able to pay taxes in silver, indicating exposure to trade. Halperin (1987, chapter 7) cites evidence that nonelite segments of the population consumed some traded goods and that several cities undertook extensive construction projects for cathedrals and other public edifices during the Mongol period.

Janet Abu-Lughod (1989) has presented a vivid picture of a non-hegemonic or horizontally linked "world system" from 1250 to 1350, the period of the *Pax Mongolica*, which covers essentially all of our seven regions. The links extended in successive steps all the way from the British Isles and Spain in the west to China, Korea, and Japan in the east, and from Bergen and Novgorod in the north to the Indonesian archipelago in the south. Indeed, it extended even further west than this, to Iceland, which imported grain in exchange for woolen cloth, and even in a more tenuous form to Greenland, which while isolated and largely self-sufficient did on occasion send walrus tusks or polar bear skins to Iceland or Norway (Phillips 1998, chapter 9). Lopez (1971, p. 108) reports that one company based in Lucca actually sent agents there to collect papal tithes. Although only items with a high ratio of value to weight such as spices, silk, furs, and slaves were traded over long distances, there were fairly extensive regional markets for bulk items such as grain, olive oil, and timber. The physical and institutional infrastructure to support this trade in the form of transportation and credit systems was also well developed, and travelers such as Ibn Battuta, Polo, and various papal envoys showed how relatively easy and safe it was to cover enormous distances.

In addition to the testimony of Marco Polo and the papal envoys there is the information provided in the commercial handbook published by the Florentine Francesco Balducci Pegolotti in the early 1340s. According to the *Practica della Mercatura*, the land route from Crimea to Beijing was "perfectly safe, whether by day or by night" (Rossabi 1990, p. 356), and given the Italian presence in and around the Black Sea it was largely Italians who availed themselves of the opportunities which the Mongol conquests represented. The journey might be relatively safe, but it was still a long one: it took between eight and eleven months to reach China from Crimea (Phillips 1998, p. 100). Nonetheless, it was possible to make huge profits by cutting out the middleman. According to Pegolotti, travel costs and customs duties for a caravan might amount to some 3,500 florins, while the merchandise could be sold for 25,000 florins (Rossabi 1990, pp. 356–57). Italians were thus attracted in large numbers to Persia and the Kipchak steppes, while enough of their compatriots became established in China that Franciscans built a *fondaco* in Quanzhou in which to house Catholic merchants (Lopez 1952, pp. 312–13; 1987, pp. 352–53). In 1323 a bishopric was established in Quanzhou, although Franciscan missionaries such as Odoric of Pordenone (who was accompanied on his travels by one James of Hibernia, and the account of whose travels appears to have been plagiarized in the fourteenth-century English work *Mandeville's Travels*) met with no success in their efforts to convert the Chinese (Phillips 1998, chapter 5).

David Abulafia (1987, pp. 447–48) suggests that Europeans came to China to purchase not just traditional Chinese luxury exports such as silk but Southeast Asian spices as well, which were shipped north to the mainland before being purchased by Christian (and Muslim) merchants. Given the natural cost advantages which sea transport had over land transport during this period, this is a remarkable testament to the integration of the Eurasian economy during this period, although there were inevitably losers, notably in Egypt. The Venetians did not send a single convoy to Egypt between 1323 and 1345 (Lopez 1987, p. 387): the *Pax Mongolica* thus exacted an economic cost on the Muslim World, following the far graver costs imposed by Mongol wars. The Italians paid for their purchases with "gems, live horses, mechanical clocks and fountains, fine linen and woolen cloth" (ibid., p. 353). Some also tried even more direct routes to access Eastern spices, with several Italians being recorded as having ventured into India during this period (Phillips 1998, p. 103). According to Phillips (p. 238) a group of Genoese sailors hatched a plan in 1290 to sail down the Tigris and gain access to the Indian Ocean that way.

It was not just goods but also people, techniques, and ideas that moved freely across all parts of the known world for the first time. For example, both the New Testament as well as the Christian Psalter were translated into the Tartar language by John of Monte Corvino (Abu-Lughod 1989, p. 168). Information flows, however, proved far more influential in the opposite direction. Technological change, which was already under way in Western Europe, probably received a further boost by the diffusion of Chinese inventions during this period, a case that was vigorously argued by Needham (1954). But the most compelling testament to the international integration achieved by the *Pax Mongolica* comes in the form of price data cited by Lopez (1987, p. 353): apparently, Chinese silk sold in Italy during this period for no more than three times its purchase price in China.

When did "globalization" begin? While the answer depends on the definition used, a strong case can be made that it began with the unification of the central Eurasian landmass by the Mongol conquests and the reactions this aroused in the sedentary civilizations that they were launched against. Each civilization previously had been aware of the others, but only as isolated entities, not as interactive components of a unified system. In Europe even the legends of "Prester John," the mythical Christian hero in the East who was wrongly identified with Genghis Khan and other non-Muslim nomad conquerors, served to provide a unified geopolitical framework, encouraging the thought of opening an eastern front against Islam, and so arousing the desire to establish contact, by sea or land, with these realms beyond Islam for religious, military, and commercial purposes. Frustrated by their Venetian rivals on land, the Genoese contemplated an end run around Africa in the late thirteenth century, leading to the lost voyage of the Vivaldi brothers in 1291. Yet another Genoese would launch a similar attempt two centuries later. As Adshead (1993, p. 77) puts it, "if Europe came to dominate the world, it was possibly because Europe first perceived there was a world to dominate. There is a straight line from Marco Polo to Christopher Columbus, the eastward looking Venetian to the westward looking Genoese."

Eurasia on the Eve of the Black Death

The relative position of our seven regional units in 1350 was altered considerably from what it had been in 1000. Western Europe, which had been a backward "hinterland" to Byzantium and the Islamic World at the start of the millennium, had developed a highly productive agricultural base, leading to a surge in population, and had also undergone what Robert Lopez (1971) called the "Commercial Revolution," with Italian cities taking the lead in extending the range and diversity of their trade over both sea and land, and also making important technical innovations in the textile industries as well as shipbuilding and navigational techniques. The merchant communities of Greeks, Syrians, and Jews that were so prominent in the conduct of long-distance trade in 1000 had largely given way to the thrusting competition of the Venetians and Genoese, backed up by armed force where necessary. Shipping in the Mediterranean, which had been dominated by Byzantium and the Muslims, was now mainly in Italian hands. Their reach extended from the English Channel to the Black Sea by 1350, with the frequency and speed of voyages enhanced by the adoption of the compass and other nautical innovations.

As we have seen, long-distance trade exposed Western merchants to a variety of sophisticated financial practices, but it also gave them the incentive to adopt such practices themselves. Thus the Commercial Revolution, which involved not just trade with Asia but an increase in the burgeoning intra-European trade that we described in the previous chapter, stimulated a variety of important innovations in Europe. These included not just the bills of exchange that we have already encountered, but deposit banking, insurance, and "commercial and banking accounting, which gradually changes from scribbled memos to separate columns for credit and debt, and ultimately to rigorous double entry bookkeeping" (ibid., p. 107). Intra-European commerce promoted specialization during this period, both industrial and agricultural, with beneficial effects on the European standard of living. Urbanization was an integral part of this process, with towns specializing in manufacturing and exchanging their produce for imported food (Rosenberg and Birdzell 1986, pp. 78–80). Thus commerce "passed from the fringe to the very centre of everyday life" in Europe, and "became the driving force of economic progress" (Lopez 1967, p. 126; see also Greif 2006, pp. 23–27).

The Islamic World, on the other hand, seemed already to be undergoing an economic malaise, extending from the Iberian Peninsula, where it had been pushed back by the Christian advance, all the way to Iraq and Iran in the east, where it staggered under the Mongol onslaught. It is true that there was a gradual recovery after the initial devastation but there is no doubt that Baghdad, Bukhara, Samarkand, and other flourishing cities had long passed their peak. Only the North African states, and Egypt and Syria under the Mamluks, still exercised formidable political and military power. However, the wealth of the Mamluk state had become increasingly parasitical on rents from the transit trade in spices and other oriental products, while the *Pax Mongolica* diverted trade away from the Red Sea and toward the overland route. Byzantium suffered major catastrophes during the period 1000–1350, from the loss of western Anatolia to the Turks to the occupation of Constantinople itself by the Latin Crusaders from 1204 to 1261. Even after the restoration of the Byzantine emperors, control of the economic life of the empire was passing increasingly to the Genoese and Venetians. Despite having made such a promising beginning under the cultural aegis of the Orthodox Church, Kievan Rus fell victim to the Mongols, and its successor states had become the vassals and tax collectors of their steppe overlords of the Golden Horde.

The most dramatic change of the period was the domination of the Eurasian landmass from the Urals to the Pacific by the Turco-Mongol nomads of Central Asia. In 1000 they had established the Khazar Empire in the west bordering on Byzantium, Kievan Russia, and the Islamic World, and the Khitan and Tangut Empires in the east bordering on Sung China. By 1350 they had conquered all of China in the east, Iraq and Iran in the west, and reduced the Russian principalities to vassal status. In addition Delhi and the fertile north Indian plains were ruled by Turkic dynasties of slave soldiers, and the Mamluks ruling over Egypt and Syria were themselves mainly Kipchak Turks. Japan and Java had been invaded unsuccessfully by sea while raids had been conducted into Burma and Vietnam on the Southeast Asian mainland.

The Islamic World, however, was able to turn military defeat into cultural victory by the conversion of the Il-Khans and the Golden Horde to Islam, despite their earlier adherence to shamanism and experimentation with Buddhism and Nestorian Christianity. Also, as we have seen, the Crusaders had been expelled from their footholds in Palestine and Syria. Thus the territorial extent of the *Dar-al-Islam* was maintained and even extended to the northern half of India under the Delhi sultanate, with the only losses being in the Iberian Peninsula. By incorporating the vigorous and militant Turkic steppe nomads into its cultural fold, Islam was thus able to absorb and transcend the Mongol onslaught that had done such damage in the thirteenth century. The Mongols in Persia and the Russian borderlands were themselves absorbed imperceptibly into the larger Turkic populations with which they were associated and to whom they had close cultural and linguistic affinities.

THE BLACK DEATH

The integration of the *Pax Mongolica* had the tragic consequence of promoting what Le Roy Ladurie (1981) called "the unification of the globe by disease" or the formation of a "microbian common market." There was not only the conceptual unification of the world along with the economic, as pointed out previously, but also a biological unification. Bacteria and viruses, long localized to particular regions, were transferred and mingled by the movement of humans and animals over long distances, as for instance occurred with the operations of the Mongol cavalry. According to McNeill (1998) the plague germs were transmitted by Mongol troops from the Burma–Yunnan border to Central Asia, and eventually to the Genoese trading station of Kaffa (Feodosiya) on the Black Sea in 1347.[2] An oft-repeated story is that the khan of the Golden Horde Janibeg ordered infected corpses to be catapulted into Kaffa when he laid siege to it in 1347, from where the plague was transmitted by a Genoese vessel to Messina in Sicily. It rapidly spread to ports around the Mediterranean and all across Europe, Egypt, and Syria as well. The overall European death rate was estimated at between a quarter and a third, with the rate being higher in more densely populated regions in the west, and much lower in the emptier east (McEvedy and Jones 1978, p. 25). Carlo Cipolla (1994, p. 131) states that the plague killed about 25 million out of a total population of 80 million in Europe during the period 1348–51. It recurred in waves of mostly diminishing intensity until the end of the sixteenth century. It was undoubtedly the greatest catastrophe to strike the Western World during the last millennium, not even excluding the two world wars of the twentieth century. The effect on the Islamic World, according to Dols (1977), was at least as severe, if not even more so. The rest of this chapter will examine the consequences of the catastrophe and the subsequent recovery on the volume and pattern of world trade.

[2]Whether these germs were the bubonic plague germ, pasteurella pestis, or another disease is now a matter of hot controversy: for very different recent opinions on the matter, see Cohn (2003) and Benedictow (2004). Without taking a position on this biological debate, we will in what follows refer interchangeably to the "Black Death" and the "plague."

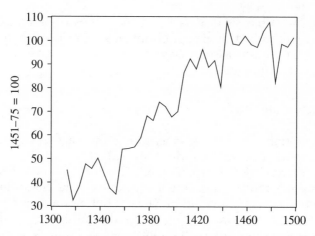

FIGURE 3.2. Real English building wages, 1300–1500
(laborers, 1451–75 = 100). *Source:* Munro (2004).

In analyzing the economic consequences of the Black Death, it is apparent that the impact effect would be a drastic decline in total production but a rise in per capita real income and wealth, since land and physical capital remain unchanged and the livestock population was apparently unaffected by the plague.[3] With diminishing returns to labor, we would expect a rise in the real wage and thus a decline in the rent per acre and the return to physical capital. Furthermore (by the well-known Rybczynski theorem in trade theory), we would expect a rise in the relative price of labor-intensive goods and a fall in the relative price of land-intensive goods, since the output of the former would contract and that of the latter expand if relative product prices were held constant. With per capita income rising we would also expect a boom in markets for luxury goods and a relative decline in markets for more basic goods such as food and other necessities.

With these simple neoclassical predictions in mind we can turn to the historical literature on the subject to find whether they are borne out or not, focusing on the European evidence. If these predictions are accurate, then a major debate between Lopez and Miskimin (1962) and Cipolla (1964) would be easy to resolve. The first two authors

---

[3]The analysis which follows draws heavily on Findlay and Lundahl (2003, 2006). Obviously, these predictions apply to regions where land was scarce, such as Western Europe and China, but not as much in frontier societies such as Central Asia, where land was in effectively unlimited supply and the marginal product of labor was relatively invariant.

spoke about the "depression of the Renaissance" since the cultural flowering of the next century and a half was accompanied by a fall in population, production, and trade around 1350 and only a gradual recovery afterwards. Cipolla, on the other hand, points toward evidence of per capita improvement. The "per capita thesis" is stated sharply by Bridbury (1962, p. 91) when he observed that England, and by implication the rest of Western Europe that suffered the effects of the plague, "was given a sort of Marshall Aid on a stupendous scale" (see also Hatcher 1977).

The basic facts seem to accord with our theoretical expectations and the per capita thesis. Figure 3.2 shows John Munro's (2004) data for English building laborers' real wages during the fourteenth and fifteenth centuries. As can be seen, the data suggest a sharp rise in English real wages from the middle of the fourteenth century. Real wages continued rising for about a century, so that by the middle of the fifteenth century laborers were earning more than twice as much in real terms as they had been doing on the eve of the Black Death.[4] These wage trends were not confined to England. Earl Hamilton's (1936, p. 186) real wage data for Navarre show that laborers' real wages more than doubled there between the early 1350s and 1401–5, before subsequently declining by about one-fifth. A contemporary Florentine observer, Matteo Villani, complained in 1363 that "serving girls and…stable boys want at least 12 florins per year, and the most arrogant among them 18 or 24 florins per year, and so also nurses and minor artisans working with their hands want three times or nearly the usual pay" (cited in Herlihy 1997, pp. 48–49). At the same time he also complained of rampant inflation, but his comments that "the common people, by reason of the abundance and superfluity which they found, would no longer work at their accustomed trades; they wanted the dearest and most delicate foods…while children and common women clad themselves in all the fair and costly garments of the illustrious who had died" (pp. 47–48) suggest that the living standards of the poor on balance improved there as well.[5] Finally, it seems clear that urban real wages increased by as much as 100% in Egypt, Byzantium, and the Balkans as well as in Western Europe (Ashtor 1976a; Pamuk 2005).

---

[4] Clark's (2005) data show much the same thing, as well as a decline in wages during the population expansion of the thirteenth century.

[5] An important exception to this trend in the literature is provided by Munro (2004), who finds that real building wages in Bruges fell by some 30% between 1349–50 and 1356–60, and only started rising thereafter, reaching a peak in 1401–5 (by which stage they were some 15% higher than the 1349–50 level).

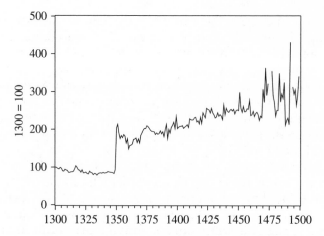

FIGURE 3.3. English wage–rental ratio, 1300–1500 (1300 = 100).
Source: data graciously provided by Greg Clark.

Figure 3.3 shows that labor gained not only in absolute but in relative terms as well. As can be seen, the ratio of English wages to land rents declined steadily from 1300 to 1350, but the Black Death led to an immediate doubling of the ratio of wages to land rents, followed by a steady increase for the following century. Towns grew larger in the wake of the plague, in contrast with the experience following the Plague of Justinian, reflecting the positive effects of increasing living standards on urbanization, which more than compensated for the negative effects of a declining population. Thus Bautier (1971, p. 187) states that the population of Paris grew from about 100,000 at the beginning of the fourteenth century to about 300,000 by the sixteenth. That of Lübeck rose from 15,000 around 1300 to 25,000 in the fifteenth century; Hamburg from 5,000 around 1300 to 16,000 around 1450; Bremen from 12,000 before the plague to 17,000 around 1400; and Danzig from 2,000 in 1300 to 20,000 by the middle of the fifteenth century (ibid.).

Within agriculture there was an expansion of land-intensive activities such as sheep and cattle rearing, relative to cereal cultivation. Other things being equal (in particular, demand), this should have led to a decline in the relative price of animal products, such as wool. This decline, together with the high-income elasticity of demand for high-quality woolen textiles, produced a long-sustained boom in the woolen cloth industry, the leading manufacturing sector of the Middle Ages. Figure 3.4(a) shows that the price of woolen cloth rose steadily

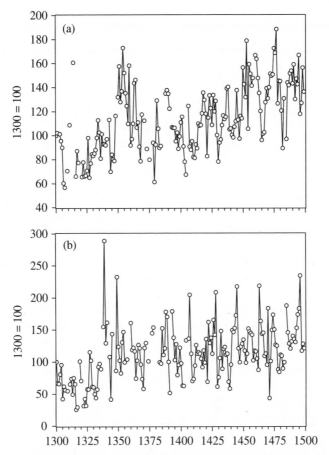

FIGURE 3.4. Relative commodity price trends, England 1300–1500 (1300 = 100):
(a) woolen cloth to wool price ratio; (b) wine and port to wheat price ratio.
Source: data graciously provided by Greg Clark.

relative to wool between 1350 and 1500, and while this presumably
reflected in part higher labor costs, it is no surprise that the industry
grew so impressively during this period, with weaving concentrated in
the towns of Flanders, and finishing and dyeing in Florence and other
northern Italian cities. Taxation of raw wool exports by Edward III to
finance his wars in France gave "effective protection" to the woolen
textile industry in England, as pointed out long ago by Eileen Power
(1941, p. 101), and stimulated a shift in the composition of exports
from raw wool to cloth, at the expense of Flanders.

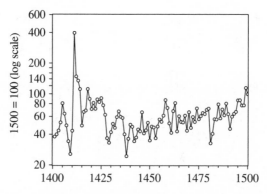

FIGURE 3.5. Annual English pepper prices 1401–1500, relative to grain (1500 = 100). *Source:* O'Rourke and Williamson (forthcoming).

The high income-elasticity of demand for wine and beer led to a rise in their relative price (figure 3.4(b)) as well, which in turn prompted an extension of vineyards and barley at the expense of wheat. Of greater importance to intercontinental trade was the effect of rising living standards on relative Asian spice prices: as would be expected, they rose sharply. Hamilton's (1936, pp. 267–69) data indicate that the price of Asian spices in Navarre doubled relative to agricultural commodities in the quarter century following the plague, and Greg Clark's data suggest that something similar happened in England, with low relative spice prices during the *Pax Mongolica* being followed by much higher relative prices from the 1340s onwards. Figure 3.5 shows that relative pepper prices in England rose across the fifteenth century, although this trend is somewhat obscured by a remarkable spike in pepper prices around 1411 or so, which lingered on during the rest of the decade and the 1420s. Once that spike, to which we will return below, has been accounted for, the upward trend in pepper prices is unmistakable. The same is true of real pepper prices in Vienna and the Netherlands, although the upward trend in the latter case was only weakly statistically significant (O'Rourke and Williamson forthcoming).

The Black Death had monetary consequences in Europe as well, memorably summed up by David Herlihy in the statement that "men were dying, but coins were not."[6] In terms of the well-known Fisher equation ($MV = PQ$), MV (the money supply multiplied by velocity) was initially unchanged, but output Q had declined as a result of the

[6]Herlihy (1967, p. 125), cited in Munro (2004, p. 1037).

decline in population, and so prices P had to rise. The result was what Munro (2004, p. 1037) termed the "sudden eruption of quite horrendous inflation," with the price of commodities rising sharply relative to silver. This fall in the relative price of silver in turn led to a reduction in silver (and gold) production in Europe (Nef 1987, p. 721), which coincided as we have seen with an increase in European demand for Eastern trade goods. These were largely paid for with silver: the net impact therefore was a decline in the European stock of silver coins, which led to John Day speaking of "the Great Bullion Famine of the Fifteenth Century" (Day 1978).[7] Lopez, Miskimin, and Udovitch (1970) trace the flow of bullion from England to Egypt by way of Italy between 1350 and 1500, and find that whatever Egypt accumulated from the West it eventually lost to India and the Far East. A particularly heavy drain on the Mamluk money supply was the cost of replenishing their own ranks with fresh imports of young male slaves from the steppes through the Black Sea. With each slave costing between 50 and 140 gold dinars, importing an estimated 2,000 slaves annually cost between 100,000 and 280,000 gold dinars in the 1420s.

Over time, the rise in European living standards should have prompted a recovery in the population, for familiar Malthusian reasons, and thus in European output levels (chapter 6 will discuss the Malthusian model in greater detail). With output rising, and the supply of silver in the economy falling, the price level should have eventually started to decline, with a prolonged period of deflation succeeding the initial burst of inflation. This should have gone on until such time as the increased relative price of silver prompted a recovery in silver mining, with a consequent rise in the price level. Thus, the simple general equilibrium model presented in Findlay and Lundahl (2003) predicts that the European price level should have initially increased after the Black Death; then declined, as a result of the Bullion Famine; and finally increased again.

This is exactly what seems to have happened. Figure 3.6 provides Northern Italian grain prices, expressed in terms of silver. Rising prices in the late fourteenth century are followed by a sharp price decline that lasts until the 1460s, when it is succeeded by an unmistakable if more modest price increase. According to Nef (1987, p. 735), there was a "boom in mining and metallurgy" between 1460 and 1530, with annual central European silver output rising perhaps more than fivefold, and

---

[7] See also Miskimin (1975) and Spufford (1988, chapters 14–16). For a contrary view, see Sussman (1998).

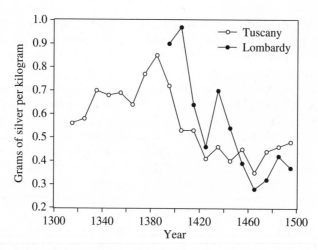

FIGURE 3.6. Northern Italian grain prices, 1310–1500 (grams of silver per kilogram). *Source:* Malanima (2002), available at http://gpih.ucdavis.edu/ Datafilelist.htm.

Munro (2003) provides compelling new evidence of the size of this boom, which "vastly exceeded the scale of Spanish–American silver imports for the first half of the sixteenth century" (p. 10). According to Munro, the fact that this boom did not provoke significant inflation can be explained by the fact that silver was being continuously drained to the east as a result of trade, and that the European economy was by this time expanding along with population, implying that an increasing quantity of money was required merely to prevent prices falling.[8]

Of course, as population gradually recovered, the Malthusian model predicts that living standards should have declined, and in principle the economy could simply have recovered its initial equilibrium (Findlay and Lundahl 2006). But this is to ignore the role of path dependence in the real world: as David Herlihy (1997) persuasively argues in his brilliant book, the experience of higher living standards, and an increase in the share of the population which was propertied, meant that a higher proportion of the European population was regulated by preventive checks as opposed to positive checks after the crisis. If this translated into a later age of marriage for females, then Europe's population could have continued to grow without living standards collapsing to their original level. In addition, he argues that labor scarcity prompted technological change, symbolized by Gutenberg's

[8]In addition, mining output accelerated sharply only after 1510.

printing press, which could satisfy the growing demand for books more efficiently than old methods based on scribes (p. 50). Another example of labor-saving technological progress for Herlihy was firearms, which again implicitly substituted capital for relatively expensive soldiers (p. 51).

Stephan Epstein (2000) provides another, political reason why the plague may have benefited Western Europe in the long run. According to him, the decentralized governance of the feudal economy was an obstacle to growth, since local jurisdictions taxed trade, and "the major influence on the rate of innovation was the cost of trade" (p. 49), in accordance with Smith's dictum that the division of labor is limited by the extent of the market. Epstein provides evidence that "agricultural innovation appears to have been inversely correlated with the intensity of seigniorial rights, and rural industrial growth was inversely correlated with the jurisdictional powers of towns and lords" (p. 51). In this context, "the Black Death emerges as an exogenous event which contributed to the feudal economy's transition from a low-level 'equilibrium trap' to a higher growth path by sharply intensifying pressures that had been building up for centuries," namely a move toward more centralized states, at war with each other and thus requiring state-level taxation and state-level administrative structures. "By shifting the bargaining power between land and labor so rapidly...the fourteenth-century pandemic turned a comparatively smooth evolutionary process into a wave of Schumpeterian 'creative destruction'.... Supported by a wealthier peasant elite...aspiring rulers increased the jurisdictional integration of their territories, making markets more competitive, stimulating commercialization and setting the stage for the long sixteenth-century boom" (pp. 54–55).

According to McEvedy and Jones (1978, p. 18), Europe's population grew from 60 million in 1400 to 81 million in 1500. English real wages remained very high throughout the fifteenth century (figure 3.2), despite an increase in the English population of some 50% (ibid., p. 43). Similarly, Hamilton's data suggest that real wages were historically high in Navarre during the first half of the fifteenth century, even though the Iberian population rose from 6.5 to 7.75 million over the course of the century (ibid., p. 105). More generally, Pamuk (2005) concludes that real wages remained above their pre-plague levels until the sixteenth century, not just in Western Europe but across the Mediterranean world, while Allen (2001) has shown that England and the Low Countries even managed to avoid declining real wages in the longer run as well.

Thus, the fifteenth century was one in which Europe experienced both an increase in its population and high living standards. Limited though they are, these data bear out the picture of an initially smaller but substantially richer European population, with a proportionately reduced output and trade in necessities but with a sharp increase in imports of luxury items such as northern furs and Eastern spices. The next section examines the consequences of this development for trade between Western and Eastern Europe.

TRADE BETWEEN WESTERN AND EASTERN EUROPE, 1350–1500

The Hanseatic League, an association of north German towns organized to protect their joint commercial interests in foreign markets, dominated the trade of the Baltic and the North Sea during the period 1350–1500. The League from the beginning to the end of its existence was mainly concerned with the two-way flow of trade between eastern and northwestern Europe along the axis Novgorod–Reval–Lübeck–Hamburg–Bruges–London (Dollinger 1970, chapter 10). Along this main stream of trade furs and wax from the north of Russia and Finland were the main products moving westwards, while Flemish cloth and salt from north Germany and the Bay of Biscay were the principal items traveling eastwards. In addition, copper and iron from Sweden, fish from Norway and Scania, and grain and timber from Prussia and Poland were other major commodities added to the stream from north and south of the east–west Novgorod–London axis. It can be seen that the trade could be characterized as an exchange of raw materials and other primary products from Russia, Finland, the eastern Baltic areas, and Scandinavia for western manufactures, particularly Flemish woolen cloth.

Statistical series are unfortunately scarce but there are some scattered indicators of the expansion of trade between 1350 and 1500. Dollinger (p. 215) reports that the trade of Lübeck in the Baltic rose from 153,000 marks in 1368 to 660,000 marks in 1492. Since prices fell sharply, perhaps as much as 50% over this period, this means that the increase in the volume of trade was possibly twice as high again. Hanseatic exports of English cloths rose from 6,000 in 1400 to more than 15,000 by 1480.

Furs from the northern forests and tundra were obtained by Finnish and Russian hunters and collected at the eastern Baltic ports. The most valuable was sable, sold in Venice for 82 ducats per 100 pelts at the beginning of the fifteenth century. Marten and beaver were sold at 30 and 14 ducats, while lynx, squirrel, otters, and weasel skins fetched prices in the low single digits for 100 pelts. Furs were clearly "prestige" or "status" goods, and the scale of demand indicates the extent to which the wealthier segments of medieval Europe, and also the Mamluk elite of the Islamic World to which many of these items were reexported, were willing and able to indulge in luxury and display. Dollinger (p. 235), who gives the price data quoted above, also reports that one Hanseatic merchant family alone imported into Flanders more than 300,000 pelts over the period 1403–15 from Danzig, Riga, and Reval. One convoy of three ships sailed from Riga to Bruges with 450,000 pelts, in addition to wax and linen of equal value to the furs.

Wax was obtained from bees in the northern forests and collected for sale to the Hanseatic and other merchants. The demand for candles to be used in religious services was presumably stimulated by the experience of the Black Death. Amber, for use as jewelry, was another valuable luxury item, the supply of which was lucrative enough to be monopolized by the knights of the Teutonic Order, the most powerful military and political entity in Prussia and the eastern Baltic area at the time.

During most of this period the Hansa dominated the trade of Scandinavia. Norway relied on grain imports from the Baltic provided by the League through their trading post at Bergen in exchange for dried codfish. The League used its influence over the grain supply to wring trade concessions out of Norway, though it respected the agreement not to trade north of Bergen. German merchants were also prominent in the commerce of Stockholm, and the League was the channel through which the supplies of copper and high-quality iron from Sweden entered the European market. Denmark supplied cattle and butter at this time, although the powerful Danish kings on occasion threatened Lübeck and other towns of the League with their naval forces. The main economic activity linking the League and Scandinavia, however, was the great salted herring industry of Scania in northeastern Denmark. Enormous quantities of salt, imported from the Bay of Biscay by large fleets of Hanseatic ships, were an essential input into the process of curing and preserving the herring caught on the shores of the Baltic (Crouzet 2001, p. 30, footnote 28).

Timber from Scandinavia, Russia, and the eastern Baltic lands was another valuable export, along with the related supply of potash and resin. Timber and hemp for use as cordage were essential inputs for the shipbuilding industries of Holland, England, and the cities of the League itself. Timber, iron, and copper were also strategic goods necessary for warships and their armament. Even the bow staves of the English archers in the Hundred Years' War were apparently imported from the forests of Eastern Europe.

Grain from Pomerania became increasingly essential to feed not only Norway but also Flanders and Holland, permitting them to specialize in the manufacture and export of woolen cloth using wool from England and Spain as the essential input. It is thus apparent that medieval northern Europe had developed an extensive pattern of specialization and interdependence between the lands of the North Sea and the Atlantic on the west and the Baltic in the east. The Hanseatic League gained its importance through the control it attempted to exercise as the sole intermediary between these diverse geographic areas. Control of the narrow Danish straits and the overland route across the Jutland peninsula linking Lübeck and Hamburg was therefore crucial, and the numerous wars that were fought by the League during this period testify to this fact. The League's objective was to prevent the Dutch and English from breaking into the Baltic and the Scandinavians from breaking out. They succeeded for about a century and a half before succumbing finally to the Dutch.

Wine, and to a lesser extent beer, were also important in medieval European trade. Specialization in viticulture developed early, and Bordeaux and Burgundy, Alsace and the Moselle were major exporting regions. Rhenish wines were exported all around Germany and the Baltic, and French wines were popular in England and the Low Countries. Beer was produced in most German towns, with Hamburg and Wismar being the biggest exporters.

What of the economic consequences of this northern trade between Eastern and Western Europe? The recovery of population and the labor force after the Black Death would, by simple factor proportions reasoning along Heckscher–Ohlin lines, raise the relative price of land-intensive goods such as grain and livestock products, together with the rent per acre of land, and lower that of labor-intensive goods such as manufactures along with the real wage. This would in turn imply an improvement in the terms of trade of the grain-exporting Eastern countries, leading to an extension of the area under cultivation and a growth of exports. These predictions seem to have been borne out in Poland, Prussia, and even to some extent in Denmark. As Postan (1970), Malowist (1966), and many others have pointed out, this had momentous social and political consequences. The nobility and gentry in all these lands, who were in any event benefiting from rising rents, were able to use their command of both military force and political influence over weak central states to bind the peasantry even more firmly to the soil in a "second serfdom," and thus expand their rents correspondingly further. Domestic manufacturing and handicrafts, and therefore the prosperity and influence of the towns, should have declined in these countries, while wholesale and retail trade should have been taken up increasingly by foreign merchants, particularly if they were better organized and financed than their domestic counterparts. Again there is abundant evidence that this is exactly what happened.

The difference in factor proportions between Eastern and Western Europe can thus go a long way toward explaining the otherwise puzzling fact, noted by many observers, of why the same cause—population recovery after the Black Death—could produce such widely divergent sociopolitical outcomes as the "second serfdom" in the former case and the decline of feudalism and the rise of towns in the latter. In each region the impact effect of the plague was to raise wages, lower land rents, and hence increase the demand on the part of landowners for serfdom. The different experiences of Eastern and Western Europe must therefore be due to differences in the "supply" of serfdom, with rulers in the former region more willing to accede to landowners' demands than their counterparts in the latter. Trade and population recovery favored urban interests in the west and rural interests in the east. To the extent that these economic gains translated into political gains as well, this can help explain the different institutional supply responses in the two regions.[9]

A major aspect of the trade of northwest Europe with the Hanseatic League was the monetary imbalance against the former, involving the transfer of silver to the north German cities. Where did this silver go? Some of it undoubtedly went to Novgorod and Smolensk to pay for the expensive furs, amber, and wax that were so much in demand in the west. In turn the Russian principalities themselves used the silver at least partly to pay tribute to the Golden Horde, although this would become less of a factor as the period progressed, as we will see shortly. The German burghers, however, also had a strong propensity to purchase luxury products from the south of Europe, chiefly Italy. The overland route through Nuremburg and Frankfurt to Milan thus redirected the silver drained from England, France, and the Low Countries to the Italian cities of Milan, Florence, Genoa, Lucca, and Venice. The Italians also supplied northwest Europe directly by sea, with Venetian and Genoese galleys calling regularly at London, Bruges, and other northern ports. The luxury products that the Italians sold were chiefly the high-quality woolens of Florence, the silks and brocades of Lucca, and the finely crafted armor and weapons manufactured at Milan.

---

[9]Allen (1998) and Domar (1970), among many others, make several of these points. England remains a puzzle, however, since it was not heavily urbanized.

In addition there were also of course the spices and other oriental products that Venice and Genoa obtained from their trade with the Islamic World, and which were increasingly demanded by Europeans as their incomes rose. In order to analyze this trade, we need to turn our attention to geopolitical developments in Central and East Asia.

OVERLAND TRADE, 1350–1500: THE AFTERMATH OF THE *PAX MONGOLICA*

The *Pax Mongolica* disintegrated as a result of the demise of the Il-Khan regime in Persia in 1335, the unrelated internal conflicts of the Mongol states in Central Asia, and the fall of the Yüan dynasty to the native Chinese Ming in 1368. While the traditional trade patterns between nomadic and sedentary peoples, such as the exchange of horses and camels for tea and silk, continued, the absence of imperial rule, even if only loosely unified between the different components of the Mongol Empire, had momentous geopolitical consequences that in turn had major repercussions on the future patterns of world trade.

The end of the *Pax Mongolica* spelled the end of the relative ease with which European merchants had been able to move throughout Eurasia. Foreigners were expelled from China, and there were massacres of Europeans in Persia and Turkestan to name just two examples. Thus it was that "the eastern frontier of south European trade gradually receded from the sea of China to the edge of the Mediterranean, losing even there the secure shelters of the Italian commercial colonies," and that European merchants found themselves once more dependent on "the Egyptian bottle-neck" (Lopez 1987, pp. 383, 387). Briefly, it seemed that the status quo ante might be restored by the great Central Asian conqueror, Timur (Tamerlane). Ethnically Turkic but politically affiliated with the Chaghatai Mongol Khans, he launched a series of attacks on surrounding areas, nomad and sedentary alike, causing great destruction and amassing a huge amount of plunder. His capital of Samarkand and other cities of the region were the beneficiaries of these fruits of conquest, reflected in splendid architecture and the construction of observatories and libraries. Adshead (1993) claims that there was an underlying logic to his apparently destructive activities, namely the securing of the southern Silk Road and the diversion of the caravan trade to this route from the alternative northern route controlled by the Golden Horde. His destruction of Sarai, the Horde's capital on the Volga and the hub of its commerce, is explained as a calculated move to further this aim.

Similarly, his conquest of the Mediterranean port of Aleppo in Syria from the Mamluks is interpreted as the securing of a western terminus for this trade route, and the conquest of China that he was planning at his death in 1405 as the acquisition of the source of the goods that traveled westward along the Road.

Certainly, in Europe "Tamerlane seemed to many a new Chingis Khan who would restore peace through destruction and commerce through peace in the immense territories he subdued," and he was all the more welcome as a result of the advances of the Ottoman Turks, who were expanding into the Balkans and threatening Constantinople at this time (Lopez 1987, pp. 388–89). The crushing defeat that the forces of the Ottoman Sultan Bayezid (Marlowe's Bejazet) suffered at his hands at Ankara in 1402 postponed the fall of Constantinople by fifty years. With his death in 1405, however, the dream would vanish, the Ottoman advance would continue, Constantinople itself would fall in 1453 to Sultan Mehmed II "the Conqueror," and European–Asian trade would once again revert to the traditional sea routes described earlier.

However, European exclusion from Asia did not imply that the overland trade as a whole declined or stagnated. As we will see, the fifteenth century was the "Age of Commerce" in Southeast Asia, fueled by the expansion of China under the Ming and the recovery of Europe and the Mediterranean from the Black Death. It would therefore be surprising if prosperity at both ends of the old Silk Road did not sustain a corresponding continuance or even expansion of the overland trade in parallel with the growth of the overseas trade. To be sure, Europeans no longer participated directly in this trade, but this was a relatively minor detail in an era when Europe was still a bit player in the economic life of Asia. Thus, an extremely valuable paper by Morris Rossabi (1990) has pointed out that the Central Asian caravan trade did not decline but actually flourished throughout the fifteenth century. Despite the fall of the Yüan, and the Mongol Empire as a whole except for the Golden Horde, the successor states in Central Asia, Iran, and Turkey generally maintained peace and security along the trade routes.

As we have seen, Timur was extremely concerned to keep open the central land route from China to the west, and his descendants, in particular Shahrukh and Ulugh Beg, ruling in the prosperous caravan cities of Herat and Samarkand, were anxious to attract trade to and through their lands in order to sustain their ambitious building programs and scientific projects, such as the great observatory of Ulugh Beg in Samarkand. The Islamicized Turco-Mongol rulers of the oasis cities of Hami and Turfan toward the eastern end of the Silk Road were eager to trade their horses and camels for silk, metals, and other manufactures from China, sending numerous "tribute" embassies or trade missions in disguise to China. Turfan alone sent no fewer than fifty-four between 1407 and 1502 (ibid., pp. 358–59). Persian cities such as Shiraz and Isfahan also sent diplomatic and trade missions. There are records of Chinese officials being sent on diplomatic and "fact-finding" missions to the Islamic lands of Southwest Asia. The establishment of the Ottoman Empire by the middle of the fifteenth century also added to peace and security along the trade routes, and merchants from as far away as Turkey, Arabia, and even Egypt traveled to China during the fifteenth century (ibid.).

THE EMERGENCE OF RUSSIA

As noted earlier the Golden Horde did not impose direct rule on the Russian principalities that they dominated. Instead they extracted tribute and manipulated the individual vassal states to maintain their suzerainty. The disruption caused by the Black Death meant that the hold of the Horde on its Russian vassals was weakened, and the ravages of Timur dealt it another crippling blow. While the initial beneficiary was the rising Grand Duchy of Lithuania, the greatest beneficiary in the long run was the strongest of the Russian principalities, Moscow.

Here the reign of Ivan III "the Great" (1462–1505), the grandfather of Ivan the Terrible, was of fundamental significance. Ivan III consolidated or "gathered" the Russian lands, hitherto divided between other city-states or republics and principalities, under Muscovite sovereignty. In addition he pushed back the penetration of the Roman Catholic Duchy of Lithuania and the German knights of the Livonian Order on Russia's western borders, opening trade routes to Eastern and central Europe and to the Baltic. The subjugation of the great trading republic of Novgorod in 1478 in particular greatly enhanced the wealth and power of Muscovy. Novgorod had controlled vast stretches of territory over which it collected the furs and forest products that it sold to the Hanseatic League and other Western merchants, and these lands were now distributed to Ivan's loyal followers. By a shrewd mixture of force and diplomacy he was also able to extend Muscovite influence over the Tartar Khanates of the Crimea and Kazan and the remnant of the Golden Horde known as the Great Horde, thus gaining access to the regions bordering the Caspian and the Black Sea. The fall of Constantinople to the Ottoman Turks in 1453 meant that he was the only ruling Eastern Orthodox monarch of his time and his marriage to Sofia, niece of the last Byzantine emperor, allowed him to claim the Byzantine heritage, with Moscow as the third and last Rome.

These considerable achievements were largely the result of his fiscal and military reorganization of the Muscovite state, based on a new "middle service class" that was granted estates and control over serfs in return for providing a mobile and disciplined cavalry force capable of standing up to both the Lithuanian and Livonian knights and the Tartar horsemen of the steppe. "By the end of Ivan III's reign Moscow had become an important commercial center, whose merchants joined their own northern lands with Kazan and the southern market centers of the Black Sea to form a single commercial network" (Martin 1995, p. 322). Ivan III was succeeded by his son Vassily III (1505–33), also an able ruler if not as great a one as his extraordinary father. Vassily managed to hold on to his father's gains and extended them by subjugating another prosperous Russian trading republic, Pskov, and also wresting the major town and fortress of Smolensk from the Lithuanians. Much of his reign was spent in conflict with his father's allies, the Crimean Tartars, and with Kazan, while the wars with Lithuania continued in the west. Relations with the Ottoman Empire did, however, develop positively, based on the ability of Moscow to provide Istanbul with the valuable sable and ermine furs that were prized at the court as ceremonial prestige goods. One of the sources of contention with the Crimean Tartars was that they were losing the middleman role that they had successfully played between the Muscovites and the Ottomans, as the two great powers established increasingly direct bilateral relations. Crummey (1987) points out that the area ruled by Muscovy increased more than threefold between the ascension of Ivan III in 1462 and the death of Vassily III in 1533, in the process transforming it from merely an "ambitious principality" into a "nation-state of enormous size." Eventually the Russian Empire would serve to unify most of northern Eurasia, thus once again giving Europeans direct access to the Asian caravan trade, as we will see in chapter 5.

THE MIDDLE EAST, THE MEDITERRANEAN, AND INTERNATIONAL TRADE, 1350–1500

Not surprisingly, centuries of conflict over the Holy Land, Europe's flirtation with the Mongols, and its abandonment of the traditional Red Sea trade during the *Pax Mongolica* had not endeared the Venetians and other infidel merchants to the Egyptian sultans. Moreover, the

Islamic World, which had exhibited such prosperity and magnificence at the turn of the millennium, was by now in the throes of a prolonged economic stagnation and decline, exacerbated by the Black Death and its continuing demographic repercussions. Mamluk rule continued in Egypt and Syria, but the Circassian Mamluks who took over from the earlier Turkish Mamluks in 1382 adopted ruthlessly predatory policies toward almost all forms of economic activity in their domains. They not only continued the traditional exploitation of the peasantry, but also introduced extortionate taxes and forced sales on industrial production and commerce. The monetary stability of the earlier dynasties was broken by the introduction of copper money on a larger scale. Agricultural production declined as a result of the falling labor force, failure to maintain the infrastructure for irrigation and Bedouin depredations, and a number of industries, from textiles to sugar refining and paper, shrank as the result of excessive taxation and competition from European imports. The revenues squeezed out of the economy by the Mamluks, supplemented by their rents from the transit trade in spices, were largely spent on luxury consumption by the elite and costly wars against the revolting Bedouin tribes and the increasingly powerful Ottoman Turks, while the late fourteenth century was also marked by the ravages of Timur in Syria. Ashtor (1976a, chapter 8), Levanoni (1995, chapter 4), and many other authorities present a very melancholy picture of the economic state of the Islamic World at this time.

Symptomatic of the relative decline of the Islamic World, and the relative rise of Western Europe, is the gradual reversal of the trade patterns that had traditionally prevailed between the two partners (Ashtor 1983, 1992, chapter 1). As we have seen, at the beginning of the millennium European exports had largely consisted of relatively unprocessed goods, with one or two well-documented exceptions such as Frankish swords, in return for high-value manufactures and luxury goods. Now, however, industrial decline in the Mamluk regions meant that it was Europe which better fit the traditional image of a "core" economic region, while the Muslim World found itself playing the role of "periphery" to a greater and greater extent. In textiles, the automatic spindle, treadle loom, and water-driven fulling mill were all adopted in Europe during the thirteenth century, but not in the Muslim World. Abulafia (1987) offers the telling example of fustian, a mixture of linen and wool produced and exported by Italy that took its name from the linen industry of Fustat or Old Cairo that had once been the major supplier of the Mediterranean world. Similar import substitution, followed by eventual export back to the original source of the imports, also took place in other European industries, such as silk. Italians bought alkali ash from Syria to manufacture glass and soap, and Venetian Murano glass displaced Syrian glass as the industry leader. Papermaking also advanced substantially in Europe relative to the Muslim World. The cultivation of cotton and to a lesser extent sugarcane for export was one of the few positive features of the Mamluk economy during this period, but even this success story foreshadowed the emergence of a "colonial" relationship with respect to Europe later on.

This picture of the consequences of the Black Death of course contrasts dramatically with the very positive outcome for Western Europe that we have described earlier, emphasizing the rise in real wages and per capita incomes and the recovery of population and output to their previous levels. Why did the same exogenous demographic shock produce such sharply divergent outcomes? Ashtor speculates that the rise in real wages in Egypt and Syria following the Black Death was one reason for Mamluk industrial decline, but this hardly seems a convincing explanation, since as we have seen real wages rose in Europe as well, with apparently beneficial long-run effects.

An alternative perspective is provided by a recent study on the differential effects of the plague in Egypt and England (Borsch 2005). Borsch's account of the impact on England is similar in essentials to that given in our earlier section for Western Europe as a whole, which conforms to the predictions of a simple neo-Malthusian model with competitive markets for goods, land, and labor. In Mamluk Egypt, by contrast, the Mamluk system of nonhereditary assignment of lands to military commanders, only for the duration of their office, meant that as individuals each landowner had no incentive to make productive long-term investments, while all had a collective self-interest as members of the same armed ruling class in maintaining their rents. They thus responded to labor scarcity with harsh measures against the peasantry to maintain their rents at the expense of the latter, and when this proved insufficient extended their depredations to urban artisans and merchants. A further very important difference was that Egyptian agriculture was based on the control and allocation of the Nile floods through a complex system of central and local irrigation works. Maintaining rents in the short-term therefore came at the expense not only of the peasantry, but of the upkeep of public works such as the irrigation system as well.

The troubles unleashed by the plague also led to intensification of Bedouin raids on settled lands, despite savage reprisals by the Mamluk regime. As a result of all these factors, Borsch (2005, p. 15) claims that while in Egypt population declined by as much as 50%, agricultural output fell by no less than 68%. Clearly, the contrast with England and the rest of Western Europe was dramatic indeed. If per capita incomes actually *fell* as a result of the plague, then the Malthusian model would generate further demographic contraction rather than the self-correcting recovery that was displayed in Western Europe. In addition the recurrences of the plague, sixteen in Egypt and fifteen in Syria between the 1360s and the early 1500s, seem to have been much more frequent and severe than they were in Western Europe (Levanoni 1995, p. 137).

If per capita incomes fell in Egypt, but land rents were maintained and urban wages increased (Pamuk 2005), this must have implied sharply deteriorating living standards for the peasantry. This should have given them an incentive to abandon cultivation of marketable crops in favor of subsistence cultivation, or flee into the towns or surrounding deserts, and this in turn should have lowered land rents and urban wages. If the Mamluks succeeded in maintaining rents, therefore, this must ultimately have been because Egyptian peasants were not all that mobile, despite the evidence of rural to urban flight cited by Borsch (2005, pp. 49–52) and implied by Garcin (1998, p. 314), who says that the population of Cairo remained stable despite the decline in the total population. For Abu-Lughod (1989, p. 238), the lesser mobility of Egyptian peasants, relative to their Western European counterparts, is in fact a key difference between the two regions during this period.

In his classic analysis of the causes of serfdom and slavery, Evsey Domar (1970, pp. 28–29) asks why serfdom was not reinstated in Western Europe after the Black Death, when clearly landowners would have benefited from forcing rural workers to accept lower living standards. His answer is that "serfdom could not be restored unless the landowners were reasonably united in their pressure on the government, and unless the latter was willing and able to do their bidding." These conditions, apparently, were not met in England. There were some attempts by Parliament to reduce peasant mobility, but these proved ineffective. On the other hand, the Mamluk regime, dominated as it was by a landowning military elite, was willing to back up landlord attempts to maintain or raise rents with legal action and violence (Borsch 2005, pp. 48–49, 59–62).

Lower intersectoral mobility would have impeded industrial growth in Egypt. Harsh taxation would have been a further burden on the sector. Both factors can thus help to explain the decline of the Muslim World's industrial sector, relative to Western Europe's, during this period. In addition, the semiarid climate made Egyptian agriculture dependent on stable maintenance of the irrigation system, which the predatory Mamluk institutional structure was not able to provide under the impact of a demographic crisis that was even more severe and prolonged than in Western Europe. As Levanoni (1995) and Garcin (1998) have amply documented, the attempt to maintain their incomes in spite of the fall in population and output led to deep divisions and conflicts between the sultan, the senior emirs, and the unruly new recruits, that severely compromised the military effectiveness and discipline of this alien ruling class. Mamluk Egypt thus never fully recovered from the Black Death, in terms of population, prosperity, political cohesion, or military prowess.

All this meant that European merchants wishing to buy spices in Alexandria were faced with a partner in the Mamluk state that was anxious to squeeze the maximum amount of profit from them and their local counterparts. Not content with the traditional revenue from taxes on the transit trade in spices, the Sultan Barsbay, who ruled from 1422 to 1438, attempted to impose a state monopoly to raise revenues even further. The Karimi merchants who had handled the trade, making fortunes for themselves while also contributing generously to the state coffers, were effectively put out of business by his measures. The Venetians and other European purchasers of the spices resisted his attempts to force them to pay exorbitant prices and his efforts ended in failure according to Ashtor (1983, chapter 5). Nonetheless, fiscal pressure ensured that the incentive for Egypt to maximize its profits persisted throughout the remainder of the century. Thus in 1480, the sultan demanded that he be paid 110 ducats for a *sporta* of pepper, when the market price was only 50 ducats. The Venetians refused, but were subsequently refused permission to leave until they had paid 70 (Lopez 1987, p. 388).

Trade in the Mediterranean during the period was dominated by the ongoing rivalry between Venice and Genoa. The main commodities that the European merchants desired were pepper and ginger, but the more valuable cloves and nutmeg were growing in importance. As Ashtor (1978) has emphasized, raw cotton was increasingly sought after as an input to the textile industry established in southern Germany, central Europe, and Italy. In return, the main export to the Islamic World was woolen cloth, both the high-quality products of Florence and Flanders but also cheaper varieties from Catalonia and France. Metals, particularly copper, were important exports as well. Olive oil from Spain and North Africa was exported to Egypt and Syria by the Italian cities, whose dominance in shipping enabled them to encroach on trade in goods produced within the Islamic World itself.

Throughout the period Venice sent regular convoys of both galleys and cogs to Alexandria and Beirut. While the number of convoys remained fairly stable on average, despite fluctuations (ibid.), the volume of trade increased because the capacity of the cogs and galleys was significantly greater in the later years. The ascendancy of Venice in the spice trade, according to Ashtor, was based on her access to silver and copper from central Europe that was much in demand by the Mamluks, and also to her well-established markets for spices in Germany and northern Europe, through her links with Nuremburg. Another factor was the more aggressive resistance to Barsbay of the Genoese and Catalans, which left them as the less preferred partners when the attempt at state monopoly was implicitly abandoned after his death in 1438. In addition, the Catalans were prone to piracy, which tended to hamper their trade when the Muslim powers took reprisals.

The pattern of Genoese trade in the Mediterranean was different from that of Venice. Her strength lay in her colonies at Pera near Constantinople and at Chios in the Aegean. She had a monopoly of alum exports from the main producing region, Phocaea in Asia Minor, which she exported directly to Flanders, where it was an essential input for the dyeing of cloth. Spice purchases from Alexandria and Damascus were also shipped directly to Southampton and Sluys in Flanders. Chios was the main source of mastic used in paints and perfumes and exported to both Europe and the Islamic World. Slaves obtained in the Black Sea area continued to be exported to the Mamluks in Egypt. Cotton was obtained by Genoa mainly from Turkey and exported to the main centers of the textile industry in Europe. Although Venice and Genoa were the major players, many other European cities and states took an active part in the trade of the Levant and the Mediterranean. Catalan merchants from Barcelona and Valencia were prominent, exporting their own woolen cloth and olive oil from Spain to Egypt and Syria. Amalfi, Pisa, and other Italian cities, and Ragusa on the eastern shore of the Adriatic, were involved as well.

The close of the fifteenth century in the Mediterranean world as a whole can be seen as marking a historic turning point, in which the arena of classical antiquity and its offshoot, Islamic civilization, underwent a crisis and transformation reflecting deep-seated shifts in underlying economic and social forces in favor of northwestern Europe and the Atlantic that would become apparent in the next century. In Western Europe this shift away from Italy and the Mediterranean and toward the Low Countries and the Iberian Peninsula is a familiar one, but associated with it was a much less familiar shift in the Islamic World. The Mamluks, ruling over Egypt and "Greater Syria" (including Lebanon, Palestine, and Transjordan), as well as the holy cities of Mecca and Medina in the Hijaz, constituted the most powerful state in the Islamic World between the fall of the Abbasid caliphate in 1258 and the fall of Constantinople to the Ottomans in 1453. The Mamluks and Ottomans were both Sunni Muslim, and both elites had their roots in the steppes of western Central Asia, but they were clearly destined to be rivals for the leadership of the Islamic World.

As Carl F. Petry (1994) has pointed out, however, the two states differed fundamentally in that the older Mamluk state wished to preserve the status quo, while the new Ottoman state was expansive and dynamic. The inherent conservatism of the Mamluk state, according to David Ayalon's (1956) classic study, was notably, and fatally, reflected in the attitude of its warrior ruling class toward the use of gunpowder and firearms. As expert horsemen with unrivaled skills in using the bow and the lance, they were hostile and unreceptive to the new military technology based on these innovations, with only auxiliary units being equipped with firearms, and artillery used only for coastal defense rather than in the field. The Ottomans, with their greater exposure to conflict with European powers in the Balkans and central Europe, were far more progressive in arming their elite Janissary infantry with muskets, and used cannon to great effect not only in sieges, as at Constantinople, but in the field as well. Their artillery proved decisive in defeating the rising Safavid dynasty of Shah Ismail at the Battle of Chaldiran in 1515, and in 1516 and 1517 they inflicted the same fate on the Mamluk armies in Syria and Egypt. The entire Mamluk kingdom was incorporated into the empire of Sultan Selim *Yavuz*, or Selim the Grim (1512-20) as he is known in the West, although the Mamluks themselves survived as an influential group within the empire.

Southeast Asia and China, 1350-1500

We turn now to the ultimate source of the spices that were sold by the Muslim World to Christian Europe, namely Southeast Asia, and to the relationship between that region and China. The fifteenth century was one of expansion driven mainly by demand for pepper and spices from China in the east, supplemented by the western trade to the Red Sea and the Persian Gulf, reflecting the demand from the Islamic World and an increasingly prosperous Western Europe. Thus, Anthony Reid (1993a, chapter 1) refers to the 1400-1650 period in Southeast Asian history as "the Age of Commerce." This in itself is a welcome antidote to the traditional Eurocentric view that associates commerce in Asia with the "Vasco da Gama Epoch" that only begins at the end of the fifteenth century. After noting the slump in the spice trade in the middle of the fourteenth century due to the ravages of the Black Death and the fall of the Mongol Empire, Reid associates the onset of his Age of Commerce with the series of great voyages launched from 1405 onwards by the Ming dynasty under the command of the Muslim admiral Zheng He (or Cheng Ho).

Many accounts of the Ming voyages by Western writers consider them purely as demonstrations of the power and might of the new dynasty and ignore their economic impact. It is interesting therefore that a modern Chinese scholar, T'ien Ju-kang (1981), stresses that Zheng He's voyages brought back enormous quantities of pepper from Southeast Asia and the Malabar Coast. He states (p. 187) that "in China, the change in the value of pepper from being a precious commodity to one in common use came about as a result of Cheng Ho's (Zheng He's) voyages." According to Reid (1993a, p. 12), "the expeditions undoubtedly stimulated Southeast Asian production of crops for the China market." Indeed, it was around this time that pepper plants from Malabar in southern India were introduced into northern Sumatra, from where pepper was exported to China. Pepper was an imperial monopoly under the Ming, who used it, along with sandalwood and other valuable imports, instead of silver or paper money, to remunerate hundreds of thousands of soldiers and civil servants. After the cessation of the voyages, pepper imports continued to be abundant as a result of private trade and tribute payments, leading to an over tenfold drop in price by the early seventeenth century. Apart from pepper, cloves and sappanwood were important commodities in this trade.

The fifteenth century was the heyday of Melaka as the classic Malay "port-polity," as identified by Kathirithamby-Wells and Villiers (1990, chapter 1), under a native potentate who kept his harbor open to merchants from all quarters of the globe. Such political entities were located on rivers, giving them access to an agrarian hinterland, at or near a seacoast giving them access to the arteries of international trade. Trade served as the major source of revenue sustaining the ruling elite. The polity could itself be the source of major exportable products, or alternatively be an entrepôt through which the products of other regions were transshipped. In this sense Melaka can be thought of as the successor of Srivijaya, and a predecessor of Singapore, as the major port-polity of the Southeast Asian region. Its historical origins are obscure. It is supposed to have been founded at the site of a fishing village around 1402 by a certain Paramesvara, allegedly a prince of the Javanese Sailendra royal family born at Palembang in Sumatra. He apparently gained control of both sides of the Straits and was recognized as the ruler of Melaka by the Ming dynasty with whom he opened diplomatic relations. Significantly, Zheng He called at Melaka in 1409 on the third of the celebrated Ming voyages.

Islam was beginning to spread in Sumatra at this time, with the port-kingdom of Pasai being the first state with a known Muslim ruler, and the Hindu Paramesvara was supposed to have converted before his death in 1424 in order to secure a trade agreement with Pasai. Subsequent rulers apparently reverted to Hinduism before the definitive adoption of Islam by the middle of the fifteenth century. The expansion of east–west trade, particularly in spices in return for silver, cloth, and porcelain, sustained the emergence and growth of Melaka as the premier entrepôt of Southeast Asia, on the basis of its location connecting the Indian Ocean and the South China Sea, between the alternating northeast and southwest monsoon winds. Islam spread as far as the Spice Islands in the wake of the growth of Melaka's trade. By the time it fell to the Portuguese in 1511 Melaka had a population estimated at between 100,000 and 200,000, making it the largest urban center in Southeast Asia (Thomaz 1993).

Trade taxes provided the state with most of its revenues since there was no agricultural production other than vegetables and valuable fruits such as durians and mangosteens, all the rice required being imported from Burma, Siam, or Java free of duty. The total value of trade around 1511 was estimated at between 1 and 2 million Portuguese cruzados. Melaka issued a tin coinage but all currencies were freely traded in the markets. The sultan himself had his own fleet and conducted trade on his own account, as well as in partnership with private traders, apparently without any attempt to disadvantage foreign or local private sector competition. Each major community, such as the Gujaratis, Tamils, Chinese, and Javanese, had its own head or *shahbandar* in charge of their transactions, and responsible to the centrally appointed royal official, the *bendahara*. Around 1516 there were said to be 1,000 Gujaratis, over 4,000 Bengalis, Arabs, and Persians, 1,000 Tamils, and several thousand Javanese. The state had a standing army and navy of mercenaries, supplemented in time of war by levies from the surrounding territories owing allegiance to the sultan. A significant community in Melaka was the *orang laut* or sea nomads, who formed the core of the naval contingents and the ruling elite of the state. The atmosphere at Melaka appears to have been remarkably cosmopolitan. The Islam practiced was not very strict, and was denounced for its laxity by more orthodox Muslims from the Middle East.

The Portuguese apothecary and diplomat Tome Pires, who visited Melaka shortly after the occupation in 1511, claimed that eighty-four languages could be heard spoken in a single day. Pires (1990), in book 6 of his work, gives a fascinatingly detailed account of the trade of Melaka. According to him, at least one hundred large ships came to Melaka every year with very valuable cargoes. Of this total there were approximately five each from Gujarat, the Coromandel Coast, and Bengal, about fifteen from the Lower Burma port of Pegu, around thirty from Siam, ten from China, ten from Palembang, and the rest from various ports in the islands and the Far East. The harbor had warehouses to hold the goods securely until they could be disposed of, and all the necessary institutions to ensure that trade could take place smoothly and securely. We learn that merchants from the Red Sea and the Persian Gulf took their goods to Cambay in Gujarat before proceeding to Melaka, and that "those from Cairo bring the merchandise brought by the galleasses from Venice, to wit, many arms, scarlet-in-grain, colored woolen cloths, coral, copper, quicksilver, vermilion, nails, silver, glass and other beads, and golden glassware." The Cambay ships each had cargoes that he valued at 70,000–80,000 cruzados, including thirty kinds of cloth "much valued in these parts." The return cargoes were cloves, nutmeg, mace, sandalwood, "enormous quantities of white silk," tin, and birds valued for their feathers as plumes.

Pires notes the interdependence of the two great ports, declaring that "the Cambay merchants make Melaka their chief trading center" and that "Melaka cannot live without Cambay, or Cambay without Melaka, if they are to be very rich and prosperous." Tamil merchants known as Klings also brought large quantities of cloth, which were exchanged for sandalwood, camphor, alum, spices, pearls, and gold. These Klings, according to Pires "have all the merchandise and more of the trade of Melaka than any other nation." The greatest of these Tamil merchants was the famous Nina Chatu, who befriended the Portuguese when they first came to Melaka in 1509 and was appointed *bendahara* after their takeover in 1511, committing suicide after they replaced him with a Malay prince to appease the local populace. Pires ends his account of Melaka with a rapturously enthusiastic paean to the port and its potential, not only as the best base for trade in the world because of its incomparable location, but also for victory in the struggle against Islam, since "merchandise favors our faith," and in the commercial competition against its main European rival, because "whoever is lord of Melaka has his hand on the throat of Venice."

Despite its dominance over the Straits, Melaka could not avoid acknowledging some loose form of dependence on the much more

TABLE 3.1. Seaborne tribute missions to China, 1369–1509
(numbers of missions).

Period	Siam	Cambodia	Champa	Java	Melaka	Pasaia
1369–99	33	13	25	11		1
1400–9	11	4	5	8	3	3
1410–19	6	3	9	6	8	7
1420–29	10		9	16	5	5
1430–39	4		10	5	3	3
1440–49	3		9	7	2	
1450–59	2		3	3	3	
1460–69	1		4	3	2	1
1470–79	4		3		1	
1480–89	3		3			3
1490–99	3		3	2		
1500–9	1		2		2	

Source: Reid (1999, table 1, p. 87).

heavily populated state of Ayutthaya in Siam that was able to dominate the Malay Peninsula militarily from its northern end. Ayutthaya was situated near the mouth of the Chao Phraya River, which flowed into the Gulf of Siam. It thus had access to fertile rice plains as well as an outlet to the sea for foreign trade, giving it a formidable combination of manpower and agrarian as well as commercial revenues. The state was founded in 1351 by a ruler of mixed royal Thai and mercantile Chinese descent, a circumstance that reflected the dual basis that was to be characteristic of this important Southeast Asian state. As table 3.1, taken from Reid (1999) shows, Ayutthaya responded energetically to the opportunity to trade with China at the start of the Ming dynasty in 1368, sending sixty seaborne "tribute" missions in the sixty years from 1369 to 1429, more than any other Southeast Asian state, though Champa and Java also sent more than forty each in the same period.

Drawing on cultural influences from the early civilization of Angkor to the east, Ayutthaya developed as a highly centralized bureaucratic state, with separate hierarchies of civil and military officials and allocations of manpower and other resources to specified functions. During the fifteenth century it was able to extend its power to the borders of Burma and Laos and also over the important ports of Mergui and Tenasserim, giving it outlets on the Bay of Bengal. Its major export in addition to rice and tin from the Malay Peninsula was deerskins, very much in demand in China, Japan, and the Ryukyu Islands. The administration of foreign trade, even though under ulti-mate royal control, was entrusted to officials of foreign origin, among them Persian and Indian Muslims in addition to Chinese and Sino-Siamese with mercantile backgrounds and experience. The kingdom maintained active contacts with China, which it acknowledged as a suzerain, as well as with India and the Middle East and all the Malay and Indonesian states.

The natural competitors of Ayutthaya in the fifteenth century were the Shans, to whom they were ethnically and linguistically related, divided into numerous petty states, the Mon kingdom of Pegu in Lower Burma founded in 1356, and the Burmese kingdom of Ava, the much diminished successor state of the Pagan Empire that fell in the thirteenth century, founded in 1364. Pegu was very actively involved in the trade of Melaka and the Bay of Bengal and its teak made it a major shipbuilding center for the entire Southeast Asian world. The large vessels that carried cargo to Melaka and other ports in Southeast Asia were often themselves sold at their destinations. Pegu also exported "Martaban jars," popular all over the Southeast Asian world as containers for water, oil, and grains. Pegu's income from foreign trade enabled its rulers in the fifteenth century to contest on better than equal terms with the inland agrarian Burmese kingdom of Ava which lacked an outlet to the sea. On the other hand Ava had substantial revenues from the productive irrigated areas of the Dry Zone in central Burma, enabling it to support a larger population than the swamps of the lower reaches of the Irrawaddy, Sittang, and Salween Rivers ruled by Pegu.

Separated from Ava and Pegu by the Arakan Yoma mountain range was the kingdom of Arakan, extending southeastward along the coast from Bengal with which it had close economic and cultural contacts despite the religious differences between Buddhism and Islam. The capital of this kingdom, Mrauk-U, founded in 1433 and located upriver in a fertile rice plain with access to the sea, also controlled the important port and cotton textile center of Chittagong in Bengal from 1459 until it lost it to the Mughals in 1666, thus giving it a diversified economic and revenue base during this period when it enjoyed its greatest power and prosperity. Bengal cotton textiles were as we have seen much sought after throughout Southeast Asia and could be traded inland and around the Bay for other goods, including rubies from Upper Burma and imports of Chinese goods brought down the Irrawaddy from Yunnan. The Arakanese maintained a powerful fleet of war galleys, specializing in naval operations in the shallow waters of creeks and rivers, which they used in raids for booty and slaves in Bengal that were another lucrative source of revenue.

Vietnam had been a province of China for almost all of the first millennium. Consequently, it is no surprise that the early Ming, with their interest in overseas contacts, attempted to restore Chinese suzerainty over this recalcitrant area by an invasion in 1407, ostensibly to remove a usurper but in reality to impose direct rule. The Vietnamese, as always, resisted and a new Le dynasty established by the leader of the national revolt arose in 1428 with its capital at Hanoi. The Ming recognized the Le as kings of Annam ("Pacified South") after payment of tribute, saving face all round and restoring relations to the traditional basis of nominal submission but effective independence. The most notable ruler of the new dynasty was Le Thanh Ton (1460–97), who conquered the Champa kingdom to the south in 1471, thus extending the realm to comprise the Mekong delta and the site of the modern Saigon in addition to the traditional base of the Red River delta, the two joined by the long coastal strip east of the Annam mountain range.

Therefore, apart from Melaka there were many other regional centers such as Arakan, Pegu, Ayutthaya, and various northern Javanese coastal states that prospered during this period. Political competition and warfare were by no means unknown but it is notable that no states with imperial claims emerged in Southeast Asia in this century. The power and glory of Pagan, Angkor, and Majapahit had all receded into history, and no new contenders had yet arisen. While Melaka and several other Indonesian and Malay ports were engaged in long-distance trade, their need for local goods stimulated rice production and shipbuilding activities in Burma and Thailand as well. Thus the long-distance trade in spices, Indian cotton textiles, and Chinese silks and ceramics was supplemented in the Southeast Asian states by intraregional trade in rice, timber, and other necessities, ensuring an efficient international specialization. There are no quantitative estimates of total Southeast Asian exports during the fifteenth century, but it seems clear that overall spice exports rose (Reid 1990).

The Ming dynasty turned its back on overseas contacts after ca. 1430, and imposed extensive prohibitions and regulations on foreign trade. The ships and the yards at which they were built ceased to exist and the technology of long-distance maritime navigation was beginning to fade away from disuse. The explanation given for these apparently irrational acts is usually the power struggle between the traditional Confucian mandarins, with their agrarian-based value system and concentration on the nomadic threat from Central Asia, and the palace eunuch faction to which Zheng He himself belonged, which was interested in the projection of Ming influence overseas, in which the former group secured a complete victory. The raids by the so-called Japanese *wako* pirates, who were in fact mostly disaffected Chinese, on the coastal areas was another reason why the Ming bureaucracy was averse to foreign trade. Security against their inroads was sought by even stricter controls on foreign trade, which was increasingly confined to the traditional tribute system. In this system trade could only be conducted in the context of tribute missions from recognized vassal states, with the volume and types of goods strictly regulated.

One interesting consequence was the emerging importance of the Ryukyu Islands under King Sho Hashi, who encouraged southern Chinese merchants to settle near Okinawa and conduct trade with Japan, China, and Southeast Asia, thus providing an important link between these major markets (Sakamaki 1964; Reid 1990). Table 3.1 shows that tribute missions to China from Java, Siam, Champa, and elsewhere continued during the fifteenth century, after the inward turn of the Ming, although with decreasing frequency. Thus, there were eleven tribute missions from Siam in the first decade of the century and ten during the 1420s, but no more than four during any subsequent decade, and this pattern was repeated elsewhere. China did not become autarkic during this period, but she was clearly more closed than she had been before.

QUANTIFYING THE LATE MEDIEVAL SPICE TRADE

We end this chapter with some quantitative information on the extent of the spice trade during the fifteenth century, since these are some of the earliest data on intercontinental trade available to us, and since the spice trade was a geopolitically important one. According to Wake (1986), European pepper imports were around 1,000 tons a year in 1400, with Venice supplying about 60% of the total. Imports of spices other than pepper were between 470 and 550 tons, with Venice importing less than half the total. By 1500 Europe's pepper imports had risen modestly to about 1,200 tons, with the share of Venice falling below 60%. For spices other than pepper, including the much more valuable items such as cloves and nutmeg, Europe's imports rose far more rapidly to between 1,200 and 1,350 tons a year, with the share of Venice rising to over 60%. Thus Venice more than compensated for her loss of market share in pepper by a significant gain in the much more lucrative trade in the fine spices.

From the previous discussion it seems likely that this fifteenth-century increase in imports reflected growing European demand rather than easier trading conditions. Pepper price evidence suggests that this was indeed the case. Frederick Lane (1968) and Eliyahu Ashtor (1969, 1973, 1976b) have provided evidence that nominal spice prices, and in particular pepper prices, fell during the fifteenth century in Venice and the Near East. However, it is relative prices that matter in indicating the economic scarcity or abundance of a commodity, and neither author provides direct evidence on this. Indeed, Ashtor (1969) suggests that part of the explanation for falling spice prices was a general deflationary price trend in the Near East, which would mirror the deflationary trend in Europe pointed to earlier. But in any event, even if real spice prices were falling in Venice and the Near East during this period, figure 3.5 shows that this finding can*not* be generalized to the rest of Europe, since real (i.e., grain-deflated) pepper prices rose in England, as well as in the Netherlands, Flanders, and Austria, over the course of the century (O'Rourke and Williamson forthcoming).

The spike in spice prices in the second decade of the fifteenth century is suggestive, for it coincides precisely with the Zheng He expeditions. Indeed, the year 1411 saw the invasion of Ceylon (Sri Lanka) and the capture of one of the local kings (Wade 2004, p. 16). We have already seen that these missions bought up significant quantities of spices and pepper, and it seems plausible that this could have translated into a large percentage decline in the residual supply that could be shipped to Europe, given the dominant role of the Chinese end market at that time. (Indeed, European clove imports declined from 22 to 14 tonnes between the 1390s and 1400s (Bulbeck et al. 1998, p. 54).) If true, this hypothesis would serve to underline the utter dependence of Europe on Asian market conditions during this period, and its peripheral status within the international economy. Asia, not Europe, still dictated the pace of intercontinental trade.[10]

This would soon change, however, as a result of the forces that we have explored in this chapter. We have seen how the Black Death increased European living standards, and thus the demand for Asian trade goods, exactly at the moment that overland trade with Asia once again became impossible for Western Europeans. Rising prices of pepper and other luxury goods were only to be expected under such conditions, as was the increased exploitation of European consumers by Muslim and Venetian middlemen, who should have raised their

[10] If Edward Gibbon is to be believed, and we would certainly like to believe him, then this is not the first time that events in East Asia directly influenced British relative prices. According to him, "in the year 1238, the inhabitants of Gothia (Sweden) and Frise were prevented, by their fear of the Tartars, from sending, as usual, their ships to the herring fishery on the coast of England; and as there was no exportation, forty or fifty of these fish were sold for a shilling.... It is whimsical enough, that the orders of a Mogul khan, who reigned on the borders of China, should have lowered the price of herrings in the English market" (Gibbon 1907, p. 148).

price–cost margins in response to increased levels of demand. In this way, the contrast between the falling spice prices of Egypt and Venice and the higher prices experienced in the major importing centers of northwestern Europe becomes easily understandable.

All this, as well as the closing of the medieval European frontier (Lewis 1958b), increased the incentive of non-Venetians to find a way around the Muslim middleman, who blocked direct access to both Asian spices and African gold, an aim which as we have seen Europeans had held since the thirteenth century at the latest. And this economic incentive was supplemented by the cultural and geopolitical incentive to return to Cathay, a desire kept alive by the travelers' tales produced during the *Pax Mongolica*. As J. R. S. Phillips (1998, p. 246) puts it, "With only a little exaggeration we might say that the ultimate legacy of the Asian and Eastern European conquests of Genghis Khan and his followers in the thirteenth century was the mutual discovery of Europeans and of the Native American peoples at the end of the fifteenth."

Chapter 4

WORLD TRADE 1500–1650: OLD WORLD TRADE AND NEW WORLD SILVER

ADAM SMITH, with what J. H. Elliott (1970, p. 1) called his "robust Scottish forthrightness," bluntly declared in his great work that "the discovery of America, and that of a passage to the East Indies by the Cape of Good Hope, are the two greatest and most important events recorded in the history of mankind." It might be fashionable today to denounce this view as yet another shocking example of the mortal academic sin of Eurocentrism. There can be no serious denial, however, that the voyages Smith referred to marked one of the major turning points in world history, ending once and for all the isolation of the Americas from the Old World of the Afro-Eurasian Ecumene. The voyages of Columbus and da Gama in the last decade of the fifteenth century were completed by Magellan's circumnavigation of the globe in 1521. Fifty years later the Spanish founded the city of Manila. The arrival there of the first galleon laden with silver from Acapulco marked the "origin of world trade" in the literal sense of the phrase, as noted by Flynn and Giráldez (1995, p. 201), since it was only then that goods passed completely around the globe in exchange for each other across the vast distances of the Atlantic and Pacific Oceans.

These epochal events raise the perennial questions of why it was the Iberian states of Portugal, Castile, and Aragon, rather than the commercially more advanced Italian city-states, the Flemish, or the rising power of France that took the lead in these momentous ventures. What were the motives of the Iberian states in undertaking the risks and the expense of these voyages into the unknown? What were the consequences for each of the regions of the Old World of the discovery of the New? What impact did the discovery of American silver have on the international economy? What was the reason for the Iberian powers being largely supplanted by Britain and the Dutch? Did the rise of the slave trade between Africa and the New World have any causal connection to the appearance of the Industrial Revolution of the eighteenth century? These and other related issues will be pursued in this and subsequent chapters.

One key feature of the next three centuries with which we will necessarily have to be concerned is the incessant warfare that characterized the era, not only between the European powers on that continent itself but overseas as well, with each other but also against the indigenous peoples, states, and empires that they encountered. These conflicts reflected a number of novel features of early modern warfare that have been described as a "Military Revolution" (Roberts 1967; Parker 1988).[1] The concept has been applied to a complex and interlocking set of developments in strategy, tactics, equipment, weaponry, fortifications, recruitment, training, and organization of armies and navies. These resulted in a substantial rise in the scale of armed forces, both in absolute terms and relative to total human and material resources available, in greater discipline and coordination between different units and services of these forces, and in increased professionalism of the officer corps at all levels. The crucial period in which the revolution occurred was taken to be 1560–1660 in the original formulation, but the dates have been extended both backward in time to as early as the fourteenth century and forward to as late as the turn of the nineteenth century.

The increase in the scale and cost of the armed forces was only possible because of the growth in the population and wealth of the states of early modern Europe, and the growing ability of these states to tap into that wealth. Growing military costs were also reflected in the significant reduction in the number of independent political units within that continent (Tilly 1975, chapter 1), and overseas in the subordination to Europe of 35% of the world's land surface by 1800 (Headrick 1981, p. 3). The conquistadores in the New World, the Portuguese and Dutch in the Indian Ocean and Southeast Asia, and the sepoy armies of the English and French East India Companies all manifested, in one way or another, the distinctive "comparative advantage in violence" that the Military Revolution conferred on the early modern European powers. However, we will also be emphasizing the fact that the new military technologies were exported to the rest of the world, leading to similar processes of political centralization, and also to similar "military-fiscal" problems, as states attempted to find the revenue to meet spiraling defense costs (Bayly 2004, pp. 91–92). Plunder and monopoly trade rents offered one way to meet these costs, exploitation of the peasantry another, financial innovation a third. How successfully states managed these challenges would largely determine their economic and political futures, and in some cases even their continued survival.

[1] A number of the most influential articles on the subject are conveniently available in Rogers (1995).

PORTUGAL, THE ATLANTIC, AND THE INDIAN OCEAN

"The Portuguese were the first Europeans to understand that the ocean is not a limit, but the universal waterway that unites mankind" as Lord Acton (1961) says in the second of his *Lectures on Modern History*, on "the New World." This primacy he attributes to the fact that the country was hemmed in by Spain, leaving no outlet but the Atlantic for the energies and ambitions of its restless nobility. The Portuguese kingdom itself was the product of the crusading spirit of the *Reconquista*, the capital Lisbon having been captured from the Moors in 1147 by a group of English, Flemish, and German crusaders on their way to the Holy Land on behalf of the founding ruler Afonso Henriques. This spirit was kept vigorously alive in subsequent conflicts, not only in the Iberian Peninsula but also later in North Africa. The high point of Portuguese arms in these wars was the capture in 1415 of Ceuta from the Berber Marinids by João I, the founder of the ruling house of Avis. Ceuta was not only captured but was held after the repulse of a joint force of the Marinids and the Nasrids of Granada in 1419. This victory not only gave the new dynasty great prestige in the Christian world, but also provided a base for further military and commercial operations in Morocco and beyond.

Distinguishing himself at the capture of Ceuta was the twenty-one-year-old Infante Dom Henrique, better known to generations of schoolchildren in the English-speaking world as "Prince Henry the Navigator," the fifth son of João and his English queen Philippa of Lancaster. Rewarded for his efforts by appointments as Governor of the Algarve and Grand Master of the knightly Order of Christ, the Infante used the resources of these and other offices and privileges accorded to him to promote a series of voyages to the Atlantic islands and the western coast of Africa. An immediate and irresistible lure for Henry was the "Golden Trade of the Moors," the attempt to get by sea to the source of the gold from the *Bilad as-Sudan* (Fernández-Armesto 2006, pp. 132–34). Raiding coastal settlements for slaves or Muslims who could then be ransomed was another important motivation (Newitt 2005, p. 15). According to Russell (2001, pp. 120–21) Henry further hoped to show that the crusade against Islam could be conducted just as effectively "on the Atlantic coasts of Saharan and sub-Saharan Africa as in the Mediterranean world."

The motive for the Portuguese expansion of the fifteenth century seems to have been an inextricable mixture of religious zeal, geopolitical grand strategy, and commercial profit, with Islam as the main adversary in all these spheres. According to Boxer (1975, p. 18), "the four main motives which inspired the Portuguese leaders... were in chronological but in overlapping order and in varying degree: (i) crusading zeal against the Muslims, (ii) the desire for Guinea gold, (iii) the quest for Prester John, (iv) the search for Oriental spices." Political rivalry with Castile was another important motivating factor (Newitt 2005). Initially, trade and plunder in and around Africa, involving gold, slaves, and other commodities, was the major economic goal, but by the late fifteenth century a more distant, but even more tempting, prospect emerged: that of outflanking Venice and the Mamluk sultans of Egypt, and breaking their joint monopoly of the spice trade by getting directly to the sources of supply. From the perspective of grand strategy the ventures could then be seen as an encirclement of the Islamic World, outflanking the Mamluks and Ottomans instead of engaging in an endless frontal stalemate on land in the Balkans and at sea in the Mediterranean. As we have noted, intertwined with these very long-term but quite rational considerations was the persistent legend of Prester John, the mythical Christian ruler of a kingdom in the East who could be an invaluable ally in the battle against the Muslims if only his realm could somehow be reached. According to an oft-repeated story, when da Gama's ships reached Calicut and were asked "What the devil has brought you here?" the reply was: "We have come to seek Christians and spices" (Boxer 1975, p. 37).

While such lofty aims may have inspired Portuguese efforts at various times, many of the operations that the Infante actually engaged in were of a more mundane and even sordid character, even by the standards of the day. Prominent among these was the initiation of a growing slave trade, with Africans sold in Europe as domestic servants, and natives of the Canary Islands sent to Madeira to work on sugar plantations set up with largely Genoese capital. Henry's monopoly rights to engage in and profit from this trade were granted by Pope Nicholas V himself. After his death in 1460 the newly discovered Cape Verde Islands were devoted to sugar plantations based on imported African slave labor, an important forerunner of the model soon to be adopted in the Caribbean. The discoverer and developer of these islands was a Genoese, Antonio da Noli, who had obtained his permit from the Navigator, thus making the latter in a sense the patron and founder of Atlantic slavery in its most odious form.

In 1468 a Lisbon merchant, Fernão Gomes, was granted a five-year monopoly on trade with Africa on condition that he extend the exploration of the coast southwards by one hundred leagues (a little over three hundred miles) each year. He achieved this and more, passing the lands named the Ivory Coast (Côte d'Ivoire), the Gold

Coast (Ghana), and the Slave Coast (Togo and Dahomey). In 1474 the young Infante Dom João, a nephew of the Navigator who was to ascend the throne as João II in 1481, was placed in charge of overseas exploration. According to A. H. de Oliveira Marques (1976, p. 218) it is this Dom João rather than his uncle the Navigator who should be regarded as the true architect of the future Portuguese Empire, with a clear and firm objective of reaching India by circumnavigating the southern extremity of the African continent. Under his leadership two notable voyages were conducted in the 1480s, passing the mouth of the Congo River and what is now known as Angola. In 1488 a major milestone was attained when Bartolemeu Dias ultimately found the southern tip of Africa, rounding the appropriately named Cape of Good Hope. After this it was a mere matter of time before the prize of India would be reached. This was delayed by the death of João II in 1495 and factional disputes at the court, until the epoch-making voyage of Vasco da Gama finally left Lisbon in 1497 under the auspices of the new king Dom Manuel I, known as "the Fortunate," a cousin of his illustrious predecessor and with comparable energy and enthusiasm for exploration and empire building.

Clear evidence of the strategic perception of João II is provided by the fact that, in 1487, the same year that Dias departed on his voyage that rounded the Cape, an "undercover" intelligence-gathering mission was sent overland to Egypt and the Arabian Peninsula. Two agents, posing as merchants, visited Cairo, Alexandria, and Aden. One of them seems to have disappeared from history but the other, Pêro da Covilhã, who could speak Arabic, made his way in an Arab vessel to the Malabar Coast of India where he obtained valuable information on the major ports, including Calicut. He then proceeded to the Christian kingdom of Ethiopia, the reality behind the legend of Prester John. Da Covilhã settled in Ethiopia, where he was made a district governor by the emperor Eskender although forbidden to leave the country, but not before handing a detailed report on the political and commercial situation in the western Indian Ocean to a Jewish emissary dispatched from Lisbon. This intelligence was probably available to the da Gama expedition, and thus da Gama had a fair idea of what to expect after he rounded the Cape and made his way up the eastern coast of Africa.

At this point it would be useful to consider the nautical technology underlying these Portuguese voyages. Navigation in the Mediterranean and the coastal waters of northern and western Europe had proceeded empirically, with the compass rose and rhumb lines of *portolan* charts serving to set courses between given points and with the positions of familiar landmarks noted. Longer-distance voyages in the open sea to unknown destinations required more scientifically grounded knowledge of astronomy and geography to be successfully undertaken, and here the revival of classical learning that took place in the Renaissance played an indispensable role, much of it transmitted through the intermediation of Jewish and Muslim scholars. João II actively promoted research into such highly relevant topics as methods of calculating latitude by observing the height of the sun at midday. Mapmakers drew upon the knowledge of European travelers to the East, from Marco Polo to another Venetian, Niccolò dei Conti, who spent the years from 1419 to 1444 traveling widely in the Middle East, India, and Southeast Asia. Equipped with the best available navigational knowledge of his day, da Gama was able to swing wide westward into the Atlantic to avoid the currents and doldrums of the Gulf of Guinea and to take advantage of the trade winds before turning east, making an accurate landfall on the southwest coast of Africa before rounding the Cape.

Such a voyage probably would not have been feasible for the European ships of the beginning of the fifteenth century, which saw remarkable progress in shipbuilding techniques. According to Parry (1964, chapter 3), on whose account we draw in what follows, Mediterranean ship design was influenced in this period by two sets of long-standing outside influences. A first crucial innovation, which had occurred several centuries before in the wake of the Arab invasions, was the adoption of the Arab triangular fore-and-aft lateen sail that was much more flexible with respect to the direction of the wind than the old Roman square-rigged sails. The latter could not progress against a headwind and were not sufficiently maneuverable. On the other hand, square-rigged ships could be much larger than purely lateen-rigged vessels, which were too small for long-distance voyages. A second outside influence came from northwestern Europe, whose cogs had retained the square rig but improved on its design relative to the Roman original. These ships were reintroduced to the Mediterranean after the Crusades, becoming the standard form of transport for large cargoes. The fifteenth century saw a burst of innovation combining the best elements of both traditions, for example adding additional masts with lateen sails to the square-rigged ships. There emerged "a wide range of mongrel types" (p. 79), of which the two most important were the larger three-masted carracks, of up to 600 tons or even more, square-rigged but with lateen mizzens; and the famous caravels, which were lateen-based, but which might also include one or two square-rigged masts. There was also a range of intermediate vessels, and explorers typically made use of "balanced fleets including—as Vasco da Gama's and Cabral's both did—one or two caravels, which they employed for dispatch-carrying, inshore reconnaissance, and other odd jobs which later admirals would entrust to frigates" (p. 82). It was these ships, emerging "through a strenuous process of experiment and change," that made what Parry calls the "Age of Reconnaissance" possible.

On da Gama's voyage the two main ships, the flagship *São Gabriel* and the *São Rafael*, were of intermediate size while a third support vessel, the *Berrio*, was a caravel of 50 tons. On the outward journey they picked up a local Muslim pilot at Malinde on the coast of what is now Kenya for the final crossing to Calicut. This pilot was said to have been the famous Ahmad ibn Majid of Oman, author of a major Arabic treatise on navigation, but Subrahmanyam (1997, pp. 121–28) argues convincingly that it could not have been this exalted personage and was probably a Gujarati. The identification was hardly plausible to begin with, since it relied on an operatic coincidence of two heroic figures from entirely different worlds happening to meet by chance in an East African port at just the right historical moment.

Calicut, at which they landed in May 1498, was the major port on the Malabar Coast and a great entrepôt. The ruler was a Hindu bearing the title of Samudri Raja or Sea King, which the Portuguese corrupted to Zamorin, by which these rulers are referred to in most Western accounts. Most of the trade was in the hands of Muslim merchants, both from the Middle East as well as native-born Gujaratis and Mapillas, who seem to have had complete freedom of worship so long as they obeyed the ban on cow slaughter. The Mapillas were descendants of Arab immigrants, mostly sailors, and lower-caste Indian women. Pepper grown extensively in the hinterland was the main direct export product along with ginger, but goods of every conceivable kind were available for reexport in either direction. The infrastructure necessary for trade, both physical such as docks and warehousing facilities, as well as banking and financial services, was available in abundance, and there was a scrupulous and impartial legal system and relatively light fees and customs duties to encourage the maximum volume of commerce.

The overall political situation in India at this time was one of transition. The dominant state had been the formidable Turkic slave dynasties of the Delhi sultanate, but this had decayed and been replaced by the weaker Afghan dynasty of the Lodis in the middle of the fifteenth century, before they were defeated by Babur, the founder of the Mughal dynasty in 1526. Central and south India were contested between the powerful Hindu kingdom of Vijayanagar and

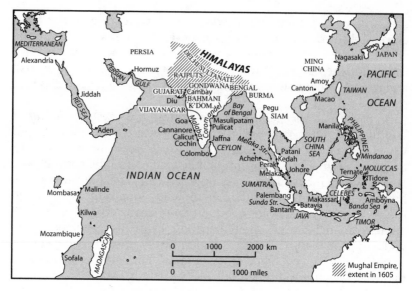

FIGURE 4.1. The Indian Ocean.

a Muslim state known as the Bahmani sultanate, both of which had broken off from the Delhi sultanate as it declined in the fourteenth century. Further north up the western coast was another wealthy Muslim sultanate, Gujarat, where the great cotton textile center and port of Cambay was located. In the east, Bengal was also under an independent Muslim ruler.

The main trading centers on the west coast at this time were Cambay and Calicut, but Goa, Cananore, and Cochin were also of some importance. All of these ports were crowded with ships from Hormuz and Aden, at the entrances to the Persian Gulf and the Red Sea respectively. The single most important commodity imported into India was one which we have already encountered, namely Persian and Arabian horses for the cavalries of the warring Indian states. Another "strategic war-animal" was the elephant trained for fighting, exported from Sri Lanka along with cinnamon and pearls. Silks, carpets, and dyestuffs were next in importance to horses as exports from Persia. The East African ports of Mombasa, Malinde, Kilwa, and Sofala sent ivory, ebony, slaves, and gold in return mostly for cotton textiles from Gujarat. Cloves, nutmeg, and mace from the Bandas and Moluccas were unloaded in the Malabar ports for transshipment westwards. Bengal and the Coromandel Coast on the eastern side of the peninsula exported cotton cloth to Melaka and other Southeast Asian ports in return for spices and porcelain from China. Tamil merchants such as the Chettiars were particularly prominent in this eastern half of the Indian Ocean trade (see figure 4.1). Many of the port cities depended on imports of rice, which was supplied by Java and Pegu. None of the Indian Ocean states seriously attempted to control or regulate trade to move relative prices in their favor, most duties and fees being for revenue purposes only. In fact the "separation of market and state" seemed remarkably pronounced, and except for piracy there seemed to be complete freedom of the seas, so that the *Mare Liberum* that Hugo Grotius would soon be advocating for European waters was achieved in the East before being disrupted by the Portuguese.

In the aftermath of da Gama's return from Calicut, Dom Manuel styled himself "Lord of the Conquest, Navigation and Commerce of Ethiopia, Arabia, Persia and India," and the Portuguese interpreted this to mean the right to monopolize and regulate all shipping and commerce in the eastern seas, and in particular the spice trade. Muslim traders and vessels were regarded as enemies and subject to seizure, confiscation, or destruction unless exempted by license, the so-called *cartaz*, on payment of the appropriate fee. The fee itself was negligible, but the vessel was obliged to put in at a Portuguese-controlled port, pay duties on its cargo, and post a bond to call in at the same port on the return journey to pay duties again on the new cargo it acquired (Pearson 1987, p. 38). To sustain this extravagant policy the *Estado da India*, as the Portuguese overseas regime was called, attempted to establish a ring of fortified coastal strong points across the Indian Ocean from Melaka in the east to Hormuz and Aden in the west. Afonso de Albuquerque, generally regarded as the architect of the scheme and who served as governor in the formative years from 1510 to 1515, captured Goa as the central base in 1510, Melaka in 1511, and Hormuz in 1514. His attempt on Aden in 1513 failed, however, and with it the entire Portuguese attempt at a monopoly of the export of spices to Europe, since the Red Sea remained open to Muslim shipping. Despite some major naval victories, such as one over a Mamluk fleet off Diu in 1509, the Portuguese did not have sufficient ships or men to be able to enforce the monopoly scheme in the absence of control over Aden.

Boxer (1975, pp. 52–53) states that the population of Portugal in the sixteenth century was not much above 1,250,000, and that there were probably no more than about 10,000 able-bodied Portuguese males in service in the east at any one time, though Subrahmanyam and Thomaz (1991, p. 318) cite an estimate of 14,000 to 16,000 for the last quarter of the sixteenth century. Resort was had to the growing

Eurasian population and to native crews and levies to make up the deficiency. The number of ships in any single year was never above three hundred, according to this same authority. Losses of both ships and men by the *Estado da India* were very heavy as a result of weather, disease, and warfare. Eventually, a compromise was worked out whereby Muslim merchants and rulers would pay moderate levels of "protection money" to the Portuguese when it was unavoidable, while private Portuguese traders engaged in the profitable local carrying trade in partnership with native Muslims and Hindus.

Despite these problems with the enforcement of their grandiose schemes the success achieved by the Portuguese was remarkable by any standards. Among the reasons often cited for this success is the familiar one of disunity among their opponents. Cochin and Cannanore, for example, collaborated against their rival the Zamorin of Calicut, before themselves falling prey to the Portuguese. The powerful Hindu state of Vijayanagar was glad to have its cavalry mounts supplied exclusively by the Portuguese after they had taken both Hormuz, where the Persian horses were loaded to cross the Arabian Sea, and Goa, where they were brought ashore for delivery inland. The Muslim sultanates of the Deccan, such as Bijapur, which had lost Goa to the Portuguese, eventually combined and destroyed their great Hindu rival state in 1565, sending the lucrative horse trade into a temporary slump. In the Indonesian archipelago rivalries between the Muslim sultanates also worked to the advantage of the Portuguese. One Asian state against which they made no headway, however, was China. Attempts to use force in the South China Sea in the 1520s were defeated by the Ming coastal squadrons, and as we will see access to the port of Macao was only obtained in the 1550s after a deal was made with local Chinese officials.

Another popular explanation for the Portuguese success in eastern waters is their use of firearms, particularly the effective use of cannon on board oceangoing vessels. Despite the fact that the Indian states were acquainted with artillery on land, they were generally not able to deploy it at sea. The Mamluks were famous for scorning the use of firearms but the Ottomans, who as we have seen supplanted the Mamluks in 1517, inheriting their interest in the Red Sea trade, had no such inhibitions. Turkish vessels at times inflicted considerable damage on Portuguese shipping and bases. On the whole, however, the land-based Asian rulers, like the sultan of Gujarat, seem to have believed that "wars by sea are the affairs of merchants, and of no concern to the prestige of kings" (Pearson 1987, p. 56). There is no doubt that a concerted effort by any of the more powerful Indian states could have driven the Portuguese out of their bases, but none of them seems to have seen it in their interest. It was only the smaller trading states and communities of the Malabar Coast that had their interests diametrically opposed to those of the Portuguese, forcing them to engage in all-out war when their only alternative was capitulation to Portuguese demands. Thus Calicut lost out to Cochin, and the Mapillas were defeated, but only after a gallant struggle.

The capture of Melaka in 1511 initially disrupted the traditional pattern of Indian Ocean trade, based on the dominant position of that port city and its liberal trading regime. Tamil merchants continued to trade at Melaka (Das Gupta 1999, p. 251), but Muslim Gujaratis opened an alternative route through Acheh at the northwestern tip of Sumatra, down the west coast and through the Sunda Straits to Bantam in northwestern Java. From Acheh, pepper was exported through the Maldives to the Red Sea and ultimately to Venice. In addition, pepper could be moved within India, and up the west coast to Gujarat, from where export to the Red Sea was possible despite Portuguese patrols. The failure to take Aden thus continued to haunt the *Estado*.

Boxer (1969) cites numerous Portuguese and other European sources to show that the vessels that were engaged in the Acheh–Red Sea trade were "tall ships" of the same type as the Portuguese great carracks, and comparable if not even larger in size and armament and identical in sails and rigging. They seem to have carried large numbers of Turkish, Arab, Abyssinian, and other mercenaries for protection and gave as good as they got in occasional battles with Portuguese warships that attempted to intercept them, for example in 1562 and 1565 (ibid.). Since the Portuguese built their ships on the west coast of India, we seem to have here a clear example of a successful transfer of technology from West to East. Acheh was a major thorn in the Portuguese side, with frequent attacks on Melaka compounding the damage caused by the diversion of the spice trade. There were numerous calls for an all-out assault on Acheh to solve the problem, but the regime in Goa could never find the resources to mount such an expensive operation.

Another endemic problem that the *Estado da India* was never able to resolve was the conflict between the interests of its officials as servants of the crown on the one hand, and as military leaders or private traders on their own account on the other. The *Estado* could obviously not be a modern Weberian bureaucracy with a tightly structured set of rules and procedures that ensured smooth functioning in the interests of the state alone. As Newitt (1980) points out, Portugal had made a promising start in the development of bureaucratic state enterprise in the *Casa da Guine*, which was set up to administer military operations and trade relations in West Africa in the second half of the fifteenth century. A greatly expanded version of this organization, the *Casa da India*, was set up to perform the same role in the Indian Ocean. The much vaster scale and distances involved, and the attendant problems of communication, made it in practice impossible to work as originally envisaged. An exchange of letters took two months in West Africa, but two years between Lisbon and Goa. The scale of the enterprise relative to Portugal's financial resources also meant that prompt and regular payment for salaries, maintenance, and working capital could never be assured. Another problem was the shortage of trained manpower necessary for the task of running the empire. Unlike Castile, which had over thirty universities to train literate and numerate recruits, Portugal had only Coimbra, later supplemented by the Jesuit college of Evora. Under these circumstances it is not surprising that an alternative model had to be resorted to in practice. The prototype of this model was provided by the colonization of the Atlantic islands that we have noted already.

This alternative conformed to a more traditional or medieval patri-monial-feudal form, where the ruler delegated power to members of the nobility or trusted individuals of lesser rank, it being understood that they would use the offices to maintain themselves and their kinsmen and followers in their accustomed lifestyles, while at the same time meeting their responsibilities to monarch and state. The values, training, and ethos of these *fidalgos* were biased toward honor and renown from military exploits and patronage to kinsfolk and retinues, which might of course have been entirely rational in the context of the society in which they lived. As was common practice in early modern Europe, offices were freely bought and sold, at prices reflecting the rents that could be extracted from them (Pearson 1987, chapter 3). Thus in 1618 the post of judge in the customs house of Goa was sold for more than twice what was paid for the captaincy of the entire city. The captaincies of the forts of Hormuz and Diu, through which the very profitable trade of the Persian Gulf and Gujarat passed, were sold for fourteen and five times as much respectively as the captaincy of the capital, Goa, itself. The terms of these offices were usually quite short, seldom exceeding three years, so the incentive was to squeeze the maximum rents out in the given time rather than pursue any longer-term objectives for the benefit of the state. Under these circumstances it is not surprising that the strict rules of monopoly enforcement of the spice trade were often breached. Newitt (1980, p. 26) cites the case of Sofala in 1548, where there was not a single tusk available for the royal export monopoly on ivory, while the captain of the port was shipping huge quantities on his own account. Portuguese officials in Malabar bought pepper on their own account, at prices above the low prices they offered growers in their capacity as administrators of the royal spice monopoly. Pearson (1987, p. 67) even goes so far as to speculate that the failure to take Aden could, perhaps, be explained by the fact that closing the Red Sea would severely restrict the opportunities for corruptly permitting forbidden Muslim cargo and shipping to get through.

The strongest and most insidious incentive that the crown relied on to solve its "principal–agent problem" in the *Estado da India* was the opportunity to plunder. Within a territorial empire, officers of the state have an obligation to preserve the lives and property of the subject peoples, provided they submit and pay the stipulated taxes and tribute to the state, out of the proceeds of which the officers are rewarded. The seaborne empire of the Portuguese was of an entirely different type. The few fortresses and ports that they held did not contain large numbers of non-Christian natives who could be taxed. Muslim or pagan states, tribes, and individuals were all, however, subject to predation of one form or another by the *Estado* and its servants. Strong points on shore could be fed and supported by raids on neighboring territory, and fleets at sea maintained by the prizes and booty taken, as Vasco da Gama himself pointed out (Newitt 1980, p. 21). Recalcitrant states and cities offered particularly good opportunities for organized plunder. Thus when Francisco de Almeida, the first viceroy, stormed Mombasa in 1505 he divided the city into quarters with the officer in charge of each having the right to dispose of all goods and persons seized therein after an appropriate cut for the state.

One problem with the reliance on plunder as a tool of empire building was that the opportunities in a given area were soon exhausted, requiring an extension of the "plunder frontier" for the momentum to be sustained. As Newitt (p. 16) says, "it was the movement of the plunder frontier which attracted men to ever-new regions and to make further discoveries. In other words plunder was the prime motive force of 'discovery'." After the initial gains from seizing wealth, recourse had to be taken to more mundane opportunities, such as the collection of fees and dues and commercial trading profits. The demands of the *fidalgo* class could not, however, be satisfied within these limits, and so the state turned increasingly to the seizure of territory wherever possible. Mughal India and Ming China were too strong to provide any opportunities in this regard, but Angola and Mozambique, as well as Ceylon, were more vulnerable to encroachment. These additions probably added more to the cost of the empire than they did to its revenues, though they did satisfy the demands of the *fidalgos* for an aristocratic lifestyle.

Pearson (1987, chapter 2) poses an interesting counterfactual proposition: what if the *Estado* had simply relied on peaceful economic competition in the spice trade, relying on the cost advantage of the Cape route rather than on the expensive and ultimately unsuccessful attempt to impose a monopoly by force of arms? He cites figures from the eminent Portuguese economic historian Vitorino Magalhães-Godinho to show that the price difference between the cost of pepper in Lisbon and Malabar would yield a gross margin of 260% and a net margin of 152% after wastage and transport costs had been allowed for. On this basis he concludes that peaceful trade could have been much more profitable than the militaristic monopoly policy with its heavy outlays on fortresses and war fleets. He also argues that the Dutch and British East India Companies, in the seventeenth century, did not attempt to impose monopolies by force in India, though the Dutch did so on an extensive scale in the Moluccas and Java, as we will see. The reason for this alternative peaceful policy not being pursued by the Portuguese was of course the influence of the crusading tradition and the feudal ethos of the *fidalgo* class.

Attractive though it is, the counterfactual seems implausible to us. As we have seen, the *Estado* relied explicitly on plunder as a tool for its trading operations, as a major part of the potential remuneration of its employees, and as a source of working capital. Completely peaceful trade could only have been possible with a much higher initial capitalization. Unlike the United Provinces and Britain in 1600, Portugal in 1500 was a poor country without the resources of the Amsterdam and London capital markets. In 1500 capital would have had to be borrowed from the Genoese and Florentines at what would doubtless have been a very heavy risk premium. Furthermore, the silver influx from the New World that was pouring into Europe in 1600, and which was utilized by the East India Companies to purchase spices for resale in Europe, had not even begun in 1500. It would therefore seem that reliance on its comparative advantage in violence was a necessary part of the initial Portuguese effort in the sixteenth century, the cost advantage of the Cape route by itself not being sufficient.

By the end of the sixteenth century, a multicentered or polycentric equilibrium had emerged in the Indian Ocean trade, replacing the earlier one based on the dominance of Melaka. Portuguese Melaka now had to share not only with Acheh and Bantam, but also as we will see with other centers such as Makassar. The factories and fortresses that the Portuguese established in Ternate, Tidore, Amboyna, East Timor, and other places could not prevent native, Chinese, and Indian merchants from engaging in and even expanding their trade. The only viable option was for the Portuguese to join them, not as agents of the crown as at Melaka, but in private trade on their own account and in joint ventures with the non-Westerners. In fact "Portuguese" came increasingly to mean Eurasians of either Indian or Indonesian origin, as Das Gupta (1999) points out. The new equilibrium was thus not that different in Asia from the old, although as we will see later there had been important changes at the European end of the trade routes.

Indeed, a growing recognition that what was once known as the "Vasco da Gama Epoch" (Panikkar 1953) was not that different from what had gone before as regards Asian spice markets, and that the European tail was not yet wagging the Asian dog, has been one of the main themes of recent literature on early modern Asian maritime history (Wills 1993; O'Rourke and Williamson forthcoming). Prior to da Gama, European imports had accounted for at most one quarter of Asian spice production, and Asians remained the dominant consumers throughout the sixteenth century (Reid 1993a, p. 19; Pearson 1996, p. xxiii). According to Kieniewicz (1969), only about 30% of Malabar pepper production went to Lisbon in 1515, with the remaining 70% being consumed by Asians; while only 55% of Malabar production shipped west between 1504 and 1549 went to Lisbon, the rest going to the Levant. While Malabar pepper supplies grew by some 7 or 8% per annum during the sixteenth century, this was a result of "growing demand for pepper in India, China, Persia and the countries ruled by the Ottoman Empire" rather than anything happening in Europe (ibid., pp. 61–62). Thus, Europeans were still only consuming a quarter of Asian pepper output as late as 1600 (Pearson 1996, p. xxviii), while European imports accounted for just 7% of clove production in 1510–19 and 17% in 1570–79 (Bulbeck et al. 1998, p. 54). In economic terms, the Portuguese century in Asia was still largely Asian, and while Europeans might compete over the profits to be made from the spice trade, this competition should be thought of as a battle over the markups to be charged to European consumers over an Asian supply price that was still mainly set, as it had always been, by the interactions of Asian producers and consumers. Things would be very different in the New World.

Spain, Portugal, and the New World

Every schoolchild knows, or at least used to, that Christopher Columbus was a Genoese who peddled his project of sailing west to reach
the Indies to several European powers, including the Portuguese,
before it was finally taken up by Ferdinand of Aragon and Isabella
of Castile, the joint monarchs of Spain (see figure 4.2). Why did they
do so? Aragon was by tradition a Mediterranean power, with a strong
urban mercantile interest, particularly in Catalonia. Castile, on the
other hand, was a land-abundant pastoral society, with an economy
based on sheep rearing and the export of wool, and a ruling class
of *hidalgos* with a crusading warrior ethos formed by the *Reconquista*.
Unlike Portugal, neither realm would have seemed a likely candidate to
undertake a risky Atlantic venture. As J. H. Elliott (2002, chapter 1) has
pointed out, however, Castile's wool trade with her northern European
partners had involved her in a growing commercial network, with
Genoese merchants and bankers prominent in Seville. The wool trade
also got Castile engaged in Atlantic navigation. The occupation and
colonization of the Canary Islands, and North African campaigns
against the Moors, prepared the monarchs to take further steps
overseas. We must also remember that the great event of 1492 was
not what we think it is now, but the fall of the last Muslim stronghold
of Granada and the completion of the *Reconquista*, which must have
led to a further surge of confidence.

The voyages of Columbus to the Caribbean were soon followed
by settlements in the large islands of Hispaniola and Cuba. In 1513
Vasco Núñez de Balboa famously saw the Pacific while "silent upon a
peak in Darien" after he had begun the occupation of the Isthmus of
Panama,[2] which was completed by the ruthless Pedro Arias Dávila, at
whose orders he was executed. By 1521 Hernán Cortés had destroyed
the Aztec Empire and occupied the capital Tenochtitlán that became
Mexico City with just six hundred men, sixteen horses, and a large
number of allied Indian forces, while in the 1530s the empire of
the Incas in Peru was overthrown by Francisco Pizarro, with barely
one hundred men and thirty-seven horses. Expeditions were sent to
the regions of what are now Chile, Argentina, and Paraguay in the
next decade. Ports were established at Santo Domingo, Havana, and
Cartagena, and at Callao on the Pacific coast of Peru to serve the capital
of Lima. The monarch was represented in the colonies by two viceroys:
one for Mexico or New Spain residing in Mexico City, and one for Peru
or New Castile residing in Lima.

[2]We know. See Beach (1934) and Wicker (1956).

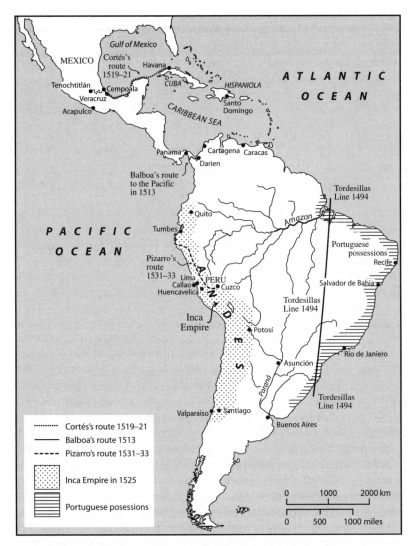

FIGURE 4.2. Latin America and the Iberian conquests.

Most of these remarkable results were achieved not by officials of the crown but by what Parry (1966, p. 54) calls "a few thousand down-at-heel swordsmen" mostly from the frontier region of Estremadura, known to history as the *conquistadores*. The reasons given for their astonishing success have ranged from the possession of firearms, steel weapons, and horses, all unknown to the natives, disunity and

demoralization on the part of the latter, the ferocious determination and fighting spirit of the men themselves, and the vision and
ability of their leaders, particularly Cortés. Crucially, exposure of the
indigenous peoples to the germs of the Old World wrought havoc
on their numbers, which declined precipitously as a result of waves
of smallpox, typhus, measles, and other diseases, adding to their
disorganization and the success of the conquest. Estimates of the
extent of the population decline vary considerably, but whatever the
correct figure, it was shockingly high. To take an extreme and highly
contested example, Henry Dobyns has estimated that as many as
95% of the Native American population may have been wiped out
by European diseases (cited in Livi-Bacci 2006, p. 204). As Livi-Bacci
points out, there is a logical link between estimates of the population
decline and views as to the causes of that decline, for if the population
really fell by several tens of millions, then it would seem that germs
are a more plausible explanation for this than the depredations of a
relatively small number of conquistadores. In fact, Livi-Bacci provides
plausible evidence that germs were not the only factor at work, but
that Spanish violence, as well as "a weakening of reproduction, and
expulsion and forced migration of the indigenous people into hiding
or into inhospitable areas were also powerful factors in the decline.
Behind the demise of the Indians lay not only the blind determination
of germs, but also no less deadly human forces" (pp. 226–27).

The numbers of Spaniards in the New World were small but the
import of horses, cattle, sheep, and pigs soon led to rapid increases
in the stocks of these animals in an environment that was new but
very favorable to them. What Crosby (2003) has vividly termed the
"Columbian Exchange" also involved flows in the opposite direction
of maize, tobacco, and the potato, all of which were to have at least
equally significant consequences for the Old World as the animals had
for the New. Wheat, sugar cane, and cotton were Old World imports
into the New that would later be exported back in vast quantities, with
major economic consequences. While the demographic impact of the
Columbian Exchange, or the Magellan Exchange as McNeill (1998)
has termed the transfer of species across the Pacific, was profoundly
negative for the New World, it was unambiguously positive for Eurasia
(Crosby 2003, chapter 5). The new, high-yielding American crops
would eventually lead to demographic expansion in regions as far
apart as China and Ireland. As Crosby (2003, p. 199), in an oft-cited
passage,[3] puts it, "while men who stormed Tenochtitlán with Cortes

[3]By, among others, Flynn and Giráldez (2004), who put great emphasis on this
intercontinental trade in DNA in their account of "when globalization began."

TABLE 4.1. Old World population, 1500–1820 (millions).

	1500	1600	1700	1820
China	103,000	160,000	138,000	381,000
India	110,000	135,000	165,000	209,000
Southwest Asia	17,800	21,400	20,800	25,147
Territory of former U.S.S.R.	16,950	20,700	26,550	54,765
Eastern Europe	13,500	16,950	18,800	36,457
Western Europe	57,268	73,778	81,460	133,040
Africa	46,610	55,320	61,080	74,236

Source: Maddison (2003).

still lived, peanuts were swelling in the sandy loams near Shanghai; maize was turning fields green in south China, and the sweet potato was on its way to becoming the poor man's staple in Fukien."

Population data for this period are obviously largely based on guess-work, but it is clear that the population of the Afro-Eurasian Ecumene grew rapidly in the centuries after Columbus. According to table 4.1, China's population grew by some 50% during the sixteenth century, declined over the course of the seventeenth, and then exploded during the eighteenth, almost tripling between 1700 and 1820. In India, Europe, and Africa the population grew more steadily, almost doubling over the course of the three centuries in the two former regions, and increasing by more than 50% in the latter. The Chinese boom followed the "second agricultural revolution" of the seventeenth and eighteenth centuries, based on the introduction of maize, peanuts, and sweet potatoes. In Ireland, the potato-based population boom of the eighteenth and early nineteenth centuries was only halted by the arrival of another New World import, *phytophthora infestans*, in 1845 (Ó Gráda 1999).

Spanish penetration of America in these early decades can be interpreted as a "frontier of settlement" moving behind a "frontier of plunder," which shifted from the Caribbean islands to central Mexico and Peru before the two converged around the middle of the sixteenth century. The first two decades in the islands saw pure predation on and destruction of the relatively primitive native population, until oppor-tunities were exhausted by the capture of the gold stocks possessed by the Indians and the virtual disappearance of the people themselves. The resources obtained in this way financed the early expeditions to the mainland that encountered the more advanced Aztec and Inca Empires, where in each case an aristocracy of warriors and priests extracted tribute from sedentary peasant populations. In essence

Cortés and Pizarro each replaced a ruling native elite by a Spanish one, both living off the exploitation of the subjugated peasants. The terrible toll inflicted on the peasant populations by the conquest, however, drastically reduced the surplus income from the land accruing to the new Spanish rulers. Livestock rearing on open ranges and land formerly tilled by the now shrinking peasant populations provided a substitute source of income for the new owners. The discovery of the huge silver deposits in Mexico and Peru in the 1540s created a major increase in the demand for meat to feed the mineworkers, and was also a huge source of profit to the settler population and of revenues to the crown. Rather than depending on inflows of capital from Spain to finance investments in the New World, it was rather the case that the quick fortunes made there became available to fund state expenditure and private projects in Spain itself.

Macleod (1984, p. 356) says that for the first forty years after 1492 "people formed the main cargoes out from Europe." The numbers, mostly involving Spaniards, were between 200,000 and 300,000 for the sixteenth century and 450,000 for the seventeenth. The early settlers were not prepared to live on maize, beans, and cassava and so wheat, wine, and olive oil were initially exported from Spain, but were eventually displaced because of import substitution and dietary shifts as the settlers adjusted to their new environment. The main return cargo of the *Carrera de Indias*, as the transatlantic link was called, was gold for the first fifty years. Trade between Spain and the New World was subject to the monopoly enjoyed by the Seville merchant guild known as the *consulado*. All exports and imports were licensed by them and administered by the *Casa de Contratacion* or "House of Trade," which maintained the warehouses and docks, regulated the ships and crews, and collected taxes and dues, including the *quinto* or royal fifth on the value of all the goods traded overseas. Despite being located several miles up the winding Guadalquivir River, Seville was a sensible choice as the hub of global Spanish trade. Her rich agricultural hinterland could readily provision the ships for their long voyages and the large community of Italian bankers, mostly Genoese, was a ready source of finance. Heavy taxes and tight regulations meant, however, that there were ample opportunities for smuggling and contraband that were eagerly taken by other European powers, in particular the Dutch and British. Even more dangerous to the treasure fleets of the *Carrera* was outright piracy by the audacious mariners of these northern rival states, such as Piet Heyn and Francis Drake.

The trade between Seville and Spanish America has been described and measured in the greatest imaginable detail in the monumental

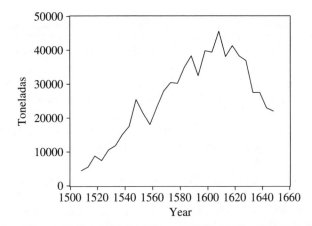

FIGURE 4.3. Volume of trade to and from the Spanish Indies,
1506–1650 (toneladas). *Source:* Phillips (1990, pp. 43–44).

eight-volume study by Huguette and Pierre Chaunu (1955–59), based
on the detailed records of the individual voyages of about 25,000 ships
between 1504 and 1650.[4] Knowing which ships sailed each year and
the tonnage of each ship, an approximate measure of the volume of
freight carried each year across the Atlantic in both directions can
be constructed and a detailed time series for 1504–1650 obtained.
Figure 4.3 graphs their results, based on the summary data provided
in Phillips (1990, pp. 43–44). It shows more or less steady growth until
around 1620, with the exception of a lull in the 1550s and a sharp drop
following the catastrophe of the Spanish Armada in 1588. From 1620
to 1650 there was a decline in tonnage that was more than made up for
in terms of value, according to the Chaunus, as the wheat, wine, and
oil exported from Spain were replaced by more expensive textiles and
other manufactures obtained from Italy, Holland, and England. This
reflected the dietary import substitution in the colonies referred to
above. The Chaunus (1974, p. 120) cite the example of "the triumphant
implantation of the vine beside the Pacific, in the oases of the dry
Peruvian coast, despite the ineffectual prohibitions obtained by the
Andalusian aristocracy from a docile Spanish government."

The Chaunus interpret the seventeenth century in New Spain as
a period of consolidation and growth based on the home market,
as opposed to the outward-looking or export-led sixteenth century
based heavily on the exploitation of the silver mines of Mexico and

[4]For an English-language summary see Chaunu and Chaunu (1974).

Peru. They do not accept that the more inward-looking or autarkic seventeenth century was in any sense a period of retrogression; in fact, they say it was "quite the opposite." This is interesting in light of the well-known thesis of a European or even worldwide "Crisis of the Seventeenth Century," originally advanced by Eric Hobsbawm (1954). Independently of Hobsbawm, specialists on Latin America such as Woodrow Borah and Murdo Macleod had asserted that there were signs of a depression in New Spain in the seventeenth century, on the basis of demographic stagnation, labor force shortages, and production problems in industry and agriculture. However, TePaske and Klein (1981) find that revenues from several treasuries in New Spain trended upward over the course of the seventeenth century, not downward, with silver production also rising, though there were some fluctuations. This is obviously inconsistent with the crisis theory, as applied to New Spain.

Carla Rahn Phillips (1990) has assembled much of the available evidence on the Atlantic trade of the Iberian empires from 1500–1750 and we draw heavily on her work in what follows. It is convenient to begin with some major primary exports other than the precious metals, since these are often overlooked. Among the earliest and most interesting of these were cattle hides. This export trade is a revealing precursor of the pattern of transatlantic trade that was to emerge more fully in later centuries. Livestock rearing is obviously a land-intensive activity. In Spain and the rest of Europe pasture for cattle had to compete with sheep and tillage, while it was virtually free in the open spaces of the larger Caribbean islands, Mexico, and Central America (Macleod 1984, p. 360). The carcasses were left to rot after the animals were skinned since there was as yet no significant domestic demand for beef, and export was impossible without refrigeration. The export of hides rose from an annual average of about 27,000 in the period 1561–65 to a peak of 134,000 in 1581–85, before falling back to 32,000 in the 1650s and less than 10,000 in the closing decade of the century. This decline could reflect the growth both of tillage competing for now scarcer land, and of domestic consumption during this second and more inward-looking century in colonial development. The annual average value of the export of hides was about 78 million maravedis in the late sixteenth century, about twice the value of annual sugar exports from Spanish America (Phillips 1990, p. 79).

Cochineal, a red dye obtained from cactus-eating insects, was a surprisingly valuable export item in this period, worth 125 million maravedis a year, while indigo brought in 30 million maravedis a year. Total exports of all these commodities, other than precious metals, from the American colonies to Spain came to about 320 million maravedis, with cochineal accounting for no less than 42% of the total (ibid.). Outward-bound merchandise exports from Seville were worth about three times as much again and were thus of the order of about 900 million maravedis (p. 83). Almost all of this 1.2 billion maravedis worth of annual merchandise trade in both directions, however, was only worthwhile because of the precious metals, mainly silver after the middle decades of the sixteenth century, that were exported from the colonies to Seville during this period. As the Chaunus (1974, p. 121) say, "the economic madness of transporting at enormous cost products of little value, and highly unsuitable for long-distance transport, between Spain and America, was only possible because of the very high profitability of the silver mines in the New World." What do we know about the volume and value of these precious metal exports that were the driving force of so many of the age's economic and political developments?

Beginning with gold, Phillips (1990, p. 83) cites an estimate due to Chaunu that between 23 and 27 tonnes were shipped to Spain from the Americas before 1525. Most of this was plundered from the inhabitants of the Caribbean islands and the Aztecs, while gold was later mined from mostly alluvial deposits. Production and export went through a series of short cycles as successive areas were exploited and abandoned, beginning with Santo Domingo, which peaked in 1510, followed by Puerto Rico, Cuba, and Panama peaking in 1520, then Mexico, and finally Peru about the middle of the century. Far more important, however, was the discovery in ca. 1545 of the vast "silver mountain" at Potosí in the Andean highlands of what is now Bolivia. The mine was located at a very high altitude of over 12,000 feet and assembling the necessary labor force was a major problem. The Viceroy of Peru instituted a system known as the *mita*, whereby one-seventh of the males between 18 and 50 in each province were drafted annually for service in the mine, obtaining in this way a labor force of 13,500 men with a third of them working at any one time (Bakewell 1984, p. 125). The remaining workers were free labor working for wages despite the arduous conditions. The total population of Potosí was about 160,000, making it the largest concentration of population in Spanish America and one of the largest in the world outside China.

Figure 4.4 reproduces Ward Barrett's figures for the total American production and exports of precious metals. Earlier works, such as Hamilton (1934), had shown American shipments to Europe falling in the seventeenth century, one of the factors that Hobsbawm pointed to in his famous article as evidence of crisis, but Barrett accepts the

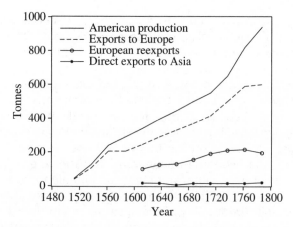

FIGURE 4.4. American production and exports of precious metals, 1501–1800 (annual averages, tonnes). *Source:* Barrett (1990, pp. 242–43).

verdict of Michel Morineau (1985) that exports in fact kept rising, and most experts now seem to accept this (e.g., Pearson 2001). His data show output rising from some 45 tonnes of silver equivalent a year in the first quarter of the sixteenth century to 125 tonnes in the second quarter, 230 tonnes in the third quarter, and 290 tonnes in the last quarter. This massive increase in production, and hence exports, would not have been possible without a major technological change, the mercury amalgam process, to separate the metal from the ore. Mercury was conveniently available from Huencavelica in Peru, and was also imported from Almaden in Spain. About 20–30% of the officially registered bullion that crossed the Atlantic belonged to the crown as a result of the *quinto*, and was worth about 24 billion maravedis in total from 1555 to 1600 (Phillips 1990, p. 85).

Turning to Portugal, its entry into the New World was a fortuitous one. During his voyage to India in 1500 the commander Pedro Álvares Cabral swung sufficiently far west into the Atlantic to make a landing in what we now know as Brazil, but which he thought was another island. The name given to the area came from the brazilwood trees that grew there in abundance, the source of a valuable dyestuff. Exploitation of the brazilwood and other natural resources was first contracted out to a consortium of merchants, but there was then direct crown control, from 1506 to 1534, based on the establishment of royal factories or trading centers and licensing of private trade with the native population. French vessels also attempted to enter the trade, leading to conflicts with the Portuguese. In 1534 there was a drastic shift of policy toward the familiar model of the Atlantic islands. Twelve captaincies were created granting extensive stretches of the coast to each one, with the right to venture as far into the interior as desired. The captain had wide powers over the land assigned, with the obligation to remit specified shares of taxes and other income to the crown. From 1549 onwards the crown appointed a governor to coordinate the activities of the settlers, and to prevent the French and other interlopers from gaining a foothold. Forceful methods were also used against the Indian tribes, who were largely exterminated during this period.

The cultivation of sugar cane soon became the economic mainstay of these territories, with *engenhos* or mills spreading over the country-side surrounded by cane fields. With the booming demand in Europe, growth was very rapid. Johnson (1984, table 1, p. 279) indicates that in 1570 there was a white population of 20,000 in Brazil with 60 sugar mills, while in 1585 the corresponding figures were almost 30,000 and 120. Production of sugar increased rapidly, reaching 15–20,000 tonnes from over 200 mills in the 1620s according to Mauro (1984, p. 457), who also reports that there were 13–15,000 African slaves in Brazil in 1600 and that an annual average of 4,000 a year were being imported in the first half of the seventeenth century. They constituted about 70% of the labor force of the sugar mills. Associated with sugar in the New World was thus the familiar complement of slavery, which as we have seen had long been a feature of sugar production. At this time, most of the slaves were being imported from Angola on the southwest coast of Africa, with the death rate of the slaves on the small overloaded vessels often exceeding 50%. Pernambuco was the fastest growing and most prosperous of the original captaincies, with 41% of the white population and 55% of the mills in 1585. The planters of this region became noted for spending their profits lavishly on luxury imports from the motherland. Bahia was another prosperous region and the attractive site of Rio de Janeiro, initially developed by the French, was captured from them in 1565 and developed rapidly thereafter.

The Pacific and East Asia

The expanse of water that Balboa saw from his peak in Darien and claimed for the crown of Castile was known at the time as the *Mar del Sur* or South Sea. He could not have had any idea of its vast extent, or of what lay within it or on the opposite shores, though he would of course have known that eventually one must arrive at Asia. The voyage of Magellan, a tough Portuguese veteran of his country's forays in the Indian Ocean but now in Spanish service, was aimed at reaching the Spice Islands from the opposite direction to that taken by the Portuguese. There does not seem to have been any original objective of a circumnavigation of the globe for its own sake, only a pragmatic search for an alternate trade route. Departing in 1519 with four ships and 237 men, the circumnavigation was completed in 1522 by only one ship, the *Victoria*, and 18 men under the command of Sebastián del Cano, Magellan himself having been killed in a skirmish on the island of Cebu before a landing was made on the island of Tidore and a valuable cargo of spices collected. Del Cano was awarded a coat of arms, suitably displaying cinnamon, nutmeg, and cloves, surmounted by a globe proclaiming him the First Circumnavigator.

Exploitation of the Spice Islands did not prove easy since the Portuguese were already installed on the rival island of Ternate. Hostilities broke out between the Christian rivals, each aided by a local Muslim ally in the person of the respective sultans of Ternate and Tidore. The disputes were not confined to the military, commercial, and political levels but extended to cosmography as well, since by the Treaty of Tordesillas of 1494 the pope had divided the newly discovered lands of the world between the two Iberian powers based on a meridian 270 leagues west of the Cape Verde Islands, with Spain getting everything to the west and Portugal everything to the east. The question was, which side of this Tordesillas Line, extended around the globe, did the Spice Islands lie on? Realizing that whatever his legal claims might be the Portuguese had the advantage of the proximity of Melaka, Charles V wisely settled for the sum of 350,000 ducats by the Treaty of Saragossa in 1529, to the disgust of many of his subjects.

O. H. K. Spate (1979) entitled the first volume of his great history of the Pacific *The Spanish Lake* and so it was, despite many challenges, for almost two centuries after Magellan. It is not clear, however, what immediate economic advantage the Spanish Empire derived from all the heroic voyages her mariners made in the vast expanse of these waters in search of treasure, spices, and souls for conversion to the true faith. The only lucrative opportunity, but one that was to persist for centuries, was the exchange of American silver for Chinese silks, with many other items of lesser value thrown in, taking place through Manila in the Philippines, the only Spanish colony in the Pacific. The islands were claimed and named in honor of the future Philip II in 1542, but effective occupation and settlement only began with the expedition of Miguel López de Legazpi that was sent out from Mexico in 1564.

Legazpi seized the site of Manila with its splendid natural harbor from a native Muslim ruler in 1571, and extended control over most of the main islands before his death in 1572. A significant exception was Mindanao with a formidable Muslim presence that has persisted to this day. Conversion to Christianity, under the enlightened leadership of the Augustinian friar and explorer Andrés de Urdaneta, proceeded rapidly. Many Chinese were already attracted to the islands before the Spanish arrival, but the appearance of the galleons from Acapulco at Manila from 1571 onwards was a transformational event in the history of world trade, inducing a large inflow of Chinese immigrants from the mainland despite the necessity of purchasing permits from the Spanish authorities to do so legally. The walled city contained the Spanish administrators, soldiers, and clergy together with their Filipino Christian converts, surrounded by a much larger extramural Chinese community of artisans and traders, only a few of whom converted. With the Ming dynasty in full control of the Chinese mainland, and frequent incursions by formidable Chinese pirates and warlords, it is not surprising that the immigrant Chinese population, indispensable as it was to the economic viability of Manila, came to be feared as a sort of potential "fifth column" by the Spanish administration.

The attitude of the Ming authorities to foreign trade and contact with foreigners in general has now to be looked at. The openness toward overseas contacts in the first decades of the fifteenth century, when the great voyages of Zheng He were undertaken, was long a thing of the past. The potential gains from trade between Southeast Asia and China were so great, however, that the opportunities for skimming revenue and collecting bribes was too great for officials in Guangdong and other coastal regions to resist. It was within this framework of officially illegal but tacitly sanctioned trade that the Portuguese began to operate after they took Melaka in 1511.

After some initially clumsy and futile attempts to force their way into the China trade the Portuguese finally hit on an effective compromise, worked out by two eminently sensible men, a private Portuguese merchant, Leonel de Sousa, and a Chinese official named Wang Po. As recounted in Wills (1998), the Portuguese were given a place on the Pearl River estuary to construct warehouses and build a church, but had no direct access to any source of food other than what the Chinese would permit them. In addition to an annual fee, taxes were paid on the trade, or at least some part of it, with the revenue shared between the local officials and the central government. The Portuguese were not supposed to permit any outsiders, particularly the dangerous

Japanese, to enter their narrowly prescribed zone. This was the origin in 1557 of the celebrated Portuguese outpost of Macao, which only reverted officially to China more than four centuries later.

Fortunately for the Portuguese a veritable bonanza or "middleman's paradise" opened up for them to exploit with respect to Sino-Japanese trade. China had a very strong comparative advantage in silk, both in its raw form and as fabric and apparel, greatly desired by the Japanese despite their own large domestic sector since that was of inferior quality. Japan at this time was opening up very productive silver mines and demand for that metal was high in China for both monetary and other uses. The problem was how to effect this mutually agreeable transfer, since the Ming authorities were loath to either permit Japanese to come to China or Chinese to go to Japan, for what we would today call "national security" reasons. Thus both Manila and Macao had the same opportunity to provide the Chinese with silver in exchange for their silk, Manila with the galleons from Acapulco, and Macao with silver from Japan.

Every year at least one "great ship," carracks of 1,600 or even 2,000 tons, built of Malabar teak, would sail from Goa to Melaka laden with Indian cloth and other manufactures. These were sold for spices, sandalwood, and other Southeast Asian products, which were then shipped to Macao, where they were exchanged for silks. The ship would then head for Japanese ports, where the silks would be sold for silver, which was then transported back to Macao. Finally, spices were again purchased in Melaka to take back to Goa, from where they could be sent by other ships to Europe around the Cape. The beauty of this arrangement was that the Portuguese input in material terms was practically zero, other than bearing the undoubtedly high risk of the voyages and providing the necessary "managerial services." The ships were built in India and the crews, including the pilots, were largely Asians or Africans, while the goods traded were all or mostly of Asian origin.

The profits of a single voyage were regarded as sufficient to set up the license-holder for life. Every year up to 1618 "The Great Ship from Amacon," as the English called the carrack sailing from Macao, would carry loads of Chinese raw silk and textiles to Nagasaki, bringing back between 18 and 20 tonnes of silver according to Boxer (1959, p. 7). After 1618 it was found preferable to replace the single great ship each year by six or seven smaller and faster vessels known as galliots, to avoid interception by heavily armed Dutch and British ships that were attempting to supplant the Portuguese in the lucrative China–Japan trade. Boxer (1959, p. 169) says that "the profits derived from the Macao–Japan trade were still formidable down to the end" and the quantity of silver exported may even have been three times as high in 1639 as in the early 1600s. Atwell (1998, p. 399) cites the Jesuit father João Rodrigues, the favorite interpreter of Tokugawa Ieyasu, as saying that in the 1540s even the gentry seldom wore silk, whereas by the time of Hideyoshi (the 1580s and 1590s) "the whole nation wears silk robes; even peasants and their wives have silk sashes and the better off among them have silken robes."

Japan during the second half of the sixteenth century was emerging from her prolonged *Sengoku Jidai* or "Country at War" period, when various feudal lords were contending to replace the enfeebled Ashikaga Shogunate that had been in power since the fourteenth century. The most successful of these contenders was the great warlord Oda Nobunaga, who maintained good relations with Jesuit missionaries and Portuguese merchants. The Japanese had adopted firearms immediately following their first appearance in the island of Tanegashima, where two Portuguese armed with arquebuses were shipwrecked in 1543. These guns were purchased by the local ruler, copies made by his armorer, and soon the weapon was adopted and used in battle by most of the contending forces. The rapid spread of firearms increased the decisiveness of battles and Nobunaga made effective use of them to defeat his main rivals before he was assassinated in 1582 by a treacherous general. As John Whitney Hall (1970, p. 138) says, "the importation of the musket probably hastened by several decades the ultimate unification of the country."

The other import that the Portuguese brought to Japan was Christianity, and Saint Francis Xavier and a small band of Jesuits enjoyed remarkable success in making converts, including many influential leaders. Saint Francis was greatly impressed by the Japanese, saying that they were "the best people so far discovered and it seems to me that among unbelievers no people can be found to excel them" (Sansom 1973, p. 115). In their turn the Japanese also seem to have had great respect for some of the Jesuit missionaries and *fidalgos* whom they met, whose values of personal honor and martial prowess were in conformity with their own *samurai* ethos. A prominent feudal lord, Omura Sumitada in Kyushu, the first Japanese of his rank to be converted to Christianity, gave the Portuguese the site of the harbor of Nagasaki in 1571, the same year that the Spanish founded Manila. Nobunaga himself was hospitable to the Jesuits, perhaps seeing them as a counterweight to the influence of the Buddhist sects that were his most detested enemies.

Nobunaga was succeeded by the even greater figure of Toyotomi Hideyoshi, who essentially completed the political unification of the country by the time of his death in 1598. The final consolidation came, however, after Tokugawa Ieyasu defeated all remaining opposition in 1600, installing a Shogunate that was to last till the Meiji Restoration of 1868. The Japanese economy appears to have grown rapidly in response to this process of national unification (Yamamura 1981). Consolidation of domains and rationalization of property rights gave peasants more independence and incentive to increase agricultural productivity, and commerce benefited from the abolition of tolls and improved transport. The notable increase in Japanese demand for higher quality silk from China thus becomes explicable, and accounts for the profitability of the Macao–Nagasaki voyages.

A fatal blow to this trade was struck, however, when the Tokugawa established their seclusion policy in the 1630s and violently expelled all Christian missions, limiting Western contact to a few Dutchmen on the tiny island of Deshima outside Nagasaki. The complex interaction of the Portuguese and the Japanese during what has been called "the Christian century" of that country's history went through three phases. From the 1540s to the late 1580s the Japanese were eager to trade and were also receptive to the religious and cultural influence of their visitors. In 1587 Hideyoshi appears to have suddenly realized that, however great the benefits of trade might be, the preaching of the Jesuits might undermine the foundations of the country's cultural and social institutions. He therefore attempted in the remaining years of his rule to separate trade from missionary activity, permitting the former but banning the latter, although without consistently strict enforcement, which was also the approach taken by the first two Tokugawa Shoguns until 1623. The third Shogun Iemitsu (1623–51), however, apparently came to the view that since the Portuguese were bringing priests into the country disguised as traders or other laymen, thereby threatening the political stability of the country, they should be excluded completely, with foreign trade confined to Dutch and Chinese traders at Nagasaki. The peasant revolt in 1637 known as the Shimabara Rebellion, in which the battle cry of the Japanese Christian warriors fighting on the peasant side was "*Santiago*" (Saint James), must also have been seen as confirming the inherent danger of the imported religion. Alternatively, Sansom (1963, chapter 4) offers the interesting view that the exclusion policy was really a device to secure a monopoly of foreign trade for the Shogunate, and to prevent potential rival feudal lords from enriching themselves by this means. The exclusion was of course a tremendous blow to Macao but that resilient trading city was able to survive, turning for an alternative source of silver to Manila. As Parry (1967, p. 210) says, Manila was "the meeting ground, halfway round the world, of the heirs of Columbus and Vasco da Gama; a triumph of maritime communication in defiance of probability."

Transpacific trade was essentially confined to that conducted between the Spanish American colonies and China through Manila, a trade long identified with the legendary *Manila Galleon*, which is also the title of the classic account by W. L. Schurz (1939) of this unique episode in the history of global commerce. The basic exchange between the two continents was Chinese silk, as well as porcelain and Southeast Asian spices to some extent, for the silver that was pouring out of the mines of Potosí and Mexico. Chinese traders, mostly from the southern ports of Amoy (Hsia-men) and Canton, took raw silk, fabrics, and apparel to Manila, where these cargoes were sold for silver and carried back for sale in the New World.

The problem for the Spanish authorities, both in the Peninsula and the American colonies, was what volume of this trade would be in their best interest. There was a silk industry not only in Spain but also in Mexico, successfully introduced by Cortés himself soon after the conquest. There was thus the predictable demand for protection by both the metropolitan and colonial branches of the industry. Furthermore, there was reluctance for too much silver to be diverted across the Pacific, since this meant less for the urgent needs of trade and war in Europe. Not to permit any trade at all, however, would doom the Philippines to extinction, since there was no other viable economic option to sustain this most westerly jewel in the Spanish crown. The compromise solution was to permit trade, but to restrict it to a prescribed level, permitting survival of the import-competing silk industry at both locations and keeping the diversion of silver to the Pacific within limits, while at the same time providing the incentive necessary to induce a sufficient number of colonists to settle in a dangerous and unhealthy environment for Europeans.

The regulated system was introduced in 1593, after an initial period of relative freedom from 1571. The value of the cargo to be loaded at Manila was not to exceed an amount known as the *permiso*, fixed at 250,000 pesos at Manila prices and twice that amount for the value of final sale at Acapulco prices. As Schurz (1939, p. 155) succinctly explains, "this had the force of an export quota for the colony and served the double purpose of limiting the competition of Chinese silks with those of Spanish manufacture in the Mexican market and of restricting the passage of Mexican silver to China." The level of the *permiso* was unchanged until 1702 when it was raised to 300,000 pesos at Manila and again twice that at Acapulco. The rate of return at official values was thus capped at 100%, before subtraction of taxes and duties and discounting for the not inconsiderable risks of loss due to storms or piracy. Increasing the value of the goods shipped above the permitted level would of course increase total profits proportionally, but leave the rate of return unchanged, assuming Acapulco prices to be double Manila prices as before.

Allocation of these rents (that is to say, of cargo space on the galleon) was a source of immense patronage, jealously fought over by the governors and other crown and municipal officials and members of the Spanish merchant community. Schurz recounts in amusing detail how they were assigned to various segments of Manila society, ranging from merchants to civil servants, military officers, pensioners, widows and orphans, and last but by no means least the representatives of various religious and charitable organizations. As can readily be imagined, overloading was rampant to the point of endangering the safety of the vessels and increasing the risk of loss or capture, by cutting down the space necessary for spare nautical equipment and munitions for defense. By contrast the return voyage from Acapulco to Manila was "virtually in ballast" as Schurz says because the silks were paid for largely in silver, of an obviously much higher ratio of value to weight. The number of passengers, however, was typically greater to Manila than to Acapulco, as the population in the Philippines steadily grew.

The demand for the silks and other Asian goods brought to the deep harbor of Acapulco by the galleons was intense. Officially, the only buyers permitted at Acapulco were the inhabitants of the Viceroyalty of New Spain, but it proved impossible to prevent the people from the other Viceroyalty of Peru from entering as well, and even going so far as to place orders in Manila itself through their agents. A good part of the silk arriving in Acapulco around 1600 was taken from Vera Cruz to Spain itself (Parry 1967, p. 209), a remarkable tribute to the low cost and high quality of a commodity that was still competitive after crossing the Pacific and Atlantic combined. All European visitors to Mexico City and Lima were astonished at the extent to which the people, including *mestizos* and even Indians, were dressed in silk, while the better off Spaniards displayed a level of luxury beyond anything that could be seen in the capitals of Europe.

The Mexican silk industry only saved itself from being wiped out by using Chinese raw silk as an input. Atwell (1998, p. 409) cites a source in which it is claimed that raw Chinese silk imported from Manila kept 14,000 weavers working in Mexico City and Puebla. It is little wonder that Schurz (p. 190) claims that the profit rate on the galleon trade was between 100 and 300%, instead of the permitted level of a little more than 80%. Notables such as governors and viceroys made enormous fortunes on the privileged access they had to the scarce cargo space. Schurz cites the instance of a well-known sixteenth-century navigator who started with 200 ducats worth of Spanish and Flemish goods that he was able to convert in Manila to 1,400 ducats worth of silk merchandise, on which he made a clear profit of 2,500 ducats after selling it in Acapulco. The demand of other European countries for Chinese silk reduced the profitability of the galleon trade in later centuries, but it nevertheless continued up to 1815.

The Dutch Rise to Primacy in World Trade

The last decade of the sixteenth century saw the emergence of the Dutch as a major actor in the world economy, displacing the Portuguese and the Spanish within a few decades and holding their primacy well into the eighteenth century before eventually losing it to the British. The seven northern provinces of the seventeen comprising the Spanish possessions in the Netherlands had revolted against what was felt to be the oppressive rule of Philip II at the end of the 1560s. They formed the Union of Utrecht as a sort of defensive alliance in 1579, and declared their independence from Habsburg Spain in 1581. The southern provinces, including the highly developed Flanders and Brabant, roughly corresponding to what is now Belgium, were brought back within the Spanish and Catholic fold but only after considerable emigration of wealthy and skilled dissenters to the north. Antwerp in Brabant, which had been the major emporium in that part of Europe from before the fifteenth century, was largely ruined by the hostilities and the prolonged blockade of the Scheldt by the Dutch, and was soon overtaken by Amsterdam in Holland, by far the most populous and wealthiest of the seven United Provinces. The population of Amsterdam rose from about 50,000 in 1600 to double that in 1620 and 200,000 by 1650.

The Dutch Republic was a merchant oligarchy, somewhat like Venice but much more than a mere city-state, with a population of between 1 and 2 million, about the same as Portugal, and with a diverse and productive hinterland. Executive leadership in the new state largely came from the House of Orange, descendants of William the Silent (died 1584), regarded as the "father of the nation." They held the office of Stadholder in Holland, Zeeland, and Utrecht and also commanded the Dutch armed forces. The main federal institution was the States General that met at The Hague. The main asset of the upstart republic was its economic system, certainly the most productive and efficient in Europe at that time, with Italy having passed its peak in the preceding century. Agriculture was concentrated on high-value-added activities such as livestock and dairy farming rather than tillage, releasing a high proportion of the labor force for industry and services. The strongest initial comparative advantage of the Dutch economy was in shipping, particularly to the Baltic, the so-called "mother trade" from which all the others sprang. Most of the grain exported from the Baltic regions was carried in Dutch ships to Amsterdam and reexported from there to other parts of Europe, including the Mediterranean. The herring fisheries of the North Sea were another great staple of the Dutch, using the large vessel known as the herring bus, a sort of floating factory in which the catch was gutted, salted, and packed.

Considerable strides were also made in manufacturing, partly at the expense of older and more established centers in Flanders and other parts of the Spanish Netherlands. Thus Hondshoote had been the major producer of the "new draperies," lighter woolen cloth made from long staple wool. The conflict with Spain sent thousands of skilled workers and entrepreneurs from this town to Leyden in Holland, which doubled its population from 1580 to 1600 and more than doubled its output of these textiles over the same period. By 1664 Leyden was producing 144,000 pieces a year and van Houtte (1977, p. 162) states that "at this time Leyden was the outstanding manufacturing center for wool in Europe and perhaps in the world." These Dutch cloths were soon being exported to the Baltic as well as to Mediterranean markets. Flemish refugees also established Haarlem as an important linen producer. Shipbuilding to replace depreciation of the huge fleet and also for export was another major component of the industrial sector, with 250–350 ships a year produced around 1650. A notable nautical innovation was the *fluit*, a vessel designed to maximize cargo carrying capacity and minimize labor cost at the expense of speed. It was these vessels, introduced in the 1590s and built in the shipyards of Hoorn, which kept Dutch freight rates so low in the bulk carrying trades as to drive most competitors out of the market. One reason why *fluits* could economize on labor was that they were unarmed, or only very lightly armed. This meant, however, that they required naval escorts when sailing in dangerous waters, a nice example of the dependence of Plenty on Power during this period. In contrast to this Dutch division of labor between civilian and military shipping, English and other merchant ships continued to be heavily and expensively armed. According to George Downing, whom we will encounter in the next chapter, "If theire Merchant men have constant Convoy and the

English Merchant men must be both Merchant and man of warr, he cannot sayle at so easy a rate as a Hollander, and consequently all the Trade must still dayly more and more fall to the Hollanders" (Barbour 1930, p. 281).

As we will see later, an important new sector of foreign trade that the Dutch penetrated after 1590 was with Russia, not through the Baltic but north of Norway to Archangel. This route involved exchanging luxury products such as wine, spices, silk, and expensive woolen cloth for furs, leather, and caviar, which were in turn reexported all over Europe. The Dutch replaced the English as the leaders in this high-value trade by 1610, according to Jonathan Israel (1989, p. 44), who attaches great importance to this breakthrough as marking a significant step up from merely being a low-cost shipper, since it required the capital and trading connections necessary to assemble a wide range of expensive commodities for resale purposes. Many elite merchants from other parts of Europe, including so-called "New Christians" from Iberia, began to operate in the new state, attracted by the commercial opportunities and religious toleration.

Essential to this high-value carrying trade was access to the Lisbon spice market, which was under Spanish control after the union of the Iberian crowns in 1580. Access could be cut off at any time by embargoes, and was in 1585 and 1595. The only viable long-term solution was to go to the source, the East Indies themselves, thus doing to the Portuguese what they had themselves done to Venice and Egypt a century earlier. Accordingly, in 1594 a "Company of Far Lands" was organized by a group of Amsterdam merchants, and a fleet of four ships sent to the eastern seas, returning in 1597 with the loss of one ship and many lives but with enough pepper for the voyage to be regarded as a success (Boxer 1973, pp. 24–26). With this encouragement, two fleets with a total of twenty-two ships left in 1598, one of which, commanded by Jacob van Neck, returned with eight ships and sufficient spices to turn a profit of 400%, causing the bells of Amsterdam to peal with joy. With the thirst for profits mounting, sixty-five ships left in 1601. It soon became apparent, however, that the bubble was causing pepper prices to rise sharply at the source, over 100% in six years according to Israel (1989, p. 68), and fall in Europe.

The situation cried out for the organization of an effective monopoly, but how was this to be achieved? The problem was solved at the federal level by the States General, the leading role in the negotiations being taken by the remarkable Johan van Oldenbarneveldt, a prominent statesman from South Holland. A chartered company was formed in 1602, the *Vereenigde Oost-Indische Compagnie* or VOC, with a board of seventeen directors, the famous *Heeren XVII*. Amsterdam, the major source of capital, had eight directors, Zeeland had four, and the North Quarter (Hoorn and Enkhuizen) and South Holland (Delft and Rotterdam) two each. The seventeenth directorship was to rotate between Zeeland, the North Quarter, and South Holland, thus preventing Amsterdam from having a guaranteed majority while acknowledging its preeminent position, which was also indicated by the headquarters of the company being located there.

The VOC was awarded a monopoly east of the Cape of Good Hope and west of the Straits of Magellan for an initial period of twenty-one years. The *Heeren XVII* had the power to wage defensive war, to construct fortresses and strongholds, and to enter into treaties and alliances in the vast zone covered by its monopoly. The VOC has thus rightly been said to have been "virtually a state within a state" (Boxer 1973, p. 26). It was a unique combination of commercial and political power, of a kind never seen before. It is true that Venice, Genoa, and the Hanseatic League employed considerable naval power, but they were only city-states without the full resources of a genuine nation-state, such as the Dutch Republic undoubtedly was despite the small size of its population. Once the extraordinary institutional basis of the VOC was created in 1602, it was soon deployed with remarkable success in the East Indies. By the middle of the century and the end of the eighty-year "war of liberation" from the Habsburgs in 1648, the Dutch were the dominant European power in the trade between Asia and Europe and in the intra-Asian carrying trade, far outstripping their established Iberian rivals. Much of the credit for this success has to go to the fourth and certainly the greatest of the VOC's governors-general in the Indies, Jan Pieterszoon Coen (1587–1629). His statement to the directors soon after he took up his duties that "we cannot make war without trade nor trade without war" is an entirely accurate statement of the relationship between war and trade in the mercantilist era, and Coen proved himself to be equally ruthless and proficient at both.

As we have seen in the previous sections, trade in the Indian Ocean and the Pacific had settled into a stable pattern by the early 1600s. The Portuguese held Goa, Hormuz, Melaka, and Macao and the Spanish held Manila as fortified bases and harbors, but with more spices going overland to Europe than around the Cape at this time there could be no question of any monopoly being held by the *Estado da India* in these commodities. The acutely penetrating geostrategic mind of the young Coen saw this situation as clearly ripe for a takeover bid of global proportions. His native country had fought the Iberian superpower to a standstill on its own soil and was building up sufficient naval resources to break into the ring of fortified trading posts from Hormuz to Manila, by seizing them directly or establishing competitors that would divert their trade. Furthermore, instead of passively waiting for supplies to appear, a more forward policy could extract spices at the source from the native growers at low prices, if rival native and foreign buyers could be kept away by force, and exported to Europe at relatively low volumes but high margins of profit. Judiciously selected Dutch settlers could be set up for business at various locations in Asia, engaging in the huge volume of the intra-Asian carrying trade, the profits from which could provide the annual working capital for the trade to turn over, without the expensive necessity of obtaining silver bullion or specie in Europe from the Spanish or their Italian creditors. With all the details of this vision set down in memoranda to the *Heeren XVII*, it is perhaps little wonder that they made him governor-general at the age of thirty.

The bulk of the spice trade was in pepper, a vine that grows relatively easily over a wide area in the tropics, from Malabar to Sumatra and Java. Its supply was therefore impossible to monopolize, and a cartel was also obviously impossible to organize and maintain. With cloves and even more with nutmeg and mace, on the other hand, the possibilities were much greater. The nutmeg tree required such a specific combination of soil, temperature, and rainfall to flourish that it could only grow in the five small Banda Islands. At least since the early sixteenth century demand was sufficient for the islands to have become specialized in the supply of these spices, importing sago, rice, and cloth in exchange. Cloves were also restricted in the area over which they grew at this time, mainly the small islands of Ternate and Tidore west of the large island of Halmahera, as well as Amboyna and Ceram, collectively known as the Moluccas. Villiers (1990, p. 93) reports that the successive markups on clove prices were remarkable, with the price in Melaka 30 times higher than at the source in the Moluccas, in India 100 times higher, and in Lisbon at times of scarcity as much as 240 times higher. For nutmeg the ratios were even greater. Milton (1999, p. 6) reports that 10 lb. of nutmeg could be bought in the Bandas for less than one English penny, while the same amount would sell for seventy shillings, or 840 pence!

The Dutch visited all these islands in the early VOC voyages and contracts were obtained from the native chiefs, obliging them not to sell to any buyers other than the VOC itself. Thus when representatives of the British East India Company (EIC) appeared in the Moluccas a little later and started to buy the spices at more favorable prices, the Dutch regarded them as interlopers and the native chiefs as violators of the sanctity of contract, and hence felt justified in using force against both parties when they refused to desist. In 1616 the Dutch occupied all of the Bandas in force, with only the tiny island of Pulau Run holding out with a small group of East India Company men led by the factor Nicholas Courthope. He was eventually killed in 1620 after a gallant defense, a colorful account of which is given in Giles Milton's (1999) *Nathaniel's Nutmeg*. Coen carried out an utterly ruthless and despicable campaign of "ethnic cleansing" against the Bandanese, killing or deporting virtually the entire population and replacing them with imported slaves and Dutch settlers to supply the nutmeg.

Amboyna was the scene of another very unpleasant Anglo-Dutch episode, the massacre, or more correctly judicial murder, of the British community of the EIC and their Japanese employees for an alleged plot to seize the fortress on the island, as confessed to by them, but only under excruciating torture. The output of cloves was limited to Amboyna itself, while trees in other islands were uprooted to keep the supply restricted to what was thought to be the monopolistically optimal level. The *Heeren XVII* wrung its hands and acted "shocked, shocked" at Coen's brutality in the Bandas, but he could claim that all he was doing was executing the monopoly policy that they had sanctioned. Even aside from the obvious immorality of Coen's actions, contemporaries and historians have questioned the rationality and cost of his policy in the long run. The meticulous and fair-minded scholar Meilink-Roelofsz (1962) has argued that supply was too short in some subsequent years, and is doubtful whether the expense on warfare and suppression could have been offset by sufficient profits on the very limited volume of trade in cloves, nutmeg, and mace.

The sultan of Bantam took advantage of the Anglo-Dutch hostilities to take over the coastal state of Jakarta, on the north coast of Java, where the VOC had a settlement and trading post. Returning with his fleet in 1619 from Amboyna, where he had gone to evade a stronger British naval force, Coen took the city by storm with himself in the lead and burnt it to the ground. He founded the new capital of the VOC on its site, naming it Batavia after the ancestral Teutonic forebears of the Dutch. The city was laid out with streets and canals on the Dutch pattern and soon attracted a considerable native and Chinese population, in a manner very similar to Manila. It would serve as the capital of the Dutch Empire in the East Indies till after World War II. Coen ended his first term as governor-general in 1623 and went back to Holland, but returned for a second term in 1627. The founding of Batavia was a challenge to Sultan Agung of the powerful state of Mataram in central Java, and he laid siege to the new city with a large force and almost succeeded in taking it. Coen died suddenly in Batavia during the siege in 1629, probably of dysentery, at the age of forty-two. The siege was eventually relieved and the conflict between Batavia and Mataram came to an end later in the century when the latter, along with Bantam, essentially became a dependency of the VOC regime.

Coen's expansionist policies continued under his able protégé Antonie van Diemen, who finally conquered Melaka from the Portuguese in 1641 with the aid of the sultan of Johore, and were given a major boost when peace with Spain finally arrived in 1648. The end of this struggle implied the greater availability of two essential "inputs" for the VOC's trade: soldiers and silver. No less than 10,500 seasoned veterans of the war against Spain were hired and sent to serve the company in the period 1648–52, while the flow of silver to Batavia was raised from about 8 million guilders in previous decades to almost 12 million guilders during 1650–60 (Israel 1989, p. 245 and table 5.17).

The Dutch initiated the takeover of Ceylon from Portuguese control in 1638 by forming an alliance with Rajasinha II, the ruler of the inland kingdom of Kandy. With its augmented resources the VOC was able to capture Colombo from the Portuguese in 1656 with a force of two thousand Dutch troops and Sinhalese auxiliaries, and soon gained control of the entire island. They took Jaffna in 1657 and annexed the domains of their erstwhile ally, the king of Kandy, giving the Company the ability to successfully monopolize the valuable cinnamon trade, and control the profitable export of elephants to the Mughal Empire and other Indian states. VOC forces captured a string of Portuguese forts and trading stations on the Malabar Coast in the early 1660s, including Cochin in 1663. Only Goa and Macao, which they had saved from a determined Dutch assault in 1622, now remained of Portugal's Asian strongholds, with the exception of Timor and Solor in the Lesser Sundas. In the East Indies the VOC completely excluded the English from the Banda Islands, and the Spanish from Ternate and Tidore, and consolidated their position in Java and Sumatra. They conquered, in an alliance with its Bugis rivals, the powerful sultanate of Makassar on the island of Sulawesi (Celebes) in the late 1660s, preventing it from trading with English or other competitors, and thus raising their own profits from the trade in cloves and other spices, eliminating surplus production on some occasions by the forcible removal of the populations of the cultivating areas.

The VOC campaigns against Kandy and Makassar are interesting examples of early European imperialism in Asia, marking a departure from the original Portuguese pattern and presaging English and French activities a century and more later. Thus while the Portuguese were for the most part content to establish fortresses and trading posts at strategic locations and rely on sea-power alone in the attempt to control trade, the VOC was prepared to go a step further in the establishment of monopoly power by physically dominating the areas in which commodities such as nutmeg, cloves, and cinnamon were produced. As Sinnappah Arasaratnam (1988, p. xx) says, "the territorial expansion of the Dutch in Asia was a direct result of their commercial policy." These substantial gains more than compensated for setbacks in the Far East, where the Tokugawa seclusion policy implied the cessation of Japanese silver supplies, while the Dutch were expelled from Taiwan in 1661. The lesson for future Asian nationalism in these events is clear. Where there was a strong unified Asian state such as Tokugawa Japan or Qing China, the Europeans could be confined to the margins of mutually beneficial commerce, but where the Asian lands were divided by internal rivalries as in the Indonesian Archipelago or Ceylon they could fall prey to a rapacious European power.

Cloth from the eastern Coromandel Coast of India was the commodity most in demand in exchange for spices in the archipelago. The VOC accordingly set up two "factories" or trading stations in the region, at Masulipatam and Pulicat, in the first decade of the seventeenth century. As Raychaudhuri (1962, p. 16) points out, the Deccan sultan was anxious to receive the VOC into his realm, as evidenced by the fact that he exempted the company from a 12% stamp duty on cloth that all other purchasers, even local merchants, had to pay, in a manner reminiscent of the present practice of many developing countries attempting to attract foreign investment. This did not, however, prevent his rapacious officials and other local authorities from harassing the company in various ways to extort bribes. Other hindrances were the almost constant warfare and periodic famines that afflicted the region. Despite these difficulties the supply of the cloth itself was highly elastic, with purchases constrained only by the capital that the company could muster each year in the form of precious metals, the only acceptable means of payment.[5] Exports of cloth rose steadily over the century, going not only for the purchase of spices in the islands but to Europe and even Japan and Persia as well, making the Coromandel cotton textiles a truly global commodity handled by the VOC. The share of Coromandel cloth and other textile items as a share of total sales in Amsterdam rose from 17% in 1648–50 to 43% in 1698–1700, which means that it had outstripped spices and pepper, which fell from a combined total of 58% to 37% over the same period (Glamann 1958,

[5]The higher are elasticities of supply and demand, the more responsive are producers and consumers to price changes. For an example of how such elasticities can matter for economic outcomes, see figure 6.5 and the accompanying discussion.

p. 14). The "left arm" of the VOC, as the Coromandel trade used to be called, thus eventually became stronger than the "right arm" of the spice trade from the archipelago.

Cloth was by no means the only item exported by the Dutch from Coromandel. Indigo was another commodity in strong demand both in Europe and Asia, the cultivation of which the company attempted to encourage in the area. Perhaps the most surprising item, however, was gunpowder manufactured from local sources of saltpeter, which according to Raychaudhuri supplied not only the company's substantial requirements but was exported to Europe to meet the demand generated by the Thirty Years' War as well. A trade in slaves, fed by frequent outbreaks of famine, also developed but did not reach significant proportions despite Coen's efforts to promote it. A local Hindu warlord refused offers for him to supply slaves, saying that he thought it was a great sin in the eyes of the gods. In this case at least the Hindu gods were more merciful than the Calvinist God of Coen. The Coromandel stations also served as a convenient base for promoting trade with Bengal, Burma, Siam, and the Malay Peninsula.

The first fifty years of the VOC were thus clearly a remarkable success. The number of ships returning each decade from Asia to their home ports rose steadily from 50 in the second decade of the century to 103 by the sixth and 156 by the last, while share prices on the Amsterdam Exchange rose almost fourfold between 1625 and 1648 (Israel 1989, tables 4.8 and 5.19). According to de Vries and van der Woude (1997, p. 396), total dividend payments by the VOC to 1650 were eight times the original investment, and the annual rate of return to a shareholder who held till 1650 was 27%.

Dutch intercontinental trade in this era was by no means confined to the VOC and Asia. From the 1590s onwards the Dutch were active in the Atlantic as well, both on the west coast of Africa and the east coast of the Americas. On the Guinea Coast Dutch ships traded initially for gold and ivory before later taking part actively in the slave trade. War with Spain cut off access to salt for the herring trade in Portuguese and Spanish waters, but large fleets were sent to exploit extensive deposits on the Venezuelan coast and in the Caribbean before vigorous Spanish countermeasures put a stop to them, with Dutch seamen often being executed as criminal interlopers. In North America the Dutch bartered axes and knives with the natives for beaver and otter furs, and in the Caribbean they did the same for hides. As in the case of the East Indies, competition between Dutch traders sharply reduced profit margins in all these trades and the familiar remedy of forming an integrated joint stock company was adopted, namely the West-Indische Compagnie

(WIC). The WIC was established nineteen years after the VOC in 1621, with an even larger initial capital and a board of nineteen directors, referred to of course as the *Heeren XIX*.

The Thirty Years' War was raging in Europe at this time, and the WIC in the Atlantic had to face the full might of Habsburg Spain and Portugal. It had some notable initial successes. In West Africa the price for gold on the Guinea Coast in terms of copper utensils was cut in half by the ending of competition (Israel 1989, p. 161). In the Caribbean Admiral Piet Heyn captured the Spanish treasure fleet off the coast of Cuba in 1628, netting 11 million guilders (ibid., p. 162). On the other side of the ledger Flemish privateers based in Dunkirk frequently caused havoc with Dutch shipping, destroying or capturing hundreds of herring busses, and were sometimes able to snare much richer prizes such as eight richly laden merchantmen from Archangel in 1642 (ibid., pp. 136–37). According to Parker (1979, p. 198) over 1800 mainly Dutch vessels were seized or destroyed by the privateers from 1626 to 1634. Israel reports that Dutch shipping from the Baltic to the Mediterranean fell by over 90% in the first seven years of the 1620s.

Bahia, the main Portuguese outpost in Brazil, was captured by the Dutch in 1624 but was promptly recaptured by a large joint Iberian fleet a year later. The Dutch gained another foothold at Recife in Pernambuco in 1630 and proceeded to actively develop sugar estates using slaves from West Africa. According to Israel (1989, pp. 163, 169) the Dutch sold over 23,000 slaves in their Brazilian territories from 1636 to 1645 while raising the export of sugar from 3,600 chests in 1638 to a peak of 9,500 in 1643. Shortly thereafter, however, the entire Dutch position in Brazil collapsed when the inhabitants in their territories, mainly Africans, Indians, and *mestizos*, revolted with the aid of their brethren in the southern Brazilian region still held by Portugal, and succeeded in driving out the Dutch by 1654. In 1647 the WIC estimated a profit of 400,000 florins in Brazil, but spent 1,100,000 florins on defense (Parker 1979, p. 195). After this debacle the WIC gave up the attempt to bolster its trade in the New World by military force and relied henceforth on peaceful if unethical means instead, finding a niche in exporting slaves across the Atlantic from West Africa.

Boxer (1975, p. 106) claimed that the seventeenth-century conflict between the Dutch Republic and the Habsburg Iberian powers was more deserving of being called World War I than the usual one of 1914–18, since it was "waged in four continents and on seven seas." The costs of the war, by whatever name, were truly staggering as clearly revealed by Geoffrey Parker (1979, chapter 10). The Southern Netherlands, particularly the provinces of Flanders and Brabant that

had been in the forefront of European economic development since
the Middle Ages, were devastated by war and blockades. They did
make a respectable recovery but did not regain their leading position
in Europe until the Industrial Revolution in the nineteenth century.
Spain wore itself out in the conflict, the treasure of the Indies being
spent many times over on the large military forces it had to maintain
in the Netherlands. Parker (1979) reports that royal receipts from the
Indies during 1571–75 amounted to about 4 million ducats, whereas
expenditure on the army of Flanders in the same period came to
9 million ducats, and on the Mediterranean fleet to 5 million ducats, a
deficit of 10 million that had to be made good by merciless taxation in
Castile itself and recourse to massive borrowing from the Genoese and
other, mainly Italian, bankers. The national debt rose from 36 million
ducats when Philip II ascended the throne in 1556 to 85 million at
his death in 1598, and to 180 million by 1667. The burden of the war
on the Portuguese, whose rivalry with the Dutch was exacerbated by
the union of the crowns in 1580, was particularly devastating since, as
we have seen, it cost them the most valuable portions of their Asian
empire. When they broke away from Spain in 1640 it was too late, since
the Dutch had surged so far ahead.

Dutch success emerges clearly from the available figures on shipping. Figure 4.5 draws on Jan de Vries's invaluable survey to show
the number of ships departing for Asia per decade from Portugal,
the Netherlands, England, France, and other European countries.
Since not all of these ships returned to Europe, some being used for
commercial or military purposes in Asian waters, and others lost, and
since ships varied in size both across countries and over time, the
figure also shows the tonnage that returned from Asia to Europe over
the same period. As can be seen, the Portuguese enjoyed a complete
monopoly of the Cape route throughout most of the sixteenth century.
While the number of ships they sent out to Asia declined more or less
continuously over the course of the century, from 151 ships during the
first decade to just 43 during the 1590s, this was compensated for by
an increase in the average size of ships (from 283.3 tons in the 1500s
to 1144.2 tons in the 1590s) and an increase in the percentage of ships
returning to Portugal from 58% to 93% over the same period. The
result, as the figure shows, was that the tonnage returned to Lisbon
grew slowly but steadily over the century, only declining in the 1590s,
which was the decade the Dutch first made their appearance in Asian
waters.

From that moment onward, the Dutch were sending more ships to
Asia than the Portuguese or anyone else, and this advantage persisted

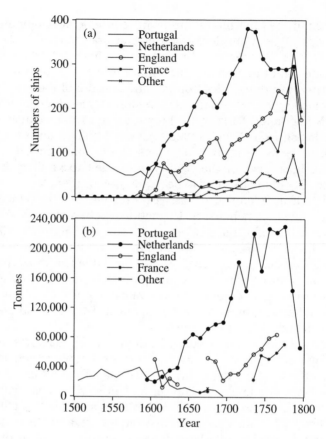

FIGURE 4.5. Trade around the Cape, 1500–1800: (a) numbers of ships sailing to Asia per decade; (b) tonnage returned to Europe. *Source:* de Vries (2003).

for almost two centuries, until the 1780s. Since Dutch (and Portuguese) ships tended be larger than either English or French ones, the Dutch advantage in numbers of ships sailing translated into an even larger advantage in terms of tonnage returned to Europe. As for the Portuguese, the tonnage returned to Lisbon declined steadily throughout the seventeenth century. Already by mid century, they were no longer a serious competitor on the Cape route which they had pioneered a century and a half earlier. Primacy in the intercontinental trade between Europe and Asia had clearly shifted to the VOC and the Dutch Republic, although they were already finding it necessary to contend with their English rivals in order to maintain it.

As Parker (1979, p. 191) demonstrates, the Dutch did not achieve their victory easily. Resisting the huge Spanish armies required vast sums annually, rising from 3 million florins in 1591 to 9 million in 1607, 13 million in 1622, and 19 million in 1640. Taxes had to be raised and the public debt of the province of Holland alone was 153 million florins in 1651. One great difference with Spain, however, was that most of this debt was borrowed in Amsterdam and held internally, paying interest rates that *fell* from 10% in the 1600s to 5% in the 1640s and 4% after 1651, thanks to the high propensity to save of the Dutch, despite the opulent lifestyle of the merchant princes and the Regent class.

The VOC as we have seen was eventually highly profitable, but it took decades for its military and commercial infrastructure to be built up, while the WIC was a losing proposition for almost every year of its existence. Indeed it is possible to argue that, for all its glamor and prestige, long-distance intercontinental trade contributed less to the true prosperity of the Dutch Golden Age than the humdrum "mother trade" of the Baltic and the herring fisheries. Of the 4,300 ships that the Dutch operated in 1634, the fishing fleet accounted for 2,250, the Baltic and Mediterranean fleets for 1,750, and the East and West Indies for only 300 ships (ibid., p. 196). We must therefore never lose sight of the fact that intra-European and no doubt intra-Asian trade in the early modern era were far greater in volume and value than the spices, silks, and slaves that crossed the oceans of the world. To do this, however, should not be to deny the importance of what was achieved in the 1500–1650 era, in creating the beginnings of a truly global economy.

Russia, Sweden, and the Baltic, 1500–1650

Before leaving Europe, it is worthwhile pausing to pick up the threads of the story of Russia's gradual rise to prominence as a major Eurasian power, since this represented yet another striking example of European expansionism during this period. As we have seen, under the reigns of Ivan III and Vassily III the Grand Duchy of Muscovy made enormous gains, so that when Ivan IV (1533–84) inherited his father's throne as a three-year-old infant, he was the ruler of what was now a powerful nation-state. His youthful elevation provoked an extended power struggle between various aristocratic factions that ended with his coronation as Tsar or Caesar of all Russia, and not merely as Grand Prince of Muscovy, in 1547. Ivan claimed to be the heir of the Byzantine emperors and head of the "third Rome," but despite these pretensions he is better known to history as Ivan *Grozny* ("the Terrible"). Early in his reign the army was strengthened with the establishment of regiments of musketeers, the famous *streltsy*, to supplement the traditional cavalry, while the artillery park and siege train was also enhanced. These measures paid off in securing the great victory over the Khanate of Kazan in the middle Volga region in 1552, which opened the way east to Siberia and down the Volga to Astrakhan on the Caspian Sea. Many Tartar nobles were taken into Russian service at this juncture, augmenting the cavalry forces that Ivan was able to deploy against independent Tartar tribes and in the war that he subsequently launched against Livonia in the west.

The conquests of the Kazan, and later the Astrakhan Khanates, were considered as victories of the Orthodox Christian Crusade against the infidel Muslims. These conquests involved Muscovy in prolonged conflicts with the Crimean Tartars and the Ottoman Empire on its southern borders. In the east, however, "the conquest of Kazan initiated a process that resulted in the annexation of all of Siberia" (Martin 1995, p. 354). The annexation of Siberia was in turn the factor most responsible for turning the land-locked medieval Muscovy into the great empire of Peter and Catherine the Great. A noble family, the Stroganovs, was licensed by Ivan to colonize and collect furs beyond the frontiers of Kazan, and a detachment of Cossacks defeated the khan of Sibir in 1582, laying open the vast expanse of Siberia to Russian expansion and colonization. Small numbers of hunters and trappers, followed by troops and settlers, gradually worked their way eastwards along a string of forts and trading posts, reaching the Pacific at Okhotsk by the 1640s. The valuable sable, ermine, and other pelts were mostly collected as tribute from the native tribes, whose resistance to Russian exploitation was easily and brutally overcome.

While the initiative was private, the government in Moscow oversaw the process through a specialized *Prikaz* or department for Siberia created in 1637, making sure that the state received a tenth of the best pelts as its revenue. The goal was not the acquisition of territory for cultivation and intensive settlement, but rather the extraction of wealth by means of the fur trade, with troops, administrators, and settlers merely providing the infrastructure required to obtain the fur supplies. The gathering of furs paid no attention to considerations of ecological sustainability, simply moving the process further and further east when supplies were exhausted. By the nineteenth century the furry El Dorado was a frozen wilderness, useful only as a place of exile for convicts and political dissidents. During the late seventeenth and eighteenth centuries, however, Siberian furs were a major source of wealth for the Russian Empire. The Russian population of Siberia rose from 169,000 adult males in 1719 to 412,000 in 1792 (Perdue 2005, p. 89).

To the west, the great ports such as Reval (Tallinn) and Riga were virtually free cities or merchant republics, while the knights of the Livonian Order had declined considerably from the formidable fighting force they once were. Thus the Russian attack launched in 1558 met with considerable initial success, taking Dorpat and Narva even though failing before Riga and Reval. No sooner had Narva fallen to Ivan than ships from across Northern Europe swarmed there to do business with him and were welcomed (Kirchner 1966). Ivan used Narva not only as an outlet for Russia's traditional exports such as furs, but also to import weapons and military supplies. The trade turnover was so abundant and varied that prices of most items including precious metals were reportedly lower there than in other Baltic ports. The volume of trade at Narva was reflected in the large increase in the number of ships from there passing through the Sound at Elsinore, at least 76 in 1567, and Kirchner asserts that the trade there must have involved hundreds of ships a year, rivaling that of Riga, the largest port in the eastern Baltic.

There was thus a scramble to share in the trade possibilities that the Russian intrusion opened up. The resulting rivalries led to the outbreak of the Northern Seven Years' War (1563–70), in which Sweden, which took over Reval in 1561, was ranged against Denmark, Poland–Lithuania, and Lübeck, the major port city of the Hanseatic League. Russia remained neutral, with Narva flourishing from being open to commerce from all quarters. However, ultimately none of Russia's powerful competitors were willing to stand idly by while she made these important gains. Denmark, Sweden and most importantly Poland–Lithuania all intervened, with the result that Ivan soon found himself involved in protracted hostilities along an extended western front. The Crimean Tartars also took advantage of the situation to launch a devastating raid on Moscow in 1571. Poland and Lithuania merged into a dual monarchy or commonwealth by the Treaty of Lublin in 1569, and elected Stephen Batory (1576–86), Prince of Transylvania, to rule over them. He turned out to be a formidable military leader, threatening Russia's western defenses at a number of points. The Swedes gained control of most of the coastline around the Gulf of Finland, and Narva fell to them in 1581.

Peace had to be made with Poland–Lithuania at the Truce of Yam Zapolskii in 1582, restoring the prewar borders, and separately with the Swedes, acknowledging the highly unfavorable status quo for the

Russian side. It took almost a century and a half for the Baltic window
to be opened again by Peter the Great. If only Russia had been able to
hold on to Narva and consolidate its position there, one could argue,
as Kirchner does, that the Westernization of the country could have
been accelerated by that amount of time. Instead the seventeenth
was almost a lost century in Russian history, marked by a successful
expansion to Siberia and the east as we have noted, but at the expense
of a further "Asiaticization" of its sociopolitical structure (Kirchner
1966, p. 76), in the sense of a greater centralization of despotic power
than in the West.

The reign of Ivan IV, after its promising beginning, descended into
an ongoing eruption of violence and repression. Russian historians
of both the Tsarist and Soviet eras have attempted to justify even
his most bizarre and sadistic acts as motivated by *raison d'état*, as
somehow necessary steps in the creation of an effective nation-state
capable of standing up to the numerous external threats confronting
it. As Richard Hellie (1986) and Isabel de Madariaga (2005) both point
out, however, it is difficult to see any necessity for the execution and
torture of thousands of innocent people, and in the case of the alleged
rebellion of Novgorod, the massacre of an entire city, in the interest
of social progress. The acute paranoia of an absolute monarch is a
much more plausible explanation for these senseless and gratuitously
cruel acts that mercifully ended with his death in 1584. It is also hard
to argue *raison d'état* when much of the country was devastated
and ruined for at least a generation during the resulting chaos of
disputed successions, false pretenders, peasant rebellions, and foreign
invasions known in Russian history as the "Time of Troubles," events
that were set in train to a large extent as a consequence of the
atrocities that Ivan IV himself was personally responsible for. Russia
did, however, slowly begin to recover under the new dynasty of the
Romanovs, who came to power in 1613, to the acclamation of an
aroused populace that had driven an occupying Polish army out of
Moscow.

The rest of the seventeenth century continued to be marked
by the protracted three-cornered struggle between Russia, Poland–
Lithuania, and Sweden. The conflict between Russia and Poland–
Lithuania was over which power would dominate Eastern Europe,
more specifically the lands of the present states of Belarus and Ukraine.
Smolensk was recaptured by the Poles in 1611 but then permanently
recovered by the Russians in 1654. The great Cossack rebellion of
the 1650s led by Bogdan Khmelnitsky devastated Poland and enabled
Russia to obtain Kiev and all of Ukraine east of the Dnieper by the Truce

of Andrusovo in 1667, with the acquisition confirmed by another treaty in 1686. By this time it had become clear that the composite Roman Catholic Commonwealth simply could not muster sufficient unity and resources to match its autocratic Orthodox enemy.

Sweden was another formidable opponent. Despite a population of not much more than 1 million, this state was experiencing its *Stormaktstid* or "Age of Greatness" as the dominant power of northern Europe and the Baltic. The foundations of its power had been laid by the prudent stewardship of Gustav I Vasa (1523–60), which enabled his successors to resist the Danes and begin to establish an empire in Finland, Livonia, and Estonia, achievements crowned by the brilliant military and diplomatic accomplishments of his grandson Gustav II Adolf (1611–32). Offsetting the disadvantages of its relatively poor soil and meager agricultural resources, Sweden had rich deposits of copper and iron ore that not only provided its own armed forces with the "sinews of war" but could also be used to finance imports of civilian necessities like grain and salt in times of emergency. A relatively open society of rural gentry, peasant proprietors, and urban burghers, supplemented by an influx of talented foreign businessmen and soldiers mostly from Germany, the Netherlands, and Scotland, provided the necessary human resources for the imperial mission.

Michael Roberts (1979, chapter 1) has contrasted the views of what he calls the Old School of Swedish historians with those of the so-called New School. For the former, the national security of a vulnerable state in a hostile environment was the main aim of Sweden's empire-building ventures. The latter stressed the predominance of an economic motive, namely the desire to secure a monopoly of the lucrative Baltic trade, from Russia at the eastern end to Denmark and the Sound at the western, leading to the necessity of controlling key ports such as Narva, Reval, Memel, Riga, and Danzig and their hinterlands. Roberts and others have argued convincingly that the evidence does not support a strict and narrow economic interpretation of Swedish policy, while trade and customs duties were never absent from consideration either. The issue is essentially the same one as the "Power versus Plenty" debate on mercantilism that was disposed of by Jacob Viner (1948), and that will be a main focus of the following chapter: simply put, achieving either aim would promote further achievement of the other. It is thus safe to say that the Swedish objective was a *dominium maris Baltici*, since that was necessary for the achievement of both national security and economic supremacy in the long run, regardless of whichever one was given primacy.

Pitch, tar, hemp, and timber, all necessary inputs for the expanding navies and mercantile marines of the Dutch and English, and which

Norway, Finland, and Russia could all supply in abundance, were the main items of Baltic export, while manufactured goods and Eastern products were the main imports along with the traditional salt, cod, and herring. Among the Baltic ports Danzig at the mouth of the Vistula was the main outlet for Polish grain exports and the entry point for imports from Western Europe that were sold upstream and deep into the interior in exchange for them. Grain was clearly the main export, constituting 70–80% of the total value, but Danzig was also the outlet for Hungarian copper, lead, and iron, and goods from Lithuania and Russia that were shipped on the Niemen or via Königsberg (Attman 1973, pp. 57–66). The main destination of Danzig's exports in the fifteenth century was Lübeck, but in the sixteenth it was largely the Netherlands, while England also became important in the seventeenth. The English Eastland Company had its trading station at the small port of Elbing from 1580 to 1628, but thereafter moved to Danzig.

Which of the several contenders would establish hegemony over this prosperous Baltic trading world? The cities of the Hanseatic League still had their fleets and trading networks but they did not control their hinterlands and lacked the necessary financial and military resources to compete with the rising nation-states of the region. Like the knights of the Teutonic and Livonian Orders they were increasingly becoming medieval relics in an early modern age. They could compete with or even dominate Novgorod and Pskov when these were republican city-states, but not after their absorption by the expanding Muscovite Leviathan. The Dutch Republic could carry the bulk of the shipping in the Baltic, but she was preoccupied with fending off her Habsburg overlords at home and with her colonial empire in the East and West Indies, and had more to gain by simply trading with all parties.

The struggle for the dominion of the Baltic in the seventeenth century was thus won by the Sweden of Gustav II Adolf, which decisively eclipsed Christian IV's Denmark as the leading Scandinavian power during and after the Thirty Years' War (1618–48). This shift in the two kingdoms' relative power was symbolized by Sweden's capture of Scania in 1658, giving it joint control with Denmark of the narrow straits separating the North and Baltic Seas. Poland–Lithuania was also significantly set back, with the war launched against her by Charles X (1654–60) of Sweden from 1655 to 1660 referred to in Polish history as the period of "the Deluge," though she did experience a recovery before the disastrous partitions that she suffered at the hands of Russia, Prussia, and Austria later in the eighteenth century. The trade of Danzig declined after the "Deluge," losing out relative to other ports such as Reval and Riga that belonged to the victorious Swedes.

Despite these military successes, Sweden never achieved the monopolistic control over the Baltic trade that she coveted. This was
largely due to the opening of a new sea route, and a new chapter in the
history of world trade, when an English ship commanded by Richard
Chancellor anchored on Russia's Arctic shore on a bay in the White Sea
in 1553. The ship was the sole survivor of three that were attempting
to find a northeast passage to China and the East Indies. Chancellor
and members of his crew made their way to Moscow and an audience
with the Tsar, who was quick to note the potential gains from trade.
Despite the fact that it was icebound for most of the year, a profitable
trade was developed by the newly formed Muscovy Company at the
port of Archangel. Russia exported goods such as rope, wax, tallow,
skins, furs, and timber for masts. Flax and hemp, two very important
Russian exports, were mostly shipped from the Baltic ports, while
grain was only shipped from Archangel when prices were very high,
since it was only then that the high freight charges of the Arctic route
could be borne. Imports were cloth and cotton fabrics, metal products,
weapons and war materials, wine, salt, and precious metals.

In 1587 no fewer than ten ships from Archangel returned to England,
and in the 1590s fourteen or fifteen "tall merchant ships yearly" are
reported as sailing to and from the port on the White Sea. However,
it did not take long for the Dutch to overtake the English in the
Archangel trade, as we have seen (Israel 1989, pp. 43–48). In 1600
thirteen Dutch ships docked at Archangel along with twelve English
ones, but by 1604 the corresponding numbers were seventeen and
nine. Thereafter the Dutch continued to pull away. The reasons for the
Dutch success were their greater command over financial resources
and access to East Indian spices, enabling them to better service the
Russian market with larger and sturdier vessels for the demanding
Arctic route, and establish trading stations in Moscow and Vologda
to store the necessary inventories. They were also able to provide
superior dyed and finished woolen cloth, and had greater supplies of
silver to meet the deficits in the value of Western trade with Russia. An
indignant Tsar Alexis (1645–76), the father of Peter the Great, expelled
the English in 1649 for having committed the outrage of decapitating
their sovereign. This was the early ascendant phase of Dutch economic
primacy, as we have already noted in connection with Anglo-Dutch
competition in the East Indies, and it was manifested in the Arctic
waters as well. We should also note the strong evidence of the extent
of globalization achieved by the early seventeenth century, since East
Indian spices and New World silver were both crucial factors in this
most northerly of European trades.

In addition to this northern route, overland trade across Poland between Eastern and Western Europe expanded in the sixteenth century and continued to grow despite setbacks in the seventeenth. Vast herds of cattle were driven from the extensive plains of Ukraine, Hungary, Moldavia, and Wallachia for slaughter in western towns such as Augsburg, Nuremburg, Regensburg, and Ulm, passing through Lublin, Kraków, Poznan, and Breslau along the way. Russian furs, skins, and leather, as well as Russian and Polish wax, were also sent overland from Novgorod and Pskov to centers such as Leipzig, where there was a well-known fair at which these goods were disposed of for Western products.

Attman (1973, chapter 3) emphasizes, despite considerable opinion to the contrary, that there was a "unity of the Russian market" since most of the goods involved could be, and often were, transported on all three routes, via the White Sea, the Baltic ports, and overland across Poland–Lithuania. Attman's contention, first advanced in a 1944 paper, is strongly supported by Arne Öhberg (1955). He points to the Archangel route as being the crucial factor preventing the Swedes from imposing their long-dreamed-of monopoly on Russian overseas trade with the West. Thus, during the Thirty Years' War when Gustav II Adolf and his Chancellor Axel Oxenstierna were attempting to monopolize the supply of Baltic grain to the Amsterdam market by their stranglehold on the Vistula, the resulting spike in grain prices drew exports of grain from Archangel, foiling the attempt. Sweden systematically attempted to divert the Archangel trade to the Baltic ports that they controlled by reducing customs duties to as low as 2%, to which the Russians responded by raising their export duties to offset this inducement to their merchants to abandon the northern route. Swedish diplomatic efforts to persuade the Russians to shift their Archangel trade to the Baltic ports were rejected, since the Russians were not willing to accept the risk that Sweden would take advantage of them if they did so, despite earnest assurances to the contrary. According to Öhberg (p. 162) "the White Sea route was a permanent factor of insecurity with which the Swedish government had to reckon in any action it took concerning Baltic trade."

SOUTHEAST ASIA DURING THE AGE OF COMMERCE

We now examine some of the implications of the Voyages of Discovery for the region which had all along been the unwitting object of European desire, namely Southeast Asia. In order to gain a proper perspective we need to examine the period 1500–1650 from the standpoint of Southeast Asia itself, instead of from that of the *Estado da India*, the East India Company, or the VOC as we have up to now, or as if "from the deck of a Dutch ship," as it was once famously put by J. C. van Leur (1955). We will thus explore the fortunes of the political entities of Southeast Asia, both on the mainland and in the archipelago, taking into account their interactions with India, China, and the Europeans. The impact of the Age of Commerce on Southeast Asia went far beyond trade, affecting not only the balance of power between states and regions but even so fundamental a cultural sphere as religion, with the spread of Islam and Christianity, and to a certain extent Theravada Buddhism as well, being associated with the expansion of commerce (Reid 1993b). As in the Japanese case, a key consequence of the European presence was the rapid spread of European military technology, leading to more conclusive military engagements and aiding the establishment of centralized political control over wider areas.

The small Burmese hill kingdom of Taungngu on the borders of Ava and Pegu was able, under two great warrior-kings, Tabinshwehti (1531–50) and Bayinnaung (1551–81), to conquer first Pegu and then Ava, and thus to combine the revenues from both seaborne commerce and agriculture. They established a formidable empire that defeated and sacked Ayutthaya in 1564 and 1569, reducing it to vassal status, along with Chieng Mai in what is now northern Thailand and most of what is now Laos. Bayinnaung thus became the ruler of the largest empire in Southeast Asian history. He greatly impressed European observers, one of whom, the Venetian merchant Caesar Fredericke said: "He has not any army or power by sea, but in the land, for people, dominions, gold and silver, he far exceeds the power of the Great Turk in treasure and strength" (Harvey 1925, p. 176).[6]

This Second Burmese Empire, as Htin Aung (1967, chapter 6) calls it, however, proved to be ephemeral. The Siamese and Laotian parts were separated from Burma by mountain ranges that were difficult to traverse, and no unified administration could be set up over the empire as a whole. The component centers were entrusted to the unreliable care of royal relatives and in 1599 the splendid capital Pegu was taken, sacked, and burnt by an alliance between the king of Arakan, with a large force of Portuguese mercenaries, and the governor of Taungngu. The Burmese part of the empire was restored under two grandsons

[6]On the other hand, Harvey felt that the Venetian was exaggerating greatly in comparing Bayinnaung to the Ottoman sultan, who at that time would have been none other than Suleyman the Magnificent himself.

of Bayinnaung: Anaukhpetlun (1605–28) and Thalun (1629–48). The decision of the latter to move the capital from Pegu on the coast to Ava, inland up the Irrawaddy, in 1634 has been subsequently interpreted as a fateful turning away from the remarkable "openness" of the golden age of Tabinshwehti and Bayinnaung, and a return to a more "closed" and inward-looking agrarian polity that eventually fell an easy prey to the British. However, Lieberman (1991, 1993) has made a strong case that this was a rational decision to consolidate the agrarian base and land revenues, while at the same time continuing to obtain revenues from overseas trade and the lucrative overland trade with China.

Among the many Portuguese mercenaries and adventurers who appear in Southeast Asia in these times, one of the most colorful was Felipe de Brito, who began his career in the service of the king of Arakan, sailing with his flotilla in the attack on Pegu in 1599. After this he was placed in command, with some fifty other Portuguese, of the important seaport of Syriam in the Irrawaddy Delta. Realizing its considerable commercial potential, it did not take de Brito long to operate independently from his Arakanese master, levying customs duties on coastal shipping and building up a force of Portuguese, *mestizos*, and Indian Muslims. To strengthen his position further he went to Goa to obtain recognition from the Viceroy, returning with reinforcements and six ships as well as the Viceroy's half-Javanese niece Dona Luisa de Saldanha as his bride. Syriam had a church and two Jesuit priests busily converting the heathen, and de Brito unwisely took to looting and despoiling Buddhist shrines, melting down sacred bronze bells to make cannon. He also diverted coastal shipping forcibly to Syriam, in effect monopolizing the supply of overseas imports to the interior, as well as conducting plundering forays on inland centers. Anaukhpetlun finally had enough and in 1612 besieged and captured Syriam before reinforcements could arrive from Goa and Arakan. De Brito was impaled as a punishment for his sacrilege, taking three days to die, and the unfortunate Dona Luisa was sold into slavery. The surviving Portuguese and many Muslim mercenaries were settled at villages in the interior and their descendants continued to serve in the artillery arm of the royal Burmese armies as late as the nineteenth century. Despite this episode, Anaukhpetlun was interested in maintaining the flow of trade and several diplomatic overtures were made to the Dutch and British, to Acheh, and even to Goa, but without any significant effect.

In Siam, the Portuguese opened diplomatic and commercial relations with Ayutthaya immediately after their occupation of Melaka, and were soon involved as mercenaries and military advisers to the armed forces of the kingdom, particularly regarding artillery. The leader of the Thai revival following the disaster of 1569 was the young crown prince Naresuan, who had spent his youth at the Burmese court and gained a reputation as a warrior fighting against rebels on its behalf, before he returned to Ayutthaya, becoming king in 1590. Until his death in 1605 Naresuan campaigned successfully against both the Burmese and Cambodians, regaining Chiengmai and capturing the ports of Tavoy and Tenasserim from the Burmese, thus gaining access to the Bay of Bengal. An important feature of his reign was the expansion of international trade, to the east with Taiwan, China, Japan, and the Ryukyu Islands, and to the west with Sumatra, India, and the Middle East. Deerskins, rice, forest products, and tin were the major exports, as well as elephants to the Indian courts. He developed a strong navy, even offering to defend the Ming from the invasion of Korea by Hideyoshi in 1592 that threatened China. The armed forces were strengthened by importing firearms from the Portuguese and steel swords and halberds from Japan. Siam was an important destination for the Japanese "Red Seal" ships, licensed to trade by the Tokugawa before their adoption of the seclusion policy in the 1630s. Reid (1999, p. 93) indicates that it received thirty-six of these ships in the period 1604–16, more than any other Southeast Asian destination (although Cambodia, Cochinchina, and Luzon in the Philippines were all important destinations as well).

In their prolonged struggles with each other, both the Thai and Burmese kingdoms relied extensively on Portuguese mercenaries, arquebuses, and cannon in addition to the traditional war-elephants, with the pachyderms also used as mounts for arquebusiers and "jingals" or small cannon.[7] Though evenly matched against each other, these regimes, with revenues from overseas trade and access to advanced military technology, were easily able to dominate their more backward hinterlands, so that the Age of Commerce was responsible for the creation of powerful centralized mainland states in both Burma and Siam. The link between Plenty and Power can be seen at work in Vietnam as well. As we saw in the previous chapter, Le Thanh Ton had captured the south in 1471, but the unified kingdom proved too difficult to hold together. A separation took place between the northern kingdom of Tongking, with its capital at Hanoi and ruled by the Trinh clan, and the southern segment of Cochinchina, with its capital at Hue and ruled by the rival Nguyen clan. The Le were still

[7]Lieberman (1980) provides an excellent account of the role of both firearms and of the Portuguese mercenaries in the Burmese conquests.

recognized as the rightful rulers of the entire kingdom by China, but were now reduced to being mere puppets of the Trinh.

Commercial influences were much more pronounced in Cochinchina, with the port of Hoi An (Faifo) becoming one of the busiest centers of international trade between 1570 and 1630, and particularly in the 1620s. This port was the main entrepôt for the exchange of Japanese and Chinese products for each other (because of the Ming ban on direct trade with Japan), and of both for Southeast Asian goods of all kinds. It was founded by Nguyen Hoang (1558–1613), one of the most imaginative and far-sighted leaders of his clan, to provide the economic base for the new Cochinchinese state by tolls on visiting ships. These revenues enabled the Nguyen to acquire cannon and other firearms from the Portuguese, helping them to prevail against the more populous Tongking state of their Trinh rivals, who despite being supported by the Dutch were much less inclined to depend on foreign trade (Li 1998).

Turning now to the islands, Portuguese rule over Melaka was not accepted as legitimate, either by Ming China or by the Muslim traders who used to frequent the port, and Melaka's trade was as we have seen dispersed to a number of new centers that emerged as a result. One such center was Bantam, whose location in northwestern Java not only gave it access to the abundant supplies of pepper from southeast Sumatra, but also control over shipping passing through the Sunda Straits. It could thus play a dual role, not only as an entrepôt between the Middle East and India in the west and the Spice Islands and China in the east, but also as a major source of pepper. The ruling sultans enjoyed substantial revenues by buying pepper cheap from the hinterlands and selling it dear in the port, as well as taxing the entrepôt trade. These revenues enabled them to maintain strong naval and land forces, and also to engage in extensive long-distance trade of their own in both the Indian Ocean and the South China Sea. The arrival of the Dutch and the English after 1600 increased the demand for pepper and other goods and thus should have benefited Bantam, but the VOC, while complaining loudly about the monopolistic practices of the sultan, used their naval power by blockades and other means to restore the balance. Coen, wanting to divert trade to Batavia, went so far as to seize Chinese junks sailing from Bantam, forcing them to resell their pepper at low prices and even kidnapping the crews to work on VOC plantations until restrained by headquarters in Amsterdam (Meilink-Roelofsz 1962, p. 253). Hostilities between Bantam and the Dutch were frequent, sometimes even threatening the security of Batavia. Sultan Abulfatah Agung (1651–83) was a particularly firm opponent of the

VOC, but the Dutch were able to intervene in a civil war that broke out between the sultan and his son to capture Bantam and reduce it to a dependency in 1683, installing the son as a puppet ruler (Ricklefs 1993, pp. 78–80). All other Europeans were banned from trading in Bantam and the English EIC had to move its operations to Bencoolen on the west coast of Sumatra.

The counterpart to Bantam in the eastern end of the Indonesian Archipelago was Makassar, on the southwestern limb of the island of Sulawesi (Celebes). This state was a composite body that fused together two distinct polities, a warlike agrarian kingdom, Gowa, and a small maritime trading principality, Tallo. The hinterland produced a surplus of rice that was exchanged for nutmeg, mace, and cloves at Melaka or the Spice Islands. These were in turn traded for cloth, porcelain, and other manufactured goods from China, India, and elsewhere. Much of this trade was in the hands of Muslim Malay merchants who had fled eastwards to avoid the pressure of the Portuguese and later the Dutch. They were welcomed by the local rulers and seemed to have enjoyed "extraterritorial" rights for their persons and property. There was also an extensive trade in slaves, with much of the demand coming from pepper plantations in Java and Sumatra. Makassar's location, midway between the Straits of Melaka and the Spice Islands, made it an entrepôt for such valuable goods as sandalwood from Timor and tortoiseshell and other marine products collected by the *orang laut* we encountered in chapter 3.

The trading opportunities attracted both European and Asian traders, all of whom were welcomed on an admirable "nondiscriminatory" basis by the remarkably tolerant locals. Weights and measures were standardized and a stable gold coinage issued. The fusion of the two component realms became particularly close in the 1590s when Matoaya, the king of Tallo, also became the chancellor or prime minister of the king of Gowa, who was his nephew. This remarkable man, whose career and achievements as well as those of his son are portrayed with great sympathy and insight by Anthony Reid (1999, chapters 6 and 7), was the architect of Makassar's golden age in the first half of the seventeenth century. Importuned by both Muslims and Christians to abandon the traditional animism of his people and convert to one or other of their respective "true faiths," Matoaya chose Islam in 1603, but of a particularly tolerant and eclectic kind, while his nephew would rule as Sultan Ala'uddin after his death. The people followed suit, not without some reluctance, but without any use of force by the rulers.

While these events were taking place, as we have seen the VOC was carrying out its genocidal policy in the Bandas and Moluccas and attempting to impose its monopoly on all trade in nutmeg, mace, and cloves. The only outlet for "smuggled" spices was Makassar, which thus grew in importance to the Portuguese and the English EIC, as well as to Asian traders. The English regarded their Makassar factory as "one of the especiallest flowers in our garden" (Kathirithamby-Wells and Villiers 1990, p. 151). When the Dutch demanded that Makassar cease all trade with the Spice Islands, Sultan Ala'uddin replied with a ringing statement of the principle of *Mare Liberum* that could not have been put better by Hugo Grotius himself:

> God made the land and the sea; the land he divided among men and the sea he gave them in common. It has never been heard that anyone should be forbidden to sail the sea. If you seek to do that you will take the bread from the mouths of people.

This open-door free trade policy naturally brought merchants from everywhere to Makassar, including Portuguese in increasing numbers as the Dutch threat to Melaka mounted. Despite their loyal adherence to Islam, the local rulers permitted the establishment of Christian churches in Makassar, which even became the headquarters of various monastic orders after the fall of Melaka to the Dutch in 1641. Matoaya had died in 1637 followed soon after by Sultan Ala'uddin, but the partnership was renewed in the next generation by Matoaya's son Pattingaloang as chancellor, and by Ala'uddin's son Sultan Mohammed Said. Pattingaloang was a truly extraordinary figure, fluent in Portuguese and with a knowledge of French and Spanish as well as Arabic and Malay. He was deeply interested in mathematics and Western science and technology. Not surprisingly in light of Dutch hostility he was anxious to acquire the latest weapons and techniques of fortification from the English and Portuguese. With this upgrading of their equipment added to their legendary warrior spirit, the Makassarese, "the fighting cocks of the east" as the Dutch called them, were very formidable enemies, even to European powers. The VOC, however, was relentless, realizing that the only way to achieve the long sought after monopoly of the spice trade would be by eliminating Makassar as an independent power. The Dutch therefore built an alliance with a disaffected Bugis warrior prince named Arung Palakka, who had come to Batavia with his followers after a failed rebellion in Sulawesi. In service with the VOC army in Java he apparently acquired great expertise not only in the use, but also in the manufacture of firearms. With his aid, the VOC conquered Makassar in two hard-fought campaigns in 1667 and 1669, deposing the sultan and expelling all their European competitors. Arung Palakka was installed as a king in southern Sulawesi, where he ruled autocratically until his death in 1696. The VOC spice monopoly in the eastern Archipelago was finally secure.

Another formidable militarized trading state that appeared in Southeast Asia during the Age of Commerce was Acheh in northern Sumatra. This state came into prominence just as the Portuguese entered the Straits and conquered Melaka. Sultan Alauddin Riayat Shah al-Kahar (1539–71) established Acheh as a major competitor to Melaka in the pepper trade, sending at least five large ships each year to the Red Sea carrying as much as the Portuguese were able to send by the Cape route (Reid 1975, p. 46). He also established diplomatic relations with the Ottoman Empire in 1567, obtaining technical assistance in the casting and use of heavy artillery, and threatening Melaka repeatedly. The commercial emporium of Bandar Acheh, better known to the world after the terrible tsunami of 2004, developed around his palace and was inhabited by traders from all over the Islamic and Southeast Asian worlds. Sultan Iskander Muda (1607–36) came close to achieving a complete royal monopoly of the pepper trade, expelling British and Dutch traders. He used his trade revenues to build up an extremely formidable military machine, including a fleet of huge war galleys each carrying 600–800 men and several cannon, an artillery park with several giant guns, cavalry and elephant corps, and large numbers of conscript infantry.

Iskander Muda waged war successfully on Johore, Pahang, Kedah, Perak, and other Malay states as well as strengthening his hold on the other ports in Sumatra. He was also successful against the Portuguese in a number of clashes on land and sea. His main objective was to drive the Portuguese out of Melaka and in 1629 he attacked it with several hundred ships, one of them a monster galley named "the Terror of the Universe" and carrying one hundred guns, which Reid (1993a, p. 233) claims to have been the largest wooden vessel ever built, and over 20,000 men. He besieged the city for three months from the landward side but the entire armada was captured or destroyed by a Portuguese relief squadron, supported by Malay allies from Johore and Patani, and most of the besieging troops were killed or captured. The defeat of Acheh by the Portuguese was a boon to the Dutch, who would otherwise have had to contend themselves with this formidable enemy. The year 1629 was thus a real turning point for VOC hegemony in Southeast Asia (ibid., p. 274), since this was also the year in which they decisively defeated Sultan Agung of Mataram. Twelve years later the Portuguese would lose Melaka to the Dutch, aided by the same Johore that had helped to save it from Iskander Muda, a nice lesson in Southeast Asian realpolitik.

TABLE 4.2. European clove imports, 1490–1657 (annual averages, tons).

| Year | Portuguese | | | Dutch and English | Muslim Routes |
	Official	Private	Total		
1490–99					50
1500–9	12	2	14		14
1510–19	11	4	15		3
1520–29	45	15	60		2
1530–39	33	11	44		6
1540–49	45	15	60		5
1550–59	40	15	55		10
1560–69	25	10	35		35
1570–79	30	10	40		35
1580–89	100	40	140		30
1590–99	80	30	110		30
1620–22	2	1	3	280	2
1638				290	0
1653–57	0	0	0	174	0

Source: Bulbeck et al. (1998, table 2.4, p. 32).

As we saw in the last chapter, the fifteenth century was a period of rapid trade expansion in Southeast Asia. All this changed abruptly with the Portuguese irruption and the fall of Melaka in 1511. As Reid (1990, p. 7) observes, "the period immediately following the European discovery of the sea route to Asia in 1498 ... was a very bad one in economic terms for the lands below the winds," since the Portuguese "began to sink or plunder every spice ship they encountered." Estimated annual average exports of cloves, nutmeg, and mace fell from 74, 37, and 17 tonnes respectively in 1496–99 to 38, 6, and 2.5 tonnes in 1503–5, a depression that lasted according to Reid for the first three decades of the sixteenth century. Subsequently, however, there was a revival of pepper and spice exports to the Red Sea by Gujarati merchants sailing from Acheh. By the 1560s the Red Sea shipments were exceeding those of the Portuguese, although both were expanding in absolute terms, with the customs revenue of Melaka, reflecting private and official Portuguese exports, doubling from 10 million *reals* annually in the 1540s to 20 million in the 1580s (ibid., p. 9). Table 4.2 shows that by the end of the sixteenth century total European clove imports were roughly three times as high as in the 1490s.

The Spanish capture of Manila in 1571 and the entry of the English and Dutch Companies onto the scene in the early 1600s led to the 1570–1630 period becoming the climax of the boom in the Southeast Asian spice trade. Intense competition between all three European

TABLE 4.3. Southeast Asian pepper exports, 1500–1659 (tons).

Year	Europe and Middle East	China	India, Japan, America	Total
1500–9	50	500	400	950
1510–19	100	500	400	1000
1520–29	200	500	400	1100
1530–39	300	500	500	1300
1540–49	600	500	600	1700
1550–59	700	500	700	1900
1560–69	1300	700	700	2700
1570–79	1300	900	800	3000
1580–89	1400	900	900	3200
1590–99	1400	1000	1000	3400
1600–9	2000	1000	1000	4000
1610–19	1500	1000	1000	3500
1620–29	1500	1200	1100	3800
1630–39	1400	1200	1200	3800
1640–49	2100	400	1300	3800
1650–59	2200	400	1400	4000

Source: Bulbeck et al. (1998, table 3.7, p. 86).

trading states resulted in relatively low prices for European consumers and a peak in European consumption levels of over 200 tonnes of cloves, 200 tonnes of nutmeg, and 70–80 tonnes of mace in the 1620s (ibid., p. 14). The successful VOC monopoly for nutmeg and mace thereafter restricted supplies and raised prices in Europe. The VOC was less successful in its attempt to monopolize the supply of cloves, but nevertheless was able to restrict supply in areas under its own control and destroy clove trees outside, doubling the price in Europe and trebling it in India. Table 4.2 shows that European clove imports rose very sharply between 1580 and 1638, before falling significantly in the 1650s. Pepper fetched only a fraction of the price of the fine Moluccan spices, but its much greater volume made it the major export commodity during Southeast Asia's Age of Commerce. As table 4.3 shows, total annual pepper exports from Southeast Asia roughly quadrupled between the first decades of the sixteenth and seventeenth centuries, with exports to China and "other regions" (i.e., India, Japan, and the Americas) roughly doubling, and exports to Europe and the Middle East simply exploding.

The boom was driven not only from the west by European demand and the influx of New World silver, but by strong demand from China and Japan as well. After 1567 the Ming permitted licensed trade with Southeast Asia, at a volume increasing from fifty large junks a year to over one hundred by the 1590s. The Japanese could exchange their silver for Chinese silk and locally produced deerskins and other forest products in Southeast Asian ports such as Manila, Ayutthaya, and Hoi An in Cochinchina, with 355 "vermilion seal" ships sailing there between 1604 and 1635, when they abruptly ceased with the introduction of the seclusion policy. Cochinchina received 87 of these ships, and Manila and Ayutthaya about 55 each (ibid., p. 10). This loosening of restrictions stimulated more Chinese trade and migration into the region, until the process was interrupted by the turbulence associated with the fall of the Ming in the middle of the seventeenth century. Wang Gungwu (2000, p. 29) considers that "the two decades from the 1620s to the fall of the Ming dynasty in 1644 marked the peak of free-ranging Chinese commercial activity in Southeast Asia before modern times." He gives three reasons for the extraordinary success of private Chinese traders, mainly Hokkiens from Fujian Province, during this period: first, the absence of strong control from the center due to the crises the Ming dynasty was facing; second, the withdrawal of Japanese competition due to the seclusion policy the Tokugawa adopted in 1635; and third, the conflict between the Dutch and their Iberian rivals that gave an opening to the Chinese.

The Cape Route, Venice, and the Middle East

We now turn to some of the economic implications of the European "Voyages of Discovery." As we have seen, an aim of the Iberian explorers had been to circumvent the Venetian and Muslim middlemen who had traditionally controlled European imports from Asia, and those middlemen were not slow in realizing the potential threat which da Gama's exploits posed to their interests. Thus, the Venetian ambassador in Cairo greeted the news with the statement that the opening of the Cape route was a "causa de grande ruina del Stato Veneto" (Magalhães-Godinho 1953, p. 283), while Girolamo Priuli wrote that the loss of the spice trade would be for Venice "like the loss of milk to a new-born babe" (Braudel 1975, p. 543). The fact that in the centuries that followed the economic center of gravity in Europe gradually shifted away from the Mediterranean might suggest that these observers were right, and that the Cape route did indeed deal a mortal blow to economic life in southeast Europe and the Middle East. However, historians have shown that on closer inspection the story is more complicated than this.

Following their conquest of Egypt in 1517, the Ottomans faced the same problem as their Mamluk predecessors of how to ensure that spices and raw silk would continue to flow through either the Red Sea or Basra, which the Ottomans took over in 1546, and not be diverted south around the Cape or north to Russia by the Volga route. With the Portuguese ensconced in Hormuz and the Ottomans in Basra, the entire length of the Persian Gulf became a bone of contention between them. Numerous violent battles were fought, on both land and sea, with inconclusive results, the Ottomans remaining secure in their control of the Red Sea but unable to dominate the Persian Gulf (Özbaran 1994, chapter 13). A war fleet was assembled at Suez, which was the main Ottoman naval base, and Aden and the Yemen were occupied to guard the entrance to the Red Sea from the Portuguese. Since Portuguese penetration of the Red Sea would have endangered the holy cities of Mecca and Medina, the Ottoman sultan had a religious duty as well as economic and political reasons to block any such attempt.

After their bitter inconclusive rivalry in the Persian Gulf, the Portuguese and Ottomans eventually found it to be in their mutual interest to cooperate (ibid.). The Portuguese permitted Indian spices, indigo, and cotton textiles to reach Basra, while Arabian horses were collected there for shipment to India through Hormuz. As a result, spices became increasingly available at Aleppo and Bursa, as well as at Tripoli and Beirut. Hence the position of Venice in the spice trade was restored by the middle of the century and continued to expand after that, a remarkable recovery indeed and due in large measure to the military prowess of its great Muslim ally. This of course did not prevent the Venetians and Ottomans from fighting each other on numerous occasions in the same century over such issues as Cyprus and Crete.

There is little doubt that had it not been for the Ottoman intervention, the Portuguese attempt at a spice monopoly would have been successful. As pointed out earlier, the emergence of Acheh as a source for Indonesian spices, and the active Gujarati merchant shipping, also helped revive the Red Sea route, and with it the fortunes of Venice and the Ottoman Empire. We have already seen that the Ottomans sent technical and military assistance to the sultan of Acheh, helping him to threaten Portuguese Melaka. An Ottoman naval assault at Diu in Gujarat in 1538 had to be called off but alarmed the Portuguese, as did the seizure of Basra. Fortunately for them, other conflicts in the Mediterranean diverted Ottoman resources away from the Indian Ocean at this critical time. The military alliance with Acheh eventually faded after the Ottoman naval defeat at Lepanto in 1571 and the death of the sultan of Acheh a few years later, but the spices continued to flow into the Red Sea.

Venice thus initially survived the discovery of the Cape Route (Lane 1933, 1940). Does this resilience of the old trade routes imply that the Portuguese discovery of the Cape route had no impact on European spice markets during the sixteenth century? Lane (1968, p. 597) argued that not only did the Cape route not displace Venice, it did not even lead to lower spice prices in Europe. Rather, it led to higher spice prices, presumably because of the increasing costs which Portuguese predation in the Indian Ocean implied for merchants operating there (which would be consistent with the dip in European imports immediately after 1500). O'Rourke and Williamson (forthcoming) show that this argument is incorrect, in that it relies on nominal spice prices, which were rising along with all other European prices as a result (as we shall see) of the influx of New World silver. As they show, *real* (i.e., grain-deflated) pepper prices fell sharply across Europe during the sixteenth century, following (as we saw in the previous chapter) a century during which they had been on the rise throughout northern Europe. Moreover, real prices fell for cinnamon, cloves, ginger, incense, and mace as well as for pepper. The Cape route did, therefore, help to integrate European and Asian markets, and presumably the fact that the Venetians and Ottomans fought their way back into the spice trade in the late sixteenth century can only have strengthened this integration, since it would have increased competition, lowered profit margins, and brought European prices even closer to Asian levels (ibid.).

Moreover, one can argue that the Cape route also helped to increase market integration *within* Europe, by overturning old monopolies and increasing competition. In the fifteenth century, German merchants wishing to buy Asian goods from Venice had to do so in Venice itself, where they were obliged to stay in the *Fondaco dei Tedeschi* and buy and sell under the supervision of the Venetian government. By contrast, beginning in 1501 the Portuguese began to dispose of their "Atlantic" pepper in Antwerp. The Fuggers and other prominent German merchant houses switched their orders to Antwerp from Venice, with Lyons serving as a subsidiary distribution center, and Kristof Glamann (1974) states that pepper prices in Antwerp fell to their lowest point in the second decade of the sixteenth century. The Portuguese initially operated the pepper market as a royal monopoly with the annual supplies sold "*en bloc* or in large lots for the king's account" (ibid., p. 486), but in 1577 they reorganized their policy, permitting private contractors to bid for the right to participate in the market. Konrad Rot, an Augsburg merchant, attempted to put together a consortium involving the rulers of Saxony and Denmark, among others, to bid for these rights and thus monopolize the entire market for Portuguese pepper, but was unable to secure the necessary funds to fulfill the ambitious scheme. Another even more ambitious project, to jointly monopolize both the Portuguese and Venetian supplies, was broached on separate occasions by each of the parties to the other but never came to fruition, "a dream never realized but nonetheless pursued in the sixteenth century" (ibid., p. 486). The net result was that overall competition remained higher than it had been prior to da Gama's voyages.

It was not the Portuguese, but the Dutch and English who finally put paid to Venice's traditional preeminence in the spice trade. By the 1620s Amsterdam, followed by London, had displaced Antwerp as the main source of pepper for Western Europe. According to Wake (1979, p. 389), "a new level of prices now ruled on the European market. In terms of silver prices this was approximately 30% to 40% below the import price maintained by the Portuguese in the preceding century. This was sufficient to end the Levantine trade of the Venetians and other Mediterranean importers." The competition between the VOC and the English East India Company in pepper was the main factor driving prices down and consumption up in European markets. The Dutch and English companies were engaged in a fiercely competitive non-zero-sum game, each attempting to gain market share at the other's expense by increasing supplies. As Douglas Irwin (1991) has shown, the VOC was facilitated in this by its incentive mechanisms, which led decision makers to maximize revenue rather than profits, implying that they were willing to supply greater quantities than their British counterparts. In the process, however, both sides drove pepper prices down to below 60 florins per 100 Dutch pounds by the 1650s (Glamann 1974, p. 484), and prices only rarely rose above this level for the rest of the century and beyond. Despite the Anglo-Dutch competition, Wake maintains that the Portuguese, unlike the Venetians and other Mediterranean suppliers, were able to continue actively in both the pepper trade and increasingly also even in the fine spice trade. This of course increased still further the competitive pressures in these markets.

Our focus on competition receives indirect support from the evidence for those fine spices, namely cloves, nutmeg, and mace, for which competition was less intense. As we have seen, unlike the case of pepper, where the sources of supply were so diversified that buyers

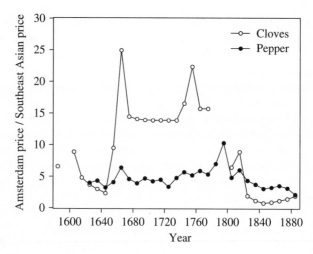

FIGURE 4.6. Spice markups, Amsterdam versus Southeast Asia, 1580–1890 (Amsterdam price / Southeast Asian price). *Source:* Bulbeck et al. (1998).

had to pay a competitive price, the VOC could sustain monopsonistic control in the Moluccas for nutmeg and mace.[8] The picture that emerges from Glamann's (1958, chapter V) summary of this policy is one of profit-maximizing price discrimination between the Asian and European markets: as he says (p. 93), "by controlling the islands the Company could fix an arbitrarily low price of delivery, so that the gross profit from the spices became overwhelming, often more than 1000%."

Figure 4.6 shows the dramatic effects of this monopsony policy. In the 1580s, when Asian spices still reached Amsterdam via the Portuguese (or via the traditional Levantine overland routes), clove prices were six and a half times higher in Amsterdam than in Southeast Asia. The margin was almost nine during the first decade of the seventeenth century, immediately following the establishment of the VOC, but it then slipped in subsequent decades to between two and five. Establishment of full control over the sources of supply had an immediate effect on the VOC's profits: the price margin rose to 9.5 in the 1650s, and an extraordinary 25 in the 1660s, before falling back to an equilibrium level of around 14 or 15, which was to last more or less unchanged until the 1770s. The contrast with pepper is striking:

[8]Monopsony: a state of the market in which there is effectively a single buyer or consumer for a particular product, who is therefore in a position to influence its price; a consumer in this position (Oxford English Dictionary).

margins for this spice lay between 3 and 4 until well into the nineteenth century, barring occasional rises during times of warfare. This was almost exactly the same as the margins realized for cloves after the establishment of the VOC as a serious competitor in the Asian trade, but before it succeeded in controlling clove supplies at their source (that is, during the 1610s through the 1640s). The importance of market structure emerges clearly from these data.

Another important economic link between Venice and the Ottoman Empire was the sale of high-quality Venetian woolen cloth to the latter. In the course of the seventeenth century, however, the Dutch and English, yet again, displaced Venice and other Italian producers in the Levantine markets for these key manufactured goods. Charles Wilson (1960, p. 212) pithily accounts for this by observing that "the Turks wanted cheap, light cloths. The Venetians offered dear, heavy ones." Constricted by guild regulations, Venice insisted on maintaining high quality and high prices. Meanwhile, northerners lowered quality and price and also resorted to such unscrupulous devices as smuggling and counterfeiting by putting Venetian markings on their own cheaper products, practices that are still familiar today (Rapp 1975). According to Rapp, "it was the invasion of the Mediterranean, not the exploitation of the Atlantic, that produced the Golden Ages of Amsterdam and London" (p. 501), while he attributes the success of the English to "a sort of revolution in marketing" that provided the Levantine consumers with what looked like fine woolen cloth, but which was much cheaper as a result of the inferior quality and quantity of raw material inputs.

This "invasion" of the northern powers into the trade and navigation of the eastern Mediterranean had as a political and diplomatic background their common enmity, with the Ottomans, to the great Catholic power of Spain and the Habsburgs, who were allied with the papacy. After their defeat in 1571 at Lepanto, the Ottomans were anxious for the support of the Protestant English and Dutch, both strong naval powers threatened by the common enemy Philip II. A trade agreement or "capitulation" of 1580 gave the English the right to trade freely in Ottoman ports for a payment of only 3% customs duty, instead of the customary 5% that the Venetians and French had to pay. The Levant Company, formed by a group of English "Barbary merchants," provided the framework under which England exported its woolen cloth not only to Ottoman markets but further east as well, in exchange for imports of raw silk, wine, and currants. Another key English export was war materials such as tin, lead, and steel as well as arms. In addition to depriving Venice of its market for high-quality woolen cloth, the English also replaced her in the Mediterranean carrying trade for the Ottoman Empire. The Dutch entry into the Levant trade followed the English pattern with a lag, with their corresponding capitulation secured in 1612, and with a similar structure of exports and imports. According to Israel (1989, pp. 149–56) the Dutch trade in the Mediterranean entered a severe decline after the resumption of hostilities with Spain in 1621, but eventually revived and flourished after the end of the war in 1648.

Bob Allen (2003a) has recently provided econometric evidence suggesting that Venice's loss was indeed England's gain, and that the growth of productivity in these "new draperies" was a major factor in English economic success during the early modern period. "It provided a strong boost to urbanization, and the growth of rural industry. Through these effects, the success of the new draperies was responsible for a large proportion of the growth in TFP in agriculture as farmers successfully responded to the greater demand for food, wool and labour. Without [this] seventeenth century success, wages, agricultural productivity, and city size would all have been lower in 1800" (ibid., p. 431).[9]

The main industrial sector of the Ottoman economy was silk. The town of Bursa, located just to the south of the Sea of Marmara, had long been both a manufacturing center for silk fabrics and an emporium where Western manufactured goods of all kinds, but particularly woolen cloth, were exchanged for Persian raw silk as well as spices and other Indian goods. Inalcik (1994, p. 227) states that there were about one thousand silk looms operating in Bursa around 1500, weaving about 36 tons of raw silk annually, while at least six caravans a year brought about 120 tonnes of raw silk from the east. This implies that around two-thirds of the raw silk arriving at Bursa was destined for Europe. The "vertical" interdependence between the Safavid and Ottoman economies created by the silk trade was a temptation to each party to conduct economic warfare against the other by declaring either an import or an export embargo. Selim the Grim caused havoc in his own domains and in Italy with an import embargo that was eventually lifted by his son Suleyman when he came to power in 1520. At the other end, Shah Abbas the Great imposed an export monopoly, hoping to divert supplies away from the overland routes and toward the Cape, but he was similarly unsuccessful, his successor and grandson Shah Safi restoring open trade in 1629.

[9]The Encyclopaedia Britannica defines econometrics as "the statistical and mathematical analysis of economic relationships." Total factor productivity, or TFP, is a measure of the level of technology in a sector or country.

Bursa serviced important north–south trade routes as well as the more familiar east–west ones. Eastern goods were sent overland from Bursa to Brasov on the border between Wallachia and Transylvania, and from the ports of Akkerman and Kilia on the northern shore of the Black Sea to Lwów in eastern Poland by Ottoman and Balkan merchants, from where they were passed on to northern Europe. Rich silk brocades from Bursa were apparently the favored clothing of the Polish and even Swedish elites during these times. In return woolen cloth, metalware, and other European manufactures were sent in the opposite direction. These trade links notwithstanding, Poland and the Ottomans competed fiercely for control over the region between the Dnieper and the Dniester, with the Christian rulers of Moldavia caught in between the two great powers.

The old Genoese trading center of Kaffa continued to be important under the Ottomans, serving in particular to link Istanbul with the rising power of Muscovy, the major source of furs that were much in demand by the court. The Black Sea during this period was very much an Ottoman lake, much more so than it had been a Byzantine one, since the Ottomans did not permit the Genoese or other powers to fortify their trading settlements. The provisioning of Istanbul required grain, fish, and livestock exports in abundance from the Crimea, and the slave trade was also very important. The nomadic tribes of the Crimean steppes found slave raiding on the settled populations of Poland, Russia, and the Circassian region such a profitable supplement to the raising of livestock that Inalcik (1994, p. 284) says it became the mainstay of their economy, with at least 10,000 slaves being exported every year during the entire 1500–1650 period. Anatolian exports to balance these imports consisted of primary products such as wine, nuts, and fruit, but locally produced coarse cotton textiles were another major item, displaying the complementarity of the northern and southern shores of the Black Sea. Despite these many other activities, the reexport of Indian spices, particularly pepper, continued to be a mainstay of the trade. As Inalcik (p. 343) observes, "geographic and economic conditions, transport costs in particular, resulted in a separate zone for spice on a line east of Vienna and Italy." Thus, while the Cape route could serve the needs of Western Europe, there was a vast zone in Eastern and central Europe, the Balkans, and the Ottoman domains that remained, the needs of which were met by the Levant trade.

The Islamic World in these times exhibited once again, as in the original Golden Age of Islam, a high degree of international factor mobility within the common cultural framework of Islamic law and religion. Persian poets graced the courts not only of the Safavids, but even more those of the great Mughals (Savory 1980). Turkish merchants had colonies in distant Sumatra as well as the ports of Gujarat, while Indian merchants and bankers could be found in Iran, Turkey, and even Russia. Ottoman mercenaries and military experts moved all over the Islamic World, diffusing their knowledge of firearms and how to use them. Architecture, painting, ceramics, and the decorative arts were all enriched by cross-cultural contacts, not only within the Islamic World but across the great religious divides as well.

SILVER, SILK, AND SPICES

While a key impulse leading to the international integration of the sixteenth and seventeenth centuries was the lure of the spice trade, it was the flood of silver released around the globe by the mines of the New World that was the lifeblood of the "circulatory system" of the world economy, as Fernand Braudel (1975, p. 569) has called it, with "a steady flow of gold and silver coins of every description, traveling from west to east, following the rotation of the Earth, carrying along with them a wide range of commodities as a kind of supplementary currency, and loosing in the opposite direction a rich and varied stream of different commodities and precious goods from east to west." This silver chain that girdled the globe had many individual links, each of which deserves to be noted and examined in its own right.

Starting in Western Europe with the Baltic trade, there was a persistent deficit in the exchange of Western wine, cloth, and other manufactures for imports of eastern primary products such as grain, timber, and furs, which was settled with silver obtained increasingly from the Americas. This silver in turn tended to be drained further to the east in exchange for Persian silk and other luxury products from the Middle East. The Levant trade of Europe through the Mediterranean also resulted in an outflow of silver to purchase Eastern spices through the Red Sea and the Persian Gulf. Finally, the Cape Route, initiated by the Portuguese but subsequently used by all the European trading nations, resulted in a further outflow of silver in exchange for spices, silk, and cotton textiles. American silver also reached Asia directly via Manila, as we have seen, where it was exchanged for silk and other luxury Chinese goods, while Japan was another major source of silver, which was again exchanged largely for Chinese silk through the intermediation of European traders.

What were the amounts of silver involved in these flows? Not surprisingly, there is much debate about the absolute and even relative magnitudes of the various flows, but recent scholarship has helped to clarify several key issues. We turn first to what was unquestionably the largest flow of silver during the early modern period, that between the Americas and Europe. Barrett (1990) gives figures for American silver production of 17,000 tonnes for the sixteenth century, 34,000 for the seventeenth, and 51,000 for the eighteenth. Of this total, around 85% was shipped to Europe in the first three-quarters of the sixteenth century, but the share fell to between 70% and 75% between 1576 and 1775. Thus, there was an annual average import into Europe from the Americas of 205 tonnes of silver and equivalent in the period 1551–1600, 245 tonnes for 1601–25, and 290 tonnes for 1626–50.

Of these amounts, Barrett's data give 100 and 125 tonnes being reexported from Europe during 1601–25 and 1626–50 respectively, while 145 and 165 tonnes, or 59% and 57%, were retained within Europe. Barrett's European export data are largely based on the work of Artur Attman, and the figures have been criticized by Pearson (2001) for underestimating European reexports, and consequently overstating the extent to which American silver was retained within Europe. As Pearson notes, Attman himself described his European export figures as "very conservative" (Attman 1986, p. 115). On the other hand, even allowing for such biases it would seem difficult to sustain the claim that Europe merely played an intermediary role in the world silver trade, importing it from America and promptly reexporting it all again. European demand for silver, if only to provide the liquidity necessary to accompany its not inconsiderable economic growth during this period, seems to have been important in its own right.

Europe is not the only "sink" for silver during this period that has often been overlooked. Figure 4.4 indicated a growing gap between New World silver production and silver exports after the middle of the sixteenth century, suggesting that increasing amounts of silver were being used to support growing American economies as well. Corresponding to this was increasing interregional transfers within the Spanish Empire, all of which is, as Grafe and Irigoin (2006) point out, at odds with caricatures of a predatory and absolutist Spanish state ruthlessly siphoning resources from its colonies.

Flows from America to the Philippines amounted to around 17 tonnes per annum during the first half of the seventeenth century, if TePaske (1983, reproduced in Barrett 1990, p. 251) is to be believed, to 38 tons per annum according to von Glahn (1996a, p. 438), or to as much as 50 tons per annum according to Flynn and Giráldez (1995). Another major source of silver was, as we have seen, Japan, which was a major producer during this period, particularly during the years from 1560 to 1640. A technological innovation introduced from Korea, the so-called "ash-blowing" process for separating silver from lead after smelting, increased output dramatically at mines in the western Iwami province of Japan and became widely adopted according to Yamamura and Kamiki (1983). They note, interestingly, that the mercury amalgam process used at Potosí was known to the Japanese as a result of contact with Spanish missionaries, but was not employed because of the local unavailability of mercury.

Panel (a) of table 4.4 gives von Glahn's (1996b, pp. 133–41) figures for Chinese silver imports in the late sixteenth and early seventeenth centuries (converted into annual averages), as well as the earlier estimates of Yamamura and Kamiki (1983). Three sources of supply are distinguished: Japan, the New World (via the Philippines), and Europe (via India). As can be seen, the big difference between the two sets of estimates is the relative role of Japanese supply during 1600–45, with the Yamamura–Kamiki estimates implying that the vast majority of Chinese imports were supplied from Japan in the first half of the seventeenth century. As Pearson (2001, p. 38) notes, if these figures are to be believed, then for the eighty years from 1560 to 1640 Japanese silver exports to China would represent 36% of New World production, a very high proportion indeed. We therefore tend to side with von Glahn's estimates, as do other authorities such as de Vries (2003). These show Japan supplying somewhere around one-half of Chinese imports between 1550 and 1645, with the figure being closer to 60% in the late sixteenth century. The New World supplied between one-quarter and one-third of China's silver requirements, and about one-sixth came from Europe via India, on the assumption that about one-half of the silver which was exported from Europe to India was eventually passed on to China (von Glahn 1996b, p. 135). For the period 1600–45, the last years of the Ming dynasty before it was overthrown by the Manchus, von Glahn estimates annual Chinese silver imports of about 111 tonnes a year, more than twice as high as in the earlier period. Taking the two periods together, China imported 7,300 tonnes of silver from all sources, a truly massive figure.

Why did China import so much silver? The proximate answer is that the very high value placed on silver relative to gold in China, noted by many contemporary commentators, could imply a ratio as low as 5:1 for the relative price of the same weight of the two metals, whereas it was around 12:1 in Europe. Naturally, this led to silver flowing to China.

TABLE 4.4. Chinese and Indian silver imports, 1550–1645
(annual averages, tonnes).

(a) Chinese imports

Source and carriers	1550–1600	1601–45
Japan		
Portuguese	14.8–18.4	14.4
Chinese	9.0	13.3
"Vermillion-seal"	0.0	18.7
Dutch	0.0	7.6
Smugglers	?	?
Subtotal	23.8–27.4+	54.0
(Yamamura–Kamiki estimate)	27.0–39.0	133.3–166.7
New World/Philippines		
Chinese	11.7	13.8
Portuguese	0.0	1.7
Smugglers	?	22.9
Subtotal	11.7	38.3
(Yamamura–Kamiki estimate)	8.4	20.0
Indian Ocean/Europe	7.6	18.9
Total	43.1–46.7+	111.3+
(Yamamura–Kamiki estimate)	35.4–47.4	153.3–186.7

(b) Indian imports

Source	1588–1602	1630–45	1679–85
Persian Gulf	27.8	25	30
Isfahan–Agra	10	5	10
Red Sea	75	40	56
Portuguese	11.2	3	0
English	0	5.2	25.1
Dutch	0	6.6	9.7
Total	124	84.8	130.8

Source: von Glahn (1996b, table 13, p. 140) and Haider (1996, table 9, p. 323).

At a deeper level, the high price of silver in China was due to the very limited local production and a strong demand for silver bullion as a medium of exchange and tax payments, due to the collapse of the paper currency and the bronze coinage of the Ming dynasty (Flynn and Giráldez 1995). This caused the private sector and the government itself to rely increasingly on silver bullion for all transactions, and scarce local supply in turn implied that the silver had mostly to be imported. The rising Chinese demand for silver coincided with rising supply in the Americas and Japan, with large-scale trade being the inevitable result.

The Chinese dependence on foreign sources of silver has led some prominent scholars to assert that it was a sudden, sharp, and exogenous decline in silver imports that was responsible for the collapse of the Ming dynasty in 1644, and its replacement by the Manchu Qing dynasty that lasted until 1911 (Adshead 1973; Atwell 1982, 1986; Wakeman 1986). In this version of events the fall of the Ming was a result of the global "seventeenth-century crisis" that we have already encountered. A crude summary of the argument is that the regime had become so dependent on silver imports as the basis of its monetary and fiscal system that the sudden fall in imports due to the Tokugawa expulsion of the Portuguese and the ban on licensed Japanese exports to China, and concomitant interruptions of the flow of New World silver to Manila, led to a serious fiscal crisis. Declines in revenue and hence military expenditures, as well as rural discontent with the measures designed to compensate for the revenue shortfall, enabled the Manchus to overthrow the Ming. At the theoretical level the thesis suffers from the usual fallacy that historians attempting to use the quantity theory of money have been all too prone to, namely confusing the role of the *stock* of money as the key determinant of the price level and nominal income, with the *flow* of silver imports that is merely the increment in this stock. The thesis that it was a shortage of silver that led to the fall of the Ming has been convincingly refuted, at the most basic empirical level, by Maloughney and Xia (1989) and von Glahn (1996a,b). There was *no* decline in total silver imports before 1644, since the Portuguese expulsion from Nagasaki was fully compensated for by increases in imports by the Dutch and native Chinese traders, while in the case of Manila unofficial supplies more than made up for the decline in officially sanctioned shipments.

Apart from China, the other great Asian sink for American silver in this period was Mughal India. Najaf Haider (1996, table 9, p. 323) provides a valuable quantitative analysis of the sources of the Mughal Empire's silver imports, reproduced in table 4.4(b). Due to the scarcity of data, he gives detailed estimates only for three subperiods, 1588–1602, 1630–45, and 1679–85. For the first interval he estimates an annual inflow of 124 tonnes, of which more than half came from the Red Sea, bringing silver from Ottoman and Safavid territories, while almost one-quarter came from the Persian Gulf (two-thirds of the approximately 42 tonnes exported from the port of Hormuz annually).

The remainder came via the overland route from Iran to Agra through Kandahar, and via the Cape Route courtesy of the Portuguese. Imports were around one-third lower during the next subperiod, 1630–45, with the Red Sea flow almost halving. By 1679–85 there was a recovery to an annual average inflow of 130.8 tonnes, with the share transported by the Dutch and English Companies rising substantially, while the Portuguese dropped out. Thus, it would appear that the Mughal Empire imported on the order of 100 tonnes of silver per annum during this period, although the amount fluctuated considerably. India's gross imports were thus substantially larger than China's in the late sixteenth century, and the same order of magnitude as China's in the early seventeenth century. It is important, however, to stress that these Indian import figures are gross, since Indian silver was also shipped further east, ending up in China.

Figure 4.7 summarizes the current state of knowledge on intercontinental silver flows, as expertly surveyed by Jan de Vries (2003). The figure reproduces his two flow diagrams giving production, trade, and absorption of precious metals in two periods, 1600–50 and 1725–50. He accepts Barrett's figures for American production and exports to Europe, Attman's data for European exports (which as we have seen may be an underestimate), and von Glahn's estimates of Japanese silver exports. He remains agnostic, on the other hand, about the relative merits of the estimates by TePaske and by Flynn and Giráldez of flows via the Philippines. The data for South and East Asian absorption are calculated as being equal to the sum of the flows from Japan, from the Philippines, and from Europe via the Cape route, and are equal to between 91 and 126 tonnes per annum during 1600–50.[10]

As can be seen from the figure, during the first half of the seventeenth century flows around the Cape constituted a comparatively small share of total flows, amounting to less than 6% of European imports from America, or just 4% of American production. Flows of silver from Western Europe to the Levant were more than twice as high, and flows to the Baltic were more than three times as high. Silver flows around the Cape were also lower than the direct exports of silver to Manila, less than one-third the size if the Flynn and Giráldez estimate is accepted. This is all consistent with the late-sixteenth-century revival of the old overland trade routes that we highlighted earlier. The figure also shows the extent to which European trade with China was facilitated by Japanese silver: Japanese silver flows to China were nearly four times

[10] Note, however, that if the Indian data in table 4.4 are correct, South and East Asian absorption must have been much greater than this.

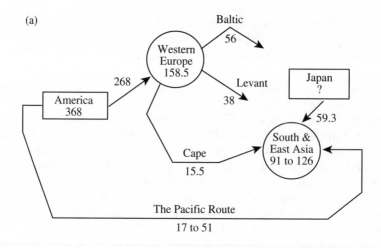

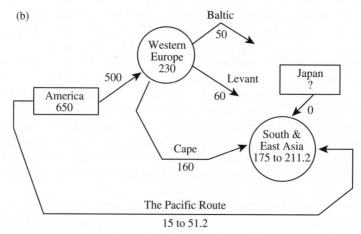

FIGURE 4.7. Intercontinental silver flows, early seventeenth and eighteenth centuries (kilograms per annum): (a) 1600–50; (b) 1725–50. *Source:* de Vries (2003, figure 2.3a,b). Note: the figures in rectangles (exporting regions) represent production, while the figures in circles (importing regions) represent domestic absorption.

as large as European exports via the Cape. As de Vries (2003, p. 82) puts it, "a commitment to intra-Asian trading achieved major economies in the European 'specie cost' of Asian goods."

The figure also shows that by the second quarter of the eighteenth century, when the Cape route was at its peak, the simple-minded view of American silver being shipped first to Europe, and then to Asia via the Cape, was much closer to being true than during the seventeenth century. By that time three-quarters of American silver was being shipped to Europe. Of that total, almost one-third was shipped to Asia via the Cape, or almost 50% more than was exported from Western Europe to the Baltic and Levant combined. It was in this period that the great European trading companies most clearly dominated Europe– Asian trade, to such an extent that they had become South and East Asia's major source of silver (flows via Manila having remained roughly constant since the early seventeenth century, and flows from Japan having dried up altogether).

What were the economic effects of these enormous silver flows? We want to distinguish here between the effects at the western and eastern ends of the Eurasian landmass. As the preceding discussion has made clear, there was a crucial difference between the nature of silver imports in the two regions. In Western Europe, silver imports can essentially be viewed as an exogenous shock, boosting the local silver supply and hence the local money supply. In East Asia, on the other hand, silver imports were an endogenous response to price differentials, and might therefore be expected to have had quite different economic effects. In what follows we explore the economic consequences of New World silver, first for Europe, next for the main importing regions (China and India), and finally for the intermediate zone comprised of the Ottoman and Persian Empires, as well as Russia.

In Europe, and especially in Iberia, where the shock first hit, the predictable effect of New World silver imports was to lower the relative price of silver, or in other words to raise the general price level. According to the monetary approach to the balance of payments, the process should have worked as follows (Flynn 1996, chapter 1). First, the Iberian money supply increased exogenously, boosting Iberian consumer prices. Next, cross-border trade in goods should have led to prices elsewhere in Western Europe, and particularly in neighboring states, increasing. Finally, this price increase should have raised nominal incomes elsewhere, in the process raising nominal money demand and provoking silver imports from Iberia (since in this model money always flows to where it is demanded). In a modern globalized world in which commodity markets are perfectly integrated, this process of inflation transmission should have occurred rapidly, and price levels should have remained roughly equal across Europe. In the context of early modern Europe, in which goods markets were indeed linked with each other, but in which trade was still extremely costly, the process should have taken longer, and substantial and persistent dis- equilibrium price gaps might be expected to have opened up between

Iberia and more remote regions. Douglas Fisher (1989) finds plausible econometric evidence linking European price increases in this period to the inflow of New World silver, via the monetary approach to the balance of payments mechanism outlined above.

In East Asia, on the other hand, silver flowed into the economy endogenously, to satisfy a growing demand for silver that was linked in China to the use of silver bullion as the main medium of exchange. This demand was presumably strengthened by the demographic impact of the "Magellan Exchange," which as we have seen led to a sixteenth-century Chinese population boom, and thus to an expanding economy and an increased demand for money. Finally, the sixteenth century saw "rapid advances in the commercialization of China's domestic economy" (von Glahn 1996b, p. 142), which also required additional money supplies. The role of the imported silver was thus to provide liquidity for an expanding real economy; in terms of the well-known Cambridge version of the quantity theory, where the money supply M is equal to kPY, the rise in M was induced by a growing income Y, rather than being an exogenous phenomenon, and insofar as the rising money supply had anything more than a passive or facilitating role in the economy, it was presumably to boost k, the index of the degree to which the economy was "monetized," along with Y, rather than prices P. Indeed, there is not much evidence of a rising price level in China during the period; while rice prices drifted very slowly upwards during the sixteenth century, land prices seem to have declined (although rice prices did increase substantially during the early seventeenth century, before declining again after 1660 or so) (von Glahn 1996b, pp. 158–59, 242).

As in China, silver was largely used in India for monetary purposes. According to Irfan Habib (1982, p. 360), "the Mughal Empire could well boast of one of the finest coined currencies of the contemporary world, a trimetallic currency of great uniformity and purity, with the silver rupee as the basic coin." Gold coins were rare and used mostly for ceremonial purposes, while copper coins were used for smaller transactions. Silver could be coined freely at the numerous Mughal mints on payment of a small fee, and the value of the rupee had a slight premium over its silver content, reflecting confidence in its purity. Since India had no domestic sources of silver supply during this period, it is assumed that imports were the only basis for the coinage. It is also believed that virtually all of the imported silver was coined, with only gold being hoarded in bullion form. During the reign of Akbar (1556–1605) silver replaced copper currencies in importance in urban and later even in rural areas, being used by the state to pay officials and military officers (rather than grants of land), while at the same time land revenues were also required to be paid in cash rather than in kind (Moosvi 1987). Silver was thus the basis for a notably increased monetization of the Mughal economy. This monetization undoubtedly reflected the increasing economic integration of the empire, particularly of the trade-oriented western coastal region with the agrarian hinterland of the center and the north.

In a pioneering study Aziza Hasan (1969) used the Mughal coins surviving in the collections of major museums as the basis for estimating an index of currency output. Hasan's index triples from ca. 1590 to 1640, after which it declines until ca. 1685, but it is still double the 1590 level at that point. An important objective of her research was to examine whether any evidence could be found of links with the inflow of American silver into Europe. Comparing the movements of her index with Hamilton's figures for silver imports into Spain, she finds a close correspondence, with a lag of some ten to twenty years, "so regularly indeed that the fluctuations in the volume of silver imports into Spain could be faithfully reflected in the Indian imports of silver and the currency output of Mughal mints." In an important subsequent contribution, Shireen Moosvi (1987) confirmed the rise in currency output, and calculated that while French annual output of coined silver was about 75 tonnes in the 1631–60 period, the Mughal annual average from 1556–1705 was double that at about 152 tonnes, not at all unreasonably high in light of the fact that the Indian population was about 130 million, as compared with about 20 million for France.

Thus far, we have seen that silver had very different effects in Europe, China, and India. In Europe, it led to inflation, while in South and East Asia it sustained growing and increasingly monetized and commercialized economies. But what of the regions that lay in between, and through which the silver passed along the traditional trade routes between Europe and Asia? Did the silver lead to inflation, did it facilitate commercialization, or did it merely transit these territories, leaving no particular mark on their economies? We conclude this section by looking at three key intermediaries: Persia, the Ottoman Empire, and Russia.

The role of Iran in the world economy during this period is particularly interesting. The Safavid dynasty was established by the youthful and charismatic Shah Ismail (1501–24) at the outset of the period and reached its zenith under Shah Abbas I (1588–1629). It was the Safavids who firmly established the Shia branch of Islam in Iran, and created the foundations of the modern Iranian state and nation after centuries of domination by Arab, Mongol, and Turkic rulers. Iran's central location, along the major east–west and north–south trade routes of western Eurasia, meant that it was a crossroads for the flow of goods and precious metals in all directions. Locally produced raw silk supplied not only Persian requirements for the weaving of brocade and taffeta, but also, as we have seen, the needs of the flourishing silk industries of Turkey and Italy. This gave Iran a favorable balance of trade with the west that was partly drained by its deficit with India and the East Indies arising from imports of cotton textiles, indigo, sugar, and spices, despite the lucrative export of cavalry horses, dyestuffs for the Indian cotton textile industry, and a wide variety of nuts, fruits, and other processed foods. This persistent feature of Iranian trade, a trade surplus in the west partly offset by a deficit in the east, led to a famous description of it by a prominent European resident in Isfahan in 1660, the French cleric Raphael du Mans, as quoted by Haider (2002, p. 197):

> Persia is like a big caravanserai which has only two doors, the one on the side of Turkey by which silver from the west enters... the other door of exit is Bandar Abbas or Gombroon in the Persian Gulf for going to the Indies, to Surat, where all the silver of the world unloads, and from there as if fallen into an abyss, it does not re-emerge.

However, the fact that Persia ran a trade surplus in the mid seventeenth century (Ferrier 1986, p. 489) suggests that at least some of the silver that entered the empire was retained domestically.

The economy of Iran, particularly during the reign of Shah Abbas, was an interesting blend of market forces, reflecting the activities of a sophisticated merchant class of native Persians, Indians, and most prominently Armenians, within a framework of vigorous and extensive state intervention motivated by the thirst for revenue and a strong mercantilist desire for the enhancement of national wealth and power (Matthee 1999, chapter 3). The Armenian merchant community of Julfa was resettled in a special quarter, known as "New Julfa," of the magnificent new capital of Isfahan and given extensive privileges in return for their services to the state in the commercial, financial, and diplomatic spheres, a role that continued well into modern times. What we would now call "import substitution" projects were undertaken by Shah Abbas for the production of indigo, cotton, and rice, and he even attempted to halt the drain of specie for pilgrimages to Mecca, in Ottoman territory, by developing a competing Shia site for the veneration of Imam Reza at Mashad. Royal factories for the production of silk and other textiles were established in most major towns, and measures were taken to improve the transport and communications infrastructure. All this points to a Persian economy that was expanding and becoming more commercialized, suggesting that Persia did indeed retain some silver during this period to facilitate the process.

As we have seen, the bitter rivalry of the Shia Safavids with the Sunni Ottomans frequently led to difficulties with the westward export of silk and other goods from Iran through the major Syrian entrepôt of Aleppo. Considerable efforts were therefore made to develop alternative routes to western markets, one through Astrakhan and up the Volga to the Baltic, and the other the maritime route from the Persian Gulf and around the Cape, as urged by the English and Dutch East India Companies. To this end an English fleet helped Abbas to capture Hormuz from the Portuguese, with Dutch connivance, in 1622. However, better relations were eventually established with the Ottomans in recognition of their mutual interest in maintaining the westward flow of silk, and so the maritime and Volga routes were ultimately unable to displace the westward route to the Levant.

The Ottoman Empire was also at the crossroads between east and west of the global circulation of silver that was unleashed by the Voyages of Discovery. This very fact, in the opinion of Omer Lutfi Barkan (1975), was responsible for the decline and ultimate collapse of the hitherto highly stable Ottoman economic, social, and political system. The Ottoman economic regime, extending across Anatolia, the Balkans, Egypt, and North Africa was, in Barkan's opinion (p. 4), "basically one of imperial self-sufficiency." After the Voyages of Discovery, however, the expanding European Atlantic economy undermined this system. Consistent with the monetary approach to the balance of payments, the rise in European prices meant that commodities such as "wheat, copper, wool and the like" were "sucked out of Ottoman markets," ruining traditional industries and causing social dislocation among the artisan classes and the countryside as well as unrest and dissatisfaction in key military units. Thus if the Ottoman Empire was "the sick man of Europe" in the nineteenth century, it was not the contemporaneous Industrial Revolution that was responsible for the sickness, according to Barkan, but the Price Revolution of the sixteenth century that had already caused the lingering malaise.

Barkan's highly influential article has recently received a respectful but very critical review by Şevket Pamuk (2000, chapter 7) in his authoritative work on Ottoman monetary history. Pamuk finds smaller price rises than had Barkan; thus prices in terms of silver rose to a peak about 80–100% higher than in 1490 in the first quarter of the seventeenth century, whereas Barkan reported a rise of 165% over

1490 by 1605. Prices in terms of silver then *fell* according to Pamuk, until they were only about 20% higher in 1700 than they had been in 1490. Pamuk also contests the thesis that the Price Revolution was responsible for the empire's fiscal, military, and industrial difficulties, stressing the role of other factors such as the notable increase in warfare on many fronts and the associated military and fiscal burdens, as well as the traditionalism of agricultural and industrial organization that made these sectors unable to adapt to change. Nevertheless, while "in many ways...the Middle East was only a transit zone for these intercontinental bullion flows" (Pamuk 1994, p. 959), the evidence suggests that prices there did rise during the sixteenth century, while there is also strong evidence that the Ottoman economy was becoming more monetized during this period, and that "demand for money was growing but this demand could be met by increased supplies of silver."

Silver thus had an effect on the Ottoman and Persian Empires, raising prices in the former, and coinciding with (and perhaps facilitating) an increase in commercial activity in both. As we have seen, there was an active trade in northeastern Europe during this period, and thus it is not surprising that the silver influx even reached as far as Poland, Russia, and the Baltic regions, despite their distance from the regular east–west trade routes. As Marian Malowist (1958, p. 27) says, "the old view that Baltic trade lost its importance in the age of the great discoveries has long become untenable. On the contrary we now know that the Baltic countries became both the source of western raw materials and a market for their exports, thus facilitating their relatively rapid industrialization." We have also seen that there was a net export of silver from west to east in this era. While some of it was transmitted further east to Persia and the Ottoman lands, enough remained to monetize the local economies as well, as documented by Blum (1956).

In summary, the discovery of New World silver had a major impact on the economies of Eurasia, stimulating price rises, and facilitating both monetization and commercialization. Its most basic function was to increase intra-Eurasian trade, both within "national" economies and between them, and this is hardly surprising given silver's medium of exchange function. The increased availability of silver, and its tendency to flow east in response to higher prices, offers one way to understand the late-sixteenth-century revival of overland trade between Asia and Europe, and this increased trade in itself would have benefited Russia, Persia, and the Ottoman Empire, even in the absence of any increased monetization in those regions. In this way, the New World brought Eurasia closer to itself. Silver also played a crucial role in facilitating the activities of the European trading companies in Asia, with profound political consequences not just for Southeast Asia (as we have seen) but ultimately for India as well (chapter 5).

The New World would ultimately have an even more profound economic impact on the Old World than this, by leading to qualitatively new forms of intercontinental trade that were motivated above all by the Americas' vast endowments of land. However, for this trade to take off, the American colonists had to solve the key problem facing them, namely a shortage of affordable labor; and while as we have seen they hit almost immediately on the solution to this problem—slavery—it took time to build up the institutional framework necessary to supply the European market efficiently.

The implications of this can be seen in figure 4.8, which provides real (i.e., rye-deflated) prices for pepper and sugar in the Netherlands during the sixteenth and seventeenth centuries. The contrast between the two series is striking. As we have seen, real pepper prices started falling shortly after the Voyages of Discovery, eventually stabilizing at a historically low level some time in the mid seventeenth century. Sugar prices, however, rose very sharply throughout the sixteenth century, indicating that the growing Brazilian sugar exports documented earlier were insufficient to meet the demands of the European market: scarce labor still made for inelastic New World supply. The result was an ever-increasing incentive for settlers to supply Europe with sugar and other "tropical groceries," and hence an ever-increasing incentive to ship slaves across the Atlantic. It was only in the 1590s or so that the balance started to shift decisively in favor of European consumers (and, we might add, against the unfortunate Africans sold into slavery). It was thus toward the end of the sixteenth century, just as the Dutch and English were preparing to make their mark in the Indian Ocean, that the Age of Silver began to make way for the Age of Sugar and Slaves, that the Atlantic started to supplant the Indian Ocean in economic importance, and that the triangular trade which will be a focal point of the next chapter became a key driving force within the world economy.

This period of gradual economic transition coincided with a political one as well. The middle of the seventeenth century marked a major watershed in early modern history. In Europe the devastatingly disruptive Thirty Years' War came to an end, with the Peace of Westphalia in 1648 ushering in a new era in international relations. Russia was extending its frontier eastwards in the Siberian forest belt and had already reached the Pacific by 1648, while the Manchu Qing Empire was busily extending its own frontiers westwards into Central Asia after overthrowing the Ming in 1644. Japan was beginning its long

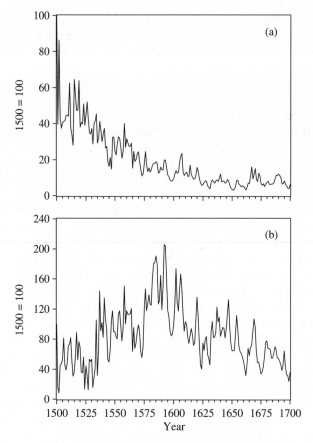

FIGURE 4.8. Real Dutch prices of (a) pepper and (b) sugar, 1500–1700
(1500 = 100). *Source:* van Zanden (2005).

but by no means unproductive seclusion from the rest of the world
under the Tokugawa. The Islamic "gunpowder empires" were showing
some signs of strain and tension but were still formidable on land.
In Southeast Asia the Dutch were extending their control over the
Indonesian archipelago and Ceylon after capturing Melaka in 1641,
while Burma and Siam were establishing powerful kingdoms with the
help of Portuguese mercenaries and military technology.

The growing network of world trade was to be the matrix within
which there eventually emerged a truly transformative breakthrough
to modernity. The Industrial Revolution was now little more than a
century away.

Chapter 5

WORLD TRADE 1650–1780: THE AGE OF MERCANTILISM

THE PERIOD FROM the middle of the seventeenth to the early nineteenth century saw a prolonged struggle among the leading European powers to control the resources, territory, and trade of the New World. The labor force of many of these New World societies was not confined to the relatively thin trickle of European immigrants and the native Americans within their domains, but soon came to include in growing numbers slaves imported from West Africa, marking a major increase in the engagement of this continent with the world economy. Table 5.1 shows the astonishing increase in this inhuman trade (Curtin 1969; Eltis 2001). A little more than 250,000 slaves were shipped across the Atlantic during the sixteenth century, but more than five times that number were transported during the seventeenth century, and by the close of the following century almost two million souls were being sent to the Americas every quarter century. In total more than 11 million Africans were forcibly moved to the New World between the sixteenth and the mid nineteenth centuries. The Portuguese, who as we have seen were early sugar producers, maintained their head start in the slave trade if not in other spheres of economic activity, and were responsible for almost half the total slave trade, while the British accounted for more than a quarter (and were the most active slavers during the heyday of the trade, the eighteenth century).

From the complex interactions of these diverse sources, there emerged what could be called an Atlantic System, linking four continents by an ocean and comprised of a northern Anglo-Dutch–French segment, a central Spanish–Mexican zone, and a southern Luso-Brazilian zone, all connected with each other and with Africa via multiple webs of economic relationships. The abundance of natural resources of this "Great Frontier," as Walter Prescott Webb (1952) called it, meant that the trading activities of the European powers came increasingly to involve imports from and exports to the New World. The prevailing mercantilist doctrine of those times viewed the struggle

TABLE 5.1. Volume of transatlantic slave trade, 1519–1867
(by nationality of carrier, thousands).

Period	Portuguese	British	French	Dutch	Spanish	U.S.	Other	All nations
1519–1600	264.1	2.0	0.0	0.0	0.0	0.0	0.0	0.0
1601–1650	439.5	23.0	0.0	41.0	0.0	0.0	0.0	503.5
1651–1675	53.7	115.2	5.9	64.8	0.0	0.0	0.2	239.8
1676–1700	161.1	243.3	34.1	56.1	0.0	0.0	15.4	510.0
1701–1725	378.3	380.9	106.3	65.5	11.0	0.0	16.7	958.6
1726–1750	405.6	490.5	253.9	109.2	44.5	0.0	7.6	1,311.3
1751–1775	472.9	859.1	321.5	148.0	1.0	89.1	13.4	1,905.2
1776–1800	626.2	741.3	419.5	40.8	8.6	54.3	30.4	1,921.1
1801–1825	871.6	257	217.9	2.3	204.8	81.1	10.5	1,645.1
1826–1850	1,247.7	0.0	94.1	0.0	279.2	0.0	0.0	1,621.0
1851–1867	154.2	0.0	3.2	0.0	23.4	0.0	0.0	180.7
All years	5,074.9	3,112.3	1,456.4	527.7	517.0	280.0	94.2	11,062.4
Percent of trade	45.9	28.3	13.2	4.8	4.7	2.5	0.9	100.0

Source: Eltis (2001, table VII, supplement materials).
Available at http://oieahc.wm.edu/wmq/Jan01/Eltis.htm.

for wealth as a zero-sum game, and each of the powers looked upon its colonies as suppliers of raw materials and markets for manufactures of the "mother country" alone, with foreign interlopers to be excluded by force if necessary. Hence, there was frequent conflict during this period, often in the New World itself. Success in these wars would go to the states that could best muster the fiscal resources necessary to provide effective naval and military forces, so that Power would be the means to secure Plenty, which in turn would provide Power with its sinews, in terms of the classic formulation of mercantilist policy by Jacob Viner (1948). This relationship between Power and Plenty in what has been called the "age of mercantilism" is what provides the unifying theme of this chapter.

Most of the rivalries of the age of mercantilism were about which national company could gain control of a given market or trading area, such as the spice trade of Southeast Asia, or entry and exit into the Baltic. The aim was to exert monopoly control over a given trade, thus gaining monopoly profits, which in turn would increase the state's financial ability to successfully wage war, thus enhancing its mercantilist trade objectives. Such logic was hardly new, since as we have seen many previous states, including Srivijaya, Mamluk and Ottoman Egypt, Venice, and the *Estado da India* had more or less successfully attempted to pursue similar policies. Given this "zero-sum" focus on the international division of monopoly rents, classical arguments regarding the gains from trade to all parties under peaceful conditions of perfect competition did not apply. The much derided stress on the necessity of acquiring stocks of precious metals could be defended as essential in light of the necessity to finance deficits in the Baltic trade for naval stores, or acquire working capital for the lucrative trade of the East India companies with Asia (Wilson 1949).

Of course, within the context of a national ideology such as early modern mercantilism, the opportunities for what is now known as "rent-seeking" behavior by special interest groups such as colonial projectors and chartered companies would be rife, and Ekelund and Tollison (1981) have usefully applied this conceptual model to the historical experience of England and France. Apart from a very brief discussion (pp. 12–13) of general trends from 1600 to 1750, however, they largely ignore the international context of the age of mercantilism that is the concern here. One has to ask, what was a realistic counterfactual for an individual European nation state choosing to unilaterally embrace peaceful free trade? In the absence of anything resembling an effective collective security mechanism, or a clearly defined hegemonic power, military defeat and exclusion from foreign markets seems to us as plausible an answer as any. The issue of what constitutes a plausible counterfactual is obviously relevant to any rigorous cost–benefit assessment of mercantilist policies, as is the question of whether the state involved ended up winning or losing its wars. With the obvious exception of the American War of Independence, Britain by and large won its wars during this period, with important implications for the future of the international economy, and so its rise to international prominence will necessarily be an important theme of this chapter.

Origins of the British Empire: Trade, Plunder, and Settlement

Everyone has heard that the British Empire was supposed to have been acquired in "a fit of absence of mind," even if they are unlikely to know the source of the quote, the Victorian imperial historian J. R. Seeley. The context for Seeley's quip was his protest against the tendency of English historiography to concentrate on the extension of liberty at home rather than expansion abroad, which he regarded as the real driving force of national development since Elizabethan times. First published to widespread acclaim in 1883, his slim volume on *The Expansion of England* remains a vivid and forceful statement of this theme (Seeley 1971). What he actually said (p. 12) was: "We seem, as it were, to have conquered and peopled half the world in a fit of absence of mind," meaning that this was the impression one might gather from conventional histories of eighteenth-century Britain, that "make too much of the mere parliamentary wrangling and the agitations about liberty," when the real history of the nation was its quite conscious and explicit acquisition of an empire overseas, so that in the eighteenth century "the history of England was not in England but in America and Asia."

As in the case of the Iberian powers and the *Reconquista*, the process of English expansion began with an "internal colonialism," slowly absorbing the "Celtic fringe" of the Welsh, Scots, and Irish into what was eventually to become the United Kingdom of Great Britain and Ireland. The Scottish and English crowns were joined in the person of King James the Sixth and First, and the kingdoms themselves merged in the Act of Union of 1707. The incorporation of the Irish was a more difficult and bloodier affair, with particularly brutal episodes during the regimes of Elizabeth, who felt it necessary to "bring in that rude and barbarous nation to civility," and of Oliver Cromwell and the joint reign of William and Mary. Some of the most notable Elizabethans who engaged in early plundering raids and colonial projects in the New World, such as Sir Humphrey Gilbert and Sir Walter Raleigh, first came into prominence by the perpetration in Ireland of what would now be regarded as flagrant atrocities. As J. H. Elliott (1990, p. 50) says, "Ireland for the English, like Andalusia for the Spaniards, served as a useful laboratory for developing the ideas and techniques which would make possible the subsequent establishment of overseas empire."

Kenneth Andrews (1984, p. 356) has pointed out that "in the course of English overseas expansion trade, plunder and settlement were closely interwoven," with plunder initially taking pride of place. He goes on to observe that between 1550 and 1630 the nation's shipping tonnage more than doubled, and that the special strength of this fleet was its "aptitude for warfare and predation," so well illustrated offensively in the piratical raids of Drake and Hawkins, and defensively against the Spanish Armada in 1588. Settlement took longer to develop, beginning with Virginia and New England on the mainland and with St. Kitts, Nevis, Antigua, Montserrat, and Barbados in the West Indies between 1600 and 1632, followed by the major acquisition of Jamaica from the Spanish by Cromwell in 1655. The profitability of sugar cultivation in the Caribbean islands meant that they were more attractive for investment and exploitation than the mainland settlements, and the population there rose far more rapidly, particularly because of the importation of African slaves. Indeed, according to Beckles (1998, p. 222), "by 1640 the English had gained a demographic advantage in the Caribbean over other European nations."

Migration of Europeans to the British mainland areas and the West Indian islands between 1601 and 1700 was fairly balanced, at around 177,000 persons in each case, but in the case of Africans there was a huge disparity, with only about 12,000 being sent to the mainland and 237,000 to the Caribbean (Games 2002, table 2.1, p. 41). By 1800 the corresponding migration totals from 1600 were 752,000 Europeans and 287,000 Africans to the mainland, and 290,000 Europeans and as many as 2,045,000 Africans to the Caribbean. All the African migrants were of course slaves, and of the Europeans Games says (p. 41) that no fewer than 75% of them were indentured servants or convicts. This reliance on coerced labor, such a feature of New World agriculture, may in part reflect the extreme land abundance of these societies, which implied roughly constant returns to labor and hence low or even zero rents for landowners reliant on expensive free workers (Domar 1970). It may also, paradoxically, have reflected "the development of freedom at home, including individual property rights," since this "permitted Europeans to expand their rights in persons beyond Europe. European freedom at home was thus the prerequisite for European-directed slavery abroad" (Drescher 2004, p. 33).[1]

Table 5.2 shows that, while population totals in the two regions were similarly small in 1650, the North American total was more than four and a half times higher than the West Indian by 1770, at nearly 2.3 million. Slaves accounted for 90% of the West Indian population by the eighteenth century, but for just a fifth of the population of North America. The West Indian slave population was far smaller than the total number of slaves shipped there, indicating that very high levels of slave mortality required constant slave inflows to replenish supply. On the other hand, it would seem that the mainland slave population was becoming self-sustaining. The data also clearly indicate the very high levels of natural increase among North American whites, as well as the very low levels of natural increase (and indeed out-migration) among those whites who migrated to the Caribbean. Astonishingly, the white population of British North America almost doubled in the twenty years between 1750 and 1770.

The relationship between trade, settlement, and plunder in the early years of the British Empire is well brought out by the example

---

[1] The literature on the causes of African slavery in the New World is too vast to be adequately summarized here. One important recent statement is Eltis (2000).

TABLE 5.2. Population of British New World Colonies, 1650–1770 (millions).

	1650	1700	1750	1770
North America				
White	53	234	964	1,816
Black	2	31	242	467
Total	55	265	1,206	2,283
Percent black	3.6	11.7	20.1	20.5
West Indies				
White	44	32	35	45
Black	15	115	295	434
Total	59	147	330	479
Percent black	25.4	78.2	89.4	90.6

Source: McCusker and Menard (1991, table 3.1, p. 54).

of Jamaica, the subject of an illuminating study by Nuala Zahedieh (1986). As she says (p. 210), "the island was a consolation prize acquired in what was little more than a state-sponsored buccaneering raid on the Spanish Indies," Cromwell's so-called "Western Design," the initial objective of which was to occupy Hispaniola but which turned to Jamaica when that expedition was bungled. Neither the Cromwellian regime nor that of Charles II was inclined to spend any further military or financial resources on the island, which had also been neglected by its Spanish possessors, but the location of the town and harbor of Port Royal and its potential as a base for privateering and contraband trade made it "a dagger pointed at the Spanish Empire." By 1670 Port Royal had over twenty ships and 2,000 men engaged in such nefarious but highly lucrative activities. The most famous and successful of these freebooters was Henry Morgan, familiar to all aficionados of Hollywood pirate movies during the era of Errol Flynn and Tyrone Power. Morgan's raid on Portobello in 1668 alone "produced plunder worth 75,000 pounds sterling, more than seven times the annual value of the island's sugar exports" (p. 216).

The Spanish settlers in the islands and mainland found it cheaper and more convenient to obtain their imports of European goods through Jamaica than to wait for the annual fleet from Seville or Cadiz as required by official regulations. Zahedieh argues that, as a result of the profits from plunder and the contraband trade, the island was awash with liquid funds that were invested in sugar plantations and other agricultural activities, making it unnecessary to raise any capital from England. She thus refutes the well-known contention of Adam Smith that colonies were a drain on the productive capital of the mother country, presenting plausible calculations that the rate of return on sugar plantations in Jamaica was of the order of 10% or more, higher than the prevailing rate of interest in England. Thus Jamaica seems to have been an ideal mercantilist colonial project, requiring no initial capital from the mother country but yielding high returns from plunder and smuggling at the expense of the enemy, and sending valuable primary exports such as sugar back to the metropolis, and in English ships to boot. Indeed a better example of the Marxian concept of "primitive accumulation" cannot be imagined, since Jamaica went on to become the largest sugar exporter in the British Empire for most of the eighteenth century, long after the days of Henry Morgan were over.

Most of the "chief and principal gentlemen and planters" who made their fortunes in Jamaica were, according to a contemporary diarist, "formerly rude and of mean birth, men of their wits, which have here advanced their fortune" (p. 214). One such man, Peter Beckford, who had been a common seaman, was the grandfather of William Beckford, the most prominent of the West Indian "nabobs," who along with his three brothers had seats in the House of Commons and was reputedly one of the wealthiest men in England in the eighteenth century. The sugar plantations of Barbados and Jamaica made the West Indies possessions so prosperous that Eric Williams (1966, p. 52) referred to them as the "hub of the British Empire, of immense importance to the grandeur and prosperity of England." One advantage for historians of the mercantilist obsession with trade is that the states of this period started collecting detailed trade statistics, and table 5.3 provides information on exports from Britain's New World colonies between 1768 and 1772. As the first panel shows, the total value of West Indian exports of sugar and related products such as molasses and rum was £3.9 million a year over the period 1768-72, of which £3.4 million went to Great Britain and the remaining £0.5 million to North America.

On the mainland the New England colonies (Massachusetts, Connecticut, New Hampshire, and Rhode Island), settled mostly by dissident Protestants from England in the 1620s, were of a very different character from the Caribbean islands. Cromwell himself referred to New England as "a cold, poor and useless place," showing no foresight about what his doughty fellow Puritans were eventually to make of their unpromising surroundings. A diversified economy of maize cultivation, fur trading, livestock rearing, fishing, and shipbuilding as well as a variety of shipping and other services led many of the

TABLE 5.3. Exports from British New World colonies, 1768–72
(pounds sterling).

Product	Great Britain	Ireland	North America	Other Europe	West Indies	Africa	Total
				West Indies			
Sugar	3,002,750		183,700				3,186,450
Rum	380,943		333,337				714,280
Molasses	222		9,648				9,870
Total	3,383,915		526,685				3,910,600
				New England			
Fish/whale	40,649			57,999	115,170	440	214,258
Livestock/meat	374			461	89,118		89,953
Wood	5,983	167		1,352	57,769		65,271
Potash	22,390	9					22,399
Grains	117	23		3,998	15,764		19,902
Rum	471	44		1,497		16,754	18,766
Other	6,991	1,018		296	247		8,552
Total	76,975	1,261		65,603	278,068	17,194	439,101
				Middle Colonies			
Grains	15,453	9,686		175,280	178,961		379,380
Flaxseed	771	35,185					35,956
Wood	2,635	4,815		3,053	18,845		29,348
Iron	24,053	695			2,921		27,669
Livestock/meat	2,142			1,199	16,692		20,033
Potash	12,233	39					12,272
Other	11,082	1,310		2,227	6,191	1,077	21,887
Total	68,369	51,730		181,759	223,610	1,077	526,545

settler families to enjoy what was called "competence," a sufficient degree of comfort if not wealth. This pattern of development made the economy of New England complementary with that of the West Indies, exporting corn, codfish, and other supplies to sustain both the free and slave populations of the islands, French and Dutch as well as English, and importing rum, molasses, and sugar. Trade was also active with the Spanish and Portuguese islands of Madeira and the Azores, involving the exchange of fish and foodstuffs for wine and salt. While early marriage and large families led to high rates of natural increase for the original immigrant population, the Native American population was devastated by disease and hostilities with the better-armed settlers, who saw this as the working of divine providence. The rapid population growth and a diversified economy led to

TABLE 5.3. *Cont.*

Product	Great Britain	Ireland	North America	Other Europe	West Indies	Africa	Total
				Destination			
				Upper South			
Tobacco	756,128						756,128
Grains	10,206	22,962		97,523	68,794		199,485
Iron	28,314	416			461		29,191
Wood	9,060	2,115		1,114	10,195		22,484
Other	23,344	3,357		526	12,368		39,595
Total	827,052	28,850		99,163	91,818		1,046,883
				Lower South			
Rice	198,590			50,982	55,961		305,533
Indigo	111,864						111,864
Deerskins	37,093						37,093
Naval stores	31,709						31,709
Wood	2,520	228		1,396	21,620		25,764
Grains	302	169		1,323	11,358		13,152
Livestock/meat	75	366		103	12,386		12,930
Other	11,877	515		365	785	362	13,904
Total	394,030	1,278		54,169	102,110	362	551,949

Source: McCusker and Menard (1991, pp. 108, 130, 160, 174, 199).

substantial urbanization and the emergence of a trading and financial sector based on Boston, with its own merchant elite, which was the entry point for British imports from where they were distributed to the other mainland colonies and the West Indies. Earnings from shipping services were almost as much as total commodity exports, at least £427,000 (McCusker and Menard 1991, p. 110). This fact leads McCusker and Menard (p. 92) to the observation that "the New Englanders became the Dutch of England's empire."

The other early mainland colonies to be developed were the Upper South of Virginia and Maryland, which soon emerged together as a classic monoculture export economy growing the "noxious weed" tobacco as a highly lucrative cash crop around Chesapeake Bay. The production of tobacco, which rapidly developed a mass market in Europe, rose from about 60,000 lb. in 1629 to 15 million pounds by 1670 and 28 million pounds by the middle of the 1680s (Horn 1998, p. 183), after which it stagnated before recovering again after 1715 and rising to about 50 million pounds by 1760. Table 5.3 shows that the Upper South exported more than any other mainland region, with total exports (annual average 1768–72) of more than £1 million. Tobacco was responsible for over three-quarters of this total, all tobacco exports going to England from where about 85% was reexported to continental Europe (McCusker and Menard 1991, p. 124).

Between New England and the Upper South were the Middle Colonies of New York and Pennsylvania, with their offshoots of New Jersey and Delaware. New York had a strong Dutch connection on the basis of its origins in the New Netherlands colony that fell to the English in 1664, and Pennsylvania had a strong Quaker connection because of its founder, William Penn. These historical initial conditions proved to be valuable links in forging trade networks with Amsterdam, the Dutch West Indies, and the widespread Quaker trading community. Agriculture in Pennsylvania also benefited from the advanced farming practices of the large number of German Protestant immigrants going to that state. Philadelphia and New York developed rapidly as mercantile and financial centers, displacing Boston well before the Revolution. Philadelphia grew to become the largest town on the mainland with a population of 35,000 in 1775, comparable to Bristol or Manchester in England. Unlike New England with its strong dependence on the West Indies, and the Chesapeake with its almost exclusive reliance upon England, the Middle Colonies were well-balanced in their export destinations, with just over 40% going to the West Indies, just over a fifth going to Britain and Ireland, and slightly more than a third going to the rest of Europe. Significantly, earnings from shipping and other services were more than £250,000 (ibid., p. 202).

The Lower South of North and South Carolina and Georgia had a different history from the other mainland colonies in that they were not founded by settlers arriving directly from England or Europe, but by immigration from the West Indies and the Upper South, the "dregs and gleanings of all other English colonies" to quote an uncharitable observer. The initial impulse came from Barbados, where the rapid growth of sugar plantations on a small island crowded out most of the indentured workers and other early immigrants. In the course of the seventeenth century about 10,000 persons left Barbados for other colonies (ibid., p. 171). They initially made a living as "the colony of a colony" (Edgar 1998), exporting foodstuffs and other supplies to support the sugar monoculture of Barbados. Later a profitable trade in deerskins was developed with the local Indians, but it was rice that formed the basis of another classic case of an export economy in South Carolina. Exports rose from 1.5 million pounds in 1710 to over 90 million pounds by the time of the Revolution. By the 1740s indigo emerged as what was called an "excellent companion commodity" to rice, in that it was complementary in input requirements. The "colony of a colony" thus came to replicate Barbados itself, with rice in place of sugar, but with both dependent on slave labor. Significantly, by the late eighteenth century the proportion of blacks had risen to over 40% (McCusker and Menard 1991, p. 172). Two-thirds of the rice exports went to Great Britain with the rest divided equally between the West Indies and Europe. All the indigo went to Great Britain.

Despite the obvious importance of agriculture and primary product exports to the thirteen mainland colonies, manufacturing was not negligible. Perkins (1988, p. 25) states that colonial iron output was 1,500 tons or 2% of world output in 1700, rising to 21,000 tons annually in 1775 and no less than 15% of world output, employing 8,000 workers in over eighty furnaces and exporting £58,000 worth of bar and pig iron annually to England. With their abundant timber supplies the mainland colonies not only exported masts for ships but also ships themselves, accounting for over one-third of the total British-registered shipping underwritten by Lloyd's (McCusker and Menard 1991, p. 81; Price 1998, p. 83).

Thanks to Walton and Shepherd (1979), on whose work table 5.3 is based, we have good data on the thirteen colonies' balance of payments on the eve of independence (annual averages 1768–72). Total commodity exports were £2.8 million, while invisible export earnings were £600,000 for shipping and £220,000 for insurance and commissions. On the debit side, there were commodity imports of £3.9 million, payments for slave imports of £200,000, and payments for indentured servants of £80,000. The overall current account deficit, once various fiscal items had been taken into account, was only around £40,000, to be financed by borrowing or export of specie, an utterly negligible amount in relation to the almost limitless potential of the economy of what was soon to become the United States of America (McCusker and Menard 1991, pp. 81–83; Perkins 1988, tables 2.1 and 2.2).

Trade between the mainland colonies, the West Indies, Great Britain, and foreign states took place within the mercantilist framework of what was known as the Old Colonial System, the basis of which was the Navigation Act, passed in 1651 by the Cromwellian Parliament but rendered more operationally effective by the Act of 1660 adopted by the Restoration Parliament, and followed by the Staple Act of 1663 and some other subsequent legislation. The purpose of this legislation was to ensure that all goods imported into England be carried in English ships or in ships of the country of origin of the imported goods. This was clearly aimed against the Dutch and their domination of the carrying trade: all trade between and with England's colonies should be carried in vessels of either English or colonial ownership. Furthermore, a list of "enumerated" commodities including sugar, tobacco, cotton, ginger, indigo, and some other dyestuffs could only be exported from English colonies to England itself, i.e., they could only reach any foreign destinations after being reexported from England.

The impact of this set of state interventions on the welfare and growth of both England and the colonies has long been an active area of research and controversy, with early cliometric studies typically finding that the burden imposed on the colonies was small (Thomas 1965; McClelland 1969; Walton 1971).[2] It is worth recalling, however, that even Adam Smith defended the Navigation Acts, on the grounds that "defense is more important than opulence," and that the merchant marine was the "nursery of seamen" and hence of recruits for the Royal Navy in time of war. For the mainland colonists, confining the conveyance of imports to English shipping meant some loss of transportation efficiency, but this was probably more than made up for by the gains from the exclusion of the Dutch from the extensive and profitable trade with the West Indies. In the case of exports of the enumerated products tobacco growers undoubtedly lost, since English and Scottish merchants reexported over 80% of their colonial purchases to France and other European countries. Sugar growers, on the other hand, enjoyed import duties three or four times as low in England as sugar from French or Dutch colonies.

MERCANTILISM, COMMERCIAL RIVALRY, AND THE ANGLO-DUTCH WARS

As we have seen in the previous chapter, the Dutch had emerged by 1650 as the leaders in global commerce on virtually all of the seas and oceans of the world. The Anglo-Dutch wars thus occurred at the very height of Dutch power. Jonathan Israel (1989, chapter 6) regards the period 1647–52 as "the Zenith" of Dutch world trade primacy, coinciding with the cessation of hostilities with Spain in 1648. This led to a drastic fall, in some cases by as much as 50%, in transport and insurance costs that enabled a substantial growth of trade, particularly in the Mediterranean. Dutch merchants could now trade on equal terms in Spain and Spanish colonies, and all their acquisitions in Asia, Africa, and the New World were recognized. Peace with Spain also

---

[2]Cliometrics consists of the application of modern economic theory and statistical techniques to the study of history.

facilitated Dutch military expansion in Southeast Asia, and with it the establishment of effective monopolies for Moluccan spices.

Lower interest rates, and better technology in the later stages of cloth manufacture, combined with easier access to Spanish wool to give an important advantage to the Dutch in this key sector. The relative fall in Dutch freight rates and the enhanced comparative advantage in woolen cloth production boosted their Baltic trade at the expense of England and the Hanseatic towns, as well as their trade with Italy and the Levant. The Dutch also became much more active in the Caribbean once the hostilities with Spain ended. It was the immediate impact of these developments on England that intensified the simmering resentment of the English and helped to set off the first Anglo-Dutch war of 1652–54.

The progress of their smaller Protestant ally had been watched by the English since late Elizabethan times with a mixture of admiration, envy, and resentment or, as Charles Wilson (1957, p. 10) put it, "a simple, primitive jealousy of the large profits which were apparently easily earned by the Dutch from their more advanced system of foreign trade." What made the Dutch success even harder to bear was that the English, with at least double the population, had much greater agricultural and industrial resources at their disposal than the Dutch. They were self-sufficient in food, with even some surplus in good years, while the Dutch had to depend on grain imports from the Baltic to meet their requirements. The English woolen cloth industry used the plentiful fleece of its own sheep, whereas the Dutch had to import their supplies from Spain. However, England exported only unfinished "white cloth," not yet dyed, to Holland where the major portion of the value added was generated. Most galling of all was the immense profit that the Dutch derived from the North Sea herring fishery, mostly in waters just off the coasts of England and Scotland.

All of these complaints found expression in the most famous tract of English mercantilism, Thomas Mun's *England's Treasure by Fforraign Trade*, written in the 1620s and 1630s but published only in 1664 on the eve of the second Anglo-Dutch war. According to Mun the elaborate edifice of Dutch commercial prosperity rested ultimately upon the English allowing them to fish as they pleased in English territorial waters, employing about one thousand herring busses and half a million men in all stages of the production process, with a catch valued conservatively at in excess of £1 million annually. As Mun put it, the United Provinces "are like a fair bird suited with goodly borrowed plumes; but if every Fowl should take his feather, this bird would rest neer naked" (cited in Wilson 1957, p. 22). The only way to ultimately

restore control over access to her own "Great Fishery" and deny the
Dutch their "borrowed plumes" was by the assertion of naval power,
putting the dependence of Plenty upon Power in the starkest possible
terms.

Meanwhile, during the reigns of James I and Charles I various
schemes were attempted to increase national involvement in the
herring fishery, but they were all thwarted by the inability of the English
to compete with the Dutch at the necessary level of commercial organization and financial backing. Similarly, the project to retain English
cloth at home for finishing and dyeing, thus generating the additional
value added rather than ceding it to the Dutch, associated with the
name of a leading London businessman, Alderman Cockayne, also
ended in failure for the same reasons. As many developing countries
have since discovered, "cutting out the middleman" and taking his
profits is not easy to do in the absence of the necessary skill, enterprise,
and capital.

England emerged from the Civil War with a strong navy and an
aggressive middle class that was ready to challenge the Dutch commercial hegemony. According to David Ormrod (1998, p. 685), "without
doubt, the driving force behind English commercial policy after 1650
was Dutch competition," while the goal of this commercial policy "can
almost be specified in a basic formula: to remove corporate monopoly
privilege where appropriate, while providing for the protection of
mercantile interests within a *single, overarching national monopoly*
granted by Parliament" (our italics). Ormrod argues that new mercantile groups in England and the American colonies were opposed
to the traditional awarding of monopolies by royal prerogative to
particular entities such as the Merchant Adventurers, pressing instead
for measures that would preserve particular trades or sectors for
national enterprise, but leave open to competition which particular
national firms could succeed and prosper within them, supported by
tariffs, subsidies, bounties, and "drawbacks" (repayment in whole or
part of import duties on reexported goods). Thus the Navigation Act
"dealt a deadly blow to the Dutch carrying trade" without granting
special privilege to any particular British concern. It was the newly
enhanced power of Parliament, acting in the collective interest of
the national mercantile class as a whole, rather than the "grace and
favor" of a monarch to a particular supplicant, that was henceforth
to be responsible for carrying out "mercantilist" economic policy in
England. Ormrod (1998, 2003) argues convincingly that this approach
was more "modern" and efficient than the particularist approaches
adopted by the Dutch Republic, which were ultimately responsible for

the loss of its economic primacy, first in the regional economy of the North Sea and ultimately in the Atlantic economy as a whole, soon after the turn of the eighteenth century.

Cromwell himself was anxious to maintain good relations with the only other Protestant republic in Europe, and even proposed a sort of Protestant alliance or league to promote common economic and security interests against Spain and the other Catholic powers, an idea that was brusquely dismissed by the more pragmatic Dutch. With the navies of both nations prowling the narrow seas between them, it is not surprising that an incident occurred in which the English navy opened fire on a Dutch fleet off Dover with the loss of two warships, claiming that they were not shown the proper respect in their home waters. Passions on both sides became inflamed and war broke out in 1652 despite the reluctance of Cromwell and leading Dutch statesmen.

The very extent and interdependence of the Dutch global trading network, the foundation of their prosperity in peacetime, made them dangerously vulnerable in time of war. Dutch admirals were required by their government to protect the corn fleet from the Baltic, the silver fleet from Spain, East Indiamen returning from Batavia, West Indiamen returning from the Caribbean, the North Sea herring fleet, and sundry other vessels besides. It is no wonder that Admirals Tromp and de Ruyter, both naval commanders of supreme quality, were disgusted with the task of convoying and protecting merchantmen and sought instead to seek out and destroy the English fleet in a decisive action. There were several major battles in the English Channel, usually ending in favor of the English because of their heavier firepower. The returning Dutch merchant fleets frequently had to sail around the north of Scotland to avoid being taken in the Channel, which added considerably to the cost. The English were able to blockade the Dutch ports successfully for long periods, thus inflicting damage on their commerce and raising the prices of bread and herring, the staples of the Dutch diet.

Eventually both sides tired of the cost and disruption caused by the war, and the Treaty of Westminster that ended it did not impose any onerous conditions on either side. The English may have had the better of the naval engagements but the final outcome was more consistent with a draw. Dutch commerce suffered more in the short term but received no lasting damage and soon revived, though its vulnerability to a rival maritime power had been clearly displayed, and the lesson was not lost on its future leaders. On the other side "English merchants could look back on the Dutch War with some satisfaction" (Wilson 1957, p. 77), and the confidence they gained was to have profound effects on future thought and policy. English naval strength continued to grow throughout the remaining years of the Cromwellian regime, with the addition of over 200 ships, so that when Charles II was restored to the throne his navy had more than ten times as large a fleet as that of his father (ibid.).

The Restoration regime did not simply continue with the naval and commercial policies of the Protectorate but strengthened them even further. The king's younger brother James, the duke of York, was appointed Lord High Admiral and as such was an ardent advocate of asserting English sea-power. Several of Cromwell's closest henchmen and advisers were not only given high office but promoted as well after they judiciously switched sides. The most significant of these Vicars of Bray was Sir George Downing, unfortunately better known because of the London street named after him than for his own remarkable achievements as an economic administrator and policy maker. A member of a Puritan family that migrated to New England and an early graduate of Harvard, he returned to England to fight on the Parliamentary side. Downing was not an original thinker but an ardent believer in the doctrines of Thomas Mun on the necessity of a balance of payments surplus which, combined with his unrivaled knowledge of Dutch commercial and financial practices, obtained while he was the English ambassador at The Hague, made him according to Wilson (1957, p. 103) the father of mercantilist practice in England. The revised Navigation Act of 1660 had the same anti-Dutch intent as that of 1651 but was streamlined and made more enforceable, since the requirements of the Act for carriage in English vessels could now be checked against a register of foreign-built ships owned by English citizens that was not previously available. Downing also designed the Staple Act that required European goods to be exported to the colonies in English ships. Realizing that simply banning the sale by the Dutch of fish in England when the national industry was still underdeveloped would be ineffective, he merely doubled the import duty. Similarly, he allowed English citizens to register Dutch-built ships until the domestic industry was able to attain self-sufficiency. Though inspired by a strong spirit of anti-Dutch economic nationalism, the new mercantile code devised by Downing was marked by a shrewd practicality that served the nation well in this formative period of her economic development, when she was attempting to "overtake and surpass" her great rival for mastery of the world's oceans and commerce. Wilson's (1957, p. 102) assessment of this phase of British economic history in the 1660s is worth quoting in full:

It is no exaggeration to see these years as a turning-point in England's economic destiny, when the old monolithic conception of the export trade in half-manufactured cloth gives way to a new conception—a foreign trade growing in scope and variety in which the new colonial regions added their new commodities. These in turn became the basis of refining and manufacturing industries in London and the west-coast ports and of a large reexport trade. The whole system rested on a growing mercantile fleet, and slowly the necessary commercial and financial mechanisms were evolved for facilitating its operations.

Wilson's contention of a decisive break in the nature of England's foreign trade in the first decade of the Restoration is independently supported by the meticulous quantitative research of Ralph Davis (1954, 1962, 1967). Before the outbreak of the Civil War 80% of England's exports were of woolen cloth to Europe, and extra-European trade was only a small fraction of the total. By 1700, however, the export of woolens had fallen to less than half the total in spite of growing rapidly in absolute terms, because of the huge increase in colonial reexports that had taken place by the end of the century. The most prominent of these colonial reexports were tobacco and sugar. It is important to note that it was the Navigation Acts that were largely responsible for funneling this colonial produce through England to the continent of Europe, since it is almost certain that the Dutch would have captured most of the carrying trade across the Atlantic with their larger and more efficient shipping industry and financial organization. This shift in the structure of English foreign trade was of such significance in the view of Davis (1967, p. 3) "that we may well attach to the period running from the English Restoration to American Independence the title of Commercial Revolution."

At the court of Charles II a strong faction emerged in favor of renewing hostilities against the Dutch while pursuing colonial trade more vigorously. It was based on an alliance between an inner circle of the king's favorites and a clique of London merchants. They found a strong supporter in the duke of York, eager for the pursuit of naval glory. The Royal African Company was formed to prospect for gold and to trade in slaves and ivory on the west coast of Africa. Extended hostilities broke out with the Dutch, though no war was as yet declared. In Asia the nutmeg island of Pulau Run continued to be a bone of contention between the respective East India Companies. Tensions were also raised by the marriage of Charles to the Portuguese princess Catherine, of the new royal house of Braganza. She brought a rich dowry in Bombay and Tangier, but in exchange the Portuguese wanted support of their remaining positions in India against Dutch encroachments. The VOC not only drove the Portuguese from their forts on the Malabar Coast but also refused English vessels the right to land. As Downing complained about the Dutch propensity to piously invoke Grotius on the freedom of the seas, "with these people it is mare liberum in the British Seas but mare clausum on the coast of Africa and in the East Indies" (quoted in Wilson 1957, p. 118).

On the mainland of North America the Dutch colony of New Amsterdam was captured by a raiding party and renamed in honor of the Lord High Admiral, though at the time it was not felt to be worth a fraction of Pulau Run. Popular feeling against the Dutch was whipped up by what would now be called the print media. When the war faction at court was searching for plausible reasons to justify a war a leading commander is reputed to have made the remark, "What matters this reason or that reason? What we want is more trade, that they now have." Sufficient cause was ultimately found for the second Anglo-Dutch war to be officially declared in 1665, despite the reluctance of wiser heads on both sides. Once again the navies were evenly matched and the battles bloody and hard-fought but without a decisive outcome. The enthusiasm for war waned in England and the Treaty of Breda that concluded it in 1667 gave the Dutch important concessions in the interpretation of the Navigation Acts, involving agreement not to board and search neutral vessels for belligerent cargoes, as the British navy had been wont to do. Permission was given for Dutch ships to import Rhenish wines and Silesian linens into England as products of the Republic's own natural hinterland. It confirmed the Dutch hold on Surinam, which became their main base of operations in the New World, and their possession of Pulau Run. The English gained recognition of their acquisition of New York, New Jersey, and Delaware as well as the retention of some forts and trading stations in West Africa.

A third Anglo-Dutch war broke out in 1672 at the instigation of the French in alliance with England. A French army of 120,000 men with some German allies invaded the Republic, while a massive Anglo-French armada of 146 ships and 34,000 men was prepared to land troops on the Dutch coast (Israel 1989, p. 293). All seemed lost since France was clearly the most powerful European power on land, and at sea the English were at least equal to the Dutch. There was a collapse of the Amsterdam financial markets with VOC shares losing half their value, and a general expectation in Europe that the days of the Republic were numbered. Almost miraculously, however, the Dutch, under the young William of Orange as Stadholder and commander of the armed forces, were able to fight the English and French to a draw at sea and prevent a French invasion of their homeland by the desperate device of opening the dikes, while Spain and Austria intervened against France. Dutch privateers took a devastating toll of English shipping, at least 700 vessels according to Israel (ibid., p. 299), many with very valuable cargoes. The thrust of subsequent English policy after she concluded a separate peace in 1674 shifted to the containment of France rather than continued rivalry with the United Provinces.

BRITAIN, FRANCE, AND THE DUTCH REPUBLIC

By an exquisite irony of the law of the jungle in the age of mercantilism, at the very moment when the big VOC fish was devouring the little fish of Kandy and Makassar in Southeast Asia, the Dutch Republic itself was attracting the baleful gaze of a very big fish indeed, the France of the young Louis XIV and his great minister Jean-Baptiste Colbert. The Dutch rise to world trade primacy did not cause resentment only in England, her natural maritime competitor, but also in France, the major outlet for her exports and reexports and a significant source of many of her imports as well. In business circles and the court there was a feeling that the "servile dependence" of the great nation on the Dutch entrepôt had gone too far and needed to be ended (ibid., p. 284). This did not imply that France should emulate particular English measures such as the Navigation Acts, since she did not have anything close to as strong a navy or merchant marine, though Colbert made strenuous efforts to improve both. The most effective weapon for France to use in a trade war was import tariffs on the large volumes of the many goods that she obtained from the Republic, such as fine woolen cloth, spices, cheese, herring, whale-oil products, and refined sugar. Israel also points out that France could hurt the Dutch in third markets, particularly Spain, Spanish America, and the Levant, by increasing her own exports of goods such as fine linens and silks to these areas in competition with Dutch exports.

Colbert was also an enthusiast for promoting investment in particular industries, one of which was sugar refining, a major sector of Dutch industry. In 1664 Colbert raised tariffs on Dutch exports to France, moderately in most cases, but more heavily on refined sugar and spices to encourage the newly created French East and West India Companies. In 1667, after the conclusion of the second Anglo-Dutch war, tariffs on fine woolen cloth and linen were doubled and on refined sugar raised by 50%, while duties on whale oil were quadrupled and on tobacco were raised as much as sevenfold (ibid., table 6.25). The Dutch retaliated by banning the import of French brandy and raising tariffs on silk and linen, provoking higher French tariffs on herring and spice imports. A full-scale trade war had clearly broken out and real war would soon follow in 1672. As we have seen, England withdrew and made a separate peace in 1674, but the Republic had to fight on against France until 1678 against great odds but with powerful allies on its side, alarmed at the prospect of domination by the Sun King. The Treaty of Nijmegen that ended the Franco-Dutch conflict gave the Republic excellent terms, including the repeal of Colbert's tariffs of 1667. In this sense the war did not achieve France's immediate economic objectives but it should not therefore be regarded as a defeat. Stoye (1969, p. 290) argues that Louis made the concessions to the Dutch in order to prise them loose from their allies in the coalition against him. This enabled him to force them to accede to the extension of French power in western, northern, and central Europe in the subsequent treaties that brought the end of all hostilities in 1679.

The entry of France as the third major player in the contest for world trade primacy clearly raised the familiar strategic problem of which two of the three players would form an alliance against the third. In the second Anglo-Dutch war the French allied with the Dutch to prevent England, which they then considered the stronger rival, from gaining hegemony. After the poor English performance, however, they seem to have regarded the Dutch as their main opponent, therefore obtaining a compliant ally in Charles II by the payment of generous subsidies, and inducing him to instigate the third Anglo-Dutch war. After the failure of that enterprise to deliver the expected knockout blow, the question of who would ally with whom was opened once again. In 1677 William of Orange, already a Stuart on his mother's side, she being the sister of Charles II, also acquired a Stuart wife in the person of Mary, daughter of the duke of York, the future James II. After the Glorious Revolution of 1688 and the joint reign of William III and Mary II, it was clear that it would be the English, in alliance with the Dutch, contesting for the primacy of world trade and empire with the France of Louis XIV. The Dutch Republic would continue to have a long innings, but she would be overshadowed by the two great powers bestriding the English Channel. The Protestant alliance, or "Protestant Capitalist International," that Cromwell had proposed to the States General of the United Provinces in 1651, and which they had scornfully rejected, had come into existence after all, vigorously opposing the power of the greatest Catholic monarch of the age, and promoting the prosperity of both the United Provinces and what was soon to be, after the Act of Union in 1707, Great Britain.

Britain and France: Commercial Expansion and the Second Hundred Years' War

Over the course of the "long" eighteenth century, defined for present purposes as the period from 1689 to 1815, no fewer than 64 years out of a total of 126 involved war between Britain and France (Seeley 1971, p. 21). The interludes of peace were therefore usually marked by jockeying for position and preparations for the next outbreak of hostilities. Much of the fighting was on the European mainland but the wars were worldwide in scope and extent, with a strong focus on North America and the West Indies on the one hand, and India on the other. While it could be argued that the main motivation for France was territory and hegemony within the continent of Europe itself, and for England the acquisition and protection of the overseas sources of her valuable colonial trades, the logic of the opposing interests dictated that Britain could not afford to let France dominate the continent, nor France let Britain expand her overseas settlements and trading stations unchecked. Thus Britain had to maintain a standing army ready for deployment on the continent, or subsidize allies to oppose the French on land, while France had also to maintain a strong navy, supplemented when necessary by fleets of privateers. This required each state to raise sufficient revenue to provide the military resources required, so that once again Plenty was needed to sustain Power, which in turn was necessary to secure the provision of Plenty. Their relative success in raising this revenue would largely determine the outcome of what Seeley (p. 24) called "a kind of Second Hundred Years' War."

France, coming later to the New World than the Iberian powers, had been forced like England to concentrate its colonial efforts on North America. Still in search of precious metals, gems, and spices, early French explorers such as Jacques Cartier were also driven by the fruitless search for a "northwest passage" to the Pacific and Asia, in ignorance of the vast extent of the northern ice cap. The first of the northern continent's resources to be exploited on a large scale was the cod fisheries of the Grand Banks off Newfoundland. Once again the Portuguese were the pioneers, but eventually fishermen from Normandy and Brittany took the lead in this major European industry, serving the large domestic market in France and relying on plentiful supplies from the Bay of Biscay to salt the "green" fish that they caught at sea. An "inshore" or "dry" branch of the cod fishing industry salted the catch ashore, and this activity was undertaken by the small settler colonies that were established in what are now the Canadian Maritime provinces of Nova Scotia and Newfoundland. The lower quality dried cod was an important export to the French West Indies to feed the slave population.

The fishing settlements attracted Native American tribes trading beaver pelts for European products, notably firearms and brandy. The main area of French settlement was along the banks of the Saint Lawrence between Quebec, founded in 1608 by Samuel de Champlain, and Montreal, which became the collection point for beaver and other furs from the western regions. While a few French colonists, the celebrated *coureurs des bois* or *voyageurs*, entered the forests themselves and went up the rivers in the birchbark canoes that they learned to make from the natives, most of the hunting and trapping was undertaken by natives over increasingly extensive areas as successive animal habitats were depleted. Competition between tribes for control over the supply of furs was made more lethal by the availability of firearms. The Algonquin tribal federation was allied to the French, while their Iroquois rivals sought support from the Dutch of New Amsterdam and later the English who replaced them.

A royal monopoly over the fur trade was granted in 1600 and taken over after 1627 by the Company of New France, established by Cardinal Richelieu to develop the French settlements in North America. Colbert placed New France itself directly under the crown in 1664, and established a new Company of the Indies to conduct trade under its auspices. New France was governed from Quebec under a strict civil, military, and ecclesiastical hierarchy, in marked contrast to the looser, decentralized structure of the British American colonies. Exploration of the interior of North America, the construction of trading posts and fortified settlements in the Illinois country, the descent of the Mississippi and the foundation of New Orleans at its mouth in 1718, and the establishment of the Province of Louisiana in 1722 meant that France appeared to control a vast arc of territory north, west, and south of the English mainland colonies, thus blocking their expansion, but she lacked the demographic base in the New World to exploit this advantage effectively. One reason for the very limited immigration to Canada from France was that both the fishing and fur interests feared that more settlers would mean larger output, higher costs, and lower prices for their exports. Another reason is that unlike England, which allowed religious dissenters to migrate to the colonies, France denied this opportunity to the Huguenots. The lack of a viable settler base meant that overhead costs of defense and administration were higher, placing additional fiscal strains on the metropolitan state.

In the West Indies the French initially shared the island of Saint-Christophe (St. Kitts) with the British, from which they went on to occupy Martinique and Guadeloupe and eventually also Saint-Domingue. After experimenting with tobacco and other crops, these islands eventually specialized in sugar grown on large plantations with African slave labor, just as in the British colonies of Barbados and Jamaica. French colonial production of sugar grew very rapidly, particularly on the extensive virgin soils of Saint-Domingue. According to Davis (1973, table 4), sugar production in the French West Indies and in the British colonies of Barbados, Jamaica, and some other smaller islands was equal in 1720 at some 24,000 tons, but by 1767 the French colonies were at 77,000 tons while the British output was 67,000 tons. Saint-Domingue accounted for 63,000 tons in 1767 compared to 36,000 tons in Jamaica, the largest British producer. Notably, the fish and fur exported from New France in 1730 amounted in value to only 7% of the value of sugar exported by the West Indian colonies (Pritchard 2004, p. 162), despite the vast disparity in the land areas of these two parts of the French Empire.

In the first quarter century after the Glorious Revolution, England fought two long wars with France, the so-called War of the Grand Alliance, or Nine Years' War, from 1689 to 1697, and the War of the Spanish Succession from 1701 to 1713. The first of these involved the efforts of William III and his Austrian and German allies to check French expansion on the mainland, and to defeat the attempt by Louis to restore James II to the throne. The war saw much heavy but inconclusive fighting that strained budgets on both sides, leading to a large increase in the level of customs duties in England. Traditionally, English foreign trade had a 5% duty on both exports and imports, and was thus a "nondistortionary" and purely revenue-raising measure. The fiscal demands of the Nine Years' War caused William and Mary to raise these duties to 15% or higher, levied on "official values" or arbitrary prices that could be much higher than actual import prices, thus giving them a significant protective effect in some cases. French imports in particular, especially the products of their leading silk and linen industries, were taxed severely, as were cotton and silk imports from India and China. Though the higher duties were initially applied to exports as well, the industries concerned, such as the politically powerful woolen industry, were able to get them reduced or entirely repealed in the 1722 tariff reforms of Sir Robert Walpole. Import duties were successively raised in subsequent wars, resulting in the system becoming increasingly protectionist over the course of the eighteenth century. England did not make any territorial or commercial gains as a result of the war, but William did secure French recognition of his crown.

During the war French naval activity in the Caribbean was mostly devoted to what was called "royal privateering" against Spanish America, whereby the king's warships were in effect rented out to private investors to raid and pillage enemy vessels and installations. The most notable of these efforts was the 1697 raid on Cartagena by a large squadron from France combined with colonial militia and buccaneers from Saint-Domingue, which yielded 10 million livres in booty, much of which was apparently invested in sugar-producing facilities on the island. The raid had the even greater significance of diverting a British fleet that was supposed to be in the Mediterranean protecting the Spanish coast, contributing to the French capture of Barcelona and forcing Spain out of the Grand Alliance against France. This led to the end of the war and the signing of the Treaty of Ryswick, by which the French claims to Saint-Domingue and Tobago were recognized by Spain (ibid., chapter 7).

Hostilities on the mainland were initiated by the Comte de Frontenac, the Governor-General of New France, using regular troops, Canadian militia, and Indian allies against settlements in New England and New York to relieve the pressure on France in the European theater (Lenman 1998, p. 152). The British response involved attacks by their Iroquois allies on French settlements resulting in clashes between them and tribes allied to the French, with both Native American sides seeking their own advantage in the control of territory and the fur trade at the expense of the other. Success in both economic and military conflicts between the European rivals depended to a large extent on their ability to provide their respective clients with goods of lower price or higher quality. Unfortunately, one tragic aspect of this competition was between French brandy and English rum, both equally destructive of the wellbeing of the native inhabitants, however effective each was in eliciting the supply of furs or military cooperation. It is generally accepted that the French were much more successful in their relations with the tribes than the English. An important French diplomatic victory at the peace treaty at Montreal in 1701 that ended the war in North America was to secure the neutrality of the Iroquois confederacy in any future war between the French and British (Eccles 1987, p. 81).

The War of the Spanish Succession was fought to prevent the Bourbons from uniting the French and Spanish crowns after the last Habsburg king of Spain, Charles II, died childless. If the wealth of Spain's vast overseas empire could be united with France's population and territorial extent in Europe within the same dynastic state, the outlook for the northern maritime powers would not be encouraging. French commercial and financial interests had already penetrated the

Spanish economy in Cadiz and secured the Asiento, the monopoly license to import 38,000 slaves into Spanish America at a price of 100 livres per head, a right that had previously belonged nominally to a Portuguese concern but was in practice exercised by a variety of European suppliers, mainly Dutch and British.

The Caribbean did not see major naval engagements during the war but there was extensive French privateering, including a spectacular raid on Rio de Janeiro in 1711, and considerable other damage to English, Dutch, and Portuguese interests. Notably, however, trade between the colonies of all the European belligerents not only continued but actually flourished, since wartime conditions made it harder for the metropolitan authorities to enforce mercantilist restrictions. The expansion of sugar cultivation on Saint-Domingue, Martinique, and Guadeloupe continued unabated and the mainland English colonies found ready markets for their produce in the French Caribbean islands. Pritchard (2004, p. 384) goes so far as to declare that "the War of the Spanish Succession, by breaking the stifling forces of regulation and control and introducing freer trade than ever before witnessed, may have been the most important stimulus to economic growth in France's colonial history." The Dutch, always anxious to carry on trade, even with their enemies in time of war, turned a blind eye to the raising of loans in Amsterdam to finance the French war effort, much to the chagrin of their English allies.

French defeats in Europe at the hands of the brilliant Allied commanders, the duke of Marlborough and Prince Eugene of Savoy, led to the sacrifice of colonial and commercial interests in the Americas at the end of the war to prevent further territorial concessions having to be made in Europe. The eastern region of French Canada known as Acadia fell to a provincial British force and was renamed Nova Scotia. This region ended up being ceded to Britain by France at the Treaty of Utrecht in 1713, along with Newfoundland and the French part of St. Kitts. Pritchard (2004, p. 401) is of the opinion that "the Treaty of Utrecht dealt any French dream of empire a serious blow from which it never recovered."

The treaty was a landmark in Britain's rise as a great power and in that of its overseas empire. The Spanish crown did go to a member of the Bourbon family, in the person of Philip V, but the treaty ensured that the French and Spanish branches of the dynasty could never be merged to rule over both kingdoms. Gibraltar, captured in 1704, was ceded to the British, giving them a key naval base that they have not relinquished to this day. A notable economic prize was the Asiento, which was secured for thirty years. Another significant by-product of the war was the Methuen Treaty with Portugal, signed in 1703, by which England had preferential access for cloth exports to Portugal in exchange for reciprocal preferences for Portuguese wine exports to England, the trade immortalized by David Ricardo's use of it to illustrate his theory of comparative advantage. By 1715 Louis XIV was dead, succeeded by his great-grandson, and the last Stuart, Queen Anne, was succeeded by the first Hanoverian, George I. The Treaty of Utrecht, which ended a quarter century of only briefly interrupted warfare between Britain and France, was followed by a quarter century of peace.

British trade with Spanish America was now supposed to be governed by the terms of the Asiento, but illegal trade continued to take place. In an effort to prevent what they regarded as blatant smuggling and contraband trade, the Spanish authorities licensed so-called *guarda-costas*, vessels manned by a motley assortment of crews including former buccaneers, to interdict foreign shipping that they suspected of engaging in illegal trade of any kind. In the course of these activities, an English captain named Robert Jenkins apparently had his ear cut off in a shipboard scuffle with a French boarding party. Seven years later he presented the severed organ pickled in a bottle of brandy to an outraged House of Commons, leading to the declaration of the only war in history named after a severed body part. A large British naval force captured Portobello but failed to do the same to Cartagena and Havana. The Anglo-Spanish conflict soon merged into an Anglo-French one after the outbreak in Europe of the War of the Austrian Succession (1740–48), which saw the French-supported Jacobite invasion of Scotland and the rising of the Highland clans in 1745 that was crushed by the Hanoverian regime at the Battle of Culloden.

In the aftermath of Utrecht there had prevailed initially a sort of geopolitical and economic equilibrium between the French and British colonies on the North American mainland that was now broken. A destabilizing factor was the growth of the settler population in Virginia that induced a movement west of the Alleghenies into the Ohio valley in search of additional farmland, financed and organized by land speculators. This agitated the Iroquois confederacy that claimed possession of these lands and alarmed the French authorities, fearing that the English might advance to the Mississippi and cut the links between Louisiana and New France. They accordingly intervened actively in the Ohio valley, constructing a string of forts and escalating the conflict with the Virginians, obliging the British government itself to send regular troops to support the colonists. A force of British regulars under General Braddock, together with a contingent of Virginia militia under the young George Washington, was ambushed by Indians allied with the French, with Braddock being killed in the encounter. By a chain of unintended consequences this set the stage for the worldwide Seven Years' War of 1756–63 (Anderson 2001; Higonnet 1968), known in American history as the French and Indian War.

The early phases of the war in North America saw some initial victories by the French and their Native American allies, but command of the Atlantic ensured that Britain, under the furiously energetic and boldly imaginative leadership of William Pitt the Elder from 1756 to 1761, could deploy more effective military force across the ocean and would ultimately prevail. The French were driven from their forts in the Ohio valley, and Louisbourg, Quebec, and Montreal all eventually fell to well-planned "combined operations" by naval and land forces, the most spectacular of which was the capture of Quebec in 1759 by James Wolfe, where both Wolfe and the French commander Montcalm were killed. Montreal fell in the following year. The Royal Navy also inflicted crushing defeats on French fleets at the Battles of Quiberon Bay on the coast of France and Lagos on the coast of Portugal in 1759. Guadeloupe and Martinique were captured in 1759 and 1762, along with several smaller islands including Dominica, Saint Lucia, and Grenada. The extended conflict in India between the two East India Companies that had been going on since the 1740s went increasingly in favor of the English. The headquarters of the French company at Pondicherry fell to the English in 1761, leading to the capture of other trading stations on the east coast of India, again largely as a result of British naval superiority. In 1758 French forts and trading stations on the Senegal and Gambia Rivers, and the island of Goree in West Africa, fell to small British naval expeditions. The Spanish Bourbons rashly formed a "Family Compact" with their French cousins and entered the war in 1762, promptly losing Cuba and the Philippines for their pains after British naval squadrons and landing forces captured Havana and Manila, while their invasion of Portugal was beaten off with the help of a British expeditionary force.

In Europe itself the fighting pitted the military genius of Frederick the Great of Prussia, supported by large British subsidies, against the huge armies deployed by his French, Austrian, and Russian enemies. Frederick was in dire straits when he was saved by the death of the Empress Elizabeth in 1762 and the subsequent withdrawal of Russia from the war. Hostilities in all theaters were eventually concluded at the Treaty of Paris in 1763. Unlike all the wars since 1689 that had ended only in relatively marginal changes to the status quo ante bellum, the Seven Years' War was a decisive triumph for Great Britain over France. All of New France was ceded to the British, who also received Florida from the Spanish, giving them command of the North American continent east of the Mississippi from Hudson's Bay to the Gulf of Mexico. Louisiana was transferred from France to Spain, and Cuba and the Philippines were also returned to her. The valuable and highly prized sugar islands in the Caribbean were returned to France, largely due to the influence of the West Indian planter lobby in Britain, which wanted Barbados and Jamaica to continue to enjoy the protection afforded by the higher import duties on foreign sugar. Despite these gains, the peace terms were bitterly denounced by Pitt after his fall from power and replacement by Lord Bute, the favorite of the new king George III, as being too favorable to France and giving them the possibility to stage a successful comeback (Plumb 1963, p. 114). The French chief minister the duc de Choiseul also made a prediction, shared even by some British leaders, to the effect that with no French presence on the continent to threaten them any longer, the American colonies would soon demand independence from Great Britain (Eccles 1987, p. 148). As it turned out, both statesmen were uncannily prescient.

It is evident from the preceding paragraph that it was the command of the oceans of the world that enabled Great Britain to achieve these astonishing feats of global force projection within a few years, while always being separated only by a narrow stretch of water from invasion by the most formidable land power in Western Europe. As we have seen, and the 1588 defeat of the Spanish Armada notwithstanding, it was only during the Anglo-Dutch wars that Britain truly emerged to naval eminence and even then she was by no means able to dominate the Dutch fleets. During the War of the Spanish Succession it took the combined strength of the English and Dutch fleets to stand up to the French navy, which had been greatly expanded by Colbert, with the French defeating an Anglo-Dutch fleet at Beachy Head in 1690 before their own defeat later at La Hogue. Indeed, the outbreak of the Seven Years' War saw a humiliating British naval defeat at Minorca in 1756, the event that led to the execution of Admiral Byng "pour encourager les autres," as Voltaire famously said.

If that was the purpose of the execution, it was certainly immensely successful since, as we have seen, British admirals proceeded to win a string of victories in the Atlantic, Pacific, and Indian Oceans without any further defeats. The aforementioned victory at Quiberon Bay in November 1759, the Trafalgar of the Seven Years' War, ended at one stroke all hope of a bold French plan to invade Britain or to challenge her any further at sea, while also sealing the fate of the French empire in Canada in the following year (Anderson 2001, chapter 43). Particularly strikingly, the capture of Manila was effected with the loss of only 26 dead by a small expedition, financed and mounted from Madras by the East India Company, of 500 British regulars and 550 Indian sepoys, transported on ten ships of the Royal Navy's Indian Ocean squadron. The casualties were much higher when Havana was taken, over 6,000 dead, but not from the Spanish resistance, which was feeble, but from an outbreak of yellow fever, reportedly causing Dr. Johnson to exclaim, "may my country never be cursed with such another conquest" (Kamen 2003, p. 482).

Recent writings by naval historians have stressed that the linchpin of British naval strategy during the Second Hundred Years' War was the regular deployment of the Western Squadron, a fleet of warships guarding the windward Western Approaches to the English Channel, well out into the Atlantic but close enough to receive instructions and intelligence from headquarters and to monitor, intercept, or blockade any potentially threatening moves by French fleets, which had their main bases at Brest and Toulon. At the same time as it was performing this primary defensive function for the home islands, the Squadron was in an excellent position to protect outward- and inward-bound British commercial shipping to the East and West Indies and to interdict, in time of war, that of its European enemies. Limited predatory or defensive missions to other seas could be and were undertaken by "detaching" components of the main squadron as necessary to the relevant waters. Furthermore, any Western European enemy such as France or Spain wishing to contest the detached force on the way to or at its destination would itself have to endeavor to leave its home ports under the watchful eyes of the Western Squadron, and risk annihilation if it was not sufficiently large.

This was the elegant and economical solution of the Royal Navy to the problem of how to reconcile its defensive and offensive objectives with the limited resources available. N. A. M. Rodger (1998) points out that 64% of Britain's naval resources in ships and men during the height of the Seven Years' War were deployed either at home or defensively in the Mediterranean, noting that "in this, the most successful war of commercial conquest that Britain ever fought, the bulk of the navy stayed at home—and by doing so, it made those conquests possible" (p. 179). Implementation of the strategy required not just an adequate supply of warships, but in addition the capability of keeping a sufficient fraction of them at sea, which was a function of the scale and efficiency of maintenance, repair, manning, and victualing systems. As Baugh (2004) points out the Royal Navy in the eighteenth century performed all these ancillary functions exceptionally well, with the result that in 1762 80% of the ships and men were at sea, an astonishingly high ratio that the French and Spanish did not come close to matching. The length of time at sea also meant that there was more experience accumulated by junior officers, and greater opportunity to assess their performance for promotion and advancement. In addition, the Royal Navy's rulebook meant that captains were obliged to engage the enemy wherever possible, implying that crews tended to be well-trained and battle-hardened (Allen 2002). Thus, even if the rival navies could match or exceed the number of ships of the line and support vessels, the Royal Navy was generally able to outperform them in action.

Navies were extremely expensive, a 74-gun ship costing £50,000 to build in 1780 when the largest factory in England cost only a tenth of that amount (Baugh 2004, p. 238). The full crew of a battle fleet could amount to 24,000 men, larger than most contemporary towns, which meant a huge strain on the supply of provisions when the entire fleet was in port (Duffy 1992, p. 66). Maintenance of this powerful military machine obviously required state expenditure and revenue on an unprecedented scale, documented by the pioneering work of John Brewer (1990) on the British fiscal-military state in *The Sinews of Power*. He finds that between 1680 and 1780 the British army and navy trebled in size (Brewer 1994, p. 57). Average annual tax revenue rose from £3.6 million during the Nine Years' War to £8.6 million during the Seven Years' War (Brewer 1990, p. 30). Rapid as this growth of tax revenue was, it could not keep pace with the growth of expenditure, the solution being found in the expansion of the National Debt from £16.7 million in 1697 to £132.6 million in 1763 (ibid.). Military spending as a percentage of total expenditure averaged about 70% in these wars,[3] but as a percentage of national income it rose from 9% in 1710 to 14% in 1760 (pp. 40–41), a figure which is high even by the standards of today, indicating the extraordinary war-fighting capabilities of the eighteenth-century British fiscal-military state. Brewer explains the fiscal efficiency of the state as a consequence of the centralization of both revenue collection and expenditure in a single authority, the Treasury, and the recruitment of highly skilled practitioners by the Excise and Customs departments.

For comparison of the fiscal efforts of Britain and France we can turn to the very striking results obtained by Mathias and O'Brien

[3]The proportion was even higher according to O'Brien (1993).

(1976). On the basis of standard stereotypes, one would have expected that France with its royal absolutism would be capable of extracting more revenue than Britain, with its constitutional monarchy and more representative political institutions. Surprisingly, however, they found that Britain extracted twice as much tax revenue in real per capita terms as did France over most of the eighteenth century, and three times as much during the Napoleonic Wars. The difference was due to the much greater reliance on a very wide range of indirect taxes on articles of consumption in Britain, and the effective collection of those taxes by officials recruited for that purpose. Crucially, "Around 1800, something like one-third of tax revenue came from customs duties levied in large part on the imports of tropical foodstuffs and alcoholic beverages. Could the central government have funded a military establishment of sufficient capability to defend the integrity of the kingdom's boundaries without a tax base that included an array of imported commodities in inelastic demand?" (O'Brien and Engerman 1991, p. 206).

This stronger tax base also enabled Britain to borrow more extensively and at lower interest rates than France, so that the fiscal burden of the many wars could be "smoothed" by the issue of the National Debt in money and capital markets presided over by the Bank of England, created in 1694. The high levels of military expenditure, and the heavy taxation and borrowing that they necessitated, can be analyzed conventionally as "crowding out" private investment and thus as being detrimental to the performance of the economy in the long run (Williamson 1984). Such an approach, however, ignores the necessity of generating and protecting overseas commerce in a mercantilist world where unilateral free trade and a pacific stance were not viable options. Thus the Dutch Republic, which clearly would have had the most to gain from a regime of free multilateral trade, had to tax itself even more severely than Britain to defend its own extensive trade.

As Pitt and Choiseul had both foreseen, for separate reasons, Britain did not have long to enjoy the apparent gains of the 1763 Treaty of Paris. The American colonies were soon in the throes of a prolonged postwar recession exacerbated by a slump in tobacco prices, arousing opposition to imperial control. Meanwhile, the war had left a "European military fiscal crisis" in its wake (Bayly 2004, pp. 92–96), with the main belligerents all having to service massive debts. In Britain, the House of Commons refused to vote higher land taxes in 1767, while the greater power of business there made it impossible for government to default on its debts, as had happened in 1672 under Charles II. Politically, it seemed much easier to transfer the tax burden to the colonies, for example, by collecting stamp duty there (McCusker 1996, pp. 360–61), especially since the government felt it necessary to maintain a strong military presence in North America. This provoked the famous outcry of "no taxation without representation," resulting in the repeal of the Stamp Act but the imposition of higher customs duties instead, together with tighter enforcement of mercantilist trade regulations as well as other unpopular measures such as the obligation to quarter the armed forces in emergencies. Another major source of dissension was the attempt by the British government to preserve the western territories from settlement to avoid clashes with the Native American tribes. The tensions finally led, by a series of well-known steps, to the Declaration of Independence in 1776 and the outbreak of the Revolutionary War.

France, stung by the humiliating defeats of the Seven Years' War, had undertaken extensive military reforms including an ambitious program of naval construction that saw naval expenditure rise from about 30 million livres a year in the 1760s to over 150 million at the end of the next decade (Kennedy 1987, p. 118). She entered the fray on the colonists' side in 1778, to be followed soon by Spain and even England's longtime ally the Dutch Republic, while the other European powers declared themselves neutral, thereby completely isolating England. France for once was free of continental entanglements in Europe and could concentrate on a naval and colonial war, while Britain of necessity had to fight an American continental war to suppress the rebellious colonists in a conflict that had many of the characteristics of an insurgency, rather than simply a conventional battle between opposing armies. The expanded French fleet, in combination with the Spanish, outnumbered the British one and was able to temporarily gain sufficient command of the Atlantic to prevent Lord Cornwallis and a large British army, besieged by George Washington and 5,800 French regulars at Yorktown on the Chesapeake Bay in 1781, from being evacuated or reinforced by sea, forcing Cornwallis to surrender. This was the decisive battle of the war that ended with the Treaty of Versailles in 1783. Washington himself handsomely acknowledged the significance of the French contribution in a letter to Admiral De Grasse in which he said, "You will have observed that whatever efforts are made by the land armies, the navy must have the casting vote in the present contest" (Lloyd 1965, p. 174). The Canadian historian W. J. Eccles (1987, p. 153) is even more explicit: "French initiative, French tactics, French ships, French guns and men achieved that unexpected and decisive victory. The Americans could not have done it on their own." The Treaty of Versailles, whereby independence was granted to the new United States of America, retained Canada and Nova Scotia in British possession and restored Florida to Spain. Louisiana would remain in Spanish hands until 1800, when it was briefly returned to France, before being sold to the United States in the Louisiana Purchase of 1803.

The size of the British armed forces deployed and the scale of military expenditure during the American Revolutionary War were both even higher than in the Seven Years' War, and the National Debt increased by another £100 million to a total of £243 million (Brewer 1990, p. 30). The war also had very severe consequences for France's much more disorderly fiscal system, where the finance minister Calonne and his predecessor Necker together borrowed over 900 million livres in the decade from 1777 to 1787 (Doyle 1988, pp. 43–52). The situation was so bad that Calonne informed Louis XVI that no fiscal remedies could be found without a complete overhaul of the society and administrative system of the ancien régime, leading to the summoning of the Estates-General in 1789 and the outbreak of the French Revolution. The last act in the drama of the Second Hundred Years' War thus began to unfold, with consequences that we will explore in chapter 7.

What were the implications of these momentous events for British and French trade? As we saw in the last section England's foreign trade was transformed in the last four decades of the seventeenth century by the explosive growth of colonial reexports, primarily of tobacco and sugar, displacing the traditional exports of woolen cloth in relative importance. These commodities were originally high-priced luxuries in European markets, but the rapid extension of cultivation in the Chesapeake region and the West Indies led to dramatic reductions in price and highly elastic responses in consumer demand, creating mass markets for both products. According to Davis (1967, p. 10) tobacco sold at 20–40 shillings a pound during the reign of James I, but at not more than a shilling during the reign of his grandson Charles II. Sugar followed a similar pattern, and the same was also true of Asian "tropical groceries" such as tea, whose price fell from 12 to 36 shillings per pound in the 1720s to between 2 and 10 shillings per pound in 1785, and which had become a working class drink by mid century. In Britain, per capita sugar consumption rose from roughly 4 pounds in 1698–99 to twice that level in the 1710s, doubled again by the 1750s, and stood at some 24 pounds by the 1790s; while tea consumption per capita quadrupled between the 1730s and 1790s (Berg 2004, pp. 366–67). The availability of these commodities gave workers an incentive

TABLE 5.4. English exports, 1699–1774 (thousands of pounds sterling).

	1699–1701	1722–24	1752–54	1772–74
Woolen goods				
Continental Europe	2,745	2,592	3,279	2,630
Ireland and Channel Islands	26	19	47	219
America and Africa	185	303	374	1,148
India and Far East	89	72	230	189
Other manufactures				
Continental Europe	456	367	647	987
Ireland and Channel Islands	60	40	168	280
America and Africa	290	376	1,197	2,533
India and Far East	22	15	408	501
Reexports (to all markets)				
Total	1,986	2,714	3,492	5,818
of which				
Calicoes	340	484	499	701
Total manufactures	746	1,116	1,145	1,562
Tobacco	421	387	953	904
Sugar	287	211	110	429
Pepper	93	44	104	110
Tea	2	267	217	295
Coffee	2	151	84	873
Rice	4	63	206	363

Source: Davis (1962, pp. 291, 302).

to shift from leisure to work, and from subsistence production to commercial activities, and scholars such as Jan De Vries (1993, 1994) and Joachim Voth (1998) have identified and measured an "Industrious Revolution" which contributed substantially to economic growth in eighteenth-century Europe (Bayly 2004, pp. 51–55).

In the eighteenth century woolen exports to the main market in continental Europe continued to expand relatively slowly, as table 5.4 (taken from Davis 1962) shows. Overseas markets, on the other hand, rose much faster. The star performer among English exports in the eighteenth century was a wide variety of miscellaneous manufactures such as "nails, axes, firearms, buckets, coaches, clocks, saddles, handkerchiefs, buttons, cordage" and other items so tedious to enumerate that the customs officials listed them simply as "Goods, several sorts," all destined for the colonies across the Atlantic. This category of English goods, listed as "other manufactures" in table 5.4, saw their exports to continental Europe almost doubling over the course of the eighteenth century, but the most important markets were overseas. Thus, exports to Africa and America grew from less than £300,000 at the start of the century to more than £2.5 million by the early 1770s, reflecting not only the progress of this sector in Britain itself but also the extension of the empire as a result of the successful prosecution of the Seven Years' War. Significantly, India and the Far East took £408,000 worth of these goods in 1752–54 and £501,000 worth in 1772–74, compared to negligible amounts in 1722–24. Continental Europe had been the largest market for these goods at the start of the century, but overseas exports were three times more important on the eve of the American Revolution.

The initial sharp decline in tobacco and sugar reexports, documented in the table, reflected the effects of French competition, and the subsequent increase the effects of victory in the Seven Years' War. Tea from China and coffee from the West Indies rose from negligible amounts to £295,000 and £873,000 respectively in 1772–74. The reexport of Indian calicoes by the East India Company to Europe and Africa grew rapidly, more than doubling to £701,000 by 1772–74. All this is clear evidence that British trade in the first three-quarters of the eighteenth century had acquired a decisively intercontinental character, in contrast with its more traditional European orientation at the end of the seventeenth century. This was particularly so with respect to the more dynamic elements of miscellaneous manufactured exports, and the reexport trade, and shows the growing importance of empire for the British economy at this time, and the role of Power in providing for Plenty.

Crouzet (1990) notes the surprising fact that French foreign trade grew even faster than English trade between 1715 and 1784. He defines total "foreign trade" as the sum of the values of exports, imports, and reexports, and finds that while English foreign trade increased in real terms by a factor of 2.4 between 1716–20 and 1784–88, French foreign trade increased over the same period by a factor of at least 3.

This faster growth allowed French foreign trade to almost catch up with Britain's by the middle of the 1780s, after being just above half of its rival's in 1716–20. However, this still left it at barely one-third of the British level in per capita terms. As regards the direction of trade, France had a large share of the trade with Spain and Spanish America, helped no doubt by the Bourbon connection, while Britain dominated the smaller Portuguese–Brazilian market, thanks to the Methuen Treaty. The main difference in the export of manufactures, however, was that France did not enjoy the growing market of the

TABLE 5.5. British and French trade, 1787–89 (thousands of pounds sterling).

	Domestic exports		Reexports		Imports	
	Britain	France	Britain	France	Britain	France
To/from own colonies,						
Africa, Asia	6,919	3,610	1,719	33	14,830	9,173
of which						
Ireland	1,569		961		3,358	
West Indies	1,761		208		5,582	8,000
Canada	781		240		268	
Asia	2,170		54		5,465	900
Africa	636		257		157	273
To/from foreign						
American colonies	617	200	2		1,096	
To/from the U.S.	2,567	56	334	5	1,246	401
To/from Europe						
and the Levant	7,741	6,750	2,797	6,921	9,958	11,964
Total	17,846	10,617	4,852	6,960	27,132	21,539

Source: Cuenca Esteban (2004, tables 2.1, 2.2, and 2.3, pp. 38–42).

British colonies on the American mainland, with the population of New France being of almost minuscule proportions in comparison. Table 5.5, taken from the work of Cuenca Esteban (2004), shows that even in 1787–89, after American independence, Britain was still exporting significant quantities of domestically produced goods to the United States, a market that France was seemingly unable to penetrate. France did enjoy rapid growth in reexports of sugar from her West Indian possessions of Martinique, Guadeloupe, and particularly Saint-Domingue. It was the competition of the much-lower-cost sugar from this source that reduced British reexports from Barbados and Jamaica. French colonial trade grew tenfold from 1716–20 to 1784–88, making it almost 40% of the total at that time. However, table 5.5 also indicates French vulnerability, in that the overwhelming majority of her colonial imports were from Saint-Domingue.

INDIA: THE DISINTEGRATION OF THE MUGHAL EMPIRE AND THE TRANSITION TO COLONIAL RULE

As the previous chapter has already indicated, the Mughal Empire was a formidably large and powerful political entity, with a population many times greater than contemporary imperial states, the Manchu Qing Empire being the only exception. Under Shah Jahan (1628–58) and his son Aurangzeb (1658–1707) the Mughals penetrated as far north as Afghanistan, as far to the east as Assam, and south almost to the tip of the peninsula. Aurangzeb conquered the Deccan sultanates of Bijapur and Golconda that had resisted all previous efforts by the dynasty to incorporate them. The frontiers of cultivation and of Islam were considerably extended, notably in Bengal, while Indian cotton textiles were sold all over the world by the European trading companies. On their northwestern frontier the Mughals maintained a stable equilibrium with the Safavids, with Kabul in their hands while Herat was held by the Safavids, and Kandahar as the bone of contention passing from one to the other. Despite these conflicts both dynasties and the Afghans benefited from the caravan trade that they all conducted with each other and with Central Asia.

Aurangzeb's long reign was the period in which the dynasty saw both its maximum territorial extent and the beginning of its downfall. A good case can be made that the two were causally related to each other by the familiar phenomenon of "imperial overstretch," expansion of an empire beyond the optimal point at which the benefits and costs of adding further territory are in balance and after which the net effect is negative (Kennedy 1987; Findlay 1996). The conquest of the Deccan sultanates, and the attempt to administer them directly, undoubtedly strained the resources of the empire, leaving it more open to rebellions and invasions in other quarters in the future. One of the major threats faced by the Mughals during this period was the emergence in the western region of Maharashtra of the Maratha confederacy, a mobile predatory state created by the audacious and charismatic warrior chieftain Shivaji Bhonsle (1674–80). After securing their home base in the lands between the Western Ghats and the coast, the Marathas under Shivaji and his successors swept to the north and east, harassing the Mughals and other Muslim and Hindu states unless bought off by the payment of at least a quarter of the regular revenues that the lands were assessed for.

Instead of allowing the Deccan sultanates to remain as buffer states against the far more lethal threat of the Marathas, Aurangzeb chose to take them over and confront the Marathas directly. This geopolitical error can perhaps be traced to his fanatical Sunni orthodoxy, which could not tolerate the Shia faith of the Deccan rulers. The Mughals' tradition of religious tolerance, established by Akbar but subverted by Aurangzeb, would have been preserved had his scholarly and humane elder brother Dara Shukoh won the succession battle between the brothers that ended with the capture and execution of the latter. As it was, Aurangzeb's persecution of non-Muslims by measures such as the reimposition of the jizya, the poll tax on unbelievers, needlessly compromised the traditional loyalty of the Rajput princes to the regime, and aroused the otherwise peaceful Sikhs and sturdy peasant Jats of northern India to fierce and prolonged resistance.

Finally, and perhaps most important of all, it was a military-fiscal crisis similar to that confronting the major European states that led to the decline of the empire (Bayly 2004). As in Europe, new military technologies had increased the cost of the incessant warfare that the empire now found itself engaged in. Meanwhile, the growing independence of provincial governors and other officials led them increasingly to retain the revenues and dues they collected for their own use, rather than transmitting them fully to the center. The loss of revenue sapped the numbers and effectiveness of the imperial armies, which of course only made it harder to prevent state revenues from declining even further. This Mughal decline was symbolized by the sudden emergence in quick succession of two remarkable Afghan warlords, Nadir Shah and Ahmad Shah Durrani. The former put an end to the Safavid dynasty in 1736, and in 1739 conducted a devastating raid on northern India and Delhi, slaughtering thousands and carrying away an enormous amount of plunder, including the fabled Peacock Throne of Shah Jahan. His raid was followed a few years later by the even more destructive forays of Ahmad Shah Durrani's Afghan Abdali tribesmen.

The increase in revenues accruing to the provincial chiefs made these positions more desirable, so that rival contenders sought the support of either the Marathas or of the European Companies in exchange for commercial privileges. It was by this means that the English East India Company was able to gain control of the rich province of Bengal in the 1750s and 1760s. The Company was formed in 1600, and granted a monopoly of English trade east of the Cape of Good Hope and west of the Straits of Magellan, originally for fifteen years. As we saw in the last chapter, the Company's initial efforts concentrated on the spice trade in the Indonesian archipelago in competition with the Dutch, in which it was not very successful. When Surat in Gujarat was chosen in 1607 as the first station in India, it was intended to serve as a base for the supply of the Indonesian trade, rather than for the trade of India itself. It was not long, however, before the advantages of Surat as "the fountainhead from whence we may draw all the trade of our East Indies; for we find here merchandise which we can take and sell in nearly all parts of these Indies and also in England" (Andrews 1984, p. 270) were realized. The hinterland of Surat supplied cotton textiles, and also indigo and saltpeter. It was a convenient port from which to sail not only to the Spice Islands in the east, but also to the Persian Gulf and the Red Sea. Furthermore, it was close to the Mughal capital of Agra, with its enormous demand for luxury goods of all kinds, where the Company also established a factory.

The Company used its naval forces not only to protect itself from the Portuguese, but also to serve as escorts for Indian ships carrying valuable cargoes to the Red Sea and the Persian Gulf as well as thousands of pilgrims to Mecca. All these services and the skillful diplomacy of the ambassador Sir Thomas Roe put the Company in the good books of the emperor Jehangir, and led to the granting of several commercial privileges. Another factory was established at the important port of Masulipatam on the east coast in 1611. Andrews (1984, p. 273) states that the English commercial penetration of the Indian subcontinent was well under way by 1630. In 1639 the site of Madras was obtained from a local ruler and Fort St. George constructed on it, to be followed in 1690 by the founding of Calcutta and the construction of Fort William. In 1668 the Company received from Charles II the future port of Bombay, which was eventually to displace Surat as its main center on the west coast. These three Company trading stations, Bombay, Madras, and Calcutta, were of course destined to become the main port cities of modern India. Madras grew rapidly and had a population of over 300,000 by 1700, while Calcutta and Bombay had 100,000 and 70,000 respectively by the middle of the eighteenth century (Smith 1981, p. 456). Each of these cities was the headquarters of an autonomous "Presidency," responsible only to the Directors in London, thus providing a necessary degree of decentralization at the expense of some loss of coordination and consistency of overall policy for the subcontinent as a whole.

In the 1680s the Company's head in London Sir Josiah Child, perhaps better known to posterity as the author of the mercantilist classic *A New Discourse of Trade*, rashly attempted to intimidate the Mughals by the use of naval power in Bengal and western India, but soon had to climb down when Aurangzeb seized the factory at Surat and threatened to expel the English from India. The Company did not attempt any further forcible interventions until the 1750s, long after the death of the formidable Aurangzeb. Trade expanded steadily after the reorganization of the Company in 1708, when two rival claimants to the original royal monopoly charter were formed into the "United Company of Merchants of England trading to the East Indies," with a capital of £1.25 million, a very large sum for the time, contributed by some 3,000 shareholders. The profit rates of the Company were always respectable, with the Company endeavoring to maintain a dividend rate of 8%, twice the rate of interest paid on bond debt (Chaudhuri 1978, p. 445).

The origins of organized French trade in India, as with so much else in ancien régime France, go back to Colbert, who launched a General Company in 1664 "to procure for the kingdom the activity of commerce and to prevent the English and the Dutch profiting from it alone, as they had done up to then" (Markovits 2004, p. 144). A French squadron was dispatched to Indian waters in 1671 but did not achieve much beyond the establishment of a trading station in the village of Pondicherry in 1674. This grew into the fortified headquarters for French trade on the subcontinent, with a population of 120,000 by 1740. Another important French station was at Chandernagore in Bengal, founded in 1688, from which valuable supplies of silk and cotton textiles were secured. Thirty vessels were sent to India between 1711 and 1716, but this was only half the English figure and one-fifth that of the Dutch (figure 4.5). After reorganization in the 1720s the French Company developed Pondicherry and the trade with India to a flourishing state. Between 1728 and 1740 the volume of its trade increased tenfold from £89,000 to £880,000, but this was still only half the British figure (Smith 1981, p. 457). The profit rate of the French Company in the 1730s was, however, 25%, significantly higher than the maximum 10% of its English rival (Markovits 2004, p. 209).

The decades of the 1740s and 1750s in India were dominated by the global Anglo-French power struggle, compounded as we have seen by Iranian and Afghan invasions in the north and by local Indian political conflicts in which the two European powers took opposing sides, resulting in an extremely confusing series of actions and counteractions by all the parties concerned. All this ultimately led to the triumph of the English, the utter defeat of the French and, even though they of course did not realize it at the time, the future subjugation of all the Indian powers to the English. The key strategic insight of Joseph Francois Dupleix, the leader of the French cause in India, was that India in the middle of the eighteenth century was vulnerable to a takeover bid by any leading European power at the low price of a small but well-trained army of native troops, led by European officers and a few regulars using modern artillery and armaments, and supplemented by skillful diplomacy to play the local potentates off against each other. By this means, wealthy local states or Mughal provinces could be ruled as mere puppets of the European companies, who could thereby gain control over lucrative local sources of revenue to finance either commercial activities or further expansion of their political influence. Unfortunately for Dupleix and for France it was Robert Clive, a young officer of the East India Company, and Britain backed by its superior financial and naval power, that ultimately succeeded with exactly the same approach that Dupleix had pioneered.

Britain's opportunity came when the Nawab of Bengal, under whose virtually independent rule the Company had been able to successfully promote its commercial interests in that province, died and was succeeded by his grandson, a young hothead named Siraj-ud-Daula who provoked the British by seizing Calcutta. Robert Clive embarked from Madras with a force of British regulars and Indian sepoys and confronted Siraj-ud-Daula and the Bengal army at Plassey in 1757. Siraj-ud-Daula was promptly killed and replaced by Mir Jafar as Nawab of Bengal, the latter being replaced in turn when he proved insufficiently responsive to British wishes. Once again, however, the British misjudged, as the new Nawab made strenuous efforts to assert his independence, calling in an army led by the Nawab of Oudh and the Mughal heir apparent Shah Alam himself. This was defeated by Company forces in the hard-fought Battle of Buxar in 1764, placing Bengal securely under British control. A treaty of 1765 with Shah Alam granted the *diwani*, the right to collect the revenue of Bengal, to the Company, and also put Oudh under a form of supervision exercised by a British Resident and military garrison. Bengal, with its substantial land revenues and extensive silk and cotton textile industries, had thus become "the British Bridgehead" for the takeover of India (Marshall 1987).

Within Bengal the Company's servants, not excluding Clive himself, indulged in an orgy of corruption that caused a scandal in England, leading to the tighter regulation of the Company by the state in a Regulating Act of 1773. Clive, whose distress over the charges leveled against him could not be assuaged even by the award of a peerage, committed suicide in 1774. Warren Hastings took up the new post of Governor-General, with authority extending to the Madras and Bombay Presidencies as well as Bengal. Hastings not only placed the administration of Bengal on a sounder footing but also contained serious threats to the British position in India from the Muslim ruler Haider Ali of the formerly Hindu state of Mysore, who was supported by the French, and from the Marathas. Hastings left India in 1785 to face impeachment and trial in England, flayed by the rhetoric of Edmund Burke that irretrievably damaged his reputation despite his eventual acquittal. His achievement, however, aptly summed up by Percival Spear (1990, p. 92), was to have "found a revenue administration and left a state."

Hastings was succeeded as Governor-General by Lord Cornwallis, fresh from his surrender to George Washington at Yorktown, who stamped out the remnants of corruption in Bengal and reformed the conditions for Company service by raising salaries and prohibiting trade on personal account in return. The Marathas and the Mysore state under Haider Ali's son Tipu Sultan, the most determined enemy that the British faced in India, were contained and defeated by the next Governor-General, the Anglo-Irish Richard (later Marquis) Wellesley. His younger brother Arthur, also in the service of the Company, gained valuable military experience fighting the Marathas, preparing him for his future incarnation as the duke of Wellington and victor of Waterloo. The British extended their power up the Ganges valley in Oudh and toward Delhi. In 1803 the Mughal emperor Shah Alam, blinded by the Afghans in 1788 and virtually powerless long before that, placed himself under British protection, symbolically confirming what by then was obvious to all, that Britain had become the real ruler of what had been the Mughal Empire.

After this extended description of the complicated political background, we can turn at last to the structure and evolution of the economic system of the Mughal Empire. The state, and therefore the towns in which most of the elite resided, was built upon the extraction of land taxes from the peasantry. "The Great Mogul consumes everything," a Florentine traveler said (Markovits 2004, p. 123), apparently referring to the extraction of vast revenues from the countryside to the center for redistribution down the chain of military and civilian officials of the regime, each with his own retinue of retainers to be supported. Tapan Raychaudhuri (1982, p. 173) says that "the Mughal Empire was an insatiable Leviathan: its impact on the economy was defined above all by its unlimited appetite for resources." According to Maddison (2001, p. 109) land taxes accounted for some 15% of national income. It is worth noting, however, that this figure was comparable to the equivalent figure in eighteenth-century England, an issue to which we will return in the next chapter. An important aspect of the Mughal taxation system was that it prescribed lower rates for land devoted to cash crops such as cotton and sugarcane than for land devoted to food grains, in a deliberate attempt to promote the commercialization of the economy. There were also incentives for bringing new land under cultivation and for the construction of infrastructure such as wells. The growth of foreign trade contributed to the revenues of the empire, raising land revenue and customs duties, and as we have seen led to bullion inflows increasing the supply of coined currency.

Despite the succession struggles and wars with the Marathas, the subcontinent as a whole benefited from a *Pax Mughalica*. There were strong regional differences in the availability of food grains, with some areas such as Bengal having large surpluses while others such as Gujarat had deficits, necessitating considerable interregional trade by both land and sea to balance demand and supply. Bengal and Gujarat were also dependent on each other for the raw materials of their major manufactured goods. The Bengal cotton textile industry imported cotton from Gujarat, and the silk weaving industry of Gujarat imported raw silk from Bengal (Prakash 2004, chapter 9). The cotton textiles traded were not just fine quality muslins largely destined for the export trade, but to a greater extent the coarse cloth worn by ordinary consumers.

As noted in the previous chapter, the fact that the Mughal Empire collected its land revenue in cash itself necessitated trade and exchange between town and country, for the farmers to obtain the cash required and for the largely urban recipients to spend it. As B. R. Grover (1994) has amply documented, these needs led to towns and regions in northern India being linked together by an extensive road system in addition to the rivers. Insurance rates were very low at about 2%, indicating a high degree of safety in moving merchandise between markets. An entire community known as the Banjaras specialized in moving goods from place to place by means of pack oxen, often in droves of thousands of these animals, reducing price gaps as a consequence. Even the frequent invasions and wars that occurred in the middle decades of the eighteenth century did not permanently disrupt the functioning of the economic system. The uniform silver coinage of very high purity, and a well-developed banking and credit system involving the use of sophisticated financial instruments such as the bill of exchange or hundi, facilitated the integration of commodity and capital markets, which was nevertheless far from being complete because of the many market imperfections of what was still a preindustrial economy.

In terms of international trade Indian merchants during this period continued to have contacts with the Red Sea and Persian Gulf ports in the west, and with Burma, Siam, and the Indonesian islands in the east. The most notable of these in the seventeenth century was the Jain merchant prince Virji Vora of Surat, reputed to be the richest man of his day with a fortune placed in the vicinity of 50 million rupees or £10 million (Gokhale 1979, chapter 7). His trading interests extended as widely as that of the East India Company itself, and the Company relied on him for loans in several critical instances. By the later eighteenth century, however, the Indian mercantile community was increasingly losing ground to the Company, being able to survive mainly as auxiliaries to its activities in international trade, while continuing to have the major role in domestic trade.

Most European traders were extremely impressed with the business acumen of the Gujarati and Tamil merchants with whom they dealt both in India and Southeast Asia. India was the manufacturing exporter par excellence of the seventeenth and almost all of the eighteenth century, with her cotton textiles much sought after in all the known continents of the world. Despite this, Habib (1980, p. 1) has stated that "it would be foolish, even if detailed evidence has not been studied, to deny that India during the seventeenth century had been definitely surpassed by Western Europe." A blunt assertion such as this, from the leading authority on the economic history of the Mughal Empire, who furthermore has impeccable radical and nationalist credentials, is a welcome antidote to the unhistorical view that it was not until the Industrial Revolution itself that there was any discernible technological gap between Western Europe and the rest of the world.[4]

Habib provides evidence that while technological adaptation was impressive in some areas, such as the introduction of New World cash crops like tobacco and maize and in shipbuilding, Mughal India, like the rest of the Islamic World, had failed to introduce basic innovations such as book-printing, mechanical clockwork, and optical improvements such as spectacles and telescopes, and had fallen behind in iron and steel technology despite its early lead in this field. He also notes that in India the abundance of cheap skilled labor served as a substitute in many areas for the lack of tools and mechanical implements of various kinds, thus providing no incentive for the introduction of machinery. Indeed, it was on the basis of lower silver wages that India remained competitive in the international textile market during the eighteenth century (Broadberry and Gupta 2005). In military technology the Mughals were good at manufacturing muskets and heavy brass cannon, but fell behind in the manufacture of lighter iron cannon that were much more efficient on the battlefield than the bronze monsters to which their rulers were prone.

The rapid decline of the empire following the death of Aurangzeb should not be construed as necessarily implying a corresponding decline in the economy. It is clearly possible that the growth of local autonomy resulting in smaller revenue transfers to the center could be accompanied by increases in real incomes retained by the peasants

---

[4]In an earlier classic article, Habib (1969) went so far as to deny that the Mughal economy had the capacity to attain an independent path to capitalism and modern economic growth.

themselves or by the local landowners or "regional gentry classes," who could become the focal points of a more decentralized and healthier pattern of development than the earlier one dominated by the full power of the Mughal Leviathan. Thus a number of authors such as C. A. Bayly (1983, 1988) have argued that the slow but perceptible growth of output and population of the seventeenth century did not cease, but continued up to the middle of the eighteenth century despite, if not even because of, the center's loss of authority. Oriented toward trade and the market, this "new middle class," which Bayly (1983, p. 15) refers to as "the intermediate classes of society—townsmen, traders, service gentry—who commanded the skills of the market and the pen," could form a convenient, if uneasy and contentious, partnership to further its commercial interests and activities with the East India Company, organizing the procurement and supply of its exports from India, collecting its revenues and even providing it with loans whenever necessary. Thus the "colonial society" that emerged in India after Plassey may not have been so much a product of the crude external deus ex machina of "colonialism" per se, but rather of a more benign evolution out of Indian society itself, once the burden of the Mughal state had been lightened in its several "successor states."

In addition to whatever other virtues it might or might not possess, this thesis has an advantage that appeals to many, namely that the Indian agents are not seen as helpless victims but as active participants in the jointly determined outcome of a historic intercultural encounter. The thesis of continuity between the precolonial and colonial regimes has, however, been rejected outright by Irfan Habib (1997, pp. 259–95) and M. Athar Ali (1993, pp. 90–99), who stress the hostility of the Company to any emergence of potential native rivals to its dominant role in the economy. The difference between the two positions may perhaps be less than it seems, with one stressing the common and the other the antagonistic aspect of what was by its very nature a complex and ambivalent relationship. Rajat Kanta Ray (1998) records both the despair of the losers, the Mughal landowners, their retainers, and the Muslim intellectuals, who lamented what they called the inqilab or "turning upside down" of their familiar world, and the enthusiastic response to the new opportunities opened up by the British takeover on the part of the emerging Bengali Hindu middle class, the so-called bhadralok, which was, however, not unmixed even at the outset with the seeds of the nationalistic opposition to colonial rule with which they were later to become involved so actively.

By what may only appear to be a coincidence, the definitive history of the English East India Company up to the establishment of its

bridgehead in Bengal has been written by one of the most distinguished contemporary members of this remarkable social group, K. N.
Chaudhuri (1978). He provides a set of detailed statistical tables of
the Company's trading activities for the period 1660–1760, giving the
value of total imports from Asia (mostly India) by the Company for
sale in England, or reexport to Europe and the rest of the world, and of
the exports of goods (but mainly precious metals) sent to Asia (again
mostly India) by the Company to pay for these imports. From 1660
to 1760 the compound growth rate of imports and exports was about
2.2% per annum, faster than either population or aggregate output
growth in Europe or Asia during this period, although there were some
pronounced swings in the series, notably a sharp decline in the 1690s.

Pepper from Malabar and Southeast Asia was important earlier in
the seventeenth century, reaching over 25% of total EIC imports in
some years, but was increasingly displaced by cotton textiles, which
dominated the shipments from India by the eighteenth century. These
Indian cotton textiles, globally distributed by the East India Company,
were without doubt one of the major success stories of the world
economy. With a very wide range of qualities and price they served the
entire spectrum of the market, from the superfine muslins of Bengal
worn by aristocratic ladies in England at one end, to the coarse blue
Coromandel cloth worn by African slaves in the Caribbean at the other.
The global matching of supplies to estimated demands for each of
such a wide range of varieties by the Company was a logistical marvel
in that preindustrial age. Orders for supplies were transmitted from
London to Calcutta, Madras, and Bombay, and contracts signed with
consortia of local merchants for delivery of the cloth by the mostly rural
weavers in the hinterlands on whatever terms they could negotiate
with the merchants. Competition from Indian cottons terrified both
the woolen industry and the silk weavers of Spitalfields in England,
provoking strong protectionist measures that slowed but did not halt
the expansion of exports from India. Textiles averaged between 60
and 80% of total EIC imports until the 1750s, when rising tea imports
(which led to the share of China reaching a third by the end of the
period) lowered the textiles share to just below 55%. Raw silk from
Bengal and China was another significant import that often exceeded
10% and sometimes even 20% of total import value. Imports of coffee
from Mokha peaked at 15–20% of total imports in the 1720s, but
thereafter fell to about 5%, while saltpeter and indigo were relatively
minor imports.

The terminal date of Chaudhuri's series is 1760, but we learn from
other sources that as a result of securing the *diwani*, the revenues

of Bengal and loans from private British residents in India, such as Company servants investing their savings, could finance the necessary purchases of textiles and other goods, making it necessary to ship out much less "treasure" from Europe than before. Indeed, the share of "treasure" in total EIC exports fell from well over 75% for most of the 1660–1760 period to a mere 30% or so at the end, coinciding with the victory at Plassey and the conquest of Bengal (Chaudhuri 1978, table C4, p. 512). The Bengal revenue of about £3 million annually (Marshall 1998, p. 492) not only helped to finance the return cargoes of Indian goods to Europe by the Company, but also covered the purchase of Chinese tea at Canton and raw cotton from Gujarat. Furthermore, Bihar and Bengal were the source of what was to prove the Company's most profitable means of financing the lucrative Chinese tea trade, namely opium, for the purchase of which the Company assumed monopoly rights in 1773 (Prakash 1998, pp. 327–36). The opium was sold in Calcutta by public auction to private traders, who then exported it to Canton, thus setting the stage for the notorious Opium Wars of the mid nineteenth century, as a result of which China itself was also reduced to a state of almost helpless dependency.

In addition to the trade of the Company itself there was also private trade by English merchants, often the Company's own servants but operating with their own capital and for their own profit. The obvious conflict of interest that this posed was a recurring theme in the history of the Company. An outright prohibition would cause resentment and lower morale, but no constraints at all would of course diminish severely the profits of the shareholders, leading to some form of compromise being adopted in practice. Many servants of the Company and other Europeans went into partnership with local Indian or Armenian traders, or took loans from them to engage in intra-Asian trade. European seamen took advantage of their superior navigational techniques to enter the carrying trade with locally built vessels, charging a premium for their more efficient and secure service.

One of the most interesting of these sea captains and private traders was Thomas Pitt (1653–1726), grandfather of Pitt the Elder, known as "Diamond" Pitt because of a stone that he acquired in India and subsequently sold to the duke of Orleans for the then huge sum of £125,000. "Diamond" Pitt began his career as captain of an interloping vessel but rose to become Governor of Fort St. George in Madras from 1697 to 1709, making his fortune by organizing several highly profitable voyages on his own account. His Indian profits financed the purchase of the famous "rotten borough" of Old Sarum, from whence his more famous grandson William was to enter the House of Commons in 1735. Another notable private trader and eventually Governor of Madras was Elihu Yale (1649–1721), who used part of the fortune that he made to endow in 1701 a well-known educational institution in Connecticut that bears his name. The prosperity of Madras was based not only on the export of cotton textiles from the Coromandel Coast, but also on the transshipment of goods from Bengal, Burma, Siam, and China to the west coast of India and to the Red Sea and Persian Gulf. The establishment of Calcutta and Fort William, however, led to the lucrative Bengal trade being diverted there so that the fortunes of Madras began to wane. Calcutta enjoyed a spectacular boom after the Clive takeover, with English private traders voyaging in increasing numbers not only directly to Canton but picking up valuable cargoes of tin and spices in the new British settlement of Penang, established in 1786, and the older center of Bencoolen in Sumatra as well (Marshall 1999).

We conclude this section by drawing attention once again to the fundamental break that occurred in the relationship between Indians and the European Companies after Plassey and the acquisition of Bengal by the British. Up to that time the Companies had had to compete with each other and the large domestic demand in the markets for cotton textiles, raw silk, indigo, saltpeter, and whatever else they wanted to buy. Whatever price reductions they received would be due to the volume of their orders and the desire of suppliers to maintain long-term relationships with important customers. Under Shah Jahan and Aurangzeb, and even their feebler successors up to the 1750s, there could have been no extended possibility of using force to coerce the local agents in any transaction. Om Prakash (1998, p. 317) has made an a priori plausible argument that since the demand for cotton textiles from Europe was probably growing faster than India's ability to supply, the terms of trade should have been moving against the Companies and in favor of the Indian merchants and weavers. This proposition receives some support from Chaudhuri's (1978, table A3) import price index for the English EIC, which rose sharply from 100 in 1664 to a peak of 155 in 1705, and remained significantly above 100 up to ca. 1725. This indicates a pattern of rapid demand growth in Europe pulling prices initially upward, until the organization of an expanded supply response led to prices falling back to something approaching their initial levels. With abundant supplies of even skilled labor and no evidence of land scarcities at this time, the supply curves for cotton textiles were presumably highly if not even perfectly elastic in the long run, hence the eventual return to the initial price.

During this precolonial period from 1600 to 1750, India did quite well in her trade with Europe through the medium of the European

Companies, exploiting her strong comparative advantage in cotton textiles to obtain the silver inflows needed to sustain and expand her monetary base on the basis of competitive market relationships. After Plassey, however, the English Company was master not only of Bengal, but with an army of no fewer than 115,000 troops (mostly sepoys, under English officers) was in a position to enforce monopoly and monopsony power against both the locals and the rival European Companies in the Coromandel Coast and the Carnatic as well (Prakash 1998). Particularly egregious was its operation of the opium monopoly in Bengal (ibid., pp. 327–36). Furthermore, the revenues of Bengal not only rendered the previous annual injections of silver by the Company into India unnecessary, but also even reversed it by what Indian nationalist writers called the "drain" of precious metals out of the country to purchase tea in China or remit profits to England. The importance of this for Britain can be seen from Cuenca Esteban's (2001, p. 58) recent finding, based on his reworking of British balance of payments statistics, that "without the accumulated credits from India transfers since 1757, Britain's financing of land warfare during the French wars could have been compromised," yet another confirmation of the role of Plenty in sustaining Power during this period.

SOUTHEAST ASIA AND THE END OF THE AGE OF COMMERCE

As noted in the previous chapter, the second half of the seventeenth century saw the Dutch consolidate their monopoly over the trade in cloves and nutmeg. From a military and political standpoint, therefore, it would seem that the VOC should have been in a favorable position to enhance its profits. From the standpoint of a strictly economic calculus of costs and benefits, however, the picture was very different. Military and administrative costs increased without corresponding increases in revenues and profits, due to the lack of incentives for the native peasants, merchants, and rulers to generate more production and trade given the VOC's monopolistic controls and attempts to secure compulsory deliveries. The market for spices in Europe was also beginning to be saturated by the second half of the seventeenth century. Indian cotton textiles, initially sought by the Companies merely as the means by which to obtain spices, were becoming more sought after than the spices themselves in European markets, and the VOC found it increasingly difficult to compete with its English rival in this more dynamic sphere of intercontinental trade.

Anthony Reid regards the middle of the seventeenth century as a "watershed" in the history of the region, with the positive trends

unleashed earlier by commercial expansion halted or reversed by stagnation ascribed to a global "seventeenth-century crisis," reinforced
within the region itself by the repressive policies of the VOC. Reid's
contention is accepted for the Malay–Indonesian world, but denied for
the mainland states of Burma, by Victor Lieberman (1993), and Siam,
by Dhiravat na Pombejra (1993). As we have seen, Lieberman maintains that the Burmese kingdom of the so-called "Restored Taungngu
Dynasty," despite shifting its capital from Pegu in the Irrawaddy Delta
to Ava further inland, was still able to extract revenues from taxes and
monopolies on trade at the coast to supplement its agrarian tax base
in the hinterland, while also engaging actively in overland trade with
China. It thus continued to expand in terms of output, population,
and mobilization of military resources, and so was able to impose
and even extend its sway over outlying areas without any significant
interruption until it was overthrown in 1752. Similarly, Pombejra
argues that while the kingdom of Ayutthaya became disenchanted
about trade involvements with the French, Dutch, and British, it
nevertheless continued to trade actively with Japan, China, India,
and the Islamic World, thus again denying any seventeenth-century
watershed. In what follows we therefore take a closer look at each
of these two powerful Asian states, before returning to the islands of
Southeast Asia and charting their relative decline during this period.

Burmese rulers during the late seventeenth and early eighteenth
centuries were mainly concerned with consolidating their internal
administration and fending off their neighbors on the borders of Siam,
Yunnan, and Manipur. In the 1740s a rebellion in Lower Burma by
the Mon expelled their Burmese governors, and swept north to take
the capital Ava itself in 1752, thus bringing the Taungngu dynasty to
an end. Resistance to the Mon invasion, led by a village headman
who displayed extraordinary gifts of political and military leadership,
united the demoralized population and remnants of the Ava forces in
opposition to the invaders. He recaptured Ava in 1753 and eventually
drove the Mon back to Lower Burma, taking the name Alaungpaya
("Future Buddha") and reigning until his death in 1760 as the founder
of the Konbaung dynasty, which was the last to rule Burma until
overthrown by the British in 1885.

Alaungpaya's rise to power coincided with the run-up to the Seven
Years' War, and in keeping with the global nature of that conflict Burma
also became indirectly involved. Dupleix, alert to any opportunity
to fish in troubled waters if it would profit him against the English,
exchanged diplomatic missions with the Mon, hoping to acquire a
pliant ally with an excellent natural harbor and shipbuilding facilities

in Syriam, de Brito's old base, thereby outflanking the British in Bengal. His representative, the Sieur de Bruno, acted as a military adviser to the Mon, and French warships fired on Burmese war-canoes in battles around Syriam and Dagon. The latter was taken and named Rangoon ("End of Strife") by Alaungpaya in 1755, as he came down the Irrawaddy to take the war into the ancestral homelands of the Mon. With the French besieged along with the Mon in Syriam, an expedition with three warships was sent from Pondicherry to relieve them. Unfortunately for the French, Alaungpaya captured the warships, took their guns and muskets for his army, conscripted the crews and junior officers to serve as gunners, and decapitated the twelve most senior officers, including the Sieur de Bruno. The French guns and crews dramatically improved the quality of the Burmese artillery against the Mon, and also in subsequent conflicts with the Siamese and Manchus in which they served as an elite corps. According to Harvey (1925, p. 231), one of them, the Chevalier Milard, became Captain of the Guard and Master of the Ordnance for the Konbaung dynasty, while many of the others ended their days in Burmese inland villages "far from the Breton cliffs and the women who waited in vain for their return," but with Burmese wives perhaps providing some consolation.

Alaungpaya captured Syriam and Pegu, wreaking death and destruction on the Mon, before turning Burmese attention once again to the irresistible Siamese target of Ayutthaya. He died before he could take it in 1760, at the untimely age of only forty-six, but it did fall in 1767 to his son Hsinbyushin ("Lord of the White Elephant," 1763–76), who destroyed the city completely and took thousands back to Burma in captivity. A more notable and constructive achievement of Burmese arms was the defeat of repeated invasions of Burma by the Manchu dynasty in the late 1760s, provoked by border disputes in the Shan States. This was followed by the resumption of cordial diplomatic relations and intensive overland trade between the two states that lasted until the British conquest (Hall 1968, pp. 412–14). Another of Alaungpaya's sons, Bodawpaya (1782–1819), extended this Third Burmese Empire (Htin Aung 1967, chapter 8) to the greatest extent in the country's history by adding Arakan and Manipur to the conquests of his father and brother, but thereby inevitably risked confrontation with that other great conquest state, the English East India Company, in the adjoining provinces of Bengal and Assam.

The VOC began operations in Siam soon after it entered eastern waters in the early seventeenth century, but was unable to do much more than gain a foothold before the reign of King Prasat Thong (1629–56), from whom the Dutch received valuable concessions for the trade in deerskins and tin, in return for naval assistance against the Burmese and Malay states. Asian nonnationals were more influential than Europeans in Siam during this period. The persecution of Japanese Christians by the Tokugawa caused many of them to seek refuge in Southeast Asia and one of these Christian samurai, Yamada Nagamasa, became head of the royal bodyguard and played an important role in the succession struggles later in the seventeenth century. Persian influence was also strong at the Ayutthaya court, and was supposedly instrumental in the coming to power of King Narai (1656–88), who was to be the most "Westernizing" of Siam's monarchs before the nineteenth century.

Narai's Persian advisers instituted a royal monopoly in 1662 over all overseas trade, creating difficulties for the Dutch who also had to face increasing competition from private European and Asian traders as well as the English East India Company. The EIC had in its employ an extraordinarily talented and ambitious young Greek by the name of Constantine Phaulkon, who came to Siam in 1678, and whose quick mastery of the Thai language brought him into contact with King Narai when he served as an interpreter. He then entered the royal service and rapidly was given control over all the foreign trade relations and foreign policy of the kingdom, eventually rising to the very top of the civil administration, holding a post equivalent to that of prime minister. He suppressed the influence of the Muslim faction at the court and developed close ties with the French East India Company, when it entered into diplomatic and commercial relations with the Siamese court, as well as with a French Jesuit mission. Embassies were exchanged between Paris and Ayutthaya and a large contingent of French troops arrived in 1687, ostensibly to guard their trading station but instead taking up positions in Bangkok, uncomfortably close to the capital itself. This understandably caused great alarm in the native court faction, who suspected, probably rightly, that Phaulkon was plotting a takeover of the state and the hapless Narai by conniving with the French. They struck swiftly, capturing and executing Phaulkon before Narai died of an illness shortly after. The leader of the coup then usurped the throne and the French withdrew their contingent without engaging in any hostilities.

The Siamese court thereafter steered clear of any entanglements with European powers until it became obliged to do so in the nineteenth century. Foreign trade, however, continued to be actively promoted, particularly with China and Japan. Much of this trade was of the entrepôt variety, with Ayutthaya serving as the conduit for Southeast Asian exports in return for Chinese and Japanese imports to the region.

The export of rice to southern China from Siam became increasingly important over the course of the eighteenth century, and Chinese immigrants and families of Chinese origin became prominent in both trade and the civil bureaucracy, where they competed for power with other extended clans of foreign origin, the "Brahmins" and the Persians (Wyatt 1984, chapter 5). The attention of the court during this time was concentrated on relations with Laos and Cambodia and so it seems to have been surprisingly unprepared for the Burmese onslaught under Alaungpaya and his heirs in the 1760s.

Once again, however, as with Naresuan after Bayinnaung, the Siamese made a rapid recovery under a charismatic leader. This time he was not the crown prince but a half-Chinese provincial governor named Phraya Taksin. He set up his capital at Thonburi on the other side of the river from Bangkok and used his contacts with his father's overseas Chinese Teochiu trading community to finance resistance to the Burmese. Within three years he had regained essentially all the lost territory of Ayutthaya and was crowned king (ibid.). He then seems to have become mentally deranged, engaging in sacrilegious and cruel behavior that alarmed both the court and the powerful Buddhist clergy, and was deposed and executed in 1782, a sorry end for a national hero. A new dynasty, the Chakri, ruling till the present day, also partly Chinese but with strong family connections to all the various factions in the bureaucracy, came to power. The founder of the dynasty, King Rama I, was a son-in-law of Taksin. The capital was shifted permanently down the river to Bangkok, closer to the sea and the outside world, in sharp contrast to the earlier Burmese move from coastal Pegu to inland Ava. In destroying Ayutthaya, therefore, the Burmese may in fact have done the Siamese an unintended favor of great historical consequence.

Finally, and more briefly, in Vietnam warfare between the southern Nguyen and the northern Trinh had exhausted both states, and a massive peasant uprising known as the Tay Son Rebellion broke out in the 1770s that threatened to put an end to both of them. The rebels were defeated on the brink of victory, however, by Nguyen Anh, with the help of a remarkable French cleric, Pigneau de Béhaine. Nguyen Anh restored the unity of the Vietnamese state, ruling as the emperor Gia Long from 1802. As with the new dynasties in Siam and Burma, tribute was paid and recognition granted in return by the Qing. The Nguyen dynasty lasted until 1955, when the monarch Bao Dai was deposed and the Republic of Vietnam proclaimed, with the unfortunate Ngo Dinh Diem as the first president.

Having taken into account the main developments on the mainland, we now describe the course of events in the archipelago. By the 1720s

Johore, as an ally of the VOC, had emerged as the dominant native state in the region of the Straits, with its capital at the port of Riau, a bustling Islamic entrepôt reminiscent of the old Melaka. A new element that emerged on the Malay political scene around this time was the role of Bugis and Makassarese refugees from Sulawesi, driven out by the dictatorial rule of Arung Palakka, which was alluded to in the previous chapter. These groups drew on their traditional prowess in both warfare and trade to make their way in the peninsula as raiders, mercenaries, traders, and settlers, in a manner strikingly reminiscent of the Vikings in Europe toward the end of the first millennium. As outsiders they could not achieve legitimacy as the sovereign rulers of Malay states, but in Johore they did become sub-kings, known as Yantuan Mudas, in whose hands the real power lay. The Bugis's downfall came when they overreached themselves by attempting to take Melaka from the VOC in 1784, being defeated by a fleet from Holland in an action in which their leader was killed. All Bugis were forced to leave Riau and Johore, leaving it and the neighboring state of Selangor briefly under Dutch control. These, however, were the last days of the VOC, due to momentous events in Europe (see chapter 7), and they were soon driven out of Riau by an attack of pirates from the Sulu Sea, leaving the harbor and environs in a state of anarchy and presaging what Andaya and Andaya (1982, p. 108) call "the Demise of the Malay Entrepôt State."

Central and eastern Java was neither peaceful nor prosperous in the eighteenth century. The VOC wanted a pliant puppet state in the interior of the island, allowing it to concentrate on trade at Batavia and along the coast. Unfortunately, however, they found that supporting their client princes against the claims of rivals and assorted rebels was a costly, draining, and frequently bloody effort as one war of succession followed another. They finally worked out a compromise by splitting Mataram into separate courts at Jogjakarta and Surakarta, with ostensibly independent native rulers watched over by Dutch Residents, while directly administering Batavia and the coasts. They did want to exercise control in certain parts of the interior over the production of coffee, sugar, indigo, and other cash crops, and for this they tended to rely more on compulsion and administrative controls over the peasantry rather than price incentives. Meanwhile, riots in Batavia in 1740 at which the Dutch themselves may have connived led to tens of thousands of Chinese being massacred, followed by a rebellion that also caused much damage and further loss of life before it was suppressed. The second half of the eighteenth century was generally more peaceful but both the VOC and Java were clearly stagnating. Ricklefs (1993, p. 105) says of this era that, "in the midst of corruption, inefficiency and financial crisis this first Dutch empire in Indonesia was gently going to sleep."

The ultimate beneficiaries of all these developments, in which they had played no direct part at all, were of course the British. As we have seen, the EIC's occupation of Bengal led to a rapid expansion of private English "country trade" to China, picking up any opportunities that arose in the Straits along the way. The island of Penang, leased to the EIC in 1786 by the sultan of Kedah in the hope of gaining British protection against the claims of his traditional Siamese overlords, now voiced assertively by the new Chakri dynasty, was a useful place to exchange Bengal cottons and opium for Malayan tin and other products that would be esteemed in Canton in exchange for tea, and also had potential as a naval base. A region of the mainland opposite the island was also leased to the British in 1800 and named Province Wellesley, another feather in the cap of that illustrious family. The demand for tin was leading to a boom in the Malay Peninsula, where it was in abundant supply, particularly in the state of Perak, providing a further impetus to immigration from the southern provinces of China, the source of most of the entrepreneurship and technical expertise in the industry. It was too late for the VOC to benefit, however, since the French occupation of Holland had forced William V to flee to England, where he placed Dutch possessions in the Far East in English hands until such time as he could return.

What of trade during the period, and of Reid's contention that the mid seventeenth century constituted a watershed for the Southeast Asian archipelago, ending the Age of Commerce that had begun a quarter of a millennium previously? Table 5.6 shows that pepper exports continued to grow until the 1670s, but that they then fell back again and had not regained this peak as late as the 1780s. Exports to India, Japan, and America held steady, and exports to China actually rose after the 1670s; it was exports to Europe that declined, presumably as a result of monopolistic Dutch practices. Figure 5.1 provides even stronger evidence of the impact of the Dutch monopoly on the Southeast Asian economy: Indonesian clove exports soared from the first decade of the sixteenth century (when they totaled 170 tons) to the 1620s (by which time they had reached 450 tons). Simultaneously, the sale price of cloves in Southeast Asia exploded, from \$35 per ton to \$1,000 per ton, an astonishing rise even in the context of the Price Revolution that we studied in chapter 4. But the Indonesian price collapsed in the 1650s as the Dutch extended their control, and reached \$206 per ton in the 1660s, a figure that was to

TABLE 5.6. Southeast Asian pepper exports, 1650–1789 (tons).

Year	Europe and Middle East	China	India, Japan, America	Total
1650–59	2,200	400	1,400	4,000
1660–69	2,900	500	1,500	4,900
1670–79	4,500	500	1,500	6,500
1680–89	2,600	600	1,500	4,700
1690–99	2,600	1,300	1,400	5,300
1700–09	1,800	1,500	1,500	4,800
1710–19	1,900	1,200	1,500	4,600
1720–29	3,600	900	1,500	6,000
1730–39	3,000	1,100	1,600	5,700
1740–49	3,600	800	1,600	6,000
1750–59	2,300	1,000	1,600	4,900
1760–69	2,700	1,200	1,700	5,600
1770–79	2,400	1,900	1,800	6,100
1780–89	2,100	2,100	1,900	6,100

Source: Bulbeck et al. (1998, table 3.7, p. 86).

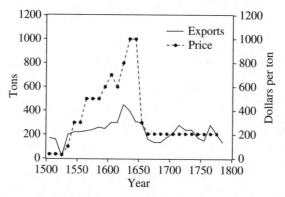

FIGURE 5.1. Indonesian clove exports and prices, 1500–1789.
Source: Bulbeck et al. (1998, table 2.15, pp. 58–59).

remain unchanged until the 1780s. This price collapse was clearly
not due to an increase in supply, since exports fell sharply, but to
the Dutch monopsonistic control we considered earlier. Presumably,
the double monopolistic squeeze of low buying prices for cash crops
and high selling prices for foodstuffs and textiles was a factor leading
Malay–Indonesian peasant producers to withdraw into subsistence
production during this period, the reverse of Europe's Industrious
Revolution.

One might object that these are data on just two, perhaps unrepresentative goods, but there is broader evidence of a decline in the archipelago's prosperity during the period. A particularly useful indicator is provided by the data on Southeast Asian imports of Indian cotton textiles from the Coromandel Coast, Gujarat, and Bengal. Imports of these "brightly-colored and finely woven" Indian cloths constituted "the best single index of commercial prosperity in the region," according to Reid (1990, p. 21), since Southeast Asian export revenues were largely spent on them. Cloth imports climbed to a peak between 1620 and 1650, during which time their value was roughly equivalent to 60 tonnes of silver per year, four times as much as in 1510 (ibid., p. 23). They then fell to only about half this amount by the 1680s, as a result of the restrictive monopolistic policy of the VOC and saturation of the European market for pepper and fine spices. While the mainland states such as Burma, Siam, and Cochinchina under their energetic new dynasties may have been able to sustain their earlier development and even expand by reorienting trade both overland and overseas with Qing China, it is apparent that the period from 1650 to 1800 was one of at least stagnation if not even decline in the living standards of the population in the main Indonesian islands and much of the Malay Peninsula. Reid (1993a, chapter 5, 1999, chapter 10) sees this period as marking the "Origins of Southeast Asian Poverty."

There are two caveats to this rather negative assessment, and both involve China. The first, as we have seen, is that the mainland states increasingly traded with China overland, and prospered accordingly. Here, Asians remained firmly in control of their own destinies. The second concerns Chinese participation in maritime trade during the period. As we will see, the Qing initially ruthlessly suppressed the coastal regions of China in their struggles against Ming loyalists, leading to sharp declines in trade and shipping. After ca. 1685, however, Chinese ships, traders, and settlers became increasingly active in Southeast Asia, particularly in Vietnam, the Philippines, and Siam but also in Java, Sumatra, and the Malay states. Communities of Ming loyalist exiles sprang up in Cambodia and Vietnam. One of these, led by the Mac family, established a virtually independent state at the port of Hatien on the east coast of the Gulf of Siam in the early 1700s and played a prominent role in Vietnamese history. As we have seen the Chinese presence was pronounced in both Manila and Batavia, the indispensable role it played in the economies of both cities being resented by the European colonizers and the indigenous people alike. The Spanish expelled all Chinese traders from the Philippines in

1755, leaving the field open to the mestizo Chinese–Filipino Roman Catholics with Spanish names to become the commercial, and subsequently professional and political, elite that they remain to this day (Reid 1996, p. 46). In Indonesia revenue farming for the VOC as well as local rulers became another activity of Chinese entrepreneurs. In Siam the role of Chinese merchants became increasingly pronounced with the shift in the direction of trade away from the West and toward China by the late seventeenth century.[5]

THE MANCHU EMPIRE

We now return to the vast Eurasian heartland, from Russia across Central Asia to China and the Far East. None of the states and peoples of these lands were directly involved in the "Voyages of Discovery" but they were all sooner or later to be confronted with the consequences, in the shape of both the rising pressure from but also the commercial possibilities opened up by the maritime powers of Western Europe, as in the case of the silver influx from the New World that we examined in the previous chapter. The main theme of the east–west interaction across Central Eurasia that we will be concerned with here, however, is the drive toward the center from both directions by the powerful new states that emerged at either end, that of the Manchu Qing dynasty in China and Muscovy in Russia. As we have seen, both China and Russia had fallen prey to the Mongol Empire, the former ruled directly by the Yüan dynasty and the latter as a submissive client state of the Golden Horde. The native Ming dynasty expelled the Mongols in 1368 but did not pursue them further into the interior after unsuccessful early attempts, relying instead on a defensive strategy behind the Great Wall to prevent future invasions by steppe nomads. It was left to the Manchus after the fall of the Ming in 1644 to initiate the "great enterprise" of conquest and colonization deep into the heart of Inner Asia at the expense of the Mongol and Turkic tribes. At the opposite extremity the rising power of Muscovy began its imperial career, as we have seen, with the conquest of the Khanate of Kazan by Ivan the Terrible in 1554, opening the way to Siberia, the riches of the fur trade, and the Pacific. Trade and war, both with the native tribes and each other, were the options of two empires on a collision course. In what follows, we first describe the rise of the Manchu Empire before turning

---

[5]See Wang (1981, 2000) and Skinner (1996) for insightful accounts of the formation of overseas Chinese "Creole" communities during this period.

to its trading relationships with the rest of the world, both by sea and over land.

Contrary to a widespread impression, the Manchu themselves were not pastoral nomads from the steppes. Their original economic system was based on a combination of livestock breeding, hunting, and agriculture on the northeastern borders of China, and they had already long been exposed to cultural influences from the great neighboring state to which they were tributaries. Their ancestors were the Jurchen, who as we saw ruled North China as the Chin dynasty from 1125 to 1234, before falling to the Mongols. Two remarkable leaders, the tribal chieftain Nurhachi (1607–26) and his son Abahai (1635–43) (later known as Hong Taiji), were the creators of a powerful military machine, partly financed by the lucrative trade in furs and the medicinal root ginseng that their location on the northeastern borders of China gave them access to.[6] They used this force to conquer Korea and subjugate most of Inner Mongolia. Eventually, with the assistance of Mongol auxiliaries and turncoat Ming generals, they took advantage of the civil war raging in China to capture Beijing in 1644, and ultimately all of China by the 1680s, after the suppression of resistance by Ming loyalists in Yunnan, southern China, and Taiwan.

The Qing maintained their separate cultural identity as a ruling elite by prohibiting intermarriage between Manchus and Chinese, but adopted traditional Chinese institutions in the administration of their empire, which was largely staffed by ethnic Chinese literati. Each ministry or department had a "dyarchic" leadership, with one Manchu and one Chinese official at the head, balancing the technical expertise of the Chinese with the presumption of greater loyalty and reliability of the Manchu. In many respects the Manchus, as outsiders to the dominant high civilization of East Asia, felt compelled to be "more Chinese than the Chinese," and the Qing appear to have been accepted by the Chinese themselves as a much less "alien" dynasty than the Mongol Yüan three centuries earlier. Even the compulsory adoption of the Manchu male hairstyle with the characteristic "queue," originally despised as a symbol of alien oppression, came to be accepted until it was rejected again after the growth of nationalism in the late nineteenth century. The history of the Qing is a remarkable example of how an ethnic group of less than 1 million people was able to rule successfully over the most populous nation in the world without losing its distinct social, cultural, and political identity from 1644 to 1911.

---

[6]The starting dates of both reigns are here taken to be the year they became khan.

CHINA'S OVERSEAS TRADE

As we have seen, international trade in the South China Sea, and even across the Pacific with Manila, was flourishing under the late Ming despite the negative attitude that the dynasty itself had toward it. The Portuguese at Macao, and the Dutch with their Japanese connections, were adding to the vigorous activities of Chinese merchants from the southern coastal provinces of Fujian and Guangdong in the trade with Southeast Asia at the height of that region's Age of Commerce. It is therefore unsurprising that the trading communities of these provinces were not eager to accede to Manchu rule. The region was dominated at this time by the remarkable Zheng family, which controlled powerful fleets that could serve equally to engage in piracy, or to purport to suppress it in the service of the Ming state after the head of the family, Zheng Zhilong (1604–61), was appointed as a sort of high admiral with authority to patrol the southern coasts. This man had been to Macao in his youth, learnt Portuguese, and had even been baptized a Christian under the name Nicholas Gaspard Iquan. He served as an interpreter for the Portuguese and the Dutch but made his fortune as the agent of Li Tan (or Li Dan), founder of a trading empire connected with the Ryukyu Islands and Japan and known to Europeans as "Captain China" (Clements 2005, pp. 18–25). Zheng acquired control of Li Tan's assets in Japan and Taiwan on his death in 1625, which he used to strengthen his position in Amoy and South China. Li Tan had apparently been a galley slave of the Spanish in Manila before becoming head of the Chinese mercantile community at Hirado on the southern island of Kyushu. He was also paid handsomely to serve as a sort of lobbyist for the East India Company with the Chinese authorities. He thus appears to have had personal contact and connections with all the major actors of the East Asian trading world of his day, and personified the Sino-Japanese "silk for silver" trade described in the previous chapter (Wills 1979). The Manchus gave Zheng Zhilong the option of retaining his position if he would renounce the Ming, which he promptly did, only to be denounced for this act by his half-Japanese son Zheng Chenggong (1623–62), better known to history as Coxinga, a Dutch corruption of one of his Chinese titles. Coxinga was born in Hirado, living with his Japanese mother before joining his father in China at the age of seven. He was given a classical education and training in martial arts, both of which were to be useful in his subsequent stormy career.

Deng (1999, p. 95) gives some scattered information on the scale of the Zheng trading operations that are quite remarkable. He says that the annual profit made on the trade with Japan alone amounted to 20 tonnes of silver, and overall was from 85 to 100 tonnes. In terms of tonnage the Zheng trade with Japan was supposedly between seven and eleven times as important as that of the Dutch. Deng also says that Zheng ships sailing to Japan could each carry over 70 tonnes of raw silk, which in view of silk's extreme lightness implies a huge size for these ships. Profits of this magnitude enabled three generations of the family to maintain 8,000 ships and 170,000 troops from the 1640s to the 1680s.

When the Manchus arrested his father on suspicion that his surrender was merely a ruse, Coxinga assumed control of the extensive family resources and used them effectively in armed resistance to the invaders, defeating their forces on land and sea and even sailing up the Yangtze in 1659 with a fleet of hundreds of vessels and tens of thousands of soldiers to seriously threaten Nanjing, before he was repulsed and forced to withdraw. Seeking a more secure base he landed his forces on Taiwan, expelling the VOC from its outpost at Fort Zeelandia after a long siege. The Manchus realized that his economic and military power on Taiwan depended on contact with the mainland and accordingly ordered a complete evacuation of a long stretch of the eastern seaboard to the extent of twenty miles inland, causing great distress to the population and setting trade back for decades. The brutal measure was nevertheless effective in achieving its strategic objective. Coxinga died in 1662, shortly after the Manchus executed his father in reprisal for his rebellion, but his son Zheng Jing (died 1681) and other surviving members of the family held out on Taiwan until it was captured in 1683 by Manchu forces commanded by a former Zheng associate, and governed henceforth as a prefecture of Fujian province. The suppression of the Zheng trading empire and the setback to the southern Chinese coastal economy undoubtedly made it easier for the Europeans in Asian trade, since they now did not have such effective competition to contend with. The Qing in principle opened all ports to trade in 1685 on payment of a 20% import duty, but in practice there were still administrative and monopolistic restrictions weighing down the expansion of commerce.

Nevertheless, according to Mazumdar (1998, p. 95), "there was an unprecedented increase in overseas trade from China." The removal of Zheng domination may itself have stimulated a rush of newcomers to enter the South China trade from the port of Amoy. Mazumdar (1998, tables 7–9, pp. 97–98) shows the number of Chinese junks calling at Batavia rising from 51 in 1684–88 to a peak of 82 in 1699–1703, far outstripping the number of junks from Macao calling there in the

same periods. She also shows even greater Chinese activity, both in
absolute terms and relative to the Dutch, on the route to Nagasaki
between the lifting of the Qing ban at the Chinese end in 1685, and the
imposition of Japanese restrictions on trade in 1715. No fewer than
540 Chinese vessels sailed to Nagasaki during 1684–88, even though
only 128 of them were allowed to land by the Japanese authorities, as
compared with just 19 Dutch ships, and Chinese ships outnumbered
their Dutch counterparts by a similar margin throughout this period.
The need for Japanese copper for purposes of coinage was a major
reason why the Qing regime was anxious for trade with Japan to
expand. Finally, Mazumdar also shows that Chinese ships calling at
Manila far outnumbered Portuguese ships during this period.

The struggle between the Zhengs and the Qing can be looked upon
as yet another instance of one of the main themes of this chapter,
the conflict between maritime trading polities and inland agrarian
ones, usually ending as in this case with the victory of the latter. One
of the great counterfactual "might have beens" of Chinese history is
what if Coxinga had been successful in taking Nanjing? What if the
Chinese scholar-officials, who had the option of safely serving the
Qing in their familiar roles or throwing in their lot with an impetuous
young rebel and pirate chieftain like Coxinga in defense of their native
Chinese dynasty, had chosen the latter? Might the Manchus have
been driven from China, or at least left the south with sufficient
autonomy to engage fully in the burgeoning international trade of the
eighteenth century, as a leader and not just acquiescing reluctantly
in a subordinate role to the European powers? The Zhengs, with their
Japanese, Portuguese, and Dutch connections and the trading network
inherited from Li Tan, were certainly wide open to all the multinational
currents that were flowing in the era of early modern globalization.
Coxinga's army itself was a multinational construct, with an elite
bodyguard of former African slaves acquired from the Portuguese, and
an even more fearsome unit of warriors known as the "Iron Men," who
wore plate armor and are plausibly supposed to have been displaced
Japanese samurai. The forces of "earthbound" China, the alliance of
northern warlords and bureaucrats, once again proved too strong for
the nascent forces of southern coastal "maritime" China at the end
of the Ming dynasty, just as they had defeated another Zheng, the
great Muslim eunuch admiral Zheng He, at its beginning. Posterity
at least has been kind to Coxinga, as it has to Zheng He, in some
compensation for his tragic life. Even the Qing honored him after his
death as a paragon of the supreme Confucian virtue for the unswerving
loyalty that he displayed toward the Ming. His victory over the Dutch

and resistance to the Manchus made him the hero of both modern Chinese regimes, and he is revered in Taiwan as the architect of its incorporation into the Chinese cultural sphere, where he is apparently even prayed to for rain by the natives (Clements 2005, p. 260). His Japanese mother and birth on Kyushu have also endeared him to the Japanese, with the Battles of Coxinga by Chikamatsu being one of the most famous puppet plays by that great master.

Chinese scholars regret that the Zhengs were not able to use their massive accumulation of mercantile capital to break out of the sterile grip of the traditional Chinese state, dominated by the landed gentry and literati classes, and launch the country on a more creative outward-looking path based on commercial enterprise and profit. Thus Zheng Zhilong could find no better use for his vast commercial empire and the powerful naval forces necessary to protect it than to place it in the service of the decadent Ming dynasty, in return for land and official rank and awards. His ambition for his gifted son was to give him the best possible classical education in preparation for a career as a scholar-official. When the Qing replaced the Ming his sole concern was to propitiate the new masters, to his son's disgust. Coxinga's own admirable loyalty to the Ming ended in defeat and tragedy, when he had the option of merely acknowledging their nominal sovereignty and maintaining his own trading regime intact in Southeast China and Taiwan, and expanding it further by participation in the booming world economy with which he was already so familiar. No Chinese regime was to embark again on a trade-oriented path of development until, ironically, another refugee state was to arise in Taiwan in the 1940s and be emulated by the rulers of the mainland in the 1980s (Cheng 1990, pp. 236–37).

Manchu power in China was consolidated and greatly extended during the long reign of the Kangxi emperor (1661–1722). China itself was pacified by the 1680s and its frontiers extended considerably into the region of the present Xinjiang ("New Territories") Province by a series of campaigns against the Mongol tribes, some of which were personally led by the emperor. The purpose of these campaigns was not so much territory for its own sake as security against the traditional fear of Mongol invasion, this time using an aggressive forward policy rather than passive reliance on the Great Wall as under the Ming. Using the traditional Chinese method of "making the barbarian fight the barbarian," Kangxi allied with the eastern Khalkha Mongol tribes to defeat and kill Galdan (1676–97), the great leader of the western Zunghar Mongols. The traditional trade of tea for horses, indispensable for the Qing cavalry, was an important element in policy toward the Mongols, both allies and enemies. Agricultural production, essential for the provision of supplies deep in the steppe, was provided by military colonies around fortified points. Kangxi's policies were essentially continued by his son the Yongzheng emperor and grandson the Qianlong emperor, the length of whose reign rivaled his own. Tibet was conquered and incorporated into the Qing Empire by 1751, thus obtaining Chinese control over the Dalai Lama and the religious sites of Tibetan Buddhism, to which both the Manchus and the Mongols adhered.

The Zunghars, after the death of their leader Galdan, were ably led by his nephew, and under him they built up a vast empire in western Mongolia stretching from Siberia to the frontiers of Tibet, threatening the eastern Khalkha Mongols, who were faithful vassals of the Qing. A war of extermination launched against the Zunghars by Qianlong in 1757 obliterated not only their state but also almost all traces of the people themselves. China reached the maximum extent in 1759 that it was ever to attain as a result, an area of 11.5 million square kilometers (Gernet 1982, p. 480). It should also be noted that, as we have already seen, the neighboring states of Korea, Burma, Siam, and Vietnam, as well as many Central Asian states and peoples, also acknowledged Qing suzerainty at this time, thus extending the sway of the dynasty to an even greater extent.

The *Pax Manchurica* saw a vast expansion of population in China from the late seventeenth to the middle of the nineteenth century. According to Maddison (1998, p. 169), the population fell from about 145 million in 1620 to 126 million in 1680, recovering to 157 million in 1710 before simply taking off, more than doubling by 1800 and almost trebling to 412 million by 1850. The cultivated area only doubled (Naquin and Rawski 1987, p. 25, table 1), but yields per acre rose because of a wider range of crops, including New World plants such as the sweet potato, maize, chilies, and peanuts, and cash crops such as tea, sugar cane, and tobacco. The sweet potato in particular made a big difference to the amount and stability of the food supply in deficit areas such as Fujian, since it could be grown on soils unsuitable to other crops and was better able to survive droughts. Tobacco, introduced from the Philippines, was also cultivated widely and the Chinese soon became addicted to what they called "dry alcohol," smoking it in pipes and later mixing it with opium.[7]

---

[7]Naquin and Rawski (1987, p. 23), however, argue that extensions of land under traditional crops, and changes in cropping patterns, were even more important than the New World plants.

The overseas trade of Qing China came to be increasingly concentrated on the port of Canton in Guangdong province in South China, particularly after 1757 when it was mandated by the Qing regime as part of its regulatory framework. Merchant associations or "monopolistic guilds" in Canton apparently dated back to the 1550s, when the government authorized particular groups to deal with foreign traders and collect revenue from them on its behalf. These groups or firms, known as *hong*, bore legal responsibility for the behavior of the foreign merchants and were entitled to deal exclusively with them in return. They became increasingly important after 1685 and the removal of the Qing ban on foreign trade. A group of thirteen such firms was formed in 1720 into the subsequently famous institution known as the Cohong, which survived despite several vicissitudes until the Opium Wars of the next century. The number of associated firms rose and fell but the Cohong maintained its identity as a sort of formally authorized cartel dealing with all foreign traders, and also with myriad local firms and merchants connecting export–import dealers with regional brokers and individual rural producers of export products such as silk, sugar, and tea. The state was represented directly by various Chinese and Manchu officials, the most important of whom, I suppose, was known as the Hoppo, representing the Imperial Household itself. The resulting situation, as anyone familiar with the notion of rent-seeking behavior would recognize, was a cornucopia of corruption, with all parties contending for their share of the gains from the monopolistically restricted trade. The Imperial Household did well out of the proceeds, its take being not just the officially collected duties but presents and donations by all the beneficiaries to assure their survival in privileged positions. The only constraints were the need to provide sufficient incentives for the local producers and foreign traders to supply and demand the goods involved (Fairbank 1969, chapter 3; Mazumdar 1998, chapter 6). Private traders, both English "country" traders from India and local Chinese outside the Cohong system, also competed vigorously for the spoils, particularly in the officially banned opium trade.

According to the French scholar Louis Dermigny, the tonnage of foreign ships trading at Canton increased by a factor of almost nine between 1719–26 and 1783–91, a huge increase by any standards (Naquin and Rawski 1987, p. 103, table 2). The commodities involved included the traditional Chinese exports of silk and porcelain, but pride of place now belonged to tea, which of course had long been grown and consumed in China, but the consumption of which expanded worldwide and particularly in England and Europe from the eighteenth century, as we have already noted. Holden Furber (1976, p. 126) reports two pounds of tea being presented to Charles II in 1664 by the Directors of the EIC, and sporadic amounts were imported in the next two decades. Chaudhuri (1978, p. 387) finds as much as 38 thousand pounds being imported by the EIC in 1690, with the difference between the average cost price of 1 shilling and the sale price of 6 shillings all being absorbed by the customs duty of 5 shillings per pound. The takeoff in demand began early in the eighteenth century, and in the seven years from 1713 to 1720 the EIC imported over 2 million pounds of tea. Growth continued to be spectacular in each of the subsequent decades, with imports of 8.9 million pounds in the 1720s, 11.7 million in the 1730s, 20.2 million in the 1740s, and 37.4 million in the 1750s, and with the corresponding sales values rising from £611,441 in the 1720s to £1,692,698 in the 1750s (ibid., p. 388, table A17). In 1760 imports of tea by the EIC were as much as 39% of all imports by the Company, almost as much as the 43% of cotton and silk textiles from all of Asia (ibid., tables C19 and C24). The tea was carried on specialized "China ships" making only one stop in India on the outward voyage and no stops at all from Canton on the return voyage, to get the tea packed Chinese fashion in zinc-lined chests to the consumer as fresh as possible. By contrast the VOC missed the opportunity to be competitive in the tea trade, buying it in Batavia instead of direct at Canton, and never getting it fast and fresh to the European markets.

The EIC's "investments" or purchases of tea in Canton were financed, as we have noted already, by the sale of Indian goods, including opium, by English private traders for silver, which was then made available to the Company for the tea purchases from the Cohong, with the traders obtaining bills on London in pounds sterling in exchange for their silver. This "Britain–China–India Trade Triangle" is the subject of a valuable paper by Tan Chung (1974). His table 2 (p. 413) shows that British exports to China to pay for these tea purchases were 52% silver in 1761–70, a share which fell sharply until 1800 and became negligible thereafter. The share of Indian goods, on the other hand, rose from 24% in 1761–70 to over 50% in the next three decades, and then sharply upward to 83% in 1821–30. Table 4 (p. 419) shows the annual average shipment of Indian opium to China rising from 2,000 chests (of 149 pounds each) in the 1790s to 3,800 and 4,400 in the first and second decades of the nineteenth century, and then exploding to 11,400 and 24,300 chests in the 1820s and 1830s respectively. In 1821 the opium import by China was worth 9 million Spanish dollars compared with Chinese tea exports to Britain worth 8.4 million Spanish dollars (p. 420).

The most striking finding, however, is that, contrary to widespread belief, opium exports from India were not necessary for the EIC to balance its trade with China. Tan's table 5 (p. 420) shows that from 1792 to 1795 British–Indian exports to China excluding opium exceeded the annual "investment" of the Company in tea and other Chinese goods by an average of over £200,000 annually. Indian cotton exports from Bombay were the biggest contributor in this regard. He says (p. 421) that "if opium were to play such a limited role of balancing Britain's China trade, not many chests of it would have been traded in the eighteenth century and it would have been totally given up in the nineteenth century." Mazumdar (1998, p. 105) also asserts that "until 1823, raw cotton was the most valuable Indian export to China—more valuable than opium." Indian cotton exports, an input for the Chinese textiles known as "nankeen," were more than adequate according to Tan to finance the purchase of Chinese tea, without recourse to opium with its destructive consequences for the moral and social fabric of Chinese society.

The boom in tea exports, 50–70% of which came from Fujian province (Naquin and Rawski 1987, p. 170), brought seasonal migrant labor and enterprise into that province from other regions, while production was financed by loans from the merchant community in a sort of putting-out or proto-industrial system (Gardella 1990, pp. 333–42). Local landowners, including Buddhist and Taoist monasteries in the mountainous hinterland, played a generally passive role, simply renting out the land without any decision-making or risk-taking in the production process. The organization of the tea trade appears to have had a quite sophisticated or "modern" flavor, with written contracts stipulating quality and quantity to be delivered, terms of payment, and penalties for default. While labor for planting and picking the tea was relatively unskilled, the later stages of processing the crop for the market required a variety of specialized skills. Gardella (1990, p. 332) observes that supplies could have been expanded more rapidly if demand had not been constrained by the monopolistic pricing policies of the EIC at the consuming end in European markets.

The growth of tea output naturally led to land being diverted from rice production, leading to the necessity of imports not only from other parts of China, but from Southeast Asia, particularly Siam and Cochinchina, as well. This phenomenon, whereby tea exports to Europe stimulated the intra-Asian rice trade, constitutes a nice example of triangular trade in addition to the more familiar Atlantic one, which we will consider at length in the next chapter. Trade relations between Ayutthaya and South China, as we have seen, extended back to the origins of the former state and were particularly active during the time of the Zheng regime. Coxinga imported tin and saltpeter for military use in exchange for Japanese silver and lead, and in 1665 his son Zheng Jing sent twenty junks to Southeast Asia, of which ten went to Siam (Viraphol 1977, p. 45). The removal of the Qing ban on foreign trade saw a surge in the junk trade between the Chinese ports of Amoy, Canton, and Ningpo and Southeast Asian ports. In Siam Chinese merchants from Fujian province were actively involved both as private merchants and court officials and their numbers, as noted by several European observers, seem to have increased greatly. The substantial trade between China, Siam, and Japan in these years was dominated by Chinese merchants, captains, and crews, many in the service of the Ayutthaya court, who exported deerskins and other Southeast Asian products as well as Chinese goods to Nagasaki, primarily in exchange for imports of copper.

Despite drawing substantial revenue from all this overseas trade, however, the Qing regime restored the official ban in 1717. The main reasons appear to have been suspicion that the growing numbers and prosperity of the Chinese communities in Southeast Asia were a potential "fifth column," and loss of food grains and strategic raw materials such as ship timber, due to the fact that half of the junks sailing abroad each year never seemed to return. Trade continued despite the ban but was nevertheless set back as a result. The hardship caused was apparently so severe that the plea of the Qing viceroy for the coastal regions to have the ban removed was granted in 1727 and lasted for forty years. The shortage of rice in South China, combined with its cheapness and relative abundance in Siam, seems to have been the most important factor responsible for the lifting of the ban. At least 110 ships a year sailed from Amoy and Canton, mostly to Siam and the Malay Peninsula, according to Viraphol (1977, p. 72), who also notes (p. 73) that "in the final analysis, the regeneration of the Sino-Siamese trade in the period between the 1720s and the 1760s owed most to the importation of rice from Siam into Southeast China, the single most tangible factor for the rescinding of the second overseas travel and trade ban." The rice trade was encouraged by the Qing emperors by the grant of tariff concessions, as well as awards and ranks to merchants and officials engaged in the trade (ibid., chapter 5). The pattern of trade between South China and Siam conformed to a standard "factor proportions" framework, with the relatively labor-abundant provinces of Fujian and Guangdong exporting labor-intensive manufactures such as earthen and metalware and textiles, in return for land-intensive natural-resource products such as rice and sappanwood from Siam, as well as tin from the Malay Peninsula.

CHINESE AND RUSSIAN OVERLAND TRADE

It is now time to turn our attention to the no less important question of China's overland trade. As we saw in chapter 3, the overland caravan trade held up relatively well in the century and a half following the collapse of the *Pax Mongolica*, but in the sixteenth century there was a notable decline and disruption of the trade. This decline has usually been attributed, in rather Eurocentric fashion, to the discovery of the Cape route, the hypothesis being that the overland trade could not compete with the lower cost of shipping goods around the Cape. Rossabi (1990, p. 351) argues persuasively, however, that the Cape route competition by itself was not the only, or even the main, cause of the decline in the long-distance caravan trade across Central Asia. He considers the political disruption and instability that broke out along the overland route from the early 1500s onwards to be the most significant factor. In particular, the disintegration of the Timurid Empire at the hands of the nomadic Uzbeks and Kazakhs meant that Samarkand, Herat, and the other great caravan cities of Transoxiana and Khurasan were no longer the magnets that they once were for the overland trade, the new nomadic powers being more interested in pillage and booty than in trade. In Persia the new Safavid dynasty of Shah Ismail took time to consolidate power and was soon locked in violent struggles with both the Uzbeks and the Ottomans, while its adoption of the Shia branch of Islam made it inhospitable to Sunni merchants and aroused even fiercer opposition from the firmly Sunni Ottomans. The oasis cities of Kashgar, Yarkand, Hami, and Turfan were raided by the Kazakhs and other nomadic tribes, while also becoming bitterly divided internally by religious and sectarian disputes between adherents of the orthodox clergy on the one hand and followers of Sufi orders, who were themselves divided into warring camps, on the other. Only two missions were sent to China from Central Asia between 1600 and 1630 (ibid., p. 363), and missions from Turfan, so frequent in the fifteenth century, were also greatly reduced in number.[8]

---

[8]A somewhat related debate regards the relative efficiency of the European Companies and traditional Asian trade. Niels Steensgaard (1974), following van Leur (1955), viewed traditional Asian trade as being of the "peddling" type, a mere transfer of superfluities between different regions carried on by small-scale operators with very limited capital. The *Estado da India*, though operating at a much larger scale and over much longer distances, and with more advanced nautical technology, was in his view also an essentially premodern "redistributive enterprise," in that its motivation was more that of a feudal lord collecting tolls, tribute, and plunder than a commercial organization characterized by profit and rational business calculation. By contrast,

By the late sixteenth and early seventeenth centuries the Ming dynasty entered a period of chronic instability marked by massive corruption and violent peasant rebellions, leading ultimately as we have seen to its downfall by the 1640s. The Kansu Corridor in the northwest, through which the caravans had to pass on their journey to the west, was hit particularly hard by severe droughts and associated peasant unrest. These difficulties were further exacerbated by the fact that many of the people in this area were Muslims, who were supported in their opposition to the Ming by their coreligionists from the oases and the steppes. Mongol and Manchu hostility to the Ming was another element in the challenges that proved impossible for the Ming to overcome. The new Qing rulers themselves were no more acceptable to all the rebellious elements, so that the instability did not decline even several decades after the fall of the Ming. As we have seen, the Qing emperors from Kangxi to Qianlong were engaged in a fierce struggle with the Zunghar Mongols in Inner and Central Asia, which ended only with the virtual extinction of the Zunghars in the 1750s. The relentless warfare in the steppes for almost a century was clearly not conducive to the long-distance caravan trade along the traditional southern Silk Road route. It was overseas trade that brought silver into Qing China in return for her tea, silk, and porcelain, while the traditional trade of tea for horses and camels from the steppes faced severe restrictions and disruptions.

A major new overland trade partner for Qing China, as well as a potentially dangerous political competitor, was, however, beginning to emerge with the penetration of the Russians eastwards into the Siberian taiga and forests in search of the abundant furs that they extracted from the native tribes. As we have seen, the Russians reached the Pacific at about the same time that the Qing took over China.

---

the Dutch and British East India Companies represented the appearance of unfettered market forces. Steensgaard's work was severely criticized by Meilink-Roelofsz (1980), who pointed out that "peddling" is a characterization which hardly applies to the sophisticated organization of Melaka, and of the Gujarati, Tamil, and other Asian merchants trading there, not to speak of the very astute Chinese engaged in commerce all over Southeast Asia. She also questions the thesis of a "modern" and highly "rational" VOC, pointing to its inaccurate accounting methods, often excessive and ineffective use of force by a bloated military establishment, and failure to achieve its main objective of a tight monopoly over Asian trade, except for the very limited and costly efforts in relation to mace and nutmeg in the Moluccas. To be fair, Steensgaard was aware of such points, citing (pp. 25–26) the example of an Armenian merchant, Hovhaness, operating between Basra, Isfahan, and Surat from 1682 to 1693, who meticulously kept track of complicated transactions involving different coins and measures that he handled with "the greatest of ease."

The Zunghars desperately sought an alliance with this powerful state but the Russians had no desire to alienate the Manchus, with whom they were anxious to conduct trade, offering their precious furs in exchange for tea, silk, and other Chinese goods. Diplomatic relations were opened, leading to the landmark Treaties of Nerchinsk in 1689 and Kiakhta in 1728 between the two major powers at either end of the Eurasian landmass.

The initial, inevitable collision between the Russian eastward penetration and the western borders of Qing dynasty China took place in the valley of the Amur River on the fringes of southern Siberia and northern Manchuria in the 1640s. The Russians wanted to use this fertile valley as a source of food supplies for the fur traders, but the local tribes paid tribute to the Qing, who as a result did not allow this. After some clashes the two sides signed the Treaty of Nerchinsk, by which the Russians agreed to withdraw from the Amur region while the border was fixed to the north. In return for these territorial concessions the Russians received the right to trade their furs for silk and other Chinese goods. The two sides also agreed under whose "sphere of influence" the various local tribes including the Mongols would fall. In particular the Russians agreed not to ally with the dangerous Zunghars. Remarkably, the language in which the diplomatic negotiations were officially conducted was Latin, with two European Jesuits acting for the Qing, and a Polish officer in their service for the Russian side (Perdue 2005, p. 167). The Treaty permitted one state caravan every three years to Beijing, bringing furs to be exchanged for silk and other products. According to Foust (1961, p. 479), the forty years from 1689 to 1728 saw fifty Russian caravans to Beijing, including the ten official state caravans, with the remainder unofficial private caravans, indicating that the trade must have been profitable. The surge of fur exports seems to have led to a glut and price declines. Peter the Great apparently wanted to create a well-regulated monopolistic company on a joint stock basis to remedy the situation but nothing came of the idea.

A new Sino-Russian agreement, the Treaty of Kiakhta, was signed in 1727, establishing a durable framework for the conduct of the overland trade between the two powers that lasted until 1860 (Mancall 1964, p. 24). One state caravan to Beijing every three years continued to be permitted, but it was supplemented by the establishment of Kiakhta, on the border between Russian territory in Siberia and Chinese territory in Mongolia, as a center for regular private trade by merchants from both sides. Russian merchants and officials resided at Kiakhta, while their Chinese counterparts were located nearby, but on the other side of the border at a site called Mai-mai-cheng (literally "buy–sell town"). This private trade soon eclipsed the cumbersome system of state caravans to Beijing, the last of which was in 1755, before being formally ended by Catherine the Great (1762–96) in the first year of her reign, presumably as a result of her belief in free trade as befitting a monarch of the Age of Enlightenment. By "free trade" the enlightened despot did not of course mean the absence of taxes on trade, if only for revenue purposes. She made the somewhat startling pronouncement, quoted by Foust (1969, p. 281), that "where there is trade there are customshouses. The purpose of trade is the export and import of goods to the benefit of the state." In any event, both private traders and the state treasury did well as a consequence of the Treaty of Kiakhta. The value of the furs exported from Kiakhta to China rose from about 400,000 silver rubles in 1735 to almost 1.2 million in 1759 (Mancall 1964, p. 25). By 1802 the total trade turnover at Kiakhta was nearly 9 million rubles, yielding revenue to the state of 900,000 rubles (Foust 1969, p. 352, table 1). The state apparently realized that instead of sending crown caravans to Beijing with their very high overhead costs, a much more "enlightened" or rational policy was to leave the trade in private hands but collect substantial revenue from duties set at a reasonable rate of approximately 10% of turnover.

This "Kiakhta Trade" was a significant, though little known, aspect of world trade in the eighteenth century. The paper of this title by Mark Mancall (1964), on which most of the account here draws, is therefore an extremely valuable contribution, while Foust (1969) provides an excellent detailed account of the diplomatic and political background. Mancall notes that the trade expanded greatly from the 1760s to the end of the eighteenth century, with furs as the major export from the Russian side, at first constituting 85% of the total value of exports before falling to about 75% at the end of the century. At the height of the trade, beaver and sea otter furs were in the greatest demand, causing supplies to be sought from as far as the Kamchatka Peninsula and the Kurile Islands, and eventually even the Aleutians and Alaska. The Chinese demand was so great that Russian merchants resorted to importing North American pelts for reexport through Kiakhta. Woolen cloth was the next most important export to China from the Russian side, and again recourse had to be sought from reexports to augment insufficient Russian supplies. Peter the Great had inaugurated the Russian woolen industry but despite considerable growth in the eighteenth century it could not fully cover even internal demand. By 1850, however, Russian supplies had risen sufficiently to satisfy the Chinese demand of 1.5 million yards, and accounted for 65% of Russian exports to China, as compared with just 23% for furs. Mancall (1964, p. 28) notes that the East India Company was not able to sell woolen cloth successfully at Canton, and speculates plausibly that this was because the Kiakhta source was closer to the North China market where the extreme cold would have created the greatest demand.

On the Chinese side the major export at first was the nankeen cotton cloth, which even served as the numéraire in the calculation of relative prices in what was essentially a bilaterally balanced barter trade. Silk fabrics were initially also an important Chinese export, but a vigorous import substitution program in Russia eroded its importance quite rapidly, falling from about 24% of total exports in 1751 to half that by the end of the century. An unusual but important Chinese export item was rhubarb, in such great demand in Russia for its medicinal properties that its internal distribution was a state monopoly until 1782. What eventually became the dominant Chinese export to Russia, however, was tea. Russians were introduced to tea drinking by contact with the Mongols, and the opening of the trading station at Kiakhta further encouraged Russian consumption. From the 1760s to 1785 it constituted only 15% of total imports, but just as in the case of the overseas trade through Canton it exploded toward the close of the century, and by 1825 was 87% of total Russian imports from China, rising to 95% by 1850. Mancall gives some useful figures on the relative importance of China in total Russian trade. In the second half of the eighteenth century, Russian foreign trade grew substantially, from about 19 million rubles a year in 1758–60 to almost 60 million rubles in 1792. The Chinese share remained stable at about 7–8% of the total, while constituting about two-thirds of Russia's total Asian trade. The Chinese share of Russian customs revenue was, however, disproportionately higher at about 38% of the total in 1775 (453,200 silver rubles).

It is interesting to compare the overland trade at Kiakhta with the overseas trade at Canton during these years. As we have seen, tea was the main commodity exported by China at both locations. The scale of the Canton trade, however, seems to have been much greater, at 23 million pounds as compared with 2.5 million at Kiakhta in 1800 (Gardella 1990, pp. 331, 334). The qualities of the teas sold in these markets were also different, with high-quality teas for the Russian market balanced by low-quality brick tea for the Siberian market at Kiakhta, while Canton exported mainly medium-quality teas for the British and European market, the price per pound averaging out at about the same in the two places. Kiakhta dominated Canton in the import of furs, with evidence of a linkage between the two markets, since imports at Canton rose when the Kiakhta trade was interrupted on certain occasions. In terms of Chinese imports of woolen cloth Kiakhta had an annual average of 856,000 silver taels in 1802–4, more than twice as much as the annual average at Canton in the last years of the eighteenth century (Mancall 1964, p. 44). Mancall also reports that the Sino-Russian trade at Kiakhta seems to have been conducted in an amicable and respectful manner, in sharp contrast to the mutual hostility and incomprehension between the British and Chinese at Canton. British observers noticed this, but conveniently tended to explain it as a consequence of their Russian counterparts being "half-Asiatics" themselves. Certainly, the history of the Kiakhta trade gives a very different picture of Qing attitudes toward Westerners, and diplomatic and trade relations with them, than the familiar stereotypes of arrogance and ignorance conveyed by their Anglo-Saxon interlocutors (chapter 6).

As we have seen, the exhaustion of fur supplies in Siberia led Russians as far afield as the Aleutians and Alaska in search of fresh supplies. To handle this extension of the Siberian trade a Russian–American company was formed, with its headquarters in Irkutsk. Foust (1969, p. 318) calls it "the first joint-stock, limited liability, imperially sanctioned company in Russian history." Provisioning the Aleutian and Alaskan colonies of hunters and trappers, and sending the pelts to Chinese markets, presented immense problems in the icy northern seas. British and American competition through Canton also had to be faced. The solution to all these problems was for Russia to have access to Chinese ports, both to supply the Alaskan outposts and to sell the furs in the Chinese markets. Their attempts to do this by sending a ship to Canton with furs to sell were firmly rebuffed by the Qing, who did not permit the vessel to discharge its cargo. The Russians had to operate solely within the Kiakhta system, which was doomed, as the Russians themselves clearly foresaw, to fall victim to the growing overseas trade. An attempt to "open" Japan to the entry of Russian vessels in 1804 was also summarily rejected by the Tokugawa. Finally, an ambitious embassy was dispatched from Irkutsk to negotiate either an opening of Chinese ports to Russian shipping, or permission for overland caravans to enter the interior of China, but it did not even succeed in reaching Beijing. The nineteenth century thus opened on an anxious note for Russian trade with the Far East.

Simultaneously, however, Russia was strengthening her position as a great European power as well. A decisive thrust toward the "Westernization" of Russia was made by Peter the Great (1682–1725) in the first quarter of the eighteenth century. Peter ended Sweden's short-lived "Age of Greatness" by his defeat of the warrior-king Charles XII (1697–1718) in the Great Northern War, not only recovering Narva as a "window to the west" but adding Riga and Reval as well. In addition he built St. Petersburg on the swampy banks of the Neva at enormous human cost to consolidate the Russian presence on the shores of the Baltic. Catherine the Great further enhanced Russia as a great power by expansion in the south at the expense of the Tartar Khanates and the Ottoman Empire, and to the west at the expense of Poland and Lithuania, with the former Grand Duchy being entirely incorporated within the Russian Empire along with substantial portions of Poland. Under the terms of the Treaty of Kutchuk-Kainardji of 1774, the Ottomans granted Russia navigation rights in both the Black Sea and the Straits, allowing Russian ships direct access to the Mediterranean.

Alexander Gerschenkron (1970, lecture 3) interprets the Petrine drive as a particularly extreme case of mercantilist state intervention, in which, according to his familiar scheme, the greater the extent of "relative backwardness" the greater is the intensity of the institutional effort to overcome it (Gerschenkron 1962). It is in this light that he sees Peter's measures to build roads, bridges, and canals, attempting to link the Baltic to the Volga and the Caspian, and other such ambitious projects aimed at creating a unified national economic system. Industrialization was geared toward the needs of warfare with the Sweden of Charles XII, representing the Western model that was to be "overtaken and surpassed" in the language of his Bolshevik successors, as well as with the Ottomans and Safavids: hence the stress that Peter placed on iron and steel, gunpowder, shipbuilding, and so on in his industrialization program. The role of foreign trade was to provide the export surpluses needed to pay for essential military-industrial inputs from the West, as well as the numerous foreign experts and technicians that Peter hired.

As Arcadius Kahan (1974) points out, access to the Baltic ports reduced transport costs for both Russian exports and imports by comparison with the previous reliance on Archangel, and this factor alone must have stimulated foreign trade significantly in the Petrine era. He concludes that "the recognition of greatly expanded foreign trade as a means of overcoming Russia's economic backwardness and its cultural isolation was the main legacy of Petrine foreign trade policies" (ibid., p. 236). In another contribution, Kahan (1985, p. 163) declares that "foreign trade in Russia during the eighteenth century was one of the important engines of economic growth. It had a major impact on the commercialization of agriculture, the growth of

TABLE 5.7. Composition of Russian exports, 1710–95 (percent).

	1710	1769	1793–95
Crops	37.8	50.5	43.1
Hemp	34.4	18.8	20.2
Flax	3.3	11.3	12.6
Linseed and hempseed	0.04	3.5	3.4
Grains	2.9	16.9	6.9
Livestock products	50.5	12.5	18.1
Tallow	11.4	5.0	11.3
Hides	39.0	7.5	6.8
Forest products	5.1	4.5	4.2
Industrial goods	3.3	22.8	22.2
Iron		9.8	12.0
Linen textiles	3.3	13.0	10.2
Total accounted for	96.7	90.3	87.6

Source: Kahan (1985, table 4.2, p. 168).

industry, the expansion of the money supply, and the accumulation of capital." Foreign trade experienced a remarkable fifteenfold expansion in real terms from the beginning to the end of the eighteenth century. The growth of Russian exports was particularly rapid between 1742 and 1793, over tenfold in terms of value and six and a half times in real terms. On a per capita basis Russian export volumes thus grew threefold, despite a doubling of the population from 18 million to 37 million over this period (ibid., p. 265).

Table 5.7 gives the commodity composition of Russian exports during the eighteenth century. Russian exports were for the most part bulk goods with a low ratio of value to weight, such as hemp and flax, wax and tallow, hides, skins and leather, pitch and tar, timber, and increasingly over time grain and bar iron. Thus, with the exception of grain, her exports were mainly intermediate inputs for the manufacturing industries and shipping of the more developed economies of Western Europe. Evidence of some industrialization emerges from these figures, since iron was not exported in 1710 but accounted for 12% of total exports in 1793–95, while the share of linen textiles, some of which were used to clothe slaves in the New World, rose from 3 to 10% over the same period. Iron was produced in state factories or by privately owned enterprises in the Urals region, with low labor and fuel costs offsetting the high transport costs to Western markets. Here the supply of credit by British buyers of Russian iron was an important factor in the growth of exports.

Competition with Swedish iron for the British and other Western markets was intense, with Sweden having the better quality and Russia the lower price. Russia overtook Sweden as the main source of imported iron for Britain by the 1760s. However, as Kahan (1985, p. 186) says, "Russia's leading role in the eighteenth-century European iron market is largely a well-kept secret known primarily to specialized historians."

The Dutch were the most important trading partner around 1700, only to be surpassed by the British by the 1730s and 1740s, reflecting the shift in economic primacy that was becoming so evident. The main outlet in 1700 as we have seen was Archangel on the White Sea, displaced increasingly by Riga and St. Petersburg, while the Black Sea ports were to become increasingly important later in the century for grain exports to the Mediterranean. In the east we have already noted the growing trade with China through Kiakhta. All the overseas trade was carried in foreign bottoms, the Russian merchant marine being practically nonexistent.

Russian imports in the eighteenth century reflected the highly skewed income distribution resulting from the social composition of the country. The nobility, gentry, and merchant elite, largely concentrated in St. Petersburg, spent lavishly on luxury textiles and "colonial" products such as spices, sugar, and beverages, which together constituted about 40% of imports. Industrial inputs such as dyestuffs and other raw materials, largely for the growing textile industry, constituted another 40%. St. Petersburg was the main port of entry for these imports but was also the outlet for exports from a vast hinterland, since the Neva, at the mouth of which it was located, was connected by canals to the main Russian river systems all the way to the Caspian. As court and administrative capital, as well as Russia's leading port soon after its foundation in 1703, it reflected the will and vision of Peter the Great, so aptly captured in both the famous statue, dedicated laconically "To Peter I from Catherine II," and Pushkin's poem "The Bronze Horseman." Riga was the second port in importance, but lost some trade to its Prussian rivals Königsberg and Memel because Russian import duties were higher. Archangel continued to be an outlet for Siberian goods but declined relative to the Baltic ports.

If Archangel had been Russia's "window to the west," then Astrakhan, at the estuary of the Volga on the Caspian Sea, was Russia's "window to the east." The capture of this city in 1556 stimulated the growth of a substantial Russian trade with Iran. The main commodity was silk, in both raw and finished form, which was exported from Iran for consumption within Russia as well as for reexport to Western Europe.

This trade was largely in the hands of Armenian merchants, who as we saw in the previous chapter were granted a sort of state monopoly by Shah Abbas, which was also recognized by Russia. The Armenians were well-placed to conduct this trade since they had members of their community residing in Russia and Poland as well as in Iran. The continuous conflict with the Ottoman Empire, as we have seen, led the Safavids to seek alternative outlets for their silk exports. The transit trade in silk peaked by the 1740s, but Russia imported increasing quantities of raw silk from Iran for its own silk textile industry. Cotton, both as raw material and fabric, along with carpets, were other Iranian exports to Russia. In return Russia sent furs and reexports of European goods like woolen cloth. The balance of trade with Iran appears to have been negative, thus draining further to the east the silver that Russia earned on its surplus in the Baltic trade with Western Europe.

Astrakhan was also the base from ca. 1620 onwards for a small but active community of Indian merchants, who were part of an extensive network stretching from Lahore and Multan to Kandahar, Isfahan, and Bukhara, linking northern India with Afghanistan, Iran, Central Asia, and Russia (Dale 1994). These Indian merchants brought Russian products, including luxury items such as sable furs, Borzoi hounds, and gyrfalcons, to the Mughal elite and also engaged in money lending. They penetrated the Volga basin and the interior of Russia as far as Moscow, arousing the ire of native Russian merchants who could not compete against their command of financial resources and sophisticated business practices. The Russian state did not act effectively on these complaints, since the Indian merchant community generated substantial revenue from customs duties. Indian cotton fabrics were exported to Russia by the Dutch and British East India Companies through Archangel and the Baltic ports rather than by these Indian merchants, possibly due to the greater insecurity of the overland trade routes. A lucrative Russian trade was also carried on through Orenberg, a fort and trading station founded in the 1740s on the Ural River, with the nomadic peoples of the Central Asian steppes. Large flocks of sheep were imported from this region, serving as the source for the large volume of tallow exported by Russia to England and Scotland for making soap and candles, reflecting the reach of early modern globalization from Glasgow to the Kirghiz Steppes, and Russia's role within it.

Conclusion

By the middle of the eighteenth century, the international economy had been transformed out of all recognition from the system that had existed at the beginning of the millennium. Most importantly, America was no longer an isolated landmass, but an integral component of the international economy, trading directly with Asia, Africa, and Europe. The one (inhabited) continent remaining isolated from the others was Australasia, but that would soon change. The first British settlement in Australia was founded in 1788, in which year there were approximately 1,000 colonists and 29 sheep recorded in New South Wales. By 1821 the number of sheep had grown to 250,000, and by 1838 it had grown to 3,100,000 (Vamplew 1987, pp. 25, 107). Western Europe was no longer a peripheral player on the margins of Eurasia, but had become the center of the new world economic system, with political control over large parts of America, South and Southeast Asia, and trading posts in East Asia and sub-Saharan Africa. Many of the empty cells in table 2.1 had now been filled in. Most obviously, Western Europe was now directly connected to all other regions, while Eastern Europe was now directly connected to East Asia and North America via Russia's Siberian possessions.

According to O'Rourke and Williamson (2002a), Europe's trade with the rest of the world grew throughout the early modern period, including during the seventeenth century, which is sometimes regarded as crisis-ridden. They find average growth rates of 1.26% per annum during the sixteenth century, 0.66% per annum during the seventeenth, and 1.26% growth during the eighteenth, or 1.06% per annum overall. The results are consistent with Jan de Vries's (2003) more recent calculation of tonnage returned from Asia to Europe: according to him this grew at 1.01% per annum during the sixteenth century, 1.24% during the seventeenth, 1.16% during the eighteenth, and at 1.1% overall. An average growth rate of 1% per annum, or thereabouts, over a period of three centuries may not seem particularly impressive when compared with what was soon to come, but it was surely impressive relative to what had gone before. According to Angus Maddison (2003), Chinese and Western European GDP both grew at roughly 0.4% per annum between 1500 and 1820, while Indian GDP growth was slightly less than half that level. Ratios of intercontinental trade to GDP were thus increasing in Eurasia in the three centuries following da Gama.

Figure 5.2 offers a simple framework to think about the sources of trade growth during this or any other period. MM is the import demand function in a region (that is, domestic demand minus domestic supply). It slopes downward, indicating that countries import less as the home market price they face (p) increases. SS is the export supply function (foreign supply minus foreign demand) in the other region, with export supply rising as the price abroad (p^*) increases.

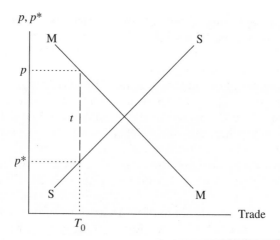

FIGURE 5.2. The sources of trade growth.

In the absence of trade barriers caused by transport costs, monopolies, wars, or insecurity, international commodity markets would be perfectly integrated: prices would be the same at home and abroad, determined by the intersection of the two schedules. Trade barriers of all sorts drive a wedge (t) between export and import prices. In this framework, trade can increase either because of a decline in trade barriers, or because of an outward shift in import demand, or because of an outward shift in export supply.

If trade growth is being driven by declining trade barriers, then the wedge t in figure 5.2 will fall, and the price in the exporting region p^* will rise relative to the import price p; that is to say, there will be commodity price convergence. We saw some evidence in chapter 4 that the initial impact of the Cape route was to bring European and Asian markets closer together, but this process does not seem to have been sustained. As figure 4.6 showed, there is absolutely no evidence of commodity price convergence between the Netherlands and Southeast Asia during the seventeenth and eighteenth centuries, a reflection of the VOC's monopolistic practices. O'Rourke and Williamson (2002b) show that this finding can be generalized to other commodities for which we currently have the necessary price evidence: for example, the gap between the price paid by the English EIC for cloth in India and the price that it received for this cloth in London remained remarkably constant, at about 100%, between 1660 and 1760. Moreover, the same was true of Anglo-Indian price gaps for silk, coffee, tea, and indigo, implying that outward shifts in supply and demand were primarily responsible for trade growth between 1600 and 1800. According to O'Rourke and Williamson (2002a), demand shifts were more important than supply shifts, accounting for between a half and two-thirds of the growth in European imports during the early modern period.

Why were price gaps so stable? One possible explanation is that the period did not see the extent of technological improvements in shipbuilding that had characterized the fifteenth century, and that would characterize the nineteenth.

Menard (1991) has shown that there is *no* evidence of systematically declining freight rates on transatlantic routes during this period, consistent with this hypothesis. Another is that mercantilism was to blame: not just monopolistic practices keeping intercontinental price gaps artificially high, but also the warfare which as we have seen was an ever-present feature of the period. There seems to be price evidence supporting this second view also, since Euro-Asian commodity price gaps rose during the first and second Anglo-Dutch wars and the Seven Years' War (figure 4.6), while prices of imported goods rose in Peru during the War of the Spanish Succession and the War of Jenkins' Ear between Spain and Britain (Brown 1990, pp. 183–85).

Further evidence that trade costs of all sorts were still a significant impediment to trade comes from the evidence on what sorts of goods were being shipped across the oceans at this time. As table 5.8 shows, the vast majority of European overseas imports were high value-to-weight commodities, which could bear the cost of transport because they were not produced in Europe. True, there had been an evolution over time in the range of goods transported. As we have seen, the most important early transfers across the Atlantic and the Pacific involved trade in DNA: one boat sufficed to ship species between previously isolated continents, often with dramatic consequences. Silver was the next New World export of importance, again an extremely valuable commodity, while spices retained their traditional importance in Euro-Asian trade. Some time around the middle of the seventeenth century, Indian textiles started to dominate in the Companies' imports from Asia, but again these were often luxury items, and certainly the European textile industry could not as yet compete with its Indian counterpart. Meanwhile, silver was beginning to be displaced in relative importance by "colonial goods" such as sugar and tobacco in the New World's exports, but again these were commodities that could not easily be grown in the temperate climate of Western Europe. Intercontinental trade was gradually involving bulkier and bulkier commodities, but it did not as yet, for the most part, involve large-scale trade in bulky items such as grain or iron which could be as easily produced on either side of the ocean.

TABLE 5.8. Composition of European overseas imports, 1513–1780.

(a) Imports from Asia to Lisbon, 1513–1610 (% by weight)

	1513–19	1523–31	1547–48	1587–88	1600–3	1608–10
Pepper	80.0	84.0	89.0	68.0	65	69.0
Other spices	18.4	15.6	9.6	11.6	16.2	10.9
Indigo	0.0	0.0	0.0	8.4	4.4	7.7
Textiles	0.2	0.0	0.0	10.5	12.2	7.8
Misc.	1.4	0.4	1.4	1.5	2.2	4.6
Total	100.0	100.0	100.0	100.0	100.0	100.0

(b) Imports of VOC into Europe, 1619–1780 (% by invoice value)

	1619–21	1648–50	1668–70	1698–1700	1738–40	1778–80
Pepper	56.5	50.4	30.5	11.2	8.1	9
Other spices	17.6	17.9	12.1	11.7	6.1	3.1
Textiles	16.1	14.2	36.5	54.7	41.1	49.5
Tea and coffee				4.2	32.2	27.2
Drugs, perfumes, and dye-stuffs	9.8	8.5	5.8	8.3	2.8	1.8
Sugar		6.4	4.2	0.2	3.7	0.6
Saltpeter		2.1	5.1	3.9	2.6	4.4
Metals	0.1	0.5	5.7	5.3	1.1	2.7
Misc.		0.2	0.1	0.4	2.3	1.7
Total	100.0	100.0	100.0	100.0	100.0	100.0

The technological and geopolitical underpinnings of globalization were thus much weaker before 1800 than they would be afterwards. Nevertheless, the fact remains that Europe's trade with the rest of the world grew substantially in the three centuries after 1500. Moreover, there seems to be a clear statistical link between transoceanic trade and prosperity during this period. According to Acemoglu et al. (2005, p. 549), the urbanization rate in the "Atlantic" European economies (England, France, the Netherlands, Portugal, and Spain) was just 10.1% in 1500, less than in the rest of Western Europe (11.4%) or Asia (11.5%). By 1700, urbanization was higher in Atlantic Europe (14.5%) than in either of the other two regions (13.1% in the rest of Western Europe and 11.6% in Asia), and the margin was even higher by 1800 (19.8% versus 16.9% and just 8.9% in Asia). GDP statistics show the same pattern of disproportionate growth in the five overseas colonial powers whose fortunes we have been exploring in this and the previous chapter. Similarly, Allen (2003a) finds a strong statistical relationship between trade and growth in early modern Europe, concluding that "the intercontinental trade boom was a key development that propelled north-

TABLE 5.8. *Cont.*

(c) Imports of English East India Company into Europe, 1668–1760
(% of invoice value)

	1668–70	1698–1700	1738–40	1758–60
Pepper	25.25	7.02	3.37	4.37
Textiles	56.61	73.98	69.58	53.51
Raw silk	0.6	7.09	10.89	12.27
Tea	0.03	1.13	10.22	25.23
Coffee	0.44	1.93	2.65	
Indigo	4.25	2.82		
Saltpeter	7.67	1.51	1.85	2.97
Misc.	5.15	4.52	1.44	1.65
Total	100.00	100.00	100.00	100.00

(d) Estimated annual sales of colonial imports,
England and Netherlands, 1751–54

	Total sales (1000 pesos)	Percentage of sales From Asia	Of total
Textiles	6,750	41.7	21.1
Pepper	1,100	6.8	3.4
Tea	2,800	17.3	8.7
Coffee	1,000	6.2	3.1
Spices	1,850	11.4	5.8
Misc.	2,700	16.7	8.4
Total from Asia	16,200	100.0	50.5
		From America	Of total
Sugar	8,050	50.8	25.1
Tobacco	3,700	23.3	11.5
Misc.	4,100	25.9	12.8
Total from America	15,850	100.0	49.5
Total overseas imports	32,050		100.0

Source: Prakash (1998, pp. 36, 115, 120) and Steensgaard (1990, p. 12).

western Europe forwards" (p. 432). Indeed, his results suggest that over half of England's urbanization during this period can be attributed to growing trade, and hence to British imperialism (p. 431).

Allen treats each nation's trade as an essentially exogenous variable, reflecting the importance of military might in grabbing trade for individual states. As he says (p. 414), "some countries were successful in the race for empire, while others were not." His conclusion that, in the geopolitical context of the time, it was best to do well in this race is one that we wholeheartedly agree with. We are not arguing that warfare was good for growth in itself. Indeed, as Mokyr (2002, p. 280) points out, "Italy after 1490, the Spanish Netherlands after 1580, Germany and central Europe after 1620, Ireland after 1650, and Sweden after 1700 are just a few examples of societies whose prosperity was severely damaged by the direct impact of armed conflict." Southeast Asians, enslaved Africans, and the unfortunate inhabitants of the Americas provide other examples of populations who clearly lost out as a result of European imperialism during this period. Nor are we denying that free trade would have been preferable to the bilateral restrictions of mercantilism: as we will see in chapter 7, the removal of these restrictions, and the generally peaceful environment of the time, was one factor underlying the nineteenth-century's extraordinary trade boom. We are saying that in a zero-sum (or even negative sum) mercantilist world, it was important to win one's wars, that Power was indeed important in providing for Plenty, and that the Royal Navy brought economic as well as military benefits to Great Britain. As David Ormrod (2003, p. 341) puts it, "the limits to growth in the premodern period were determined by geopolitics: by state power and the extent of naval protection available for merchant shipping in distant waters."

What, if any, were the links between trade and empire as described in the present chapter, and the event that defined the transition to economic modernity, namely the Industrial Revolution? It is to this subject that we turn next.

Chapter 6

TRADE AND THE INDUSTRIAL REVOLUTION

AMONG ALL THE CRUCIAL EPISODES that have been regarded as separating "modernity" from previous times, the most familiar and enduring has been the Industrial Revolution, which was long taken to have occurred in England at some time in the late eighteenth or early nineteenth centuries. Every schoolboy, at least in the British Empire, was taught that a "wave of gadgets" had been introduced by ingenious mechanics and entrepreneurs into coal mining, iron and steel, cotton spinning and weaving, and other industries, mostly located in the north of England, that eventually transformed economic life in Europe and the overseas territories of European settlement, but left behind great multitudes of the less fortunate in Asia, Africa, and Latin America that were not yet equipped with the necessary institutions to adopt the new technology. The same schoolboys also obtained the impression, from Dickens and other writers, that the Industrial Revolution, at least in its early stages, was a grim and heartless process in which "dark satanic mills" reduced workers, including women and children, to cruel deprivation and exploitation at the hands of Gradgrind, Bounderby, and others of their ilk. When the schoolboys grew up and went to university they would read T. S. Ashton's classic little volume (Ashton 1948), which would fill in the historical details with the relevant statistics and disabuse them of the thought that the Industrial Revolution was anything other than a monumental blessing to humanity, or at least those members of it who were of European extraction. Any remaining unconvinced by this thesis would be referred to *Capitalism and the Historians* (Hayek 1954), where they would be forced to confront the question of why, if the rural landscape was as idyllic as in its portrayal by artists and poets, so many people were drawn to Birmingham and Manchester to work in those very same dark, satanic mills.

If any of the schoolboys chose to pursue graduate studies in economics and went to, say, MIT in the late 1950s, they would have encountered Walt Whitman Rostow, engaged in generalizing the Industrial Revolution into a theory of *The Stages of Economic Growth* (Rostow 1960). In this schema the central stage was described by the aeronautical metaphor of a "takeoff," defined as a compressed period of one or two decades in which there would be a sharp, discontinuous increase in the rate of growth of national income accompanied by an approximate doubling of the rate of national savings and the emergence of a "leading sector" setting the pace for the rest of the economy to follow. The first, paradigmatic takeoff was of course the British Industrial Revolution, dated daringly by Rostow to 1783–1802. At about the same time the classic account of the technological aspects of the Industrial Revolution was presented by David Landes (1969) in his *Prometheus Unbound.*

Meanwhile, however, the "new economic history" or Cliometric School was turning its attention to the Industrial Revolution. There had already been criticism of Rostow's insistence on a sharp disconti-nuity in growth and savings rates from scholars such as Phyllis Deane and Simon Kuznets (in Rostow 1963), since these were difficult to match with the historical record in Britain and elsewhere, but now more careful macroeconomic calculations reinforced this skepticism. A graduate student of the 1980s would thus have learned that there were no sudden breaks or shifts in any of the relevant rates and ratios, so that the climactic event itself appeared to dissolve into a long, slow, gradual but sustained increase in the standard of living, accompanying an admittedly unprecedented increase in population. The new revisionist account of the Industrial Revolution is presented most authoritatively in the work of Crafts and Harley (e.g., Harley 1982; Crafts 1985; Crafts and Harley 1992). Cuenca Esteban (1994) is probably the most influential critique of the new macroeconomic data, while the strongest defense of the traditional view is Landes (1999), in which the "dead horse" kicks back vigorously at its detractors.

The extent of the revision in the estimated growth rates is summa-rized in table 6.1. As can be seen, the old estimates of GDP growth by Deane and Cole (1967) for the period 1760–1830 have been revised downward by approximately two-thirds, so that growth is now thought to have averaged less than 0.2% per annum during the last four decades of the eighteenth century, and only 0.5% per annum during the subsequent thirty years. Growth in the relatively dynamic industrial sector was more rapid, and has been revised downward by less: the new estimates for the late eighteenth century range from 1.6 to 2.6% per annum, and there seems to be consensus that industrial output growth accelerated to over 3% per annum after 1800, although this is still less than the 4.4% estimate of Deane and Cole.

TABLE 6.1. Estimates of British industrial and GDP growth, 1761–1860
(percent per annum).

	Author	1700–60	1760–1800	1800–30	1830–70
(a)	Deane and Cole (1967)	0.44	0.52	1.61	1.98
(a)	Crafts	0.3	0.17	0.52	1.98
(b)	Hoffmann (1955)	0.67	2.45	2.7	3.1
(b)	Deane and Cole (1967)	0.74	1.24	4.4	2.9
(b)	Harley	N.a.	1.6	3.2	N.a.
(b)	Crafts	0.62	1.96	3	N.a.
(b)	Cuenca Esteban (1994)	N.a.	2.61	3.18	N.a.

Source: Mokyr (2004, table 1.1, p. 4); (a) national income per capita; (b) industrial production. N.a. = not available.

Even more alarming for scholars used to thinking in terms of dramatic breakthroughs and waves of gadgets are the figures on technological change, or total factor productivity (TFP) growth. Even the earliest estimates due to Feinstein (1981) implied very low rates of TFP growth during the late eighteenth century, the heroic age according to traditional accounts. What the revisionists (Crafts 1985; Crafts and Harley 1992; Antràs and Voth 2003) have succeeded in doing, using a number of methods, is to greatly reduce TFP growth estimates for the early nineteenth century as well, from well over 1% per annum to roughly 0.5%. Moreover, recent scholarship has shown that the aggregate growth rate had been steadily increasing since the beginning of the eighteenth century. Thus, "the origins of modern economic growth extended over a longer time period and a wider geographical area than are traditionally encompassed in studies of the Industrial Revolution" (Harley and Crafts 2000, pp. 820–21).

The question thus arises, was the Industrial Revolution revolutionary? Most scholars agree that there are a number of qualitative features of the late eighteenth and early nineteenth centuries that justify labeling that period as "revolutionary."[1] First, these low figures for aggregate growth conceal as much as they reveal, in that the leading sectors of the Industrial Revolution initially represented only a small share of the aggregate economy, and thus had only a small influence on the aggregate numbers. Growth was extremely fast in key sectors such as metallurgy and, especially, cotton textiles: between 1770 and 1815, Harley's figures show the cotton industry growing at 7% per annum, the iron industry at 3%, and the coal industry at 2.5%, with

[1] For an excellent introduction to the vast literature on the subject, see Mokyr (1999), whose approach we largely adopt in what follows.

TABLE 6.2. British exports, 1784–1856, by product group (percent).

Period	1784–86	1794–96	1804–6	1814–16
Cotton goods	6	15.6	42.3	42.1
Woolen goods	29.2	23.9	16.4	17.7
Other textiles	10.6	10.6	7.4	8.2
Other manufactures	38.3	37.4	23.8	17.5
Foodstuffs and raw materials	15.9	12.5	10	14.5
Total (£000)	12,690	21,770	37,535	44,474
Period	1824–26	1834–36	1844–46	1854–56
Cotton goods	47.8	48.5	44.2	34.1
Woolen goods	16.3	15.2	14.2	10.5
Other textiles	9.1	9.8	10.9	12.7
Other manufactures	19.2	17.6	18.7	23.8
Foodstuffs and raw materials	7.6	8.9	12	18.9
Total (£000)	35,298	46,193	58,420	102,501

Source: Davis (1979, table 2, p. 15).

other industries growing at around 1% (Crafts and Harley 1992, p. 713). Second, and as a consequence of this, the period saw rapid structural change. Agriculture's share of British male employment fell from 61% in 1700 to 53% in 1760, 41% in 1800, and 29% in 1841 (Crafts 1985, table 3.6, p. 62). Within industry, the share of the modern sectors, such as cotton textiles, rose, while that of traditional sectors, such as the woolen, linen, and leather industries, fell. In 1752–54, the leading sector of the Industrial Revolution, cotton textiles, accounted for just 1.3% of total English exports, while the share of woolen textiles was 61.9% (O'Brien and Engerman 1991, table 3, p. 184). As table 6.2 shows, by the first decade of the nineteenth century the share of cotton goods was over 40%, while the share of woolens had declined to under 20%.

The third major reason for concluding that the Industrial Revolution was indeed revolutionary is that living standards did not collapse, although the British population was growing rapidly. This break in traditional Malthusian relationships between factor endowments and real wages marked a profound rupture with the past (Crafts and Harley 1992, p. 704), and economic historians have long appreciated its significance (for an important recent account, see Clark (2007a)). As Wrigley and Schofield (1989, p. 412) say, "perhaps for the first time in the history of any country other than a land of recent settlement rapid population growth took place concurrently with rising living standards. A basic feature of the human condition had changed." According to Wrigley

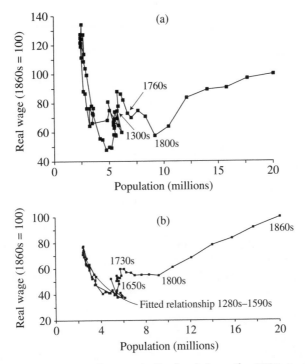

FIGURE 6.1. Population and wages in England, from the 1280s to the 1860s: (a) Phelps-Brown and Hopkins (1981) wages; (b) Clark (2005) wages. *Source:* Clark (2005, figures 3 and 5, pp. 1310, 1312).

(2004, tables 3.1, 3.2, and 3.4), the English population rose from 5.2 million in 1701 to 5.9 million in 1751, 8.6 million in 1801, and 14.9 million in 1841. The main reason for the increase was not a decline in mortality, as one might be inclined to suppose, but an increase in marital fertility, partly reflecting a fall in the average age of marriage for females from 26 years in the early 1700s to 23 years by 1830–37.

Based on past experience this should have led to a collapse in English living standards, consistent with the predictions of the Malthusian model that we used when analyzing the consequences of the Black Death in chapter 3. In this model, with capital, land, and technology given, there are diminishing returns to labor, implying that as population grows labor productivity and real wages decline. However, figure 6.1 (taken from Clark 2005) shows that the traditional negative Malthusian relationship between real wages and population started breaking down in either the late seventeenth or the late eighteenth

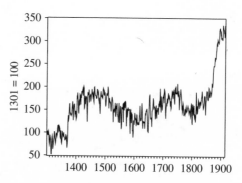

FIGURE 6.2. Real wages in London, 1301–1913 (1301 = 100).
Source: Allen (2001).

centuries, depending on which real wage series one believes in.[2] Before then, wages and population lay along a tightly defined if notional negatively sloped schedule, but then the economy started moving away from this schedule, so that higher levels of population could coincide with higher real wages, or at least real wages that were not declining, or not declining as fast as would have been expected based on past experience. The early nineteenth century appears as a particularly distinct break in both these series, in that from then on both population *and* real wages were increasing, whichever wage series one uses (Allen 2001; Clark 2005; Feinstein 1998). The great achievement of the British Industrial Revolution was thus that it permitted a massive population expansion without any decline in living standards, suggesting that old Malthusian constraints were being overcome.

Figure 6.2 offers another way of appreciating just how dramatic the nineteenth-century breakthrough was. For centuries, real wages had experienced pronounced cycles around a broadly constant trend, which is consistent with the Malthusian model's long-run predictions. The model assumes that the mortality rate is a decreasing and the fertility rate an increasing function of per capita income. This yields a critical value of per capita income at which the two rates are equal and the population therefore stationary. Any discrete increase in capital, land, or technology, no matter how large, would eventually

[2]Wrigley and Schofield (1989, p. 410) have a very similar graph, in which 1781 emerges as a crucial turning point. Their graph is reproduced in Landes (1999), who also stresses the importance of this break with the past. Note also that the Low Countries were able to combine constant real wages with a rising population during the early modern period, an indication that this "great escape" was not limited to Britain (Allen 2001).

only result in a larger population at the same standard of living. While per capita income would increase in the short run, in the long run this would induce an increase in population, and per capita income would decline to its long-run level due to the operation of diminishing returns, as the growing population pressed against a fixed endowment of land and natural resources. For centuries the model seems to have fitted the facts reasonably well, but in the nineteenth century stagnation was permanently replaced by dramatic sustained growth. In this figure, based on Allen (2001), the break occurs around 1870, while Clark (2005) presents a similar series but with the break occurring around 1815. In this light, the frequently intemperate debates between Industrial Revolution "optimists" and "pessimists" boil down to a question of timing, with the bigger picture being the dramatic and unambiguous nineteenth-century break with the past.

While a suitably updated Malthusian model does a good job of explaining the preindustrial period (Clark 2007a), it cannot explain the constant growth that followed. To do so, we can usefully turn to Solow's (1956) benchmark neoclassical growth model, or the many endogenous growth models that have succeeded it.[3] The Solow model differs from the Malthusian in two major respects. In terms of demography the positive relationship between population growth and per capita income is replaced by the assumption that population growth is invariant with respect to per capita income. Second, the given level of technology in the Malthusian model, which can change discretely but not incessantly, is replaced by the assumption of a fixed exogenous rate of "labor-augmenting" technical progress. Under these assumptions it can be shown that the economy will enjoy a "steady-state" growth rate equal to the sum of the two exogenous rates of population growth and technical progress, while per capita growth will be due to technological progress alone. Thus the transition from Malthus to Solow is marked both by a "demographic transition" in which the population growth rate ceases to vary endogenously (and positively) with per capita income and instead becomes an exogenous constant, and a "technological revolution" in which the jerky, episodic nature of technical progress in the Malthusian model is replaced by continuous progress at a constant rate.

[3] "Explanation" of the breakthrough episode itself, of course, still presents formidable difficulties of interpretation and analysis, both for economic history and economic theory. Obviously, any attempt to provide such an explanation will have to move beyond the Solow model by endogenizing both technological progress and fertility decisions. A particularly influential paper trying to do just this is Galor and Weil (2000), while Galor (2005) provides an invaluable overview of the current literature on the transition to modern economic growth.

Can such a transition be at least loosely identified with an actual episode in economic history such as the Industrial Revolution in England? The answer appears to be yes, although the transition happened in stages, and part of the transition happened in the later nineteenth century. Figure 6.1 showed that the traditional negative relationship between income and population started breaking down in the seventeenth or eighteenth centuries, indicating perhaps a steady improvement in technology over that period which then accelerated in the nineteenth century (Clark 2007a, chapter 11). On the other hand, the rapid growth in population during the eighteenth and nineteenth centuries is consistent with Malthus, in that it can plausibly be attributed to slightly better real incomes inducing earlier formation of separate households by young married couples in conformity with the "European marriage pattern" (Hajnal 1965). Eventually, some time after the 1870s, the increase in fertility was replaced with a decline in fertility, indicating a definitive breakdown in the Malthusian demographic model, or at least in the upward-sloping Malthusian fertility function. This at last meant that the benefits of technical progress were no longer diluted by higher population growth, allowing the emergence of "modern economic growth" and more rapidly rising living standards (Galor and Weil 2000; Galor 2005). All things considered, it would seem that there is still plenty of life left in the dead horse.

Technological change was crucial in allowing industrializing economies to escape from the Malthusian trap, and the fourth reason for considering the Industrial Revolution to have been, after all, revolutionary, is the extent of technological progress during the period (Mokyr 1990, 1999, 2004, 2005a). This progress is best illustrated with reference to the canonical leading sector of the period, namely cotton textiles. As we have already seen, Indian calicos and muslins were for a long time profitable imports into Europe for both the British and Dutch East India Companies. They were in fact so successful in competing with woolens in the home market that the woolen industry agitated successfully for protection against imports of cotton fabrics from India, Persia, and China, imposing a prohibition in 1700 and extending it in 1721, only to be later hoist with its own petard when the domestic cotton industry that arose in Lancashire as a result ended up as a far more successful competitor. As Mantoux (1962, p. 203) observes, the ancient woolen industry "by its blind passion for monopoly, stirred up that competition that it tried to kill a few years later: for it is from the prohibition of 1700 that the success of English-made cotton goods, as a substitute for Indian fabrics, can be said to date." Thus (p. 104), "the seeds [of the cotton textile industry, and therefore in a sense of the Industrial Revolution itself] were in fact brought to England in the ships of the East India Company," while the new industry was "a child of the East India trade" (p. 203). Mantoux furthermore points out (p. 204) that the new cotton textile industry had "instead of privileges, all the advantages of freedom" and was therefore "a field for inventions and for every kind of initiative" making all conditions favorable for it to emerge as the first modern machine industry.

The cotton textile industry (as well as the manufacture of "new draperies," referred to in chapter 4) had been established by refugees from Antwerp, who had fled after the infamous "Spanish Fury" of 1576, when over seven thousand inhabitants were killed, and after the siege and capture of the town by Habsburg forces in 1585. The immigrants first settled around Norwich in East Anglia before the industry was drawn to Lancashire and the vicinity of Manchester by ca. 1640. The yarn they spun was either too coarse or too weak and therefore needed to be mixed with linen to make it sufficiently strong. The resulting mixture of cotton and linen was called fustian, and was deemed to be exempt from the ban on the manufacture of pure cotton fabrics imposed in 1721, and which lasted until 1774. The Lancashire climate was held to be particularly favorable to the spinning of cotton and proximity to the major port of Liverpool meant that raw cotton supplies could conveniently be brought not only from Smyrna (Izmir) in Turkey but also increasingly from the Caribbean, Brazil, and the New World. The fustian was printed with designs after the Indian fashion and found ready markets in connection with the slave trade on the western coast of Africa and in the slave plantation societies of the New World.

Despite these successes the cotton textile industry would have remained of only minor importance were it not for the extraordinary series of technical innovations in spinning and weaving that occurred with increasing frequency from the second half of the eighteenth century. The first major innovation was in weaving: the flying shuttle of John Kay was introduced in 1735, which effectively doubled the output of a single weaver. There followed three key innovations on the spinning side: the spinning jenny of James Hargreaves, the water frame of Richard Arkwright, and the mule of Samuel Crompton, which would eventually lead to Richard Roberts's self-acting or automatic mule, invented in 1825 and introduced in the 1830s. The huge increase in spinning productivity created an imbalance on the weaving side, despite the invention of a power loom by Edmund Cartwright in the 1780s, because several technical shortcomings still had to be overcome that were not fully resolved until the 1820s. A crucial breakthrough came when steam engines were used as the power source for both spinning and weaving. By 1835 steam power was providing 30,000 of the 40,000 horsepower used in the industry as a whole, with the rest relying on water (Chapman 1972, table 1, p. 19). According to Chapman, the number of operative hours to process 100 lb. (45 kilograms) of cotton was over 50,000 for spinning by hand in India. In England it was cut to only 2,000 by the 1779 invention of Crompton's mule, and fell to 300 by 1795 and 135 by 1825, compared with 40 in 1972 at the time of publication of Chapman's study.

Spinning and weaving were not the only stages of cotton textile production to experience major technical innovations. Bleaching the woven cloth was at first accomplished by immersing it in sour milk to provide lactic acid, a lengthy and inefficient process that was improved first by the use of sulfuric acid, produced industrially in Scotland by the 1750s, and later and even more significantly by the use of bleaching powder, another early example of an industrial chemical. Dyeing and printing were also mechanized (ibid., p. 25). As a result of all these innovations and the substantial markets at home and abroad, the cotton textile industry was not only contributing a rapidly increasing share of national income; the technical innovations that were first made in cotton were applied to the woolen, linen, and silk industries as well, while the cotton textile industry stimulated growth in the chemical and engineering industries via its demand for intermediate inputs such as sulfuric acid and bleaching powder, and for capital goods such as looms and spindles (ibid.). All things considered, Rostow's original characterization of cotton textiles as the leading sector of the British Industrial Revolution appears to have been well-founded.

Continuous technological change, not just in textiles but in metallurgy and other sectors as well, directly helped Britain escape from the Malthusian trap, but it did so indirectly as well. First, as has been emphasized by E. A. Wrigley (1988) in one of the most important contributions on the subject in recent years, the new technologies of the Industrial Revolution, and in particular the steam engine, were based on coal. Previously economies had relied on "organic" sources of energy, that is to say on human or animal power, or wood. They were thus ultimately dependent on the fertility of the Earth's surface, which provided sustenance to man and beast, as well as the forests from which the wood was procured. Alternative energy sources depended on the vagaries of wind and waterpower that were specific to time and place. It is not surprising that Malthusian constraints should have been tightly binding in an era when land had to provide not just food, fibers (i.e., the raw materials for textiles), and building materials, but fuel as well (Pomeranz 2000). Britain in the eighteenth century, however, running out of forests, was fortunate enough to have coal available in abundance below the surface of the Earth, and the new technologies allowed it to tap for the first time in a prolonged and systematic way the vast reserves of subterranean fossil fuels that the world has been drawing on ever since to sustain its continuing growth of population and production. As Wrigley (1988, 2000) himself points out, the fact that these reserves now provided an additional elastically supplied input into production, along with land, helps explain the breakdown of traditional short-run Malthusian relationships between population and living standards, which depend crucially on land and other factors of production being in fixed supply (Mokyr 2004, p. 18).

The Industrial Revolution also helped Europe overcome Malthusian constraints from the middle of the nineteenth century onward, by providing new transportation technologies that brought Europe closer to the vast land endowments of the New World. This not only enabled Europe to import ever-increasing quantities of elastically supplied food and raw materials, but allowed it to send large numbers of people overseas at a time when its own population was growing rapidly. In this manner, Europe's effective land endowment was augmented, at precisely the time when it was experiencing a population explosion (Pomeranz 2000, chapter 6). As Galor and Weil (2000, p. 826) put it, "By easing the land constraint at a crucial point—when income per capita had begun to rise rapidly, but before the demographic transition had gotten under way—the 'ghost acres' of the New World provided a window of time, which allowed Europe to pull decisively away from the Malthusian equilibrium."[4] Elastically supplied New World land and elastically supplied coal are thus two vital components of any explanation of how Europe escaped the curse of diminishing returns during this period, with technological change increasing the importance of both.

Figure 6.3 shows the Crafts–Harley index of total British industrial production, as well as an index of raw cotton imports, a good indicator of activity in the cotton textiles sector (and an equally good reminder of the vital importance of New World land for British growth, even before the advent of the steamship and railroad). As can be seen, there was a sharp acceleration in raw cotton imports in the 1780s, and cotton textiles output grew far more rapidly than total industrial output until

[4]The concept of "ghost acres," originally due to Georg Borgstrom, was popularized among economic historians by Eric Jones (2003).

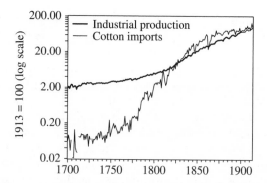

FIGURE 6.3. British industrial output and cotton imports, 1700–1913 (1913 = 100). *Source:* Crafts and Harley (1992, table A3.1, pp. 725–27) and Mitchell (1988, pp. 330–31, 334–35).

the mid nineteenth century. The figure also shows that there was a clear acceleration in the rate of overall industrial growth some time around 1820. As we will see in the next chapter, this acceleration coincides with the end of the Revolutionary and Napoleonic Wars with France, and simple trade theory suggests that the trade disruption associated with these wars should have favored British agriculture at the expense of British industry. The move from war to peace thus offers one explanation for the timing of this acceleration.[5] Another explanation is simply that, as we have seen, the most rapidly growing sectors of the new industrial economy, such as cotton textiles, were initially a small share of the whole, and that it was only after a number of decades that their weight in the overall economy was such that their growth would have an appreciable effect on the overall statistics.[6] In any event, it is clear that the Industrial Revolution only became widespread enough to have an appreciable impact on the aggregate British and European economy during the century between Waterloo and the Great War. Industry still accounted for less than 30% of male

[5] Williamson (1984) argues the case strongly.

[6] Indeed, debates regarding the precise rate of growth during the Industrial Revolution hinge mainly on the weight of the cotton textiles sector in total output at various periods (see Cuenca Esteban 1994, 1995; Crafts and Harley 1992; Harley and Crafts 1995). It should be noted, however, that some authors (e.g., Temin 1997) vigorously dispute the claim that technological change was limited to just a few sectors during this period, arguing that Britain did indeed become "the workshop of the world, not just the cotton factory of the world" (p. 80). In the long run, this is indisputably correct, implying that, as with the "standard of living debate," this is a debate largely about timing.

TABLE 6.3. Per capita levels of industrialization, 1750–1913
(U.K. in 1900 = 100; 1913 boundaries).

Country	1750	1800	1860	1913
Austria–Hungary	7	7	11	32
Belgium	9	10	28	88
France	9	9	20	59
Germany	8	8	15	85
Italy	8	8	10	26
Russia	6	6	8	20
Spain	7	7	11	22
Sweden	7	8	15	67
Switzerland	7	10	26	87
United Kingdom	10	16	64	115
Canada	N.a.	5	7	46
United States	4	9	21	126
Japan	7	7	7	20
China	8	6	4	3
India	7	6	3	2
Brazil	N.a.	N.a.	4	7
Mexico	N.a.	N.a.	5	7

Source: Bairoch (1982, p. 281). N.a. = not available.

employment in 1800, but this proportion had risen to 47% by 1840, and would reach 54% in 1910 (Crafts 1985, p. 62).

Gradually, the new technologies spread to the northwestern European continent, despite the initial attempts of the British government to prevent this by prohibiting the export of machinery and skilled workmen. Table 6.3 gives Paul Bairoch's (1982) estimates of per capita industrialization between 1750 and 1913. While the basis for such estimates is necessarily slender, the further back one goes in time, the trends are sufficiently dramatic to be worth taking seriously. The table shows Britain pulling ahead of its European competitors in the second half of the eighteenth century, and further increasing its lead over the next sixty years. Belgium (an independent country since 1830) and Switzerland were early emulators, as was France, but even so, until mid century their per capita industrialization lagged far behind that of the United Kingdom. In the second half of the nineteenth century, however, there was a substantial convergence of these early emulators (particularly Belgium, Germany, and Switzerland) on Britain, which was actually overtaken by the United States; the table also shows industrialization spreading gradually to Eastern Europe and Japan.

Because the Industrial Revolution began in Europe, and only slowly diffused to the rest of the world, a dramatic gap began to open up between industrialization in Europe and elsewhere. According to table 6.3, China and India actually deindustrialized between 1750 and World War I. While they had enjoyed per capita industrialization levels of between 70 and 80% of Britain's in 1750, a forty- or even fiftyfold gap had opened up by 1913. While the precise figures are certainly open to question, the available evidence clearly indicates that India deindustrialized during the nineteenth century, and that Indian and Chinese per capita incomes stagnated or declined between the turn of the century and 1870 (chapter 7). For example, the share of the Indian labor force employed in industry declined from 15 to 18% in 1800 to around 10% in 1900 (Roy 2000, cited in Clingingsmith and Williamson 2004, p. 9).

The result was a growing asymmetry in the world economy, with Europe accounting for an increasing share of world industrial output. According to Bairoch (1982, p. 296), in 1750 the developing world accounted for three-quarters of world manufacturing output, with China accounting for nearly a third, and India for a quarter. Even if these figures are a massive overestimate, there can be no doubt of Asia's declining share in industrial output over the course of the eighteenth and nineteenth centuries. In 1913, for which we have good data, India's share was just 1.4%, China's share was just 3.6%, and the share of Europe and her British offshoots was a staggering 89.8% (ibid.).[7]

What can explain Europe's takeoff to nineteenth-century growth, and what explains the Great Divergence that ensued? What was the role of trade and empire in these developments, and why was it Western Europe that experienced the takeoff first, when as we have seen the region was a relatively peripheral backwater at the start of the second millennium? The following sections will attempt to provide some answers to these questions, beginning with an account of British trade patterns during the Industrial Revolution.

TRADE DURING THE INDUSTRIAL REVOLUTION

Ralph Davis (1979) is the most convenient and helpful source on the role of foreign trade, and in particular that of the cotton textile trade, in the Industrial Revolution (see also Crouzet 1980). His data, reproduced in table 6.4, show that cotton goods exports rose continuously for every decade from the 1780s to the 1850s with the exception of the 1820s,

---

[7] By "British offshoots," here and later in the book, we will mean the Anglo-Saxon settler economies of North America and Australasia.

the annual average rising from about £250,000 in 1784–86 to almost £12 million in 1854–56. The growth rates in the volume of cotton goods exports (i.e., exports measured at "official values" or constant prices) were truly remarkable: 39%, 84%, 71%, and 68% in the four decades from 1815 to 1855 (table 8, p. 20). As we saw in table 6.2, this implied that the share of cotton goods in total exports rose from 6% in 1784–86 to 42% in 1804–6 and 48% at its peak in 1834–36. After this the share fell to 34% by 1854–56 as metallurgical and engineering products surged, but the absolute level continued to grow. Europe took between 40 and 60% of British exports for the first half of the nineteenth century, but in 1854–56 the share of Asia and Africa (39%) exceeded that of Europe (29%) for the first time, reflecting the success of import substitution in the more advanced European economies and the rise in economic importance of India and other colonies.

An interesting comparison that Davis makes is between "old" (Europe, the United States, Canada, the West Indies) and "new" (Asia including the Near East, Africa, Australia, and Latin America) markets. Sales to the old markets fluctuated slightly around the £15 million level for the first half of the nineteenth century, but sales to the new markets rose very rapidly from a mere £680,000 in 1804–6 to nearly £19 million in 1854–56, substantially more than sales to the old markets. The growth of the cotton textile industry in Europe was based on replacing imports of British cotton fabric with imports of British cotton yarn. Thus European imports of British cotton fabric remained roughly constant over the first half of the nineteenth century while imports of British cotton yarn increased by over 250% (table 5, p. 17). France and Switzerland became self-sufficient in cotton textiles by the 1830s and began exporting to neighboring countries soon afterward (p. 17). Similarly, the share of America and Australia in British cotton exports was 50% in the early nineteenth century but fell steadily to between a third and a quarter by the middle of the century. This decline reflected import substitution by the New England cotton textile industry in the United States, based on the same raw cotton that was the main input in the British industry, as well as the slow impoverishment of the colonies in the West Indies by rising competition in the world sugar market.

Among Britain's other exports, woolen goods exports continued to generally rise over the first half of the nineteenth century in absolute terms, although as we have seen in table 6.2 they declined steadily as a share of total exports. Traditional exports of metals and metalware rose modestly up to the 1840s, but in the next decade there was a huge surge in exports of iron products related to railway construction, including steam locomotives, rolling stock, and rails. These went first

TABLE 6.4. Exports of cotton goods, 1784–1856, by destination (thousands of pounds sterling).

Period	1784–86	1794–96	1804–6	1814–16
Europe	310	761	7,224	11,386
%	*40.5*	*22.4*	*45.5*	*60.8*
Asia and Africa	164	199	683	346
%	*21.4*	*5.9*	*4.3*	*1.8*
America and Australia	292	2,432	7,964	7,010
%	*38.1*	*71.7*	*50.2*	*37.4*
Old markets	766	3,384	15,192	17,040
%	*100.0*	*99.8*	*95.7*	*90.9*
New markets	0.0	8.0	679.0	1,702.0
%	*0.0*	*0.2*	*4.3*	*9.1*
Total	766	3,392	15,871	18,742
Period	1824–26	1834–36	1844–46	1854–56
Europe	8,682	10,612	10,153	10,263
%	*51.4*	*47.4*	*39.3*	*29.4*
Asia and Africa	1,707	4,056	9,356	13,831
%	*10.1*	*18.1*	*36.2*	*39.6*
America and Australia	6,490	7,730	6,326	10,814
%	*38.5*	*34.5*	*24.5*	*31.0*
Old markets	12,313	15,037	13,246	15,954
%	*72.9*	*67.1*	*51.3*	*45.7*
New markets	4,566.0	7,361.0	12,589.0	18,954.0
%	*27.1*	*32.9*	*48.7*	*54.3*
Total	16,879	22,398	25,835	34,908

Source: Davis (1979, tables 3 and 9, pp. 15, 21). Old markets are Europe, U.S.A., Canada, and the West Indies. New markets are Asia, Africa, Australia, and Latin America.

to Europe in the 1840s and then to America in the 1850s, which took over half of the total overseas sales in 1854, with India picking up some of the slack after that. These export sales reflected Britain's dominant position in world pig iron production at mid century, with an output of over 2 million tons, five times that of France and ten times that of Germany (p. 28).

Britain's trade with the advanced industrial countries of Europe went through an interesting evolution. The lead in mechanized spinning and the earlier stages of other manufacturing processes that Britain acquired early in the nineteenth century made its partners concentrate initially on the less mechanized later stages of production, so that a "vertical" division of labor appeared with these countries importing industrial raw materials and semifinished goods such as cotton and worsted yarn, iron billets, bars, and girders as intermediate inputs from Britain. In addition British firms had developed organized markets for raw cotton, wool, and hides so that a substantial reexport trade in these items also grew up. The share of British exports to Europe accounted for by raw materials and textile yarns rose steadily from 17% in the 1780s to 57% by the 1850s (table 21, p. 34). On the other hand Europe's share of Britain's finished goods exports fell from 36% in the 1780s to 21% in the 1850s. Thus Britain's trade with an industrial Europe largely involved the export of some finished manufactures, but mainly semifinished intermediate inputs, in return for other finished manufactures, together with some primary products like wheat, wine, and timber. To the less developed regions of the world, however, Britain exported finished manufactures in exchange for primary products, mainly foodstuffs and raw materials of agricultural origin like tea, coffee, and sugar.

As we have seen, the reexport trade in colonial produce had long been a mainstay of Britain's overseas commerce, constituting about a third of total exports for the first three-quarters of the eighteenth century (p. 31). These figures directly reflected the successes of the mercantilist phase of the evolution of Britain's foreign trade, such as the influence of the Navigation Acts and the victories and annexations of the Seven Years' War. The loss of the North American colonies led to a severe slump in the reexport trade as sugar, tobacco, rice, and other produce were now sent directly to Europe instead of through British ports. The trade revived during the long struggle with France, when British rule of the seas meant that she was able to channel most of these products toward herself for reexport to final destinations, but the subsequent peace once again led to the restoration of direct links between European centers and the sources of supply. An entirely new form of the reexport trade got under way now, however, as Britain became the natural hub or collection point for the vast amounts of primary and semifinished products that European industrialization was now requiring. Between 1794–96 and 1854–56 the share of reexports in total exports fell from 24% to 17%, but reexports more than tripled in total value from less than £7 million to over £21 million (p. 33). Rather than the compulsion of the Navigation Acts, which were repealed in 1849, the new trade reflected Britain's emerging comparative advantage as a center for the distribution of a wide range of raw materials from all over the world, including Brazil and the newly independent former Spanish colonies in Latin America.

Britain's total imports rose over sevenfold from £20.3 million in 1784–86 to £151.8 million in 1854–56 (table 6.5). The composition of these imports changed significantly. Manufactures had been almost a third of total imports in 1700, but the strong industrial growth of the eighteenth century reduced this share to 10.5% in 1784–86 and to less than 2% in the 1810s and 1820s, although the share had recovered slightly to 5% by 1854–56. The share of raw materials rose from 47% in 1784–86 to a peak of 68% by 1834–36, before stabilizing at about 60% in the next two decades. The share of foodstuffs fell slightly from about 42% to about 35% over the period as a whole. These foodstuff imports consisted of "temperate zone" products such as grain and meat from Europe on the one hand, and "tropical" commodities such as tea, coffee, cocoa, and sugar on the other. As Davis points out (p. 37) the prices of these tropical goods were falling substantially as rising supplies arrived from overseas territories at increasingly lower transport costs. However, supplies of temperate zone foodstuffs from the distant sources of North America and Ukraine only became plentiful after the railways had opened up the interiors of these vast spaces and the steamship lowered ocean freight rates even further (chapter 7). In the interim, Britain had to rely on imports from Europe, and especially from Ireland, as Brinley Thomas (1985) has emphasized. Thomas estimates that imports from Ireland as late as the 1830s were equivalent to 13% of English agricultural output, and more than 85% of total English imports of grains, meat, butter, and livestock: thus "Irish land was being called in to alleviate the mounting pressures on English land" (pp. 741–42).

The origin of the raw material imports underwent significant changes. The traditional reliance on the Baltic for timber and naval stores shifted to Canada, while Australia was becoming increasingly important as a source for wool, and entirely new products like jute from India and palm oil from West Africa began to make their appearance (Davis 1979, p. 38). The share of total raw material imports that came from Europe fell from 65.7% in 1784–86 to 30.8% by 1854–56. However, Europe became a relatively more important source of manufactured goods, with its share increasing from 36% in 1784–86 to 84% in 1854–56, as the rising tide of European industrialization began to flow in while Asian textiles declined rapidly.

Cotton, sugar, and tea were among the major imports throughout the entire period, with sugar being initially at the top, where it had been for one hundred and fifty years, but being replaced by cotton from the 1820s onward. The increasing consumption of these goods that we documented in chapter 5 for the eighteenth century seems to have continued between the 1780s and 1850s. The Caribbean islands were the main source of sugar but Mauritius, acquired from France

TABLE 6.5. British imports, 1784–1856, by product group (percent).

Period	1784–86	1794–96	1804–6	1814–16
Manufactures	10.5	7.1	3.4	1.1
Raw materials	47.0	44.7	54.2	56.2
Temperate foodstuffs	2.6	6.4	5.7	3.2
Wines spirits	7.5	8.3	6.3	5.8
Tea, coffee, cocoa	13.5	12.0	12.7	11.4
Sugar	12.8	17.3	13.6	17.2
Other foodstuffs	6.1	4.1	4.1	5.0
Total (£000)	20,386	34,326	50,619	64,741

Period	1824–26	1834–36	1844–46	1854–56
Manufactures	1.6	2.7	4.3	5.1
Raw materials	62.3	67.8	62.3	59.0
Temperate foodstuffs	4.2	2.9	10.3	15.4
Wines spirits	6.8	5.7	3.9	3.7
Tea, coffee, cocoa	9.0	6.9	4.6	4.5
Sugar	11.8	10.1	9.9	7.2
Other foodstuffs	4.3	3.8	4.8	5.1
Total (£000)	56,975	70,265	81,963	151,581

Source: Davis (1979, tables 23 and 24, pp. 36–37).

during the Napoleonic Wars, and India also provided further supplies. Retained imports of sugar increased more than fourfold between 1784–86 and 1854–56, reflecting a population increase from 9 to 21 million and a 150% increase in the annual per capita consumption to the remarkable level of about 35 lb. (ibid., p. 45). Sugar was of course strongly complementary in demand with tea, the consumption of which rose even more rapidly than sugar over the period from 1784 to 1856. Consumption per head almost trebled to about 3.2 lb., while retained imports increased by a factor of almost six (p. 47) despite an import duty of almost 100% for most of the period. As Davis (p. 47) says, "From a rare and expensive luxury at the beginning of the eighteenth century, tea had become a small indulgence of masses of people as regular organized traffic with China lowered the cost; and then in the era of cheap supplies after 1784 it was generally adopted into the diet of all classes, down to the poorest farm laborers and nailmakers."

These trends, which reflected Britain's growing specialization in manufacturing, implied that Britain was becoming a much more open economy during this period. According to Crafts (1985, p. 131), exports accounted for 8.4% of British GDP in 1700, for 14.6% in 1760, for 9.4% in 1780, for 15.7% in 1801, for 14.3% in 1831, and for

19.6% in 1851. Exports were particularly important in manufacturing: Cuenca Esteban (1997) has recently found that exports accounted for a continuously rising share of British industrial output between the 1720s and 1851. Exports accounted for 13% of industrial output in 1700, if the data in figure 6.3 are accepted, but for 18% in 1760, for 25% in 1780, for 40% in 1801, and for 49% in 1831. Several authors (e.g., Thomas 1985; Harley and Crafts 2000; Clark 2007b) have pointed out that this growing openness and specialization were the inevitable consequences of Britain's rapid population growth during the period, or at least afforded the only prospect that the growth could be sustained. As Brinley Thomas (1985, p. 731) put it, "How could this unprecedented swarming of people on a small, offshore island be made consistent with a rising standard of living? It was impossible on the fixed area of English cultivable land, whatever miracles English technological progress in agriculture might accomplish. The way out was for England (through a transportation revolution and international trade) to endow itself with the equivalent of a vast extension of its own land base." In other words, population growth and a limited land endowment necessarily implied large-scale imports of food and raw materials, which necessarily had to be paid for with exports of manufactured goods. Trade and industrialization were thus essential for British population growth, which in turn was essential in securing Britain's military dominance during the nineteenth century (Clark 2007b). Furthermore, by making Britain dependent on foreign food supplies, population growth and specialization in manufacturing gave Britain a strong strategic incentive to ensure a smoothly functioning international trade system (Offer 1989).

Trade, Overseas Expansion, and the Industrial Revolution

One of the most enduring controversies in economic history has opposed those who believe that the roots of the Industrial Revolution lay primarily within the nature of British, or more broadly European, society during the Age of Enlightenment, and those who feel that Europe's relationships with the rest of the world were a crucial ingredient helping her make the crucial breakthrough. The debate is ideologically tinged, since as we have seen at great length in the previous two chapters, Europe's relationships with the rest of the world had been forged largely as a result of violence. It is thus closely related to the answers various authors have posed to David Landes's (1990) famous question, "Why are we so rich and they so poor?" "We" in this case is taken to mean citizens of Europe and her British offshoots, with the Japanese perhaps qualifying as honorary Europeans for this purpose. As Landes says (p. 1), there are two traditional responses to the question. The first holds that "we are so good and they so bad: that is, we are hardworking, knowledgable, educated, well-governed, efficacious and productive"; the second that "we are so bad and they so good: we are greedy, ruthless, exploitative, aggressive..." The first explanation would stress European financial development, the Glorious Revolution, Francis Bacon, or the great thinkers of the *Lumières*; the second would stress monopolistic exploitation of the periphery, plunder, or slavery.

The debate is also related to a more technical economic one about whether the sources of growth during the British Industrial Revolution are to be found more on the side of supply or of demand (Mokyr 1977). Did growth primarily result from domestic inventiveness, or did foreign market demand (and hence, implicitly, Britain's American colonies from which an increasing share of that demand now arose) provide an exogenous boost to growth? Finally, the debate is related to different theoretical perspectives on the sources of growth that have been held over the past half century by economic historians. Some have stressed profits as the engine of growth, following Marx and other classical economists; others have stressed demand (even though the Keynesian framework is designed to explain short-run fluctuations rather than long-run growth rates); still others have focused on technological change, as in the Solow model; and several cliometricians have eschewed any sort of dynamic analysis, preferring to focus on static resource allocation questions instead.

Landes comments on the answers to the question he poses that "it is not clear to me that one line of argument necessarily precludes the other" (Landes 1990, p. 1). We strongly agree with this assessment, just as we would argue that it does not make a lot of sense to assert that either supply or demand was the sole factor underlying the Industrial Revolution. Certainly, it is easy to dispose of the argument that an exogenous boost in demand pulled up British output during the late eighteenth and early nineteenth centuries. If that were the case, then in terms of figure 5.2 British industrial growth would have been due to an outward shift in the foreign import demand schedule MM, and the relative price of British industrial output would have increased.[8] However, a striking characteristic of Britain's foreign trade

---

[8]Moreover, the breakthrough to modern economic growth in the First Industrial Nation would then be explained by prior growth elsewhere (Mokyr 1977).

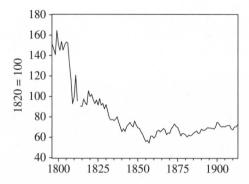

FIGURE 6.4. British terms of trade, 1796–1913 (1820 = 100).
Source: based on data in Imlah (1958) and Cuenca Esteban (1997).

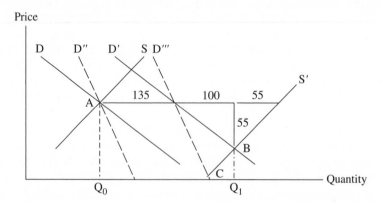

FIGURE 6.5. Demand versus supply during the Industrial Revolution.

during the Industrial Revolution was the substantial deterioration in her terms of trade until some time in mid century (figure 6.4), when they started to recover slightly, as a result of declining transport costs which as we will see raised everyone's terms of trade. This is not just at odds with the predictions of a simple Keynesian explanation of the Industrial Revolution; it might also seem surprising to those who adopt some variant of a model of an industrial "core" area brutally exploiting a helplessly dependent primary-producing "periphery," or more simply of a hegemonic imperial state wringing tribute from its colonial territories.

From the perspective of the standard theory of international trade, however, this is exactly what we should expect. If one economy, for whatever reason, starts to grow more rapidly than its trading partners, and furthermore concentrates much of this growth in the export-rather than the import-competing sector, the supply of these exports is going to increase faster than the demand for them by the more slowly growing partner countries, and so the relative price of the exports in world markets must fall for equilibrium to be maintained. In the case of Britain at the time of the Industrial Revolution, the pattern of technological change was heavily biased toward the cotton textiles sector, where so many of the major innovations first occurred. By the 1780s Britain had already more or less completed the import substitution process at the expense of hand-spun and hand-woven cotton textiles from India. There was therefore clearly going to be a substantial and growing exportable surplus of the new machine manufactures on the world market that had to be sold at steadily declining relative prices in return for her imports of mainly foodstuffs and raw materials.

A supply and demand diagram, which is a simplified version of the general equilibrium model presented in Findlay (1982), can help to make the point (figure 6.5). According to Crafts and Harley (1992), industrial output rose by roughly 235% between 1780 and 1831, while GDP rose by roughly 135%.[9] Assuming an income-elasticity of demand of unity, and assuming that foreign incomes rose at the same rate as British incomes, the demand for British manufactures at constant prices thus rose by about 135%, illustrated by the outward shift of demand from D to D' (ignore D'' and D''' for now). If the supply curve for industrial goods had been vertical, it would have shifted out by a full 235%, so as to intersect the new demand curve at the new equilibrium, denoted by point B. The available data on the British terms of trade suggest that, at this point, relative manufactured goods prices were 55% lower than in the initial equilibrium A.[10] If the elasticity of supply equaled unity, on the other hand, the supply curve would have shifted out (at constant prices) by 290% (= 135 + 100 + 55), far more than the 135% outward shift in demand. While this exercise is obviously highly approximate, the fact that Britain's terms of trade fell significantly clearly implies that British supply curves must have been shifting out more rapidly than the demand curves for British manufactured goods during this time. One important implication is that Britain's gains from

[9] Given the very approximate nature of this exercise, we prefer using round numbers for ease of exposition.

[10] This calculation is based on a heroic, if not foolhardy, splicing together of the very different terms of trade series given in Deane and Cole (1967) and figure 6.4. Given the nature of the exercise we have once again preferred round numbers to any pretence of accuracy.

the unprecedented degree of technological progress that she achieved during the Industrial Revolution were shared to a considerable extent with her trading partners, as a result of the substantially improved terms of trade that they consequently enjoyed (Clark 2007b). The possible exception is India, which had been the world's leading exporter of cotton textiles on the basis of traditional labor-intensive technology. It was this influx of machine-made Lancashire cotton textiles that brought about the deindustrialization of India, a topic that continues to be controversial up to the present day.

Overseas demand was not the exogenous driving force behind British industrial output growth. Does it follow that trade was irrelevant to that growth? The most visible impact of the Industrial Revolution on the import side of Britain's trade balance was of course the surge in raw cotton to feed the unprecedented expansion of the Lancashire textile industry. Retained imports of raw cotton rose from 16 million pounds in 1784–86 to 803 million pounds in 1854–56, or by a factor of fifty (figure 6.3). The main source in the late eighteenth century was the West Indies, but the limited area of the Caribbean islands soon led to their displacement by the vast spaces of the United States and Brazil. In 1854–56 the United States was supplying more than three-quarters of all imports (Mitchell 1988, p. 334), as a consequence of Eli Whitney's invention of the cotton gin in the 1790s and the rapid extension of the frontier of cultivation, which reduced the price per pound from 16¼ pence in 1804–6 to a mere 5¾ pence in 1854–56 (Davis 1979, table 26, p. 41). "Cotton in fact was an essential support of British prosperity—and had to be imported, at whatever the current market price, not merely because it was a component in a fabric with a great consumer demand, but because huge investments and a great number of working families in Britain were dependent on it to maintain their returns and livelihoods" (p. 40).

The link between the Industrial Revolution and the extension of the slave plantations in the New World on which the essential raw material was cultivated could not therefore be more obvious, carrying with it the uncomfortable implication that the Revolution itself would not, or at least might not, have occurred at the time and place that it did had it not been for the Atlantic "triangular trade" connecting flows of raw cotton from the Americas with exports of cotton textiles from Lancashire and the supply of slaves from the west coast of Africa. The links between the Industrial Revolution and the Atlantic slave trade were the subject of *Capitalism and Slavery*, the famous book by Eric Williams (1966), who later became the Prime Minister of Trinidad and Tobago. Rather than resting his case on the direct technological linkage between industry in Manchester and the slave plantations of the New World, Williams chose to advance a more subtle and much more difficult thesis to prove, that to a substantial extent it was the *profits* of the Atlantic slave trade that *financed* the Industrial Revolution. In the preface to his book Williams (1966) described it as "strictly an economic study of the role of Negro slavery and the slave trade in providing the capital which financed the Industrial Revolution in England and of mature industrial capitalism in destroying the slave system." Williams's own evidence was largely of an anecdotal nature, citing numerous particular instances in which individuals or families with known connections to the slave trade made investments in manufacturing or associated activities such as building railways or canals.

The "Williams Thesis," as it has come to be known, has haunted the historiography of the Industrial Revolution. Earlier British historians of the imperial school, anxious to defend the honor of the Anglo-Saxons and their economic achievements, have belittled Williams's arguments as mere mythmaking by an embittered black intellectual, incapable of the sober study of economic history.[11] In their view slavery may indeed have been morally deplorable, though one cannot be sure of even that, but it was certainly not of major economic significance to any aspect of the British economy. Reference is also made to the views of Adam Smith that plantation slavery in the New World was part of the unproductive, monopolistic and mercantilist "Old Colonial System," an incubus on the vital force of free enterprise associated with the expansion of the "home trades" that was the true engine of British economic growth in the eighteenth century.

This notion that plantation slavery was an inefficient, archaic remnant of bygone eras was of course famously demolished by the earliest cliometricians, most notably by Robert Fogel and Stanley Engerman (1974) in *Time on the Cross*. "New" economic historians, for the most part liberal Americans, have treated Williams more respectfully, if not without a tinge of patronization. Their main intellectual weapon deployed against Williams has been to divide any estimate of the role of the slave trade by British or even European national income, thereby ensuring that it is reduced to insignificance. For example, Stanley Engerman (1972) estimated that in 1770 slave trade profits amounted to 0.54% of British national income, 7.8% of total investment, and 38.9% of total commercial and industrial investment. Whether these

---

[11] See Sheridan (1987) for an informative appraisal of the early reactions to *Capitalism and Slavery*.

figures are large or small seems to largely depend upon the eye of the beholder. Solow (1985) considered them to be high or at least not low enough to dismiss the thesis purely on this ground, and made some alternative calculations arguing that West Indian investments based on an elastic supply of cheap slave labor gave much higher returns than would have been available at home.

Inspired by Engerman's example, Patrick O'Brien (1982) advanced a broader critique of the Williams Thesis, arguing on the basis of further statistical ratios that far from being central to the activities of the industrial "core" of the British or European economy, "the periphery was peripheral." The contention and the catchy phrase itself have since been widely cited, including in the most recent and authoritative textbook treatment of the subject (Harley 2004, p. 198). On the other hand, as pointed out in Findlay (1990, p. 26), the figures presented by O'Brien in table 1 of his paper "appear to be as high as the most enthusiastic Williams supporter could hope for." For 1784–86 he gives an estimate of £5.66 million for profits in trade with the periphery, as compared with just £10.30 million for total gross investment in the British economy, or over 50%. For 1824–26 the corresponding figures are £15.95 million for colonial profits and £34.30 million for gross investment, only slightly under 50%. O'Brien (1982, p. 9) asserts that "a hypothetical British edict abolishing the slave trade in 1607, rather than two centuries later, could not have made that much difference to the levels of wealth and income achieved in Western Europe in 1807." However, he does not offer any suggestions regarding which countries, sectors, raw materials, and markets would have substituted for Britain, the Lancashire cotton textile industry, cotton from the Americas, and Britain's overseas possessions and the United States, all of which were dependent on African slave labor.

As various authors have pointed out, it is problematic to dismiss something like the slave trade on the basis that the profits derived from it were but a small share of national income. Consistent application of this argument could of course prove that the Industrial Revolution itself is a myth, since as we have seen the share of modern industry during that era was itself only a small proportion of British national income. Paul Mantoux (1962, p. 103) was well aware of this problem of not confusing size with significance: "if we may borrow an analogy from natural science, only a negligible quantity of ferment is needed to effect a radical change in a considerable volume of matter. The action of foreign trade upon the mechanism of production may be difficult to show, but it is not impossible to trace." On the other hand, most economists and economic historians would nowadays agree that Williams's focus on profits was misplaced, since in the long run it is technological progress rather than capital accumulation that is responsible for sustained per capita income growth. As we have already seen, the key technological innovations were clearly the work of British inventors and entrepreneurs, operating within a broader European environment in which new techniques and applications were rapidly diffused from country to country and from one branch of industry to another. In this sense the Industrial Revolution was clearly not the result of an influx of capital into cotton textile manufacturing from any source whatever, no matter how large.

Keynesian and Marxist theoretical models, with their focus on demand and profits respectively, are poorly suited to explore the role of trade in the Industrial Revolution. So too are static neoclassical trade models. In cliometric's early days, its practitioners enjoyed considerable success by pointing out that Harberger triangles, estimated in the context of such models, were small. It followed that the impact of trade policies was small as well. Thus Thomas and McCloskey (1981), in a memorable if nonquantitative contribution, argue that, by the miracle of substitutability, a British economy closed to foreign trade would have produced much less cotton, but much more beer, at a minimal welfare loss. In a far less dogmatic and more nuanced contribution, Harley (2004) discusses various mechanisms that might have linked trade to industrialization and growth in Britain during this period, but even he cannot resist the temptation to play the old trick of multiplying two fractions by each other to obtain an even smaller fraction, and in this manner obtain the result that "self-sufficiency in 1860…would have cost Britain only…about 6 per cent of national income…no trivial sum, to be sure, but measured against the whole rise in output per worker of roughly 80 per cent from 1855 to 1913, only one thirteenth of the story" (ibid., pp. 194–95). However, comparative static trade models cannot, by definition, say anything about the impact of trade on growth, and to show that the British economy as it stood in 1860, with the Industrial Revolution already firmly entrenched, would have suffered a small welfare loss had it not been able to trade at all is not only unconvincing on its own terms, but evidently raises the question of what forces were required to bring the economy to that state in the first place.

We would thus argue that a lot of the debate on the links between trade and the Industrial Revolution has been posed in the wrong terms, largely reflecting inappropriate theoretical frameworks. For example, the Marxist stress on profits has led many writers to concentrate on the role of sugar plantations in the Caribbean, when this may not in fact be the right place to look (Eltis and Engerman 2000). Furthermore, posing the question in "either/or" terms seems to us to be profoundly unhelpful. Domestic inventiveness was required to make the technological breakthroughs of the period, but the key question for us is what would have been the effects of those breakthroughs in the absence of international trade, and what would this in turn have implied for future technological progress.

The British economic growth spurt of the eighteenth century was of course by no means the first in economic history. Even though statistics are hard to come by, we have ourselves noted in this volume numerous episodes of remarkable economic expansion. Examples include the Golden Age of Islam in the last centuries of the first millennium, the impressive upsurge in China under the Sung dynasty in the eleventh and twelfth centuries, the general prosperity of the Eurasian landmass under the *Pax Mongolica*, the rapid recovery in Europe led by the Italian city-states after the Black Death, the export-led boom during the Age of Commerce in Southeast Asia from 1400 to 1650, the Dutch Golden Age of the seventeenth century, and the great Qing expansion in eighteenth-century China, to name only some of the most notable "efflorescences" of world history, in the terminology of Jack Goldstone (2002). None of these episodes however, with the possible exception of the Dutch boom in the seventeenth century, resulted in a *sustained* increase in per capita income.

As Mokyr (2004) points out, what really marks out the Industrial Revolution from previous efflorescences was the fact that this burst of creativity did not peter out, but was sustained for the duration of the nineteenth century and beyond. Previous efflorescences, whether based on technological progress or commercialization, all inevitably ran into diminishing returns for a number of reasons (although in the case of the Sung and Southeast Asian efflorescences, one could certainly point to outside intervention by Mongols or Dutchmen as an important factor). We have already seen how a Malthusian society experiencing a one-off burst of technological innovation must in the end run up against the constraints of limited land and natural resources and so reach the limits of its possible expansion. Alternatively, consider a society experiencing "Smithian growth," which can be defined as the expansion of economic activity accompanying the extension of specialization and the division of labor, caused by a widening of markets due to the removal of artificial barriers, possibly along with a succession of discrete innovations in agriculture, manufacturing, and transport. Once all the relevant connections between locations have been forged, and no further gains from specialization are possible, such Smithian growth will inevitably end (Kelly 1997).

We argue that international trade was a key reason why the British Industrial Revolution was different. The argument comes in two parts. First, a given domestic stimulus to growth, such as the new technologies of the Industrial Revolution, led to a greater rise in incomes as a result of the opportunities afforded by international trade. By helping the economy escape from resource constraints, trade ensured that technological change translated into a more sustained growth experience than would otherwise have been possible. Second, the extent of technological change itself depended at least to some extent on the openness of the economy to trade. Both arguments rely crucially on the well-known fact that trade systematically raises the elasticities of supply and demand facing an economy. Nevertheless, it is useful to consider each in turn.

Our first claim is that the remarkable innovations of the Industrial Revolution would not have had the deep and sustained consequences that they did if British industry had not operated within the global framework of sources of raw materials and markets for finished products that had been developed during the heyday of mercantilism and the Navigation Acts, and consolidated by the victories in the long series of wars against the Dutch and French. Slavery and the plantation economy of the New World, supplying first sugar and then cotton, the two major British imports for over two hundred years, was an integral part of this Atlantic System. "New" economic historians pride themselves on the use of counterfactual thought experiments to examine historical questions, such as the economic significance of the introduction of the railroad. It is therefore somewhat surprising that virtually no one has attempted a counterfactual study of what would have happened to the Lancashire cotton textile industry if there had not been any British colonies or slavery in the New World. Would India and Egypt, or free white labor in the Americas, have been able to fill the gap? Would some other industry, or country, have quickly emerged to take the place of cotton manufacturing in England? What would have happened to Lancashire had overseas markets not been available to it, or if it had had to source all its raw materials supplies at home? And what in turn would this have implied for the British economy as a whole?

In order to consider such questions, a general equilibrium model of the Atlantic economy as a whole is needed, such as the one provided by Findlay (1990), inspired by the pioneering contribution of Darity (1982). The model has three regions. Britain (or Europe) produces manufactures with capital and labor, which is assumed to be in fixed supply, and a primary intermediate input such as raw cotton that is worked up into fabric, or raw sugar that is refined for final consumption. America (or the New World) produces the raw material that is exported and used as the intermediate input into manufacturing in Britain, in exchange for manufactures. It produces this raw material with slave labor imported from Africa at a rising marginal cost, and land that is in fixed supply. Africa exports slaves in exchange for imports of manufactures. Each region's trade is balanced overall, on a multilateral basis. Capital is in perfectly elastic supply at a constant rate of interest, equal to the rate of time preference in Britain and America. The slave population in America has a death rate higher than its birth rate, so an annual flow of imports is needed from Africa to keep the slave population constant.

What is the impact of the Industrial Revolution in the context of this model? Following our previous discussion, the Industrial Revolution is modeled as a positive technological shock, increasing the efficiency with which capital and labor in Britain convert the imported raw material into final manufactured output. The consequent increase in British industrial output raises the demand for the American raw material, and hence the price of the raw material increases, improving the terms of trade of America. The output of the raw material and the steady-state slave population in America go up, as do the price and export of slaves from Africa (since increased raw material output raises the demand for slave labor). An increase in the labor force in Britain would have a similar expansionary effect on all the endogenous variables of the Atlantic System, by boosting British industrial output. An increase in the supply of land in America would also have an expansionary effect on the whole system, but would reduce the price of the raw material by increasing its supply and turn the terms of trade against America and in favor of Britain. Any expansion in Britain or America raises the price and supply of slaves from Africa, and so turns the terms of trade in favor of slave-exporting African states such as Dahomey and Benin.

These qualitative "predictions" find support in the factual record. As table 5.1 showed, the transatlantic slave trade reached a peak during the last third of the eighteenth century: no less than 17% of the 11 million Africans forcibly removed to the New World met their fate during the period traditionally viewed as the "heroic phase" of the early Industrial Revolution. Eltis and Jennings (1988) report that Britain's terms of trade with Africa fell from 112 in 1750 to 40 in 1800 (that is to say, the price of slaves in terms of imported manufactures rose by a factor of two and a half), while Curtin (1975) calculates that the terms of trade of the Senegambia region rose from 100 in

1680 to 475 in 1780, while the proportion of slaves in total exports rose from 55% to 86%. Thus the Atlantic slave trade, and the slave plantations of the southern United States, were hardly unprofitable and inefficient operations dying under their own weight before each was forcibly ended by the British abolition and the American Civil War respectively, but were instead actually at their peaks during the Industrial Revolution, mainly due to the voracious appetite for raw cotton and other intermediate inputs. As Eltis and Jennings (1988, p. 959) observe, "If the slave trade had not been abolished the impact of overseas trade on Africa would have been larger in the nineteenth century...rising European needs for raw materials from plantations would have prompted an expansion of the traffic that might well have dwarfed the nineteenth-century migration from Europe...slave prices would have increased substantially but this would not have prevented massive expansion of the traffic."

The model predicts an expansion of British manufactured exports as a result of the Industrial Revolution, in part to pay for these increased imports of raw materials, and here again as we have seen it accords with reality, with export growth being particularly rapid in the leading cotton textiles sector. There is also abundant evidence in support of the model's predictions that the Industrial Revolution should have increased the New World's exports and improved its terms of trade. Figure 6.3 has already shown that Britain's imports of raw cotton grew at spectacular rates, and the statistics on U.S. exports naturally mirror this finding. From a mere 189,000 lb. in 1791, U.S. raw cotton exports rose to nearly 21 million pounds by 1801 and nearly 93 million pounds by 1810 (North 1966, table B-IV, p. 231). According to North (1966) the volume of both U.S. exports and U.S. imports grew sharply from the 1790s (when figures become available) onwards, although there was a very sharp decline associated with the Napoleonic Wars from 1808 to 1814 to which we will return in the next chapter. Meanwhile, the U.S. terms of trade improved from 100 to 162 over the course of the 1790s, and while war led to a subsequent decline here as well, terms of trade improvement resumed in 1815 (ibid.).

Britain continued to benefit from cheap raw cotton supplied by the United States long after the abolition of the Atlantic slave trade in 1807, since as noted in chapter 5 the slave plantations there could prosper and expand with a labor force that did not require replenishment from Africa to continue growing. As we have seen, the share of cotton textiles in British exports peaked in 1834–36 and had fallen to about a third by the outbreak of the American Civil War in 1861. That event provides a nice illustration of the interconnectedness of the world economy, and of the historical relevance of our model: its effect on British cotton textile exports, by disrupting raw materials supplies, was no less than 40%, with the value falling from about £50 million in 1861 to £30 million in 1864. Recovery was rapid, however, and the absolute value of cotton textile exports kept on rising all the way until 1912–13, reaching a peak of £125 million (Schlote 1952, table 15, p. 151).

The model suggests that the British economy was intimately interconnected during this period not just with America, but with Africa as well. Table 6.6, taken from Inikori (2002), dramatizes the African link by providing estimates of the share of American export commodities produced by African slave labor between the Voyages of Discovery and the middle of the nineteenth century. As can be seen, the share had risen to an enormous 80% by the eighteenth century. The model thus enables us to see how British manufacturing, American agriculture, and the African slave trade were all deeply interrelated. Assume for now that technological change had taken place in Britain as before. If British industry had been forced to source its raw materials domestically, rather than import them, this would have implied a rapidly increasing cost of raw materials, as increasing levels of demand came face to face with a limited domestic land endowment. In this manner, the ghost acres of the New World (Jones 2003; Pomeranz 2000) had a crucial effect, permitting the expansion of British industry without driving up raw materials costs to prohibitive levels. This is of course a variant of the argument that we have already encountered, concerning the role of trade in helping Europe escape from Malthusian constraints, but the model allows us to see that African labor was important as well as New World land. The very fact that New World land was so abundant, and that it was still so costly to get there, meant that free labor would be scarce and expensive there, and above all inelastically supplied. African slaves were not only cheaper than free labor, but could be easily imported in response to growing demand. The New World implied elastic supplies of land, and Africa implied elastic supplies of labor: the net effect was an elastic supply of raw materials, implying that the Industrial Revolution drove up raw materials prices by far less than would have been the case in a closed economy. In turn, this implied that industrial growth could continue for longer, without being choked off by rising input costs.

Trade also had important implications for British manufacturers on the demand side. Demand may not have been the prime mover of industrial growth, but trade prevented cotton textile and other export prices from *falling much faster* than they would have done had the British economy been closed. There is no doubt at all that external

TABLE 6.6. Share of American "export commodities"
produced by Africans, 1501–1850.

Period	Production of export by commodities (£000)	Share produced Africans (%)
1501–50	1,286	54.0
1551–1600	3,764	55.5
1601–50	6,268	69.0
1651–70	7,970	69.1
1711–60	14,142	80.6
1761–80	21,903	82.5
1781–1800	39,119	79.9
1848–50	89,204	68.8

Source: Inikori (2002, table 4.7, p. 197).

demand cushioned the fall in price by shifting the demand curve facing Britain's producers of exportable goods much further to the right than would otherwise have been the case. It also, crucially, made demand much more elastic than if only the home market was open to them. This implied that a given supply increase translated into a greater increase in output, and a lower price decline, than in a closed economy. In terms of figure 6.5, imagine that supply shifted out as before, and that demand also shifted out by 135% at constant prices, but now let demand be more price inelastic, shifting from D″ to D‴ instead of from D to D′. Clearly, the net effect is a much smaller increase in output than before, and a much larger decline in price, with the equilibrium shifting from A to C instead of from A to B. In recent years much has been made of the export-oriented development strategy of the four East Asian "newly industrializing countries" or NICs, namely Hong Kong, Singapore, South Korea, and Taiwan, the example of which is said to have inspired Deng Xiaoping in his decision to have China follow an "open door" policy. In this sense one might well say that Britain at the turn of the nineteenth century was "the first NIC." Dismissals of the role of demand during its industrialization reflect in our view a failure to think in the appropriate counterfactual terms. On both the supply and the demand sides, trade increased elasticities, meaning that a given domestic impulse (in this case, technological change) propelled the British economy much farther than would otherwise have been the case.

Second, in the absence of trade the incentives facing innovators would have been less favorable during the late eighteenth and early nineteenth centuries, and thus supply would have shifted out by less in the first place (Findlay 1982, 1990). Although we still lack a universally accepted theory of technological progress, it seems clear that any sensible model would yield the result that if Britain had been closed to trade, the Industrial Revolution could not have been sustained. The technological breakthroughs associated with it were not made in the name of pure knowledge, but in pursuit of profit. Indeed, profits were required if inventors were to break even, let alone prosper, since as Robert Allen (2006) has pointed out innovators such as Richard Arkwright had to spend considerable sums of money, obtained from venture capitalists, in order to bring their ideas to fruition. High fixed costs of innovation meant that innovators required profits to survive, and larger markets obviously helped innovators recoup those fixed costs. Grossman and Helpman (1991, pp. 242–46) point out that, in general, a larger market has offsetting effects on inventors' incentives: it means larger potential profits, but also more potential competitors. At least in the initial stages of the Industrial Revolution, when it was the British alone that were forging ahead, the first effect would have clearly dominated the second.

It might be objected that, however large these fixed costs were, they were surely not so large for an individual firm that they could not have been recouped by selling to the domestic market alone. Once again, we would stress that trade mattered as much by raising demand elasticities as by shifting the demand curve outwards, and this increased the incentive to innovate even in a context where firms were individually small. In an important recent theoretical contribution, Desmet and Parente (2006) show that larger markets imply more elastic demand curves for individual monopolistically competitive firms.[12] The implication is that an innovation that reduces price will lead to a greater increase in sales and revenue, which makes it more likely that firms will choose to implement costly innovations in the first place. Moreover, at the industry level trade increases elasticities as well, as we have seen. Absent trade, input costs would have risen, and output prices would have declined, more rapidly than would otherwise have been the case, and this would hardly have increased the profitability of investing in new textile technology. Furthermore, Grossman and Helpman (1991) emphasize that trade also boosts innovation by facilitating the transmission of ideas. We have already come across many examples of techniques and ideas being transmitted internationally during the course of this book, and Mokyr (2002, 2005b) emphasizes the extent to which both the Scientific Revolution

[12]Aficionados will note that they derive this result in a model using Lancaster (1979) ideal preferences.

of the seventeenth century and the Enlightenment of the eighteenth century were European rather than British phenomena. Openness to the world—to its ideas, its raw materials, and its markets—was essential in producing the British takeoff.

The argument finds support in the available data on British trade. We have already seen how Britain exported an increasing share of both total output and, especially, industrial output during the eighteenth and early nineteenth centuries. By 1815, no less than 60% of output in the crucial cotton textiles sector was being exported (Harley 1999, p. 187). Even more important to our argument, which stresses the ability of elastic overseas demand to absorb additional British output, is the fact that in the late eighteenth and early nineteenth centuries, a very large share of *additional* output was exported. According to Crafts (1985, p. 131), increases in exports were equivalent to 21% of the total increase in GDP between 1780 and 1801, while Cuenca Esteban (1997, p. 881) estimates that as much as "50 to 79 percent of additional industrial production could have been exported in the much debated period 1780 to 1801," a somewhat higher figure than the already very sizable 46.2% implicit in Crafts's figures (O'Brien and Engerman 1991, p. 188). In textiles, 60% of additional output was exported between 1815 and 1841, if Harley's (1999, p. 187) data are to be believed. Furthermore, by the late eighteenth century manufacturing was spreading across Western Europe, and English manufacturers were finding themselves increasingly excluded from markets in Germany, France, Sweden, and elsewhere (Davis 1962). Not surprisingly, therefore, between 1780 and 1801 the Americas accounted for roughly 60% of additional British exports (O'Brien and Engerman 1991, p. 186)

British innovators were thus crucially dependent on overseas markets as their industries expanded. The implication, in a mercantilist world in which nations systematically excluded their enemies from protected markets, is that British military success over the French and other European rivals was an important ingredient in explaining her subsequent rise to economic prominence. The robustness of the argument can be "tested" by exploring how well it does at answering two very different questions. First, why was it that Britain, rather than another European country, made the transition to modern economic growth first? Second, why did the Industrial Revolution occur in Europe rather than in Asia?[13]

---

[13] We are following various authors, including Jones (2003) and Mokyr (2002, 2005a), in distinguishing between these two questions.

WHY BRITAIN? WHY EUROPE AND NOT ASIA?

Why Britain?

The question of why the Industrial Revolution should have taken place in Great Britain has always invited speculation without providing any fully satisfactory explanation. In the terminology of old-fashioned history textbooks, there is a familiar list of fairly obvious "proximate causes," while attempts to locate the deeper or more fundamental causes have generally ended up by invoking "the English genius" or the spirit of sturdy Anglo-Saxon individualism that was presumably brought over by Hengist and Horsa from the depths of the Germanic woods (Macfarlane 1979, p. 170, citing Montesquieu). Max Hartwell (1967, p. 59) lists as proximate causes favorable capital accumulation due to high savings and a low and falling rate of interest, technical inventions, fortunate natural resource endowments such as abundant coal and iron ore, laissez-faire policies, market expansion associated with increase of population, agricultural productivity and foreign trade, and finally a set of "miscellaneous" factors such as success in foreign wars and a string of good harvests in the 1730s and 1740s. Popular explanations with earlier economic historians were of the "Adam Smith plus the steam engine" variety, with the effect of the great treatise of 1776 sweeping away the restrictive remnants of medieval and mercantilist regulation and unleashing the forces of free enterprise and competition that led to the burst of technical innovation.

Among the most astute observers, and certainly the most concerned, of English economic performance in the eighteenth century were their great rivals the French. François Crouzet (1981) has provided a fascinating glimpse of French views on the sources of England's wealth, drawing not only on the writings of Physiocratic economists but on reports and memoranda prepared by diplomats and officials in the Foreign Ministry and Ministry of the Marine. "*Rien de nouveau sous le soleil*" is indeed all that one can say, since there is an almost exact correspondence between what Crouzet reports and the reaction of American commentators in the 1980s toward the emergence of Japan: the same mixture of admiration, envy, suspicion, and hostility. Despite accusations of perfidy and unfair practice, however, the commentators cited by Crouzet generally offered a clear and penetrating assessment of the strengths of the British economy of the eighteenth century that could hardly be bettered today, and were to some extent more on the mark than Adam Smith himself, with his strong ideological axe to grind against mercantilism and neglect of innovation in manufacturing (Koebner 1959, p. 382).

The French writers noted that England had an area only one-quarter that of France, and yet had a population that was almost half, and a total trade that was twice as great, along with an enormous shipping fleet and the ability to carry and service a much larger public debt. As early as the 1740s French officials were warning that, with the expansion of the Royal Navy and her increasing domination of overseas trade, England was planning to dispossess France of her colonies in the Americas and to confine her to purely internal trade, while in the 1780s they noted British designs upon the trade of China and East Asia. The one factor that Crouzet says they kept stressing was Britain's foreign trade, said to have been "immense," "enormous," and "prodigious." Voltaire, called the "father of Anglomania" by Ian Buruma (1998), linked Britain's success in trade with the freedom of her constitution, which he saw as mutually reinforcing each other in a virtuous circle: "trade, which has made richer the citizens of England, has helped to make them free, and this freedom has, in turn, enlarged trade."[14] Meanwhile an official of the French Foreign Ministry declared in 1738 that "trade makes the wealth of England which owes to it her navy and the multiplication of her manufactures" (Crouzet 1981, pp. 63–64). Thus the French were well aware of what Patrick O'Brien has called the "naval-industrial complex" of Hanoverian England.

Crouzet quotes Voltaire once again: "What made the power of England is that all the parties have ... combined since the time of Elizabeth to promote trade. The same Parliament, which had the head of its King cut off, busied itself with maritime projects, like in the most untroubled times. The blood of Charles I was still warm, when that Parliament, though almost entirely made up of fanatics, passed in 1650 [actually 1651] the famous Navigation Act" (ibid., p. 65). The French mercantilists complained bitterly about England's protectionist policies, but admired them for their efficacy and wondered why their own country could not emulate them. Measures such as banning or imposing high duties on the import of foreign manufactures, admitting raw materials duty-free (a nice acknowledgement of the importance of "effective protection"), allowing the duty-free export of manufactures, and banning the export of domestic raw materials such as wool, were regarded as the height of mercantilist sophistication and responsible for England's success. The same French official who made these observations, Étienne de Silhouette, also wrote that "the riches which the English attract from America, from their own colonies and also from Brazil, are the foundations of their power" (ibid., p. 67).

[14]For a recent version of the same argument, see Acemoglu et al. (2005).

What was later called the "Americanization" of British trade in the eighteenth century did not pass unnoticed by the French, whose own colonial aspirations were to suffer for it, as we saw in the last chapter.

Foreign trade was not the only area in which the French felt that they lagged behind England. The fact that real wages were higher in Britain but yet did not seem to place the country at a disadvantage in trade puzzled many, but the better minds clearly realized that this was due to higher productivity across a wide range of activities. It was even stated that "an English workman does more work than six Frenchmen, and does it better, so that the country can withstand foreign competition despite the dearness of labor" (ibid., p. 69). In 1786 the Marquis de Custine commented on "the fire-engines [perfected by M. Watt] used everywhere to drive machinery which simplifies labor" and which was "put in motion by burning coal that is dirt cheap in all the provinces. It serves as substitute for a great deal of waterpower and drives mills to spin and card cotton, which thanks to it can be attended by children." It was also noted that in contrast to the French bias toward luxury industries the English manufactures tended to cater to the mass market, and so had a broader base for expansion. Of course, catering to the mass market required markets, including markets overseas.

Behind all of these particular advantages the French observers stressed the benign influence of Britain's political and social institutions: the security of person and property, the freedom of the press, decentralized local administration in contrast to French centralization under the *intendants*, the relative frugality of the court, and above all the role of parliament in promoting and fostering all forms of trade and economic activity. The high status enjoyed by merchants in England, and the willingness of even the nobility to participate in trade, were also given much weight in accounting for the superiority of British economic performance by French observers. Religious tolerance was also seen as working to England's economic advantage, as in the case of the numerous Huguenots who had transferred their knowledge, skills, and capital from France after the Revocation of the Edict of Nantes in 1685. It is also interesting, as Crouzet points out, that the criticism of the French ancien régime, quite explicit in many of the writings quoted, came not only from *philosophes* and independent writers but also from officials within the French administration itself.

What can economic historians say with the benefit of hindsight? First, as already noted, the intellectual developments leading up to the Industrial Revolution, such as the Scientific Revolution and the Enlightenment, were phenomena that spanned Western Europe, and thus cannot explain the fact that Britain "came first." As Mokyr (2005a, p. 1126) says, "many if not most of the technological elements of the Industrial Revolution were the result of a joint international effort in which French, German, Scandinavian, Italian, American and other 'western' innovators collaborated, swapped knowledge, corresponded, met one another, and read each others' work." Second, we join with authors such as Allen (2006) and Clark (2007a) in doubting whether British success can really be attributed to superior institutions, put in place by the Glorious Revolution, which supposedly placed limits on government, secured property rights there, and thus facilitated investment and growth. Quinn (2001) has shown that while risk premia on English government debt disappeared after the Nine Years' War, *private* interest rates, which are presumably what private investors cared about, actually increased. Similarly, Clark (1996) finds no links between political events such as the Glorious Revolution and private interest rates between 1540 and 1837, while in a subsequent work he finds no effect of the Glorious Revolution on British total factor productivity growth either (Clark 2007a, chapter 11). As Allen (2006) notes, work by Jean-Laurent Rosenthal (1990) further undermines this "New Whig" interpretation of economic history. Far from it being the case that French property rights were insufficiently strong, it turns out that they were if anything too well-defined, with the implication that landowners under the ancien régime could block beneficial infrastructural improvements, such as irrigation works.[15]

Nor is it the case that Britain enjoyed the supposed benefits of an unusually small government, since as we noted in the previous chapter Britain extracted far more from each taxpayer than did France for most of the eighteenth century. Indeed, the period from 1688 to 1815 saw a remarkable expansion in the share of national expenditure undertaken by the state, although the estimates of different authors vary. Government's share rose from a tiny percentage in 1688 to nearly a fifth before Waterloo according to O'Brien (1988, p. 3), and hovered around 10% for much of the eighteenth century. Clark (2007a, table 7.3) puts the tax take (including church taxes) at 14–16% during the century following 1760, while Crouzet's (1993) figures suggest that British taxation accounted for roughly 20% of national income for much of the eighteenth century, while the French government's take hovered between 10 and 13%.[16] Recent work by economic historians

---

[15]Another strong critique of the "New Whig" view is provided by Epstein (2000).
[16]Cited in Bonney (2004, pp. 202–3).

has therefore undermined the "Washington Consensus" view that small government and low taxes were the basis for British success, and that these were both underpinned by representative government. Reviewing the evidence, Hoffman and Norberg (1994, pp. 299–310) are quite explicit, and their conclusions are worth quoting at length:

> Presuming that the English path was the only road to freedom, historians have assumed that representative institutions, such as the English Parliament, were the people's sole defense against a ravenous, absolutist fisc. They have portrayed the monarchs of continental Europe robbing their downtrodden subjects and riding roughshod over property and liberty.... So ingrained is this distinctly English view of early modern state building that much of it passes for common sense.... The notion that those who are freest are taxed least does not hold up in the light of comparative history. If we compare the rates of taxation in Spain, France, England, and the Netherlands, we find that in the absolutist states, Spain and France, taxation was relatively light.... In the end, representative institutions, not absolute monarchy, proved superior in revenue extraction...liberty was a necessary precondition for the emergence of a strong state, a state of wealth and power.

Why might this have been the case? Van Zanden and Prak (2006) point out that while there may be advantages to individuals pooling their resources via the state in order to procure various collective goods, there are a variety of practical problems that have to be overcome first. Potential taxpayers need to be reassured that the state, thus empowered, will not turn against them, while there is also the temptation on the part of individuals to "free ride," leaving others to pay for the collective goods while they themselves enjoy the benefits. For Van Zanden and Prak, citizenship provided the means by which these "agency problems" could be overcome, with citizenship being defined as "an enforceable mutual relationship between an actor and state agents" (Tilly 1996, p. 8). Citizens had to pay taxes, but also had the right to participate in the political process that ultimately determined how those taxes would be administered and spent. Elected officials also had political rights and obligations, implying that "taxes had to be levied on a fair basis, had to be transparent, and that citizens who were coerced to pay had to be treated with respect." The upshot was that states based on citizenship rather than coercion could actually levy more taxes, not fewer.

What might these desirable collective goods have been? In an era where the Military Revolution had greatly increased the cost of maintaining armies, where no supranational organization existed to keep the peace, and where states routinely used military force to exclude each other's products from protected markets, there are no prizes for guessing correctly. An overwhelming share of British government expenditure, an astonishing 83% according to O'Brien (1993), was for military purposes.[17] As a share of national income, military expenditure of about 16% (80% of 20%) far outstripped that of private capital formation (ibid., p. 135). Of this military expenditure no less than 60% was allocated to the Royal Navy (p. 138). Britannia thus undoubtedly ruled the waves but at a rather hefty price, involving highly regressive taxation and a massive growth of the national debt.

Whether the results were worth it or not continues to be a matter of controversy. We noted evidence in chapter 5 that showed trade and economic prosperity being clearly linked in the early modern period, suggesting that it was in a nation's interest to secure markets for itself rather than see them lost to its economic and military rivals. We have also argued at length that, for a small European country like Britain, overseas markets were vital if its Industrial Revolution was to be sustained. The extension of the empire, with its concomitant growth of overseas markets for manufactures and of sources of raw material supplies, were of course exactly what the mercantilists were urging, the use of Power in order to secure Plenty. From this point of view the era from 1688 to 1815 was undoubtedly a triumphant success, with the Dutch overtaken and the French humbled. Adam Smith and his liberal followers to the present day, however, would, and have, argued that much of this expenditure was wasted, unnecessarily crowding out more productive private investment. The assumption of course is that the markets and raw material supplies that the private sector relied on would have existed regardless. Any conclusive assessment of the opposing viewpoints would have to undertake a vast and mind-boggling exercise in counterfactual history: what if there had been no empire at all? Part of this exercise would have to be an appraisal of what the Dutch and French responses would have been to a purely defensive posture by Great Britain. It would be difficult to argue that they would not have striven to supplant the British imperial enterprise by an expansion of their own, to the disadvantage of the counterfactually passive British. Universal free trade would presumably have been even better for Britain than trade with its colonies, based on costly military victories, but this was hardly a realistic alternative during the early modern period. In any case all that we know is that there was a long and fierce contest for economic primacy between the three leading

[17] As we saw in the previous chapter, Brewer's (1990) estimate is somewhat lower.

European powers that ended in an unalloyed triumph for the British. To contend that the expenditures and policies of the Hanoverian state that secured this outcome nevertheless reduced the welfare of the British people seems somewhat academic, and is in any case not provable in the absence of the aforementioned, and rather forbidding, counterfactual thought experiment.

Pending such an exercise, and given the importance of trade for the Industrial Revolution, it seems reasonable to conclude that British military successes overseas played an important role in explaining why Britain, rather than France, was so successful and precocious an industrializer.[18] To this it might reasonably be objected that the United States won its independence at precisely the moment when the Industrial Revolution started to gain momentum, but this seems to us to neglect the importance of what economists term "path dependence" in determining bilateral trade patterns. There are a number of theoretical reasons why a history of trade between pairs of countries will predispose them to trade more with each other in the future. It might be that there are one-off costs associated with breaking into a market for the first time and that once these costs have been sunk subsequent trade is facilitated. Alternatively, a history of trade between individual merchants, producers, and retailers might lead to trust being built up between them, thus lowering the cost of trade. Whatever the reason in principle, in practice it is clear that trade between pairs of countries becomes self-perpetuating (Eichengreen and Irwin 1998), while a vast empirical literature has established that even today a history of past colonial ties continues to foster trade between former colonies and colonizers (e.g., Rauch and Trindade 2002). Furthermore, even after independence the United States remained an English-speaking country, whose white inhabitants hailed mostly from the British Isles. The empirical trade literature has also unambiguously established that a shared language promotes trade, presumably by reducing transactions costs, while ethnic Chinese networks have been shown to facilitate trade in the late twentieth century (ibid.). Britain's colonial history thus continued to boost its trade with the United States, long after the Treaty of Versailles. In 1821, and shortly after a war that had opposed the United States and Britain, no less than 44% of U.S. imports came from Britain, while just 7% came from France (Carter et al. 2006).

[18]This is of course not to deny the potential role of other factors, such as Britain's abundant coal reserves, although even here one could argue, as Bob Allen (2006) does, that the growth in Britain's coal industry was largely a result of the growth of London, itself a function of the trade boom.

Why Europe and Not Asia?

The question of why the Industrial Revolution occurred in Britain, rather than say France or the Netherlands, is surely much less fundamental than the more general question of why Europe made this transition to modern growth first, rather than Asia or the Islamic World. As we have seen at some length in our opening chapters, the Islamic World and Sung China initially had much more advanced economic systems than Western Europe. Market organization, monetary systems, and manufacturing technology were all more highly developed outside Western Europe than inside it. Western Europe had nothing to compare in terms of urbanization, for example, with Baghdad and Cairo, or K'ai-feng and Hang-chou. We also saw that the Islamic World was from the beginning of the millennium in direct contact with all the regions of the then known world, whereas Western Europe was only acquainted with Eastern Europe and the Islamic World, and with both to only a very limited extent. In terms of scientific knowledge and philosophical speculation it was the Islamic World that inherited the achievements of classical antiquity, which were passed to Europe largely by being translated from Arabic into Latin by scholars in al-Andalus.

Yet, as we have also seen, it did not take many centuries before Europe was drawing level with and then surpassing the Islamic World in commercial sophistication and agricultural and industrial technology. What was happening in the rest of the world while the West was "rising"? An earlier Western historiography had a simple answer: nothing! In the tradition of Hegel's *Philosophy of History* and Marx's "Asiatic Mode of Production," they argued that the history of the non-Western peoples was merely a sorry tale of a succession of "Oriental Despots," exercising absolute power over terrorized populations on the basis of their control of essential irrigation works, blocking any progress toward representative institutions and individual initiative. Economic development in the long run was impossible if any successful merchant or entrepreneur could have his property confiscated without any hope of legal redress. Cruel and relentless as it might have been, it was the predatory expansionism of the West that was performing the historically necessary function of "battering down the Chinese Walls" of stagnant Asian societies, as Marx said, counting on the railways introduced into India by the British to end the millennial isolation of self-sufficient Indian villages and eventually launch them into a progressive future that they could not have attained but for the colonial intrusion. Later Western writers, inspired by Marx but without his hard unsentimental logic, have argued that all societies if left to themselves would presumably follow similar paths of social development, but that the non-European societies were prevented from doing so by the predatory imperialism of the West, whose "primitive accumulation" drained them of their resources to ensure its own hegemony. Thus left-wing sympathy and solidarity with the Third World does not necessarily preclude an equally Eurocentric vision.

The notion of an unchanging East also marks the enormously influential work of the greatest of all social scientists of the twentieth century, Max Weber. Combining immense erudition with penetrating theoretical acumen, Weber produced in his various works what may be called a comparative sociology of global development, embracing not only the link between the Protestant ethic and the rise of capitalism in the West but also the role of religion in China and India and why those regions did not undergo a comparable transition. In the West he saw an evolution toward the increasing "rationalization" of all forms of social interaction, separating the private from the public sphere and driven by an "inner-worldly asceticism" that eventually resulted in the emergence of capitalism and impersonal "rational legal" bureaucracy that transformed nature and traditional society. The East, however, developed rationality only to the point of adapting behavior to existing external circumstances, rather than attaining "mastery" over them and making the world anew as the West had done after the Reformation and the Industrial Revolution. Nature and the social world could only be propitiated by "magic" and ritual as in Confucianism, or escaped from to secure personal spiritual fulfillment by asceticism in Hinduism and Buddhism. Weber was aware of considerable business activity and commercial acumen in China and India, but he claimed that only in the West had rational bookkeeping and capital accounting been developed, without which economic life could not be said to have a truly rational basis.

Weber's studies appeared when India had long been a British colony and China was barely emerging from the decadence of the last days of the Qing into warlordism and social disorder. Only Japan had begun a successful economic and social transformation, but the West dealt with the Japanese, like South Africa in the days of apartheid, by treating them as honorary Westerners while continuing to be skeptical at best regarding whether the Indians or Chinese would ever be able to fully develop and enter the modern age. Since his time and particularly in the last two decades, this attitude has of course been completely reversed, with many in the West now afraid that the rapid expansion of the Chinese and Indian economies is threatening their economic security. Weber's influence remains so great, however, that the recent *Cambridge Companion to Weber* (Turner 2000) still repeats his views on China and India with very little criticism.

The point of our extensive recounting of the experiences of our seven regions, however, has been to show that all seven, and not only Western Europe, underwent significant economic and political change, both internally and in terms of contacts with each other during both peace and war. Technology, population, and sociopolitical organization were not fixed and stable in *any* of the regions. Major innovations such as early ripening rice in China or the eastern crops introduced into the Middle East during the Golden Age of Islam raised productivity and increased populations according to the Malthusian demographic-economic model that we have consistently applied to both east and west in the Eurasian landmass, while warfare and plagues drastically dislocated societies and reduced their populations. The reason that China and India have always had such relatively huge populations is a sign of their long-run economic success prior to the Industrial Revolution, and not of failure.

Indian cotton textiles and Chinese silk and porcelain were the world's leading manufactured exports as late as the eighteenth century, i.e., until the Industrial Revolution. Indian merchants from both coasts plied the Indian Ocean for over one thousand years and competed on at least equal terms with the East India Companies until well into the eighteenth century. The Ottoman, Safavid, and Mughal Empires, as well as that of the Manchu Qing dynasty of China, were not mere tyrannies expressing the will of a single despot but complex exercises in multiethnic state building, far more intricate than that of the Habsburgs. All four were formidable military machines, sustained by productive agrarian economies, and leavened by considerable commerce both internal and external, which were impervious to Western intrusion until the eighteenth century. Far from being reluctant to trade, the Southeast Asian states all eagerly embraced it between themselves, and with China and the Islamic World, long before the "Age of Commerce," which as Anthony Reid points out was in any case inaugurated in Southeast Asia *not* by Vasco da Gama, but almost one hundred years earlier by the Ming voyages of Zheng He. When they came into contact with the Portuguese they were not merely passive participants in trade, but actively used the firearms and mercenary services that the *feringhi* were able to provide to launch extensive empire-building activities of their own.

The eminent cultural anthropologist Jack Goody (1996) has submitted Weber's entire doctrine of a lack of rationality in the East to a devastating critique. He points to the fact that the keeping of books and accounts had a long history in the Mediterranean world, and that (as noted in chapter 3) Italian merchants acquired their acquaintance with these methods from trading with the Islamic World. He goes on to cite numerous instances of rational and purposive business activity from ancient times in India and China down to the early modern era. Business practices in both East and West have evolved over long periods, and it is surely illegitimate to pick one point in time when the West was undoubtedly ahead and imply an absolute qualitative difference by the use of the words "scientific" or "rational" to describe its practices, implying that those of the East did not rise above mere common sense.

Similarly, Sinologists such as Mark Elvin (1984) have pointed out that using a single unchanging "ideal type" to characterize Chinese society over two millennia is not a fruitful research strategy. It cannot explain why different regions in China at the same time, or the same region at different times, should produce different outcomes if the only available explanatory device is a fixed unchanging mentality shared by all the individual actors at all times and places. Francis Bacon, as is well-known, considered the three greatest inventions of his age as the compass, the printing press, and gunpowder, all of which are indubitably Chinese, even if, as some contend, they were independently rediscovered much later in Europe. In the early fourteenth century there was a mechanized device used for spinning hemp in China that was very similar to one used for spinning raw silk at the same time at Lucca and Bologna in Italy (Elvin 1989).[19] The great Ming voyages of Zheng He in the early fifteenth century eclipsed the already impressive maritime achievements of the Sung, and the scale of the Qing expansion in the eighteenth century was spectacular. Thus even if China did not generate an industrial revolution comparable to that of the eighteenth century in Britain, these achievements by themselves are sufficient to render the Weberian thesis of a lack of "rationality" in Chinese society quite untenable. Certainly, a society that constructed the Great Wall and the Grand Canal, and launched the Ming voyages, could hardly be accused of never having achieved at any time a "mastery" of nature.

Nor do stereotypical depictions of Asian "Leviathan" states as compared with limited European governments stand up to scrutiny, since

[19]Allen (2006) would argue that low Chinese wages, rather than a lack of Chinese "rationality," was the reason why this machine was not embraced in China: while that society had the *capability* to industrialize, it lacked the *incentive*. The reasons for China's failure to industrialize remain a subject of controversy (see Mokyr 2005b).

as already noted countries such as Britain and the Netherlands had governments that were *large* by the standards of the day. While as we saw in the last chapter the Mughal Empire at its height commanded a similar share of the state's resources as did eighteenth-century Britain, it was an exception in the non-European world. Feuerwerker (1984, p. 300) estimates that the share of tax revenue in national income was between 6 and 8% in Ming China ca. 1550 and was between 4 and 8% two centuries later. The share was less than 4.5% in the Ottoman Empire throughout the early modern period (Clark 2007a, table 7.3) and was a mere 2–3% during the late eighteenth century (Pamuk 2004, p. 243). Finally, attempts to explain European success by pointing to more liberal economic policies there also seem doomed to failure, at least with respect to the trade sphere that has been the focus of this volume. By early modern standards, the Indian Ocean which the Europeans encountered was a laissez-faire paradise, with ports such as Calicut and Melaka adopting much more liberal policies than any European state of the time. As we have seen, the Europeans did not bring free trade to Asia in the wake of da Gama, but monopolistic trade restrictions backed up with the threat of violence. More generally, there is no evidence that more market-friendly policies led to more efficient commodity markets in early modern Europe. In an important recent paper, Keller and Shiue (forthcoming) analyze European and Chinese grain markets from the seventeenth to the nineteenth century, and find that Chinese markets were as efficient as their European counterparts as late as 1780. It was after the Industrial Revolution, not before, that European markets pulled ahead of Chinese ones.

It is, unfortunately, easier to criticize others than to build up a convincing answer to what is after all one of the most enduring questions in social science. There seem to us to be a number of points worth emphasizing, however. First, monocausal explanations are entirely unsatisfactory, something upon which most of the major participants in the debate nowadays are in agreement. A second, obviously related point is that we need to make a sharp distinction between factors that were necessary for European growth, and ones which were sufficient. A great many factors may indeed have been necessary for the "rise of the West," but they cannot have been sufficient, since in many cases we can find the same conditions applying in other regions of the world as well. Third, if the focus is on "why Asia did not rise," rather than on "why Europe rose," then very different explanations are going to be required to account for the experiences of economies and societies as different from each other as the Chinese Empire, the Muslim World, or Southeast Asia.

Fourth, as we have seen the various regions of the world did not develop in isolation, but profoundly influenced each other, through trade, war, missionary activity, and a host of other channels. Explanations that treat each region as if it were an island, with a set of characteristics evolving in isolation from the others, miss a large part of the picture. Europe's links with the rest of the world were crucial in explaining its own development, and thus the takeoff to modern growth cannot be understood without reference to such factors as the transmission of technology from Asia to Europe, or European overseas expansion. In turn, these phenomena can only be understood as the outcome of a variety of long-run historical processes. Goody (1996, p. 41) exactly sums up our own approach when he says that "Capitalism must be seen as the result not of a sudden cataclysm but of a long series of events, some of which took place outside of the confines of Western Europe, especially before the Renaissance. The situation appears to be recurring today, when new developments in productive systems are taking place in the East. Societies that are in the vanguard (modernizing) at one point give way to others at another; the pendulum swings. Looked at over the longer span of time, no one region is solely responsible for the birth of modern society."

What can we say about the role of trade in promoting growth, in the context of these broader debates? First, it is obvious that many of the efflorescences that we have come across had their roots in trade expansion, commercialization, and a growing division of labor. This is obviously true in cases such as Southeast Asia's Age of Commerce, or the European Commercial Revolution, but it is true of episodes such as the Sung economic miracle as well. As noted in chapter 2 the Sung miracle was largely driven by growing commercialization and specialization, linked to the development of extensive inland waterways. Interestingly, in light of our earlier arguments concerning Britain, Morgan Kelly (1997, p. 955) has argued that "Market expansion not only caused output to grow by permitting increased specialization; it also increased the incentives for innovation.... The adoption of early ripening strains of rice in the eleventh century...would not have been worthwhile in a subsistence economy without the means of transporting the increased surplus to markets.... Similarly, most of the quadrupling of iron output during the eleventh century was accounted for by a few very large ironworks in northeastern China.... [This] caused the rapid deforestation of northeastern China...and provided both the inducement and the resources to develop bituminous coke as an alternative fuel source."

The Asian record thus confirms that trade and growth were intimately linked. However, the Chinese example also teaches us that access to markets was not a *sufficient* condition for a takeoff to modern growth, since the Chinese market was large enough to have provided would-be entrepreneurs with all the consumers they could possibly have desired. Selling to domestic consumers only was not an option in a small economy like Britain, and thus international trade was a necessary condition for growth there. To explain the absence of a Chinese takeoff, however, historians need to look for other explanatory factors, particularly since as we have seen early modern Chinese markets were well-integrated by European standards.

Another explanatory factor that may indeed have been necessary for European success, but cannot have been sufficient, is the intensely competitive European "states system," which we have already alluded to on a number of occasions (Jones 2003). The political fragmentation of Europe, with a number of competing states not dominated by a single center, meant that there was more room for the exercise of choice between alternative social, political, and economic policies as well as competition between states for military and economic supremacy (ibid.). The free cities of Europe, so rightly singled out by Weber as a vital element in its distinctive character and future trajectory, and in particular the Italian city-states of the Commercial Revolution, added a further luster to the era of expansion that started to slow down only early in the fourteenth century, before it was struck by the catastrophe of the Black Death.

We find unpersuasive the notion that competition between European states led to a beneficial fiscal "race to the bottom," with mobile labor and capital placing limits on the ability of governments to impose taxes, since as we have seen taxes were high in Britain on the eve of the Industrial Revolution, not low. On the other hand, it is surely true that political fragmentation made it more difficult to suppress inconvenient ideas, and that exit options made for a more robust "intellectual market" in Europe than in a counterfactual unified continent. Even better, a common European culture ensured that ideas could flow smoothly across frontiers, even when their originators could not. Thus the European "states system" may indeed have been a contributory factor to the Scientific Revolution of the seventeenth century, and the Enlightenment of the eighteenth, both of which were undoubtedly important impulses underlying Europe's subsequent growth takeoff (Jones 2003; Mokyr 2002, 2005a, 2006).

The European "states system" also, clearly, ensured that European states remained competitive militarily. To scholars such as Jones for whom the system is an important key to Europe's long-run success, China provides the natural comparison. Thus, China's failure to produce modern guns (Landes 2006) can be taken as an illustration of what could happen to societies lacking the stimulating pressures of military competition. However, even if this characterization of China is granted, political fragmentation *was* a feature of both South and Southeast Asia. The fact that, as we have seen, new military technologies were rapidly adopted by Southeast Asian states can on one level be taken as support for Jones's stress on competition as a force for change. On the other hand, as noted in chapter 4, political fragmentation was one of the factors that allowed a succession of small European states to dominate the Indian coastline, and ultimately the interior as well. Moreover, the Muslim World had since 750 been characterized by the same combination of fierce interstate competition and a shared culture which were apparently so beneficial in Western Europe, and yet it too eventually fell into relative decline. A willingness to slaughter one's coreligionists was not, it seems, a sufficient condition for a takeoff any more than was a sufficiently large market.

Geography seems to us to be one reason why interstate competition favored Western Europe disproportionately. Its peripheral location on the western edge of Eurasia had protected it from the Mongols, while Muslim cities such as Baghdad and Damascus were devastated by Genghis Khan's successors. The Mongol "shock" was, as we have seen, as positive for Western Europe in its effects as it was negative for the Muslim World. At other times, Europe's location placed it at the mercy of Muslim middlemen, giving Europeans a strong incentive to engage in maritime exploration. Geography alone gave whichever power controlled the Red Sea and the Persian Gulf the ability to earn substantial rents on the transit trade. Western Europe, however, was a terminus rather than a transit point on east–west trade routes, implying that states seeking new trade-based sources of revenue would have to pursue aggressive military strategies in order to obtain them. Naval power, in particular, would be required to gain control over shipping lanes or those regions producing spices or other luxury trade goods. Indeed, naval power was required in order to grab whatever rents remained to be extracted once Asian imports had been purchased in Alexandria or Beirut, since other European states had to be excluded, by force, from competing for the Mediterranean trade. Together with the more general strategic importance of first the Mediterranean, and then the Atlantic, this meant that Europeans enjoyed a pronounced military edge at sea, developing sailing ships that were essentially floating gun platforms. This combination of "guns and sails" (Cipolla 1965) was as we have seen an important factor in establishing European hegemony over Asia. Just as important, according to Felipe Fernández-Armesto (2006), was the Europeans' privileged access to "the favourable winds and currents" of the Atlantic, which was the "highway to the rest of the world." By contrast, the conditions facing Asian navigators were much less favorable: as Fernández-Armesto succinctly puts it, "To start worldwide ventures, it was vital to be in the right place" (p. 149).

An even more important geographical advantage enjoyed by Europe was of course its relative proximity to America. Western Europe was far more likely to "stumble across" this vast continent than any of our other world regions, and the competitive pursuit of Plenty in support of Power ensured that Europeans would not be long in exploiting American resources to the best of their ability. In support of the "military competition" thesis, the fact that the Ottomans faced enemies on multiple fronts, hemmed in between the Safavids, Russians, and Western Europeans, might help explain why they remained relatively competitive militarily for so long, why they were so willing to make use of foreign technical expertise, and why their economic and political institutions displayed a considerable capacity for innovation (Pamuk 2004). But the Ottomans' geographical location also meant that territorial expansion was impossible beyond a certain point. The Sahara was no substitute for the Atlantic, and the relatively easy pickings of the New World would go to the Western powers. This not only gifted the Atlantic economies with the vast resources of the "Great Frontier" (Webb 1952); it may also have helped preserve the European states system itself by providing it with "an essential safety valve" (Jones 2003, p. 108).

The ways in which different regions responded to common shocks is another factor that seems to us worth emphasizing. We have already noted how the Mongol shock had very different effects on the Muslim and European Worlds. Similarly, as we noted in chapter 3, it seems as though the Western European response to the Black Death was in the long run more beneficial than that of the Muslim World. Recent work by economic historians has shown that while real wages rose across Europe, and in Istanbul and Cairo as well, after the plague, those wage gains were retained to a far greater extent in northwestern Europe than elsewhere (Pamuk 2005, 2006). We also saw that it was during the late Middle Ages that economic relationships between the Islamic World and Western Europe were reversed, with the former switching from being an exporter of manufactured goods to being an exporter of primary products. Chapter 3 speculated that this was in part due to the different responses of the two regions to the temporary increase in real wages (and the temporary decline in rents) caused by the plague. In northwestern Europe, high wages led to favorable demographic responses which helped to "lock in" temporary wage gains, and arguably promoted a variety of labor-saving innovations as well (Herlihy 1997). By contrast, the plague weakened the fiscal foundations of the Mamluk state, leading to a damaging shift toward the taxation of trade and commerce there. Indeed, its main source of revenue in the fourteenth and fifteenth centuries was increasingly the taxation of the transit trade with Venice and other Italian cities in spices through the Red Sea, the growth of which was created by the post-Black Death boom in Europe. It does not appear to be entirely coincidental that the Portuguese discovery of the Cape Route in 1498 was followed soon after, in 1517, by the fall of the Mamluks to the Ottomans.

What seems clear from the historical record is that the European advantage over Asia had been slowly building up over a long period. That this was the case is implicit in the new data on growth during the Industrial Revolution (since if growth was slower during the late eighteenth century than previously thought, then European incomes must have been higher before the Industrial Revolution than previously thought as well). Recent work by Robert Allen and other scholars on long-run real wage trends have also confirmed that living standards were higher in northwest Europe than in Asia (or the rest of Europe) before Britain's takeoff to modern growth (Broadberry and Gupta 2006).[20] Clearly, there were forces internal to Western Europe that had been promoting growth since the turn of the millennium, as well as beneficial external influences on the region, such as the transfer of technology and science from Asia and the Muslim World. In a fascinating recent contribution, for example, Buringh and van Zanden (2006) show that European book production rose at roughly 1% per annum between the sixth and eighteenth centuries, from an annual production of roughly 120 manuscripts over the course of the sixth century to the 20 million books printed in 1790 (p. 11). There was particularly rapid growth during the eighth and ninth centuries, in the first quarter of the second millennium, during the recovery from the effects of the Black Death, and again after Gutenberg's invention of movable-type printing in the mid fifteenth century.

Clearly, a variety of factors internal to European society must have been responsible for these long-run trends. We hope, however, that the reader will have been convinced of the important role that trade played in assisting this development, throughout both the medieval and early modern periods: the interactions between world regions

[20] According to Allen (2007), Indian real wages were as high as English ones as late as the seventeenth century, but then fell behind in the eighteenth, so that by 1800 English living standards were far higher.

were crucial in determining outcomes. Even an author such as Mokyr (2005b, p. 339), for whom the roots of the Industrial Revolution are to be found very clearly in the Scientific Revolution and the Enlightenment, argues that "the Enlightenment had roots in the commercial capitalism of the later middle ages and the sixteenth century," and long-distance trade was as we have seen intimately connected with the latter phenomenon. Moreover, in addition to the mechanisms that we have been stressing, there were surely others that mattered as well. For example, the political importance of trade during the mercantilist era empowered merchants, giving rise to legislation that was favorable to commercial interests (Acemoglu et al. 2005). Imports of tropical products not only augmented the government's tax base, but also gave workers new reasons to earn money, thus helping to fuel an "Industrious Revolution" (de Vries 1993, 1994). Overall, it is hard not to conclude that European overseas expansion was a vital ingredient in her long-run success. Some final words, therefore, seem in order about why it was that Europe ended up dominating Asia militarily and politically, rather than vice versa.

While it is true that Europe experienced a "Military Revolution" in the seventeenth century, the Ming voyages emphatically demonstrated that China, at least during the early fifteenth century, possessed the capability for overseas expansion. While the *capability* was there, however, the *incentive* was lacking, since the necessity to give priority to the defense of the land frontiers was plausibly deemed more imperative by the rival faction at court, and since China was relatively self-sufficient, as least compared with Western Europe—another key geographical factor, in our view. Indeed, as we saw in the previous chapter, while the European states were projecting their power overseas in the Americas and South Asia, China under the Qing dynasty was engaged in a vast westward campaign to crush the Zunghar Mongols, to ensure that there would never be any future threat from that familiar quarter. Thus it is perhaps not to the point to enquire why China did not emulate the European powers by engaging in attempts to expand markets and secure raw materials overseas. The giraffe that Zheng He supposedly brought back to China was no doubt a welcome addition to the Imperial zoo, but was hardly of sufficient strategic importance to warrant an ongoing commitment to maritime exploration. The Mongol threat was a distant memory in Western Europe but an ever-present danger on their western borders to the rulers of China. They did not realize that a new and greater danger had already appeared on their eastern shores and they made no preparations to face it.

In 1793 George III sent the veteran imperialist Lord Macartney, with many years of experience in India and the Caribbean, on a famously fruitless embassy to the Qianlong emperor. Macartney, foreshadowing Max Weber, shrugged off the failure of his mission and observed in his journal that "the Empire of China is an old, crazy first-rate man-of-war, which a fortunate succession of able and vigilant officers has managed to keep afloat for these one hundred and fifty years past, and to overawe their neighbors merely by her bulk and appearance," but with lesser men at the helm she would surely drift until "dashed to pieces on the shore" (Spence 1990, p. 123). So spoke the restlessly rational West against what it regarded as the placidly complacent East, but "history is full of contrived corridors" and the last word has not yet been written on this long encounter.

CONCLUSION

The success of the European Industrial Revolution is intimately connected with trade and overseas expansion, which reached a crescendo after the last great achievement of Europe's "Middle Ages," the Voyages of Discovery. In turn, those voyages have clear historical antecedents, notably the Viking impulse to explore the North Atlantic, but also in such episodes as the Crusades, overland contacts with East Asia during the *Pax Mongolica*, and the ill-fated journey of the Vivaldi brothers (Phillips 1998). This characteristically European urge resulted not just from Europe's desire for Asian trade goods, but also from her geographical location, which left her at the mercy of whichever powers controlled the Red Sea, the Persian Gulf, and the approaches of the Black Sea. In this sense, Mohammed was as much responsible for da Gama as for Charlemagne.

While the origins of the Industrial Revolution were inextricably linked with the centuries-old development of the international economy, which previous chapters have surveyed, it would in turn go on to revolutionize the international trading system, through a number of key channels. It opened up huge economic asymmetries in the world economy, revolutionized international transport, and helped to cement the geopolitical dominance of Europe over Africa and Asia. The Industrial Revolution was not only in large measure explained by the history of trade which we have studied thus far; it is the key to understanding the subsequent history of trade to which we will now turn our attention.

Chapter 7

WORLD TRADE 1780–1914: THE GREAT SPECIALIZATION

BY THE MID EIGHTEENTH CENTURY there was a well-developed international trading system that linked almost all the continents through trade, as shown in chapter 5. Traditional Euro-Asian trade was still important, and the Atlantic had now become a bridge rather than a barrier, linking Europe with her colonies in the Americas, and linking both continents with African markets and slave supplies. These well-defined patterns of intercontinental trade, which had been centuries in the making, would be permanently disrupted in the decades following 1780, which saw a series of profound shocks to the international system. First, there was a major economic one: the Industrial Revolution, which was the focus of the previous chapter, and which will loom large throughout the remainder of the book. Second, the beginning of the period experienced a worldwide military conflict, which severely disrupted trade. Third, independence movements in the Americas deprived the European powers of most of their colonies there. And fourth, in 1807 the British government abolished the slave trade between Africa and its overseas colonies, following a similar move by Denmark in 1803 (Engerman 1981, pp. 4–5). The United States also banned the transatlantic slave trade in 1807, while Britain went on to try to prevent other powers from shipping slaves across the Atlantic.

These four shocks interacted in such a way that the international economy of the "nineteenth century," by which we will generally mean the period 1815–1914, would be fundamentally different from what had gone before. In terms of the matrix in table 2.1, the three centuries from 1500 to 1800 were largely concerned with filling in cells that had previously been blank. From now on, however, and as a result of the Industrial Revolution, the *intensity* of these interactions would increase at a historically unprecedented rate. Furthermore, because the Industrial Revolution was at first limited to Western Europe and her British offshoots, the structure of international trade and the international division of labor would change dramatically, becoming far more asymmetric than had ever been the case before. It is during this period that it begins to make sense to divide the world into "North" and "South," or employ terms such as the "Third World," and while such expressions obviously oversimplify, concealing more than they reveal, we will begin to use them in this chapter when it is convenient to do so. Corresponding to this growing economic asymmetry was a political one, as European empires expanded across the globe, implying that events in Europe now had a disproportionate influence on the world as a whole. We thus begin the chapter with an account of a European conflict that had worldwide ramifications, namely the Revolutionary and Napoleonic Wars opposing Britain and her old enemy, France.

War and Revolution[1]

We saw in chapter 5 that the mercantilist period was characterized by frequent wars that disrupted international trade. We also saw that these wars led to severe fiscal crises for the states involved, which in turn led to the outbreak of the American and French Revolutions. There followed a far larger conflagration than previous mercantilist wars, into which an additional ideological dimension had now been injected. In 1792, France declared war on Austria and Prussia, and on February 1 of the following year she declared war on Great Britain. The ensuing conflict between the two countries lasted until 1815, with just two brief interludes of peace, the first from the Peace of Amiens in March 1802 until the renewal of war in May 1803, and the second during 1814–15.

Almost immediately, France banned imports of many British goods, and in October 1793 she banned all British manufactures. Meanwhile, the British blockaded the French coast. As Eli Heckscher (1922) emphasized, measures of this kind were motivated by mercantilist reasoning, and in particular the desire to prevent the enemy from earning precious metals via exports.[2] This was in sharp contrast with policy during the two world wars of the twentieth century, when as we shall see, the belligerents attempted to deprive their opponents of *imports* such as food and munitions. The blockades of the 1790s, as well as the later Continental Blockade, thus had a distinctly eighteenth-century flavor. Famously, in 1810, when Britain was suffering from a

---

[1] The following three sections draw heavily on O'Rourke (2006).

[2] The exception being that food exports were occasionally banned when domestic food supplies were scarce.

poor harvest but France had food in abundance, Napoleon authorized food exports to its enemy accounting for roughly 13% of English grain consumption in that year (Olson 1963, p. 65). Such a policy stance, based on the hope that one's opponent could be brought to its knees by supplying it with food in return for gold, relied on the assumption that Britain needed trade surpluses to finance its war effort on the European continent. It ignored the possibility that the war effort could be financed via continental lending to Britain (Neal 1990, p. 205), and invites counterfactual speculation as to what would have happened had Napoleon instead attempted to starve out the British (Rose 1902; Heckscher 1922; Olson 1963).

From the beginning, neutral European states found themselves caught up in this trade conflict, despite their natural desire to continue trading with both sides. An early response by the Baltic powers was to form a "League of Armed Neutrality," in December 1800, under which Russia, Sweden, Prussia, and Denmark agreed to provide naval protection for their merchant shipping.[3] The British responded with a ban on trade with the League (apart from Prussia) and launched a naval attack on Copenhagen, leading to the League being dissolved in 1801. On the other hand, the early years of the war were good ones for the merchant marine of the neutral United States, which found a lucrative niche transporting French colonial goods to France. The result was a boom in American reexports, although whether this boom translated into broader benefits for the U.S. economy, or merely served to "crowd out" exports of American-produced goods, is a subject of debate (North 1966; Adams 1980; Goldin and Lewis 1980).

Napoleon's attempts to undermine the British manufacturing sector were enhanced by his military victories over Austria and Russia in 1805, and Prussia in 1806. In November 1806, he issued the "Berlin Decree," which proclaimed the British Isles to be under blockade, an imaginative policy stance given the crushing naval victory that had been obtained by the Royal Navy at Trafalgar the previous year. More seriously, the Decree banned all trade in British goods, and stated that ships arriving directly from Britain or her colonies were to be barred from French ports. Crucially, the French were now able to apply this policy not just in France, but also in such vassal states as Spain, Naples, and Holland. In 1807 the extent of the Continental Blockade was further widened, following Napoleon's defeat of Russia at Friedland and the Treaty of Tilsit. This led to Russia and Prussia joining the

---

[3]This succeeded a similar arrangement between the two Scandinavian countries in 1794.

Continental Blockade, and enabled Napoleon to turn his attention to Portugal, which was successfully invaded later the same year. Fearing that Napoleon would force Denmark into a military alliance, the British invaded Denmark and seized her navy, which not surprisingly led to Denmark (and Norway) entering into an alliance with France and joining the blockade. Finally, Sweden was forced to join in 1810.

In this manner the European neutrals were obliged to take sides in the trade dispute. Next it would be the turn of the United States. In November 1807 the British responded to Napoleon's policies by issuing a series of "Orders in Council," under which neutral ships carrying goods from enemy colonies directly to their mother countries could be seized. They could still carry goods from enemy colonies to their own home ports, or from enemy colonies to British ports, or from British ports to enemy ports. What this meant in practice was that neutral, and in particular American, vessels would have to put into British ports if they wanted to ship goods from, say, French colonies to France. Napoleon's counterresponse was to declare that any neutral ship putting into a British port could be seized. At this stage, American merchants were faced with an impossible dilemma: no matter what they did, if they attempted to carry French colonial goods to France their ships would inevitably be seized by either the British or the French. In December 1807, Thomas Jefferson's government reacted by closing its ports to all belligerent shipping, and by forbidding American ships to leave these ports. This so-called "Embargo Act" was repealed in 1809, and replaced with a Non-Intercourse Act which banned trade only with Britain and France, as well as their colonies, and which was applied with varying degrees of severity over the succeeding years (Heaton 1941).

The year 1810 was to prove the high-water mark for Napoleon's Continental Blockade. On December 31 of that year, Tsar Alexander opened Russian ports to neutral ships. This was one of the factors that ultimately led to Napoleon's disastrous invasion of Russia in June 1812, which ended in a costly and humiliating retreat. There followed a devastating military defeat at the hands of the Russians and their Allies at Leipzig in 1813, and by early 1814 France itself was invaded. The blockade legislation was finally repealed following Napoleon's abdication in 1814, having effectively collapsed in the summer of 1813. On the other hand, in 1812 continuing friction over trade, as well as the pressing into British service of seamen aboard U.S. vessels, led to the United States declaring war on Britain. There followed a British blockade of the U.S. coastline, which was greatly strengthened in 1814, when military victory over Napoleon allowed the Royal Navy to redeploy its forces there. The "War of 1812" would last until Christmas Eve, 1814, when a peace treaty was signed in Ghent. Famously, news of the treaty reached New Orleans too late to avert a final battle there on January 8, an indication of how fragmented the world still was in many ways.

THE REVOLUTIONARY AND NAPOLEONIC WARS: SHORT-RUN IMPLICATIONS

In a classic book, Eli Heckscher (1922) argued that the Continental Blockade, and similar policies adopted by the British and Americans, had no great effect on the international trading system, as a result of smuggling and corruption among the public officials who were supposed to enforce the trade restrictions. On the other hand, Crouzet (1987) argued that the blockade was effective from mid 1807 to mid 1808, and again from the spring of 1810 until the winter of 1812, while both Frankel (1982) and Irwin (2005) have shown that the Jefferson Embargo *did* severely restrict American foreign trade. The available data on the volume of trade suggest that French imports were sharply reduced during the Embargo period, and that both U.S. imports and exports fell dramatically, especially during 1814. Relative to their (quadratic) trends, French and American imports were down by slightly more than 50% during 1807–14, and U.S. exports were down by slightly more than a third, while British trade volumes were affected only marginally, and in a statistically insignificant way (O'Rourke 2006, table 1, p. 129). On the other hand, such evidence would presumably not convince Heckscher, since these official statistics do not include smuggled goods.

Relative prices, on the other hand, provide a good indicator of the scarcity of imported goods, and table 7.1 provides some summary evidence on what happened to the prices of imported goods, relative to export goods, in various countries during the conflict. In each case, the table gives the percentage by which relative import prices exceeded their long-run trends during the war as a whole, as well as during the blockade period of 1807–14. As can be seen, relative import prices in Europe and the Americas increased substantially, particularly during the blockades. Within Europe, the traditional exchange of British manufactures for continental food and raw materials was disrupted, leading to an increase in the relative price of wheat in Britain, and of textiles in France. But the really dramatic price movements involved goods traded between continents. Thus, the price of pepper relative

TABLE 7.1. Price impact of Napoleonic Wars (percentage increase in relative price above quadratic trend).

Relative price	Country	War	Blockade
(a) Intra-European			
Wheat/textiles	Britain	19.03	41.35
Textiles/wheat	France	16.58	19.84
Textiles/wheat	Germany	6.74	5.71
(b) Europe–Asia			
Pepper/wheat	France	66.53	216.36
	Britain	−27.22	−8.21
	Holland	1.41	119.46
Pepper/textiles	France	19.10	109.82
	Britain	−13.37	29.74
	Holland	15.13	167.37
(c) Europe–Americas			
Sugar/wheat	France	63.31	195.03
	Britain	16.31	−2.90
	Holland	17.87	165.10
	Germany	2.43	143.09
Raw cotton/wheat	France	−6.46	114.28
	Britain	−10.96	−26.17
	Holland	−9.47	11.45
	Germany	−28.7	67.89
Sugar/textiles	France	26.70	125.59
	Britain	38.44	37.25
	Holland	25.27	214.64
	Germany	−4.04	129.95
Raw cotton/textiles	France	−19.76	78.81
	Britain	6.43	4.93
	Holland	−2.31	31.23
	Germany	−33.2	58.82
Textiles/raw cotton	U.S.A.	106.01	182.51
Wine/raw cotton	U.S.A.	28.59	137.05
Rouen cloth/silver	Peru (Arequipa)	12.92	91.58
Paper/silver	Peru (Arequipa)	53.19	120.79
Paper/silver	Peru (Lima)	46.87	111.77

Source: O'Rourke (2006).

to wheat doubled in Holland during 1807–14, and trebled in France, with similarly large relative price increases on the European mainland for American goods such as raw cotton and sugar. Notably, import prices in Germany increased only during the blockade period, when Napoleon's regime extended eastwards across the Rhine; and the relative prices of non-European imports did not rise by much in Britain, which makes sense given the Royal Navy's control over the high seas. Also notable are the large increases in relative import prices in both the United States and Latin America, where naval warfare between Spain and Britain (1796–1802 and 1804–8) seriously disrupted trade.

What had started as a purely European conflict thus also had substantial consequences for the non-European parts of the world. Another example of these wider intercontinental effects is provided by Lovejoy and Richardson's (1995) data on slave prices deflated by the cost of imported trade goods, both in West Africa, where British slaving had been heavily concentrated, and further south, in Angola. If their prewar (1788–92) level is taken to equal 100, real West African slave prices stood at 91.6 during 1793–97, 122 during 1798–1802, 132.5 during 1803–7, but only 74.3 during 1808–14, and 40.3 during 1815–20. The prices then recovered to 57.6 in the early 1820s, and to 90.1 in the late 1820s. The timing of the price decline suggests strongly that the British and U.S. abolition of the slave trade was the most important force driving it, an impression strengthened by the evidence that Angolan slave prices were stable after 1808 (ibid., table 3, p. 113). On the other hand, the postwar recovery in slave prices suggests an independent effect for the war in lowering relative export prices in Africa as well.

For a small number of countries we have more systematic data on the terms of trade during the conflict, and these are reproduced in figure 7.1 (where the shaded areas refer to 1807–14). The data show a sizable deterioration in the Swedish terms of trade (i.e., a rise in relative import prices), a very sharp deterioration in the United States, especially during 1814, and an enormous deterioration in France between 1807 and 1814 (following an improvement during the Peace of Amiens). The British terms of trade also deteriorated, but by much less. In turn, these shocks presumably inflicted substantial welfare losses on the countries concerned. Irwin (2005) estimates that U.S. welfare declined by some 5% during Jefferson's Embargo, while O'Rourke (2007a) estimates annual welfare losses of 4–5% for the United States between 1807 and 1814, of around 2–3% for France during the same period, and of between 1 and 2% for Britain.

THE REVOLUTIONARY AND NAPOLEONIC WARS:
LONG-RUN IMPLICATIONS

It seems clear that the wars of 1792–1815 had a substantial and disruptive effect on international trade around the globe, but they also

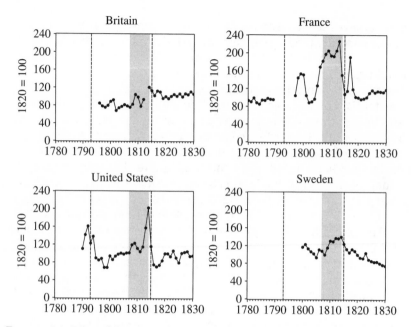

FIGURE 7.1. Price of imports relative to exports, 1780–1830 (1820 = 100). The lines refer to 1793 and 1815, and the shaded areas refer to 1807–14. *Source:* Imlah (1958), Schön (1984), Cuenca Esteban (2004), and North (1966).

had a variety of longer-run implications that would shape the political context for international trade policy over the next century. On the one hand, the blockades gave rise to protectionist lobby groups in key Northern economies, who had benefited from trade disruption, and who would do everything in their power to impede any subsequent moves toward free trade. On the other hand, the wars brought an end to several trade-restricting features of the eighteenth-century mercantilist international system.

We will begin with the negative effects of the wars on nineteenth-century international integration. In Britain, landed interests had benefited from the rise in agricultural prices, with rents rising substantially. After the war, landlord lobbying led to the 1815 Corn Law, which effectively excluded foreign grain from British markets for most of the following seven years. While this law was gradually relaxed in the succeeding decades, it was only finally repealed in 1846. When Europe eventually moved toward freer trade in the late nineteenth century, this was largely as a result of Britain's example. Might Britain have liberalized earlier had the Napoleonic Wars not intervened?

Such an argument assumes that industrialization (which would have proceeded more rapidly in the absence of the war (see Williamson 1984)) would have led to the emergence of powerful export interests, which would have eventually triumphed as their political power grew. Would the extension of the franchise favoring urban interests, and thus the free trade cause, have predated the 1832 Reform Act, had war not occurred? (Surely the Revolution and succeeding wars did nothing to hasten liberal reforms in Britain.) Alternatively, might landlords have diversified into non-agricultural interests earlier, and been co-opted by the free trade side as eventually happened (Schonhardt-Bailey 1991)?

While it is near impossible to provide definitive answers to such questions, a hint that the Napoleonic Wars did significantly delay the advent of free trade in Britain can be found with the passage of the Eden Treaty between Britain and France in 1786. This treaty "put an end to the hundred years' commercial war" between the two countries, abolishing prohibitions on imports, and reducing tariffs generally, "usually down to 10 or 15 per cent" (Heckscher 1922, p. 20). It is true that, even in the absence of war between the two countries, this treaty might eventually have lapsed. Heckscher (1922, pp. 20–23) reports that the treaty led to widespread complaints from a variety of French industries, notably the French textile industry, and one can certainly speculate that this pressure would eventually have born fruit. On the other hand, the new postrevolutionary French tariff of 1791 contained only moderate additional protection, despite widespread protectionist pressure. It was only in early 1793, when tensions between the two countries were mounting, and shortly before war broke out between them, that the French denounced the Eden Treaty. Moreover, it was the French who denounced the Treaty, not the British, whose leaders had at this stage already been influenced by the ideas of Adam Smith and other economic liberals. There is thus a prima facie case that the French and Napoleonic Wars delayed the adoption of free trade policies in Britain, maybe even by several decades.[4]

In France, the distributional effects of the blockades were more complex. Many traditional French industries had been intimately bound up with the eighteenth-century Atlantic economy, and were naturally severely damaged. These included industries processing colonial goods, such as sugar refining, industries serving overseas markets, such as linen, and industries directly involved with shipping,

[4]A counterargument might be that British hegemony, and thus war ending with British victory over the French, might have been required for the widespread trade liberalization of the nineteenth century: see below.

such as shipbuilding, rope-making, and sail-making (Crouzet 1964). On the other hand, import-substituting industries such as cotton textiles presumably benefited from the absence of British competition, despite the increase in raw cotton prices. Thus, the output of machine-spun yarn quadrupled between 1806 and 1810, with a spectacular growth in the number of spindles in northern and eastern French cities such as Lille and Mulhouse, as well as in regions under French control such as present-day Belgium and Saxony, where the number of mule spindles rose from 13,000 in 1806 to 256,000 in 1813 (ibid., p. 576). Chabert (1949, pp. 347–49) reports that profits rose more rapidly during the war in France than any other category of income, and that this was true of the textile industry despite its high raw materials costs: he reports several cases of cotton spinners and other industrialists who made large fortunes during the wars. The location of French industry thus shifted, away from the Atlantic coast toward inland regions, and its orientation also changed, from an outward-looking to an import-competing, inward-looking one. After the war, such sectors would consistently lobby for protection, and they generally obtained it.

One particularly striking example of this phenomenon is the European beet sugar industry. A German chemist, Andreas Marggraf, had succeeded in obtaining sugar crystals from beet in 1747, and the first refineries were producing sugar by the turn of the century. In 1811, faced with the growing scarcity of sugar, Napoleon issued a decree promoting beet cultivation through a variety of means, leading to a rapid growth in the number of factories. This new industry, which eventually spread to several other Northern Hemisphere countries, would soon become dependent on government subsidies and protection, since tropical producers retained important underlying cost advantages. Indeed, government production and export subsidies became so prevalent that in 1902 nine European countries (who represented not only Northern beet sugar interests, but Southern cane interests by virtue of their colonial empires) signed the first international primary commodity agreement, the Brussels Convention, which aimed at abolishing sugar subsidies (Taussig 1903; Viner 1923, pp. 178–86).

In this sector, therefore, wartime import substitution had not only a long-run effect on subsequent trade policies, but also a large negative impact on tropical sugar producers, particularly from the 1870s onwards. Between 1860 and 1900, European countries increased their share of world trade in sugar from zero to 60%. World beet sugar production rose by 188% between 1882 and 1900, as compared with a rise in cane sugar production of 86%. By 1902, free market sugar prices had declined to little more than a third of their 1880 level (Stover 1970, pp. 55–56). This came on top of the blow that West Indian plantations (but not their unfortunate workers) had suffered in the 1830s, when all slaves in British colonies had been emancipated, and as we will see later the Caribbean was one of the worst-performing regions of the world during the late nineteenth century (Hanson 1980, pp. 83, 103; Curtin 1954, p. 158). At the time of writing this book, North–South disagreement regarding Northern protection for its sugar industry was still one of the main obstacles facing world trade negotiators in the Doha Trade Round, held under the auspices of the WTO, and which was suspended in July 2006.

In the United States, the combination of expensive textiles and cheaper-than-usual raw cotton gave a great boost to the cotton industry. The number of cotton spindles there grew from 2,000 in 1790 (compared with over 2 million in Britain) to just 8,000 in 1809, but to 94,000 in 1810 and 333,000 in 1817 (Rosenbloom 2004, table 12.1, p. 366). However, the industry experienced severe difficulties with the end of the war. The result was that New England textile manufacturers such as Francis Lowell successfully sought protection, with the 1816 tariff bill effectively excluding low-cost Indian fabrics from the American market (Temin 1988). In years to come Northern industrialists would consistently lobby for protection, and against the free trade interests of the slave-owning agricultural South. The United States would be protectionist until well into the twentieth century.

The wars thus gave rise to successful protectionist lobby groups in several countries. However, they also led to geopolitical changes that would greatly facilitate the emergence of the highly globalized economy of the late nineteenth century. First, the wars led to a collapse in continental European power in the Americas, following Britain's earlier loss of the United States. The trend started in 1791, when slaves in Saint-Domingue, France's most important sugar colony, revolted. Despite being invaded by both Britain and France, Haiti succeeded in gaining its independence in 1804. In Latin America, Napoleon's invasion of Iberia was followed by a series of revolutions over the course of the following decade. By the 1820s independent republics (an independent empire in the case of Brazil) had been established across the continent, with the Spanish retaining possession of just Cuba and Puerto Rico.

As we will see, these newly independent states would go on to impose high tariffs, but at the same time the old mercantilist restrictions governing trade with the Iberian colonies now lapsed. The effect was dramatic: the share of British manufactured exports going to Latin America rose from 0.06% during the mid 1780s to 3.3% in

1804–6, 6.3% during 1814–6, and 15% in the mid 1820s (Davis 1979, p. 88). Something very similar happened in Asia. The Dutch VOC was severely weakened by the fourth Anglo-Dutch war of 1780–84, losing half its ships, and became "a ward of the state" (de Vries and van der Woude 1997, p. 455). Following the French invasion of 1795, the VOC was taken over by the new Batavian Republic regime, but war made trade with Asia next to impossible, and the VOC was dissolved in 1799. In 1806, a historic milestone was reached when a Dutch government permitted free trade with Asia for the first time since 1602, although war continued to hinder such trade in practice (ibid., p. 456). Meanwhile, in Britain wartime scarcity and social unrest undermined the argument for the English East India Company's privileges, and the company lost its Indian trade monopoly in 1813 (Webster 1990).

These wars were disastrous for the Netherlands. When the Continental Blockade was adopted in 1806, the screw tightened even further on the Dutch merchant navy, which had until then "managed to sustain itself by using flags of convenience, nurturing connections with the neutral American merchant fleet, and generally living by its wits," but now found all such activities being rigorously clamped down upon (de Vries and van der Woude 1997, p. 685). Although Dutch independence was restored in 1814, the nation's relative military and trading strength had been dealt a sizable and lasting blow. On the other hand, what was bad for the VOC was necessarily good for Southeast Asian exports. Bulbeck et al. (1998) document Southeast Asian trade in four key regional exports, cloves, pepper, sugar, and coffee, and find that the 1780s marked a positive turning point for Southeast Asian exports. Thus, export growth averaged an impressive 4.6% per annum during 1780–1829 (p. 15), which was by far superior to the rates achieved previously. It is true that trade during the wars was unstable, owing to the disruption of shipping and the French occupation of the Netherlands in 1795. Export growth in real terms fell to a mere 0.1% per annum in the 1810s, before increasing to 11% per annum in the 1820s. Javanese sugar barely reached Europe during 1790–1816, while the same was true for the island's coffee exports after 1794 (pp. 118, 147). However, while exports to Europe declined during the wars, Chinese and, especially, American ships could now buy spices directly in Southeast Asia, and ship them to their home markets. With sugar and coffee production in Saint-Domingue disrupted by the slave rebellion there, there was an abundant demand for the region's output.

Price data also suggest that the ending of the VOC monopoly had a positive effect on the Southeast Asian economy. Both clove and pepper prices rose relative to silver by between a third and a half between the 1770s and the first two decades of the nineteenth century. This picture of rising export prices during the wars is at odds with the pattern of falling relative export prices (or rising relative import prices) elsewhere, but is what would be expected with the ending of a centuries-old monopsony. The experience of Southeast Asia during this period thus reinforces Reid's argument, reviewed in chapter 5, that Southeast Asian decline after 1650 was due to VOC restrictions (O'Rourke 2006; Reid 1999).

The initial impact of the wars on the Dutch East Indies was liberal politically as well as economically. The Dutch state, rather than the VOC, now ran the territory, and Governor-General Daendels, who took over the colony in 1808, started reforming and modernizing it. His aims included trying to introduce a strict distinction between merchant interests and the bureaucracy, attacking the privileges, which were seen as feudal, of the native elite, and building new roads. When the British conquered the colony in 1811, Daendels was replaced by Thomas Stamford Raffles, who replaced the existing panoply of taxes with a land tax designed to provide local landowners with more flexibility and greater incentives. In 1816, the British, and Raffles, were replaced once again by colonial representatives of the Kingdom of the Netherlands, and the new governor, G. G. Van der Capellen, continued in a generally modernizing vein until the mid 1820s. For example, it is from this period onward that the Dutch state began systematically collecting statistical data about its Southeast Asian possessions (van Zanden 2004).

The French wars thus saw the end of many mercantilist restrictions associated with early modern European colonialism. In consequence, international trade would be conducted on a far more multilateral basis than had been the case during the early modern period, with tariffs replacing such restrictions as the protective weapon of choice. Furthermore, this new, more multilateral era would have one clear hegemonic power, at least insofar as naval power was concerned. Once Britain had finally switched to free trade, by mid century, the Royal Navy would provide a guarantee of open international trading conditions for everyone.

Finally, the wars of 1792–1815 were so costly that they led to a remarkably durable political settlement in Europe, instituted by the Congress of Vienna. According to Paul Schroeder, the new political equilibrium arose from "a mutual consensus on norms and rules, respect for law, and an overall balance among the various actors in terms of rights, security, status, claims, duties and satisfactions rather than power" (Schroeder 1992, p. 694). The system, which relied on "the restoration of the rule of law, beginning with its foundation, the security and legitimacy of all thrones" (ibid., p. 696), held a series of congresses and conferences which essentially managed to keep the peace between the European Great Powers for forty years, until the Crimean War of the 1850s. While that conflict fatally undermined the system, and was followed by a series of wars associated with Italian and German unification, and while the "nineteenth century" would ultimately end with the disaster of 1914–18, the fact remains that battlefield deaths as a proportion of Europe's population were seven times higher in the eighteenth century than they were in the nineteenth (Schroeder 1994, p. vii). The nineteenth century was in fact a remarkably peaceful one in the context of Europe's bloody history, and this was important in an era when, as we shall see, Europe increasingly dominated the rest of the world politically as well as economically. This broadly favorable political context in turn provided a framework within which the new transportation technologies unleashed by the Industrial Revolution could permanently transform the nature of international trade.

The Industrial Revolution and Transportation Technology[5]

If intercontinental trade was at the heart of the incentives which led to the exploits of da Gama and Columbus, and if these exploits in turn implied to a sequence of events which would prove crucial in triggering, or at least sustaining, the Industrial Revolution, then it is not less true that the Industrial Revolution would go on to utterly transform the nature of the intercontinental trading system which had been so central to its genesis. It did so in two main ways. First, the Industrial Revolution created a massive asymmetry within the world economic system, with Europe and her British offshoots embarking on a path of sustained per capita income growth, associated with industrialization and a rapid increase in both their share of world population, and their relative military and political power. How the world responded to this unprecedented economic shock is the major theme of any international economic history of the nineteenth and twentieth centuries, and will be dealt with in this and subsequent chapters. Second, the worldwide impact of this shock, especially insofar as it was reflected in the nature of intercontinental trade, was greatly magnified

[5]This section draws heavily on O'Rourke and Williamson (1999, chapter 3).

by the fact that the new technologies of the Industrial Revolution, and in particular the steam engine, would integrate international commodity (and factor) markets as never before. In this section we will outline the major breakthroughs in transportation technology which occurred in the late eighteenth and early nineteenth centuries, and go on to argue that these would open national economies to intercontinental trade in ways that differed radically from what had gone before.

Previous globalizations had been largely geopolitical in their origins, associated with violence and conquest, from the early Arab conquests to the *Pax Mongolica* to the European empires of the early modern period. The globalization of the nineteenth century, by contrast, would be largely driven by technology, and in this as in much else it was a new and unprecedented phenomenon. This is not to say, however, that violence and conquest would not continue to be features of the relationship between European powers, on the one hand, and Asian and African states and peoples on the other. The new technologies of the Industrial Revolution greatly enhanced the preexisting comparative advantage in violence that the West already enjoyed, lowering the cost and extending the reach of empire, as will be noted later in this chapter.

The transport revolutions of the nineteenth century were preceded by the improvement of roads in more affluent countries such as Britain, France, and the United States. Better surfaces, such as those developed by John Macadam, could speed travel considerably. For example, the time it took to travel from Manchester to London fell from four or five days in 1780 to thirty-six hours in 1820 (Girard 1966, p. 216). However, even on the new highways horse-drawn carriages were an expensive option, especially in larger and less densely settled countries such as the United States. Where they were practical, canals offered transport that was from a quarter to half the price of roads (ibid., p. 223). After the middle of the eighteenth century, canal construction was far more important than turnpike construction in Britain, where the length of navigable waterways quadrupled between 1750 and 1820 (Cameron 1989, p. 172). On the European mainland, there was major canal construction in France, as well as improvements along the river Rhine, where the Congress of Vienna recognized the freedom of navigation that had been established under Napoleon (Girard 1966, p. 224). It was in the United States, however, that inland waterways were most successful. The construction of the Erie Canal between 1817 and 1825 reduced the cost of transport between Buffalo and New York by 85%, and cut the journey time from twenty-one to eight days (ibid.).

Inland waterways were the initial beneficiaries of the first key transport-related invention of the nineteenth century, the steamship. In the first half of the century, steamships were mainly used on rivers (such as the Ohio and Mississippi in the United States, and the Rhone and the Rhine in Europe), the Great Lakes, and inland seas such as the Baltic and the Mediterranean. Such routes enabled them to pick up coal or timber along the way, something that was impossible on the high seas (ibid., p. 225). A key innovation, however, was the screw propeller, which allowed for bigger ships, and ultimately for lighter iron hulls. Steamships were crossing the Atlantic by the 1830s, and regular services to West and South Africa had begun by the 1850s. In 1866, the "Blue Funnel" Line started a regular service linking Mauritius, Penang, Singapore, Hong Kong, and Shanghai (Latham 1978, p. 27). Until 1860 steamers mainly carried high-value goods similar to those carried by airplanes today, like passengers and mail (Cameron 1989, p. 206). As late as 1874, steamships carried 90% of the cotton, ginger, indigo, rapeseed, and tea, 99% of the cowhides, and 100% of the teelseed from Calcutta to Britain, but only 20% of the jute and one-third of the rice (Fletcher 1958, p. 561). Ultimately, however, a series of incremental innovations such as the compound engine made steamships more efficient, expanding the range of goods that they could profitably transport. Shah Mohammed and Williamson (2004, pp. 191–94) calculate that total factor productivity rose by about 1.6% per annum on the United Kingdom–Bombay route over the four decades prior to World War I.

The opening of the 101-mile-long Suez Canal on November 17, 1869, by the French Empress Eugenie, "brought Asia some 4,000 miles nearer to Europe," cutting the distance between Britain and Bombay from 10,667 miles to 6,224 miles, and between Britain and Calcutta from 11,900 miles to 8,083 miles (Latham 1978). Just as important, the Canal further aided the new steamship technology (Fletcher 1958). Up to that point, Far Eastern trade was still dominated by sail. In the absence of sufficient coaling stations around the coast, the trip around Africa by steamer required carrying too much coal. The compound engine reduced fuel requirements, and the Suez Canal made it possible to pick up coal at Gibraltar, Malta, Port Said, and Aden. Not only did the Canal make it possible for steamships to compete on Asian routes, but it was of no use to sailing ships, which would have to be towed through it, and which also had to contend with unfavorable wind conditions at the other end. Indeed, the first sailing ship to make the journey, the *Noel*, was wrecked on the first evening after it emerged from the Canal (Latham 1978, p. 27; Fletcher 1958, p. 558). In consequence, there was an immediate and dramatic shift toward the construction of steamships in the major shipyards of the world (Girard 1966, p. 248).

The other major nineteenth-century development in transportation was the railroad. The Liverpool–Manchester line opened in 1830, and early European emulators included Belgium, France, and Germany. The growth in railway mileage during the late nineteenth century was phenomenal, particularly in the United States, where trains would play a major role in creating a national market. By 1869, a transcontinental line linked the East and West Coasts of the United States. The Canadian transcontinental railway was completed in 1885 and the trans-Siberian railway in 1903. The decades prior to World War I saw an explosion of railway building, largely financed by British capital, in countries such as Argentina, India, Australia, and China. In 1913, Asia accounted for almost 10% of the world's railway network, and India, with nearly three-quarters of the Asian total, ranked an impressive fourth in the world in terms of total railway mileage (Latham 1978, p. 22; Hurd 1975, p. 266). The African share of the total was much smaller (at just 4%), but a substantial network was constructed in South Africa, and both the French and the British were active in building railways elsewhere on the African continent, often for strategic reasons (Latham 1978).

What was the impact of these transport innovations on the cost of moving goods between countries? Nominal freight rates fell dramatically, but what we are interested in is the real cost of transporting commodities. The best way to measure this is to collect freight rates for particular commodities on particular routes, and express these rates as a percentage of the price of the commodity in question, in either the export or the import market. Not only are such "freight factors" (North 1958, p. 538) directly comparable with ad valorem tariffs, which are also expressed in percentage terms, and are also barriers to trade; they can be used to compare transport costs across different routes, as well as over time.

North (1958) provided data for wheat imports into Britain on five routes: the Baltic, the Black Sea, the East Coast of the United States, South America, and Australia. Freight rates only started falling substantially some time after mid century, with the period after 1870 or so emerging as one of sustained transport cost declines. The timing is not that dissimilar from that provided by Knick Harley's (1988) index of British ocean freight rates, which remains relatively constant between 1740 and 1840, before dropping by about 70% between 1840 and 1910. What mattered, however, was the cost of transporting goods between producers and consumers, and this typically depended on overland costs as well as on ocean freight rates. Based on the pioneering work of Knick Harley (1980, 1990), it is possible to divide the Chicago to Liverpool wheat freight factor into its constituent parts: Chicago to New York City, and New York to Liverpool. Between 1866 and 1870 it cost 17.2% of the Chicago wheat price to ship a bushel of wheat to New York, but just 11.6% of the Chicago price to ship it on from New York to Liverpool. By 1909–13, these freight factors had declined to 5.5% and 4.7% respectively.[6] Thus, the 18.6 percentage point decline in the freight factor during this period can be decomposed into an 11.7 percentage point decline in the Chicago to New York component, and a 6.9 percentage point decline in the transoceanic component. Overland transport remained much more expensive than ocean transport. It follows that railways and canals did more of the work in integrating global commodity markets during this period than the steamships that have been the traditional focus of economic historians.

Table 7.2 presents decadal freight factors from North (1958), Yasuba (1978), Stemmer (1989), Persson (2004), Harley (1980, 1989, 1990), and Williamson (2002). The Mediterranean coal export freight factor fell particularly dramatically: it exceeded 200% until 1870 or so, but had declined to 53.8% by 1910. The table also shows that the oft-studied North Atlantic grain trade understates worldwide transport cost declines during this period. Wheat freight factors from the East Coast of the United States to Britain were low to begin with, and thus did not have far to decline. Freight factors from the Black Sea, Latin America, and (most of all) from inland locations were initially higher, and fell further. For example, the tramp charter rate for shipping rice from Rangoon to Europe fell from 74 to 18% of the Rangoon price between 1882 and 1914 (Williamson 2002, p. 60).

More recently, Shah Mohammed and Williamson (2004) have revisited the data underlying the Isserlis (1938) British freight rate series, and have produced a series of route-specific freight rate indices, deflated by the relevant commodity prices.[7] They confirm the earlier impression of sharp declines in real freight rates between 1870 and 1913: declines of 50% or more are not uncommon in this sample of routes. It seems clear that the four decades leading up to World War I did indeed witness an unprecedented, dramatic, and worldwide decline in intercontinental transport costs—especially when declines in overland rates are taken into account.

[6]Gold dollar wheat price (#2 spring) from Harley (1980, pp. 246–47); freight rate is the sum of the lake and canal freight rate from Chicago to New York City (Statistical Abstract of the United States, various issues) and the New York City to Liverpool ocean freight rate given in Harley (1990, p. 167) (all sums are converted when necessary into paper dollars using Officer (2006)).

[7]The series are, however, reported in index form rather than as freight factors.

TABLE 7.2. Freight factors, 1820–1910 (percent).

	Commodity	From	To	Basis
(1)	Wheat	Baltic	Britain	Import
(2)	Wheat	Black Sea	Britain	Import
(3)	Wheat	East Coast U.S.	Britain	Import
(4)	Wheat	New York	Britain	Export
(5)	Wheat	New York	Britain	Import
(6)	Wheat	Chicago	Britain	Export
(7)	Wheat	South America	Britain	Import
(8)	Wheat	Rio de la Plata	U.K.	Import
(9)	Wheat	Australia	Britain	Import
(10)	Coal	Britain	Genoa	Export
(11)	Coal	Nagasaki	Shanghai	Export
(12)	Copper ore	West coast, South America	U.K.	Import
(13)	Guano	West coast, South America	U.K. or European Continent	Import
(14)	Nitrate	West coast, South America	U.K. or European Continent	Import
(15)	Coffee	Brazil	U.K. or European Continent	Import
(16)	Salted hides	Rio de la Plata	U.K.	Import
(17)	Wool	Rio de la Plata	U.K.	Import
(18)	Rice	Rangoon	Europe	Export

	1820	1830	1840	1850	1860	1870	1880	1890	1900	1910
(1)	8.0	7.1	7.2		6.8	9.6	4.5	3.5	5.9	3.4
(2)	15.5	16.3			15.0	17.3	9.2	9.7	10.8	6.8
(3)		10.3		7.5	10.9	8.1	8.6	5.0	8.2	3.2
(4)				10.5					6.9	
(5)				9.4					6.2	
(6)						33.0	21.7	13.3	15.9	7.4
(7)							15.6	18.5		7.4
(8)								15.4		6.9
(9)								22.3	26.7	15.4
(10)			213.1	224.5	246.1	194.0	163.1	69.7	64.5	53.8
(11)							84.0	57.0	35.0	20.0
(12)					21.3			7.8		
(13)					24.9			18.5		
(14)					34.1			23.0		9.7
(15)					5.2			2.0		1.5
(16)					3.1			3.8		
(17)					1.3			1.3		
(18)							73.8			18.1

Source: Rows (1)–(3), (7), (9): North (1958, pp. 550–52). Rows (4)–(5): Persson (2004, p. 141). Row (6): see footnote 6. Rows (8), (12)–(17): Stemmer (1989, p. 31). Row (10): Harley (1989, pp. 334–36), Mediterranean route; British export price from Mitchell (1988, pp. 748–49). Row (11): Yasuba (1978, p. 29). Row (18): Williamson (2002, p. 60) (data for 1882 and 1914).

BULK COMMODITIES AND HECKSCHER–OHLIN EFFECTS[8]

Figure 5.2 showed that when transport costs decline, trade volumes increase, other things being equal. But the transport revolutions of the nineteenth century did not just lead to greater quantities of goods

[8]This section draws on O'Rourke (2001) and O'Rourke and Williamson (1999, 2005).

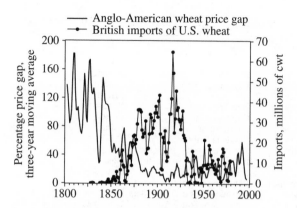

FIGURE 7.2. Anglo-American wheat trade, 1800–2000.
Source: O'Rourke and Williamson (2005, figure 3, p. 10).

being traded; they also led to a greater variety of goods being traded, and this had profound implications for the world economy. When intercontinental transport costs were very high, it was only economical to transport goods with high value-to-weight ratios across the oceans. Very often, these were goods that commanded a high price in the destination continent because they were not produced there at all, or only in very small quantities. In other words, when these goods were imported, they did not displace local production to any great extent: that is, they were wholly or largely *noncompeting*. Table 5.8 showed that throughout the sixteenth and early seventeenth centuries, pepper, other spices, and indigo constituted the bulk of Portuguese imports from Asia, while in the eighteenth century imports of tea and coffee became important in both the Dutch and English cases. Indeed, as late as the middle of the eighteenth century a small number of commodities that were clearly noncompeting (pepper, tea, coffee, spices, sugar, and tobacco) accounted for 57.6% of European imports from the Americas and Asia.[9]

This would change dramatically in the nineteenth century. Figure 7.2 plots the Anglo-American wheat price gap, as well as British imports of U.S. wheat, over the past two centuries. As can be seen, the

[9]An exception to this general rule is provided by Indian cotton textiles, which as we have seen became an increasingly important European import during the seventeenth and eighteenth centuries. The key difference between cotton textiles and commodities like pepper is that, while cotton textiles originated in India, they could be imitated by European producers, which is exactly what eventually happened: an early example of industry's inherently footloose nature.

price gap fluctuated widely, around an average of about 100%, up to 1840 or so, after which it collapsed in dramatic fashion, and this was at precisely the same time that Britain started importing wheat from the U.S. The timing coincides neatly with the decline in transport costs from about mid century documented in the previous section, and particularly with Harley's (1988) freight rate index. Over the course of the nineteenth century, transoceanic trade in bulk commodities such as grains, metals, and textiles became more and more common. One implication was that long-distance trade now began to displace domestic producers in large numbers, be they Indian textile producers or European farmers. European land found itself in direct competition with the vast and fertile land endowments of the New World, while Indian weavers found themselves outcompeted by European technology and capital. The result was that long-distance trade began to have economy-wide effects on the allocation of resources, and hence on factor prices and the distribution of income, just as two Swedish observers of the period, Eli Heckscher and Bertil Ohlin, predicted (Flam and Flanders 1991; O'Rourke et al. 1996; O'Rourke and Williamson 1999, chapter 4).

Figure 7.3 makes the point clearly, for one European economy, Britain. From 1500 onward the land–labor ratio trended downward, as population grew, but land endowments remained fixed. In a textbook closed economy, where commodity and factor prices are determined by domestic supply and demand, this should have had two effects. First, the demand for food should have risen relative to the supply of food, and the relative price of food should thus have gone up. Second, the ratio of wages to land rents should have declined, as labor became more abundant and land scarcer. As can be seen in figure 7.3(a), both these predictions held true for the period prior to 1840: the price of food rose relative to the price of manufactures, and the wage-to-rent ratio declined. After 1840, however, the story was very different (figure 7.3(b)). Despite the fact that a rising population continued to press against a fixed land endowment, and at an accelerating rate, the relative price of food stopped rising, and eventually started to fall, while the ratio of wages to land rents started to rise.

In other words, at some point in the decades following 1815, British commodity and factor prices stopped being determined primarily by British endowments of land and labor, and this reflects the opening up of the British economy to long-distance trade in competing commodities such as grain. Domestic relative prices were now increasingly determined by world market conditions, rather than by domestic supply and demand. As transport costs fell, food supplies from the New

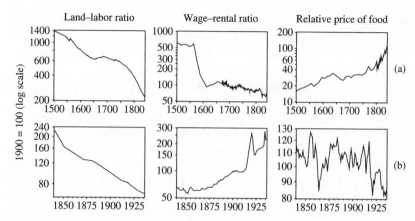

FIGURE 7.3. Endowments and relative prices, Britain 1500–1936 (1900 = 100):
(a) 1500–1840; (b) 1840–1936. *Source:* O'Rourke and Williamson (2005).

World and Ukraine prevented British food prices from rising further,
and eventually led them to fall. In turn, the decline in relative food
prices put downward pressure on British land prices and land rents,
while cheap food benefited British workers.

It was not just in Britain that trade began to have this impact
on economy-wide factor prices and income distribution. We have
abundant evidence on late-nineteenth-century relative factor prices,
compiled by O'Rourke et al. (1996) and Jeffrey Williamson, in a series
of papers summarized in Williamson (2002). These papers present
data on w/r, the ratio of the unskilled, urban wage to the returns
to agricultural land. This was the key relative factor price in an era
when agriculture was still an important component of the economy,
and in which intercontinental trade was largely dominated by the
exchange of resource- and land-intensive products for labor-intensive
products such as manufactured goods. The stylized fact which motivated Heckscher and Ohlin was one of the land-abundant New World
exchanging food for European manufactured goods, and their logic
suggests that in times of globalization, w/r should have converged
internationally. In land-abundant New World economies, where w/r
was high, it should have declined, and in land-scarce European
economies, where w/r was low, it should have increased. In absolute
terms, European wages (which were low, as a result of the limited land
available per worker) should have caught up with New World wages
(which were high, as a result of the New World's vast land and resource
endowments), while low New World land prices should have caught

up with high European land prices. By and large, these predictions hold good for the late nineteenth century (O'Rourke and Williamson 1999, chapter 4).

Moreover, those Third World countries that participated in the late-nineteenth-century global economy experienced similar trends (Williamson 2002, table 3, p. 73). In land-scarce economies such as Japan, Korea, and Taiwan, the wage–rental ratio increased substantially, while it fell sharply in land-abundant food-exporting nations and regions such as Argentina, Uruguay, Burma, Siam, Egypt, and the Punjab. Finally, econometrics and simulation exercises indicate that commodity market integration was indeed a key factor driving these international factor price trends (O'Rourke and Williamson 1994, 1999; O'Rourke et al. 1996).

As we will see, this fact had crucial implications for the nature of trade politics. Before 1815, as previous chapters have documented extensively, international trade had been seen by governments as a means of extracting rents, by driving a wedge between the prices paid to producers in one location and those paid by consumers in another. The question then was who was going to get these rents, and as we have seen the result was international competition between overseas trading companies, and frequent warfare in the age of mercantilism. Trade-related conflict was thus inherently *inter*national in nature. Cheaper transportation and intercontinental trade in competing goods implied that the politics of trade would now also involve *intra*national conflict, between those groups in society who gained as a result of intercontinental trade and those who lost.[10] Where the losers were sufficiently powerful politically, the result was defensive tariffs, designed to insulate them from the negative effects of declining transport costs. We will see later how these political pressures would play out in practice over the course of the late nineteenth century.

NINETEENTH-CENTURY IMPERIALISM

There is one further factor that was favorable to nineteenth-century globalization that we need to address at this stage, however briefly. The Industrial Revolution not only led to the economic asymmetries that will be the focus of much of this chapter and the next, but to

---

[10]Indeed, it would mean that international conflict over who would "get the rents" would become less and less important. Trying to monopolize the spice trade was difficult enough, but trying to monopolize the grain trade would have been merely silly.

military and political asymmetries as well. Three European states in particular, the United Kingdom, France, and Russia, exploited these asymmetries to expand into Asia and Africa over the course of the nineteenth century. They did so not just at the expense of local rulers, but also of weaker imperial rivals such as the Ottomans, who lost out in North Africa to the British and French, in the Black Sea region to the Russians, and in the Balkans to the forces unleashed by nineteenth-century European nationalism, with Greece gaining independence as early as 1832. Meanwhile another "European" power, namely the British offshoot of the United States, was embarking on a rather similar program of imperial expansion, mostly at the expense of native American tribes.

As we noted earlier, the ability of the European powers to extend their sway so drastically was greatly assisted by the new technologies of the Industrial Revolution. According to Headrick (1981, p. 3), Europe increased the proportion of the Earth's surface it controlled from 37% in 1800 to 67% in 1878, and 84% by 1914. He attributes this dramatic expansion to the interaction of two factors: the power of the new technology, and commercial and geopolitical motives for domination over the land and resources of Asia and Africa. Headrick divides the process into three successive phases: penetration, conquest, and incorporation into the expanding world economy, through the provision of transport and communications infrastructure. A surprisingly important role in the first of these phases was played by shallow-draft armed steamboats sailing up rivers such as the Irrawaddy in the Anglo-Burmese wars and the Yangtze in the Opium Wars, and easily overcoming the war-canoes and war-junks sent against them. In the second half of the nineteenth century the breech-loading rifle and the machine gun rendered most battles against colonial forces hopelessly one-sided affairs. Perhaps as important as greater firepower, however, was the prophylactic use of quinine, discovered by the Jesuits in Latin America, against malaria, enabling the safe penetration and conquest of large tracts of Africa and Asia by European traders, missionaries, soldiers, and administrators.

By and large, the Europeans used the power thus acquired to impose freer trading conditions on the rest of the world. The most infamous example is probably the Opium Wars that Britain waged against China during 1839–42 and 1856–60. The East India Company had lost its remaining monopoly, on trade with China, in 1833 as a result of pressure from merchants wishing to boost sales of textiles and opium there. When the Chinese banned opium imports in 1839, war was declared, with China being easily defeated by a small British military force. Under the Treaty of Nanking (1842), Britain was granted Hong Kong, five ports including Shanghai were opened to free trade, and Chinese tariffs were fixed at just 5%. The excuse for the second war came when the Chinese boarded a British vessel, the *Arrow*. The French joined in this war on the British side, and the resulting Treaty of Tientsin opened more foreign ports as well as the Yangtze River to international commerce, and legalized the opium trade (Cain and Hopkins 2002, pp. 282, 362–63). As we will see later, China was not the only nominally independent Asian country to have free trade forced upon it during this period.

Formal empire was also proceeding apace in Asia. In India, yet another Anglo-Irishman, Lord Moira, was appointed governor-general of Bengal in 1813. Under his command the East India Company defeated the Gurkhas of Nepal, as well as the Pindari horsemen who periodically raided British-held territory. During the latter war he also defeated various Pindari allies, notably the Maratha ruler or *peshwa*, as well as Najpur and Indore. In 1818 Rajasthan accepted the suzerainty of the EIC. By 1820 all India as far as the frontiers of the Punjab had been brought under British control. Raffles set up a British colony in Singapore in 1819, Britain acquired Melaka in 1824, and over the rest of the century it gradually gained control over what would become known as British Malaya. The British also conquered most of the Burmese coastline in 1826 (Lloyd 1996, pp. 147–48) as a result of the first Anglo-Burmese war. There followed a series of further acquisitions in mid century: Sind, the Punjab, Berar, and Oudh. The final chapter came in 1857, when the Bengal army mutinied, captured Delhi, and proclaimed its allegiance to Bahadur Shah II, the elderly Mughal leader. After a brutal struggle the revolt was suppressed, the British government took over responsibility for running India from the EIC, and Bahadur was exiled to Rangoon, Lower Burma having been occupied and annexed in the second Anglo-Burmese war of 1852.

Meanwhile, in a move which would come back to haunt the Western powers in the following century, the French gained control over Cambodia, Laos, Cochinchina, and ultimately all of Vietnam. In turn, the establishment of what became known as French Indochina was one of the factors prompting the British to conquer all of Burma in 1885, bringing the last Burmese royal dynasty to an end, after which they ran the country as an Indian province, although it always retained its separate identity. By this stage the only independent state remaining in Southeast Asia was Siam, which served as a convenient neutral buffer state between the French and British possessions in the region (ibid., pp. 233–34); and even Siam eventually lost its Laotian possessions to the French.

In North Africa, Algeria, Tunisia, and Tripolitania had all established de facto independence from the Ottoman Empire early in the eighteenth century, although formally they remained under Turkish suzerainty. The nineteenth century would see all three states, as well as Morocco (which had never succumbed to the Ottomans) and Egypt, falling under European domination. In April 1827, the last of the Algerian *deys*, Huseyn, struck the French consul Deval with a fly-whisk, in anger at France's failure to repay moneys owed as a result of grain purchases between 1793 and 1798. After three years of blockades and unsuccessful negotiations, the French government invaded Algeria in 1830, and "France found itself engaged in a colonial enterprise which it had neither really wanted nor seriously prepared" (Raymond 1970, p. 285). By 1847, the Algerian resistance leader, Abd El-Kader, had finally been forced to surrender, and Algeria became a French settler colony.

The invasion unsettled the existing political equilibrium throughout North Africa. While the rulers of Tunis initially welcomed the defeat of their Algerian rivals, Tunisia gradually fell more and more under European influence, and a French protectorate was established there in 1881. Morocco found itself at war with the French in 1844, when Abd El-Kader sought refuge there, and with the Spanish in 1859 as a result of a dispute regarding the boundaries of Ceuta. In 1912 Morocco also became a French protectorate. In Tripolitania, the Ottomans reestablished direct rule in 1835, but eventually lost the colony following the war with Italy of 1911–12. Finally, in Egypt Ottoman weakness had already been revealed in 1798, when Napoleon successfully invaded Egypt: it took the intervention of the British in 1801 to restore Ottoman power there. Even more strikingly, when the Albanian governor of Egypt, Muhammad 'Ali, invaded Syria in 1831, his military successes threatened the very existence of the Ottoman Empire itself, which had to be bailed out by the Russians in 1833 and the British and Austrians in 1840 (Holt 1970, pp. 383–84). French and British influence, both economic and political, then increased in Egypt, where as a result of the Suez Canal they now had vital financial and strategic interests, until the British established a de facto protectorate there in 1882.

In sub-Saharan Africa, the British already held the Cape Colony, which they had seized from the Dutch in 1806, and were granted permanently at the Congress of Vienna. They also had several bases in West Africa, notably in Freetown in Sierra Leone from which the Royal Navy attempted to interdict the slave trade, and to which it returned liberated slaves. In the late nineteenth century, adventurers such as Cecil Rhodes and George Goldie would use these bases as platforms from which to mount gigantic land grabs on behalf of private companies, with the government subsequently stepping in to establish formal British rule in the territories thus seized. Eventually, virtually the entire continent was partitioned between various European powers, in the so-called "Scramble for Africa" of the period from 1880 onwards (Pakenham 1991). The British and French were to the fore in this, but the most infamous example of European brutality in Africa remains the "Congo Free State" ruled by Leopold II, king of Belgium, control of which was eventually transferred to the Belgian state as a result of international outrage at the treatment of its inhabitants. From this period on, African markets became increasingly important for European manufacturers. Thus, Africa accounted for less than 3% of British exports in the mid nineteenth century, but for 4.3% in 1890 and 8.3% in 1906 (Cain and Hopkins 2002, p. 309).

While France and Britain expanded their empires overseas, Russia expanded hers overland. To the west, she acquired control over Finland in 1809 (from Sweden), Bessarabia in 1812 (from the Ottomans), and Poland (as a result of the Third Partition of 1795 and the Congress of Vienna of 1815). However, from that point onwards her gains would exclusively be made in the east and the south (although she intervened on several occasions on behalf of fellow Slavs such as the Serbs and Bulgarians, who were rebelling against Ottoman rule). There were early advances in the Caucasus, including Georgia (1801), northern Azerbaijan (1813), and Yerevan (1828), the latter two regions being seized from Persia. The Chechens were only subdued in 1859, however, and the Circassians in 1864, after decades of brutal conflict (Longworth 2005, pp. 200–7). Progress was easier in Central Asia, where the Russians consolidated their control over Kazakhstan, and advanced into Turkistan, taking Chimkent, Tashkent, Samarkand, Khiva, Kokand, and Bukhara (ibid., pp. 216–17). The process eventually led to clashes with Afghan forces in 1885, and to a crisis with Britain which, alarmed by Russian expansion, had already secretly helped the Circassians during the 1830s and openly come to the aid of the Ottomans during the Crimean War of 1853–56. The ensuing negotiations led to Anglo-Russian agreement about their respective spheres of influence, and halted Russian expansion in this direction.

Further to the east, however, Russian imperialism kept up its momentum, occupying Sakhalin, as well as the adjacent mainland south of the Amur River, where it constructed the naval base of Vladivostok that would eventually become the terminus of the trans-Siberian railway. The Amur region was acquired from the Chinese, and yet the Russians managed to keep on good terms with that nation, eventually establishing a sphere of influence in Manchuria and obtaining the right to connect Vladivostok to the trans-Siberian railway through there. As we will see, this process eventually led to conflict with the rising power in the region, Japan.

Americans pride themselves, and perhaps rightly so, on their "exceptionalism" compared with the European countries from which most of their ancestors emigrated. Thus they often tend to assume that while Europeans established a succession of empires by the unjust conquest of Asian and African peoples and territories, they themselves have expanded peacefully within their own natural boundaries, intervening abroad only to defeat tyrannies and defend the liberty of less fortunate others. When they think of the founders of the national myth, the Puritans of New England, they prefer not to think of them falling "on their knees, and then upon the aborigines," but rather of a "shining city on a hill," springing from "the fresh, green breast of the New World." Indeed, much of the westward expansion of the early United States was by purchase of territory: Louisiana from Napoleon in 1803 for $15 million, Florida from the Spanish in 1819 for $5 million, and Alaska from the Russians in 1867 for $7 million. "Never did a state buy so much for so little," as Raymond Aron (1974, p. xxviii) wryly remarks.

But violence and conquest were by no means eschewed, with native Americans as the main victims. There was also the 1846–48 war against Mexico, a "disgraceful affair" as Hugh Brogan (1986, p. 305) calls it, which acquired the vast extent of Arizona, New Mexico, Utah, Colorado, Nevada, and California for the young "imperial republic." The war itself had largely been provoked by the 1845 annexation of a willing Republic of Texas, set up by American settlers who had successfully rebelled against Mexico and declared its independence in 1836. The 1823 Monroe Doctrine, declaring the Western Hemisphere out of bounds to intervention by European powers, was in effect declaring it a sphere of influence of the United States, with no explicit reference to the wishes of the Latin American colonials, then rebelling themselves against the Spanish Empire. The Doctrine could only be sustained by the power of the Royal Navy, which prevented potential European rivals from any possibility of action across the Atlantic, a nice instance of "free-riding" by the weaker partner of a coalition on the stronger. The reciprocal "concession" was for the United States to refrain from any interventions in Europe, in conformity with George Washington's warnings against entangling alliances with foreign powers.

The westward expansion of the United States across the continent, facilitated by the railroads and fueled by rising immigration from Europe, was particularly rapid in the decades following the end of the Civil War in 1865, with native Americans being swept aside with contemptuous ease, although they resisted bravely. The frontier was officially declared closed in 1890, which implied that henceforth the land–labor ratio would be falling, setting in a stage of diminishing returns. There followed the depression of 1893 and widespread labor agitation, and populist agrarian agitation against the deflationary monetary policies associated with the gold standard. In addition, Germany, Russia, and Japan were asserting their increasing influence in the world, based on their rapid industrialization, arousing fears that the United States would fall behind in what was believed to be a ruthless Darwinian struggle for economic and political supremacy.

As Richard Hofstadter (1967, chapter 5) has explained brilliantly, this national mood, a mixture of anxiety, belligerence, and belief in the "Manifest Destiny" of the United States to lead the world, found its outlet in the Spanish–American War of 1898. The war began with the best of intentions, to assist Cuban rebels against Spanish oppression, and was touched off by the as yet unexplained explosion of the USS *Maine* in Havana. The U.S. Navy and an expeditionary force that included Theodore Roosevelt and his "Rough Riders," who took part in a famous charge at the Battle of San Juan Hill, soon defeated the Spanish forces. An unfounded fear that a Spanish fleet from the Philippines might attack the West Coast of the United States led to an American Far Eastern Squadron, under the command of Commodore George Dewey, being dispatched from Hong Kong, which destroyed the Spanish fleet in Manila Bay without the loss of a single man. By a familiar logic, or rather illogic, of war the victorious American naval squadron had to be "protected" from land-based enemy action by an occupying force, setting off hostilities with rebellious Filipinos intent on securing their own independence from Spain. Thus a war by America to liberate the Cubans from Spanish oppression ended with America engaged in the brutal suppression of a Filipino insurgency. Once acquired, the usual arguments for holding on to the fruits of conquest were made, namely that the Filipinos were unable to govern themselves and that, besides, the islands were valuable as a gateway to the illusory riches of the China market. Protestant missionaries were also anxious to save the Filipinos from the wrong sort of Christianity, while resistance by Muslim Filipinos, known as Moros, was particularly fierce and sustained, and was only suppressed with particular brutality. The unintended consequence of all these actions was the acquisition of Cuba, Puerto Rico, the Philippines, and Guam.

Hawaii was also annexed to the United States in 1898. The islands, discovered by Captain James Cook in 1778, had been used as a port of call for whalers, and developed a sugar industry on the basis of American capital and mainly immigrant labor in the second half of the nineteenth century. The 1876 Reciprocity Treaty gave Hawaiian sugar duty-free access to the U.S. market, raising the prices which its producers received. As a result of this, the Hawaiian sugar acreage rose more than tenfold between 1870 and 1890, stimulating a large inflow of Chinese and Japanese labor, and giving the largely American plantation owners a powerful vested interest in continued preferential access to the American market (La Croix and Grandy 1997, pp. 172–73). Increased dependence of the Hawaiian economy on the United States in turn increased U.S. bargaining power, which is how Pearl Harbor came to be conceded to the United States in 1887, much to the distress of France and Britain. The harbor proved useful to the Americans during the Spanish–American War, but native Hawaiians resented this concession, creating a split between native and planter opinion. When the McKinley tariff of 1890 abolished American sugar duties, replacing them with a domestic production subsidy which benefited U.S. producers, but not Hawaiian plantations, this set the stage for a decisive split between the two sides, since it gave planters a powerful incentive to bring about the incorporation of Hawaii within the United States (ibid.). The last native ruler of Hawaii, Queen Lili'uokalani, made vain attempts to resist American domination, but was deposed in 1893, after which a republic was declared before the eventual annexation five years later.

An 1876 report of the U.S. House Committee on Ways and Means asserted bluntly that "the Pacific Ocean is an American Ocean...the future great highway between ourselves and the hundreds of millions of Asiatics who look to us for commerce, civilization, and Christianity" (ibid., p. 168). Consistent with this belief, the United States took the lead in opening up Japan to trade with the West when Commodore Perry entered Tokyo Bay, uninvited, in 1853, setting off Japan's remarkable drive to modernization after the Meiji Restoration of 1868. Trade and missionary activity in China led public opinion in the United States to develop strong feelings of sympathy for the country and people. Thus when Secretary of State John Hay in 1899 urged Japan and the European great powers to maintain an "Open Door" to trade and investment by all foreign nations, and respect the "territorial and administrative integrity of China" instead of carving it up into separate spheres of influence, this was highly popular at home, even though it was honored more often in the breach than in the observance, even by the United States itself. Finally, with colonial possessions in both the Atlantic and the Pacific, it was natural for the United States to pursue a project for linking the two oceans by a canal across the narrow Isthmus of Panama. When difficulties with Colombia, on whose territory the site was located, arose regarding permission to construct the Canal, it was a simple matter to arrange a "revolution" that established the independent Republic of Panama, which signed a 99-year lease for $10 million and an annual payment of $250,000, ratified by the U.S. Senate in 1904. The Canal was eventually turned over to Panama at the end of 1999.

All of these empires typically forced free trade policies on their newly conquered territories, and promoted railroad construction for both economic and strategic reasons. Imperialism was thus a major driver of nineteenth-century globalization.[11] The technologies of the Industrial Revolution were the other major driver of globalization during the period, as we have seen. By contrast, where countries were free to choose their own trade policy, and especially in the self-governing republics and dominions of the New World, tariffs remained generally high between Waterloo and the Great War.

Nineteenth-Century Trade Policy[12]

Nineteenth-century trade policies varied dramatically between continents. In Europe, the broad picture is one of gradual liberalization until the 1870s, which reinforced the impact of declining transport costs, followed by a protectionist backlash which muted (but did not overturn) the integrating effects of the new transport technologies. In the Americas, and to a lesser extent in Australasia, tariffs were high throughout the nineteenth century. As we have seen, Western powers imposed free trade on China, and something similar happened both in those territories absorbed into European empires, as well as in other states in Asia and Africa that managed to retain their independence.

In the immediate aftermath of the Napoleonic Wars, European trade policies were almost universally protectionist. The initial exceptions to this general rule were smaller countries such as the Netherlands,

---

[11] In his well-known book, Niall Ferguson has gone so far as to coin the phrase "Anglobalization" to describe the phenomenon, claiming that "no organization in history has done more to promote the free movement of goods, capital and labour than the British Empire in the nineteenth and early twentieth centuries" (Ferguson 2003, p. xxi).

[12] This section draws heavily on O'Rourke and Williamson (1999, chapters 3, 6), who in turn largely rely on Bairoch (1989), the standard reference on European trade policy in this period.

which adopted a relatively liberal trade policy in 1819, and Denmark, which had already abolished import prohibitions and adopted low tariffs as early as 1797. The first major economy to liberalize was Britain, where power was shifting to export-oriented urban interests. A series of liberal reforms in the 1820s and 1830s were followed by Robert Peel's momentous decision to abolish the Corn Laws in 1846, and move the United Kingdom to a unilateral free trade policy stance, against the objections of landlords and much of his own Tory party (Schonhardt-Bailey 2006; O'Rourke and Williamson 1999, chapter 5). What was true for Britain was true for other countries as well. The years after 1846 saw further moves toward liberalization in countries such as Austria–Hungary, Spain, the Netherlands, Belgium, Sweden, Norway, and Denmark (Bairoch 1989, pp. 20–36). As Accominotti and Flandreau (2006) show, average tariffs were falling throughout the 1850s in the major European powers.

A further breakthrough came in 1860, with the Anglo-French Cobden–Chevalier Treaty. This treaty abolished all French import prohibitions as well as the British export duty on coal, and lowered British tariffs on wine. The treaty also established most-favored-nation (MFN) relations between the two countries, and laid the basis for a series of further bilateral trade deals between the countries of Western Europe, all of which incorporated an MFN clause. Even though tariff-cutting was already underway in Europe by the time of the treaty (ibid.), the nondiscriminatory nature of the MFN principle greatly strengthened the multilateral nature of the nineteenth-century trade regime, to which we drew attention earlier in connection with the demise of eighteenth-century mercantilist privileges. MFN clauses also implied that bilateral concessions were automatically generalized to all participants in this network of treaties, which must have speeded up tariff reductions during this period. According to Bairoch (1989), average tariffs on the European mainland had fallen to some 9–12% by the mid 1870s, by which stage "Germany had virtually become a free trade country" (p. 41).

Until the 1870s, therefore, European trade policy trends were reinforcing the impact of transport cost declines. Things would soon change, however, as a result of the growing impact of intercontinental trade on factor prices highlighted earlier. The turning point came in the late 1870s and 1880s, when the impact of cheap New World and Russian grain began to make itself felt in European markets: for example, real British land rents fell by over 50% between 1870 and 1913. Almost all of this British decline can be attributed to international commodity market integration (O'Rourke and Williamson

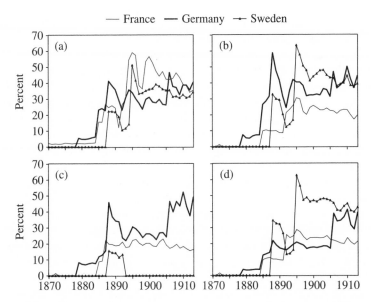

FIGURE 7.4. European grain tariffs 1870–1913 (ad valorem equivalent, percent): (a) wheat, (b) rye, (c) oats, (d) barley. *Source:* data underlying O'Rourke (1997).

1994). More generally, by the late nineteenth century, international trade was having a profound impact on income distribution, lowering the incomes of landowners relative to those of workers throughout Europe (Lindert and Williamson 2003). Wherever landed interests were powerful enough, the legislative reaction was predictable. In Germany, Bismarck protected both agriculture and industry in 1879; in France, tariffs were raised in the 1880s, and again in 1892; in Sweden, agricultural protection was reimposed in 1888 and industrial protection was increased in 1892; in Italy, moderate tariffs were imposed in 1878, followed by more severe tariffs in 1887 (although this was not enough to prevent mass emigration from the countryside (see Kindleberger 1951)).

Figure 7.4 gives ad valorem equivalent tariffs for the four major European grains (wheat, barley, oats, and rye) in three countries (France, Germany, and Sweden). The figure shows that protection was particularly high for wheat in France, for rye and oats in Germany, and for rye and barley in Sweden. Which grains were favored reflected political considerations: wheat was a key output of France's farming community, while Prussia's Junkers specialized in rye. In all three countries, tariffs on individual grains at times exceeded 50%. By any standard this represented heavy protection.

There was thus a common pattern across Western Europe of liberalization followed by a reversion to protection, prompted by the distributional effects of the grain invasion. There were exceptions; for example, liberalization was both shorter and less dramatic in Iberia. Some small countries remained relatively liberal: the Netherlands, Belgium, Switzerland, and Denmark, which managed to transform itself from a grain-exporter to a grain-importing exporter of animal products (ibid.). Most importantly, the United Kingdom also maintained free trade, despite the efforts of the Colonial Secretary, Joseph Chamberlain. In 1903 he made a speech in Birmingham in which he proposed that the British Empire become a preferential trading area, which would have required, of necessity, that the United Kingdom impose tariffs on nonempire countries. This speech marked the beginning of an intense debate on trade policy in Britain, which lasted until 1906, when a general election victory for the Liberals guaranteed that Britain would remain a free trader until the outbreak of war in 1914.

Exactly why not all countries reverted to agricultural protection has sparked an enormous political science literature (e.g., Gourevitch 1986; Rogowski 1989). Economic considerations were surely important: it turns out that countries such as Denmark and the United Kingdom which retained agricultural free trade were less vulnerable to the price and rent reductions which globalization implied. In the Danish case grain prices had been low to begin with, while the country was exceptionally well-suited to meet the growing demands of the British breakfast table, in part due to the success of its cooperative societies. In the British case, agriculture had already shrunk significantly and further decline had little impact on the overall economy (O'Rourke 1997, 2007b). Elsewhere, it seems that globalization undermined itself. Moreover, this switch toward protectionism would turn out to be permanent. Countries such as Germany, and in particular France, would remain strongly in favor of agricultural protection for the remainder of the millennium (Tracy 1989).

New World landowners benefited from exports, and thus they tended to be in favor of free trade. However, this does not mean that trade policy was more liberal in the New World than in Europe, since New World manufacturers wanted protection from European competition. As we saw above, in the United States the infant industries that sprang up during the French Wars had formed the basis for a long-standing Northern pro-tariff lobby. As a result of their efforts, the U.S. tariff on imported cotton textiles rose from around 20% in the aftermath of the 1816 tariff bill to almost 60% in the early 1840s. These interests were, however, opposed by Southern exporters of goods such as cotton and tobacco, who occasionally got the upper hand. For example, the Walker tariff of 1846 reduced protection on cotton textiles to 25% ad valorem, and the tariff was further reduced in 1857 to 24% (Irwin and Temin 2001, pp. 780–81). North–South tension over trade policy was a constant feature of American politics before the Civil War, and with Northern victory in that conflict the stage was set for consistently high tariffs. They had already been raised significantly during the war for revenue purposes, but Republican domination of Congress ensured that they would remain exceptionally high afterwards. For example, the U.S. average manufacturing tariff amounted to 44% in 1913 (League of Nations 1927, p. 15). A further indication of the protectionist nature of U.S. trade policy during the period is that, unlike most European countries, it did not subscribe to the unconditional MFN principle, which meant that it was not obliged to extend to third parties concessions which it made in a particular bilateral treaty.[13]

In Canada, support for protectionism increased after Britain's move to free trade in 1846, which removed Canada's privileged position in her major export market. It further strengthened after the U.S. Civil War, and the consequent rise in tariffs south of the border. In 1878 the Conservatives were elected on a protectionist ("National Policy") platform: the new tariff law passed in 1878 imposed tariffs on agricultural goods of between 20 and 50%, and industrial tariffs of between 20 and 30%. Tariff rates would continue to rise in the years to come, with Canada remaining protectionist for the rest of the nineteenth century (Bairoch 1989, p. 148). In Australia, pressure for protection grew in the colony of Victoria from the mid 1850s, following a decline in gold production and a consequent fall in mining employment (ibid., p. 146). The Victoria tariff bill of 1865 allowed for maximum ad valorem tariffs of 10%, but by 1893, after a succession of tariff increases, the maximum rates stood at 45% (Siriwardana 1991, p. 47). The other Australian colonies had always been less inclined to protectionism than Victoria, and the first federal tariff of 1902 was a compromise between the two sides. However, protection was greatly strengthened in 1906 and 1908 (Bairoch 1989, pp. 146–47), largely due to the stance of Australia's powerful Labor Party. New Zealand was more liberal than either Canada or Australia, but the tariff of 1888

[13]Unless, that is, those third parties extended to the United States the same concessions as had been afforded it under the treaty in question. On this conditional MFN policy, see Viner (1924).

led to average import tariffs doubling to around 20%, and subsequent tariff legislation continued the upward trend (ibid., p. 149).

As mentioned earlier, the initial effect of Latin American independence was the abolition of the colonial restrictions that had tied the continent's trade to Iberia. Shortly thereafter, however, Latin American tariffs started rising (Coatsworth and Williamson 2004). To take just two examples, the first Mexican tariff law, in 1821, imposed a 25% ad valorem tariff on all imports. Tariffs were raised substantially in 1823, and averaged 45% during the 1840s. Meanwhile, in Argentina tariffs averaged 21% in 1822 and 31% in 1836. While the third quarter of the nineteenth century saw an easing of protection in Latin America, tariffs rose again in the final quarter. Argentina increased tariffs from the 1870s onwards, as did Brazil (Bairoch 1989, pp. 150–53).

The need to raise revenue had been the main traditional motive behind Latin American tariffs. Tariffs accounted for no less than 58% of government revenue in eleven Latin American states during the seven decades after 1820 (Coatsworth and Williamson 2004, p. 26). The years following independence saw more than thirty international and civil wars in the area, implying high revenue needs, while undeveloped states and low population densities made other sources of revenue unreliable. Initially, therefore, political instability was the major factor underlying Latin American tariffs, and yet the return to greater political stability later in the century did not herald a return to lower tariff rates. Rather, the growing power of urban interests led to a deliberate attempt to boost local industry via protection. For example, the stated aim of the 1879 Brazilian tariff act was to protect domestic industry. The upshot was that by the end of the supposedly liberal belle époque, Latin America had the highest tariffs in the world. By 1913 average tariffs were almost 35% in Uruguay, almost 40% in Brazil, and over 45% in Venezuela (Bulmer-Thomas 2003, p. 139).

The picture was very different in Africa and Asia. European colonies typically had broadly free trade policies imposed upon them, the self-governing (and white) colonies mentioned earlier being the main exception. Elsewhere, independent countries were forced to follow suit, as we have seen in the case of China. This was a major pro-globalization shock in countries that had previously been relatively closed. For example, according to Paul Bairoch (1989, p. 156), China's exports in 1840 amounted to just $7 per 100 inhabitants, as opposed to $43 for the rest of Asia, $420 for Europe excluding Russia, $460 for Latin America, and $920 for the United Kingdom. It was only in the 1920s that China was accorded the right to once again set her own trade policy. Japan had been even more closed than China, but Commodore Perry's

1853 expedition led to an initial treaty which opened up two ports to foreign trade, and a further treaty in 1858 under which Japan limited herself to 5% tariffs on both imports and exports (ibid., p. 157). In less than a decade, she had switched from something close to autarky to virtual free trade, a dramatic change by any standards (Bernhofen and Brown 2004). In the subsequent fifteen years Japan's foreign trade rose seventy times, to 7% of national income (Huber 1971, p. 614). While Japan was allowed to gradually increase tariffs beginning in 1899, tariffs remained mostly low prior to 1911, when the first autonomous (and protectionist) tariff was introduced (Bairoch 1989, p. 157).

Other Asian nations had similar experiences. Thailand adopted a 3% tariff limit in 1855, while Korea started integrating economically with Japan long before being formally annexed in 1910. India and Indonesia had the liberal policies of their British and Dutch colonial masters imposed upon them as well. Russian pressure led to Iran being restricted to a maximum of 5% ad valorem duties from the early nineteenth century, and the country only regained tariff independence in 1928. The Ottoman Empire is the exception that proves the rule: her tariffs increased during the period, but this was due to the fact that they had previously been limited to 3% ad valorem following treaties signed with European powers during the early modern period, as we saw in chapter 4. An 1838 treaty with the United Kingdom allowed the empire to raise her tariffs to 5%, but at the cost of abolishing her monopolies and prohibitions. By the start of the Great War the Ottomans had been allowed to raise their tariffs to 11%, a modest degree of protection by comparison with the levels prevailing in Europe and the "regions of recent settlement," as the Americas and Australasia were known (ibid., pp. 158–60).

As we have seen, most of Africa was incorporated into the empires of various European nations during the late nineteenth century, and while the trade policies followed by the different powers varied greatly, the net effect was to substantially open the continent to international trade (ibid., pp. 103–27). As would be expected, the most liberal policies were those imposed by the British, whose colonies typically adopted low tariffs that were (after mid century) typically nondiscriminatory. French colonies' tariff policies usually discriminated more in favor of French products. In several cases (e.g., Algeria, Tunisia, and Indochina) their policies were "assimilated" with those of the mother country, meaning that they adopted French tariff policies, and that French products entered duty-free into the colonies (although the reverse tended not to be true, save in the case of Algeria). Italian and Portuguese colonies typically discriminated in favor of the colonial power, while the Belgian Congo in principle practiced a free trade policy. Some colonies, clearly, were more open to trade than others. In all cases, however, openness vis-à-vis the colonizer meant a far greater exposure to trade than would have been the case otherwise, particularly given European investments in transport infrastructure.

Table 7.3 provides an overview of tariff policies during the late nineteenth century, giving average duties on manufactured goods in 1875 and 1913. Tariffs were—uniquely—zero in Britain, and were very low in Asia, aside from Japan, which as mentioned had by 1913 regained its tariff independence and was using this to promote industrialization. In general industrial tariffs rose during the late nineteenth century in Europe (Denmark, Austria–Hungary, and the Netherlands being exceptions), and, as figure 7.4 indicated, so did agricultural tariffs: there was indeed a tariff backlash in continental Europe during this period (O'Rourke and Williamson 1999). In several European countries industrial tariffs approached or exceeded 20%. Tariffs were higher again in Canada and the United States, and were extremely high in Latin American countries such as Brazil, Colombia, and Mexico, where they were of the order of 50%. While trade policy and imperialism served to reinforce the impact of falling transport costs in the United Kingdom, Africa, and Asia, technology and politics worked in opposite directions elsewhere.[14]

COMMODITY MARKET INTEGRATION, 1815–1914

What impact did these technological and political developments have on international commodity markets? On balance, it appears that the new transport technologies were so cost-reducing that their effects swamped those of rising European and American protectionism. As we saw in chapter 5, overall intercontinental trade grew at a little over 1% per annum between 1500 and 1800. By contrast, since the end of the Napoleonic Wars it has grown at an average rate of about 3.5% per annum (Maddison 1995), although there have been sizable fluctuations in this rate over time. Despite roughly similar export growth rates, the nineteenth century was more globalizing than the

---

[14] We prefer evidence on sectoral tariffs to the frequently used average tariff, defined as the ratio of customs revenues to total imports. The latter measure does not distinguish between revenue and protective tariffs, and is subject to severe index number problems (see Irwin 1993a; Anderson and Neary 2005). By contrast, the League of Nations data in table 7.3 are unweighted averages, while Bairoch's data are more impressionistic estimates of typical or average manufacturing tariffs.

TABLE 7.3. Average tariffs on manufactured imports, 1875 and 1913
(ad valorem equivalents, percent).

	1875 (1)	1913 (2)
U.K.	0	0
Asia		
China		4–5
India		4
Iran		3–4
Japan		25–30
Thailand		2–3
Turkey		5–10
Europe		
Austria–Hungary	15–20	18
Belgium	9–10	9
Denmark	15–20	14
France	12–15	20
Germany	4–6	13
Italy	8–10	18
Netherlands	3–5	4
Norway	2–4	
Spain	15–20	41
Sweden	3–5	20
Switzerland	4–6	9
Dominions		
Australia		16
Canada		26
New Zealand		15–20
U.S.A.		44
Latin America		
Argentina		28
Brazil		50–70
Colombia		40–60
Mexico		40–50

Source: (1) Bairoch (1989, table 5, p. 42); (2) League of Nations (1927, p. 15); except for Brazil, China, Colombia, Iran, Japan, Mexico, New Zealand, Thailand, Turkey (Bairoch 1989, table 16, p. 139).

twentieth, in that the ratio of exports to GDP grew far more rapidly before 1913 than afterwards (since world trade growth was roughly equal in both periods, but world income growth was twice as high in the latter). According to Maddison (1995, p. 38, 2001, p. 127), the ratio of merchandise exports to GDP was just 1% for the world in 1820, but 7.9% in 1913.

Quantity evidence thus suggests that the nineteenth century marks a dramatic break with the past. The same picture emerges when we look at intercontinental commodity price convergence. As we have seen, there was little or no intercontinental price convergence prior to 1800. For example, figure 4.6 showed little or no price convergence for cloves and pepper between Southeast Asia and the Netherlands prior to the Napoleonic Wars. However, that figure also showed dramatic price convergence along this route for the two commodities once the wars had ended. The Amsterdam–Sumatra pepper price ratio fell from 4.4 in the 1820s (around the same level as in the 1630s) to around 2.1 in the 1880s; the coffee price ratio fell from 15.7 in the 1800s to 2.2 in the 1840s and to 1.2 in the 1880s; and the clove price ratio, which had exceeded 10 between the 1660s and 1770s, stood at 8.9 in the 1810s, but at just 1.9 in the 1820s (O'Rourke and Williamson 2002b).

There exists a vast array of evidence documenting intercontinental price convergence more generally during the nineteenth century. Figure 7.2 showed Anglo-American wheat price gaps collapsing after 1840 or so, while in a recent paper David Jacks concludes that there is evidence of a "truly international market for wheat from around 1835" (Jacks 2005, p. 399). His evidence is particularly important, since to date the literature has tended to focus on the period between 1870 and 1913, whereas in fact "much of the action in price convergence seems to have taken place well before mid-century" (ibid.). International integration seems to have progressed throughout the nineteenth century, rather than being a feature of the late nineteenth century alone. Nor was it restricted to the international wheat market. Because of the well-documented nature of both economies, Anglo-American price convergence has been extensively studied: London–Cincinnati price differentials for bacon were 92.5% in 1870, over 100 in 1880, 92.3 in 1895, but 17.9 in 1913 (O'Rourke and Williamson 1994, p. 900). Price gaps for manufactured goods (which were initially dearer in the United States) were falling as well: from 13.7% in 1870 to –3.6% in 1913 for cotton textiles, from 75 to 20.6% for iron bars, from 85.2 to 19.3% for pig iron, and from 32.7 to –0.1% for copper (ibid.).

Moreover, price convergence was not limited to the North Atlantic economy. Liverpool cotton prices exceeded their Alexandria equivalents by 42.1% in 1824–32 and by 40.8% during 1863–67, but by just 5.3% during the last decade of the nineteenth century (Issawi 1966, pp. 447–48). Meanwhile, in Asia, as we have seen, trade policy strengthened the impact of technological developments. The

Liverpool–Bombay cotton price gap fell from 57% to 20% between 1873 and 1913, while the London–Calcutta jute price gap fell from 35% to 4% and the London–Rangoon rice price gap fell from 93% to 26% (Collins 1996, table 4). Relative price changes were even more dramatic in Japan after it opened up in 1858. Its two main exports were raw silk and tea (the latter having been introduced to the country by the Dutch in the early nineteenth century). Between 1846–55 and 1871–79, the price of raw silk rose by 50% in Japan, where it had been relatively low, but by just 19% in world markets, while the price of cheap tea rose by 64% in Japan, but by just 10% elsewhere (Huber 1971, p. 618). Meanwhile, the bar iron price gap between Japan and London fell from 468% to 115%; the nail price gap between Osaka and Hamburg fell from 400% to 32%; the ginned cotton price gap vis-à-vis Manchester fell from 106% to 1%, the cotton yarn price gap fell from 175% to 51%, and the cotton cloth price gap fell from 160% to 32%; and the refined sugar price gap vis-à-vis Hamburg fell from 271% to 39% (ibid., p. 620).

Commodity market integration in the late nineteenth century was thus worldwide in its extent. Indeed, Williamson (2002) argues that Third World economies were becoming more rapidly integrated with the rest of the world than rich countries during the late nineteenth century. This is of course what you would expect, given the European tariff backlash of the late nineteenth century: O'Rourke (1997) shows that grain tariffs were sufficiently high to seriously impede price convergence between countries such as France and Germany, on the one hand, and grain-exporting regions on the other. Where no such backlash was permitted, price convergence was correspondingly more impressive. Nor was the effect limited to transoceanic price gaps, since the railroad had similar effects in the interiors of continents. Jacob Metzer (1974) documents an impressive decline in grain price dispersion within Russia after 1870, while John Hurd (1975) does the same for India, and Williamson (1974, p. 259) provides similar evidence for the United States. As we saw earlier, railways played a crucial role in integrating markets worldwide as well as nationally, linking peasant producers in the interior to coastal ports, and thus to consumers overseas.

One further dimension of this integration bears mentioning. As we have seen, the beginning of the nineteenth century saw the end of mercantilist attempts to monopolize bilateral trade routes between "mother countries" and colonies, while the MFN principle further advanced the cause of multilateral, as opposed to bilateral, trade by opposing discriminatory trade policies. As figure 7.5 shows, the outcome was an international trading system that was indeed profoundly

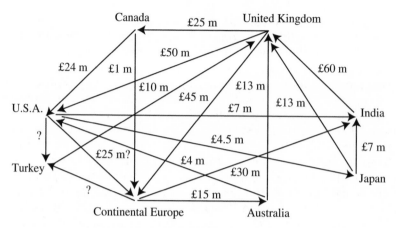

FigURE 7.5. World pattern of settlements, 1910. *Source:* Saul (1960, p. 58).

multilateral, with countries and regions running up surpluses with some partners which they then used to pay off deficits elsewhere. A particularly well-known example is India, which ran surpluses on its trade with continental Europe, the United States, Japan, and China (the latter not being included in the figure) in order to settle a large deficit with the United Kingdom. The United Kingdom, in turn, relied on its surpluses with India (and, to a lesser extent, with Australia, Japan, the Ottoman Empire, and China) to finance its deficits vis-à-vis continental Europe and the United States (Saul 1960, pp. 57–58). The United States's surpluses vis-à-vis Britain and Canada were offset by its deficits vis-à-vis continental Europe, Japan, and India; and so on. As A. J. Latham (1978, pp. 67–70) points out, Asia thus played a crucial role in the international trading system, in that the United Kingdom's unilateral commitment to free trade, which underpinned the system as a whole, would have been difficult to sustain had it not been able to offset its growing deficits vis-à-vis the other industrial economies by means of its surpluses with the East.

In turn, the multilateral system relied on convertible currencies, and thus on national and international monetary stability, which in the late nineteenth century was provided by the gold standard. This did not abolish exchange rate fluctuations, since exchange rates could fluctuate within a narrow band defined by the cost of transporting gold, and countries could and did move onto and off gold. However, the gold standard limited exchange rate fluctuations between countries, and recent econometric work clearly shows that gold standard adherence promoted trade between countries. López-Córdova and Meissner

(2003) conclude that trade between pairs of countries may have been boosted by some 30% when both countries were on gold, and both Estevadeordal et al. (2003) and Flandreau and Maurel (2005) concur that gold standard membership promoted trade (although there is disagreement regarding both the size of the effect and the mechanism explaining it). An implication is that the gradual spread of the gold standard during the late nineteenth century was one of the factors underlying that period's trade boom.

COMPLEMENTARY FACTOR FLOWS AND THE GREAT FRONTIER

The late nineteenth century did not just see unparalleled commodity market integration: it was marked by unprecedented international factor flows as well. Indeed, as far as migration is concerned, the late nineteenth century seems to have been more globalized than today. Although barriers to immigration were being erected by the end of the period (Timmer and Williamson 1998; O'Rourke and Williamson 1999, chapter 10; Hatton and Williamson 2005), by and large the late nineteenth century stands out as a relatively liberal interlude in terms of migration policy, and falling transport costs eventually led to huge migration flows (roughly 60 million Europeans emigrated to the New World between 1820 and 1914).

At the beginning of the century, transport costs remained high, free labor flows were still small, and intercontinental migration was dominated by slavery. During the 1820s, free immigration into the Americas averaged a mere 15,380 per annum, compared with a slave inflow of 60,250 per annum. By the 1840s, the free inflow had increased to 178,530 per annum (and the slave inflow had declined to 44,510 per annum (Chiswick and Hatton 2003, p. 68)), although it was not until the 1880s that more Europeans had migrated, cumulatively, than Africans (Eltis 1983, p. 255). In the third quarter of the nineteenth century, European intercontinental emigration averaged around 300,000 per annum. The numbers more than doubled in the next two decades, and rose to more than 1 million per annum after 1900 (Chiswick and Hatton 2003, figure 2.1, p. 69), with Italians and Eastern Europeans adding to the traditional outflow from northwest Europe.

There was also substantial emigration from India and China during the period (Hatton and Williamson 2005, chapter 7): 6.3 million Indians settled abroad between 1834 and 1937, with 13.6% of them going to the Caribbean, the Pacific, and Africa. Most went to other Asian countries, however, and in particular to Ceylon, Malaya, and (especially) Burma. Similarly, 8.2 million Chinese were living abroad in 1922, but again most of these were in Asia. Given the size of the two countries' populations, these numbers represented low emigration rates, with poverty traps preventing would-be emigrants from leaving (ibid.). Nonetheless, these migration flows could be considerable from the point of view of the recipient countries. For example, in 1911 nearly 30% of the Malayan population was Chinese, and a further 10% was Indian (Latham 1978, p. 109).

As for intercontinental capital flows, these were also substantial (Obstfeld and Taylor 2004). Foreign investments were 7% of world GDP in 1870 but almost 20% on the eve of World War I, a figure that was not equaled until roughly 1980 (p. 55). Between 1870 and 1914, Britain exported capital at an average rate of 4.5% of its GDP, and as much as 8–10% during lending booms, while inflows were just as important in such major borrowing nations as Argentina, Australia, and Canada (pp. 59–60). A crucial technological innovation facilitating the integration of international capital markets was the telegraph, with the first transoceanic line (between Ireland and Newfoundland) being inaugurated in 1865. For the first time ever, information could cross oceans within the space of a day, greatly facilitating financial arbitrage. The telegraph led to immediate declines in intercontinental price gaps for financial assets, and seems to have promoted commodity trade as well. It allowed tramp ships to respond far more flexibly to demands for their services, and was crucial in coordinating the activities of railroads (Garbade and Silber 1978; Lew and Cater 2006).

The common characteristic of both these factor flows is that they were directed toward land-abundant and resource-abundant regions. Clearly, the European mass migrations to the New World fall into this category, but so do the Indian migrations to Burma, for example (where the British government was trying to reclaim swamp and jungle, so as to increase rice production). As far as capital flows were concerned, two-thirds of British overseas investment in 1907–13 went to the "regions of recent settlement" (Taylor and Williamson 1994, table 1, p. 350). It was not the case that capital chased cheap labor (since the "regions of recent settlement" were high-wage destinations); rather, both labor and capital chased cheap land.

The Voyages of Discovery had increased the per capita European land endowment by a factor of six (Jones 2003, p. 83; Webb 1952), but in order for this windfall to have its full economic impact the land had to be brought into cultivation, and the produce of the land had to be transported to consumers in the great urban centers of Europe and the New World. New species, silver, and colonial goods had all had a major impact on Eurasia, as we have seen, but the Americas would only realize their full potential in the world economy when ships leaving their shores were filled with such humble everyday items as wheat or beef. Clearing and cultivating the land involved heavy investments of labor and capital, and only made economic sense if railroads were available to transport the resultant output to lucrative but distant markets. In turn, constructing railroads also required heavy investments of labor and capital, while the new populations who settled the frontier needed towns, roads, and other social infrastructure. Providing these required still more labor and capital. New World economies were labor and capital scarce. Thus, in order for them to extend their frontiers they needed to import European factors of production, and in turn such investments only made sense if the agricultural output produced on the frontier had a ready market in Europe. Thus, three of the most notable features of the late-nineteenth-century international economy—the growth of intercontinental trade, the extension of New World frontiers, and intercontinental factor flows—were deeply interrelated with each other.

There is abundant empirical evidence documenting these interrelationships. For example, about 70% of late-nineteenth-century British overseas investments went into railroads, municipal sewage, and other social overhead investments required in rapidly expanding frontier societies. Railroads alone accounted for about 41% of the total in 1913 (Feis 1930, p. 27). Second, as Knick Harley (1978, 1980) has convincingly shown, frontier expansion was intimately linked with the extension of wheat cultivation. The expansion of the area under crops in the United States was a positive function of the wheat price: as wheat prices rose, more land came under cultivation (Harley 1978). Moreover, railroad construction in the New World moved in long cycles, with peaks in railroad construction coinciding with peaks in European factor exports to the New World. Furthermore, these peaks in railroad construction tended to be preceded by peaks in wheat prices (Harley 1980). Long swings in European emigration and capital exports to the New World can thus be explained as follows: high wheat prices provided an incentive for railroad construction and frontier expansion, which in turn led to intercontinental factor flows. As the new land was cultivated and started to produce wheat, which was transported to the coasts by railroad and hence to Europe, wheat supplies in urban areas rose and wheat prices fell. This lowered the incentive to extend the frontier further, but eventually, once supplies had stopped rising, and further urban growth had led to increased demand, wheat prices once again rose and the cycle was repeated.

This process of extensive growth in the frontier economies, fueled by an expansion in the inputs of land, labor, and capital, relied to a large extent on open European markets, since investments in transport infrastructure and frontier extension were geared toward supplying Europe with agricultural products: not just grain, but meat, wool, and dairy products as well. Eighteenth-century New World exports had also consisted of agricultural output, but the commodities involved were for the most part warm-climate goods that could not easily be produced in Europe. The New World's late-nineteenth-century exports, by contrast, largely involved temperate zone agricultural goods, which competed directly with European crops, and were thus as we have seen potentially menaced with trade sanctions. In this context, the fact that the largest European market, Britain, was kept open throughout the late nineteenth century (and that her Navy kept the high seas free for international commerce) played a critical role in keeping the international system functioning.

It is worth speculating about the ways in which this interrelated system would have been different if any of these links had broken down.[15] If British markets had not remained open, it would have been less attractive financially to invest in railways and frontier extension. The frontier economies would thus have grown more slowly, and would have pulled in fewer European immigrants, which in turn would have meant slower European wage growth. The frontier economies would also have grown more slowly if they had had to rely on their own savings, rather than being able to borrow from British investors. If the frontier had not expanded, then European grain prices would have been higher than they actually were, European workers would have had to pay more for their food, and European working-class living standards would again have grown less rapidly than they actually did.[16] Finally, and as we have seen, British markets might not have remained open had it not been for the trade surpluses which Britain was running vis-à-vis Asia. Britain and her empire thus lay at the heart of the international economic system.

It seems that the complex web of intercontinental trade and factor flows that emerged in the half century prior to World War I was to the mutual benefit of Europe and her New World offshoots. Although globalization led to losers as well as winners (notably European farmers

[15]For a theoretical model which incorporates intercontinental trade, an endogenous New World frontier, and international factor flows, see Findlay (1993, 1995, chapter 5).

[16]To take one particularly dramatic example, O'Rourke and Williamson (1994) find that declining transport costs can explain over 40% of the growth in British real wages during the late nineteenth century.

faced with growing food imports, and New World workers faced with growing labor market competition as a result of mass immigration), the international economy spurred a faster expansion of the frontiers and led to extensive growth in the Americas and Australasia. As we argued in the previous chapter, elastic overseas land supplies and declining transport costs were key factors—along with the gradual spread of the Industrial Revolution, and the consequent emergence of modern economic growth—allowing Europe's population to grow at an expanding rate, without running into resource constraints, higher food prices, and lower living standards for the poor. But what were the implications of this new world order for the rest of the world?

TRADE AND THE GLOBAL DIVISION OF LABOR

By 1913, international commodity markets were vastly more integrated than they had been in 1750, world trade accounted for a far higher share of world output, and a far broader range of goods, including commodities with a high bulk-to-value ratio, were being transported between continents. These trends, in combination with rapid industrialization in northwest Europe and the British offshoots, had a dramatic impact on the worldwide division of labor, as European industry outcompeted its rivals elsewhere. By the late nineteenth century there was a stark distinction between industrial and primary-producing economies: the "Great Specialization," as Dennis Robertson once memorably termed it (Robertson 1938, p. 6).

According to the available figures (given in table 7.4), primary products accounted for slightly less than two-thirds of total world exports in the late nineteenth century. For example, in 1913 food accounted for 29% of world exports, agricultural raw materials for 21%, and minerals for 14% (Yates 1959, pp. 222–23). The United Kingdom and northwest Europe were net importers of primary products and net exporters of manufactured goods. North America still exported primary products, but rapid industrialization there was leading to a more balanced trade in manufactures over time. Indeed, the United States switched to being a net exporter of manufactured goods shortly before World War I, by which stage it had become the world's leading industrial nation (Wright 1990; Irwin 2003). Meanwhile, Australasia, Latin America, and Africa exported virtually no manufactured goods, and Asian exports were overwhelmingly composed of primary products. For example, according to Lamartine Yates (1959, p. 250), primary products accounted for more than three-quarters of India's exports

TABLE 7.4. World trade, 1876–80 and 1913 (millions of dollars).

| | Primary products | | | | | |
| Region | 1876–80 | | | 1913 | | |
	Exports	Imports	Balance	Exports	Imports	Balance
U.S.A. and Canada	600	330	+270	2,101	1,542	+559
U.K.	117	1,362	−1,245	760	2,596	−1,836
NW Europe	840	1,800	−960	3,064	5,894	−2,830
Other Europe	750	515	+235	1,793	1,689	+104
Australasia	1,413	575	+838	455	129	+326
Latin America				1,531	595	+936
Africa				680	307	+373
Asia				1,792	949	+843
Total	3,720	4,582	−862	12,176	13,701	−1,525

| | Manufactures | | | | | |
| Region | 1876–80 | | | 1913 | | |
	Exports	Imports	Balance	Exports	Imports	Balance
U.S.A. and Canada	100	190	−90	734	891	−157
U.K.	865	225	+640	1,751	601	+1,150
NW Europe	1,080	450	+630	3,318	1,795	+1,523
Other Europe	210	330	−120	578	1,133	−555
Australasia	35	1,285	−1,250	9	370	−361
Latin America				51	879	−828
Africa				26	451	−425
Asia				461	1,247	−786
Total	2,290	2,480	−190	6,928	7,367	−439

Source: P. Lamartine Yates (1959, pp. 226–32). Note that world trade does not balance due to unrecorded trade.

in 1913. By contrast, textiles had still accounted for more than half of the English East India Company's exports to Europe in the late 1750s (table 5.8(c)). By 1811–12 the share of piece goods in India's exports had declined to 33%. The figure was 14.3% just three years later, and only 3.7% in 1850–51. The decline in India's industrial status is well measured by her share of the competitive West African market for cotton cloth (Inikori 2002, pp. 439–47). Up to and during the Napoleonic Wars the value of sales (by British traders) of Indian cloth to West Africa generally exceeded the value of English cloth sales. However, by the 1820s matters had decisively swung in favor of Lancashire, and by mid century Indian sales to West Africa were negligible. Between 1827 and 1830, Indian products accounted for 29%

of the quantity of cotton cloth sold in West Africa by British traders. The figure was just 7% in the 1830s, and 4% in the 1840s (Inikori, p. 447). By 1910–11 the share of cotton goods in total Indian exports had increased to 6%, but this was dwarfed by the share of *raw* cotton in exports (17.2%) (Chaudhuri 1983, pp. 842, 844).

Increasingly, therefore, intercontinental trade involved Europe exporting industrial commodities, in exchange for food and raw materials from the rest of the world. African and Asian countries not only exported a lower proportion of manufactured goods than they had done in previous centuries, but their exports were overwhelmingly directed toward the industrialized economies. It is important to recognize, as Hanson (1980) emphasizes, that this "North–South" or center–periphery distinction (with the periphery being dependent on center markets) only holds throughout the nineteenth century if the United States is defined as being part of the center, since the share of the United Kingdom in developing countries' exports declined rapidly in the years after 1880 (from 40% in 1880 to 24% two decades later), while the share of North America and the rest of Europe increased. Overall, however, his figures show the center thus defined taking 73% of developing country exports in 1840, 74% in 1880, and 70% in 1900 (p. 55), while Bairoch and Etemad (1985, p. 23) have 72% of developing world exports going to the center in 1900 and 78% in 1913.

This dependence on the center was more pronounced for primary products than for manufactured exports. According to Lamartine Yates (1959, p. 58), roughly 85% of developing country primary exports went to industrial economies in 1913, but over one-third of their industrial exports went to other "nonindustrial" countries. His figures also suggest that developing countries increased their share of world industrial exports over the late nineteenth century, from 3% in the late 1870s to 8% in 1913 (and these figures do not include Japan, which is classified here with the industrial countries). By the end of the period, therefore, the first signs of the reindustrialization of the Third World were already beginning to manifest themselves, and this would become one of the great trends of world trade in the late twentieth century.

Broadly speaking, however, it is not inaccurate to view world trade in the nineteenth century in North–South terms, with the rich and industrialized North exporting industrial goods in return for the primary exports of the poor and agricultural South. This was certainly truer in the late nineteenth century than it had been before, and truer than it has been since World War II as well. The biggest caveat concerning this simple characterization was that the New World was both rich and increasingly industrial, but was also a major exporter of primary products—indeed, the industrialized world accounted for more than half of all primary exports throughout the late nineteenth century (ibid.), with the Americas and Australasia being largely responsible for this. Nonetheless, the Industrial Revolution meant that the world was now far more asymmetrical than it had been prior to 1750 or so, both in terms of the underlying economic structures of the North and South, and in terms of the resultant trade patterns. The question now is, did this intercontinental trade benefit or harm the nonindustrial world, and did it exacerbate or smooth out the income differences that had emerged between different regions of the world?

TRADE, TROPICAL FRONTIERS, AND THE GREAT DIVERGENCE

Table 7.5 gives Angus Maddison's (2003) estimates of GDP per capita in the major regions of the world. The final row of the table gives one measure of international income inequality, the Theil inequality coefficient, taken from Bourguignon and Morrisson (2002). As can be seen, international income inequality rose dramatically during the nineteenth century, with the Theil inequality coefficient almost quintupling. In 1820, the richest region in the world (Western Europe) had a per capita GDP just 81% higher than the world average, while the poorest region in the world, Africa, had a per capita income almost two-thirds the world average. Western European per capita incomes were thus less than three times those of Africans. By 1913, the situation was very different. Western European per capita income was 127% higher than the world average, and more than five times the per capita income of Africa. Per capita incomes in the British offshoots were 243% higher than the world average, and more than eight times those in Africa.

In other words, the nineteenth century saw a massive divergence of living standards between the different regions of the world, even though within the rich Atlantic economies there was some convergence of living standards, and especially of real wages (O'Rourke and Williamson 1999, chapter 2; Williamson 1995; Pritchett 1997). It is important to realize, however, that on the whole this "Great Divergence" was due to the industrial countries pulling ahead, rather than to the poorer regions getting poorer—at least from the middle of the nineteenth century onwards, which is when the transport revolution really started to make itself felt. To take one particularly well-documented example, the Gold Coast (now Ghana) saw its exports

TABLE 7.5. Income and regional inequality, 1820–1913
(GDP per capita in 1990 international Geary–Khamis dollars).

Region	1820	1870	1913
Western Europe	1,204	1,960	3,458
Eastern Europe	683	937	1,695
British offshoots	1,202	2,419	5,233
Latin America	692	681	1,481
Japan	669	737	1,387
Asia, excl. Japan	577	550	658
Africa	420	500	637
World	667	875	1,525
Theil inequality coefficient	0.061	0.188	0.299[a]

Source: Maddison (2003, p. 262) and Bourguignon and Morrisson (2002, p. 734). [a]Data for 1910.

(in constant 1911 prices) rise from £872,000 in 1891 to £3,612,000 in 1911, or at 7.4% per annum, with the result that its GDP rose at 1.9% per annum between 1891 and 1901, and at 3.8% per annum in the subsequent decade (Latham 1978, p. 135). According to Arthur Lewis (1970, pp. 30–31), "the period 1880–1913 has to be regarded as one in which many tropical countries grew as rapidly as many of the industrial countries"—not just the Gold Coast, but also countries such as Burma, Thailand, Malaya, and Ceylon. According to Maddison's data (table 7.5), average African incomes rose some 20% between 1820 and 1870, and by an additional 27% between 1870 and the Great War. Asian incomes rose some 20% during the late nineteenth century, although they had fallen back very slightly (by roughly 5%) in the half century following Waterloo. And while Latin American incomes remained stagnant in the first half of the period (falling by some 1.6%) they rose spectacularly (by 114%) in the second. Over the period 1820–1913 as a whole, therefore, divergence was *not* due to Third World impoverishment, but to very rapid income growth in Europe, North America, and Australasia. In turn, this income growth was due to the spread of modern industrialization, which as table 6.3 showed was extremely uneven.

Did the combination of Northern industrialization and international trade slow or hasten Southern growth? Generations of scholars have identified two possibilities. The first, pessimistic, view is that Northern industrialization harmed the South, by lowering the prices its manufacturers could receive for their output, and thus forcing them out of business. This would represent a problem, rather than

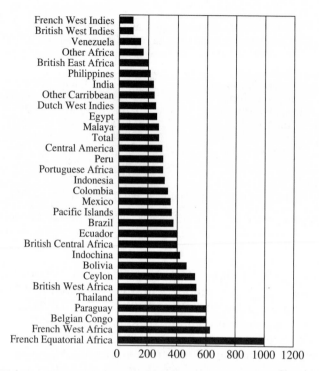

FIGURE 7.6. Tropical trade growth, 1883–1913 (1913 exports, 1883 = 100, current dollars). *Source:* Lewis (1969, p. 48).

a beneficial reallocation of resources, if for some reason there were growth-promoting externalities associated with manufacturing activities.[17] The second, optimistic, view is that Northern industrialization served as an "engine of growth" for Southern economies, by providing them with buoyant markets for their primary exports, and capital goods and loans to expand their capital stocks. Clearly, either mechanism would have been amplified by the decline in transport costs, the open markets of the United Kingdom, and the forced liberalization of Asia and Africa, which we documented earlier.

Figure 7.6 shows that there was indeed rapid export growth across the tropics during the late nineteenth century. Between 1883 and 1913, exports (in current prices) doubled or more than doubled everywhere in the tropics, barring the British and French West Indies, Venezuela,

[17]That is to say, if manufacturing promoted society-wide economic growth in a way that was not taken into account by the manufacturers themselves.

and "Other Africa," which includes territories and states such as Sudan, Ethiopia, Eritrea, and Liberia. Export growth was often dramatic (albeit in many cases from a very small base): exports quadrupled or more in Central and West Africa, Indochina, Thailand, Ceylon, Bolivia, and Paraguay. According to Lewis (1969, p. 10) the slow growers were, with one exception, either former sugar colonies (thus, the Caribbean as a whole performed poorly), or countries with unstable or "medieval" governments (e.g., Venezuela, Haiti, or Ethiopia). The one exception is India, of which more later. According to Maddison (2001, p. 127), export growth was particularly high in Africa, where it averaged 4.4% per annum (in real terms) between 1870 and 1913, well above the world average of 3.4%, with the result that the export to GDP ratio there almost quadrupled, from 5.8% to 20%. Export growth from Latin America was closer to the world average, averaging 3.3%, while export growth from Asia was slower again, at 2.8%.[18] In some countries, such as China, trade was probably not big enough to have important economy-wide effects, a point emphasized by John Hanson (1980). If Maddison's data are to be believed, however, it *was* sizable enough in Africa, Latin America, and individual countries in Asia, and grew rapidly enough as well, that the "engine of growth" hypothesis cannot be automatically discounted.

However, pessimists would counter that rapid primary product export growth is to be expected in countries undergoing deindustrialization, since otherwise they would not be able to pay for manufactured imports. Indeed, according to the well-known "Dutch Disease" argument, which we have already encountered in previous chapters, a rapid boom in primary exports could cause deindustrialization by drawing labor and other resources into the primary-producing sector, thereby forcing up costs in manufacturing (Corden and Neary 1982). There are a number of points to be made here. First, there are some tropical countries during this period, such as Ghana or Burma, for which it is difficult to take an autarkic, industrializing counterfactual seriously. Never having had a large industrial sector to begin with, the negative deindustrialization effects of primary export growth must have been minimal there, and booming exports must have had a positive effect on balance. Second, the logic underlying the Dutch Disease argument assumes scarce resources: more primary production therefore inevitably implies less manufacturing. As we will see, however, many of the participants in the nineteenth-century's

---

[18] Arthur Lewis's (1981) data also show rapid overall growth in tropical exports: 3% per annum between 1870 and 1913, as compared with a 3.2% world growth rate.

tropical export boom could draw upon effectively unlimited resources, in the shape of elastic supplies of both land and labor. The result was widespread extensive growth, that is to say, growth in output caused by growing inputs of land and labor (Reynolds 1985). The downside of this was that, since population grew rapidly as well as output, and effective land–labor ratios remained relatively constant, there was a limit to how much per capita incomes could rise. This can obviously help in explaining why these countries, despite their rapid overall growth, nevertheless in per capita terms fell further behind the industrializing core, which was experiencing rapid intensive growth based on capital accumulation and technical progress. There was an upside as well, however, since elastic factor supplies must have implied minimal crowding out of domestic manufacturing, assuming that any had existed beforehand.

This stress on elastic supplies of land and labor was a key feature of W. Arthur Lewis's writings on the late-nineteenth-century international economy (e.g., Lewis 1978a). A crucial factor explaining tropical growth during this period was for him the availability of unused land: in effect, there were tropical frontiers which were being extended during this period, corresponding to the temperate zone frontiers in the Americas and Australasia discussed earlier (Lewis 1969, pp. 22–23). Lewis's logic is that risk-averse peasant farmers continued to grow food for their families. In order to produce crops for export, they required additional land. And so, in regions such as sub-Saharan Africa, Burma, Thailand, and Indonesia, where empty land existed, primary exports, produced by peasants, boomed. In other areas, such as Latin America or the Philippines, surplus land existed but was owned by large landowners, and so the export supply response there depended on the behavior of estate and plantation owners. By contrast, in India land was already scarce, and so the export supply response to the impulse provided by Northern demand was muted. Moreover, limited resources made India more vulnerable to Dutch Disease problems, particularly since, as we have been emphasizing, India had traditionally been a relatively industrialized economy.

Findlay and Lundahl (1999) survey the literature on resource-led growth during this period, and find considerable qualitative evidence backing the basic Lewis hypotheses. For example, Siam and Burma are two classic examples of peasant economies that grew on the basis of a massive increase in rice exports. In Burma, growth was fueled by a migration into the sparsely populated south of peasants from Upper and Central Burma, and from Southern India. This was largely a result of British government policy, which provided subsidies to

Indian migrants, and improved the Burmese transport infrastructure (Aye Hlaing 1964, pp. 32–36). Between 1852 and 1915, the area under rice cultivation increased by a factor of eight (ibid., p. 6), and Burma became the world's leading rice exporter. According to Aye Hlaing (1964, p. 51, appendix A), this was sufficient to imply growing per capita incomes (at a rate of 0.8% per annum) during the first three decades of the twentieth century. In Siam also, growth was facilitated by the cultivation of previously unused land and the construction of transport infrastructure, financed by British capital. The result was a fifteenfold increase in rice exports between the 1850s and 1913, with China and Malaya being the main markets.

Rice was indigenous to Southeast Asia; in the Gold Coast the main export, cocoa, was introduced only in the 1860s. Between 1891 and 1913, cocoa exports rose from 50 pounds to 50,600 tons (Holmes 1970, p. 151). Here also the growth of the export crop was fueled by the clearing of forests and the migration of peasants south (Hill 1963), although railways were not an issue here since the producing areas lay close to the coast (Holmes 1970, p. 152). As in the Burmese case, there is evidence that per capita incomes grew in the Gold Coast, as previously noted.

Abundant supplies of uncultivated land were also an important factor in the rapid growth of coffee exports from Brazil, Costa Rica, and Colombia. In the latter two cases smallholders were dominant, while plantations were more important in Brazil. Famously, banana plantations later developed along the Costa Rican railway lines that were built to ship coffee to the coast (Gaspar 1979, pp. 21–32). Again, this was land that had previously been uncultivated. Ceylon at one stage also grew coffee, but she later switched to tea (introduced by the British in the nineteenth century) and rubber, a product that had initially been exploited in the Amazonian forests of Brazil, where it grew wild. Rubber was a smallholder product in Ceylon, unlike in Malaysia, where plantations were important, but Ceylonese tea was produced on plantations. Tamil migrants from India worked on Ceylonese tea plantations and Malayan rubber plantations. Once again, the latter made use of uncultivated lands that were serviced by railways and ports (Bruton et al. 1992, p. 178).

In nearly all these cases, the Lewis mechanism of extensive growth fueled by expanding frontiers (and in some cases by population movements as well) can be clearly discerned. In other cases the frontiers were "vertical" (Findlay and Lundahl 1999). Such was the case in Bolivia, where silver and tin exports were facilitated by the construction of railways: tin exports more than doubled during the first decade of the twentieth century (Contreras 1993, pp. 32–35). It was also the case in Chile, which was the dominant nitrate producer in the world, and whose nitrate exports grew by a factor of twelve between 1880 and 1913 (Mamalakis 1971, p. 184), and in South Africa, where diamond and gold mining were boosted by inputs of African labor and overseas capital. In other words, growth in the developing world was due to many of the same forces driving New World growth during the same period, and in particular to the interaction of international factor flows, international trade facilitated by investments in modern transportation technology, and a growing effective land endowment.

If this is so, then a question that naturally arises is: why was per capita income growth so much more impressive in the New World than in successful tropical exporters? The answer comes in two parts. First, the North American experience is radically different from that of other frontier societies, in that (as we have already noted) the United States was industrializing rapidly during this period despite being a resource-abundant exporter of primary products. This seems difficult to reconcile with Dutch Disease pessimism, as well as with the late-twentieth-century conventional wisdom that resource abundance is in fact a "curse" (Sachs and Warner 2001). Moreover, as Gavin Wright (1990) and Douglas Irwin (2003) both point out, U.S. industrial success was largely based on its natural resources, such as the vast iron ore reserves of the Mesabi Range in Minnesota that was opened up during the 1890s. Crucially, however, such natural resources were largely nontraded, due to very high transport costs before the invention of bulk carriers, and were thus used domestically to stimulate local industry, rather than being exported as in the case of raw cotton, for example. Natural resources thus "crowded in" manufacturing in North America, rather than crowding it out (Findlay and Jones 2001; Irwin 2003).

This argument does not apply to Latin America, however, whose exports mainly consisted of primary products and which enjoyed rapidly rising living standards regardless. Here, the crucial distinction with a tropical country like Burma lies in the source of the immigrant labor. In the Latin American case, immigrants arrived from Europe, where wages were already high and rising rapidly. Moreover, Latin American governments were free to tighten immigration policy when unskilled wages fell below politically acceptable levels, and Timmer and Williamson (1998) have shown that countries like Argentina did precisely this. In the Burmese case, immigrants came from South and Southeast Asia, where wages were low and relatively stagnant, and the colonial authorities actively encouraged such immigration, despite any adverse consequences it might have had on local living standards. As Arthur Lewis put it, "Given the unlimited reservoirs of Indian and Chinese labor, tropical wages and peasant incomes had to remain close to Indian and Chinese levels," whereas "the temperate settlements could attract and hold European emigrants, in competition with the United States, only by offering income levels higher than prevailed in North-West Europe" (Lewis 1978a, pp. 188, 191).

Extensive growth in a tropical context therefore implied limited increases in per capita income; but it did at least imply stagnation, or modest increases, rather than outright reductions. In some countries per capita incomes did increase, despite Lewis's radical pessimism, and this may perhaps be partly due to the fact that growth was not just caused by parallel increases in labor and land inputs, but by outside infusions of capital, transportation facilities, and market expertise as well. What about a country like India then, which had been relatively industrialized and had few internal frontiers to exploit? As figure 7.6 showed, India was an exception to the Lewis rule that exports grew strongly in nonsugar producers with stable governments. Its exports only slightly more than doubled between 1883 and 1913, placing India very much at the lower end of the growth spectrum. With a fifth of the world's population in 1820 (Maddison 2003, p. 256), we cannot dismiss the Indian experience as just one country observation among many— no more than assessments of changing world inequality toward the end of the twentieth century can ignore the Indian and Chinese experiences today (see chapter 9).

We have already seen how India lost its overseas manufacturing markets in the late eighteenth and early nineteenth centuries, becoming more and more a primary product exporter. Table 6.3 suggested massive deindustrialization, and while as we have already stressed these estimates are basically informed speculation, other evidence points in the same direction (Williamson 2006, chapter 5). For example, the share of the population in Gangetic Bihar which was "dependent on industry" fell from somewhere between 18% and 29% in 1809–13 to just 8.5% in 1901, while the yarn used in Indian handloom production fell from 419 million pounds in 1850 to 240 million pounds in 1870 (pp. 70–71).

Table 6.3 suggests that something similar happened in China over the same period. It would not be surprising therefore if income in these two giants had been stagnant or declined, at least until 1870 or so, by which time the process of deindustrialization appears to have been complete. Maddison (2003) assumes a sight decline in Indian per capita incomes between 1700 and 1820 (from $550 to $533), followed by stagnation through 1870, while in China his figures show per capita incomes stagnant between 1700 and 1820 (at $600) and then declining to $530 in 1870.[19]

Thereafter, Maddison's figures suggest a divergence in the performance of the two countries. Income per capita bottomed out in both cases, but in the Chinese case the subsequent improvements were so slight as to be almost imperceptible. By contrast, between 1870 and 1914 Indian per capita incomes grew by a third, from $533 to $709 (in 1990 prices), or at 0.65% per annum. Other evidence also suggests a more optimistic view of late-nineteenth-century Indian performance than apparent at first sight. First, as Lidman and Domrese (1970, p. 309) point out, India's relative per capita export performance looks better than its absolute performance (which is what is shown in figure 7.6), since its population growth rate in the late nineteenth century was relatively slow. Thus, for example, while Brazil's exports grew at 4.5% per annum between 1883 and 1913, and India's grew at just 2.8%, the population growth rate in the two countries was 2.3% and 0.6% respectively, implying roughly similar per capita growth rates. If agricultural exports did not grow as rapidly as elsewhere, it was precisely because the extensive growth mechanism available to other countries—filling empty land with workers, if necessary imported from overseas—was not available in the already heavily populated, and cultivated, subcontinent.

Second, by the end of the period there were some preliminary signs that the country was beginning to reindustrialize. The first successful cotton mill was established in 1856 (Wolcott 1997), and between 1880 and 1914 the number of cotton mills increased from 58 to 264, with employment increasing from 39,500 to 260,800 and yarn exports increasing from 26.7 million pounds to 198 million pounds over the same period (Lidman and Domrese 1970, p. 323). On the eve of the Great War, the Indian cotton textile industry ranked fourth in the world, while its jute industry ranked second. Coal mining was also developing, as were a number of smaller industries. Meek (1937, table IV, p. 373) calculated a crude index of "large-scale" industrial production, based on the output of six sectors: cotton, jute and woolen manufactures, paper, breweries, and iron and steel. His figures show production more than doubling between 1896–97 and 1913–14. Overall, Lidman and Domrese conclude that large-scale industrial production increased at between 4 and 5% per annum between 1880 and 1914, a respectable rate comparable to that attained in Germany during the same period.

[19] All figures are in 1990 dollars.

The criticism to be levied at India's late-nineteenth-century economic performance is thus not that growth was negative, but that it could have been a lot better. The comparison is frequently made with Japan, whose per capita GDP increased from $756 in 1874 (at 1990 prices) to $1327 in 1914, or at 1.4% per annum, and whose industrial output grew at around 7% per annum (Maddison 2003, pp. 180–82; Lidman and Domrese 1970, p. 321), or sufficiently rapidly that according to Paul Bairoch its per capita industrialization level nearly tripled between 1860 and 1913 (table 6.3).

The crucial question, however, is whether India's enforced openness can explain its failure to emulate Japan. Here, we need to make a distinction between the early nineteenth century, during which time European productivity gains in manufacturing, combined with rapid transport cost declines, *were* responsible for Indian deindustrialization (Clingingsmith and Williamson 2004), and the period from 1870 onwards which is often viewed as the classic era of nineteenth-century globalization. For the latter period, the answer to the question is "probably not." First, Japan was equally open during this period, as we have seen, and this did not prevent her from rapidly developing a manufacturing industry. Openness was not an insuperable obstacle to industrialization, it seems. Second, Latin America was independent during this period, and free to impose tariffs, but also developed on the basis of primary exports (Lewis 1978b, pp. 8–9), even though, as table 6.3 showed, industrialization in countries like Mexico and Brazil was stirring at the beginning of the twentieth century, just as it was in India. Transport cost declines were so dramatic during the nineteenth century that their effects swamped any impact that tariff policy might have had. Third, econometric studies have shown that tariffs did not boost growth in Latin America or Asia during this period, although they *were* associated with higher growth rates in Europe and her British offshoots (Clemens and Williamson 2004; Coatsworth and Williamson 2004; O'Rourke 2000), while Susan Wolcott (1997) has argued that higher tariffs would have made very little difference to the Indian textile industry in the aftermath of World War I. And finally, as stressed by Clingingsmith and Williamson (2004), India's share of world manufacturing was already slipping in the second half of the eighteenth century, before the transport revolutions of the nineteenth, suggesting that internal factors must have been driving deindustrialization as well as external competition.[20]

[20]Specifically, they suggest that deteriorating agricultural productivity resulting from the collapse of the Mughal empire drove up food prices and nominal wages, thus reducing Indian competitiveness.

The Terms of Trade

According to Bairoch and Etemad (1985, p. 52), 50% of the developing world's exports in 1911–13 consisted of food and drink, 35% consisted of raw materials, 8.5% consisted of manufactured goods, and 6.5% consisted of tobacco, opium, and precious metals. Particularly important commodities included cereals, accounting for 13.6% of classified exports, cotton (8%), coffee (7.9%), sugar (7.7%), textiles (4.7%), hides and skins (4.2%), and rubber (3.9%). To a large extent, countries specialized in particular crops following the dictates of comparative advantage (climate, land quality, and so on), with particular plants being introduced into countries that were often thousands of miles from their countries of origin in response to commercial opportunities. Producing countries were for the most part price takers on international markets, although in some cases (such as Brazilian coffee) they accounted for a sufficiently large share of the world market that in principle they possessed some monopoly power. They were thus exposed to fluctuations in world market conditions, and to changes in the prices of their major export goods.

How did these terms of trade change over time? According to the data in Lewis (1978a), the price of tropical exports relative to manufactured goods remained remarkably stable on average during the late nineteenth century. However, this evidence, and indeed most of the evidence used in the debate thus far, uses prices recorded in core markets such as London to infer trends in peripheral markets. What mattered to developing countries was the terms of trade which they themselves experienced, and in an environment of generally declining transport costs their terms of trade could have been improving even as the relative prices of their exports remained constant, or even fell, overseas (Ellsworth 1956). Recently, Jeffrey Williamson (2000, 2002, 2006) has provided evidence on the terms of trade for several developing countries for this period. His data show that individual country experiences differed greatly at any given time, reflecting the fact that they produced different export goods. The data also show that these developing countries faced terms of trade that were very volatile. This volatility could be harmful for such countries' growth prospects, by reducing foreign capital inflows (Blattman et al. 2003, 2004). On average, however, these countries' terms of trade were clearly improving over time, by nearly 10% in Japan, Korea, and Taiwan between the early 1870s and World War I, and by over 20% in Burma, Egypt, India, and Thailand (Haddas and Williamson 2003, table 2, p. 638). Clingingsmith and Williamson (2005) present even

TABLE 7.6. Primary commodity prices, 1883–1913
(deflated by manufactured goods price index; 1883 = 100).

Commodity	1883	1899	1913
Sugar	100	54.3	51.5
Tea	100	83.9	76.7
Palm oil	100	73.2	91.4
Cocoa	100	107.5	92.4
Rubber	100	98.0	96.6
Rice	100	125.2	101.9
Coffee	100	113.4	102.9
Cotton	100	78.0	131.3
Hides	100	85.0	132.3
Tobacco leaf	100	111.0	136.5
Jute	100	122.8	225.8

Source: Calculated on the basis of the data in Stover (1970, table 2.2, p. 50) and Lewis (1978a, table A.11, pp. 280–81).

longer-run data for the terms of trade of the Ottoman Empire, Egypt, and Latin America. All three series show the terms of trade improving significantly during the nineteenth century, while the Latin American series subsequently collapsed during the interwar period, of which more in chapter 8.

These average figures mask important differences in the experiences of individual commodities (table 7.6). At one end of the spectrum, relative sugar prices halved between 1883 and 1913, due to the growing levels of output, often in rich countries, and often subsidized, which we mentioned earlier. At the other end, there were marked increases in the relative prices of cotton and tobacco, while the relative price of jute more than doubled. Econometric studies have failed to find any positive impact of terms of trade growth on per capita income growth in the periphery during this period, which is probably not surprising given the extensive nature of much of that growth (Blattman et al. 2003, 2004; Williamson 2006). On the other hand, the poor performance of the sugar colonies documented earlier must have been largely due to these sharply declining sugar prices: a preview of the problems which many Third World farmers would face in the twentieth century.

CONCLUSION

Prior to the nineteenth century, intercontinental trade was relatively small scale, and largely limited to noncompeting goods, as a result of persistently high transport costs, mercantilist trade restrictions, and warfare. However, the century that followed the final defeat of Napoleon saw the world's economic structure transformed in so radical a manner that it would have been virtually unrecognizable to a late-eighteenth-century observer. The ultimate cause of this transformation was the Industrial Revolution, which started in the late eighteenth century in Britain, but which spread to the rest of what we now call the developed world over the course of the next century. The Industrial Revolution led to average living standards almost trebling in Western Europe, and more than quadrupling in the British offshoots, which had become the most prosperous region of the world by 1913 (table 7.5). Modern industry did make its appearance in Asia and Latin America toward the very end of this period: the "one million spindle mark" was reached in India in 1876, in Japan in 1898, in Brazil in 1909, and in China in 1912 (Hardach 1977, pp. 267–68). However, with the exception of Japan, these hesitant first steps were not sufficient to prevent a massive increase in the economic distance separating North and South.

It should be noted that this Japanese exception would have major political consequences, since industrialization and military strength went together during this period, as they have done since. In 1885, following a brief conflict with China, Japan obtained possession of Taiwan and the Liaodong peninsula in Manchuria. It was forced to withdraw its claims to the latter following the intervention of Russia, France, and Germany, and the Russians moved into the peninsula themselves, obtaining a 25-year lease. The stage was set for the Russo-Japanese war of 1904–5, which ended in victory for Japan, and resulted not only in her elevation to Great Power status, but to her obtaining the lease in Liaodong. Five years later, Japan would annex Korea. As we will see in the next chapter, this Japanese presence in Manchuria would have profound consequences for the world a quarter of a century later.

The Industrial Revolution led to the widespread demise of traditional industry in much of Asia not just because of the greater competitiveness of Western industry but as a result of the transport revolutions of the nineteenth century, which destroyed the natural protection which distance might once have afforded countries such as India or China. It would have taken a massive increase in tariffs, or outright import prohibitions, to counteract the effects of steamships, railroads and the Suez Canal, and it is worth speculating about how likely such policies would have been in a counterfactual world where Asia had been left to its own devices. But in any event, Western pressure forced open Asian markets, and the "Great Specialization" resulted, with Europe exporting manufactures in exchange for the primary exports of the developing world. Indeed, the technological and economic forces underlying this process were so powerful that even where resource-abundant countries had tariff autonomy—as in Latin America—and used this independence to try to boost manufacturing, the end result was still a massive increase in primary exports, counterbalanced by imports of European and North American manufactured goods.

It seems inevitable that this stark asymmetry between North and South would have to have come to an end at some stage (Robertson 1938). Eventually, the South's frontiers were bound to be exhausted, and indeed they were being exhausted by the end of this period in the New World as we have seen. With continuing population growth, diminishing returns would then set in, forcing up the price of the South's primary exports. Meanwhile, declining transport costs meant that modern industry would no longer be tied to coalfields and sources of iron ore, implying that it could spread to low-wage regions. Indeed, as we have seen, several "Southern" countries were beginning to industrialize by the end of the period. Finally, political economy considerations also suggest that the Great Specialization could not continue indefinitely. European farmers had won extensive protection by the end of this period, while governments in the Americas and Australasia were imposing heavy tariffs not just for revenue purposes, as had traditionally been the case, but with the specific goal of encouraging industrial development. Globalization backlash was an important feature of the late nineteenth century.

On the other hand, there was a range of complementary domestic policies which governments could—and did—put in place in order to shore up support for liberal international policies. Thus, Huberman and Lewchuk (2003) show that there was extensive government intervention in European labor markets in the late nineteenth century, a period that also saw a sustained rise in social transfers (Lindert 2004). A range of labor market regulations was introduced across the continent, for example, prohibiting night work for women and children, prohibiting child labor below certain ages, and introducing factory inspections. The period also saw the widespread introduction of old-age, sickness, and unemployment insurance schemes. Moreover, this "labor compact" was more widespread in the more open European economies. Huberman and Lewchuk interpret this finding as providing support for the argument that unions were persuaded to back free trade, or openness more generally, in return for pro-labor domestic policies.[21] In related work, Huberman (2004) finds that

[21] In some countries, workers backed free trade anyway because of the cheap food which it implied (see O'Rourke 1997; Bairoch 1989).

working hours in Europe and her offshoots declined between 1870 and 1913 as a result of labor legislation and union pressure, and that the decline was greatest in small open economies such as Belgium, where the Labor Party supported free trade after 1885 (Huberman, forthcoming).

To some extent, therefore, late-nineteenth-century governments successfully managed the political challenges posed by globalization, sometimes defusing protectionist demands by means of domestic legislation, and sometimes giving into them. The bottom line is that world trade grew rapidly during the nineteenth century, and commodity market integration generally deepened, despite rising tariffs in several countries. World trade might have grown more slowly after 1914 than it did before, even had war not intervened, and the political challenges facing governments might have been exacerbated; but the 1920s and 1930s would have been utterly different had it not been for the Great War. It is to that conflict, and its consequences, that we now turn.

Chapter 8

WORLD TRADE 1914-39: DEGLOBALIZATION

WORLD WAR I

WORLD WAR I BROUGHT the liberal economic order of the late nineteenth century to an abrupt halt. It thus marked the end of an era, just as the wars of 1792–1815 marked the end of eighteenth-century mercantilism. It also involved extensive efforts by both sides to blockade the others' trade: indeed, after it became clear that the German war plans which anticipated victory in the west within six weeks, allowing them to subsequently concentrate on the Eastern front, had failed, and that Allied optimism was similarly misplaced, the war became increasingly an economic struggle in which victory was ultimately determined by the resources at each side's disposal (Broadberry and Harrison 2005).

New technologies meant that the nature of the blockades was radically different from those of a century earlier. As the world's leading naval power, Britain still retained the upper hand over her continental European rivals, but her advantage was eroded in two ways. First, better artillery, mines, and submarines meant that Britain could not mount "close" blockades of enemy ports, as she had blockaded Napoleon's Atlantic ports. Rather, she was forced to maintain a "distant" blockade, preventing enemy merchant ships from reaching Germany by controlling the English Channel and the waters between Scotland and Norway. Second, submarine technology meant that Germany was able to mount a counter-blockade of the British Isles, an option that had not been available to Napoleon in practice, French rhetoric notwithstanding (Davis and Engerman 2007, chapter 5). Such distant blockades implied more contact with neutral shipping than traditional close blockades. With submarine warfare, the sinking of neutral ships was inevitable, and ultimately led to the United States being dragged into the conflict on the side of the Allies in 1917.

The British aim was to deny Germany and her allies supplies of "contraband" goods. The blockade was gradually tightened over time, with more goods (and eventually all goods) being added to the list of contraband goods, and with increasing pressure being put on Germany's neutral neighbors, such as Denmark and the Netherlands, to prevent the reexport of such goods to the Central Powers (Hardach 1977, chapter 2). Firms dealing with the enemy, and firms dealing with such firms, were blacklisted. Meanwhile, the Germans' U-boat campaign reached a climax in the spring of 1917. During that year, Allied and neutral losses of shipping amounted to 6.1 million gross tons, as compared with new construction of 2.9 million gross tons (ibid., p. 46), while 66 German U-boats sank 2,639 civilian ships, of which 1,252 were British, 708 were Allied, and 679 were neutral (for the most part, American). This implied a "kill ratio" of 40 ships sunk for every U-boat (Hugill 1993, p. 144).

Another serious interference with the open international economy of the late nineteenth century was the centralized control which even traditionally liberal governments, such as the British, imposed on trade and shipping, with scarce cargo space necessitating that governments dictate both the composition of imports through a system of quotas, and the allocation of shipping capacity. This was part of a more general shift toward massive and unprecedented government intervention in the economy. First of all, total war implied enormous increases in government expenditure. In France, Germany, and the United Kingdom, the share of government expenditure in GDP rose from 10% or under in 1913 to a third or more during the war, with the share reaching 37.1% in the United Kingdom in 1916, 49.9% in France in 1917, and 59% in Germany in 1917 (Broadberry and Harrison 2005, table 1.5, p. 15). Second, governments organized and supervised private businesses involved in the war effort, rationed food, conscripted citizens, controlled raw materials supply, and in some cases engaged directly in manufacturing (Feinstein et al. 1997, pp. 19, 189). While the controls would be dismantled and the rise in government spending curtailed in the wake of the war, the perceived success of these wartime measures would make it easier for governments to once again start intervening in the very different environment of the 1930s (Rockoff 2004).

Given the widespread nature of the prohibitions, quotas, and exchange controls adopted during the war, pointing to the tariffs levied during the conflict might seem redundant, and yet the British McKenna Tariff of 1915, designed to save on scarce shipping space, did mark an important break with the past. It imposed duties of

33⅓% on imports of luxury goods (automobiles, musical instruments, clocks, watches, and movies) and, crucially, did not impose excise taxes on equivalent domestic goods—it was thus explicitly protectionist.[1] Moreover, this shift was not reversed after the war. The Key Industries Act of 1919 protected defense-related industries, while the Safeguarding of Industries Act of 1921 protected such inessential industries as glove making and glassware (Kindleberger 1989). These acts did not represent widespread and severe protection. At the beginning of the 1930s, only £13 million worth of imports was subject to these tariffs, compared with the £138 million subject to traditional revenue duties, and a total import bill of £1,030 million (Kenwood and Lougheed 1983, p. 216). Nonetheless, they represented a break with Britain's free trade past, and also made it possible finally to introduce Imperial Preferences.

One might expect that all of this disruption would have led to a general collapse of trade. Table 8.1, which gives trade data from 1913–19, reveals a more complex pattern. In all the main European belligerents, the value of exports fell sharply, but this was not primarily a reflection of enemy policies designed to block exports. In sharp contrast with the situation during the wars of 1792–1815, countries no longer believed that the way to defeat their enemies was to prevent them from exporting, and thus earning precious metals. Rather, by the early twentieth century it was clearly understood that winning wars required abundant supplies of industrial raw materials, finished military goods, and food. The aim was thus to maximize the resources available to a country, and this meant restricting exports and, if possible, increasing imports. Blockades were meant to prevent the enemy from importing, not to prevent them from exporting. This shift in strategy is reflected in the data on trade volumes. During 1792–1815, it was imports that fell the most, but World War I saw belligerents' exports falling in a quite consistent, and often dramatic, fashion. This was what the nations concerned desired; the question was whether or not they would be able to sustain an acceptable level of imports as well.

Viewed in this light, it seems clear that the Allied blockade of Germany and her allies was more successful than the German U-boat campaign. To be sure, table 8.1 only gives nominal trade values, and this is problematic during wartime conditions, when import prices can be expected to rise. For example, when measured in tons rather than in pounds sterling, a British food import index stands at 100 in

---

[1] By contrast, late-nineteenth-century British tariffs on imported alcohol, for example, were matched by equivalent excise duties on British-produced alcohol; see the debate between Irwin (1993a) and Nye (1991).

TABLE 8.1. Trade during the Great War.

| | Major European belligerents | | | | | | | | | |
| | Austria–Hungary | | France | | Germany | | Russia | | United Kingdom | |
	Imp.	Exp.	Imp.	Exp.	Imp.	Exp.	Imp.	Exp.	Imp.	Exp.
1913	3.51	2.99	8,421	6,880	10,751	10,097	1,374.0	1,520.1	659.1	525.2
1914	2.98	2.24	6,402	4,869	8,500	7,400	1,098.0	956.1	601.1	430.7
1915	3.85	1.43	11,036	3,937	7,100	3,100	1,138.6	401.8	752.8	384.9
1916	6.09	1.63	20,640	6,214	8,400	3,800	2,451.2	577.3	850.9	506.3
1917	5.08	1.81	27,554	6,013	7,100	3,500	2,316.7	464.0	994.5	527.1
1918	3.79*	1.64*	22,306	4,723	7,100	4,700			1,285.3	501.4
1919			35,799	11,880					1,461.5	798.6

| | European overseas offshoots | | | | | | | | | |
| | Argentina | | Australia | | Canada | | South Africa | | United States | |
	Imp.	Exp.	Imp.	Exp.	Imp.	Exp.	Imp.	Exp.	Imp.	Exp.
1913	1,128	1,180	72.5	76.8	619	455	40	28	1,854	2,538
1914	733	916			456	461	34	18	1,924	2,420
1915	694	1,323	58.2	57.9	508	779	30	15	1,703	2,820
1916	832	1,302	70	64.1	846	1,179	38	24	2,424	5,554
1917	864	1,250	69.1	86.3	964	1,586	34	29	3,005	6,318
1918	1,138	1,822	55.3	75.1	920	1,269	45	31	3,102	6,402
1919	1,490	2,343	86.3	107	941	1,290	47	51	3,993	8,159

| | Asia | | | | | | | | | |
| | India | | Japan | | China | | Indochina | | Indonesia | |
	Imp.	Exp.	Imp.	Exp.	Imp.	Exp.	Imp.	Exp.	Imp.	Exp.
1913	2,022	2,574	795	716	888	628	306	345	464	671
1914	1,550	1,907	671	671	887	555	266	332	412	674
1915	1,487	2,082	636	793	708	653	224	345	390	770
1916	1,710	2,570	879	1,234	805	751	335	391	419	895
1917	1,774	2,572	1,201	1,752	856	721	374	430	385	778
1918	2,018	2,690	1,902	2,159	865	757	363	455	556	676
1919	2,371	3,503	2,501	2,379	1,008	983	751	1,051	740	2,146

*First ten months only. U.K. figures are for retained imports and domestic exports.
Austria–Hungary (billion crowns); France (million francs); Germany (billion marks); Russia (million rubles); United Kingdom (million pounds); Argentina (million paper pesos); Australia (million pounds); Canada (million dollars); South Africa (million pounds); United States (million dollars); India (million rupees); Japan (million yen); China (million Chinese dollars); Indochina (million francs); Indonesia (million guilders).
Source: Mitchell (1988, 1992, 2003a,b); Hardach (1977) (Germany); Gatrell (2005) (Russia); Schulze (2005) (Austria–Hungary).

1913, but at 89 in 1916, 75 in 1917, and 65 in 1918 (Hardach 1977, p. 124). Nonetheless, there is a sharp contrast between the steady increase in British import values during the war, and the explosion in their French counterparts, on the one hand, and the sharp decline in nominal German imports on the other.

One, albeit imperfect, way to control for shifting price levels during the war is to measure the value of imports as a share of GDP. Unfortunately, this is not possible for all countries, but the British and French data confirm that these countries managed to sustain imports at reasonably high levels during the war. In Britain, import shares fell only marginally, from 25.9% during 1910–13 to 23.5% during 1914–18. It was the export share that collapsed, from 20.1% to 12.9%. In France, the export share similarly declined, from 13.7% to 8.9%; the import share actually rose substantially, from 16.8% to 28.2%.[2] These trade deficits enabled both countries to sustain their war efforts, but required substantial borrowing from the United States. The picture was very similar in Russia: her exports fell from 1,520 million rubles in 1913 to an average of just 481 million during 1915–17 (table 8.1). Her imports increased sharply in 1916–17 (as they also did in Austria–Hungary), and the current account deteriorated.

Corresponding to these worsening trade balances among the major belligerents, exports rose in neutral European economies such as Sweden, in the "regions of recent settlement," and in other countries that could provide the European powers with food and/or raw materials. Export expansion was particularly strong in North America, where grain production increased during the war years to meet Allied demand. The United States also exported large quantities of arms, munitions, and other industrial goods. Nominal exports rose by 150% in the United States between 1913 and 1917, while the increase in Canada was even bigger, almost 250%. The U.S. export share of GDP rose from 6% in 1910–13 to 8.8% in 1914–18, and the Canadian share doubled, from an already high 14.4% to 29.2%. Although nominal import values rose during the war, after initial setbacks, both countries ran substantial trade surpluses, as table 8.1 shows.

The picture was more mixed in Latin America. The nominal value of exports fell initially in countries like Chile and Brazil, but it soon recovered, and by 1916 was well ahead of its prewar level in Argentina, Chile, and Peru. In general, countries like Chile which produced items essential for the war effort, such as grain, meat, and copper, did better than those, like Brazil, whose main export items (such as coffee) were considered as "nonessential." Latin American import values fell sharply in the early years of the war. For example, the 1915 level was just 62% of the 1913 level in Argentina, and roughly 45% in Brazil, Chile, and Peru. Since the value of exports recovered by more than the value

[2]Trade shares here and in subsequent paragraphs are based on the data underlying Jones and Obstfeld (2001), where necessary supplemented with trade data in Mitchell (1992, 1993, 1995).

of imports, the Latin Americans also tended to run trade surpluses during the war.

In Asia, Japan's nominal exports more than trebled. While her imports also rose substantially, they did so by less, and the country's trade moved from deficit to surplus (Hardach 1977, p. 261). Japan clearly became more rather than less open during the war, with her import share of GDP rising from 13.9% before the war to 14.2% during it, and her export share rising from 12.8% to 17.7%. Elsewhere in Asia, nominal export values held steady in India, and rose slightly in China and Southeast Asia. Only in India did imports fall substantially, a reflection of the subcontinent's prewar dependence on the United Kingdom for most of her manufactured imports. Nominal trade levels also held steady in South Africa, and held reasonably steady in Australia, although in the latter country economic growth implied declining trade shares.

This brief survey has revealed the somewhat surprising fact that most countries did not become unambiguously more closed to trade during the war (Germany being one of the more notable exceptions). Indeed some became unambiguously more open, in particular the United States and Japan. Nevertheless, international commodity markets suffered a serious setback during the conflict, as the cost of shipping goods between continents increased dramatically. According to Shah Mohammed and Williamson (2004), real freight rates tripled between 1910–14 and 1915–19, and this had a predictable impact on international commodity price gaps. Thus, the Liverpool–Bombay cotton price gap, which had been 20% in 1913, increased to 102% in 1917; the Liverpool–New Orleans cotton price gap increased from 12% to 43.8%; the London–Calcutta jute price gap rose from 4.4% to 106.8%, the rapeseed price gap rose from 25.3% to 161.6%, and the linseed price gap rose from 21.8% to 216.8%; the Hull–Bombay cottonseed price gap rose from 39.9% to 278%; and the London–Rangoon rice price gap increased from 26.5% to an astonishing 422.5% (Hynes and O'Rourke ongoing).

Corresponding to this wartime commodity market disintegration was a decline in the overall volume of world trade, although this is hard to document since existing indices of total world trade omit the war and the immediate postwar years. According to the United Nations's unpublished (1962) index, the volume of world trade in 1921 was 22% lower than in 1913, and it was only in 1924 that the 1913 level was exceeded (by some 1.7%). Maddison (1995) is less pessimistic: according to his data, world trade levels were some 7.4% higher in 1924 than in 1913.

Overall, it seems safe to conclude that the volume of world trade fell sharply during the conflict, if by an unknown amount.[3] As we have seen, however, such aggregate effects mask a large range of individual country experiences (as was the case during the wars of 1792–1815). This diversity is important in understanding the evolution of trade and trade policy during the interwar period.

THE AFTERMATH OF WAR

Whatever the immediate impact of World War I on international trade, its longer-term impact was disastrous. As many authors have emphasized, it changed the nature of domestic and international politics, as well as the structures of individual economies, in such a way as to make it much more difficult, if not impossible, to return to the "normalcy" of the late nineteenth century.[4] In some cases, these changes were largely a continuation of trends that had existed before the conflict, with the war serving to speed them up. In other cases, the war was clearly an exogenous driving force changing the nature of the international economy. It is often a matter of judgment as to which of these two descriptions is the more accurate, but overall the war provoked, or accelerated, so many changes that the history of the international economy over the succeeding twenty years can only be interpreted as a working out of the forces which it had set in motion.[5]

It is useful to distinguish between two types of forces. First, as in the case of the Anglo-French wars a century before, trade disruption implied a dislocation in traditional production and trade patterns, with predictable consequences for income distribution, for the nature of postwar economic adjustment, and for the political economy of trade policy. As had been the case after 1815, these consequences were almost uniformly negative for international economic integration. Second, the war had a variety of geopolitical consequences, and unlike in the nineteenth century, these did not counterbalance the aforementioned negative effects of the war, since the Treaty of Versailles was as unsuccessful in laying the foundations for a stable postwar order as the Congress of Vienna had been successful.

[3] Based on gravity equations, Glick and Taylor (2006) estimate that declining trade between adversaries led to world trade declining by some 14–18%, and that impacts on neutrals lowered world trade by a further 10–15%.

[4] The literature is too enormous to be adequately summarized here. Particularly influential contributions include Aldcroft (1977), Eichengreen (1992a,b), Feinstein et al. (1997), Hardach (1977), Kindleberger (1973), Lewis (1949), and Svennilson (1954).

[5] Our account largely follows such standard accounts as Eichengreen (1992a,b) and Feinstein et al. (1997).

There were three wartime adjustments in production that were crucial for subsequent events. First, non-European primary producers expanded their export capacity in order to meet European wartime demands, with the result that the postwar period would see downward pressure on the prices of these commodities. Second, European industries expanded during the war in order to meet the demand for war-related equipment. Once peace was reestablished, these found themselves with excess capacity. Third, the war gave a boost to non-European industrialization, in much the same way as the Revolutionary and Napoleonic Wars had boosted industrialization outside Britain.

In agriculture, the problems that arose can best be illustrated by the experience of the crucial cereals sector. The European acreage under wheat fell sharply during the war, not just in traditional wheat importers but also in exporting countries like Hungary, Poland, and what was to become the U.S.S.R. (Malenbaum 1953, table 1, pp. 236–37). In Germany, cereals output fell by half between 1913 and 1917, and the decline was even greater in France (Ritschl 2005, table 2.5, p. 49; Hautcoeur 2005, table 6.1, p. 171). But those declines were more than matched by a 15% increase in acreages outside Europe. Exports of wheat and wheat flour from the United States rose more than threefold in value between 1913 and 1918 (Eichengreen 1992a, p. 92; U.S. Department of Commerce 1975, Series U281), while the Canadian wheat acreage was 74% higher in 1919 than it had been in 1913 (Statistics Canada, Series M249[6]). Meanwhile, Southern Hemisphere grain production also increased, from a prewar average of 14.7 million tons per annum to roughly 17 millions tons during 1914–17 (with the exception of 1916, when poor harvests worldwide drove down production levels). These wartime supply responses would in time produce a supply overhang, which weighed on world grain markets throughout the 1920s. A collapse in Soviet acreages associated with the chaos following the Russian Revolution of 1917 prevented oversupply from being a problem immediately after the war, but it also helped call forth further overseas supplies. For example, in Australia the wheat acreage increased from 8.9 million in 1919–24 to 11.97 million in 1924–29 (as compared with 7.6 million in 1909–14), while the acreage increased from 16.02 million to 19.94 million in Argentina (Malenbaum 1953, table 1, pp. 236–37). As wheat acreages in the U.S.S.R. and Europe gradually recovered, and were not matched by supply reductions overseas, downward pressure on prices inevitably

---

[6]Available at www.statcan.ca/bsolc/english/bsolc?catno=11–516-X.

resulted during the 1920s. This would become a major source of trade tensions after the war (Feinstein et al. 1997, pp. 72–73).

This pattern was not confined to grains: for example, Argentine meat exports rose by more than 75% between 1913 and 1918, while U.S. meat exports rose tenfold (Eichengreen 1992a, pp. 89–92). Meanwhile, the Javan and Cuban sugar industries enjoyed rapid wartime growth as European production fell by two-thirds (Aldcroft 1977, p. 48). The non-European sugar acreage continued to expand after the war, even as European supplies were restored, and this, together with better varieties and more efficient processing, would lead to oversupply during the late 1920s (Lewis 1949, p. 46).

Second, in the belligerent countries heavy industry expanded during the war to serve the war effort. For example, British steel output rose from 7.7 million tons in 1913 to 9.5 million tons in 1918, and aircraft production rose from 245 in 1914 to 32,018 in 1918 (Broadberry and Howlett 2005, table 7.6, p. 212). Something very similar happened in Germany, where textiles production fell nearly 80% between 1913 and 1917, but where nonferrous metal production rose by over 50% (Ritschl 2005, table 2.5, p. 46). The result was that several European heavy industries, such as shipbuilding, iron and steel, and engineering, found themselves with excess capacity after the war, especially once the plants that had been damaged during the war (for example, steel plants in occupied Belgium and France) had been replaced or upgraded. Capacity in the European iron and steel industry was roughly a third to a half higher in 1927 than in 1913, although output barely rose above the 1913 level (Svennilson 1954, pp. 120–25). The war saw a near doubling of the world's shipbuilding capacity, and by the start of the 1920s there was enough shipping to last the rest of the decade (Aldcroft 1977, p. 47).

Third, since Europe was a net manufacturing exporter, the declining European exports documented in table 8.1 translated into a fall in the supply of manufactured consumer goods on world markets, leaving opportunities for other countries to begin import substitution, or (in the case of more advanced countries such as Japan and the United States) to expand their manufactured exports.

In Asia, Japan's manufacturing output rose by over a half, with her industrial base expanding in areas such as chemicals, engineering, and iron and steel. Japanese firms developed new markets in Australia, India, Southeast Asia, Africa, and Latin America, with their share of the Chinese import market rising from 20% to 36% between 1913 and 1919, and their share of the Indian cotton piece goods import market rising from less than 1% in 1913 to 21% in 1918. This came at the expense of the United Kingdom, whose share in Chinese imports fell from 16.5% to 9.5%, and whose share of the Indian cotton import market fell from 97% to 77% (ibid., pp. 37–38; Hardach 1977, p. 279). Meanwhile, despite the political chaos in China, where the Manchu dynasty had collapsed in 1911, industrialization there also continued apace, with the production of cotton yarn increasing by 150% between 1914 and 1920, iron ore production by 165%, coal production by 77%, and an overall index of industrial output exactly doubling (ibid., table 27, p. 265). In India, the cotton industry benefited from the decline in imports (imports of cotton piece goods fell from over 3 million yards in 1913 to just 1.5 million yards in 1917, and less than 1 million yards in 1918). The result was that Indian mills increased their share of the domestic market, with modern mills sharply increasing their share of local production. Thus British manufacturers were being displaced by both Japanese and Indian competitors in this crucial market during the war. The iron and steel industry also expanded in response to a collapse in imports, with the Tata Iron and Steel Company doubling its workforce between 1913–14 and 1918–19. Meanwhile, jute mills saw a substantial increase in exports, as a result of European military demand (e.g., for sandbags) (ibid., pp. 278–80). According to the League of Nations (1945a, p. 135) total industrial output was 18% higher in 1920 than in 1913.

The war gave a substantial boost to industrial activity in North America. In the United States, industrial output rose by around a half between 1914 and 1919 (Miron and Romer 1990; Davis 2004), while Canadian industrial output nearly doubled between 1915 and 1919 (Aldcroft 1977, p. 41; Hardach 1977, p. 275). Meanwhile, South African industrial output and employment tripled, providing the foundations for the country's rapid interwar industrialization (Aldcroft 1977, pp. 34–35).

The picture is more mixed in Latin America. In Argentina, industrial output and real GDP were marginally lower in 1918 than in 1913, in sharp contrast with the prewar pattern of rapid growth. This was partly a result of a decline in the importation of capital equipment and other essential inputs, something which was a problem elsewhere on the continent (Miller 1981).[7] Similarly, there seems to have been little or no overall industrial growth in Mexico between 1914 and 1918 (Mitchell 1993, p. 302). On the other hand, one index shows Brazilian manufacturing output more than doubling between 1914 and 1918 (Mitchell

[7]GDP and industrial output data based on the YZD and IND1 series in della Paolera et al. (2003).

1993, p. 304), although Leff (1969) is more pessimistic. According to Aldcroft (1977, pp. 40–41), the war spurred industrialization in Chile and Uruguay, while textile production expanded in several countries and a range of other industries sprang up across the continent, such as motor vehicle assembly in Argentina in 1916 (Hardach 1977, p. 272). However, those industries which did particularly well, such as the Argentine dairy, wool, and leather industries, were ones which relied on local raw materials, rather than industries which were displacing unavailable European goods (Miller 1981; Barbero and Rocchi 2003). Industries which were based on import-substitution tended to be fundamentally uncompetitive vis-à-vis their European competitors, and would run into difficulties after the war (Hardach 1977; Miller 1981).

This failure would in time place extra pressure on Latin American governments to continue with their prewar policies of industrial protection. Thus, the hothouse stimulation of industrial "war babies" would lead to postwar demands for industrial protection, and not just in countries such as Argentina, but in India and Australia as well (Kenwood and Lougheed 1983, pp. 185–86; Eichengreen 1992a, pp. 88–89). Indeed, the Indian cotton industry benefited from an increase in protection during the war itself, with tariffs being raised from 3.5% to 7.5% in 1917 (Hardach 1977, p. 279). Furthermore, increased overseas competition and declining export markets would lead Europeans to call for protection in the years ahead, for once lost, markets in Asia or Latin America would prove hard to recover, a further example of the path dependence in trade patterns we encountered in chapter 6. Whereas Europe had accounted for 40.8% of world manufacturing output in 1913, that share had slipped to 35.4% in 1928 (Bairoch 1982, p. 304).

All of these trends ensured that, as in 1815, there would be no shortage of agricultural and industrial interests around the world looking for protection after the war had ended. But the war had other more systemic effects as well. First, as Barry Eichengreen (1992a) among others has emphasized, the war transformed the nature of European domestic politics, with the franchise being extended in many countries, and with a large rise in the power of socialist parties. The role of trade unions was strengthened, strikes became more frequent, and in countries such as Belgium, France, Germany, and Italy proportional representation made stable government more difficult. This had several implications for postwar policy making. In particular, unemployment would become more politically costly, and this would impair the ability of governments to pursue deflationary policies, where this was required to maintain adherence to the gold standard. Moreover, with increased unionization labor markets became more rigid, while the increasing size of firms, greater government intervention, and, in some countries, a move toward less competitive product markets all meant that goods markets were becoming less flexible as well. As Feinstein et al. (1997, pp. 22–23) stress, these changes implied less flexible economies, at a time when restructuring was required, meaning that unemployment would be a constant problem after the war, in turn making trade liberalization more difficult.

Second, the war left a legacy of inter-Allied war debts, amounting to some $26.5 billion, mostly owed to the United States and Britain, and with France the largest net debtor. Furthermore, in 1921 the Reparations Commission fixed a reparations bill of $33 billion to be paid by Germany, most of which was owed to Britain and France (Aldcroft 1977, chapter 4). These financial claims not only led to tension between the Allies and Germany, symbolized by the 1923 invasion of the Ruhr by Belgium and France, but also to disputes between the United States, which insisted on being paid in full, and her former Allies. The upshot was that the sort of international cooperation that had characterized prewar relationships between the world's leading central banks was now made much more difficult (Eichengreen 1992a,b), and as we will see later, these tensions would have broader geopolitical repercussions as well.

Third, as a result of these political changes in both the domestic and international spheres, attempts by interwar governments to return to the pre-1914 gold standard were fraught with difficulties, and once the Great Depression intervened the experiment was abandoned (although a gold bloc centered on France persevered until 1936, to its considerable cost). Contemporary observers, such as Ragnar Nurske (League of Nations 1944), believed that the collapse of the gold standard and currency instability was a disaster that hastened the disintegration of the international economy. We saw evidence in chapter 7 that stable exchange rates were indeed an important factor in the growth of world trade in the late nineteenth century, and the same source (Estevadeordal et al. 2003) shows econometrically that the collapse of the gold standard in the 1930s reduced world trade levels then.

Fourth, the war led directly to the creation of new nation states in Europe (Feinstein et al. 1997, pp. 28–32), with long-lasting consequences. The Habsburg Empire was replaced by six successor states (Czechoslovakia, Poland, Romania, Yugoslavia, Austria, and Hungary); four independent countries emerged out of what had been the Russian Empire (Estonia, Finland, Latvia, and Lithuania); and in 1922

London ceded independence to the Irish Free State, which would later become the Republic of Ireland. In some cases, the formation of new states could lead to economic integration. Such was the case with Poland, which joined together regions that had formerly been under Prussian, Austrian, and Russian control (Wolf 2003). In other cases, the newly independent states pursued liberal trade policies, notably the Irish Free State, which throughout the 1920s continued the outward-oriented strategy based on agricultural exports that had been the hallmark of Irish development since the Famine of the 1840s. More often, however, legislative independence was used to pursue nationalistic economic goals. While today's nationalist leaders, in regions such as Scotland and Quebec, speak of a free-trading future (Alesina and Spolaore 1997), in the early twentieth century independence was typically costly from an economic standpoint, involving the adoption of protectionist policies (Johnson 1965). And as Broadberry and Harrison (2005) point out, even if these new countries had not initially had protectionist intentions, as the interwar world generally descended into protectionism their very existence would imply additional barriers to trade within what had formerly been large imperial customs unions. Moreover, the new borders often separated complementary industries, leading to a breakdown of the traditional interregional division of labor. For example, Hungary retained about half her prewar industry, but lost over 80% of her forests, iron ore, waterpower, salt, and copper (Aldcroft 1977, p. 28). Elsewhere,

> Austria was left with sufficient spinning mills and finishing works, but with too few looms. At the same time Czechoslovakia, where the weaving mills were located, gave protection to an infant spinning industry, and so cut off the natural outlet for Austrian yarn. Austria's famous tanneries lost their sources of skins and tanning materials; her Alpine iron works lost their coal—about half of the old coalfields having gone to Czechoslovakia and Poland. Czechoslovakia contained a high proportion of the old Austrian industries, but not a population large enough to absorb their products…. The industries in Slovakia decayed because the favours and support they used to receive from Budapest dried up.[8]

A fifth legacy of the Great War was the Communist revolution in Russia in 1917, which paved the way for an eventual Russian retreat into virtual autarky. As early as April 1918, the Soviets established a foreign trade monopoly which would eventually be run by state-owned companies, each responsible for trade in a particular range

[8]Mitrany (1936, pp. 172–73), quoted in Lewis (1949, p. 21).

of products. This was necessary given the logic of the Communist economic system, since otherwise arbitrage would render unviable the attempts by central planners to fix relative prices without taking world market forces into account. Russia's exports fell from 1,520 million rubles in 1913 to 1 million rubles in 1920, and even after the end of the civil war Russia's engagement with the rest of the world remained greatly diminished. Its share of world trade in 1926 was 1.2%, less than a third of what it had been in 1914, and such trade as it did engage in was largely a necessary consequence of the Soviet Union's need for capital goods so that it could industrialize. This inward shift would prove to be remarkably long lasting. It was only with the collapse of Communism in the 1990s that Russia would begin its reinsertion into the international economy (chapter 9). One country that was particularly affected by this was Poland, which had exported a variety of manufactured goods to Russia before the war, but found herself cut off afterwards (James 2001, p. 116, pp. 158–59; Lewis 1949, p. 21). More broadly, the Soviet experiment had wide-ranging and long-lasting political consequences across the world, as we will see.

Sixth, and finally, while historians no longer accept the argument that the conflict, and the Treaty of Versailles which followed, set the world on a path that inevitably led to war, World War I did help to create the conditions which would lead to another world war two decades later (Howard 1989). For example, the independence of the Baltic states and Poland, the latter occupying territory formerly belonging to both Germany and Russia, might have been tolerated for the time being by the defeated powers (although in the case of Russia it took an unsuccessful war with Poland to make them recognize the new status quo), but was never really accepted. Germany, which (crucially) remained a large and potentially dangerous power, resented its territorial losses, its obligation to pay reparations, and its condemnation as the guilty party, as well as the implication that it had lost the war, something which German popular opinion was loath to accept (MacMillan 2001, p. 168; Marks 2002, p. 83). Politicians such as Hitler would almost immediately start feeding upon feelings of resentment and desire for revenge. The fact that Russia was now in Communist hands would make it much more difficult for France, Britain, and Russia to act in concert to block German expansion, and also heightened Japanese feelings of vulnerability in East Asia. The decision at Versailles to cede the Shantung peninsula, birthplace of Confucius, to the Japanese provoked outrage and disillusionment with the West in China, and despite Japan's later decision to give the peninsula back, the incident provoked widespread suspicion of Japan in both Britain and the United States. At the same time, Japan's failure to have a racial equality amendment inserted into the covenant of the League of Nations would help push its subsequent policies in an anti-Western direction (MacMillan 2001), while for many officers in the Imperial Japanese Army, "the Great War had demonstrated that economic autarky was necessary in order to guarantee victory in any future conflict. For Japan, which was resource poor, this meant that if the country was to survive a future clash with a Great Power or Powers, it required a larger empire that would provide it with a much greater measure of self-sufficiency" (Best 2003, p. 60). And finally, as we will see, the economic forces which the war helped set in motion would also play a powerful role in promoting militarism in Germany and Japan, and in preventing an adequate response to this threat.

INTERWAR COMMERCIAL POLICY[9]

Not surprisingly, the end of war did not imply an end to protection, even though the newly established League of Nations had as one of its functions the restoration and maintenance of a liberal international trading environment. The British Key Industries Act of 1919, and the Safeguarding of Industries Act of 1921, have already been mentioned; the United Kingdom also passed antidumping legislation in 1921; and minimum and maximum tariff rates were four times higher in France in 1918 than they had been before the war (Kindleberger 1989, p. 162). Even more seriously, the quantitative restrictions on trade which had been put in place during the war remained prevalent in central and southeastern Europe, where trade was at first characterized by intergovernmental barter, and later by systems of import licenses, by currency restrictions, and by government trade monopolies. This was largely due to the shortages of food, raw materials, and currency problems that the new governments faced, and although the international community agreed in Brussels in 1920, and in Portorose in 1921, that such restrictions should be removed, the agreements were not acted upon (the Portorose Protocol not even being ratified by any of its signatory states). This failure was followed by the Genoa Conference of 1922, which also called for the gradual elimination of quantitative restrictions, their replacement by tariffs, and the resumption of trade treaties based on the principle of nondiscrimination,

[9]Excellent summaries of interwar commercial policies can be found in League of Nations (1942), Kindleberger (1989), and James (2001), on which this account largely draws.

TABLE 8.2. Tariffs, 1913–31 (ad valorem equivalents, percent).

(a) League of Nations indices				
	Manufactured goods		All goods	
	1913	1925	1913	1925
Argentina	28	29	26	26
Australia	16	27	17	25
Austria	18	16	18	12
Belgium	9	15	6	8
Canada	26	23	18	16
Czechoslovakia	18	27	18	19
Denmark	14	10	9	6
France	20	21	18	12
Germany	13	20	12	12
Hungary	18	27	18	23
India	4	16	4	14
Italy	18	22	17	17
Netherlands	4	6	3	4
Poland	N.a.	32	N.a.	23
Spain	41	41	33	44
Sweden	20	16	16	13
Switzerland	9	14	7	11
Yugoslavia	N.a.	23	N.a.	23
United Kingdom	N.a.	5	N.a.	4
United States	44 (25)	37	33 (17)	29

Source: (a) League of Nations (1927, p. 15, Method B1). Notes: 1913 figures for Austria, Czechoslovakia, and Hungary refer to Austria–Hungary. The figures in parentheses for the United States in (a) refer to 1914. N.a. = not available.

with no greater success. Germany did abolish its licensing system in 1925, but Poland restored import prohibitions in the same year. There followed a series of conferences organized by the League of Nations during 1927–29 which had as their explicit goal the abolition of these restrictions, but which had only limited success. Pious declarations by such gatherings would become a feature of interwar economic diplomacy. In its retrospective on the interwar period, the League of Nations itself (1942, p. 101) ruefully acknowledged the paradox that "the international conferences unanimously recommended, and the great majority of Governments repeatedly proclaimed their intention to pursue, policies designed to bring about conditions of 'freer and more equal trade'; yet never before in history were trade barriers raised so rapidly or discrimination so generally practiced." Few if any commentators have dissented from this negative assessment.

TABLE 8.2. *Cont.*

	Foodstuffs			Semi-manufactured goods			Industrial manufactured goods		
	1913	1927	1931	1913	1927	1931	1913	1927	1931
Austria	29.1	16.5	59.5	20	15.2	20.7	19.3	21	27.7
Belgium	25.5	11.8	23.7	7.6	10.5	15.5	9.5	11.6	13
Bulgaria	24.7	79	133	24.2	49.5	65	19.5	75	90
Czechoslovakia	29.1	36.3	84	20	21.7	29.5	19.3	35.8	36.5
Finland	49	57.5	102	18.8	20.2	20	37.6	17.8	22.7
France	29.2	19.1	53	25.3	24.3	31.8	16.3	25.8	29
Germany	21.8	27.4	82.5	15.3	14.5	23.4	10	19	18.3
Hungary	29.1	31.5	60	20	26.5	32.5	19.3	31.8	42.6
Italy	22	24.5	66	25	28.6	49.5	14.6	28.3	41.8
Poland	69.4	72	110	63.5	33.2	40	85	55.6	52
Romania	34.7	45.6	87.5	30	32.6	46.3	25.5	48.5	55
Spain	41.5	45.2	80.5	26	39.2	49.5	42.5	62.7	75.5
Sweden	24.2	21.5	39	25.3	18	18	24.5	20.8	23.5
Switzerland	14.7	21.5	42.2	7.3	11.5	15.2	9.3	17.6	22
Yugoslavia	31.6	43.7	75	17.2	24.7	30.5	18	28	32.8

Source: (b) Liepmann (1938, p. 413). Notes: 1913 figures for Austria, Czechoslovakia, and Hungary refer to Austria–Hungary; 1913 figures for Poland in (b) refer to Russia; 1913 figures for Yugoslavia in (b) refer to Serbia.

Meanwhile, as table 8.2 shows, high tariffs were a problem in many European countries. The data in table 8.2 come from two different sources, the League of Nations (1927) and Liepmann (1938), which use different methods, and occasionally imply different trends for particular commodity categories in individual countries. However, by the middle of the 1920s tariffs were unambiguously higher than they had been in 1913 in Bulgaria, Czechoslovakia, Germany, Hungary, Italy, Romania, Spain, Switzerland, and Yugoslavia.[10]

Protection was on the rise outside Europe as well. This was in part a response to the disturbed economic conditions following the boom of 1919–20 and the subsequent slump of 1920–21. It was also in part due to the fact that various Asian countries had recovered their ability to conduct their commercial policy in what they perceived to be their own best interests. Thus, antidumping legislation was introduced in Japan in 1920, as well as in Australia, New Zealand, and the United States in 1921. In India, revenue tariffs were increased in the aftermath of the war, and the recommendation of the 1922

[10] Czechoslovakia and Hungary are here compared with prewar Austria–Hungary, and Yugoslavia with Serbia.

Indian Fiscal Commission that the government introduce a system of "discriminating protection" led to explicitly protective tariffs being introduced in key sectors such as iron and steel, cotton textiles, and sugar (Tomlinson 1993, pp. 132–34). According to table 8.2, the average Indian tariff on manufactured goods was 16% in 1925, four times the 1913 rate. Chinese tariffs were also increased substantially when that country regained tariff autonomy in 1929 (Latham 1981, p. 108), the average tariff on all goods jumping immediately from around 4% to 8.5% according to Clemens and Williamson (2004). The same source shows the Indian average tariff rising from 4.8% in 1918 to 14.7% in 1929, the Burmese tariff rising from 10.8% to 25.3%, and the Egyptian tariff almost doubling from 9.9% to 18.7% over the same period.

In the Americas, the widespread use of specific rather than ad valorem tariffs meant that many countries started the postwar era with lower levels of tariff protection than before the conflict (since wartime inflation had raised the prices of the goods in question, thus diminishing the protective impact of the tariffs).[11] To a certain extent, postwar deflation helped to gradually restore tariffs to their prewar levels, and this was in some instances reinforced by tariff legislation, notably in 1922 when the United States, whose government was once again in Republican hands, passed the Fordney–McCumber Tariff Act, which substantially raised tariff rates. Average tariff rates were on the rise throughout the 1920s, but in large part this was merely restoring 1913 levels of protection, and in some countries, such as Brazil, the process had not been completed by the end of the decade (Bulmer-Thomas 2003, pp. 184–86). Nonetheless, table 8.2 indicates that prewar levels of protection (which had been extremely high) had been reattained in Argentina as early as 1925, and while tariffs were slightly lower in the United States than they had been in 1913, they were already considerably higher than in 1914 (the Underwood tariff of October 1913 having substantially lowered U.S. protection, while maintaining it at what was still a high level by international standards). Rapid increases in postwar tariffs were also experienced in Australia, where according to table 8.2 tariffs in 1925 were some 50% higher than in 1913.

Things would soon get worse, as a result of two factors: first, a worldwide decline in primary commodity prices in the late 1920s, and second, the cataclysmic shock that was the Great Depression, which would heighten the problems facing primary producers and create a widespread demand for industrial protection among unemployed workers and beleaguered capitalists.

[11] Specific tariffs are expressed as a fixed tax per unit of the good in question, whereas ad valorem tariffs are expressed as a percentage of the import value.

Wheat prices began to fall from 1925, as world acreages continued to expand and stocks accumulated. Western European protection made the situation of New World and Eastern European suppliers worse. While some exporting governments (the Canadians and Americans) attempted to keep domestic prices high, the Soviet Union's aim of earning sufficient revenues to pay for capital equipment imports led it to export more as prices fell, thus exacerbating the problem (Kindleberger 1973, chapter 4). The experience was similar with sugar, whose price declined during the 1920s in response to wartime expansion outside Europe and postwar European recovery. The problem was worsened by the policies of certain governments, such as the British, who subsidized domestic production, and the Japanese, who started to produce sugar in Taiwan. Countries that had prospered during the war were now in difficulties. Java found herself excluded from the Indian market by tariffs, and from the Japanese market as well: production fell by five-sixths between 1928–29 and 1932–33. Cuba was also badly hit, and saw rioting in 1928 (Kindleberger 1973, p. 94, 1989, p. 168). Wool prices dropped sharply from the middle of the decade, with serious consequences for the Australian economy, while the postwar boom encouraged increases in rubber and coffee output that eventually led to falling prices for those commodities as well.

Falling agricultural prices were a particular problem since farmers in many countries had substantial debts that were fixed in nominal terms, even though farm revenues were declining. The inevitable result was a rise in agricultural protection in countries such as Germany and France. More seriously for the world economy, American farmers were also suffering from the agricultural depression, and so in 1928 U.S. Presidential candidate Herbert Hoover promised them tariff protection. Once elected, he called a special session of Congress in early 1929 to deliver on his pledge. The Smoot–Hawley Tariff that emerged in mid 1930 protected industry as well as agriculture, and represented a substantial increase in overall protection.[12] Deflation over the course of the next two years would increase average tariffs to an even greater extent (Crucini 1994; Irwin 1998a).

In contrast to the nineteenth-century experience, the United States was now sufficiently important that the Smoot–Hawley Tariff triggered

[12] How substantial depends on how the average tariff is measured. As a share of total imports, tariff revenues in 1931 were around 18%, which as DeLong (1998) points out would have been a low tariff by nineteenth-century standards, and was less than the level attained at the start of the century (DeLong 1998, p. 358; Eichengreen 1989, p. 16). As a share of dutiable imports, however, tariff revenues were higher in 1931 and 1932 than they had been in 1900, and Irwin claims that the Smoot–Hawley Tariffs were "arguably the highest since the Civil War" (Irwin 1998c, p. 327).

a wave of tariff increases in countries such as Canada, France, Italy, Spain, and Switzerland (Kindleberger 1989; Jones 1934), although the extent to which the more general rise in tariffs which followed was due to retaliation, as opposed to various domestic causes, remains subject to dispute (Eichengreen 1989; Irwin 1998b). At a minimum, the tariff sent the signal that the rising economic and military power of the United States was unwilling to be the unilateral guarantor of open markets that the United Kingdom had been before the war, a fact which as we will see would have serious repercussions for East Asia, and the world. The *Pax Britannica* was at an end, and the Americans were not yet ready to underwrite a *Pax Americana* (Kindleberger 1973). In any event, the tariff increases were severe: by 1931, average tariffs on foodstuffs had risen to 53% in France, 59.5% in Austria, 66% in Italy, 75% in Yugoslavia, more than 80% in Czechoslovakia, Germany, Romania, and Spain, and to more than 100% in Bulgaria, Finland, and Poland (table 8.2).

By this stage, the Great Depression was also making its impact felt on trade policies worldwide. The literature on this catastrophe is too vast to be adequately summarized here, so we shall be brief.[13] The origins of the crisis are to be found in a move toward tighter monetary policy in Germany and the United States, in 1927 and 1928 respectively, designed to prevent what was seen as unsustainable stock market speculation. In Germany, the result was an immediate sharp decline in the stock market, and investment there fell almost continuously from 1927 until 1932 (Temin 1971; Ritschl 1999; Voth 2003). In the United States, the stock market and investment kept increasing until 1929, but monetary growth slowed immediately. Even more importantly, the fact that so many countries were by now back on the gold standard meant that these deflationary shocks were transmitted across the world. Being linked together via fixed exchange rates, countries found themselves having to match the American monetary tightening, since otherwise they would have lost the reserves that were required to stay on gold. Monetary growth thus slowed across the world in 1928 (Eichengreen 1992a, table 8.1, p. 223). Moreover, each time one country started to experience falling demand as a

---

[13]Classic references include Temin (1989) and Eichengreen (1992a). The "Eichengreen–Temin" view of the Great Depression is summarized, among other places, in Temin (1993) and Eichengreen and Temin (2003). Eichengreen and Temin agree with Friedman and Schwartz (1963, 1965) that the Great Depression was largely a monetary phenomenon, but regard it as an international phenomenon rather than a primarily American one, and as being due to a variety of structural factors, notably the gold standard, rather than to isolated policy mistakes.

result of these contractionary policies, and went into recession, its imports from elsewhere fell, reducing demand in its trading partners and heightening balance of payments problems there. Under the prevailing gold standard orthodoxy, the appropriate response was to engage in more deflation, in order to cut imports and restore external balance. The world's economies thus found themselves caught in a vicious circle in which each country's adjustment pushed both itself and its partners further into crisis. Furthermore, these deflationary policies required fully flexible nominal wages if they were to be successful, but as Eichengreen and Temin (2003) emphasize, the rising worker militancy that as we saw was one of the Great War's legacies made this impossible, with profoundly negative consequences for both profitability and employment. Banking crises in Germany, the United States, and elsewhere made things even worse.

Between 1929 and 1933, GDP fell by almost 30% in the United States and Canada, while industrial output fell by over 35% in the United States, Austria, Belgium, Switzerland, Czechoslovakia, and Poland, and by over 40% in Germany. In the years following 1929, unemployment would rise to over 19% in Australia and Canada, to over 23% in Belgium and Sweden, to almost 25% in the United States, and to over 30% in Denmark, Germany, the Netherlands, and Norway (Mitchell 1992, 1993, 1995). The slump lowered the demand for primary products, including those exported by the South. Between 1929 and 1931, the gold price of coffee fell by 53% in Brazil; the prices of wool and refrigerated beef fell by 72% and 53% respectively in Argentina; the price of Malaysian rubber fell by 84%; and the price of Ceylonese tea fell by 62% (ibid.). In turn, these unfavorable draws in the international "commodity lottery" (Diaz Alejandro 1984, p. 20) slashed export revenues in primary-exporting countries. Table 8.3(a) shows that export revenues fell by over 60% in Latin America and Asia between 1929 and 1932; by over 50% in Australasia, and by over 40% in Africa. There was a particularly spectacular decline in Chile (more than 85%: see League of Nations 1939), while between 1928–29 and 1932–33 the value of exports fell by 75–80% in China; by 70–75% in Bolivia, Cuba, Malaya, Peru, and El Salvador; by 65–70% in a further thirteen primary exporters, and by over 50% in a further twenty-two (Kindleberger 1973, p. 191). To make matters worse, deflation implied rising real interest rates facing debtor countries, and no further lending was forthcoming from rich countries to help tide over the developing world during the crisis (Eichengreen and Portes 1986).

The result was widespread and radical measures to cope with the pressures on the balance of payments, including currency depreciation and import controls. Beginning in 1931, all of the major

TABLE 8.3. The decline and recovery of world trade, 1929–37.

	1929	1932	1937	1929	1932	1937
(a) Regional export and import values (gold dollars, 1929 = 100)						
	Exports			Imports		
Europe including U.S.S.R.	100.0	40.8	43.8	100.0	42.8	45.9
North America	100.0	32.6	40.9	100.0	30.5	40.0
Latin America	100.0	37.2	50.1	100.0	27.7	42.8
Africa	100.0	58.5	71.3	100.0	47.4	59.6
Asia	100.0	35.8	52.0	100.0	40.7	49.7
Australasia	100.0	44.8	59.6	100.0	28.5	45.9
World	100.0	39.0	46.7	100.0	39.2	45.9
(a) Regional export and import quantities (1929 = 100)						
	Exports			Imports		
Europe including U.S.S.R.	100.0	68.5	83.0	100.0	82.0	90.5
North America	100.0	58.5	84.5	100.0	61.0	95.0
Rest of world	100.0	95.5	127.0	100.0	62.5	106.0

Source: League of Nations (1939).

Latin American countries, with the notable exception of Argentina, defaulted on their debt. Exchange controls were introduced in 1931 in Brazil, Chile, Uruguay, Colombia, Bolivia, Argentina, and Nicaragua, and these countries were followed in 1932 by Costa Rica, Ecuador, Japan, and Paraguay, in 1933 by Mexico and El Salvador, and in 1934 by Honduras, Cuba, and China (Gordon 1941, pp. 54–55). Multiple exchange rates were introduced, biased against imports, and import quotas introduced (Diaz Alejandro 1984). Meanwhile, falling prices and government policies meant that tariff protection rose sharply. According to the Clemens–Williamson tariff data, average Latin American tariffs rose from 22.2% in 1929 to 27.3% in 1932, while those in Asia rose from 11.4% to 20.7%, and those in Egypt rose from 18.7% to 37.8%.

The Depression also exacerbated protection in the North, as governments attempted to shore up declining industries. Table 8.2(b) shows a widespread increase in tariffs in Europe between 1927 and 1931, while the Clemens–Williamson average tariff data show jumps in the average tariff between 1929 and 1932 in the United States (where the increase was from 13.5% to 19.6%), the European periphery (16.4% to 26.6%), and northwest Europe (excluding the United Kingdom, the average tariff increased from 8.1% to 14.9%). In a highly symbolic rupture with her nineteenth-century past, the United Kingdom took a decisive move toward protection in 1932, establishing 10% tariffs on a wide variety of imports. For a few months, Ireland was one of the only free trade holdouts in Europe, but later that year she too succumbed as Éamon de Valera was elected, and embarked on a wholesale trade war with the United Kingdom. In opting for a policy of import substitution, Ireland was behaving like other primary producers around the periphery, and as in Latin America the policy seemed initially to be successful in insulating the economy from the worst effects of the Great Depression (Diaz Alejandro 1984; O'Rourke 1991; Neary and Ó Gráda 1991).

Furthermore, the tentative and unsatisfactory progress toward eliminating European quantitative restrictions on trade prior to the Depression was replaced by a general move to implement such measures, even in countries that had not done so during the 1920s. In France, quotas became widespread during the 1930s: according to Haberler (1943, p. 19), 58% of French imports in 1937 were covered by some sort of quantitative restriction, while the same was true of 52% of imports into Switzerland, 26% in the Netherlands, and 24% in Belgium.[14] Even worse for the international trading system, and the world, Hitler came to power in 1933 as a direct result of high unemployment rates (Stögbauer 2001), and proceeded to institute "totalitarian" quantitative controls on foreign trade reminiscent of a war economy, as part of an effort to maximize German self-sufficiency. Pending the establishment of lebensraum to the east, the Nazis overcame Germany's deficiency in primary products by taking advantage of balance of payments difficulties in southeast Europe. There, governments proved eager to export their food and minerals in return for German manufactures. This "pernicious bilateralism," as Irwin (1993b) calls it, combined with the imperial preferences of Britain (established in Ottawa in 1932) and other colonial powers, led to the complete breakdown of the MFN principle of nondiscrimination.

The process whereby policies in one country provoked restrictive countermeasures elsewhere is well illustrated by the experience in

---

[14]Irwin (1993b) makes the point that there was a trade-off between countries' adherence to monetary orthodoxy and their adherence to free trade orthodoxy: the four countries just mentioned stuck rigidly to the gold standard for much of the 1930s, leading to deflation, overvaluation, and balance of payments difficulties. Quantitative restrictions were in large measure a response to these difficulties. By contrast, quotas were less widespread in the sterling area, which had left the gold standard in 1931. In Ireland, "only" 17% of imports were covered by quantitative restrictions in 1937, while the figure was 12% in Norway, and just 8% in the United Kingdom.

India. As already noted, Australian farmers had greatly expanded wheat production during the 1920s, and this trend continued when the new Labour government instituted a "grow more wheat" campaign in 1930. Farmers there were thus very badly hit by falling wheat prices. In addition, the deteriorating terms of trade led to the country running a trade deficit, to a loss of reserves, and to worries about Australia's ability to continue servicing its debt (Eichengreen 1992a, pp. 232–36; Rothermund 1996, pp. 82–86). The response was a de facto devaluation of the Australian currency in January 1931, which helped maintain wheat exports at high levels and eased the pressure on the balance of payments. However, this policy increased the competition facing wheat producers elsewhere, and in the summer of 1931 the Indian Government, faced with the possibility of peasant unrest in the wheat-growing Punjab, decided to impose a tariff on wheat imports. In a very similar manner, the successful Japanese response to the Depression, which involved leaving the gold standard in December 1931, and allowing a massive depreciation of the yen the following year, put pressure on Indian cotton textile manufacturers, and led to heightened protection for the sector. In 1930, tariffs of 20% had been introduced on low-quality cotton textile imports, but this level was raised to 50% for non-British goods in 1932, and to 75% in 1933. Finally, the Indian sugar industry benefited from high levels of protection aimed at Javanese exports, while the Indian tea industry managed to successfully organize a policy of export restriction, which kept prices relatively high (Tomlinson 1993, p. 133; Rothermund 1996, pp. 93–95).

The shift toward protection in India and elsewhere had in turn severe political consequences in Japan, where the impulse toward autarky had already been strengthened by racist immigration restrictions in the British Empire and the United States. Business interests had persuaded the government there to restore the gold standard in 1930 and support the League's attempts to promote freer trade, but with the U.S. market now largely closed to Japanese goods such as silk (whose share in Japanese exports collapsed from 36% in 1929 to 13% in 1934), and with its gold standard commitments forcing the government to cut expenditure, support for outward-looking policies inevitably declined. When the British Empire responded to the yen's depreciation with anti-Japanese tariffs and quotas, this further damaged liberal interests and strengthened those urging the establishment of a Japanese economic bloc, building on its existing possessions in Manchuria, Taiwan, and Korea (Best 2003; Boyce 2003; Rothermund 1996, pp. 115–19).

The comparison with nineteenth-century Britain is instructive here. Britain was also an island nation, with a limited territory, and as we saw in chapter 6 its population was growing rapidly in the late eighteenth and early nineteenth centuries. The inevitable implication was large-scale food and raw material imports, paid for with manufactured exports (Harley and Crafts 2000; Clark 2007b), while in the late nineteenth century emigration to present or former colonies in the New World provided an additional safety valve. Similarly, the Japanese population grew rapidly in the early twentieth century, from 44 million in 1900 to 56 million in 1920 and 65 million in 1931 (Maddison 2003), but none of the solutions that had been available to the British then seemed open to it now. The "regions of recent settlement" refused Japanese immigration, and protection elsewhere meant that exports, and hence the ability to import, seemed threatened as well. In the context of the relatively peaceful and liberal nineteenth century, the Royal Navy had been able to ensure British interests by maintaining a relatively open trading regime for all, but this was not an appealing option in the context of the increasingly dangerous 1930s. The stage was thus set for the Japanese army to gradually take control of the country, since imperialism seemed like one way to secure adequate supplies of primary products in a world in which the international division of labor was breaking down.[15] In September 1931, the Japanese conquered Manchuria, setting up a puppet state there the following year, and withdrawing from the League of Nations in 1933. East and Southeast Asia were now set on a road that would eventually lead to war, and the Japanese "Greater East Asia Co-prosperity Sphere."

Beginning in 1932, there were several signs that at least some countries were trying to moderate, if not reverse, the increases in protectionism of the previous years, although the World Economic Conference of 1933 proved a failure. In 1932 what we now know as the three Benelux countries agreed at Ouchy to start cutting tariffs on each other's exports. This agreement came to nothing, however, as it required other countries, with whom the Ouchy group had MFN relations, to waive their MFN rights, which the United Kingdom refused to do. While the League of Nations had been a persistent advocate of the principle of nondiscrimination, it was forced to admit in 1942 that

> instead of facilitating, the clause tended to obstruct the reduction of tariffs by means of bilateral or multilateral agreements, owing to the reluctance of governments to make concessions which would be generalized by it. This was the result, mainly, of two causes: first, the refusal

[15] Note, however, that, according to Yasuba (1996), it was the Japanese military build-up which created natural resource shortages in the first place.

of the United States to reduce its own very high tariff by negotiation while claiming to benefit from any tariff reduction negotiated between European countries; secondly, the opposition of certain countries—notably the United Kingdom, the United States and the British Dominions— to derogations from strict M.F.N. practice permitting the conclusion of regional or similar agreements for tariff reduction, the benefits of which would be limited to the participants.

(League of Nations 1942, p. 119)

How to explain this distinction between the experiences of the 1860s and 1870s, when the MFN clause had helped speed up liberalization, and the interwar period, when it encouraged countries—not just the United States—to try to "free ride" by withholding tariff concessions of their own, while claiming any concessions made between other countries? One interpretation is that the 1860s wave of tariff-cutting succeeded because the bilateral MFN treaties were, initially, discriminatory: once Britain and France had granted each other concessions, the Belgians found themselves at a disadvantage in these markets, and had an incentive to conclude a treaty, and so on. Thus, the MFN treaties of the 1860s constituted an example of what Irwin (1993b, p. 112) calls "progressive" bilateralism, of the sort that Cordell Hull was advocating in the 1930s. In his submission to the 1933 London conference, Hull proposed that the MFN principle not be invoked to prevent agreements among groups of countries, but suggested that a number of conditions be attached, one of which was that such agreements be "open to the accession of all countries" (Viner 1950, p. 35).[16]

These problems did not, however, completely block all progress toward trade liberalization. The Oslo group, comprising the Ouchy three, plus Denmark, Norway, Sweden, and (eventually) Finland, had met in 1930 for discussions on tariff reform, and agreed in The

---

[16]The latter interpretation would lead to a sanguine view of regional trade agreements. On the other hand, some of the *costs* of discrimination identified by recent authors have their echoes in the historical record too. For example, the argument that in the absence of the MFN principle, countries may be reluctant to reach bilateral agreements on the grounds that their partners may reach subsequent agreements which "by granting to third countries concessions still greater than those given to themselves, and to which they would have no claim, would render nugatory the concessions which they received" (Viner 1951, p. 107; Bagwell and Staiger 1999), finds support in the failure of the United States (and Sardinia) to negotiate satisfactory trade agreements while pursuing a conditional MFN policy in the nineteenth century. It was largely as a result of this experience that the United States adopted the unconditional form of the MFN clause in 1923.

Hague in 1937 to a program of eliminating quotas between member states on the basis that this would not violate others' MFN rights, which only applied to tariffs. Most importantly, perhaps, the 1932 U.S. presidential election led to the appointment of the strongly pro-free trade Cordell Hull as Secretary of State. In 1934, the U.S. Reciprocal Trade Agreements Act delegated authority to the Executive to conclude trade agreements, which Hull proceeded to do. As Irwin (1998b) points out, this reflected a fundamental shift in U.S. trade policy making, which had traditionally involved the United States Congress setting American tariffs in a unilateral manner. In part, the shift was prompted by a growing realization that foreign tariffs were hampering U.S. recovery (ibid.). By 1939, the United States had signed twenty treaties with countries accounting for 60% of its trade, the most important of which was with the United Kingdom, and American average tariffs had declined from over 50% in the early 1930s to below 40% (ibid., p. 350). The postwar American engagement in favor of multilateral free trade did not spring up overnight, therefore, but was already beginning to emerge during the 1930s.

However, the Anglo-American treaty only came into effect in 1939, and was soon overtaken by events. With the outbreak of World War II, blockades would once again prevent trade between the belligerent powers, and submarine warfare resumed. Thus, this period ended as it had begun, with a world at war, and governments acting so as to completely impede the normal functioning of international commodity markets.

TRANSPORT COSTS

The interwar period saw a continuation of the railway construction that had characterized the preceding era, notably in the developing world. By 1937, 5.7% of the world's railway mileage was located in Africa, 10.2% in Latin America, and 10.9% in Asia (Latham 1981, p. 23). Diesel and electric locomotives were introduced, gradually replacing the traditional steam engine. In addition, the interwar period was notable for the rapid spread of motor vehicles, which initially provided transportation services in urban areas, before serving on feeder routes to the main railway lines, and eventually competing with those lines themselves. Adoption was particularly rapid in the United States: in 1921 there was one commercial motor vehicle for every 85 Americans, whereas in 1938 there was one for every 29. By contrast, the equivalent 1938 figures were 79 in Britain, 91 in France, 179 in Germany, and 497 in Japan (Hugill 1993, p. 238).

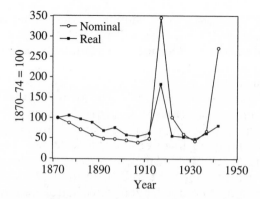

FIGURE 8.1. Freight rate indices, 1870–1944 (1870–74 = 100).
Source: Shah Mohammed and Williamson (2004, table 3, p. 188).

The growing importance of motor vehicles was in turn one of the main factors underlying the rise of petroleum as an increasingly vital energy source for the world economy. Whereas previously petroleum had largely served as a fuel for domestic lighting, it was now an essential input into modern transportation technologies, not just motor vehicles and diesel locomotives but that other defining technology of the twentieth century, the airplane, as well. Since these new technologies had military as well as civilian uses, petroleum now gained a crucial strategic importance. Moreover, oil reserves were unevenly distributed across the globe, implying an important new motive for international trade. Initially, the most important reserves were to be found in Russia and North America, but by the interwar period production was taking place in Iran and Iraq as well, under the auspices of foreign-owned companies such as the Anglo-Persian (later Anglo-Iranian) Oil Company, today's BP. The discovery of massive oil reserves in Saudi Arabia in 1948 would confirm the central importance of the Islamic World for the world's energy supply, with geopolitical repercussions that still reverberate today.

Despite these important technological breakthroughs, the picture was not so bright as regards the *costs* of intercontinental transport. Not surprisingly, freight rates shot up during World War I, before falling again, as can be seen in figure 8.1. The interwar period did see a continuation of the many incremental improvements to ocean shipping that had characterized the prewar period, such as improvements to the boilers used to convert water to steam, and the development of turboelectric transmission mechanisms, but the data suggest that this productivity growth was considerably slower during the interwar period than before the war. To be sure, according to Shah Mohammed and Williamson (2004), total factor productivity growth between 1909–11 and 1932–34 in the British tramp shipping sector was as fast if not faster than before the war, with annual TFP growth rates of 2.83% on the transatlantic route, 1.27% on the Alexandrian route, and 1.05% on the Bombay route. However, they attribute this impressive performance to war-induced technical change, since the bulk of the improvements were achieved by 1923–25.

This wartime boost to productivity in transportation was, moreover, counteracted by rising factor prices, in particular higher fuel costs and wages, and more expensive ships. As a result nominal freight rates were higher during the 1920s than they had been before the war. Although nominal freight rates would briefly regain prewar levels in the early 1930s, they then increased as the decade progressed, before once more shooting up during World War II. Had interwar productivity growth rates been maintained at their wartime levels, Shah Mohammed and Williamson (2004, pp. 194–95) conclude that nominal freight rates would have declined during the period, but this was not to be. The interwar period thus marks a sharp contrast with the continual technologically driven decline in nominal freight rates experienced during the late nineteenth century.

The interwar picture is not quite so pessimistic as regards real freight rates, since commodity prices were much higher after the war than before, and thus a given nominal freight rate translated into a lower real transport cost. Even here, however, it is clear from figure 8.1 that the war interrupted what had been a dramatic late-nineteenth-century decline in real transport costs, and that when those costs started to fall once more, it was at a slower rate than previously. Taking 1884 as 100, the Shah Mohammed–Williamson real freight index stood at 67 in 1905–9, and if the trend (assumed linear) had continued, it would have stood at just 31 in 1930–34. Instead, it stood at 58; moreover, this would prove to be the low point of real interwar transport costs, since they then started to rise again.

It would have taken a dramatic acceleration in transport cost declines to have overcome the effects of the rising trade barriers documented in the previous section. Indeed, as chapter 7 showed this was the mechanism that had led to international commodity market integration during the late nineteenth century, when tariffs had increased in Europe and much of the New World. There would be no such technological free lunch for the interwar international economy, however.

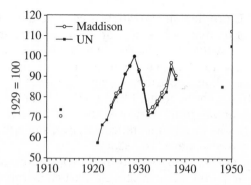

FIGURE 8.2. World trade indices, 1913–50 (1929 = 100).
Source: United Nations (1962) and Maddison (1995, p. 239).

THE VOLUME OF WORLD TRADE

What were the combined effects of the technological and political developments described above on international trade? Figure 8.2 plots two indices of world trade. The first was produced by the United Nations in 1962, in an unpublished internal report, United Nations (1962), which was a successor to earlier indices produced by Folke Hilgerdt,[17] while the second is taken from Angus Maddison (1995), building on his earlier work (Maddison 1962), which drew largely on the official data published by the League of Nations (1939). As can be seen, despite the disagreement concerning trends between 1913 and 1924 highlighted earlier, the series correspond closely for 1924–38. The volume of world trade rose by a third between 1924 and 1929, before losing all those gains in the succeeding three years. There followed a gradual recovery to 1937, although the 1929 peak was never quite reattained, before a large decline in 1938, and the undocumented but no doubt substantial collapse during the war that followed.

Overall, the period was disastrous as regards aggregate trade growth, which lay somewhere between 0.7% and 1% per annum, compared with the 3.8% growth rate between 1855 and 1913. In other words, even on the most optimistic interpretation of the available data, trade growth during the quarter century following 1913 reverted to the pre-1800 level of roughly 1% per annum, less than a third of the level during the nineteenth century. The post-1929 collapse in world trade was primarily due to a decline in manufactured goods trade: between

[17]Hilgerdt's series were used by both Lewis (1952) and Svennilson (1954). The series used here is much closer to Maddison's than the earlier series.

TABLE 8.4. Structure of trade by region, 1913–37.

	Share of primary products in exports (%)			Share of primary products in imports (%)		
	1913	1928	1937	1913	1928	1937
U.K. and Ireland	30.3	25.1	28.0	81.2	78.0	82.1
NW Europe	48.0	35.0	36.9	76.7	76.0	77.1
World	63.7	60.4	61.1	65.0	61.9	63.7
North America	74.1	61.5	55.3	63.4	68.0	72.3
Other Europe	75.6	84.1	78.8	59.9	52.0	53.0
Asia	79.5	68.9	72.8	43.2	50.3	51.2
Africa	96.3	96.4	96.3	40.5	31.1	28.4
Latin America	96.8	97.5	98.3	40.4	33.0	34.8
Australasia	98.1	97.9	96.1	25.9	26.1	26.2

Source: Yates (1959, pp. 227–30).

1929 and 1932, manufactured goods trade fell by 42%, while trade in primary products fell by just 13% (Lewis 1952). The interwar world was still clearly divided into those regions specialized in manufacturing (in particular, northwest Europe), and those whose exports consisted almost entirely of primary products, notably Africa, Latin America, and Australasia (table 8.4). Asia, southeast Europe, and North America constituted intermediate cases, with progress toward becoming more manufacturing-based being much faster in the latter region than in the former two. Thus, it was in the industrial regions—Europe and North America—that export volumes collapsed, as table 8.3(b) shows. Export volumes in the rest of the world fell less than 5% between 1929 and 1932, and by 1937 they were more than 25% higher than they had been in 1929 (whereas they were still more than 15% lower in both Europe and North America).

On the other hand, as we have seen, the nominal *value* of exports fell very substantially in all continents (table 8.3(a)). Apart from Africa, where export revenues fell by "only" 42%, export revenues fell between 55% and 70%. The contrast between the data on export quantities and those on nominal export values can be explained by the fact that export *prices* fell by most in the primary-producing regions of the world, whose terms of trade consequently deteriorated. According to Arthur Lewis (1969, pp. 49–50), the price of tropical products, relative to manufactured goods, fell by 38% between 1929 and 1932, while the price of primary products more generally fell by 30% over the same period (Grilli and Yang 1988, pp. 37–39). The League of Nations's data show the North American terms of trade improving by 11%

between 1929 and 1932, the European terms of trade by 13.3%, and the terms of trade of the rest of the world falling by 29.4%. In those Latin American countries for which there are data, between 1929 and 1933 the terms of trade fell by between 21% and 45% according to Diaz Alejandro (1984, p. 19), in sharp contrast with the improving terms of trade experienced by the continent during the late nineteenth century as a result of declining transport costs (Clingingsmith and Williamson 2005). Relatively small declines in export quantities thus coincided with large falls in export revenue. Declining export revenues, combined with a breakdown in international capital markets, of course implied that the ability to pay for imports declined. This explains why imports fell by as much in the South as in the North during the Great Depression.

Another much-remarked upon feature of the interwar trade experience is that, of this reduced trade total, a smaller proportion was multilateral in nature. Trade became more bilateral, with several blocs emerging which traded increasingly within themselves, rather than with each other. Table 8.5 gives the League of Nations's data on the role that formal or informal empires played in the trade of several leading nations. In the cases of the United Kingdom, France, Portugal, and the United States, the Depression years (1929–32) saw a marked increase in the share of their trade that took place with their overseas colonies. In the cases of Italy, Germany, and Japan, it was during 1932–38 that the tendency toward increased bilateralism was most pronounced. Thus, the share of Italy's exports going to her colonies and Ethiopia increased from just 3.6% in 1932 to nearly a quarter in 1938. Over the same period, the share of Japanese exports going to Korea and China rose from just over one-third to nearly two-thirds, while the share of Germany's exports going to southeast Europe more than trebled. Some of this growth in regionalization was the natural consequence of previous economic links between neighbors, but trade blocs also served to divert trade away from previous channels (Eichengreen and Irwin 1995), while the dramatic reorientation of the Axis Powers' trade during the 1930s bears an obvious relationship with the military strategies pursued by these countries during the period, with the causation between the former and the latter going in both directions. In the case of Japan, the strategy seems to have facilitated recovery from the Depression, in that the volume of Japanese exports roughly doubled between 1928 and 1935, while the value of its exports rose by between a quarter and a third. This was achieved despite American protectionism, which led to a fall in the share of Japanese exports going to North America from 43.8% in 1929 to 21.8% in 1935 (League of Nations 1939, pp. 33, 72).

TABLE 8.5. The share of formal and informal empire trade, 1929–38 (percent).

Trade of	Share of	In imports			In exports		
		1929	1932	1938	1929	1932	1938
U.K.	British Commonwealth, colonies, protectorates, etc.	30.2	36.4	41.9	44.4	45.4	49.9
U.S.	Philippines	2.9	6.1	4.8	1.6	2.8	2.8
France	French colonies, protectorates, and mandated territories	12	20.9	25.8	18.8	31.5	27.5
Belgium	Belgian Congo	3.9	3.8	8.3	2.6	1.3	1.9
Netherlands	Netherlands overseas territories	5.5	5	8.8	9.4	5.9	10.7
Italy	Italian colonies and Ethiopia	1.5	1.1	1.8	2.1	3.6	23.3
Portugal	Portuguese overseas territories	7.9	10.4	10.2	12.7	13.9	12.2
Japan	*Korea and Formosa*	12.3	26.2	30	16.8	21.6	32.9
	Kwantung	6	4	1.6	4.8	6.8	13.7
	Manchuria	1.9	2.7	9	2.5	1.5	8.1
	Rest of China	5.8	4	4.4	10.9	7.38	
	Total Japanese sphere of influence	26	36.9	45	35	37.2	62.7
Germany	*Bulgaria, Greece, Hungary, Romania, Turkey, Yugoslavia*	4.5	5.5	12	5	3.9	13.2
	Latin America	12.2	11.2	15.6	7.8	4.3	11.5
	Total German sphere of influence	16.7	16.7	27.6	12.8	8.2	24.7

Source: League of Nations (1939, pp. 34–35).

PRICE CONVERGENCE AND DIVERGENCE

The question which now arises is: what caused this dismal interwar performance, and, more specifically, the unprecedented collapse in world trade between 1929 and 1932? If the freight rate data in Shah Mohammed and Williamson (2004) can be believed, one candidate is ruled out, namely transport costs (figure 8.1). These fell through the early 1930s, and only started rising in the latter half of the decade, by which time the world trade recovery was already well underway. Nor can it be the case that falling trade volumes were solely due to the fact that there was less output to trade: according to Maddison's (2001) data, world trade to GDP ratios fell from around 9% at the 1929 peak to 5.5% in 1950. Finally, as table 8.4 has already suggested there is not much evidence that the decline in trade was due to the "Great Specialization" unraveling. Indeed, the overall pattern of North–South trade changed very little during the four decades following 1913, an interesting fact given the economic disintegration of the period. While the share of the South in world industrial exports had risen from 3% in the late 1870s to 8% in 1913, it barely moved during the subsequent period, standing at just 9% in the mid 1950s (Yates 1959, p. 58).[18]

The increase in restrictive trade practices was frequently invoked by contemporaries seeking to explain the collapse in world trade during the interwar period, while others pointed to the demise of the gold standard and associated currency instability. In terms of figure 5.2, the causes of the interwar trade slump must be found either in rising barriers to trade, which increased the wedge between commodity prices in importing and exporting countries, or in leftward shifts in demand and supply, due to the Great Depression. If the former effect was at work, then this should have been manifested in rising intercontinental price gaps: can these be documented for the interwar period?

In contrast to the voluminous literature documenting late-nine-teenth-century commodity market integration, there has been almost no work looking at interwar price gaps, but such evidence as we have points to a cessation of integration in some cases, and disintegration in others. Figure 8.3 shows average annual price gaps for six commodities for which we have comparable data for the pre-1914 and interwar periods. For four commodities, wheat, cotton, jute, and rice, the same route is considered in both periods, while for linseed and rapeseed the routes are slightly different, involving different embarkation points in the Indian subcontinent.[19] Four stylized facts emerge clearly from the figure. First, the late-nineteenth-century integration of interna-tional commodity markets is confirmed. Second, the figure shows the dramatic wartime disintegration of commodity markets alluded to earlier in this chapter. Third, those wartime losses were later recouped, although in the case of the London–Calcutta jute trade, never completely. And fourth, once this process of recuperation had been completed, there was no further progress toward commodity market integration, while in the cases of several commodities (rice, linseed, and rapeseed) there was disintegration from the late 1920s onwards. In the case of the London–Rangoon rice trade, for which such comparisons are possible, by the 1930s price gaps were back in the 40–50% range, where they had been in the 1890s.

[18] This reflects the underlying structure of production, since according to the Bairoch (1982, p. 304) data cited earlier, the Third World's share of manufacturing production *declined* from 7.5% in 1913 to 7.2% during 1928–38.

[19] The wheat price data concern the same grade of wheat and the same route, but the sources are different, which is why there are two series distinguished in the diagram, with two observations for 1913. As can be seen, these two observations are almost identical.

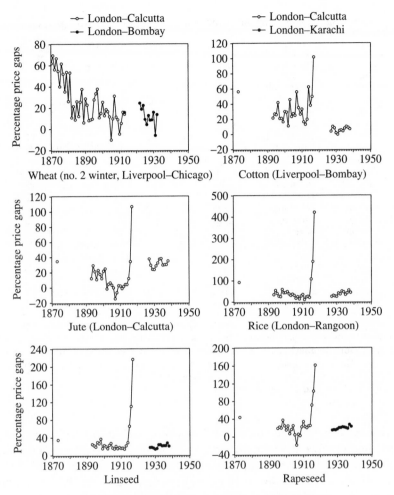

FIGURE 8.3. Percentage price gaps, 1870–1938.
Source: Hynes and O'Rourke (ongoing).

Table 8.6 gives annual percentage price gaps for twenty commodity routes between 1914 and 1937. While different routes exhibited different behaviors, some general patterns emerge from the data. First, the early to mid 1920s seem to have seen a gradual reversion to normality: for each of the six routes for which we have data, price gaps narrowed between 1922 and 1927. In the case of the wheat trade between Britain and North America, and the Liverpool–Bombay cotton trade, this was sufficient to lower 1927 price gaps below their 1913 levels, but in all

TABLE 8.6. Average annual commodity price gaps, 1913–37 (percent).

Commodity	Grade	Markets	1913	1922	1927	1929	1933	1937
Wheat	No. 2 winter	Ll–C	16.0	24.6	12.9	8.7		
Wheat	No. 1 Northern Manitoba	L–W	24.5	34.7	7.7	9.9	20.7	17.7
Wheat	Plate	L–BA	9.0	26.3	11.0	11.6	10.1	5.8
Maize	Plate	L–BA	18.7	39.3	25.3	21.0	25.5	33.6
Oats	Plate	L–BA	13.5	33.2	29.1	25.7	26.0	
Rice	Birmanie no. 4	L–R	16.0		25.9	27.7	50.4	55.3
Rice	Saigon no. 1	L–S			76.2	39.7	39.0	44.2
Rapeseed	Toria	L–K			14.7	15.1	21.8	27.3
Groundnut	Coromandel	L–M			20.5	15.2	27.1	26.6
Linseed	Bombay	L–B			17.6	16.8	23.9	27.9
Linseed	La Plata	L–BA			16.0	14.7	13.1	22.2
Cotton	Middling	Ll–NO	12.0	17.1	15.5	34.1	11.1	12.2
Cotton	Broach	Ll–B	20		4.0	8.4	5.4	8.8
Cotton	Sakellaridas	L–A			6.2	5.4	13.0	10.1
Cottonseed	Sakellaridas	L–A			17.5	19.8	23.8	24.2
Eggs	Danish	L–D			43.6	58.7	71.5	73.8
Eggs	Dutch	L–H			12.8	23.6	15.4	45.7
Butter	Danish	L–C			7.9	10.1	36.7	24.7
Coffee	Rio no. 7	NY–R	9.8	17.0	15.5	15.8	103.6	58.2
Coffee	Santos no. 4	NY–S			28.0	19.3	89.8	55.8

Ll–C, Liverpool–Chicago; L–W, London–Winnipeg; L–BA, London–Buenos Aires; L–R, London–Rangoon; L–S, London–Saigon; L–K, London–Karachi; L–M, London–Madras; L–B, London–Bombay; Ll–NO, Liverpool–New Orleans; Ll–B, Liverpool–Bombay; L–A, London–Alexandria; L–D, London–Denmark; L–H, London–Holland; L–C, London–Copenhagen; NY–R, New York–Rio; NY–S, New York–Santos.
Source: Hynes and O'Rourke (ongoing).

other cases price gaps were still higher in 1927 (and 1929) than they had been before the war. Second, the decade after 1929 was a period of disintegration: price gaps rose in 13 out of 19 cases between 1929 and 1933, and in 16 out of 18 cases between 1929 and 1937. In some instances these increases were substantial: the London–Rangoon rice price gap rose from 27.7% in 1929 to 55.3% in 1937, while the New York–Rio coffee price gap rose from 15.8% to 58.2%. The interwar combination of stagnant transport costs and rising trade barriers documented earlier meant that the quarter of a century following 1914 was a period of international commodity market disintegration, which undid many of the gains of the previous forty years, and this was particularly true of the period after 1929. The evidence thus suggests that rising trade barriers, and other forces undermining commodity market integration, were indeed a factor reducing trade volumes after 1929. According to Maddison (2001, p. 127), the Western European and Latin American trade to GDP ratios were not just lower in 1950 (8.7%

and 6%) than they had been in 1913 (14.1% and 9%): they were lower
than they had been in 1870 as well (8.8% and 9.7%).

THE GREAT DEPRESSION, THE COLLAPSE OF WORLD TRADE, AND THE DEVELOPING COUNTRIES

As we have seen, the Great Depression led to an enormous negative terms of trade shock for the developing world, whose exports
were overwhelmingly directed toward the North. However, developing
countries did well relative to the industrialized nations during this
period, at least in terms of aggregate macroeconomic indicators
(figure 8.4). There were large declines in GDP between 1929 and
1932 in Western Europe (9.1%), Latin America (13.7%), Australasia
(where the nadir was reached in 1931, with GDP 15% lower than in
1929), and above all in North America (where output kept falling until
1933, at which stage it was 28.6% lower than in 1929). Latin America's
traditional emphasis on primary exports made it vulnerable to external
shocks, and it was indeed severely affected by the Great Depression in
the first instance. However, its GDP had recovered by 1934, and by
1938 it was 20% above 1929 levels. This compares favorably with the
corresponding figures for Western Europe (13%) and North America
(where GDP was still 5% below its 1929 level). By contrast, Asia was
far less affected by the shock in the first place, with output barely
falling in South and Southeast Asia (India, Indonesia, Sri Lanka, and
Malaysia) and falling only moderately—by roughly 6%—in East Asia
(Japan, South Korea, and Taiwan), where recovery came as early as
1932, and where 1938 output was 40% above its pre-crisis level.

There are several reasons for this generally relatively impressive
performance by the developing world. One is that the terms of trade
recovered after 1932; indeed, according to Grilli and Yang (1988), they
had fully recovered by 1937. Bulmer-Thomas (2003, chapter 7) stresses
that export growth played an important role in stimulating recovery in
several Latin American states, notably Brazil, Chile, Cuba, Peru, and
Venezuela. The same seems to have been true in Japan, as we have
seen, with exports increasing not just to its Asian sphere of influence,
but to Latin America and Africa as well. A second reason, emphasized
by Diaz Alejandro (1984) in the context of Latin America, is that many
of these states also adopted a range of countercyclical policies which
helped smooth the business cycle, policies which were facilitated by
the abandonment of the gold standard, and by widespread external
debt defaults. Exchange rates were devalued in many countries besides

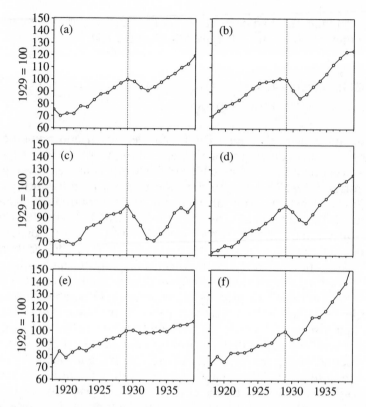

FIGURE 8.4. GDP in six regions, 1918–39 (1929 = 100): (a) Western Europe; (b) Australasia; (c) North America; (d) Latin America; (e) South and Southeast Asia; (f) East Asia. *Source:* Maddison (2003).

Australia and Japan, with real depreciations of between 30% and 90% in Argentina, Brazil, Chile, Colombia, Mexico, Peru, and Uruguay. Monetary policies were relatively expansionary, while government expenditure was maintained, and budget deficits were allowed to rise in the face of declining tax revenues. Government institutions extended credit to the private sector, while in several countries there were important public works programs, for example, extending road or irrigation networks. According to Bulmer-Thomas (2003), home demand played a crucial role in stimulating demand in Latin America between 1932 and 1939. Similarly, deficit spending largely focused on rearmament helped stimulate the Japanese recovery.

Third, many peripheral countries in Latin America and elsewhere implemented a range of policies limiting imports during the period, both quantitative restrictions on trade and higher tariffs. In the view of Bulmer-Thomas (2003, pp. 204–11), import-substituting industrialization played an important role in the recoveries of Argentina, Brazil, Chile, Colombia, Costa Rica, Mexico, and Peru, while import-substituting agricultural growth was important in Argentina, Costa Rica, Cuba, El Salvador, Guatemala, and Mexico. This was not a phenomenon unique to Latin America: the picture was rather similar in Ireland, another peripheral primary producer, where tariffs may have been beneficial in the short run to the extent that they helped lower unemployment in an era of reduced migration opportunities overseas (Neary and Ó Gráda 1991; O'Rourke 1991, 1995).

If tariffs did play such a role, they did so by switching demand toward domestically produced goods, a classic beggar-thy-neighbor policy. The fact that nearly everyone was pursuing protectionist policies during this period suggests that many of these benefits must have canceled out, and that the net effect on the world economy was negative. The consensus is that protection hurt the world economy overall, although there is a debate about whether the effect was large or small (Crucini and Kahn 1996; Irwin 1998c). However, this does *not* mean that individual countries were wrong to choose protectionism. Vamvakidis (2002) and Clemens and Williamson (2004) have employed cross-country data to show that tariffs were *positively* associated with growth across countries in the interwar period, a result in sharp contrast with the late-twentieth-century conventional wisdom that liberal trade policies are optimal, as argued by Sachs and Warner (1995) among others (see chapter 9). Free trade may indeed have been a better strategy in the late twentieth century, when core markets were relatively open. However, in an environment in which the periphery's major markets, including past and future hegemons such as the United Kingdom and the United States, were barricading themselves against imports, protection may have been the best short-run strategy. The problem with the strategy was not that it was adopted in the first place, but that it was maintained for far too long after the initial crisis had passed. Even in an enormous country like India, import substitution was reaching the limits imposed on it by the local market by the end of the 1930s (Rothermund 1996, p. 93).

Bulmer-Thomas (2003) is at pains to stress that the 1930s did not see a wholesale closing of Latin American markets to trade. Rather, export growth remained important for many countries' recoveries and development strategies. Indeed, the developing world increased its share of world exports throughout the period: Latin America's share increased from 8.3% in 1913 to 9.8% in 1928 and 10.2% in 1937, while

Africa's share increased from 3.7% to 4% to 5.3%, and Asia's increased from 11.8% to 15.5% to 16.9% (Latham 1981, p. 88). However, the interwar period marked a crucial turning point for the developing world, and particularly for Latin America. The abandonment of traditional constraints on economic policy making, such as the gold standard, would make policy experimentation easier in the future. Meanwhile, the heightened protection of the 1930s, and the consequent growth in industrial output, would increase protectionist constituencies across the continent, in similar fashion to what happened in continental Europe during Napoleon's blockade. As we will see in the next chapter, these constituencies would soon be further strengthened by the next major shock to hit the international economy, namely World War II. The result across much of Latin America was populism, with urban workers and capitalists combining to seize power from the traditionally outward-oriented landowning elites. True to their constituents' interests, populist leaders such as Perón in Argentina, Cárdenas in Mexico, or Paz Estenssoro in Bolivia promoted inward-looking policies that would prove extremely long lasting (Rothermund 1996, pp. 140–44; Rogowski 1989, pp. 74–75).

Elsewhere in the developing world, even more important political forces were set in motion by the Great Depression. The aggregate GDP effects of the slump may have been relatively minor there, but, as Dietmar Rothermund (1996) has emphasized, falling commodity prices had devastating effects on peasants producing for world markets. In some cases, the falling price of cash crops led to their retreating toward staples production and relative self-sufficiency. Elsewhere, debts and/or tax obligations—particularly poll taxes imposed by colonial rulers—meant that peasants had to continue producing for the market, but found it increasingly difficult to meet their financial obligations. The result was severe hardship, and in consequence several countries experienced political tension, rioting, or even outright rebellion. In Burma, falling rice prices and the impending collection of the poll tax led to a widespread armed peasant rebellion in December 1930, under the leadership of Saya San, that was only suppressed by the British authorities after a two-year struggle when Saya San was executed. Similarly, a peasant rebellion fueled by the same root causes took place in Vietnam in 1930–31, and was severely repressed (ibid., pp. 120–25).

African peasants were also hard pressed during the Depression, when European interests tried to shift the burden of adjustment onto native producers. Once again, poll taxes were one source of conflict, leading to political unrest in Nigeria and rioting in Togo. While the colonial administrations in both colonies reduced poll taxes in response, they actually raised them in the Ivory Coast, as European traders there obtained a reduction in export taxes on cocoa and palm kernels. The most extreme response came in the Belgian Congo, where poll taxes led to rebellions that were promptly put down, and where the authorities eventually resorted to a system of forced labor. More generally, European-owned enterprises producing plantation crops in their colonies were protected by their colonial administrators by means of quotas, or other schemes designed to support prices, but native peasant producers of cocoa or peanuts had no such help (ibid., pp. 126–35; Rogowski 1989, pp. 76–77).

The Depression thus helped pave the way for the decolonization movements of the post-1945 period, by heightening the sense of grievance of local populations. Asian nationalists would be given both intellectual and concrete support by two very different regimes, the Soviet Union and Japan. The former provided a ready-made anticolonial ideology, and communists had already been involved in both the Vietnamese uprising of 1930–31 and a Javanese revolt in 1928. The military and technological successes of the latter punctured racist notions of European superiority, and young Burmese nationalists such as Aung San, Ne Win, and U Nu would eventually turn to Japan for military support as well. Possibly the most important impact of the Depression for the future of European colonialism lay in the fact that deflationary British policies led Indian peasants to support Gandhi's National Congress party, giving it an electoral base that helped propel it to victory in the 1937 elections. From that moment on, the loss of the most important European colony was only a matter of time (Rothermund 1996, pp. 95–97, 144–48), with the less important ones inevitably following in its wake.

THE COLLAPSE OF THE OTTOMAN EMPIRE

There is one other major consequence of the Great War that we have not yet dealt with, since its ramifications were mostly felt in the late twentieth century, but which we must mention now, however briefly. The Ottoman Empire had been propped up, during its prolonged decline, by British policy seeking to preserve it as a protective barrier against what it felt were the designs against its own empire in India by Russia and other European powers. However, the 1908 revolution of the Young Turks, and subsequent political changes in Istanbul, led to the entry of Turkey into the war on the German side in 1914, an act that was to prove fatal to its survival. A British expeditionary force was sent from India to occupy the strategic port of Basra and the adjoining Ottoman province in 1914, followed by the occupation of Baghdad in 1917 and Mosul in 1918. The three Ottoman provinces of which these cities were the capitals were administered separately, and were not regarded as forming any sort of unified collective identity, though Baghdad did enjoy some precedence over the others. The combined population was about 3 million, of which more than half were Shia, about 20% Kurds (mostly in the north), and 8% a variety of Christians, Jews, and other minorities. The ruling elite, however, was mostly Sunni Arabs, who were prominent both in the Ottoman army and civil administration. The Shia communities of clerics and merchants, and several tribes in rural areas, had largely remained aloof from the Ottoman rulers, who viewed them with suspicion if not outright hostility.

The Arabs had by now become exposed to the rising tide of Arab nationalism, and resented their subordination to the Anatolian core of the Ottoman regime. The British, inspired by T. E. Lawrence, saw this Arab nationalism as a powerful card to play against the Ottomans, and held out the prospect of future emancipation in return for collaboration against the common enemy. However, Britain's ally France also had major interests in the Middle East that had to be accommodated. This was done during the course of the war by the infamous Sykes–Picot agreement, named after the two diplomats who negotiated it. Essentially, it proposed dividing the carcass of the defunct Ottoman Empire in the Levant and Fertile Crescent between France and Britain, who would control territory either directly, or indirectly via Arab states lying within their spheres of influence. There were also major concessions to Russia and France in Anatolia itself, which were rendered moot by the Russian Revolution in 1917, and Mustapha Kemal's vigorous defense of the Ottoman heartland after the Greek invasion in 1919. The French were to receive control of what are now the states of Syria and Lebanon, plus the province of Mosul, while Britain received the provinces of Baghdad and Basra, as well as Palestine. The concession of Mosul was to secure a French buffer between the British and what had been expected to be Russian holdings in Turkey itself.

The discovery of rich oil deposits, however, led to Britain acquiring Mosul in exchange for giving France a free hand in Syria and Lebanon. Palestine was split into Transjordan and the later mandated territory of Palestine, in which the Balfour Declaration of 1917 had promised the Jews a "national home." When Lenin publicized the contents of the Sykes–Picot agreement, Arab opinion was scandalized by the backtracking it represented relative to the initial British promises. The year 1920 saw joint efforts by both Shia and Sunnis to set up an independent state in Iraq, which were crushed by the British army at a loss of over 6,000 Iraqi lives, as well as of about 500 British and Indian soldiers.

All these factors led to the creation or "invention" of the state of Iraq by Winston Churchill as Colonial Secretary in 1921. Prince Faisal, the son of the sharif of Mecca, was enthroned as king of the new country in Baghdad, while Faisal's brother Abdullah was eventually crowned king of the newly created Transjordan. The new state was administered by Britain as a League of Nations mandate until 1932, when it was granted a rather circumscribed independence. The British, like the Ottomans, relied on the Sunni Arab elite to administer the country (Tripp 2000; Simon and Tejirian 2004). Faisal's grandson Faisal II was murdered in the bloody army coup d'état of 1958 that eventually led to the Baathists and Saddam Hussein, while Abdullah's descendant, also of the same name, still rules in Jordan. Another chapter in this saga would come after World War II, following a quarter of a century of increasingly vicious anti-Semitism in Europe which culminated in the Holocaust. While the 1922 census recorded just 84,000 Jews living in Palestine, there were no fewer than 800,000 Jews there in 1948, the year that the state of Israel came into existence (McEvedy and Jones 1978, p. 142). The fateful legacy of the Ottoman Empire in Israel, Jordan, Syria, Lebanon, and Iraq lives on and is yet to be finally resolved (Kedourie 1968).

Conclusion

The interwar period is a striking confirmation of the now-clichéd observation that "history matters." The Great War was a dramatic, exogenous shock to the international economic system, which did not just reinforce preexisting tendencies toward heightened protectionism. Rather, it led to an immediate disintegration of international commodity markets, a change in the domestic and international political environments, and a worldwide reallocation of economic activity that would make it difficult, even in the comparatively prosperous 1920s, to restore the prewar status quo ante. When the system was hit by a second major shock, the Great Depression, the result was wholesale protectionism, and a renewed disintegration of international commodity markets.

In turn, the breakdown of the international economic system was one important factor leading to the outbreak of World War II (Boyce 1989). Most obviously, as already noted, mass unemployment was a crucial factor propelling Hitler to power in Germany, as econometric evidence clearly shows (Stögbauer 2001). The Depression was also a primary cause of the Sudeten Germans turning to the Nazi Sudeten German Party (Marks 2002, p. 352). In Italy, the Depression was a key factor in Mussolini's decision to invade Ethiopia, which marked the end of hopes that the League of Nations might be able to provide its members with anything resembling collective security, following that organization's earlier failure to deal with Japanese adventurism in Manchuria (Boyce 2003, pp. 255–57). Finally, as we have already seen, the Depression and Western protectionism strengthened those elements within Japan who sought a policy of autarkic imperialism rather than liberal internationalism. The consequences of this would become plain when, on July 7, 1937, a minor incident at the Marco Polo Bridge outside Beijing triggered a full-scale Sino-Japanese war, and with it the beginning of World War II (Marks 2002, pp. 345–49).

Less obviously, during the crucial years of the late 1920s and early 1930s, which saw not only the invasion of Manchuria and Hitler's arrival to power, but growing Italian bellicosity as well, constant infighting among Britain, France, and the United States about economic policy—protectionism, war debts, reparations, and exchange rates—meant that they never responded effectively to counter the growing militaristic threat. Robert Boyce (1989) expertly reveals how leaders such as Chamberlain and Roosevelt came to loath each other as a result of conflicts about economic policy, and concludes his essay (pp. 88–89) in terms that may seem uncomfortably familiar today: "in the period 1929–34, economic relations declined to a state of virtual war, wherein mutual incomprehension fuelled a downward spiral in relations which left the three powers alienated from one another and incapable of addressing the problems underlying the crisis.... Long run strategic interests gave way to ostensibly short run economic necessity. And from this vantage point the gravest threats came not from the Fascist or militarist power but the other democratic powers themselves."

Chapter 9

REGLOBALIZATION: THE LATE TWENTIETH CENTURY IN HISTORICAL PERSPECTIVE

WORLD WAR II

AS WE SAW IN THE LAST CHAPTER, the world conflict that broke out in 1914 was a major factor in the international disintegration of the interwar period. It would be surprising, therefore, if the post-1945 period had seen a smooth transition toward liberalization, for it was preceded by a second world war which was even more devastating than the first, and had implications which were just as damaging for international trade. And indeed, for most of the world, the "reglobalization" for which this chapter is named would be a long time in coming.

Following the outbreak of war in Europe in 1939, trade between belligerents effectively ceased, with the fault line thus created shifting with the fortunes of war. The collapse of most of Western Europe in 1940 led to a cessation of trade between that region and Britain, while Hitler's fateful decision to invade the U.S.S.R. in June 1941 not only led to an end to trade between the two powers, and to the Axis powers being hemmed in between two front lines, but also meant that Japan was now deprived of the trans-Siberian railway as an overland route by which to import commodities (Hara 1998). Six months later, Japan launched the Pacific War against the United States, Britain, and the Netherlands, largely with the aim of gaining access to the resources of Southeast Asia. This led to Japan being limited to trading within the yen bloc. With Hitler's declaration of war on the United States, the battle lines that would persist through the end of the war were finally drawn (with a few exceptions such as the late Soviet invasion of Japan, and a series of opportunistic decisions in countries such as Argentina and Turkey to enter the war on the side of the Allies in 1945).

By 1942, there was virtually no trade between the three major blocs, German-controlled Europe (plus neutral countries such as Sweden, Switzerland, Turkey, and the two Iberian states along with their colonies), Japanese-controlled Asia, and the rest of the world. Such trade had accounted for a third of the prewar total: for example, areas which would later fall under Axis control had in 1938 accounted for over 40% of U.S. imports and around 35% of her exports (League of Nations 1945b, p. 246). Furthermore, both sides resorted to submarine warfare in an attempt to prevent their opponents from trading with their allies or colonies. As in World War I, German U-boats targeted British, Allied, and neutral shipping, largely in the Atlantic, while American submarines targeted Japanese merchant ships in the Pacific. The peak in the Atlantic campaign was reached in 1942, when 1,570 merchant ships were sunk by German U-boats, while in 1944 American submarines sank 549 Japanese merchant ships (Hugill 1993, p. 144). The effectiveness of these brutal tactics can be seen in a dramatic increase in insurance rates. For example, U.S. insurance rates on the Calcutta route had been just 2% in December 1941, but stood at 10% in March 1942, and 30% in August of that year. In the same month, U.S. insurance rates for the Egyptian route were also 30%, while they were 25% on the Red Sea, South American, and Australian routes. Mid 1942 proved to be the most difficult period for Allied shippers: while 12% of U.S. ships carrying lend-lease goods to the U.S.S.R. on the Murmansk route had been sunk in 1942, the figure declined to 1% in 1943.[1] The total Allied tonnage lost at sea in 1943 was just 44% of the corresponding figure for 1942. The result was that insurance rates also started declining in 1943: on the United States–Egypt route, for example, they were 17.5% in March, 10% in June, and 7% in October (League of Nations 1945b, pp. 279–80).

Despite these efforts, trade within each of the blocs probably increased. However, this largely took place under government control, and involved the shipment of vital military or civilian supplies. In the case of inter-Allied trade, lend-lease trade became increasingly dominant. U.S. commercial exports in 1941 had amounted to $4,279 million and lend-lease exports to $741 million. By 1943, commercial exports had shrunk in nominal terms to $2,484 million, but lend-lease exports had soared to $10,107 million (ibid., p. 247). There were also smaller "reverse lend-lease" flows of goods going from the British Commonwealth to the United States, as well as flows of "mutual aid" from countries such as Britain and Canada to allies such as the U.S.S.R., as well as to neutral countries such as Portugal or Turkey.

[1] The March 1941 Lend-Lease Act authorized the U.S. President to "sell, transfer title to, exchange, lease, lend, or otherwise dispose of" food, military equipment, and other essential supplies to "the government of any country whose defense the President deems vital to the defense of the United States."

Within Axis-controlled territory, "trade" often involved the explicit confiscation of goods by the occupiers, rather than trade in the normal sense of the word (ibid., p. 245).

As was the case during World War I, and the wars of 1792–1815, military conflict had very different effects on trade across countries. In France, both imports and exports fell sharply after 1940, with the decline in imports being more pronounced. According to the United Nations, French imports stood at just 22.2% of their 1938 level in 1942, 13.3% in 1943, and 5.6% in 1944, while the corresponding figures for exports were 50%, 46.2%, and 27.4%. This discrepancy presumably reflected France's role as a net supplier of goods for the German war effort. According to Alan Milward (1977, tables 21 and 22), French payments to Germany accounted for around 5% of German GNP in 1941–42 and for 8–9% in 1943. In the United Kingdom, by contrast, it was exports that fell by more, to less than a third of their prewar level: as during World War I, it made no sense to export more than was strictly necessary in the context of a resource-scarce war economy. The picture was different in the United States, and again mirrored the situation during the previous conflict. American exports surged, to a level nearly three times higher than in 1938, and while imports fell by a quarter between 1941 and 1942, they started recovering in 1943.

The U.S. export boom was matched by a similar one from Canada, while Argentine exports held steady during the conflict. Despite the best efforts of Nazi submarines, the trade which linked Britain to the western Atlantic played a major role in helping her successfully prosecute the conflict. By contrast, the picture regarding exports from Britain's South Asian and Australasian allies is more mixed. Ceylonese exports increased somewhat, and New Zealand exports held steady, but exports from Australia and India declined sharply (although not as sharply as exports from Japanese-occupied Indochina, which had virtually disappeared by 1945). In Europe, meanwhile, trade declined more or less across the board, with exports typically falling by 50% or more, both among neutral nations and in countries occupied by or allied with the Nazis; if the war was good business for exporters in countries such as Sweden or Denmark, it does not show up in the United Nations trade figures, at least. Finally, in Africa the picture was extremely mixed. Liberian exports exploded during the war, while elsewhere exports for the most part held fairly steady. The two major exceptions were exports from Uganda, which were nearly 50% down on prewar levels by 1943, and from French-controlled territories such as Morocco or Madagascar (where exports completely collapsed in 1942, the year the British seized the island from the Vichy French). In part, the different fortunes of various African countries depended on what sorts of commodities they exported, similar to the Latin American experience during World War I. For example, the relatively strong performance of the Belgian Congo relied on the fact that the Allies were eager to purchase its minerals, while those African countries that had depended on exports of less strategic commodities, such as palm oil, fared much worse (ibid., p. 356).

In summary, it seems that, once again, a world war did not have as uniformly devastating an effect on world trade as might have been thought, even though in Europe trade did contract sharply (and it contracted even more sharply in Japan, as the Americans tightened the noose around that nation), and even though such trade as did take place was very often qualitatively different from peacetime trade. From the various estimates which we have, it seems clear that the 1938 level of aggregate world trade had been recovered by 1949 at the latest, and that 1950 levels of world trade were roughly a fifth to a quarter higher than those in 1938 (Maddison 1995; Svennilson 1954; United Nations 1962). It should not be assumed that this was the end of the story, however, for once again the war had a variety of immediate and longer-run political and geopolitical effects that would make the task of liberalizing the postwar world economy much more difficult.

GEOPOLITICAL CONSEQUENCES: COMMUNISM, THE COLD WAR, AND DECOLONIZATION

To Western Europeans and North Americans, it seems obvious that the postwar era was one of a gradual but unmistakable trend toward ever-greater openness. This rather parochial attitude ignores the fact that in many parts of the world the war set in motion forces that would isolate countries from international markets, rather than integrate them.

In many cases, these forces were similar to those experienced after the wars of 1792–1815 and 1914–18: the trade disruption caused by the war created not just losers, but winners as well, who would use their political influence after the reestablishment of peace to try to maintain the rents which they had enjoyed during the conflict. A particularly well-known case in point is Latin America. With Britain's blockade of Nazi-occupied Europe, countries like Argentina and Brazil found that their access to continental European markets was completely disrupted, a serious matter for them given the increasing importance of German trade with Latin America before the war. Moreover, trade with Britain shrank as well, as its industry geared up for the war effort, implying a lower supply of British consumer goods available for export. War thus protected domestic industry, while states intervened to further promote industrialization, with the result that industrial growth outpaced agricultural growth almost everywhere in Latin America during the conflict (Bulmer-Thomas 2003, chapter 8). After the war had ended, urban labor and capital would argue for government protection to replace the protection that had been afforded by the war (Corbo 1992, p. 16). Whereas the late 1930s had seen attempts in several Latin American countries to liberalize trade and boost exports, the war would have a longer-lasting impact on trade policies than the Great Depression, shifting Latin America decisively toward the import-substitution strategies that would dominate much of the post-1945 period (Thorp 1992; Edwards 1994). Intellectually, this third major disruption to the international economy in three decades, following World War I and the Great Depression, made it extremely difficult for liberals to argue convincingly for an export-led growth strategy.

Similar forces could be found at work elsewhere in the developing world. Elites in regions as diverse as India and West Africa, who had benefited from wartime policies licensing trade flows, emerged as protectionists after the war, whether as industrial supporters of the Indian Congress Party, or as bureaucrats in Africa anxious to maintain and expand state power (Sachs and Warner 1995, pp. 19–20). But to this traditional mechanism was added a series of geopolitical trends that had been set in train, or accelerated, by the war, and that would dominate the political landscape of the postwar world. Three such forces stand out in particular: the spread of communism in Europe and Asia, the beginning of the Cold War, and the decolonization of much of Asia and Africa.

In Europe, the Soviet Union consolidated its control over those countries that it had liberated in the east, installing socialist governments and clamping down on democracy. This new Soviet Empire included several countries that in our schema had historically been part of Western Europe, in particular East Germany, Hungary, Poland, and Czechoslovakia. Perhaps not coincidentally, Soviet rule would be challenged particularly strenuously in these states, with uprisings in Hungary in 1956 and Czechoslovakia in 1968 being followed by the election of a Polish pope, Karol Wojtyla, in 1978, the foundation of the Solidarnosc trade union in 1980, and the collapse of the Berlin Wall in 1989. Nonetheless, we will follow conventional usage for the remainder of this chapter, and refer to the Communist and non-Communist halves of Europe as "Eastern" and "Western" Europe respectively, before reverting to our original nomenclature in chapter 10.

Meanwhile, in Korea, which had been under Japanese control since 1910, a communist regime was installed north of the thirty-eighth parallel following the Soviet incursion into the Peninsula that had begun on August 12, 1945. Some three weeks after that date Ho Chi Minh declared an independent and communist Vietnamese Republic, and proceeded to successfully resist the French attempts to defeat his Viet Minh forces that began in the following year. Even more important for world history was the conclusion of the long-standing civil war in China, which ended when Mao Zedong's Communist Party took power on the mainland in 1949. The most populous country in the world was now part of a communist bloc that stretched from the easternmost tip of Asia to central Europe.

Unlike the Mongol Empire, this formidable political bloc that now dominated northern Eurasia was a force for world economic disintegration, not integration, since communist governments were by definition hostile to free markets, both for goods and the factors of production. As we noted in the previous chapter, the very nature of the centrally planned economy, which fixed domestic relative prices at levels which bore no necessary relationship to international prices, made it necessary to insulate domestic from foreign markets by means of state trading monopolies. Moreover, by promoting the development of heavy industry throughout its sphere of influence, the Soviet system led to the breakdown of the traditional European division of labor, which had seen a largely agricultural Eastern Europe (with notable exceptions such as Czechoslovakia) exporting agricultural products to Western Europe, in exchange for industrial goods. Indeed, the fact that planners were pursuing similar policies everywhere meant that the scope for international trade between the communist countries remained limited as well, even after the formation of the Council for Mutual Economic Assistance (CMEA) in 1949, comprising Bulgaria, Czechoslovakia, Hungary, Poland, Romania, and the U.S.S.R. (and East Germany as of 1950). It was only in the 1960s that the CMEA would start significantly stimulating trade between its member states, and even then this trade creation was accompanied by trade diversion that lowered CMEA trade with the rest of the world (Pelzman 1977; Endoh 1999). Moreover, the early 1960s also saw a split between China and the Soviet bloc, reducing trade between the two sides, and trade between them virtually vanished between 1967 and 1970.

Furthermore, the new geopolitical context gave these communist economies an extra reason for not trading with the rest of the world, for since the end of the war relations between the Soviets and their former Western allies had been deteriorating sharply. It did not take long for the two major victors in World War II to discover that their postwar aims were incompatible. Stalin wanted naval bases in Turkey and the eastern Mediterranean, and to keep his troops in northern Iran, where they had been deployed by the Allies to prevent any Iranian oil from reaching Germany. He was not allowed to do any of these things by Truman, who deployed the Sixth Fleet in the eastern Mediterranean in 1946 to emphasize how unacceptable these moves were to American interests (Gaddis 2005, p. 28). American policy-makers were anxious to understand what the Soviet Union's long-term objectives were, and bombarded their embassy in Moscow to come up with answers. In a rare historical instance of the right man being in the right place at the right time, a relatively junior Foreign Service officer named George F. Kennan who was posted there answered their questions in a celebrated 8,000 word "long telegram," which Gaddis says (p. 29) "became the basis for United States strategy toward the Soviet Union throughout the rest of the Cold War." Kennan's view was that Stalin would seek to extend Communism as far to the west as possible, using all means short of war, unless checked by "a long-term, patient but firm and vigilant containment of Russian expansive tendencies," to quote from an even more famous 1947 article in Foreign Affairs that he wrote under the name "X" (Kennan 1984, p. 119). By containment Kennan did not necessarily mean military force. He saw the struggle quite clearly as one between two rival and incompatible social and political systems, and he had no doubt as to which one would succeed. He regarded the Soviet system as much weaker in terms of material and human resources, and predicted, with remarkable prescience, that the strains its rulers put upon it would lead to either the "breakup or the gradual mellowing of Soviet power." To bring this about, "the United States need only measure up to its own best traditions and prove itself worthy of preservation as a great nation" (ibid., p. 128).

The year 1947 was key, with very different implications for Eastern and Western Europe. March saw the proclamation of the Truman Doctrine, namely "the policy of the United States to support free peoples who are resisting attempted subjugation by armed minorities or by outside pressures," stated with reference to Greece and Turkey. Faced with a situation in which poor harvests and a lack of foreign exchange risked undermining Western European recovery, and potentially its democratic institutions as well, the United States's Secretary of State George Marshall announced on June 5 that the United States was ready to provide financial assistance to Europe. In return for this assistance, recipient countries had to agree to a number of promarket reforms, and coordinate their strategies for using the

American assistance, a provision which it was hoped would encourage the economic integration of Europe more generally. While the Marshall Plan took its name from that of the Secretary of State, it was Kennan who drew it up at his request (Gaddis 2005, p. 31).

This bold American initiative is correctly viewed as a key moment in Western Europe's march toward internal free trade, and a broadly liberal trade policy stance more generally. However, it was also one of the defining moments in the changing political relationship between East and West. All of Europe, including the U.S.S.R., had been invited to participate in the program, but after an initial meeting of the British, French, and Soviet foreign ministers the Soviets withdrew, on the grounds that they could not accept the American requirement of coordination across recipient countries. Nevertheless, both Poland and Czechoslovakia accepted the subsequent invitation to a conference to be held in Paris on July 12, to discuss the American initiative. This was unacceptable to Stalin, who compelled the Eastern European states to decline the invitation, thus illustrating in a very public manner the reality of life under the new political order. A series of events intervened rapidly: in early 1948 the Soviets replaced the Czech government with a more suitable alterative; on Saint Patrick's Day of the same year the United Kingdom, France, and the Benelux countries signed a mutual defense treaty in Brussels; and in June Stalin blocked all surface traffic going in and out of West Berlin, triggering the Berlin blockade.

The Cold War had begun in earnest. The year 1949 saw not only the signing of the North Atlantic Treaty, which committed the United States to the defense of Western Europe, but the passage of the U.S. Export Control Act, which gave the executive widespread powers to control exports going not just to the East, but anywhere in the world. The problem which arose in practice when trying to implement such a policy was that America's allies had to be brought on board as well, and agree which types of goods could no longer be exported to the communist bloc. This was accomplished through the establishment of CoCom, which would handle Western export controls in a multilateral fashion throughout the Cold War and was only disbanded in 1995. In 1950, following Mao's victory in China and the outbreak of the Korean War, Western European governments were sufficiently worried that they agreed with the Americans to implement a broad, or "economic," export blockade, designed to undermine communist economic development (and the United States broke off trade relations with China altogether). By 1954, however, with peace reestablished in Korea and with Stalin dead, the Europeans insisted that the blockade be restricted to narrower, "strategic" goods useful to the Soviet bloc's military efforts, and the Americans acceded to this demand (Mastanduno 1988).

Nonetheless, East–West trade was severely reduced as a result of the Cold War. Such trade had accounted for 73.8% of the East's trade in 1938, and 41.6% in 1948, but just 14% in 1953 (it accounted for 9.5%, 4.1%, and 2.1% of the West's trade in the same three years) (Foreman-Peck 1995, p. 249). Despite the relaxation in tension after 1954, and a trend toward even greater openness in the 1960s and 1970s, the conflict would continue to seriously reduce the volume of East–West trade for the next thirty-five years.

Despite Kennan's belief that the United States "need only measure up to its own best traditions" to prevail, the harsh competition of the Cold War soon created the necessity for covert operations, handled by the newly formed CIA. One of its first achievements was clandestine intervention in the 1948 Italian elections that prevented what might have been a victory for the Communists, which would have had devastating consequences for the "free world." What at first sight might have seemed another notable success was the 1953 coup that toppled the democratically elected Iranian government of Dr. Mohammed Mossadeq, which had nationalized the Anglo-Iranian Oil Company in 1951, and was felt to be vulnerable to a communist takeover. The coup against Mossadeq was acquiesced in by both the Iranian clergy and the communists, the former because they were opposed to his secularism, and the latter to his "bourgeois democratic" leanings. Both eventually paid the price for their compliance when the secret police of the Shah severely repressed them, and Ayatollah Khomeini was driven into exile in 1964. In retrospect, the overthrow of the only secular democratic regime that Iran has ever had was clearly a disaster, not only for Iran but the rest of the world. When Khomeini returned triumphantly in 1979, Iran lost the option of the sort of democracy that Mossadeq had offered, and that was so cynically deposed by CIA intrigue (Munson 1988, chapter 5). Kennan himself sadly conceded that recommending covert operations was "the greatest mistake I ever made" (Gaddis 2005, p. 164). Despite its vicissitudes, it is remarkable how successful Kennan's policy of containment turned out to be, with his predictions of either a breakup or a gradual mellowing of the Soviet system *both* coming true less than four decades after they were made.

The third major postwar trend undermining international markets was the disappearance of Europe's overseas colonies. In 1945, both Britain and France assumed that they would continue on as great imperial powers. Churchill famously proclaimed in 1942 that he had not become Prime Minister in order to preside over the dissolution of the British Empire, while in France, which was in even greater need of such reassurance, Gaston Monnerville exclaimed in May 1945 that "*Sans son empire, la France ne serait qu'un pays libéré. Avec son empire, la France est un pays vainqueur.*"[2] The hubris of such statements would soon become apparent: a mere two decades later, the two countries' empires had all but vanished, with profound consequences for the international economy.

There were several reasons for this. The conflict had weakened both countries, both financially and economically, leaving them less well equipped to wage the wars which would be required to maintain control of their colonies. The war had also involved large swathes of European colonial territory being occupied, by the Japanese in Asia, or by Germans and Americans in North Africa, leading to a decline in the prestige of the imperial power. In Asia, the Japanese openly encouraged anti-European nationalists in areas under their control, such as Aung San's Burmese Independence Army, which fought alongside them during the invasion of that country. There were proclamations of independence in Burma and the Philippines in 1943, and in Indonesia and Vietnam in 1945. The main Western victor in the war, the United States, was hostile to European imperialism, and prepared to demonstrate this in concrete ways. To take just one example, during the war Roosevelt had visited the sultan of Morocco and spoken in favor of Moroccan independence. On several occasions, this American stance was to prove of vital importance to subsequent events. Finally, news in the postwar world spread rapidly, implying that nationalist successes in one country could inspire similar revolts in different countries, and indeed in different continents.

In Asia, the aftermath of war saw Europeans returning to their former colonies, which as stated had in many cases declared independence in their absence. There followed successful wars of independence in Indonesia (1945–49), where American diplomatic pressure on the Dutch helped speed up full Indonesian independence, and in French Indochina (1946–54), where the fall of Dien Bien Phu signaled not only the military defeat of the French army against an Asian opponent in a conventional military campaign, but a striking confirmation of Europe's weakened status worldwide. The result was the creation of four independent successor states, Laos, Cambodia, and the two Vietnams north and south of the seventeenth parallel, the latter eventually being reunited in 1975 after a bloody conflict

---

[2] "Without her empire, France would only be a liberated country. With her empire, France is a victorious country."

opposing the Communist north and the United States. Malaysia was the exception that proved the rule. The British did manage to defeat the Communist insurgency there, but this was at least in part because ordinary Malaysians were convinced that the British were sincere in their stated intention to grant them independence, which they in fact did in 1957.[3]

In Africa, the peace settlement with Italy led to that country losing its colonies in Ethiopia, Eritrea, Libya, and Somaliland. Given that Italy was a vanquished enemy, this hardly seemed a portent of things to come, but there followed growing demands for independence, backed up with violence, in the French protectorates of Tunisia and Morocco, which were granted independence in March 1956. Even more seriously, in Algeria, which was regarded by the French as part of France itself, the massacres of VE Day in 1945 were eventually followed, in 1954, by a savage war between the colonial power and the Algerian FLN, which would end eight years later with Algerian independence. A distinctive feature of this war, as of many conflicts involving colonial powers in the postwar world, was that the FLN enjoyed the support of both Khrushchev and Kennedy, as well as of the growing "Third World" movement, and of the United Nations General Assembly. A similar balance of forces successfully opposed French and British attempts to seize the Suez Canal in 1956, following Egyptian President Nasser's nationalization of the Suez Canal Company. The message of the 1950s was that the days of European domination in Africa and Asia were conclusively over. Suez and Algeria were crucial turning points for European imperialism throughout Africa. Prior to 1956, the Europeans had actively (and successfully) fought against African nationalists, such as the Mau Mau in Kenya and the *indépendentistes* in Madagascar, but once Ghana became independent in 1957 the floodgates were opened, and by 1964 no fewer than twenty-seven former sub-Saharan colonies had gained their independence.

In and of itself, decolonization might not have mattered for the world economy: after all, Latin American independence a century and a half earlier had led to a liberalization of trade, at least when compared with the stifling restrictions of the colonial period. On this occasion, however, decolonization implied international economic disintegration, with the newly independent states pursuing trade policies that were very often explicitly inward-looking (much as had been the case in Eastern Europe after 1918). Sachs and Warner (1995)

---

[3] The Philippines was another exception, since the archipelago was granted independence as early as 1946.

among many other authors have succinctly summarized the reasons for this. In part the reasons are to be found in the realm of ideas: the interwar period had convinced many observers that a reliance on world export markets was dangerous, especially for countries which were excessively specialized in a small number of primary commodities. Particularly influential in this regard was the observation that, as we have seen, the terms of trade of peripheral primary product producers had collapsed during the interwar period. Scholars such as Raul Prebisch (1950) and Hans Singer (1950) mistakenly projected that collapse both backwards and forwards in time, and argued that specialization in primary products was harmful for developing countries, not just because it implied that they would suffer continuously deteriorating terms of trade, but because it deprived them of the beneficial externalities associated with industry, exemplified for many by the apparent success of the Soviet Five Year Plans.

The answer to this dilemma was industrialization based on import substitution (Corbo 1992; Krueger 1997). Thus was born the notion, long nurtured by development economists, that developing countries constituted an exception to the general rule that openness was good for growth. This notion would receive the official approval of the international community when the General Agreement on Tariffs and Trade (GATT), a body whose mission as we will see was supposed to be the fostering of open international markets, accepted that developing countries should be exempted from the free trade obligations of their richer counterparts (Krueger 1997, p. 5; Sachs and Warner 1995, p. 17). In addition to the supposed lessons of the interwar period, there was also the example of the Soviet Union, which had emerged as one of the major victors in the war, and could boast impressive growth statistics. Finally, the very fact that these were newly independent states seems to have fostered a belief that the state should assert its independence by actively pursuing "state-led industrialization" policies that were inevitably inward-looking. The fact that in many countries there were powerful interest groups that had done well out of the wartime disruption to the international economy, as noted earlier, ensured that these new ideas would find receptive audiences across the world.

Sachs and Warner also stress unfavorable macroeconomic conditions in their account. Wartime inflationary finance led to monetary overhangs, such as those which characterized the former communist economies after 1989, and just as in the latter case this made freeing up prices, an essential prerequisite to freeing trade more generally, politically costly. Later, budget deficits and balance of payments problems would lead countries in Latin America and elsewhere to impose exchange controls of one sort or another. Indeed, even a cursory reading of the classic OECD and NBER studies on Third World protectionism published in the early 1970s (Little et al. 1970; Bhagwati and Krueger 1974–78) reveals the extent to which balance of payments problems were at the origin of many if not most decisions to adopt strict quantity controls on imports. This suggests that the Third World's move away from open markets reflected systemic tensions in the world economy, rather than a series of country-specific events.

One of the underlying causes of these tensions can be found in the international monetary environment of the postwar world. In particular, newly independent countries created their own currencies, which they managed themselves: the fifteen years after World War II were thus ones of wholesale international monetary disintegration. In and of itself this would probably have reduced trade, since separate currencies appear to be an obstacle to trade.[4] But the effects of this monetary disintegration were magnified by the policy choices underlying the postwar "international economic architecture." In particular, the "Bretton Woods" system was shaped by two deeply held beliefs on the part of contemporary observers of the interwar debacle. The first was that activist macroeconomic policies, both fiscal and monetary, were crucial for countries trying to stabilize their economies. As we saw in chapter 8, this belief was entirely logical in the light of the interwar period, since it was only when countries abandoned the straightjacket of the gold standard, and adopted Keynesian policies, that they began to recover from the Depression. The second belief, which is more debatable, is that fixed exchange rates were desirable since they promoted trade. According to the proponents of this view, the breakdown of the interwar gold standard had led to a series of competitive devaluations that disrupted trading relationships, and to countries that found themselves with overvalued currencies resorting to protectionism.

In retrospect, this was a mistake. As the Mundell–Fleming model makes clear, and as Obstfeld and Taylor (2004) have emphasized in their classic account of the fall and rise of international capital markets, there is a fundamental policy trilemma which governments cannot escape. Fixed exchange rates, international capital mobility, and independent monetary policies are mutually incompatible, since the first two, by pinning down domestic interest rates, rule out the third. Thus, governments can adopt any two of these three policies, but

---

[4] A classic reference on this controversial topic is Rose (2000).

they cannot have all three at once. The Bretton Woods system chose monetary independence and fixed exchange rates; the implication was that countries had to impose capital controls, and Obstfeld and Taylor show that postwar international capital markets were indeed deeply segmented.

And herein lay the fundamental problem facing newly independent economies, seeking to manage their newly independent currencies. In order to maintain their exchange rate peg, they needed international reserves. Furthermore, in an environment in which capital was immobile across frontiers, trade deficits tended to result immediately in a loss of reserves. The trade deficit thus became a key policy problem for poor countries that should, in principle, have been continually running trade deficits and importing capital from abroad so as to catch up on richer, capital-abundant countries. If for whatever reason these countries found themselves with excess domestic demand—due to stored-up wartime inflation, for example, or to government attempts to supplement scarce domestic savings with public investment (attempts which were understandable, since, after all, international investment would not be forthcoming)—the result would be overvalued real exchange rates, a loss in competitiveness, trade deficits, and reserve losses. In such circumstances, exchange controls involving not just the capital, but also the current account, could quickly become all but inevitable. The similarity between the experience of many developing countries after 1945, and the gold bloc countries of the 1930s, which as we have seen also resorted heavily to quantitative restrictions on trade, is no coincidence.

All of these tendencies—ideology and nationalism, political economy considerations, macroeconomic imbalances, and underlying everything else the legacy of the war—were strikingly revealed in the most important of the former colonies, which as yet we have barely mentioned: British India, which gained its independence in August 1947, and was simultaneously partitioned into India and Pakistan amid great bloodshed. According to B. R. Tomlinson (1993), the strict quantitative controls which governed Indian trade immediately after independence were not so much the result of nationalist economic ideology, but were rather the direct successors of the wartime restrictions on imports that had been imposed by the colonial administration itself in 1942. Monetary financing of the war effort inevitably led to incipient inflation and balance of payments problems which persisted into the 1950s, given the government's inability to lower prices and restore competitiveness. Thus, even before the famous Five Year Plans, which started in 1952, imports were strictly licensed. When the new government embarked on an explicit policy of state-led, import-substituting industrialization, this obviously provided an additional and longer-run rationale for such restrictions. Even here, however, Tomlinson points out that the industrial licensing system, identified by Bhagwati and Srinivasan (1975) as a major factor increasing the efficiency cost of Indian protectionism, had its roots in wartime planning under the colonial Indian Government. Other factors contributing to India's inward shift included the familiar combination of ideas—the nationalist background of the new state's leaders, as well as the example of the Soviet Union—and interests, such as the growing power of Indian capitalists, and their close ties with the ruling Congress Party. The net result was that India's share of world exports, which had stood at 2.6% in 1948, was just 1.5% in 1953 and 0.7% in 1970 (ibid., p. 19).[5]

Pakistan went the way of India in its trade policy if in nothing else, implementing strict trade controls and import substitution policies. But this withdrawal from the wider current of human affairs was as nothing compared with what happened in Burma, whose peasants had in the late nineteenth century been fully engaged with world markets, as we saw in chapter 7. There, an independent constitutional republic came into being in January 1948, but a coup d'état in 1962 saw the suspension of the constitution, and the establishment of a one-party socialist system that clamped down on foreign trade.

The newly independent states of Africa followed the same trend. Ghana was, like Burma, an economy where peasant producers had responded flexibly and successfully to the opportunities provided by world markets in the late nineteenth century, but here again balance of payments difficulties led to the imposition of strict import licensing in 1961. The subsequent trade regime was succinctly summarized by J. Clark Leith (1974, p. 4) as "one of hasty introduction, difficult implementation, frequent change, organized corruption, serious shortages, and finally an attempted liberalization" imposed by a National Liberation Council following a coup d'état in 1966, and subsequently abandoned in the early 1970s. In Egypt, wartime controls on trade were maintained into the postwar period, and following the Suez Crisis in 1956 the Nasser regime embarked on a program of state-led industrialization characterized by widespread nationalization, including of the foreign trade sector (Hansen and Nashashibi 1975).

The postwar period saw an inward shift in Latin America as well, suggesting that postcolonial ideology was not the only force at work

[5]The figure in 1913 was 4.5%, but this includes Pakistan, Burma, and Ceylon (United Nations 1962).

during the period. In that continent, local industries had, as noted earlier, strengthened their economic and political position during the 1930s and World War II, as a result of the disintegration of the international economy. Export interests, on the other hand, had been severely damaged by the loss of European markets. As we have seen, the war had more long-lasting effects than either the previous war or the Great Depression, with sustained import substitution policies being embarked upon afterwards, with only a few exceptions, notably Peru until the 1960s (Bulmer-Thomas 2003, chapter 8). Protectionism in these countries received intellectual support from the United Nations's Economic Commission for Latin America (ECLA), founded in 1948 and strongly influenced by Prebisch (Corbo 1992). The result was the widespread use of very restrictive quantitative barriers to trade, as well as high tariffs. Just as in other countries attempting such policies (for example, Ireland), a growth strategy based on industries serving only the domestic market, but relying on imported inputs, led to periodic balance of payments crises, which provided an additional reason for import restrictions.

One response to the reduced effectiveness of import substitution policies, as infant industries that never became competitive internationally reached the limits imposed on them by their domestic markets, was to promote regional import substitution—hence the formation of the Latin American Free Trade Association (LAFTA) in 1961, inspired by the EEC in Europe, and comprising eleven states. However, LAFTA proved unsuccessful in abolishing tariff barriers between its member states, in contrast with the EEC, which succeeded in doing so by 1968, ten years after its foundation. Thus, a smaller group of countries set up the Andean Pact in 1969, but this fell apart when Chile left in 1976. The fact that the Central American Common Market (CACM), launched in 1960, was more successful than these two failed initiatives—the CACM had established a common external tariff by 1965—goes to show the central problem undermining South American attempts at import-substituting regionalization. The CACM economies were dominated by primary-producing exporters, selling outside the region, rather than by import-substituting manufacturers who required trade barriers in order to prosper. Not surprisingly, this made agreement on mutual trade liberalization easier to achieve, but it also presumably meant that regional liberalization was less beneficial than it would have been in the context of LAFTA.

The net result of the above was that much of the developing world became more closed to international trade, rather than more open, in the decades following World War II. The situation was in many ways the polar opposite of that which had obtained prior to World War I. As we saw in chapter 7, during the late nineteenth century European powers imposed free trade policies on much of Africa and Asia, while retaining protectionist barriers themselves (the outstanding exception being the free trading United Kingdom). The periphery was open, while the core retained the right to remain closed. During the late twentieth century, by contrast, it was the periphery that was closed, while the rich countries gradually liberalized their trade regimes. Moreover, this period of increasingly inward-looking policies lasted for a quarter of a century at least. To say that the immediate postwar years were ones of growing liberalization, therefore, is to adopt a perspective that ignores the experience of the vast majority of mankind.

THE GRADUAL RECONSTRUCTION OF THE ATLANTIC ECONOMY: 1950–70

There was one region of the world, however, which held aloof from the general drift toward protectionism: the northern Atlantic economies of Western Europe and North America, under the military and political leadership of the United States. Here, nations began, slowly but steadily, to liberalize their economies, drawing on the lessons which policy makers had learned from the experiences of the interwar period. There were several such lessons (in addition to the macroeconomic ones highlighted earlier), each of which would prove crucial for subsequent developments.

First, both the Americans and the Europeans concluded that economic integration and political cooperation within Europe were necessary in order to preserve the peace. On the American side, this led to support for European integration, which was initially manifested (as noted above) by the stipulation that the Europeans decide amongst themselves how to share out the $13 billion in Marshall Aid which would be provided by the United States over a four-year period. Initially, it was hoped that the Organisation for European Economic Co-operation, established in Paris in 1947 for this purpose, would evolve into a motor of European integration. While these initial hopes were dashed (the OEEC eventually being replaced by the Organisation for Economic Co-operation and Development in 1961, whose role was limited to that of a think tank), several other institutions soon evolved which filled the gap. Furthermore, as already noted the leverage which Marshall Aid gave the Americans enabled them to insist that the Western Europeans put in place functioning market economies, freeing up prices, bringing budget deficits under control, and taking other steps that would enable them not just to grow economically, but to move toward open trading policies with each other and with the rest of the world (Eichengreen 2007).

Second, the inability of the League of Nations to prevent the world's descent into autarky in the 1930s was seen as one of the key factors that had undermined the world economy during that period, and contributed to international geopolitical tension. It was thus decided to set up new international institutions whose job it would be to create and maintain a generally more open international economic environment. Alongside the Bretton Woods institutions, namely the IMF and IBRD (World Bank), a series of conferences negotiated a charter for an International Trade Organization (ITO), eventually signed in Havana in 1948. As is well-known, the United States never ratified the ITO charter, which was thus stillborn. However, as part of the ITO negotiation process, twenty-three nations signed the General Agreement on Tariffs and Trade in Geneva in 1947. The GATT was a vehicle designed to implement the trade policy clauses of the proposed ITO, but with the demise of the latter institution it became the framework within which countries' commercial policies would be regulated for nearly half a century, until it was replaced by the WTO in 1995.

Its basic purpose was to encourage "reciprocal and mutually advantageous arrangements directed to the substantial reduction of tariffs and other barriers to trade."[6] Despite the problems associated with the MFN clause experienced during the interwar period, nondiscrimination was the centerpiece of this Agreement (Article I), although exceptions were made for customs unions and free trade areas (Article XXIV), providing that the formation of such entities did not lead to third parties facing higher tariffs on average than they had done beforehand.[7] This exception would be invoked on several occasions over the next half century, most notably in Europe, but also (as we have seen) in the Americas. The Agreement also outlawed quotas (Article XI), although there were a number of exceptions, for example relating to agriculture and fisheries, or regarding measures taken to maintain a country's international reserves in the event of a

[6]Taken from the preamble to the Agreement, available at the GATT Digital Library (http://gatt.stanford.edu/page/home).

[7]Exceptions were also made as regards existing preferences between the United Kingdom, France, Belgium, the Netherlands, the United States, and their respective empires, past or present, as well as regards a small number of existing arrangements between neighboring states.

balance of payments crisis (Article XII). Even more striking was the recognition in Article XVIII that countries "which can only support low standards of living and are in the early stages of development" should be allowed "(a) to maintain sufficient flexibility in their tariff structure to be able to grant the tariff protection required for the establishment of a particular industry and (b) to apply quantitative restrictions for balance of payments purposes in a manner which takes full account of the continued high level of demand for imports likely to be generated by their programs of economic development." This impression of a special regime for developing countries was strengthened by the statement that "developed contracting parties do not expect reciprocity for commitments made by them in trade negotiations to reduce or remove tariffs and other barriers to the trade of less-developed contracting parties" (Article XXXVI), and the commitment that developed countries would "accord high priority to the reduction and elimination of barriers to products currently or potentially of particular export interest to less-developed contracting parties" (Article XXXVII). Sadly, while poorer countries would fully avail themselves of the various possibilities not to liberalize which the GATT thus afforded them, the richer countries would prove reluctant to fulfill their obligations under Article XXXVII, and open up sensitive domestic markets of particular interest to LDCs, such as textiles and agriculture.

As Douglas Irwin (1995) has pointed out, the initial impact of the GATT on protection worldwide was limited, if nonnegligible. The first GATT negotiation round, at which the Agreement was signed, did succeed in reaching 123 bilateral agreements which were then generalized to other member states according to the MFN principle. In the case of the most liberal country present, the United States, these agreements cut its average tariff by some 35% (p. 134). The second round, held in Annecy in the summer of 1949, led to some additional countries joining the GATT, and to some extra tariff cuts being negotiated, but when the delegates reconvened in the winter of the following year in Torquay, the process began to stall. This was in part due to the free rider effects of the MFN clause, which were at this stage beginning to be reasserted. The obvious solution, which was to move away from bilateral deals to multilateral negotiations, thus eliminating the free rider problem at the cost of increased negotiating costs (which would become steadily higher as the century progressed, and the GATT expanded in size), was only adopted in the 1960s, when the Kennedy round revitalized the GATT process.

Within the West, a key institution opening up trade during the 1950s was the European Payments Union (EPU).[8] World War II had bequeathed inconvertible currencies to Western Europe's economies, with the result that no country wanted to run a surplus with any other (since then it would have exchanged goods for inconvertible currency). This gave pairs of countries an incentive to balance trade bilaterally, and made it nearly impossible to move toward a more general, multi-lateral liberalization. The solution was to organize a system of credits and debits, held on the books of the Bank for International Settlements (BIS); now countries only had to worry about their aggregate trade deficits or surpluses. The system was oiled with hard currency provided by the United States under its Marshall Aid scheme, and participants had to agree to liberalize trade with other EPU members. The result was a rapid increase in intra-European trade, and by the end of 1958 most Western European currencies had become convertible. This in turn facilitated the agreement in 1957 to create the European Economic Community (EEC), a common market involving the three Benelux countries, plus France, Germany, and Italy, and which as noted earlier succeeded in abolishing internal tariffs by 1968; the 1960 decision to launch the European Free Trade Area (EFTA), involving the United Kingdom, Denmark, Norway, Sweden, Switzerland, Austria, and Portugal; the Anglo-Irish Free Trade Area, which came into effect in 1966; and the Kennedy round of GATT trade talks between 1964 and 1967, which lowered intra-GATT tariffs by a third.

The decades immediately succeeding World War II therefore saw a partial reconstruction of the Atlantic economy of the late nineteenth century—partial, since governments attempted to control international capital flows, and succeeded in controlling labor flows. This was a far cry from the global economy of 1914, but it was an important beginning, involving as it did the world's most advanced economies. Moreover, the move toward greater openness did not exclusively involve Western Europe and Britain's overseas offshoots. Sachs and Warner (1995) identify eight other economies that were consistently open throughout the period (Barbados, Cyprus, Hong Kong, Malaysia, Mauritius, Singapore, Thailand, and Yemen), and five others that had liberalized by 1970 (Indonesia, Japan, Jordan, South Korea, and Taiwan). Several of these countries were small and of little significance to the broader world economy, but the Southeast and East Asian economies just mentioned constitute important exceptions to the generally protectionist rule of the period. Hong Kong had always been

---

[8]The classic account of the EPU is Eichengreen (1994). See also Eichengreen (2007).

open, and Singapore pursued broadly open policies since independence. Japan was admitted to the GATT, IMF, and UN in 1955, and
abolished currency controls in 1964. In Taiwan, liberalization started in
1958, when the government started replacing quantitative restrictions
on trade with tariffs, lowering the costs of imported raw materials, and
encouraging exports. In Korea, where import licensing had been put in
place in 1946, liberalization came slightly later, with hesitant efforts in
the early 1960s being followed by a more decisive move toward lower
tariffs, and, in particular, looser quantitative trade controls after 1967.

These were not free trading economies (with the exception of Hong
Kong), still less laissez-faire economies. Countries such as Korea and
Taiwan maintained tariffs that were much higher than in the rich
countries, even after they had liberalized. In several cases East Asian
governments actively promoted exports, and the state subsidized
and coordinated investment, as well as setting up public companies
(Rodrik 1995). Nonetheless, there was a clear difference between these
countries' reliance on exports, and the import-substitution policies of
most other developing countries, and as we will see below this had
important implications both for their trade performance, and their
development generally.

POLICY DIVERGENCE: 1945–80

As we saw in chapter 8, the interwar economy found it hard to shake off
the aftereffects of the Great War. What this chapter has suggested is that
the aftereffects of World War II were just as serious and long-lasting in
most of the world, at least insofar as trade policies were concerned.
Table 9.1 makes the point by giving data, drawn from a variety of
sources, on industrial tariffs in a number of countries over the course
of the twentieth century. Of course, comparing average tariffs over
time is a risky matter, especially when calculated by different authors
using different methodologies, but nonetheless a number of stylized
facts do emerge from the table.[9] For several European countries, as
well as the British offshoots, the table clearly shows a pattern of
interwar disintegration (higher tariffs) followed by postwar integration
(lower tariffs). However, as the preceding discussion has suggested,
this pattern is largely confined to the OECD economies, since in the

[9] The classic League of Nations (1927) study upon which we rely for the 1913 and 1925
data presented unweighted average tariffs for manufactured goods, which is why we
have used unweighted manufacturing tariff averages whenever possible. Exceptions to
this general rule are noted in the table.

TABLE 9.1. Tariffs on manufactured goods, 1902–2000
(simple unweighted average, ad valorem equivalents, percent).

	1902	1913	1925	1931	1950	Early 1960s	1976	Mid 1980s	1990	2000
Argentina	(28)	28	29			(141)			14.1	16
Australia	(6)	16	27					(10)	14.1	5.3
Austria	(35)	18	16	27.7	18		11.7	9		4.3
Bangladesh	(3)	4	16						121.3	22
Belgium	(13)	9	15	13	11.2	13.1	9.1	7	8.4	4.3
Brazil		60				(99)		(44)	34.8	16.6
Bulgaria				90						11.7
Canada	(17)	26	23				12.6		10.5	4.8
China	(5)	4.5						(41)	43	16.2
Colombia		50							6.4	12
Czechoslovakia		18	27	36.5						4.6
Denmark	(18)	14	10		3.4		9.1	7	8.4	4.3
Finland			22.7				13.3			4.3
France	(34)	20	21	29	17.9	13.1	9.1	7	8.4	4.3
Germany	(25)	13	20	18.3	26.4	13.1	9.1	7	8.4	4.3
Greece	(19)				39			7	8.4	4.3
Hungary	(35)	18	27	42.6					11.7	7.1
India	(3)	4	16					(80)	83.7	31.6
Indonesia								(24)	19	8.9
Iran		3.5								7.5
Italy	(27)	18	22	41.8	25.3	13.1	9.1	7	8.4	4.3
Japan	(9)	27.5				18.0			3.9	2.9
Korea									12.6	8
Mexico		45				(22)		(17)	13.9	17.2
Netherlands	(3)	4	6		11.2	13.1	9.1	7	8.4	4.3
New Zealand	(9)	17.5							9.1	3
Nigeria									36.2	25.6
Norway	(12)				10.8		8.6		6.8	2.5
Pakistan	(3)	4	16			(93)				20.6
Philippines						(46)			19.5	7.3
Poland		N.a.	32	52					12	10.5
Portugal	(71)				18				8.4	4.3
Romania	(14)			55					17.7	16.4
Russia	(131)								8.8	10.2
South Africa	(6)								12.2	8.2
Spain	(76)	41	41	75.5					8.4	4.3
Sweden	(23)	20	16	23.5	8.5		6.0	5		4.3
Switzerland	(7)	9	14	22			3.8	3		

Source: 1902: BPP (1905). 1913, 1925: League of Nations (1927). 1931: Liepmann (1938, p. 413). 1950: Woytinsky and Woytinsky (1955, pp. 285, 292). 1964: Preeg (1970, pp. 277–78); Little et al. (1970, pp. 162–63). 1976: calculated on the basis of GATT (1980, p. 37). Mid 1980s: World Bank (1991, p. 97); for developing countries, Goldin and van der Mensbrugghe (1993). 1990 and 2000: UNCTAD (2004). Note: all figures are unweighted averages, unless figure is in parentheses. 1902 figures are weighted by U.K. exports. Early 1960s developing country data weighted by value added. 1985 developing country data import-weighted. Tariffs for 1950 and 1976 are for industrial goods; the Preeg data are for "nonagricultural products other than mineral fuels." N.a. = not available.

TABLE 9.1. *Cont.*

	1902	1913	1925	1931	1950	Early 1960s	1976	Mid 1980s	1990	2000
Taiwan						(30)			10.4	6.2
Thailand		2.5							40.9	15.8
Turkey	(8)	7.5							9.5	6.5
United Kingdom	0	0	5		23.3	18.2	9.1	7	8.4	4.3
United States	(73)	44	37		14.6	16.5	11.2	7	6.1	4
Yugoslavia		N.a.	23	32.8						13.7

rest of the world tariffs continued rising during the postwar period, to levels well above their interwar levels, let alone their pre-1914 levels. To take just two examples, as part of British India Pakistan had imposed tariffs of less than 5% before 1913 and tariffs of 16% in 1925; by the early 1960s its average tariffs on manufactured imports exceeded 90%. Meanwhile, in Argentina tariffs had increased from their pre-1939 level of a little under 30% to more than 140%. Furthermore, in these and other developing countries, such extremely high tariff rates understated the actual extent of protection, since they were supplemented, as we have seen, by a whole battery of quantitative restrictions on trade.

By the early 1970s, however, some of the underlying reasons for this rather dismal picture were beginning to unravel. In particular, international capital markets had begun to find ways around rich countries' attempts to control them, and this, together with the inherent problems involved in trying to maintain a fixed exchange rate system, led to the Bretton Woods fixed exchange rate regime collapsing in the early 1970s. In principle, this fact, together with the partial resumption of international capital flows, should have facilitated developing countries wishing to open up to international trade. In practice, however, the troubled international macroeconomic environment of the decade hardly helped would-be trade reformers in the developing world. Chile was the best-known example of a country that took the plunge, and it took a particularly unpleasant dictatorship to push the necessary reforms through. The Pinochet regime which overthrew President Allende in a violent coup in 1973 abolished exchange controls, devalued the currency and reduced average tariff levels from 94% to 10% (Maddison 2001, p. 154).[10]

[10] Elsewhere in the developing world, it seems that democracy and trade reform have gone hand in hand, perhaps for Heckscher–Ohlin reasons (since workers should favor free trade in labor-abundant countries). See Milner and Kubota (2005) and O'Rourke and Taylor (2007).

Thirty-five years after the end of World War II, the overall picture as regards world trade liberalization was disappointing. According to Sachs and Warner (1995), only around a quarter of the world's population lived in open economies. Exceptions to the general rule were few and far between: Western Europe, North America, Australasia, Japan, and a small number of other economies, most in Southeast Asia. It was only in the 1980s, and especially the 1990s, that the reglobalization of this chapter's heading would really begin.

REGLOBALIZATION: 1980–2000

There were a number of reasons why the 1980s marked a turning point for the international economy. Economists, not surprisingly, like to emphasize the role of ideas, in particular those generated by the profession itself, in overturning what had been the conventional import-substituting wisdom in much of the Third World (Krueger 1997). In this account, key academic breakthroughs include the afore-mentioned OECD and NBER studies of the late 1960s and 1970s which demonstrated empirically the inefficiency of exchange controls and other barriers to trade (Little et al. 1970; Bhagwati and Krueger 1974–78), and theoretical arguments demonstrating that, while market failures might sometimes justify government intervention, they rarely justified protectionism per se, an argument which among other things undermined the case for infant industry protection (Baldwin 1969; Bhagwati 1971). Such a reading would emphasize key political events, such as the electoral victories of Margaret Thatcher in 1979 and Ronald Reagan in the following year, and undoubtedly the rise to power of such strongly promarket politicians helped change the intellectual climate worldwide. However, both the United Kingdom and the United States were already committed to more or less free trade positions in 1980. The real action, when it came, would be elsewhere.

Beginning in 1973, the Middle East finally succeeded in doing something which the region had been incapable of since 1498: by effectively monopolizing the supplies of a commodity vital to the West, on this occasion oil, it engineered a massive improvement in its terms of trade at the expense of the rest of the world. It was this supply shock that was primarily responsible for the macroeconomic problems of the OECD economies during the 1970s, raising prices and lowering output and employment across Europe and North America. Growth rates there plummeted, and started sliding in Africa as well; but in Latin America they held steady, in large part due to the newly functional capital markets of the world, which made up for forty years of inactivity by lending governments there large amounts of money. When Reagan and Thatcher came to power, they resolved to first tackle their countries' inflationary problems, a decision that would be followed in other OECD economies over the course of the 1980s. To this end they raised domestic interest rates: the result was recession in the North, damaging the South's export opportunities, and a rise in the developing world's interest payments on its debt. This in turn implied a debt crisis across the Third World, reminiscent of the crisis of the 1930s, a fall in capital flows from North to South, and an acute budgetary problem for many developing country governments, often translating into high and increasing levels of inflation as they resorted to monetary financing.

In light of the postwar history of the developing countries, what followed may seem paradoxical. In previous decades, as we have seen, balance of payments crises had led to an increase in trade-suppressing policies, chiefly a tightening of exchange controls. As Dani Rodrik (1994, 1996) has pointed out, this was indeed the initial response of several countries in the 1980s, notably including Chile. However, as the decade progressed, and the crisis dragged on, more and more developing countries adopted "reform packages" that not only aimed to cut budget deficits and inflation, but also reduced or eliminated quantitative restrictions on trade, abolished exchange controls, and lowered tariffs. Mexico and Bolivia started liberalizing their quantitative restrictions on trade in 1985; 1988 saw major trade liberalization programs begin in Argentina and Pakistan; in 1989 it was the turn of Venezuela; and in 1990 that of Brazil and Peru (Rodrik 1994). According to the Sachs and Warner (1995) index, the majority of the world's population lived in "open" economies by 1993, and that figure does not even include the population of China, which started liberalizing in 1978, or India, which embarked on a major reform program in 1991 that would progressively open up the economy to the rest of the world over the course of the 1990s.[11]

How to explain this difference between the experience of the 1950s and 1960s, on the one hand, and the 1980s and 1990s on the other, is not altogether clear. Part of the explanation, as our discussion of the immediate postwar period suggests, lies in the different international monetary environment of the later period, and in particular the switch away from independent currencies with fixed exchange

---

[11] The Sachs–Warner criteria only rate India as being "open" by 1994. According to Wacziarg and Welch (2003), both China and India were still "closed" at the century's end.

rates to either floating rates (in the majority of cases) or currency board arrangements. In 1975, the proportion of developing countries with flexible exchange rates was just 10%; by 1997, the majority of developing countries had such an arrangement (Wolf 2004, p. 132). As Milton Friedman (1953) might have predicted, this made it easier for countries to contemplate abolishing exchange controls: if indeed the initial policy shift was in part due to the constraints imposed by fixed exchange rates and limited capital mobility, then the move to floating rates must have facilitated liberalization. It is also clearly the case that the debt crises of the 1980s were different in nature to the foreign exchange crises of earlier decades. In particular, they involved powerful creditor interests, making unilateral solutions more costly, and placing a premium on countries being able to generate export earnings, which was inconsistent with their retreating toward autarky.[12]

There is no shortage of alternative explanations to hand as well, which are not necessarily mutually exclusive. Rodrik (1994, 1996) suggests that the debt and macroeconomic crises facing developing countries were so grave that macroeconomic reform programs had become a political necessity. It then became possible for governments to "sneak in" trade reforms that would otherwise have been blocked by domestic interest groups. Implicitly, such a view accepts the independent role of ideas in driving policy changes, since if Latin American, African, or Asian governments viewed trade reform as a sufficiently good thing to want to "sneak it in," this must in part have been because they were convinced by the arguments of economists highlighted by Anne Krueger (1997). Another possibility is that international institutions such as the World Bank and IMF used the leverage which developing countries' debt problems gave them to push for trade reforms as well as macroeconomic reforms (again, this implicitly agrees with the view that ideas, in this case those ideas circulating within the international institutions, matter). Rodrik (1994) suggests that this may have been a factor in some of the smaller countries concerned, notably in Africa, but that it can hardly have mattered in the cases of economic and political giants such as Argentina, Brazil, India, Nigeria, or Pakistan.[13]

It was thus toward the end of the 1980s, or the beginning of the 1990s, that the Third World started liberalizing in earnest. It was precisely at

[12]Furthermore, unlike in the 1930s world trade and capital markets were opening up, implying that economies now had something to lose by defaulting.

[13]Experience from the European Union, successor to the EEC, suggests yet another possibility: governments may have wished to implement trade reforms, but decided to pin the blame on international organizations, who, not facing domestic electorates of their own, were well-positioned to act as scapegoats.

this time that another world-historic watershed occurred, namely the collapse of communism in Eastern Europe and the U.S.S.R., which happened in stages between 1989 and 1991, when the Soviet Union ceased to exist and was replaced by fifteen successor states. As already noted, China had started an economic reform program in 1978, which gradually liberalized the domestic economy and encouraged international trade. Now the rest of the Second World followed the Third, abolishing state trading monopolies, putting in place convertible currencies, and ultimately (in the case of most of Eastern Europe) preparing to join the European Union (EU).[14]

By the end of the century, the post-1945 return to autarky was a thing of the past in most of the world, and tariffs and other trade barriers were being reduced in all regions. Average tariffs in the developing world fell from 34.4% in the early 1980s to 21.9% in the early 1990s, and to 12.6% at the end of the century (UNCTAD GlobStat Database[15]). They fell in every region of the developing world bar South America (where they rose following the onset of the debt crisis before falling again), with particularly large falls in sub-Saharan Africa (from 33.8% to 15%), Central America and the Caribbean (from 29.5% to 8.9%), and South, East, and Southeast Asia (from 43.7% to 12.6%). Meanwhile, the average incidence of nontariff barriers (NTBs) on manufactured imports fell in Latin America from 28.4% in the mid 1980s to 1.8% in the early 1990s; it fell from 23.1% to 5.5% in East Asia; and it *increased* from 42.7% to 45.4% in sub-Saharan Africa between 1984–87 and 1988–90 (Rodrik 1999, table 1.3). Liberalization continued throughout the 1990s (including in Africa): there was a decline not just in "standard" nontariff barriers such as quotas and state trading monopolies, but in exchange controls on current account as reflected by black market foreign exchange premia as well (Martin 2001). Nor was this trend limited to developing countries: according to Coppel and Durand (1999, table 2), NTBs became less pervasive in all the major industrial economies between 1988 and 1996.[16]

This does not mean, however, that the world had reverted to free trade: far from it. There are at least three reasons for which it would be wrong to exaggerate the liberal turn which the world economy

[14]At the time this book went to press, eleven former communist countries had become part of the European Union. These were East Germany in 1990; eight further countries, including the three former Soviet Baltic Republics, in 2005; and Bulgaria and Romania in 2007.

[15]Available at http://globstat.unctad.org/html/index.html.

[16]However, the use of antidumping measures became more frequent in the EU and outside the OECD.

had taken in the last decade of the second millennium, however impressive this may have been. First, according to the data in table 9.1, average manufacturing tariffs in 2000 were still unambiguously higher than they had been before World War I in the following countries: Bangladesh, China, India, Pakistan, Thailand, and the United Kingdom. These six countries alone accounted for 44% of the world's population in 2000. Protection was also certainly higher in 2000 than it had been in former British colonies such as Nigeria or in former French colonies such as Morocco. It is safe to conclude that the majority of the world's population in 2000 lived in economies that had higher manufacturing tariffs than on the eve of the Great War.

Furthermore, emphasizing manufacturing tariffs overstates the extent to which rich countries moved toward free trade after 1945, since agricultural protection (which as we have seen triggered the move back toward protection in late-nineteenth-century Europe, as well as the protection of the late 1920s) remained extremely high in many wealthy countries in 2000, higher certainly than in 1913. Between 1997 and 1999, protection raised the prices received by farmers by 61% in Japan, 44% in the European Union, 18.5% in Canada and the United States, 28.7% in lower-income OECD economies, and by 66.7% in other OECD economies (World Bank 2001a, table 2.13).

A third reason for avoiding excessive hyperbole about the international economy in the early twenty-first century is that NTBs (such as countervailing and antidumping duties, quotas, voluntary export restraints, production subsidies, and technical barriers to trade) were *much* more important then than they had been in 1913. A particularly notorious example was the Multi-Fiber Agreement, a system of quotas put in place to protect rich countries' textile industries from Southern competition in 1974. Even though it expired in 1994, the WTO continued to manage these quotas until the end of the century and beyond. For all these reasons one cannot automatically assume that average worldwide protection was less severe at the end of the century than it was in 1913.

Given the increased importance of nontariff barriers, it is difficult to measure long-run trends in the overall stance of trade policy, although in principle measures such as the trade restrictiveness index (Anderson and Neary 2005) could do precisely this. Figure 9.1 gives World Bank estimates of overall protection in both manufacturing and agriculture during 2000–4, using the Anderson–Neary methodology (Kee et al. 2006). These are the uniform ad valorem tariffs which are equivalent to the existing configuration of tariffs and quotas, in the sense that they would restrict total imports to the same extent. As

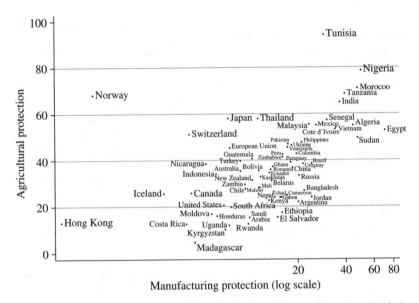

FIGURE 9.1. Levels of protection in agriculture and manufacturing, 2000–4 (percent tariff equivalent). *Source:* Kee et al. (2006).

can be seen, a sizable number of countries had industrial protection levels of 10% or less (the median being 11.7% and the mean 15.6%), but agricultural protection was much higher, with a median level of protection of 34.9% (and a mean of 35.7%). A small number of developing countries emerge as the most liberal in this sample: Uganda, Kyrgyzstan, Honduras, Moldova, Costa Rica, and Madagascar, along with Hong Kong. Rich countries generally had fairly low levels of industrial protection, but high levels of agricultural protection, Norway being an extreme example. Finally, the highest trade barriers were in developing countries, with North Africa emerging as a region that remained particularly closed. Nigeria and Tanzania also had very high levels of protection, as did India, despite its decade-long reform efforts.

INTERNATIONAL TRANSPORT COSTS

If we have dwelt at length on the political influences on international commodity market integration following the end of World War II, this is because these were the dominant influences shaping post-1945 patterns of integration and disintegration worldwide. This is the major distinction between the globalizations of the late nineteenth and late twentieth centuries: as we have seen, the former was overwhelmingly technological in origin, with falling transport costs driving commodity markets closer together, despite the best efforts of many politicians to keep them apart by imposing countervailing tariffs. The latter was much more political in origin, and involved artificial barriers which had arisen as a result of two world wars and the Great Depression being gradually dismantled. For despite the revolutionary technological advances of the period, which saw passenger air travel becoming commonplace, and men venturing as far as the Moon, the cost of transporting goods across the oceans of the world fell in real terms by surprisingly little.

To be sure, the period saw a number of important technological and organizational innovations affecting the merchant-shipping sector. The first was a by-product of the Suez crisis of 1956: with access to the Indian Ocean via the Canal seemingly at risk, shipowners began building bigger boats, and in particular huge vessels which could transport oil around the Cape. Ships of up to 35,000 tons could use the Canal, but a 100,000 ton ship was launched in 1959, and by the 1980s there were 500,000 ton ships in service. The strategy eventually worked: while initially it cost $7.50 *more* per ton of oil to transport it from the Persian Gulf to Europe around Africa rather than via Suez, by 1970 the *total* cost per ton along the African route was just $3. A second innovation was containerization, which dramatically cut port handling charges, and the time that ships had to spend in port, by up to 90%, according to one estimate (Hugill 1993, pp. 149–50). A third was the development of so-called open registry shipping, in which ships were registered in low-regulation countries such as Panama or Liberia. The resulting lower regulatory burden has been estimated as cutting costs by between 12% and 27%, while the percentage of the world's shipping tonnage registered under such flags of convenience rose from 5% in 1950 to 45% in 1995 (Hummels 1999, p. 8). Finally, specialized ships were also developed to carry chemicals, cars, and other products (World Bank 2002, pp. 103–5).

The problem is that these productivity breakthroughs were not reflected in declining freight rates. Throughout the postwar period, a series of authors documented the fact that transport costs continued to represent a serious barrier to trade, comparable with or superior to that posed by tariffs (see Waters (1970) for an early contribution). In 1976, Finger and Yeats drew attention to the fact that transport costs in the mid 1960s provided a slightly greater level of protection to U.S. industries than the tariffs of the time, despite the fact that so much media and political attention was lavished on commercial policy (Finger and Yeats 1976). They also noted that transport costs appeared to have risen between the mid 1960s and the eve of the oil shock in 1973.

Using the same sources as Finger and Yeats, and in the most careful study of post-1945 trends to date, David Hummels (1999) concludes that ocean freight rates actually increased between the 1950s and 1990s. He provides evidence regarding three types of freight rates: tramp time rates (in which a tramp freighter is employed for a fixed length of time), tramp voyage rates (in which a tramp freighter is contracted to ship a specific cargo between specific ports), and German liner freight rates (which are more representative of general cargo than the tramp rates, and which also include port costs). According to Hummels's data, nominal freight rates increased substantially over the period, with the increase being smallest for the tramp voyage rates, and largest for the liner rates.

Of course, prices in general rose during the inflationary post-1945 era. The question is, what did these movements imply for the *real* cost of shipping goods? The answer involves deflating the nominal freight rates by an appropriate deflator. Hummels shows that when deflated by GDP deflators, the liner index rises between the mid 1950s and mid 1980s, before falling back again. Using a German GDP deflator, the index never attains its initial level, even as late as 1997; deflated by the U.S. GDP deflator, it only recovers to its 1954 position by 1993. However, as both Hummels and Shah Mohammed and Williamson (2004) note, commodity price deflators are required if the purpose is to measure the ad valorem barriers to trade implied by transport costs. GDP deflators are not really suitable since these include prices of many nontraded goods and services. When Hummels deflates the tramp indices by a commodity price deflator, he finds that tramp voyage freight rates remained constant between the mid 1950s and mid 1990s, while tramp time rates increased; moreover, as already mentioned the tramp rates exclude port costs, which were sharply rising during the period.

Figure 9.2 places postwar ocean freight rates in a longer-run context, by linking them to the same series we used in chapters 7 and 8 (Shah Mohammed and Williamson 2004). The figure shows the unprecedented increase in nominal freight rates since the outbreak of World War II, and highlights the remarkably stable nature of postwar real freight rates, which is in sharp contrast with the sustained decline in

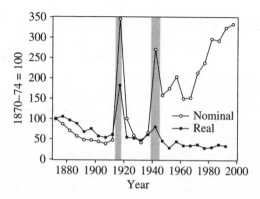

FIGURE 9.2. Tramp freight rates, 1870–1997 (1870–74 = 100). The two shaded areas represent the two world wars. *Source:* Shah Mohammed and Williamson (2004).

freight rates before 1914.[17] Moreover, other data support Hummel's conclusion that the costs of ocean transport have been stable or increasing in the postwar period (UNCTAD 2002, pp. 64, 66). While this may seem strange in light of the technological developments highlighted earlier, the explanation is to be found in rising prices of key inputs, such as fuel, wages, and shipbuilding costs (Hummels 1999, p. 13), as well as a variety of anticompetitive practices associated with both private sector and government behavior, as well as organized crime (Fink et al. 2000; Clark et al. 2004).

There are two major qualifications to this rather pessimistic picture, however. The first concerns air transport. Here, freight rates declined dramatically in the 1950s, 1960s, and 1980s, and more slowly in the 1990s. During the 1970s, when oil prices rose, air-freight rates (deflated by the U.S. GDP deflator) rose when expressed per kilogram, but fell when expressed as a percentage of the prices of goods shipped. Freight rate declines were greatest on long-distance and North American routes. The result, predictably enough, was a dramatic increase in the ratio of air to ocean shipments. Air shipments only accounted for 6.2% of U.S. imports by value in 1965, but they accounted for 24.7% in 1998 (Hummels 1999). Meanwhile, the share of air transport in U.S. exports increased from 8.3% in 1965 to 29.3% in 1994. Since air transport was more expensive than ocean transport, it was predominantly used for goods with a high value-to-weight ratio, and it was also used

[17] It is worth noting that figure 9.2 uses the tramp voyage index from 1952 onward. As noted, this is the most optimistic of the three series provided by Hummels.

over long distances relatively more than over short distances. As James Harrigan (2005) shows, this had implications for the patterns of comparative advantage observed during the 1990s, with countries that were further from the United States being more likely to send it high-value lightweight goods by airplane than countries located closer to it.

The second qualification concerns the cost-saving advantages of faster transportation. Freight rates give the cost of shipping commodities between specified ports, but do not capture the fact that it costs money to have goods locked up on boats for prolonged periods of time. Hummels (2001) estimates that each additional day that goods are spent in transit is equivalent to a 0.8% ad valorem tariff barrier for manufactured goods. The implication of the switch to air travel, as well as faster ships, is that these storage costs declined dramatically since 1950: from the equivalent of a 32% manufactured good tariff in 1950 to a 9% tariff in 1998. This clearly represents a very substantial decline in trade barriers.

Nonetheless, 9% is still a large number, certainly exceeding average U.S. tariffs in 1998. It compares with an average U.S. direct transportation cost of 10.7%: together, these two costs were equivalent to a 21% tariff at the end of the twentieth century, a considerable barrier to trade (Anderson and van Wincoop 2004, p. 704). Furthermore, there is considerable evidence that transport costs posed a much bigger problem for trade in developing countries, for example, in sub-Saharan Africa, with potentially serious implications for African trade, investment, and growth (Amjadi and Yeats 1995; Radelet and Sachs 1998).

Trends in Openness: Quantities and Prices

What were the combined effects of the technological and political developments outlined above? We begin with an overview of post-1945 world trade, before moving on to a more careful examination of regional trends.

Figure 9.3 plots the official WTO world trade index, spliced onto Arthur Lewis's (1981) series for pre-1913 trade so as to place postwar trade growth in a longer-run perspective. We link these two series using the United Nations's (1962) series for the interwar period, which was discussed in the previous chapter. The straight line on the graph extrapolates pre-1913 trends into the twentieth century, allowing us to easily compare growth rates over time. As can be seen, world trade

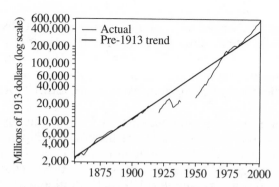

FIGURE 9.3. World exports, 1855–2000 (millions of 1913 dollars).
Source: Lewis (1981), UN (1962), and World Trade Organization.

grew more rapidly in the second half of the twentieth century than at any previous point in history: at some 5.93% per annum overall, or significantly faster than the 3.49% average growth rate prior to 1913.[18] There were two distinct phases: prior to 1973, growth averaged 7.84% per annum, but after the oil crisis it fell sharply, to 4.54%. Despite this, trade growth remained higher than before 1913 even in the 1970s; and it accelerated over time, reaching over 6% during the 1990s. Figure 9.3 also shows the effects of the world wars and Great Depression on world trade: according to these data, it was only in 1972 that world trade levels had recovered to where they would have been, had pre-1913 trends been maintained. In this respect, it took six decades for the consequences of World War I to be undone.

The fact that trade grew more rapidly than output meant, of course, that the ratio of trade to GDP tended to increase during the late twentieth century. Not surprisingly, however, given the discussion of political trends above, the timing of the move toward greater openness varied across countries and regions. Indeed, when considering the progress of international economic integration after World War II, it is crucial to take such regional differences into account, since the aggregate world trade figures we have just explored largely reflect rich-country experience, which as we have seen was atypical of much of the period.

[18] We feel comfortable in stating this since, as we have seen, world trade grew far more rapidly after 1815 than before. Export growth was particularly rapid in manufacturing, which recorded an annual export growth rate of over 9% before 1973 and over 5.5% afterwards; export growth in the mining sector plummeted after 1973, from almost 7% to just over 2% per annum, an indicator of OPEC's success in holding down oil exports; agricultural trade grew much less rapidly than manufacturing trade throughout, presumably reflecting among other things relatively high levels of agricultural protection.

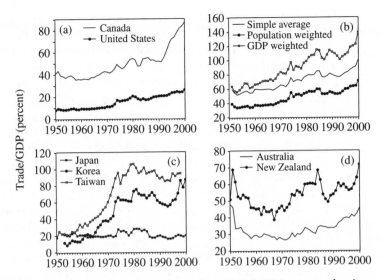

FIGURE 9.4. Trade ratios in rich countries, 1950–2000 (exports plus imports as a percentage of GDP): (a) North America; (b) Western Europe (eighteen countries); (c) East Asia; (d) Australasia. *Source:* Heston et al. (2002).

Figure 9.4 shows the evolution of trade ratios (that is to say, the ratio of exports plus imports to GDP) between 1950 and 2000 in the "West": Western Europe, the United States and Canada, Australasia, Japan, South Korea, and Taiwan.[19] Western European, Korean, Taiwanese, and American trade ratios started increasing in the 1950s (the latter only very slightly), and Canadian trade ratios started increasing in the 1960s after an initial decline. Even among this group of countries, there were important variations. In Australasia trade ratios fell during the first two decades, and only started to rise in the 1970s, while Japanese trade ratios were remarkably stable throughout. Nonetheless, these two exceptions aside, the broad impression given by figure 9.4 is one of the Western economies gradually opening up after World War II, as successive GATT agreements dismantled international barriers to trade.

This Western experience was atypical, however. There are eight developing countries whose population exceeded 100 million in 2000: China, India, Indonesia, Brazil, Pakistan, Bangladesh, Nigeria, and Mexico. Only in Indonesia did the economy start opening up as early

[19]We might have included data for Hong Kong and Singapore as well, but they only became available from 1960 onwards.

as the 1960s. Elsewhere, trade ratios either stagnated during the 1950s and 1960s (China, Pakistan, Nigeria, Bangladesh) or fell (India, Brazil, Mexico). It was not until the 1970s or 1980s that these economies' trade ratios started increasing. Figure 9.5 provides regional averages of individual countries' trade ratios, taking care to distinguish between simple averages and averages weighted by population and GDP (which are the ones we emphasize in the following discussion). As can be seen, trade ratios stagnated in Latin America until the 1970s, while they fell in Central America, sub-Saharan Africa, North Africa, and the Middle East. Only in Southeast Asia is there evidence of economies opening up during the 1960s. Elsewhere, it would be a full quarter of a century after the end of World War II, at least, before trade ratios started rising, and as often as not this followed two decades of prior decline. A common pattern seems to have been a rise in trade ratios following the first oil shock in 1973 (with the effect being particularly dramatic, as might be expected, in the oil-producing regions of the Middle East), a decline in the 1980s (particularly in Africa and Latin America), and then a rise in the 1990s, so that by the end of the century trade ratios were higher than they had been half a century earlier.

Table 9.2 places the trade ratio (or, in this case, the ratio of merchandise exports to GDP) in a longer-run perspective, providing Angus Maddison's data for a number of countries and regions between 1820 and 1998. The table highlights the unique nature of the trade expansion of the nineteenth century. As noted in chapter 7, the export ratio increased eightfold between 1820, when trade was negligible as a share of GDP, and 1913, when merchandise exports accounted for almost 8% of world GDP, and more than 16% of Western European GDP. Progress in the twentieth century was much less impressive (Krugman 1995). The table shows that merchandise exports accounted for a smaller share of world GDP in 1950 than they had done in 1913, reflecting the disintegration of the interwar period. Moreover, 1913 levels of openness (on this measure) had not been recouped as late as 1973 in the United Kingdom, Spain, Australia, Latin America, China, India, and Thailand. Indeed, they had not been recouped as late as 1992 in much of the developing world, and in particular in Latin America and India (where they had not even been recouped by 1998).

However, such quantity measures of openness can be deceiving. As Robert Feenstra (1998) and others have pointed out, the merchandise share of GDP has been shrinking in rich countries since 1913, which would tend to pull down the share of merchandise exports in GDP, irrespective of globalization trends. The growth in merchandise trade

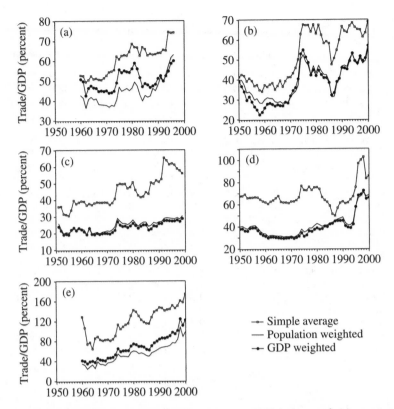

FIGURE 9.5. Trade ratios, regional averages, 1950–2000 (exports plus imports as a percentage of GDP): (a) sub-Saharan Africa (forty-one countries); (b) North Africa and the Middle East (four countries, seven from 1960); (c) Latin America (eleven countries); (d) Central America and Caribbean (nine countries); (e) Southeast Asia (five countries). *Source:* Heston et al. (2002).

over the twentieth century was thus far more impressive in rich countries relative to merchandise value added than relative to GDP (although Feenstra's table 2, which gives data for advanced countries only, shows Japanese and U.K. ratios lower in 1990 than in 1913). And other more qualitative criteria also clearly demarcate the present era from the period before World War I (Bourguignon et al. 2002): higher levels of intraindustry trade relative to interindustry trade; the emergence of new, "weightless" commodities thanks to new information technology; and, perhaps most noticeably, a rapid growth of trade in components, reflecting the increased fragmentation of firms' production processes.

TABLE 9.2. Merchandise exports as a share of GDP, 1820–1998 (percent).

	1820	1870	1913	1929	1950	1973	1992	1998
France	1.3	4.9	7.8	8.6	7.6	15.2	22.9	28.7
Germany	N.a.	9.5	16.1	12.8	6.2	23.8	32.6	38.9
Netherlands	N.a.	17.4	17.3	17.2	12.2	40.7	55.3	61.2
U.K.	3.1	12.2	17.5	13.3	11.3	14.0	21.4	25.0
Total								
Western Europe	N.a.	10.0	16.3	13.3	9.4	20.9	29.7	N.a.
Spain	1.1	3.8	8.1	5.0	3.0	5.0	13.4	23.5
U.S.S.R./Russia	N.a.	N.a.	2.9	1.6	1.3	3.8	5.1	10.6
Australia	N.a.	7.1	12.3	11.2	8.8	11.0	16.9	18.1
Canada	N.a.	12.0	12.2	15.8	13.0	19.9	27.2	N.a.
U.S.A.	2.0	2.5	3.7	3.6	3.0	4.9	8.2	10.1
Argentina	N.a.	9.4	6.8	6.1	2.4	2.1	4.3	7.0
Brazil	N.a.	12.2	9.8	6.9	3.9	2.5	4.7	5.4
Mexico	N.a.	3.9	9.1	12.5	3.0	1.9	6.4	10.7
Total								
Latin America	N.a.	9.0	9.5	9.7	6.2	4.6	6.2	N.a.
China	N.a.	0.7	1.7	1.8	2.6	1.5	2.3	4.9
India	N.a.	2.6	4.6	3.7	2.9	2.0	1.7	2.4
Indonesia	N.a.	0.9	2.2	3.6	3.4	5.1	7.4	9.0
Japan	N.a.	0.2	2.4	3.5	2.2	7.7	12.4	13.4
Korea	0.0	0.0	1.2	4.5	0.7	8.2	17.8	36.3
Taiwan	—	—	2.5	5.2	2.5	10.2	34.4	N.a.
Thailand	N.a.	2.2	6.8	6.6	7.0	4.1	11.4	13.1
Total Asia	N.a.	1.3	2.6	2.8	2.3	4.4	7.2	N.a.
World	1.0	4.6	7.9	9.0	5.5	10.5	13.5	17.2

Source: Maddison (1995, p. 38). These have been updated for some countries using Maddison (2001, p. 363), and for other countries using the raw export and GDP data given in Maddison (2001), where these produced results consistent with the earlier data series. N.a. = not available. Note: "Western Europe" here refers to countries that were not Communist during the Cold War.

This vertical specialization was first noticed by trade economists several decades ago (e.g., Findlay 1978; Helleiner 1973), but became more prominent as the century drew to a close. It sometimes took place within a single multinational company, but not necessarily so: some of the best-known examples of vertical specialization involved independent subcontractors selling to the companies under whose brand the final product would eventually be sold (Feenstra 1998, p. 36). It is important to be clear about what precisely was novel here. Clearly, it was not that different countries specialized in the production of goods at different stages of production, since the Great Specialization of the late nineteenth century involved the intercontinental exchange of food and raw materials (that is, largely unprocessed goods) for manufactures. Nor was it a dramatic increase in the share of world trade accounted for by intermediate goods, since the intermediate goods share of OECD trade actually declined between 1970 and 1992 (Hummels et al. 2001). Nor was it the fact that countries were now importing intermediate inputs, which were then used to produce other intermediates, or final products, some of which were then exported again (which is what Hummels et al. define as vertical specialization). Indeed, we emphasized in chapter 6 how the Industrial Revolution led Britain to specialize in producing intermediate inputs (such as yarn), which were then exported to textile industries in continental Europe and elsewhere.

The novelty was quantitative rather than qualitative, and lay in the *extent* to which manufacturing processes were subdivided into stages, with each stage located in a different country based, presumably, on cost minimization considerations. It is the number of times that components crossed borders in the later period that struck observers as new, but this is hard to measure systematically. According to Hummels et al., and based on a sample of countries accounting for 82% of world exports in 1990, the share of total merchandise exports reflecting vertical specialization rose from 18% in 1970 to 23.6% in 1990, while increases in such exports accounted for almost a third of the growth in the export/GDP ratio over the same period. Other measures give a similar picture: for example, Yeats (1998) found that components trade accounted for some 30% of total trade in machinery and transportation equipment in 1995, and speculated that it probably accounted for a similar proportion of total manufacturing trade.

It would be nice to supplement this quantity evidence on the growth of world trade with the sorts of price data that we have assembled for earlier periods, but systematic price evidence remains fairly elusive for the late twentieth century. There seems to be a distinction, however, between what we know about international markets for manufactured goods, and markets for agricultural and primary commodities. As far as the former are concerned, a number of recent papers appear to show international price convergence during the 1990s. Engel and Rogers (2004) find that price dispersion between European countries fell for 72 out of 101 consumer goods between 1990 and 2003, while Goldberg and Verboven (2005) document declining price dispersion in the automobile industry between 1970 and 2000, again focusing on Europe. Parsley and Wei (2002), using the same data set as Engel and Rogers, but using price data for 95 consumer goods in 83 cities worldwide, also find that price dispersion declined over the 1990s. On the other hand, official IMF and World Bank data provide no evidence of any systematic tendency toward commodity price convergence for a variety of agricultural and primary commodities (O'Rourke 2002).

These ambiguous conclusions regarding the extent of late-twentieth-century commodity market integration are consistent with an important recent paper by Baier and Bergstrand (2001), who report that income growth explains fully two-thirds of world trade growth between the late 1950s and the late 1980s, leaving only 25% to tariff reductions, and a mere 8% to transport cost declines. Strikingly, the share of trade growth due to income growth during the late twentieth century is very similar to that during the three centuries following Columbus—a period for which there is little or no evidence of intercontinental commodity price convergence (chapter 5).

Unraveling the Great Specialization

Some readers might be tempted to conclude, on the basis of the above evidence, that late-twentieth-century globalization was less than revolutionary. This would be a mistake, for the late twentieth century was in fact a period in which the nature of world trade underwent a historic change. This was above all due to the gradual spread of the Industrial Revolution to the developing world. As we have noted in the previous two chapters, the nineteenth century saw a dramatic concentration of manufacturing production in Europe and North America. Despite the growth of industry in a limited number of other countries, notably Japan, and despite the moves toward import substitution in a number of developing countries, the world economy in 1945 was still, broadly speaking, divided into an industrialized North and a nonindustrialized South. According to Paul Bairoch's data, in 1953 the developed economies (including planned economies such as the Soviet Union, but excluding Japan) accounted for 90.6% of world manufacturing output in 1953, or very slightly more than the 1913 share of 89.8% (Bairoch 1982, p. 304). Excluding Soviet bloc countries, the developed countries accounted for over 90% of the world's manufactured exports in the same year (Yates 1959, p. 228). As we have seen, corresponding to this imbalance in the structure of production was a dramatic imbalance in living standards, as well as political power. Europe's colonies were still in place in 1945, and while Britain and France had been diminished politically as a result of the war, the two big winners, the U.S.S.R. and United States, were also part of the northern, developed world.

The next fifty years would see the gradual unraveling of this traditional division of labor (UNCTAD 2003, pp. 95–96). Between 1960 and 2000, manufacturing's share of employment grew substantially in East Asia, and in the largely Muslim countries of North Africa and Southwest Asia (from roughly 8 to 15% in both cases), as well as in South Asia (from roughly 9 to 14%). Progress according to this measure was much slower in both sub-Saharan Africa (the least industrialized region of the world) and China, while the share declined (but from a relatively high level) in Latin America over the four decades as a whole. As a share of GDP, manufacturing increased from 11 to 14% in Southwest Asia and North Africa, from 15 to 27% in East Asia, from 14 to 16% in South Asia, and from 24 to 35% in China. Although the share declined slightly in sub-Saharan Africa, and substantially in Latin America (from 28 to 18%), nevertheless on this measure developing countries ended the century more industrialized than the developed world (where manufacturing's share of GDP had been declining just as it had in Latin America, from 29 to 19%).

The net result is that the industrialized countries' share of world manufacturing output fell from 88% in 1970 to 80% in 1995, while the developing countries' share almost doubled, from 12 to 20% (UNCTAD 1997, p. 82). The latter increase was mostly due to East Asia, whose share rose from 4 to 11%. The Great Divergence of the late eighteenth and nineteenth centuries had not been reversed by the close of the millennium: the rich countries still accounted for the vast majority of world manufacturing output at the close of the period. Nevertheless, a historic corner had been turned, and one that would have important implications for the structure of international trade.

Figure 9.6(a) gives the share of manufactured products in the exports of three regions: developed economies, developing countries, and the communist countries of Central and Eastern Europe, including the U.S.S.R. As can be seen, among the developing countries this share gradually rose from under 10% in 1955 to 20% in 1980, but the real change came in the 1980s and 1990s. The share was roughly 55% in 1990 and 65% in 2000; from the late 1980s onwards, the share of manufactures in exports was actually higher in the "developing world" than in the former CMEA economies. Figure 9.6(b) shows that what was true for regional exports in general was true as well for North–South trade: the last two decades of the century saw a dramatic convergence in the structure of the exports which these two regions exchanged with each other. In the North, the fact that Southern exports now consisted mostly of manufactures would eventually lead to concerns that unskilled northern workers would suffer from the

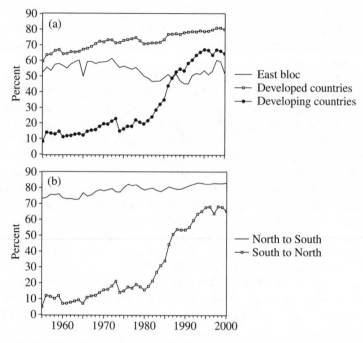

FIGURE 9.6. Manufactured products' share of exports, 1955–2000 (percent): (a) manufactured products' share of exports by region; (b) manufactured products' share of North–South trade. *Source:* UNCTAD Handbook of Statistics On-line.

increased competition, both among some economists (Wood 1994; Feenstra and Hanson 2004) and among politicians and members of the general public.

These concerns would be heightened by the fact that Southern industrialization did not just mean an increase in the share of developing country exports consisting of manufactured goods, but an increase in the South's share of world manufacturing trade as well, from just 5% in 1955 to 28% in 2000 (UNCTAD Handbook of Statistics On-line[20]). Corresponding to this increase was a decline in the share of the rich countries (from roughly 85% to around 70%), as well as in that of the economies of Central and Eastern Europe. Once again, these trends accelerated in the 1980s and 1990s.

The second half of the twentieth century also saw a gradual reduction in Southern dependence on Northern markets. The share of the

[20] Available at www.unctad.org/Templates/Page.asp?intItemID=1890&lang=1.

South's exports going to the North fell from around 70% in the late 1950s to under 60% in the 1990s. This was mostly due to a fall in the share of Southern primary product exports going northwards. The share of Southern manufactured exports destined for rich-country markets stayed fairly constant, and even increased after a dip in the early 1960s. This is an important point: in the increasingly important manufacturing sector, developing countries remained extremely dependent on northern markets.

To summarize, by the end of the twentieth century, the Great Specialization which had emerged over the course of the nineteenth century looked to be unraveling. Traditional trade patterns, which had involved rich countries exporting manufactured goods in return for the South's primary products, were being replaced with a new configuration in which two-way trade in manufactured goods did not just characterize trade between the rich countries, but trade between rich and poor as well. To be sure, this process was more advanced in some continents than in others. Table 9.3 shows dramatic progress in Latin America and South Asia, where the share of manufacturing in total merchandise exports rose from 20% and 48% in 1970 to 56% and 77% in 2000, respectively. By the end of the century, this figure had risen to more than 50% in all developing country regions with two exceptions: the Middle East and North Africa, which was heavily dependent on petroleum exports, and sub-Saharan Africa, where manufactures still accounted for less than a third of merchandise exports. Even here, however, there had been significant progress since World War II. Table 9.3 also indicates the importance of trade in commercial services, which accounted for 19% of total exports (i.e., of merchandise exports plus commercial services exports) worldwide in 2000. In 1913, services had accounted for 22% of total exports from the United Kingdom; commercial service exports accounted for 30% of U.K. exports in 2000. For the United States, the figures were 8% in 1913 and 28% in 2000 (Mitchell 1988; U.S. Department of Commerce 1975; World Bank WDI Online[21]).

Openness and Convergence in the Late Twentieth Century

The second half of the twentieth century was a period of unprecedented economic growth. According to Angus Maddison's (2003) figures, world GDP per capita rose by 185% between 1950 and 2000, or

---

[21] Available at http://publications.worldbank.org/WDI/.

TABLE 9.3. Structure of exports by region, 1970–2000.

	As percentage of: merchandise exports						total exports		
	(1)	(2)	(3)	(4)	(5)	(6)	(7)	(8)	(9)
1970									
High income	4.5	12.9	3.7	5.3	26.3	72.4	N.a.	N.a.	N.a.
Low and middle income									
Latin America and									
Caribbean	44.8	8.2	11.1	15.6	79.8	20.1	N.a.	N.a.	N.a.
South Asia	30.7	10.2	0.9	9.6	51.4	48.4	N.a.	N.a.	N.a.
1980									
High income	11.5	3.6	6.4	4.4	25.8	72.9	21.3	60.2	18.6
Low and middle income									
Latin America and									
Caribbean	27.8	3.7	41.0	9.8	82.3	17.5	70.7	15.1	14.2
Middle East and									
North Africa	4.8	2.2	83.0	4.0	94.0	7.1	87.1	6.6	6.3
South Asia	27.7	9.4	2.3	5.5	44.9	54.8	34.3	41.9	23.8
1990									
High income	8.8	2.9	4.6	3.1	19.4	78.5	15.7	63.8	20.5
Low and middle income									
East Asia and									
Pacific	15.1	5.8	12.7	2.6	36.2	60.4	32.5	54.4	13.1
Latin America and									
Caribbean	22.7	3.0	28.3	9.9	63.9	35.8	53.6	30.1	16.3
Middle East and									
North Africa	4.3	1.3	75.5	3.0	84.2	17.2	72.6	14.9	12.5
South Asia	16.1	5.1	2.4	4.2	27.8	71.1	22.3	57.0	20.7

at 2.1% per annum, and this despite a 140% increase in the world's population. When compared with the centuries of relative stagnation prior to 1800, or indeed with the modest (but, at the time, also unprecedented) growth rates of the British Industrial Revolution, or of the nineteenth century, this performance is quite simply astonishing. In the United States, which by the war's end was the undisputed economic leader of the world, accounting for 45% of world industrial output (Bairoch 1982, p. 304), growth was just above the world average for the half century as a whole, at 2.2%, but this was not where the really rapid growth was to be found.[22] Rather, a wave of "economic

---

[22] Indeed, long-run growth rates have been remarkably stable in the United States over the past century (Jones 1995): no post-1945 growth miracle here.

TABLE 9.3. *Cont.*

	As percentage of: merchandise exports						total exports		
	(1)	(2)	(3)	(4)	(5)	(6)	(7)	(8)	(9)
2000									
High income	6.6	1.7	5.0	2.5	15.8	81.2	13.0	66.5	20.5
Low and middle income									
East Asia and									
Pacific	7.8	2.1	7.2	2.0	19.1	80.3	17.0	71.3	11.7
Europe and									
Central Asia	6.0	2.8	20.9	6.3	35.9	59.6	30.1	50.0	19.8
Latin America and									
Caribbean	17.3	2.4	17.2	6.2	43.1	56.4	37.6	49.1	13.3
Middle East and									
North Africa	3.9	0.8	76.2	1.5	82.4	17.3	71.2	14.9	13.9
South Asia	12.9	1.4	4.0	2.4	20.6	77.2	15.7	58.7	25.6
Sub-Saharan									
Africa	20.2	6.2	31.5	6.7	64.6	31.3	56.5	27.4	16.1

Source: World Bank (2001b). (1) Food, (2) agricultural raw materials, (3) fuels, (4) ores and metals, (5) primary, (6) manufactures, (7) primary, (8) manufactures, (9) services. Note: the entry in column (5) is the sum of columns (1) through (4). The sum of primary and manufactured trade in columns (5) and (6) is less than 100 because of unclassified trade. The data in column (9) are for commercial service exports only. "Total" exports in columns (7) though (9) equals total merchandise exports plus commercial service exports. Columns (7) and (8) are calculated by assuming that total merchandise exports are allocated between the two categories in the same proportion as the figures in columns (5) and (6). N.a. = not available.

miracles" occurred, which led successively to Western Europe and Japan converging on the United States (above all in the 1950s and 1960s), and to the Tiger economies of East Asia (Hong Kong, Korea, Singapore, and Taiwan) doing the same in the 1960s, 1970s, and 1980s.[23]

Figure 9.7 plots regional per capita incomes relative to the United States, which can reasonably be taken to represent the "technological frontier" during the late twentieth century, and whose income thus represents the maximum feasible income level at any point in time. Figure 9.7(a) shows clearly the convergence of Japan, Western Europe, and the Tiger economies on the United States, with half-century growth rates of 5.5% per annum in the Tiger economies, 4.9% in Japan, and 2.9% in Western Europe (with growth rates among the latter group

---

[23]For a model which is consistent with these stylized facts, see Lucas (2000).

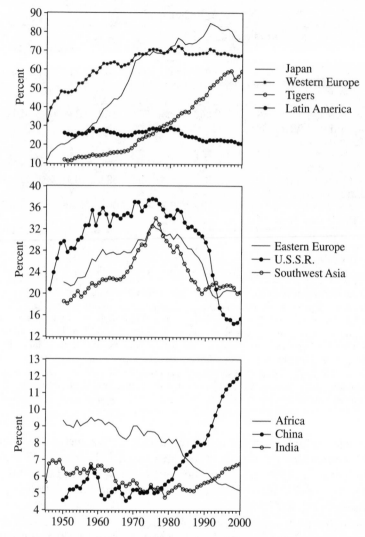

FIGURE 9.7. Regional GDP per capita, 1945–2000 (percent of U.S.A.).
Source: Maddison (2003).

of countries being highest in those economies which had been initially poorest). Figure 9.7(c) shows that China joined the convergence club in the late 1970s, as did India (if in less spectacular fashion) in the 1980s and (especially) the 1990s, after initially diverging for three decades. China's growth spurt was sufficiently impressive that its half-century

TABLE 9.4. Regional growth rates, 1960–2000
(GDP per capita, percent growth per annum).

Region	1960–73	1973–90	1990–2000
High income	4.1	2.2	1.9
Low and middle income	3.7	1.3	2.0
of which			
East Asia and Pacific	2.7	5.3	6.8
Europe and Central Asia	N.a.	N.a.	−1.1
Latin America and Caribbean	2.9	0.6	1.7
Middle East and North Africa	N.a.	N.a.	1.2
South Asia	1.1	2.6	3.2
Sub-Saharan Africa	2.3	−0.5	−0.3

Source: World Bank WDI Online. N.a. = not available.

growth rate was 4.2%, while over the fifty years as a whole Indian growth slightly exceeded that in the United States (Maddison 2003). If Western Europe, Japan, and the Tiger economies were the great success stories of the late twentieth century, the period closed amid realistic hopes that India and China would match those achievements in the decades to come, implying an unprecedented improvement in human welfare.

However, figure 9.7 and table 9.4 make it clear that there were disappointments during the period as well as successes. For example, figure 9.7 shows that while the communist economies of Eastern Europe and their Soviet master showed strong convergence on the United States until 1975, from then on their relative growth rate collapsed (indeed, as table 9.4 shows, their absolute growth turned negative during the 1990s), leaving them further behind the leader than they had been in 1950. Precisely the same was true of the oil-producing economies of Southwest Asia (although in this case the post-1970s relative collapse was not sufficient to prevent them from catching up very slightly on the United States over the half century as a whole). In the case of the former CMEA economies, their rise and decline reflected the initial success of growth strategies based on capital accumulation and industrialization, followed by the inevitable consequences of diminishing returns to capital, as in the Solow growth model, a failure to innovate, and waste associated with communism and the Cold War (Allen 2003b). The century thus ended with the hope (and, in the case of Eastern Europe, the achievement) of higher growth rates and a resumption of convergence based on a return to the market economy. In the case of Southwest Asia, it was less clear what had generated the relative slowdown in the first place, and thus what would be required to overturn it.

Even more disappointing were the cases of Latin America, and, especially, Africa. Figure 9.7 shows that neither continent managed to converge on the United States for any prolonged period of time. In the case of Latin America, there was some slight convergence during the 1950s, followed by relative stagnation through the 1970s, and divergence during the last twenty years of the century, as well as over the fifty years as a whole. The picture is even more dismal as regards Africa, which kept pace with the leader during the 1950s but thereafter fell steadily further behind, with an average half-century growth rate of less than 1% per annum. Indeed, as table 9.4 shows, sub-Saharan Africa experienced negative growth between the first oil shock and the century's end.

Comparing figures 9.4, 9.5, and 9.7, it seems clear that at this broad regional level convergence on the United States tended to be associated with a growing openness to trade. Western Europe and the Tiger economies both converged on the United States, while both became more open; in the Chinese case the move toward openness and the beginning of convergence coincided almost exactly, while Indian growth and trade both accelerated sharply during the 1990s. On the other hand, increasing openness does not appear to have guaranteed convergence, as the disappointing experience of Latin America and, especially, Africa during the 1990s demonstrates. Indeed, according to Easterly (2001), the *median* developing country growth rate across all continents was zero during 1980–99, down from 2.5% during 1960–79, and this despite the trend toward greater openness documented earlier (as well as other favorable policy trends). The broad conclusion from the regional data is thus that openness was a necessary condition for convergence on the technological frontier, but that it was by no means sufficient.

Obviously, growth depends on a wide range of variables other than exposure to trade. Standard growth models point to the importance of investment in physical and human capital, and thus to savings rates and educational systems; to the important temporary growth effects that can be associated with a rising share of the population in employment, and hence to the determinants of the labor force participation rate; and to technological progress, and hence to investment in research and development, or mechanisms enabling countries to import new technology, such as foreign direct investment. In turn, all of these variables can be influenced by government policy, the institutional environment of a country, and a host of other factors.

Furthermore, terms of trade shocks or macroeconomic disturbances can have important effects on growth rates over the short to medium run (Easterly et al. 1993).

It follows that the association between openness and growth becomes more blurred when individual country performances are examined, although many authors, such as Sachs and Warner (1995), have argued that on average there is an unmistakable positive correlation between the two variables.[24] Table 9.5 gives some sense of the complexity of individual country experience during the late twentieth century. It presents the average rich-country growth rate during three periods, 1960–73 (4.1%), 1973–90 (2.2%), and 1990–2000 (1.9%), as well as a list of the developing countries that managed to do better than this during each period. As can be seen, the list includes countries from every region: Arab countries such as Oman, Egypt, and Syria; Latin American countries such as Costa Rica and Argentina; and sub-Saharan African countries such as Mozambique, Equatorial Guinea, and Botswana, one of the world's most consistent overachievers over the period as a whole, and whose income per capita by the century's end was fourteen times higher than it had been in 1960. The table also shows that while a lot of these convergence experiences occurred in countries classified by Wacziarg and Welch (2003) as adopting open trade policies, there were also a lot of countries which managed to converge despite having trade policies classified as closed. Note, however, that very high growth rates (that is, growth rates more than three percentage points higher than the rich-country average) were almost always associated with openness: there are sixteen such cases listed in the table, of which nine were classified by Wacziarg and Welch (2003) as open, and four were unclassified. Just three cases were classified as "closed," and two of those involved China, which as we have seen was in fact dramatically opening up to trade during the periods in question, albeit from a virtually autarkic starting point.

A vast empirical literature has emerged explaining these divergent country growth performances. Not surprisingly, given what we have seen, simple monocausal relationships between openness and growth are not supported by the data. Thus, it is implausible to attribute East Asian success solely to its export orientation. Indeed, several studies have shown the crucial importance of investment in physical and human capital, as well as rising labor force participation rates, in explaining growth there (World Bank 1993; Rodrik 1995; Young 1995). To observers such as Rodrik, Alice Amsden (1989), or Robert

[24]Rodríguez and Rodrik (2001) strongly criticize this conventional wisdom.

TABLE 9.5. Developing country convergers, 1960–2000
(GDP per capita, percent growth per annum (p.a.)).

1960–73			1973–90		
Country	% p.a.	Open	Country	% p.a.	Open
Growth gap: 0–1%					
Papua New Guinea	4.2	No	Syrian Arab Republic	2.3	No
Togo	4.2	No	Tunisia	2.3	No
Panama	4.5	No	Morocco	2.4	No
Thailand	4.5	Yes	Swaziland	2.5	N.c.
Brazil	4.7	No	French Polynesia	2.6	N.c.
Barbados	5.1	Yes	Paraguay	2.6	No
			India	2.7	No
			Pakistan	3.0	No
			Seychelles	3.2	N.c.
Growth gap: 1–3%					
Lesotho	5.2	N.c.	St. Vincent and G.	3.2	N.c.
Israel	5.3	No	Sri Lanka	3.2	Yes
Korea, Rep.	5.7	Yes	Belize	3.5	N.c.
Puerto Rico	6.0	N.c.	Lesotho	3.6	N.c.
Gabon	6.6	No	Malaysia	3.8	Yes
			Solomon Islands	4.1	N.c.
			Egypt, Arab Rep.	4.2	No
			Oman	4.3	N.c.
			Indonesia	4.8	Yes
Growth gap: 3+%					
Hong Kong, China	7.3	Yes	Thailand	5.3	Yes
Singapore	7.9	Yes	Singapore	5.4	Yes
Botswana	8.8	No	Hong Kong, China	5.4	Yes
Oman	11.1	N.c.	China	6.4	No
			Korea, Rep.	6.5	Yes
			Botswana	7.2	Yes
High income growth (%):	4.1			2.2	

Source: World Bank WDI Online. Note: growth gap is growth relative to high income countries. Open means open at any time during period. N.c. means country not classified by Wacziarg and Welch (2003).

Wade (1990), government interventions designed to boost and direct investment efforts were crucial to East Asian success. Similarly, the Western European "miracle" of 1950–73 can plausibly be attributed to domestic corporatist institutions that favored wage moderation and high investment rates (Crafts and Toniolo 1996; Eichengreen 2007),

TABLE 9.5. *Cont.*

1990–2000

Country	% p.a.	Open	Country	% p.a.	Open
Growth gap: 0–1%			**Growth gap: 1–3%**		
Antigua and Barbuda	1.9	N.c.	Hong Kong, China	2.9	Yes
Benin	1.9	Yes	Bangladesh	3.0	Yes
Dominican Republic	2.0	N.c.	Belize	3.0	N.c.
Peru	2.1	Yes	Seychelles	3.0	N.c.
Syria	2.1	No	Tunisia	3.1	Yes
Papua New Guinea	2.2	No	Mozambique	3.2	Yes
Egypt, Arab Rep.	2.3	Yes	Bhutan	3.2	N.c.
Israel	2.3	Yes	Panama	3.3	Yes
Lesotho	2.3	Yes	Cape Verde	3.3	Yes
Uruguay	2.3	Yes	Sudan	3.3	N.c.
Botswana	2.3	Yes	Puerto Rico	3.3	N.c.
Iran, Islamic Rep.	2.4	No	Argentina	3.5	Yes
Tonga	2.5	N.c.	Thailand	3.5	Yes
Nepal	2.6	Yes	St. Kitts and Nevis	3.6	N.c.
Trinidad and Tobago	2.6	Yes	India	3.6	No
Bahrain	2.6	N.c.	Uganda	3.7	Yes
El Salvador	2.6	Yes	Lao PDR	3.7	N.c.
Indonesia	2.7	Yes	Sri Lanka	3.9	Yes
Grenada	2.8	N.c.	Mauritius	4.0	Yes
Costa Rica	2.9	Yes	Dominican Republic	4.1	Yes
Kiribati	2.9	N.c.	Guyana	4.5	Yes
			Malaysia	4.5	Yes
			Singapore	4.7	Yes
Growth gap: 3+%					
Chile	4.9	Yes			
Korea, Rep.	5.1	Yes			
Lebanon	5.3	N.c.			
Vietnam	5.8	N.c.			
China	8.9	No			
Equatorial Guinea	15.3	N.c.			
High income growth (%):	1.9				

and the same is true of the Irish economic miracle of the 1990s (Ó Gráda and O'Rourke 2000; Honohan and Walsh 2002). While these success stories may be due to factors other than trade liberalization, the poor performance of much of the Third World during the 1980s and 1990s may also be due to factors other than liberalization. For example, the fact that many countries liberalized in the wake of debt crises meant that their conversion to freer trade typically did not take place in promising circumstances. Even more to the point, perhaps, rich-country growth rates were less than half of what they had been in the 1960s (Easterly 2001). As we have seen, the North was still the dominant market for Southern manufactured exports, and may thus still have been an important engine of growth for Southern economies.

To an economic historian, there is a considerable sense of déjà vu about these debates. Take the issue of whether East Asian growth was due more to openness, or to domestic institutions promoting abundant and efficient investment. As we saw in chapter 6, these very same issues have been debated by economic historians in the context of the British Industrial Revolution. On the one hand, scholars such as North and Thomas (1973) have emphasized the favorable incentive structure implied by British legal and political institutions; on the other, many scholars from a variety of perspectives, such as Eric Williams (1966), Joseph Inikori (2002), or Acemoglu, Johnson, and Robinson (2005), have stressed the essential role of the Atlantic economy in spurring investment, maintaining demand, and indeed in underpinning a favorable institutional environment in the first place. Not only are the issues very similar, but the specific arguments used resemble each other as well. For example, Dani Rodrik's (1995) well-known paper, which argues against the "export-led" interpretation of Korean and Taiwanese growth, claims that initial export to GDP ratios were so small that export booms could have had only a small impact on overall output; and that there was no great increase in the relative price of exports, as would have had to have been the case if exports were the exogenous driving force behind these countries' successes. The first argument resembles those of Patrick O'Brien, Stanley Engerman, and others regarding the relatively small scale of the British traded sector; the second is precisely the test used in figure 6.5 to establish whether supply or demand shifted by more during the Industrial Revolution.

The same historical literature also helps in understanding exactly how trade enabled the East Asian Tigers and others to grow. As we argued in chapter 6, while investment and technological change may have been the keys to the British Industrial Revolution, without the possibility of trade that revolution would have been aborted. First of all, trade allowed Britain to import crucial raw materials, chief among these being raw cotton. Second, without trade output prices would have declined precipitously, as firms were forced to sell into an already saturated home market, and input prices would have soared as firms were forced to source raw materials domestically. The result would have been a collapse in profitability, and thus in investment in new capital goods and technologies. Much the same logic applies to countries such as Korea, Taiwan, or Japan during the late twentieth century, which relied heavily on imports of raw materials or capital goods (a mechanism stressed by Rodrik), and which exported a high and increasing share of their manufacturing output to the rest of the world. Trade may not have been the engine of growth for these countries, but it was the indispensable handmaiden of growth (Kravis 1970)—the wheels of growth, to pursue the automotive metaphor a little further. Indeed, this is precisely the explanation that Barry Eichengreen (2007) advances for Western Europe's convergence on the United States in the 1960s and 1970s. Domestic institutions were crucial for generating high profits and investment rates, but international institutions such as the EPU, EEC, and GATT (or the EU's Single Market Programme in the case of the Irish economic miracle) were also essential, providing reassurance to firms that once they had invested there would be a market abroad for their output, which was required if those investments were to be profitable. Trade was *not* a sufficient condition for convergence, but in the long run it was probably a necessary condition.

Conclusion

The history of late-twentieth-century international trade is a history of two worlds, and two epochs. The first epoch, which lasted roughly until 1980, saw a dramatic policy divergence between the rich countries and the rest of the world, with the former adopting ever more liberal trade policies, and the latter moving in the opposite direction. The second epoch was one of policy convergence, as increasing numbers of developing countries chose, or were forced by circumstances, to dismantle protectionist barriers and move in the direction of freer trade. That shift began in the 1980s, and came on in a rush during the 1990s. By the century's end, the ratio of world trade to GDP was higher than ever before in history.

The period saw a drastic alteration in the pre-1914 international division of labor, as the Industrial Revolution gradually spread across much of the Third World. By the end of the period, manufactures comprised a majority of exports from all regions barring Africa and the Middle East. Meanwhile, trade between developing countries rose in relative importance, although the rich countries remained the most important market for the South.

Trade was central to the various growth revolutions that ignited as regions began converging on the leading economies of North America, based on high investment rates made possible by, among other things, buoyant exports. However, the hopes which some had entertained in the 1980s, that freer trade would be sufficient to produce high levels of growth, quickly proved to be unfounded, as the experience of much of the Third World plainly showed. Domestic conditions had to be right as well if the necessary investment was to be forthcoming. But if those domestic conditions were right, then openness was an indispensable complementary policy. Of the fifty developing countries which converged on the rich countries during the 1990s, just five (Papua New Guinea, Syria, Iran, India, and China) were classified as "closed" by Wacziarg and Welch (2003), and of these five, both India and China were clearly vastly more open in 2000 than they had been twenty years previously. Import substitution may have permitted initial growth spurts in many developing countries, but eventually domestic markets became saturated and growth declined. The big economic question at the beginning of the twenty-first century was whether the strong performances of Western Europe, East Asia, China, and India over the course of the late twentieth century would eventually be replicated in Latin America, Africa, and the Middle East as well.

Chapter 10

GLOBALIZATION AT THE DAWN OF THE TWENTY-FIRST CENTURY

IF THIS SURVEY OF THE HISTORY of international trade since the year 1000 has taught the reader anything, we hope that it is this: extrapolating the immediate past into the indefinite future and calling the result a prediction is a hopeless endeavor. While the first thirty-five years following the end of World War II saw a gradual piecing together of a relatively liberal OECD economy, and the subsequent two decades broadened this trend to include most of the rest of the world, it cannot be assumed that the resultant globalization will go on indefinitely. In this concluding chapter, therefore, we provide an overview of some of the challenges which the world will face over the coming decades. We begin, however, with a brief survey of the Afro-Eurasian Ecumene at the beginning of the twenty-first century.

We began this book with a description of the seven major Eurasian "world regions" around the year 1000. How do these same regions look one thousand years later? Starting in the east, we find the Confucian East Asian societies of China, Japan, and Korea to be thriving and prosperous as before. While the lead in technology and living standards between them has passed from China to Japan, the Middle Kingdom is rapidly returning to its previous geopolitical eminence because of its vast population, rapid industrialization, and growing foreign trade. After more than a decade of stagnation, Japan has returned to growth at a modest but steady rate, with Toyota taking the lead from General Motors as the largest automobile producer in the world. South Korea has grown remarkably rapidly for the last four decades. It is an emerging power in electronics and many other manufacturing sectors, has several world-class industrial conglomerates, and enjoys the world lead in shipbuilding. North Korea, regrettably, can only make the world notice it by threatening nuclear explosions, or by driving its own people to the brink of mass starvation. The regime does not appear to be viable in the long run, and a future integration of the two Korean states would not be surprising.

As Brzezinski (1997) points out, the key question then would be what happens to the American troops currently stationed in South Korea. Their continued presence could not but be an affront to China, while their withdrawal would leave Japan feeling dangerously exposed, perhaps making it necessary for her to sharply increase her defense expenditure, and maybe even consider the acquisition of a nuclear capability. In either case the geopolitical equilibrium of the eastern end of the Eurasian landmass would be severely affected. Turning to domestic politics, Japan has had a stable democratic regime since the end of World War II while preserving its ancient monarchy, and South Korea and Taiwan have also made successful democratic transitions from military dictatorship. China, on the other hand, continues with a strongly entrenched Communist Party presiding over a state-managed capitalist economy actively engaged in the world market. This is an increasingly anomalous situation whose resolution, whatever it may be, will have momentous consequences for the region and the world.

Central Asia, with its five Islamic republics of Kazakhstan, Kyrgyzstan, Tajikistan, Turkmenistan, and Uzbekistan cut loose from the former Soviet Union, is still very underdeveloped, but is extremely well endowed with oil and natural gas. If properly handled, these could finance successful industrialization and modernization in the region. Kazakhstan's vast territory contains huge oil reserves, actively competed for by Russia, China, and the West. Ethnic Russians comprise about 37% of the population, as well as most of the country's educated and technical elite, a considerable Russian asset in this competition. Uzbekistan is the most populous of the five republics with about 25 million, and there are substantial Uzbek minorities in Afghanistan and the other Central Asian republics apart from Kazakhstan. The Turkic-speaking Uzbeks have an important ally in Turkey itself, and as the heirs to the Timurid Empire have a heightened sense of national identity, as well as a growing Islamic consciousness.

While these states have been heavily influenced by their former membership of the U.S.S.R., they are now also open to influences from elsewhere, particularly Turkey and Iran in the west and China in the east. Playing off the Russian and Chinese giants on either flank against each other, with the fraternal assistance of Turkey and Iran, is their best long-term diplomatic prospect. While China and Russia compete for influence in Central Asia, they are both acutely aware of possible contagion from this volatile region to their own Muslim minorities, in Chechnya and Xinjiang Province respectively. The United States is obviously also a major player in the area, with a desire for both energy and military bases. Several commentators have anticipated a repeat of the nineteenth-century "Great Game" between Russia and Great Britain in the region, with the United States replacing Britain, but with a newly invigorated China adding an extra dimension of complexity and unpredictability to an already combustible mix.

South Asia, divided in 1000 between a number of competing Hindu kingdoms before the establishment of first the Delhi sultanate and then the Mughal Empire, is now six states, which together have a larger population than China: the three major states of India, Pakistan, and Bangladesh in the peninsula, the island of Sri Lanka, plus the small mountain kingdoms of Nepal and Bhutan. Looking back over developments in the subcontinent since independence, an apologist for the British Raj might be forgiven for taking some satisfaction in the extent to which three legacies, cricket, the English language, and parliamentary democracy, in that order, have taken hold among its inhabitants. As we have seen, India is now growing very rapidly, following its opening up in the early 1990s from the inward-looking planned development path that it had previously followed. India's assets are its relative abundance, for such a poor country, of English-speaking skilled labor, and a very dynamic entrepreneurial class that is making it a world leader in the information technology sector. Its vigorous democratic tradition of now over sixty years gives it an advantage over China, which faces uncertainty over the future of its political system. Pakistan, while still mired in military dictatorship after failed interludes of democracy, is also stepping up its growth rate. The continuing conflict with India over Kashmir, rendered even more troubling because of the nuclear weapons that both countries now possess, is clearly a negative influence on the development of both countries, and particularly on that of Pakistan, where it is more at the center of national consciousness. Bangladesh, the former East Pakistan that seceded in 1971 with the decisive assistance of the Indian Army, has had a moderately successful economic performance over the last three decades, led by labor-intensive manufactured exports, despite unfavorable ecological circumstances and a highly corrupt if democratic political system. Sri Lanka was a prosperous primary export economy with an excellent educational system, before ethnic clashes between the Buddhist Sinhalese majority and the largely Hindu Tamil minority ripped the country apart in a vicious and still ongoing civil war that has set it back by decades.

Southeast Asia, which at the outset of the millennium was a crossroads between India and China, is once again playing its familiar role of facilitating the overseas trade of a now far more extensively and intensively globalized world, with Singapore taking the place of

Srivijaya as the crucial entrepôt of the region. Trade has brought Islam to the Malay inhabitants of Southeast Asia, and Chinese settlers to further enliven and energize its active economic life. The Indonesian archipelago, home of the Spice Islands that were so important in another era, is now the largest Muslim country in the world with a population of 200 million, while Malaysia, another Muslim state but with a large and highly prosperous Chinese minority, is one of the world's most rapidly developing economies, with its traditional primary sector now overshadowed by increasingly high-tech manufacturing. Both countries now have stable democratic political systems, Malaysia from its inception but Indonesia only after enduring two long dictatorships under Sukarno on the left and Suharto on the right. The threat from fundamentalist Islamic groups continues to exist in both countries, however, and could seriously threaten stability in the event of an economic crisis.

The largely Roman Catholic Philippines has an active if rather volatile democracy, and on the whole a creditable economic performance based on primary exports, supplemented by exports of services, and manufacturing for the home market but increasingly also for export. Buddhist Thailand, also with a history of Chinese immigration, but where integration with the native population has been much easier than in Muslim Malaysia, has also enjoyed prolonged steady growth based on primary products, increasingly overtaken by labor-intensive manufactured exports and industrialization for the home market. Both the Philippines and Thailand have small but troublesome Muslim insurgencies with which to contend. Perhaps the most remarkable Southeast Asian success story of all, however, has been the transformation of Vietnam, from the communist command economy that it was at the close of the war with the United States to the dynamic export economy, open to the capitalist world market, that it is today (although like China it still remains a one-party political dictatorship). Even Cambodia has emerged from the horrors of Pol Pot with a regime that is now open to external influences. Only Burma remains trapped in a long nightmare of stagnation, under dictatorial military rule that has now lasted for over forty years. Large offshore deposits of natural gas have made it unlikely that the regime will bow to external pressures to move toward democracy and economic reform.

As regards the relationships of the region with the rest of the world, an increasingly wealthy and powerful China will presumably imply a return to the historical pattern of an acknowledged, but very loosely enforced, primacy of the Middle Kingdom in Southeast Asia. Australia, with its increasingly lucrative trade with the Far East and Southeast

Asia, will undoubtedly continue its occasionally strained naval collaboration with Indonesia and other ASEAN countries. A possible bone of contention between China and the Southeast Asian states is the offshore oil deposits in the South China Sea. China's Yunnan Province is directly connected by the Irrawaddy with the Bay of Bengal, through a Burma ruled by a military junta that is increasingly dependent on Chinese economic and political support. It remains to be seen, not if, but when the first Chinese fleet since the squadrons of Admiral Zheng He sails through the Straits of Malacca and into the Indian Ocean.

We now turn to the most central and "connected" of our seven world regions in 1000, the Islamic World of the Middle East. At that time, as we saw, it was experiencing a "Golden Age," with a sophisticated irrigation-based agriculture and the most urbanized population in the world outside of China. After undergoing the many vicissitudes that we have traced in the previous pages the region is still central to the world's concerns, but has fallen from its former position of primacy. Per capita incomes are higher than in South or Central Asia or China, only because of the rents from the abundant oil reserves with which the region has been blessed, or perhaps cursed. The region has been the scene of many major wars since 1945: three involving Israel, in 1948, 1967, and 1973; the Algerian war of liberation against France; one between Iraq and Iran which lasted from 1980 to 1988; two between Iraq and U.S.-led coalitions in 1991 and 2003; as well as many civil wars and cross-border incursions too numerous to mention. The establishment of the state of Israel has led to successive attacks on it by coalitions of Arab states, or preemptive strikes by Israel to forestall such attacks, along with incursions into Lebanon to attack the PLO or Hezbollah. The Israeli–Palestinian conflict has been a constant source of tension in the region, with wide geopolitical ramifications. The chronically unsettled political climate caused by all these actual and potential hostilities, the negative "Dutch Disease" impact on manufacturing of high oil rents and political subsidies, and the stifling straitjacket imposed by one-party states and absolute monarchies on most forms of creativity and initiative, have resulted in low growth rates of per capita income throughout most of the region. The exception that proves the rule is Israel, though Turkey within the region and Malaysia outside it have demonstrated that Islam is not in itself an obstacle to successful modernization and development, both political and economic.

Our Eastern European region, originally dominated by the Byzantine Empire, is now essentially Russia, together with Ukraine and Belarus, successor states of the once mighty Soviet Union that lasted only from 1917 to 1991. As noted in the previous chapter, Bulgaria and Romania joined the European Union in 2007, taking them effectively out of the Russian orbit. Hopefully their absorption into "Western Europe" will not bring as many problems as did the absorption of East Germany, Hungary, Czechoslovakia, and Poland into "Eastern Europe" during the Cold War. Despite its efforts to "overtake and surpass" the capitalist West under the Five Year Plans of Stalin and his successors, Russia is no closer to this goal than it was in the days of Peter the Great. Vast reserves of oil and natural gas, as well as other minerals, have given the Russian state the means to restore centralized direction of the economy, but under a more flexible market system and with much greater private ownership than in Soviet times, as well as to play an energetic geopolitical role on the world stage. Due to its vast extent, Russia can supply energy at a lower cost than the Middle East to Western Europe at one end of the Eurasian landmass, and to China, Korea, and Japan at the other, while exercising considerable influence on its former Islamic possessions in Central Asia and on its own "near abroad." Of crucial significance in this regard is the political future of Ukraine, with its strategic location on the Black Sea, fertile soil, and population of well over 50 million, including a substantial Russian minority in the eastern regions. The "Orange Revolution" of 2004–5 seemed to signify a decisive shift to the West, but it remains to be seen how long lasting this will be. Georgia is another Black Sea state that Russia is actively seeking to retain within its sphere of influence, despite the leaning toward the West of its people and political elite. The main economic problem for Russia would now appear to be to use the earnings from its natural resource endowments to generate high and rising productivity in its modern manufacturing sectors, so as to be able to compete globally with Asia, Western Europe, and the United States, something it was never able to do as a centrally planned economy. In geopolitical terms it lags behind the United States and China, but can still play a crucial balancing role, which for the moment appears to be to cooperate with China to check U.S. power.

Relative to 1000, the most spectacular success of all has undoubtedly been Western Europe, despite the losses of its colonies during the late twentieth century. Over the centuries the region has not only been the birthplace of modern economic growth, but spawned Iberian offshoots in Latin America and, most notably, the British offshoots of Australia, New Zealand, Canada, and the United States. More recently, the region has successfully integrated its separate nation-states into a prosperous European Union. Between them the United States and the EU have only about 12% of world population, but over 40% of world GDP, a share that will, however, be falling because of the much more rapid growth of China, India, and other Asian states. The EU has enlarged itself peacefully by moving eastwards, incorporating former Soviet satellites such as Poland, Hungary, and the Baltic states into its orbit. It now embraces almost all of our Roman Catholic "Western European" world region, Bulgaria and Romania in Greek Orthodox "Eastern Europe," and Greece itself, which joined in 1981. So successful has the EU been at helping to anchor democracy and promote economic growth that several more countries outside Western Europe, including Turkey and Ukraine, wish to join it. Managing such demands, particularly in the face of mounting Russian nervousness at Western "encroachment" on what it feels to be its sphere of influence, will be a major challenge for the EU in the decades ahead, and one that it would probably rather avoid. The fact is, however, that the EU is now a Black Sea power, as well as a major importer of Central Asian and Russian energy. It will thus inevitably become involved in the politics of that region, whether it likes it or not.

The one remaining region of the Old World is sub-Saharan Africa, which as we have seen was relatively isolated from the remainder of the Afro-Eurasian Ecumene at the beginning of the second millennium, and remained hampered by relatively high transport costs at the millennium's end. During the intervening thousand years, its people had contributed massively to the prosperity of the rest of the world, particularly through the inhuman institution of slavery, which as we argued in chapter 6 was one important factor underlying the transition to modern economic growth in Europe. It is ironic, therefore, that sub-Saharan Africa remains the poorest and most underdeveloped world region at the dawn of the twenty-first century. Slavery itself presumably hampered economic development within Africa. Indeed, in a provocative recent paper Nathan Nunn (2006) finds a strong negative relationship between the number of slaves shipped from African countries between 1400 and 1900 and those countries' *current* economic development. His interpretation is that the violence that characterized the slave trade had a variety of detrimental consequences on subsequent institutional development, and hence had long-lasting effects on economic growth. Other recent papers have argued that European colonialism in Africa also damaged long-run growth there, again by damaging local institutions, based on similar econometric evidence (Acemoglu et al. 2001; Bertocchi and Canova 2002).

A much more optimistic argument is provided in a recent paper by Robert Bates, John Coatsworth, and Jeffrey Williamson (2006).

They point out that Latin America's economic performance in the first half century following its independence (roughly 1820–70) was just as dismal as Africa's post-independence performance, which has now lasted for roughly fifty years as well. Latin American per capita incomes were stagnant during these "lost decades," at a time when European incomes were, as we have seen, beginning their acceleration to modern economic growth. Bates et al. explain this poor performance as being in large part due to the incessant warfare which plagued the continent, and which we mentioned briefly in chapter 7. This is most suggestive, since Africa's poor growth during its post-1960 "lost decades" can also in large part be attributed to warfare, although clearly factors such as an unfavorable disease environment, low productivity agriculture, poor governance, and rich-country trade policies were important as well (Collier and Gunning 1999; Sachs et al. 2004). Violent conflict in Africa was in part due to proxy wars between East and West, during a "Cold War" that was often hot in the developing world. It was also due in part to border conflicts between new states, yet another negative legacy of history to the continent, or to ethnic conflict within them, with the Rwandan genocide of the 1990s providing the most horrific and best-known example. To the extent that the argument is correct there may be some hope for the future, since it may be the case that Africa will eventually settle into a new, post-imperial political equilibrium in which violence and instability will decline. Indeed, as Bates et al. report, there is some evidence that this may already be happening, with a reduction in the incidence of civil wars, and the spread of democracy on the continent. It is certainly to be hoped that they are right, since ending sub-Saharan poverty remains the single greatest developmental challenge facing humanity today.

The Future of Globalization: Economic Challenges

As we saw in chapter 9, it seemed by the end of the twentieth century as though the world might finally be heading toward a more balanced economic system, with more and more countries starting to converge on the world's technological frontier, and the "Great Specialization" becoming a thing of the past, a temporary by-product of the disequilibrium created by the Industrial Revolution two hundred years previously. Looking ahead, therefore, it seems natural to suppose that more and more countries will experience the benefits of industrialization and modern economic growth, and that trade flows will increasingly involve the mutual exchange of manufactured goods, with primary-product exports now reflecting particularly favorable resource endowments, rather than backward manufacturing sectors.

The benevolent trends that we have just described are what would be predicted if the economic system is allowed to evolve smoothly in the future, but nothing is in fact less certain. If anything, history suggests that globalization is a fragile and easily reversible process, with implications not just for international trade, but for the international division of labor and economic growth as well. To contemporary observers, the late-nineteenth-century globalization described in chapter 7 must have seemed the natural order of things, but the Great War showed how false such an assumption was. Not only was trade disrupted during the conflict itself, but the interwar era which followed saw a steady proliferation of tariff and nontariff barriers to trade in the richest countries of the world, and this was in turn followed by inward-looking antitrade policies in developing countries which lasted until the 1970s or 1980s. Even more worryingly from today's perspective, no one in 1913 saw these disasters coming (Ferguson 2005).

What sorts of stresses might emerge to test the global economy of the early twenty-first century? We can think of several, some economic and others political. One obvious potential risk in the medium to long run is that oil will become significantly dearer, for one of two reasons. The first is that world oil production will peak, and then start to decline, as has been argued by several prominent scientists (for a readable account, see Deffeyes (2001)). Such a trend, in combination with rapid Southern industrialization, would clearly lead to a dramatic and sustained rise in oil prices. The second is that current concerns over global warming will lead to the imposition of high carbon taxes. Since current transportation technologies are heavily oil-intensive, transport costs would rise under either of these scenarios, with the extent of the increase depending on how rapidly technologies evolved in response. Sufficient increases in transport costs would lead to less intercontinental trade in very bulky commodities, which would in turn be good news for some producers, such as European farmers, and bad news for others. A key policy concern would then be to ensure that those developing countries which are already hampered by relatively high transport costs not be excessively harmed by even higher ones.

Late-nineteenth-century experience is particularly instructive when thinking about a second category of potential economic stresses. That period saw continents with very different factor proportions being drawn into ever-tighter economic contact. The result was large distributional shifts favoring New World landowners and European workers, and hurting European landowners and American workers. The result, as chapter 7 showed, was agricultural protection in Europe, which persists to this day, and protection for manufacturing industries throughout the New World, as well as restrictions on immigration (O'Rourke and Williamson 1999).

In contrast, the more regional liberalization of 1945–80 mostly involved OECD economies, which were relatively similar in terms of economic development, capital–labor ratios, and living standards. Trade between them was largely intraindustry in nature, rather than being driven by strong factor endowment differences between trading partners. It thus involved less dramatic distributional consequences than late-nineteenth-century trade, and this made it easier to continue removing trade barriers. Notably, there remained one dimension along which factor endowments *were* significantly different among OECD economies, namely land–labor ratios. Not coincidentally, agriculture was exempt from the general trade liberalization of the period, suggesting that potential losers from free trade remained as powerful politically as they had been in the late nineteenth century.

As we have seen, the 1980s, and especially the 1990s, were very different in nature, involving as they did trade liberalization in much of the Third World, an increase in the South's share of manufactured exports, and a switch in the composition of North–South trade, with the South shifting from an almost exclusive reliance on exporting primary products to exporting larger volumes and a wider range of manufactured goods. Once again, therefore, globalization was linking continents with very different factor proportions, the South having substantially lower capital–labor ratios and less well-educated workforces than the North. The question which then arises is: will this recent globalization give rise to distributional shifts, in particular hurting unskilled workers in Northern economies? And if so, can we expect a political backlash on the lines of what happened during the late nineteenth century?

It is certainly true that there has been a distributional shift in rich countries against unskilled workers and in favor of the higher skilled, as the simple Heckscher–Ohlin trade theory we relied on in chapter 7 would predict. The U.S. experience is particularly well-known (and dramatic): between 1979 and 1995, real wages of workers with less than twelve years of education fell by 20.2%; real wages of workers with twelve years of education fell by 13.4%; real wages of workers with sixteen or seventeen years of education rose by 1.0%; and real wages of workers with eighteen years of education or more rose by 14% (Katz and Autor 1999, cited in Feenstra and Hanson 2004). However, international trade is just one possible cause of this rise in inequality. Technological change that was skill-using and unskilled-labor-saving would have precisely the same effect. Trying to distinguish between these two possibilities has given rise to a lively academic controversy. While much of the initial research suggested that trade has played only a small role in raising inequality, more recent work focusing on the role of imported intermediate inputs has generated larger estimates of the (negative) impact of trade on unskilled wages in rich countries.[1]

Certainly, history shows that some of the arguments made in the context of the present debate do not hold water. Thus, the argument that trade is too small a share of GDP to have a significant effect on factor prices cannot be right, since trade was typically an even smaller share of GDP in the late nineteenth century, when as we have seen commodity price convergence led to substantial distributional shifts across the world. And besides, the evidence which we saw in chapter 9 suggests that the situation is evolving so rapidly that it would be unwise to conclude too much about the future from evidence going back to the 1980s or even the 1970s, which is what of necessity most empirical studies to date have had to rely upon.

Even more relevant, perhaps, to the future of globalization is the fact that voters appear to hold opinions about trade that are precisely what would be predicted if trade were generating distributional changes in line with Heckscher–Ohlin theory. In a series of recent papers, authors such as Mayda and Rodrik (2005) and O'Rourke and Sinnott (2001) have shown that individual voter preferences are fully consistent with the predictions of Heckscher–Ohlin theory. That is, in rich (skill-abundant) countries, unskilled workers are much more protectionist than skilled workers, but this effect gets weaker in poorer countries, and disappears (or even reverses) in the very poorest countries. If unskilled workers in rich countries believe that they are being hurt by international trade, this could by itself be sufficient to produce a backlash, even if these beliefs are not accurate.

Moreover, there are signs that these attitudes are not just an artifact of opinion surveys, but are influencing politics in several rich countries. True, in the early to mid 1990s American politicians such as Pat Buchanan or Ross Perot, who attempted to garner blue-collar support by appealing to workers' fears of foreign competition, failed dismally in their electoral bids. However, in 2005 the French electorate decisively rejected a proposed European "constitutional

---

[1] The literature is too vast to be summarized here; for a flavor of recent contributions, see Collins (1998), Feenstra (2000), and Feenstra and Hanson (2004).

treaty," apparently on largely protectionist grounds. Furthermore, just as Heckscher and Ohlin would have predicted, the vote split largely on class lines, with poorer and lower-skilled workers voting against the treaty, and richer, higher-skilled workers voting in favor. The same year saw the ending of the Multi-Fiber Agreement, which as we saw had operated for years to protect Northern producers from cheap textile imports. No sooner had the MFA been phased out, than the United States moved to restrict imports of Chinese textiles, and the European Union negotiated an agreement with China limiting the growth in that country's textile exports. In the latter case, there was a clear political link between the EU's actions, and the popular distrust of globalization that had emerged in the French referendum debate. Nor was this just a European peculiarity, since shortly afterwards textile and sugar interests almost succeeded in torpedoing the United States's adoption of a Central American Free Trade Agreement.

All this suggests that the potential for a nineteenth-century-style antiglobalization backlash in rich countries cannot be ruled out in the future. As history shows, income distribution matters not just in its own right, but because of the political reactions it can provoke. The implication is that those wishing to maintain an open trading system also need to propose a range of complementary domestic policies, including but not limited to educational, training, and welfare programs, if they are to maintain political support for liberal trade policies. Indeed, as we saw earlier, late-nineteenth-century European politicians put in place precisely such programs when obtaining labor's support for free trade in countries such as Belgium (Huberman, forthcoming), and this sort of policy trade-off was at the heart of late-twentieth-century globalization in rich countries as well (Ruggie 1982; Rodrik 1998). Hays, Ehrlich, and Peinhardt (2005, pp. 473–74) summarize the argument as follows: "Because trade causes economic dislocations and exposes workers to greater risk, it generates political opposition that democratically elected leaders ignore at their peril. Thus...political leaders have had to be aware of and actively manage public support for economic openness. To do this, governments have exchanged welfare state policies that cushion their citizens from the vagaries of the international economy in return for public support for openness."

Mass immigration poses one potential threat to this arrangement, since while citizens may be happy to pay taxes so as to meet their fellow nationals' needs, they may not be so happy to pay for services provided to immigrants. Indirect support for this rather depressing proposition comes from the United States, where Alesina et al. (1999) find that public expenditure on public goods such as education and infrastructure is lower in more ethnically fragmented cities. In principle, immigrants could have either a positive or a negative effect on the fiscal health of the welfare state, depending on such things as their age profile, their skill mix, and on whether they or their children can find employment or not, but what matters politically is public perceptions. Hanson, Scheve, and Slaughter (2005) and Facchini and Mayda (2006) find evidence that individual attitudes toward immigration are influenced not just by the labor market concerns of workers but by the welfare state concerns of taxpayers. Such considerations suggest that the way in which the interaction of mass immigration and the welfare state is managed could be politically important in determining the future not just of immigration but of the future of the welfare state, and thus of globalization more generally.

THE FUTURE OF GLOBALIZATION: POLITICAL CHALLENGES

However, even if politicians *do* succeed in building the domestic policy underpinnings of continued openness, it cannot be assumed that this will be sufficient to maintain open markets. One of the lessons of history emphasized throughout this book is that the geopolitical context is crucial in determining the extent of international trade. Eurasian trade flows increased as a result of the *Pax Mongolica*, before diminishing again in the sixteenth century as a result of political turmoil; the comparatively peaceful nineteenth century saw an unprecedented trade expansion; World War I, World War II, and the Cold War all had large, negative, long-run effects on trade. The most recent globalization upswing coincided with the end of the Cold War, and took place in a period in which warfare remained all too common, but tended to be national or regional, rather than global in scope.

The major condition for a continuation of present trends, therefore, is the avoidance of a major conflict dividing the world into competing camps. The historical record thus supports historians such as Niall Ferguson (2005) who point to such geopolitical problems as imperial overstretch, international terrorism, and nuclear proliferation as being the key factors which will determine the future of globalization as we know it today. As Stephen Walt (1998, pp. 38–39) puts it, while self-congratulatory Western intellectuals could confidently proclaim "the end of history" following the defeat of communism, "History has paid little attention to this boast." As economists, we may have a lot to say about domestic "globalization backlashes," but international relations may in fact be a more relevant discipline for those wishing to understand what lies ahead for the world economy.

As readers of this book will have noted, periods of sustained expansion in world trade have tended to coincide with the infrastructure of law and order necessary to keep trade routes open being provided by a dominant "hegemon" or imperial power, as in the cases of the *Pax Mongolica* and *Pax Britannica.* After 1945 this essential role was played by the United States, at least insofar as the non-Communist world was concerned. After the collapse of the Soviet Union and China's dramatic entry into the world market, however, the question is open as to whether the *Pax Americana* can continue effectively in what is now an almost wholly globalized world economic system. Paradoxical as it may seem, the Cold War imposed a sort of discipline not only on the leaders of the two blocs themselves, but also on their respective clients, resembling as it did a global political duopoly that had evolved a set of stabilizing "rules of the game." These no longer exist in a world of one superpower monopoly and its allies, surrounded by a potentially anarchic "competitive fringe" that is not prepared to acknowledge its authority. It is no wonder that real or imagined nuclear threats from relatively minor powers such as North Korea and Iran are causing some to feel nostalgic for the bad old days of the "delicate balance of terror" (Wohlstetter 1959).

The fact that the United States is undoubtedly the dominant military power today, as well as being the world's leading economy in terms of most conventional indicators, does not in any way imply that it can impose its will unilaterally on the rest of the world. China and Russia are major powers with geopolitical objectives that conflict with those of the United States, even though they now operate within the same capitalist world market. By a remarkable irony China has displaced Japan as the leading trade partner of the United States, and its enormous savings rate, combined with a fixed dollar–yuan exchange rate, has enabled it not only to generate double-digit growth rates, but the largest foreign exchange reserves in the world. The majority of these consist of American government debt, helping the United States to run a current account deficit of more than 6% of GDP in 2006. The rapid growth of both China and India has added substantially to the demand for world energy supplies, driving up prices to the benefit of net suppliers such as the Middle East and Russia, and to the detriment of the United States and its allies in Western Europe and Japan. There is every indication that this pattern will continue into the future, unless drastic measures are taken to cut demand or find alternative sources. Thus despite its paramount position in the world economy, the United

States finds its freedom of action severely constrained by both its financial and energy dependence on rival powers.

In the light of these considerations it is perhaps not surprising that some influential voices have called for the United States to use its military power more forcefully to sustain its geopolitical dominance. In our opinion, such an approach would be fatal to the continuance of the extensive and largely benign globalization that has been achieved thus far. Since World War II the United States has fought four major conflicts, with very mixed results. The Korean War was essentially a draw, with over 50,000 American lives lost, while the Vietnam War undoubtedly ended in a defeat, with the loss of 58,000 American lives. The 1991 Gulf War to expel Iraq from Kuwait was a military success, besides being justified morally and politically. However, the 2003 invasion and occupation of Iraq has clearly been a military and political failure, with the benefits of the removal of the vicious Saddam regime being far outweighed by the enormous cost to the Iraqi people in terms of civilian casualties, destruction of infrastructure, and the disruption of their society by the unleashing of savage sectarian tensions. The only possible solace that we can draw from this ongoing sorry episode, although it will be of little comfort to the tens of thousands of families whose lives have been destroyed, is in some wise words of Raymond Aron (1974, p. 156). While these were written with reference to Vietnam, they are if anything even more cogent today: "Failure becomes success because it…teaches modesty, and prepares the way for an equilibrium among states."

Western Europe, Canada, Australia, New Zealand, and Japan are all close allies that have in the past generally followed the United States lead, despite occasional disagreements on mostly economic matters. There is no guarantee, however, that this will continue to be the case in the future, given the devastating blow to American prestige and its claims of moral leadership that has been inflicted by the U.S. occupation of Iraq since 2003. It is ironic indeed that figures such as Donald Rumsfeld and George W. Bush have done more to detach Western Europe from the United States than decades of Gaullist posturing, but that appeared to be the case at the time of writing. Rebuilding the Western Alliance in the short run will require less ideologically driven leadership on both sides of the Atlantic, but in the longer-run perceived common threats emanating from the Eurasian Heartland may serve to bring the two sides closer together again, even if unwillingly.

What might such threats involve? In the celebrated paper that he wrote over one hundred years ago, and that we have already had occasion to quote, the historical geographer and geopolitical theorist Sir Halford Mackinder (1904, p. 421) said that historians of the future "will describe the last 400 years as the Columbian epoch, and will say that it ended soon after 1900." He thought that the domination of the coastal fringes of the Eurasian landmass over its vast interior, which had been up to that time the "geographical pivot of history," would end with the relatively new invention of the transcontinental railroad, making Russia, which "replaces the Mongol Empire" (p. 436), the arbiter of the world, perhaps in alliance with Germany. Fortunately for the rest of the world, that alliance, which would have been difficult if not impossible to beat, did not emerge in either of the two world wars, and here we are over one hundred years later with the world's commerce still crossing the Atlantic and Pacific, and with both oceans patrolled by the U.S. Navy. Most of the world's manufacturing takes place in coastal regions, not only in America and Europe but also in Japan, Korea, the coastal provinces of China, Hong Kong, Taiwan, Southeast Asia, and India. So, was Mackinder wrong? The railroad has not overtaken the steamship as he imagined it would, but the oil and natural gas pipelines of the world, so necessary to sustain all that coastal manufacturing, are increasingly running overland across Central Asia. It is no longer the luxuries of the East that the West has to purchase, but the very lifeblood of manufacturing industry and transportation itself. In turn, this vital overland trade is raising familiar problems of control over bottlenecks and monopoly power.

Zbigniew Brzezinski (1997) sees the entire Eurasian landmass as the "Grand Chessboard" on which the game of power politics in the twenty-first century will be played. The "Eurasian" or "Global Balkans" is the evocative term that Brzezinski (1997, 2004) uses to denote the sub-region consisting of the five Central Asian republics, the three Caucasus states of Azerbaijan, Armenia, and Georgia, and Afghanistan. This is an area of extreme political volatility and ethnic and religious strife, compounded by competition over massive reserves of oil and natural gas. Turkey and Iran each have linguistically and ethnically related peoples in the region that they seek to influence politically, while the U.S.-led coalition's invasion of Afghanistan to overthrow the Taliban is encountering mounting interference from Pakistan among the Pashtun, and from Iran among the Farsi-speaking Tajiks in Herat and the western portions of the country. Brzezinski (1997, p. 129) sees Azerbaijan, with its strategic location on the western banks of the Caspian Sea and its huge Baku oilfields, as a geographic pivot, "the vitally important 'cork' controlling access to the 'bottle' that contains the riches of the Caspian Sea basin and Central Asia." Pipelines from

Central Asia through the Caspian, Azerbaijan, Georgia or Armenia, and Turkey could bypass Russia entirely to send vital energy supplies to Western Europe, and the Baku–Tbilisi–Ceyhan (BTC) pipeline running from the Caspian to the Mediterranean, opened in 2006, does precisely this. Similarly, oil could be exported by sea if a pipeline were constructed from Central Asia through either Iran or Afghanistan and Pakistan. The reader will recall from chapter 3 that one of Timur's strategic objectives was to divert trade from the northern Silk Road controlled by the overlords of Russia, the Golden Horde, to the southern one running through Bukhara and Samarkand, which are both in what is now Uzbekistan. The currently strained relations between the West and Iran over the latter's nuclear ambitions are undoubtedly hindering the development of trade and investment projects that could link Central Asia more firmly with the West while bypassing Russia, as in the days of the ancient Silk Road.

Turkey and Iran, the modern successors to the Ottoman and Safavid Empires, are both key players in the competition over the Global Balkans. The Turkish Mediterranean port of Ceyhan, the terminus of the BTC pipeline, is of vital interest to an EU becoming increasingly dependent on Russia for its energy supplies, making one wonder why ancient fears and prejudices are allowed to impede Turkey's entry into that organization. Similarly, if Iranian influence among the Tajiks of Central Asia is feared, then surely it would make sense to secure the cooperation of Turkey, with its influence over the more numerous Uzbeks and Turkmen. Turkey, like Russia, is now a nation-state but was once a multiethnic empire, and as such has ongoing conflicts over its own identity and future path. The cementing of Turkey even more firmly within the Western orbit seems all the more necessary, now that the invasion of Iraq has succeeded in bringing about the alignment of that country's Shia plurality with Iran, a consequence that was unintended but which should not have been unforeseen.

While widely deplored in the West, the path to power of the Iranian theocrats was, as noted earlier, paved by the West itself, as a result of the CIA-led coup of 1953. The regime is undoubtedly bent on spreading its influence in the region, but its appeal is limited to its Shia coreligionists, and is hence largely confined to sections of Iraq, Lebanon, the Persian Gulf states, western Afghanistan, where it is undoubtedly a major player, and among the Persian-speaking Tajiks of Central Asia. The oft-invoked coming "clash of civilizations" between Islam and the Christian West ignores the profound conflict between the Shia Persians and the mostly Sunni Arabs of Saudi Arabia, Egypt, and the North African states, which makes the latter natural allies of the

West in any clash with Iran. It also ignores the large, well-educated and pro-Western element within Iranian society itself. The steady nerves and cool rationality of the architects of American foreign policy in the early days of the Cold War, such as Truman, Marshall, Acheson, and Kennan, who were faced by an infinitely greater threat, would be an undoubted asset in today's United States. While the inflammatory rhetoric of Iran's elected president and his nuclear ambitions have aroused the desire in some Western quarters to invade the country and overthrow the regime, the incalculable consequences of such an action, rather than any threat posed by Iran itself, seem to us to pose the greater threat to international stability.

From a European point of view, the alternative to the "Turkish route" is the "Russian route." Somewhat optimistically, Brzezinski sees Russia as having no option other than to be incorporated into the West, and embracing both democracy and free markets, thus fulfilling the dreams of its "Westernizers" as opposed to the Slavophiles and "Eurasianists" who considered association with the materialism of the West to be corrupting to the Russian soul. Russia, however, seems clearly bent on playing an independent role in the world. Buoyed by the high prices for Russia's vast energy reserves, Vladimir Putin has been vigorously reasserting Russian influence in its "near abroad" and even further afield, while at the same time cooperating with the rising economic power of China. At the time of writing, nervous Europeans were planning the construction of the so-called "Nabucco" pipeline, which would provide a direct overland link between the BTC pipeline and Baumgarten in Austria. In response to this attempt to undermine its control over the "New Silk Route," as some journalists have called it, Russia is planning a separate pipeline under the Black Sea to Turkey, which, it hopes, will neutralize the potential threat posed by "Nabucco" by the simple expedient of linking into the latter. Additionally, the Russians are planning a further pipeline under the Baltic, with the aim of circumventing the potential bottlenecks that they face on their western borders, namely Belarus and Ukraine. This would give Russia greater control over the latter states, by allowing it to cut off supplies when necessary without halting exports to the EU. While Europeans are understandably worried by the prospect of being held to ransom by Gazprom, the Russian gas company, they should also remember that Gazprom needs markets abroad, and that the EU represents a large and powerful consumer bloc.

In the light of all these problems it would be foolish, as we noted earlier, to simply assume that the remarkable progress achieved by globalization in the last few decades will be sustained into the future.

Setbacks and disruptions from unforeseen events such as wars, revolutions, and natural catastrophes are bound to occur, along with financial crises and trade conflicts generated more directly by the process of globalization itself. Such setbacks need not inevitably imply the collapse of globalization, however, as some commentators such as John Gray (1998) imply. As in all human affairs, the choices that individual human beings make will matter, for better and for worse.

At the time of writing, a major short-run security threat seemed to be the mutual suspicion underlying relations between the West and the Muslim World. Preventing the violence in Israel, Palestine, Lebanon, and Iraq, as well as isolated terrorist attacks in the West, from degenerating into something more widespread and dangerous was the major immediate problem facing the world's leaders. In the longer run, the gradual rise of India and China to their natural roles as major economic and political superpowers was not only the best news for global human welfare in a generation, but promised to raise a variety of geopolitical challenges which as yet remain unpredictable. Indeed, history suggests that this could turn out to be the greatest geopolitical challenge facing the international system in the twenty-first century, for in the past the world has found it very difficult to adjust to the emergence of industrial "latecomers," new powers eager to play an equal role with the dominant nations of the day. Thus, German unification and industrialization during the late nineteenth century led to tensions with Britain and France over colonial and armament policy, while Japan's rise to regional prominence during the interwar period, and its search for secure sources of raw materials, ended in war against the United States and its allies. Both precedents are worrying in their implications for the twenty-first century, for similar questions are posed today, both in terms of the rights of emerging nations to rival the established powers' military capabilities (notably with regard to nuclear weapons), and in terms of the strategic importance to countries like China of ready access to oil supplies.

There is one further implication of the rise of the South that we want to mention, and that has to do with the institutions governing the international political and economic system. These reflect the state of the world in 1945, which as we have seen was unusually asymmetric, with Europe and its offshoots accounting for a historically high share of world manufacturing activity, income, and political influence. Thus, of the United Nations's five permanent Security Council members in 2000, three were European (Britain, France, and Russia), one was North American (the United States), and one was Asian (China). Strikingly, there were no permanent members from Africa or Latin America.

Even more strikingly, at the time of writing this book it seemed that several countries thought it would make sense to add a *fourth* European country, Germany, to the list, albeit alongside five other permanent members (two from Asia, two from Africa, and one from Latin America). Meanwhile, the head of the World Bank continued to be American, by tradition, while the head of the International Monetary Fund continued to be European.

Clearly, as the world becomes less asymmetric, its political institutions will have to follow suit. Managing this process will be one of the trickiest issues facing the international community in the years ahead, but it is essential if the world is to maintain a relatively open, multilateral political and trading system.

BIBLIOGRAPHY

Abraham, M. 1988. *Two Medieval Merchant Guilds of South India*. New Delhi: Manohar.

Abulafia, D. 1987. Asia, Africa and the trade of medieval Europe. In *The Cambridge Economic History of Europe*, volume II, *Trade and Industry in the Middle Ages* (ed. M. M. Postan and E. Miller), 2nd edn. Cambridge University Press.

Abu-Lughod, J. L. 1989. *Before European Hegemony: The World System AD 1250–1350*. Oxford University Press.

Accominotti, O., and M. Flandreau. 2006. Does bilateralism promote trade? Nineteenth century liberalization revisited. CEPR Discussion Paper 5423.

Acemoglu, D., S. Johnson, and J. A. Robinson. 2001. The colonial origins of comparative development: an empirical investigation. *American Economic Review* 91:1369–401.

———. 2005. The rise of Europe: Atlantic trade, institutional change and economic growth. *American Economic Review* 95:546–79.

Acton, Lord. 1961. *Lectures on Modern History*. New York: Meridian Books.

Adams, D. R., Jr. 1980. American neutrality and prosperity, 1793–1808: a reconsideration. *Journal of Economic History* 40:713–37.

Adshead, S. A. M. 1973. The seventeenth century general crisis in China. *Asian Profile* 1:271–80.

———. 1993. *Central Asia in World History*. London: Macmillan.

Aldcroft, D. H. 1977. *From Versailles to Wall Street 1919–1929*. London: Allen Lane.

Alesina, A., R. Baqir, and W. Easterly. 1999. Public goods and ethnic divisions. *Quarterly Journal of Economics* 114:1243–84.

Alesina, A., and E. Spolaore. 1997. On the number and size of nations. *Quarterly Journal of Economics* 112:1027–56.

Ali, M. A. 1993. The Mughal polity: a critique of revisionist approaches. *Modern Asian Studies* 27:699–710.

Allen, D. W. 2002. The British Navy Rules: monitoring and incompatible incentives in the age of fighting sail. *Explorations in Economic History* 39:204–31.

Allen, R. C. 1998. Urban development and agrarian change in early modern Europe. University of British Columbia Department of Economics Discussion Paper 98-19.

———. 2001. The Great Divergence in European wages and prices from the Middle Ages to the First World War. *Explorations in Economic History* 38:411–47.

———. 2003a. Progress and poverty in early modern Europe. *Economic History Review* 56:403–43.

Allen, R. C. 2003b. *Farm to Factory: A Reinterpretation of the Soviet Industrial Revolution*. Princeton University Press.

———. 2006. The British Industrial Revolution in global perspective: how commerce rather than science caused the Industrial Revolution and modern economic growth. Mimeo, Oxford University.

———. 2007. India in the Great Divergence. In *The New Comparative Economic History: Essays in Honor of Jeffrey G. Williamson* (ed. T. J. Hatton, K. H. O'Rourke, and A. M. Taylor). Cambridge, MA: MIT Press.

Amjadi, A., and A. J. Yeats. 1995. Have transport costs contributed to the relative decline of sub-Saharan African exports? Some preliminary empirical evidence. World Bank Policy Research Working Paper 1559.

Amsden, A. 1989. *Asia's Next Giant: South Korea and Late Industrialization*. Oxford University Press.

Andaya, B. W., and L. D. Andaya. 1982. *A History of Malaysia*. London: Macmillan.

Anderson, F. 2001. *Crucible of War*. New York: Vintage Books.

Anderson, J. E., and J. P. Neary. 2005. *Measuring the Restrictiveness of International Trade Policy*. Cambridge, MA: MIT Press.

Anderson, J. E., and E. van Wincoop. 2004. Trade costs. *Journal of Economic Literature* 42:691–751.

Andrews, K. R. 1984. *Trade, Plunder and Settlement: Maritime Enterprise and the Genesis of the British Empire 1480–1630*. Cambridge University Press.

Antràs, P., and H.-J. Voth. 2003. Factor prices and productivity growth during the British Industrial Revolution. *Explorations in Economic History* 40:52–77.

Arasaratnam, S. 1964. *Ceylon*. Englewood Cliffs, NJ: Prentice Hall.

———. 1988. *Dutch Power in Ceylon 1658–1687*. New Delhi: Navrang.

Aron, R. 1974. *The Imperial Republic: The United States and the World 1945–1973*. Englewood Cliffs, NJ: Prentice Hall.

Ashton, T. S. 1948. *The Industrial Revolution 1760–1830*. Oxford University Press.

Ashtor, E. 1969. *Histoire des Prix et des Salaires Dans l'Orient Médiéval*. Paris: SEVPEN.

———. 1973. La découverte de la voie maritime aux Indes et les prix des épices. In *Histoire Économique du Monde Méditerranéen 1450–1650: Mélanges en l'Honneur de Fernand Braudel*, volume I. Toulouse: Privat.

———. 1976a. *A Social and Economic History of the Near East in the Middle Ages*. Berkeley, CA: University of California Press.

———. 1976b. Spice prices in the Near East in the 15th century. *Journal of the Royal Asiatic Society* 1:26–41. (Reprinted in *Spices in the Indian Ocean World* (ed. M. N. Pearson). Gateshead: Variorum, 1996.)

Ashtor, E. 1978. *Studies in the Levantine Trade in the Middle Ages*. London: Variorum.

———. 1983. *The Levant Trade in the Middle Ages*. Princeton University Press.

———. 1992. *Technology, Industry and Trade: The Levant versus Europe 1250–1500*. Aldershot: Variorum.

Attman, A. 1973. *The Russian and Polish Markets in International Trade 1500–1650.* Institute of Economic History, Gothenburg University.

——. 1986. Precious metals and the balance of payments in international trade, 1500–1800. In *The Emergence of a World Economy 1500–1914* (ed. W. Fischer, R. M. McInnis, and J. Schneider). Wiesbaden: Franz Steiner.

Atwell, W. S. 1982. International bullion flows and the Chinese economy 1530–1650. *Past and Present* 95:68–90.

——. 1986. Some observations on the "seventeenth century crisis" in China and Japan. *Journal of Asian Studies* 45:223–44.

——. 1998. Ming China and the emerging world economy. In *The Cambridge History of China,* volume 8, *The Ming Dynasty, 1368–1644,* part 2 (ed. D. C. Twitchett and F. W. Mote). Cambridge University Press.

Ayalon, D. 1956. *Gunpowder and Firearms in the Mamluk Kingdom.* London: Vallentine Mitchell.

Aye Hlaing, U. 1964. A study of economic development of Burma, 1870–1940. Mimeo, University of Rangoon.

Bagwell, K., and R. W. Staiger. 1999. Multilateral trade negotiations, bilateral opportunism and the rules of GATT. NBER Working Paper 7071.

Baier, S. L., and J. H. Bergstrand. 2001. The growth of world trade: tariffs, transport costs, and income similarity. *Journal of International Economics* 53:1–27.

Bairoch, P. 1982. International industrialization levels from 1750 to 1980. *Journal of European Economic History* 11:269–331.

——. 1989. European trade policy, 1815–1914. In *The Cambridge Economic History of Europe,* volume VIII, *The Industrial Economies: The Development of Economic and Social Policies* (ed. P. Mathias and S. Pollard). Cambridge University Press.

Bairoch, P., and B. Etemad. 1985. *Structure par Produits des Exportations du Tiers-Monde 1830–1937.* Geneva: Droz.

Bakewell, P. 1984. Mining in colonial Spanish America. In *The Cambridge History of Latin America,* volume II, *Colonial Latin America* (ed. L. Bethell). Cambridge University Press.

Baldwin, R. E. 1969. The case against infant-industry tariff protection. *Journal of Political Economy* 77:295–305.

Barbero, M. I., and F. Rocchi. 2003. Industry. In *A New Economic History of Argentina* (ed. G. della Paolera and A. M. Taylor). Cambridge University Press.

Barbour, V. 1930. Dutch and English merchant shipping in the seventeenth century. *Economic History Review* 2:261–90.

Barkan, O. L. 1975. The price revolution of the sixteenth century: a turning point in the economic history of the Near East. *International Journal of Middle East Studies* 6:3–28.

Barraclough, G. 1976. *The Crucible of Europe: The Ninth and Tenth Centuries in European History.* Berkeley, CA: University of California Press.

Barrett, W. 1990. World bullion flows, 1450–1800. In *The Rise of Merchant Empires: Long Distance Trade in the Early Modern World 1350–1750* (ed. J. Tracy). Cambridge University Press.

Barthold, W. 1968. *Turkestan Down to the Mongol Invasion*, 3rd edn. Taipei: Southern Materials Center.

Bartlett, R. 1993. *The Making of Europe: Conquest, Colonization and Cultural Change 950–1350*. Princeton University Press.

Bates, R. H., J. H. Coatsworth, and J. G. Williamson. 2006. Lost decades: lessons from post-independence Latin America for today's Africa. NBER Working Paper 12610.

Baugh, D. A. 2004. Naval power: what gave the British Navy superiority? In *Exceptionalism and Industrialisation: Britain and Its European Rivals, 1688–1815* (ed. L. Prados de la Escosura). Cambridge University Press.

Bautier, R. 1971. *The Economic Development of Medieval Europe*. New York: Harcourt Brace Jovanovich.

Bayly, C. A. 1983. *Rulers, Townsmen and Bazaars: North Indian Society in the Age of British Expansion, 1770–1870*. Cambridge University Press.

——. 1988. *Indian Society and the Making of the British Empire*. Cambridge University Press.

——. 2004. *The Birth of the Modern World 1780–1914: Global Connections and Comparisons*. Oxford: Blackwell.

Beach, J. W. 1934. Keats's realms of gold. *PMLA* 49:246–57.

Becher, M. 2003. *Charlemagne*. New Haven, CT: Yale University Press.

Beckles, H. M. 1998. The "Hub of Empire": the Caribbean and Britain in the seventeenth century. In *The Oxford History of the British Empire*, volume I, *The Origins of Empire* (ed. N. Canny). Oxford University Press.

Benedictow, O. J. 2004. *The Black Death 1346–1353: The Complete History*. Woodbridge: Boydell Press.

Bentley, J. H. 1996. Cross-cultural interaction and periodization in world history. *American Historical Review* 101:749–70.

Berg, M. 2004. Consumption in eighteenth- and early nineteenth-century Britain. In *The Cambridge Economic History of Modern Britain*, volume I, *Industrialisation, 1700–1860* (ed. R. Floud and P. Johnson). Cambridge University Press.

Bernhofen, D. M., and J. C. Brown. 2004. A direct test of the theory of comparative advantage: the case of Japan. *Journal of Political Economy* 112:48–67.

Bertocchi, G., and F. Canova. 2002. Did colonization matter for growth? An empirical exploration into the historical causes of Africa's underdevelopment. *European Economic Review* 46:1851–71.

Best, A. 2003. Imperial Japan. In *The Origins of World War Two: The Debate Continues* (ed. R. Boyce and J. A. Maiolo). Houndmills, Basingstoke: Palgrave Macmillan.

Bhagwati, J. N. 1971. The generalised theory of distortions and welfare. In *Trade, Balance of Payments and Growth: Papers in International Economics in Honor of Charles P. Kindleberger* (ed. J. N. Bhagwati, R. W. Jones, R. A. Mundell, and J. Vanek). Amsterdam: North-Holland.

Bhagwati, J. N., and A. Krueger (eds). 1974–78. *Foreign Trade Regimes and Economic Development: A Special Conference Series on Foreign Trade Regimes and Economic Development*. New York: NBER.

Bhagwati, J. N., and T. N. Srinivasan. 1975. *India*. New York: NBER.

Bianquis, T. 1998. Autonomous Egypt from Ibn Tûlûn to Kâfûr, 868–969. In *The Cambridge History of Egypt*, volume 1, *Islamic Egypt, 640–1517* (ed. C. F. Petry). Cambridge University Press.

Blattman, C., J. Hwang, and J. G. Williamson. 2003. The terms of trade and economic growth in the periphery 1870–1938. NBER Working Paper 9940.

———. 2004. The impact of the terms of trade on economic development in the periphery, 1870–1939: volatility and secular change. NBER Working Paper 10600.

Bloch, M. 1969. The advent and triumph of the watermill. In *Land and Work in the Middle Ages: Selected Papers by Marc Bloch* (trans. J. E. Anderson). New York: Harper Torchbooks.

Blum, J. 1956. Prices in Russia in the sixteenth century. *Journal of Economic History* 16:182–99.

Blum, U., and L. Dudley. 2003. Standardised Latin and medieval economic growth. *European Review of Economic History* 7:213–38.

Blunden, C., and M. Elvin. 1983. *Cultural Atlas of China*. New York: Facts on File.

Bodde, D. 1981. *Essays on Chinese Civilization*. Princeton University Press.

Bolin, S. 1953. Mohammed, Charlemagne and Ruric. *Scandinavian Economic History Review* 1:5–39.

Bonney, R. 2004. Towards the comparative fiscal history of Britain and France during the "long" eighteenth century. In *Exceptionalism and Industrialisation: Britain and Its European Rivals, 1688–1815* (ed. L. Prados de la Escosura). Cambridge University Press.

Borsch, S. J. 2005. *The Black Death in Egypt and England*. Austin, TX: University of Texas Press.

Bourguignon, F., D. Coyle, R. Fernández, F. Giavazzi, D. Marin, K. H. O'Rourke, R. Portes, P. Seabright, A. Venables, T. Verdier, and L. A. Winters. 2002. Making sense of globalization: a guide to the economic issues. CEPR Policy Paper 8.

Bourguignon, F., and C. Morrisson. 2002. Inequality among world citizens: 1820–1992. *American Economic Review* 92:727–44.

Boussard, J. 1976. *The Civilization of Charlemagne*. New York: McGraw Hill.

Boxer, C. R. 1959. *The Great Ship from Amacon: Annals of Macao and the Old Japan Trade, 1555–1640*. Lisbon: Centro de Estudos Historicos Ultamarinos.

———. 1969. A note on Portuguese reactions to the revival of the Red Sea spice trade and the rise of Atjeh. *Journal of Southeast Asian History* 10:415–28.

———. 1973. *The Dutch Seaborne Empire 1600–1800*. Harmondsworth: Penguin Books.

Boxer, C. R. 1975. *The Portuguese Seaborne Empire: 1415–1825*. New York: Alfred A. Knopf.

Boyce, R. 1989. World war, world depression: some economic origins of the Second World War. In *Paths to War: New Essays on the Origins of the Second World War* (ed. R. Boyce and E. M. Robertson). New York: St. Martin's Press.

———. 2003. Economics. In *The Origins of World War Two: The Debate Continues* (ed. R. Boyce and J. A. Maiolo). Houndmills, Basingstoke: Palgrave Macmillan.

BPP. 1905. Second series of memoranda, statistical tables and charts prepared in the Board of Trade: with reference to various matters bearing on British and foreign trade and industrial conditions. *British Parliamentary Papers*, volume LXXXIV, Cd. 2337.

Braudel, F. 1975. *The Mediterranean and the Mediterranean World in the Age of Philip II*, volume 1. London: Collins.

Brett, M. 2001. *The Rise of the Fatimids: The World of the Mediterranean and the Middle East in the Tenth Century CE.* Leiden: Brill.

Brewer, J. 1990. *The Sinews of Power: War, Money and the English State, 1688–1783.* Cambridge, MA: Harvard University Press.

——. 1994. The eighteenth-century British state. In *An Imperial State at War: Britain from 1689 to 1815* (ed. L. Stone). London: Routledge.

Bridbury, A. R. 1962. *Economic Growth: England in the Later Middle Ages.* London: Allen and Unwin.

Broadberry, S. N., and B. Gupta. 2005. Cotton textiles and the Great Divergence: Lancashire, India and shifting competitive advantage, 1600–1850. CEPR Discussion Paper 5183.

——. 2006. The early modern Great Divergence: wages, prices and economic development in Europe and Asia, 1500–1800. *Economic History Review* 59:2–31.

Broadberry, S. N., and M. Harrison. 2005. The economics of World War I: an overview. In *The Economics of World War I* (ed. S. N. Broadberry and M. Harrison). Cambridge University Press.

Broadberry, S. N., and P. Howlett. 2005. The United Kingdom during World War I: business as usual? In *The Economics of World War I* (ed. S. N. Broadberry and M. Harrison). Cambridge University Press.

Brogan, H. 1986. *The Pelican History of the United States of America.* Harmondsworth: Penguin Books.

Brown, K. W. 1990. Price movements in eighteenth-century Peru: Arequipa. In *Essays on the Price History of Eighteenth-Century Latin America* (ed. L. L. Johnson and E. Tandeter). Albuquerque, NM: University of New Mexico Press.

Bruton, H. J. (in collaboration with G. Abeysekera, N. Sanderatne, and Z. A. Yusof). 1992. *The Political Economy of Poverty, Equity, and Growth: Sri Lanka and Malaysia.* Oxford University Press.

Brzezinski, Z. 1997. *The Grand Chessboard: American Primacy and Its Geostrategic Imperatives.* New York: Basic Books.

Brzezinski, Z. 2004. *The Choice: Global Domination or Global Leadership.* New York: Basic Books.

Bulbeck, D., A. Reid, L. C. Tan, and Y. Wu. 1998. *Southeast Asian Exports since the 14th Century: Cloves, Pepper, Coffee and Sugar.* Leiden: KITLV Press.

Bulmer-Thomas, V. 2003. *The Economic History of Latin America since Independence*, 2nd edn. Cambridge University Press.

Buringh, E., and J. L. van Zanden. 2006. Charting the "rise of the West." Manuscript and printed books in Europe, a long-term perspective from the sixth through eighteenth century. Mimeo, International Institute of Social History.

Buruma, I. 1998. *Anglomania: A European Love Affair.* New York: Random House.

Cain, P. J., and A. G. Hopkins. 2002. *British Imperialism 1688–2000,* 2nd edn. Harlow: Longman.

Cameron, R. 1989. *A Concise Economic History of the World: From Paleolithic Times to the Present.* Oxford University Press.

Carter, S., S. Gartner, M. R. Haines, A. Olmstead, R. Sutch, and G. Wright (eds). 2006. *Historical Statistics of the United States: Millennial Edition.* Cambridge University Press.

Chabert, A. 1949. *Essai sur les Mouvements des Revenus et de l'Activité Économique en France de 1798 à 1820.* Paris: Librairie des Médicis.

Chalmeta, P. 1994. An approximate picture of the economy of al-Andalus. In *The Legacy of Muslim Spain,* volume 2 (ed. Salma Khadra Jayyusi). Leiden: Brill.

Chapman, S. D. 1972. *The Cotton Industry in the Industrial Revolution.* London: Macmillan.

Chaudhuri, K. N. 1978. *The Trading World of Asia and the English East India Company 1660–1760.* Cambridge University Press.

——. 1983. Foreign trade and the balance of payments (1757–1947). In *The Cambridge Economic History of India,* volume 2, *c. 1757–c. 1970* (ed. D. Kumar). Cambridge University Press.

——. 1985. *Trade and Civilisation in the Indian Ocean: An Economic History from the Rise of Islam to 1750.* Cambridge University Press.

Chaunu, H., and P. Chaunu. 1955–59. *Séville et l'Atlantique, 1504–1650* (8 volumes). Paris: SEVPEN.

——. 1974. The Atlantic economy and the world economy. In *Essays in European Economic History 1500–1800* (ed. P. Earle). Oxford: Clarendon Press.

Cheng, K. 1990. Cheng Ch'eng-Kung's maritime expansion and early Ch'ing maritime prohibition. In *Development and Decline of Fukien Province in the 17th and 18th Centuries* (ed. E. B. Vermeer). Leiden: Brill.

Chi, C.-T. 1936. *Key Economic Areas in Chinese History.* London: Allen and Unwin.

Chiswick, B. R., and T. J. Hatton. 2003. International migration and the integration of labor markets. In *Globalization in Historical Perspective* (ed. M. D. Bordo, A. M. Taylor, and J. G. Williamson). University of Chicago Press.

Christian, D. 1998. *A History of Russia, Central Asia and Mongolia,* volume 1. Oxford: Blackwell.

Cipolla, C. M. 1964. Economic depression of the Renaissance? *Economic History Review* 16:519–24.

——. 1965. *Guns, Sails and Empires: Technological Innovation and the Early Phases of European Expansion 1400–1700.* New York: Pantheon Books.

——. 1994. *Before the Industrial Revolution: European Economy and Society 1000–1700,* 3rd edn. New York: W. W. Norton.

Clark, G. 1996. The political foundations of modern economic growth: England, 1540–1800. *Journal of Interdisciplinary History* 26:563–88.

Clark, G. 2005. The condition of the working class in England, 1209–2004. *Journal of Political Economy* 113:1307–40.

———. 2007a. *A Farewell to Alms: A Brief Economic History of the World.* Princeton University Press.

———. 2007b. What made Britannia great? How much of the rise of Britain to world dominance by 1850 does the Industrial Revolution explain? In *The New Comparative Economic History: Essays in Honor of Jeffrey G. Williamson* (ed. T. J. Hatton, K. H. O'Rourke, and A. M. Taylor). Cambridge, MA: MIT Press.

Clark, X., D. Dollar, and A. Micco. 2004. Port efficiency, maritime transport costs, and bilateral trade. *Journal of Development Economics* 75:417–50.

Clarke, H., and B. Ambrosiani. 1995. *Towns in the Viking Age,* revised edn. London: Leicester University Press.

Clemens, M. A., and J. G. Williamson. 2004. Why did the tariff–growth correlation change after 1950? *Journal of Economic Growth* 9:5–46.

Clements, J. 2005. *Coxinga and the Fall of the Ming Dynasty.* Stroud: Sutton.

Clingingsmith, D., and J. G. Williamson. 2004. India's deindustrialization under British rule: new ideas, new evidence. NBER Working Paper 10586.

———. 2005. Mughal decline, climate change, and Britain's industrial ascent: an integrated perspective on India's 18th and 19th century deindustrialization. NBER Working Paper 11730.

Coatsworth, J. H., and J. G. Williamson. 2004. Always protectionist? Latin American tariffs from independence to Great Depression. *Journal of Latin American Studies* 36:205–32.

Coedes, G. 1968. *The Indianized States of Southeast Asia,* 3rd edn. Honolulu, HI: University Press of Hawaii.

Cohn, S. K. 2003. *The Black Death Transformed: Disease and Culture in Early Renaissance Europe.* Oxford University Press.

Cole, A. H., and R. Crandall. 1964. The international scientific committee on price history. *Journal of Economic History* 24:381–88.

Collier, P., and J. W. Gunning. 1999. Why has Africa grown slowly? *Journal of Economic Perspectives* 13:3–22.

Collins, R. 1991. *Early Medieval Europe 300–1000.* New York: St. Martin's Press.

Collins, S. M. (ed.). 1998. *Imports, Exports, and the American Worker.* Washington, DC: Brookings Institution Press.

Collins, W. J. 1996. Regional labor markets in British India. Mimeo, Harvard University.

Constable, O. R. 1994. *Trade and Traders in Muslim Spain: The Commercial Realignment of the Iberian Peninsula, 900–1500.* Cambridge University Press.

Contreras, M. E. 1993. The Bolivian tin mining industry in the first half of the twentieth century. Institute of Latin American Studies Research Paper 32.

Coppel, J., and M. Durand 1999. Trends in market openness. OECD Economics Department Working Paper 221.

Corbett, M., and R. W. Lightbown. 1979. *The Comely Frontispiece: The Emblematic Title-Page in England 1550–1660.* London: Routledge & Kegan Paul.

Corbo, V. 1992. *Development Strategies and Policies in Latin America: A Historical Perspective.* San Francisco, CA: International Center for Economic Growth/ICS Press.

Corden, W. M., and J. P. Neary. 1982. Booming sector and de-industrialisation in a small open economy. *Economic Journal* 92:825–48.

Coupland, S. 1995. The Vikings in Francia and Anglo-Saxon England to 911. In *The New Cambridge Medieval History,* volume II, *c. 700–c. 900* (ed. R. McKitterick). Cambridge University Press.

Crafts, N. F. R. 1985. *British Economic Growth during the Industrial Revolution.* Oxford University Press.

Crafts, N. F. R., and C. K. Harley. 1992. Output growth and the British Industrial Revolution: a restatement of the Crafts–Harley view. *Economic History Review* 44:703–30.

Crafts, N. F. R., and G. Toniolo (eds). 1996. *Economic Growth in Europe since 1945.* Cambridge University Press.

Crosby, A. W. 2003. *The Columbian Exchange: Biological and Cultural Consequences of 1492.* Westport, CT: Praeger.

Crouzet, F. 1964. Wars, blockade, and economic change in Europe, 1792–1815. *Journal of Economic History* 24:567–88.

——. 1980. Towards an export economy: British exports during the Industrial Revolution. *Explorations in Economic History* 17:48–93.

——. 1981. The sources of England's wealth: some French views in the eighteenth century. In *Shipping, Trade and Commerce: Essays in Memory of Ralph Davis* (ed. P. L. Cottrell and D. H. Aldcroft). London: Leicester University Press.

——. 1987. *L'Economie Britannique et Le Blocus Continental,* 2nd edn. Paris: Economica.

——. 1990. England and France in the eighteenth century: a comparative analysis of two economic growths. In *Britain Ascendant: Comparative Studies in Franco-British Economic History* (ed. F. Crouzet). Cambridge University Press.

——. 1993. *La Grande Inflation. La Monnaie en France de Louis XVI à Napoléon.* Paris: Fayard.

——. 2001. *A History of the European Economy, 1000–2000.* Charlottesville, VA, and London: University Press of Virginia.

Crucini, M. J. 1994. Sources of variation in real tariff rates: the United States, 1900–1940. *American Economic Review* 84:732–43.

Crucini, M. J., and J. Kahn. 1996. Tariffs and aggregate economic activity: lessons from the Great Depression. *Journal of Monetary Economics* 38:427–67.

Crummey, R. O. 1987. *The Formation of Muscovy 1304–1613.* London and New York: Longmans.

Cuenca Esteban, J. 1994. British textile prices, 1770–1831: are British growth rates worth revising once again? *Economic History Review* 47:66–105.

——. 1995. Further evidence of falling prices of cotton cloth, 1768–1816. *Economic History Review* 48:145–50.

Cuenca Esteban, J. 1997. The rising share of British industrial exports in industrial output, 1700–1851. *Journal of Economic History* 57:879–906.

——. 2001. The British balance of payments, 1772–1820: India transfers and war finance. *Economic History Review* 54:58–86.

——. 2004. Comparative patterns of colonial trade: Britain and its rivals. In *Exceptionalism and Industrialisation: Britain and Its European Rivals, 1688–1815* (ed. L. Prados de la Escosura). Cambridge University Press.

Curtin, P. D. 1954. The British sugar duties and West Indian prosperity. *Journal of Economic History* 14:157–64.

——. 1969. *The Atlantic Slave Trade: A Census*. Madison, WI: University of Wisconsin Press.

——. 1975. *Economic Change in Pre-Colonial Africa: Senegambia in the Era of the Slave Trade*. Madison, WI: University of Wisconsin Press.

——. 1984. *Cross-Cultural Trade in World History*. Cambridge University Press.

Dale, S. F. 1994. *Indian Merchants and Eurasian Trade, 1600–1750*. Cambridge University Press.

Darity, W. A., Jr. 1982. A general equilibrium model of the eighteenth century slave trade. *Research in Economic History* 7:287–326.

Das Gupta, Arun. 1999. The maritime trade of Indonesia 1500–1800. In *India and the Indian Ocean 1500–1800* (ed. Ashin Das Gupta and M. N. Pearson). New Delhi: Oxford University Press.

Davis, J. H. 2004. An annual index of U.S. industrial production, 1790–1915. *Quarterly Journal of Economics* 119:1177–215.

Davis, L. E., and S. L. Engerman. 2007. *Naval Blockades in Peace and War: An Economic History since 1750*. Cambridge University Press.

Davis, R. 1954. English foreign trade 1660–1700. *Economic History Review* 7:150–66.

——. 1962. English foreign trade 1700–1774. *Economic History Review* 15:285–303.

——. 1967. *A Commercial Revolution: English Overseas Trade in the Seventeenth and Eighteenth Centuries*. London: Historical Association.

——. 1973. *English Overseas Trade 1500–1700*. London: Macmillan.

——. 1979. *The Industrial Revolution and British Overseas Trade*. London: Leicester University Press.

Day, J. 1978. The great bullion famine of the fifteenth century. *Past and Present* 79:3–54.

Deane, P., and W. A. Cole. 1967. *British Economic Growth 1688–1959: Trends and Structure*, 2nd edn. Cambridge University Press.

Deffeyes, K. S. 2001. *Hubbert's Peak: The Impending World Oil Shortage*. Princeton University Press.

DeLong, J. B. 1998. Trade policy and America's standard of living: a historical perspective. In *Imports, Exports, and the American Worker* (ed. S. M. Collins). Washington, DC: Brookings Institution Press.

Deng, G. 1999. *Maritime Sector, Institutions and Sea Power of Premodern China*. Westport: Greenwood Press.

Dennett, D. C. 1948. Pirenne and Muhammad. *Speculum* 23:167–90.

Desmet, K., and S. L. Parente. 2006. Bigger is better: market size, demand elasticity and resistance to technology adoption. CEPR Discussion Paper 5825.

Devisse, J. 1992. Trade and trade routes in West Africa. In *Africa from the Seventh to the Eleventh Century*, volume 3, *General History of Africa* (abridged edn, ed. I. Hrbek). Berkeley, CA: University of California Press.

Devroey, J. 2001. The economy. In *The Early Middle Ages, Europe 400–1000* (ed. R. McKitterick). Oxford University Press.

Diamond, J. 1997. *Guns, Germs, and Steel: The Fates of Human Societies*. New York: W. W. Norton.

Diaz Alejandro, C. 1984. Latin America in the 1930s. In *Latin America in the 1930s: The Role of the Periphery in World Crisis* (ed. R. Thorp). London: Macmillan.

Digby, S. 1982. The maritime trade of India. In *The Cambridge Economic History of India*, volume 1, *c. 1200–c. 1750* (ed. T. Raychaudhuri and I. Habib). Cambridge University Press.

Dollinger, P. 1970. *The German Hansa*. Stanford University Press.

Dols, M. 1977. *The Black Death in the Middle East*. Princeton University Press.

Domar, E. D. 1970. The causes of slavery or serfdom: a hypothesis. *Journal of Economic History* 30:18–32.

Doyle, W. 1988. *Origins of the French Revolution*, 2nd edn. Oxford University Press.

Drescher, S. 2004. White Atlantic? The choice for African slave labor in the plantation Americas. In *Slavery in the Development of the Americas* (ed. D. Eltis, F. D. Lewis, and K. L. Sokoloff). Cambridge University Press.

Duffy, M. 1992. The establishment of the Western Squadron as the linchpin of British Naval strategy. In *Parameters of British Naval Power 1650–1850* (ed. M. Duffy). University of Exeter Press.

Easterly, W. 2001. The lost decades: developing countries' stagnation in spite of policy reform 1980–1998. *Journal of Economic Growth* 6:135–57.

Easterly, W., M. Kremer, L. Pritchett, and L. H. Summers. 1993. Good luck or good policy? Country growth performance and temporary shocks. *Journal of Monetary Economics* 32:459–83.

Ebrey, P. B. 1996. *The Cambridge Illustrated History of China*. Cambridge University Press.

Eccles, W. J. 1987. *Essays on New France*. Oxford University Press.

Edgar, W. 1998. *South Carolina: A History*. Columbia, SC: University of South Carolina Press.

Edwards, S. 1994. Trade and industrial policy reform in Latin America. NBER Working Paper 4772.

Ehrenkreutz, A. 1981. Strategic implications of the slave trade between Genoa and Mamluk Egypt in the second half of the thirteenth century. In *The Islamic Middle East, 700–1900: Studies in Economic and Social History* (ed. A. L. Udovitch). Princeton, NJ: Darwin Press.

Eichengreen, B. 1989. The political economy of the Smoot–Hawley Tariff. *Research in Economic History* 12:1–43.

Eichengreen, B. 1992a. *Golden Fetters: The Gold Standard and the Great Depression 1919–1939*. Oxford University Press.

——. 1992b. The origins and nature of the great slump revisited. *Economic History Review* 45:213–39.

——. 1994. *Reconstructing Europe's Trade and Payments: The European Payments Union*. Manchester University Press.

——. 2007. *The European Economy since 1945: Coordinated Capitalism and Beyond*. Princeton University Press.

Eichengreen, B., and D. A. Irwin. 1995. Trade blocs, currency blocs and the reorientation of world trade in the 1930s. *Journal of International Economics* 38:1–24.

——. 1998. The role of history in bilateral trade flows. In *The Regionalization of the World Economy* (ed. J. A. Frankel). University of Chicago Press.

Eichengreen, B., and R. Portes. 1986. Debt and default in the 1930s: causes and consequences. *European Economic Review* 30:599–640.

Eichengreen, B., and P. Temin. 2003. Afterword: counterfactual histories of the Great Depression. In *The World Economy and National Economies in the Interwar Slump* (ed. T. Balderston). Houndmills, Basingstoke: Palgrave Macmillan.

Ekelund, R. B., and R. D. Tollison. 1981. *Mercantilism as a Rent-Seeking Society: Economic Regulation in Historical Perspective*. College Station, TX: Texas A&M University Press.

Elliott, J. H. 1970. *The Old World and the New 1492–1650*. Cambridge University Press.

——. 1990. The seizure of overseas territories by the European powers. In *The European Discovery of the World and Its Economic Effects on Pre-Industrial Society, 1500–1800* (ed. H. Pohl). Stuttgart: Franz Steiner.

——. 2002. *Imperial Spain 1469–1716*, revised edn. London: Penguin Books.

Ellsworth, P. T. 1956. The terms of trade between primary producing and industrial countries. *Inter-American Economic Affairs* 10:47–65.

Eltis, D. 1983. Free and coerced transatlantic migrations: some comparisons. *American Historical Review* 88:251–80.

——. 2000. *The Rise of African Slavery in the Americas*. Cambridge University Press.

Eltis, D. 2001. The volume and structure of the transatlantic slave trade: a reassessment. *William and Mary Quarterly* 58:17–46.

Eltis, D., and S. L. Engerman. 2000. The importance of slavery and the slave trade to industrializing Britain. *Journal of Economic History* 60:123–44.

Eltis, D., and L. C. Jennings. 1988. Trade between Western Africa and the Atlantic world in the pre-colonial era. *American Historical Review* 93:936–59.

Elvin, M. 1973. *The Pattern of the Chinese Past*. Stanford University Press.

——. 1984. Why China failed to create an endogenous industrial capitalism: a critique of Max Weber's explanation. *Theory and Society* 13:379–91.

——. 1989. China as a counterfactual. In *Europe and the Rise of Capitalism* (ed. J. Baechler, J. A. Hall, and M. Mann). Oxford: Blackwell.

Endoh, M. 1999. Trade creation and trade diversion in the EEC, the LAFTA and the CMEA: 1960–1994. *Applied Economics* 31:207–16.

Engel, C., and J. H. Rogers. 2004. European product market integration after the euro. *Economic Policy* 39:347–84.

Engerman, S. L. 1972. The slave trade and British capital formation in the eighteenth century: a comment on the Williams Thesis. *Business History Review* 46:430–43.

———. 1981. Some implications of the abolition of the slave trade. In *Abolition of the Atlantic Slave Trade: Origins and Effects in Europe, Africa, and the Americas* (ed. D. Eltis and J. Walvin). Madison, WI: University of Wisconsin Press.

Epstein, S. R. 2000. *Freedom and Growth: The Rise of States and Markets in Europe, 1300–1750.* London: Routledge.

Estevadeordal, A., B. Frantz, and A. M. Taylor. 2003. The rise and fall of world trade, 1870–1939. *Quarterly Journal of Economics* 118:359–407.

Facchini, G., and A. M. Mayda. 2006. Individual attitudes towards immigrants: welfare-state determinants across countries. Mimeo, University of Illinois and Georgetown University.

Fairbank, J. K. 1969. *Trade and Diplomacy on the China Coast: The Opening of the Treaty Ports, 1842–1854.* Stanford University Press.

Feenstra, R. C. 1998. Integration of trade and disintegration of production in the global economy. *Journal of Economic Perspectives* 12:31–50.

——— (ed.). 2000. *The Impact of International Trade on Wages.* University of Chicago Press/NBER.

Feenstra, R. C., and G. H. Hanson. 2004. Global production sharing and rising inequality: a survey of trade and wages. In *Handbook of International Trade,* volume I (ed. E. Kwan Choi and J. Harrigan). Oxford: Blackwell.

Feinstein, C. H. 1981. Capital accumulation and the Industrial Revolution. In *The Economic History of Britain since 1700,* volume I, *1700–1860* (ed. R. Floud and D. N. McCloskey), 1st edn. Cambridge University Press.

———. 1998. Pessimism perpetuated: real wages and the standard of living in Britain during and after the Industrial Revolution. *Journal of Economic History* 58:625–58.

Feinstein, C. H., P. Temin, and G. Toniolo. 1997. *The European Economy between the Wars.* Oxford University Press.

Feis, H. 1930. *Europe the World's Banker 1870–1914: An Account of European Foreign Investment and the Connection of World Finance with Diplomacy Before the War.* New Haven, CT: Yale University Press.

Ferguson, N. 2003. *Empire: How Britain Made the Modern World.* London: Allen Lane.

———. 2005. Sinking globalization. *Foreign Affairs* 84:64–77.

Fernández-Armesto, F. 2006. *Pathfinders: A Global History of Exploration.* Oxford University Press.

Ferrier, R. 1986. Trade from the mid-14th century to the end of the Safavid period. In *The Cambridge History of Iran,* volume 6, *The Timurid and Safavid Periods* (ed. P. Jackson and L. Lockhart). Cambridge University Press.

Feuerwerker, A. 1984. The state and the economy in Late Imperial China. *Theory and Society* 13:297–326.

Findlay, R. 1978. An "Austrian" model of international trade and interest rate equalization. *Journal of Political Economy* 86:989–1007.

——. 1982. Trade and growth in the Industrial Revolution. In *Economics in the Long View: Essays in Honor of W. W. Rostow*, volume 1, *Models and Methodology* (ed. C. P. Kindleberger and G. di Tella). London: Macmillan.

——. 1990. The triangular trade and the Atlantic economy of the eighteenth century: a simple general equilibrium model. *Essays in International Finance* no. 177 (Frank D. Graham Lecture), International Finance Section. Princeton University Press.

——. 1993. International trade and factor mobility with an endogenous land frontier: some general equilibrium implications of Christopher Columbus. In *Theory, Policy and Dynamics in International Trade: Essays in Honor of Ronald W. Jones* (ed. W. J. Ethier, E. Helpman, and J. P. Neary). Cambridge University Press.

——. 1995. *Factor Proportions, Trade and Growth*. Cambridge, MA: MIT Press.

——. 1996. Towards a model of territorial expansion and the limits of empire. In *The Political Economy of Conflict and Appropriation* (ed. M. R. Garfinkel and S. Skaperdas). Cambridge University Press.

——. 1998. The emergence of the world economy. In *Contemporary Economic Issues*, volume 3, *Trade, Payments and Debt* (ed. D. Cohen). New York: St. Martin's Press.

Findlay, R., and R. W. Jones. 2001. Input trade and the location of production. *American Economic Review* 91:29–33.

Findlay, R., and M. Lundahl. 1999. Resource-led growth—a long-term perspective: the relevance of the 1870–1914 experience for today's developing economies. WIDER Working Paper 162.

——. 2003. Towards a factor proportions approach to economic history: population, precious metals and prices from the Black Death to the price revolution. In *Bertil Ohlin: A Centenary Celebration* (ed. R. Findlay, L. Jonung, and M. Lundahl). Cambridge, MA: MIT Press.

——. 2006. Demographic shocks and the factor proportions model: from the Plague of Justinian to the Black Death. In *Eli Heckscher, Economic History and International Trade* (ed. R. Findlay, R. G. H. Henriksson, H. Lindgren, and M. Lundahl). Cambridge, MA: MIT Press.

Findlay, R., and K. H. O'Rourke. 2003. Commodity market integration, 1500–2000. In *Globalization in Historical Perspective* (ed. M. D. Bordo, A. M. Taylor, and J. G. Williamson). University of Chicago Press.

Finger, J. M., and A. J. Yeats. 1976. Effective protection by transportation costs and tariffs: a comparison of magnitudes. *Quarterly Journal of Economics* 90:169–76.

Fink, C., A. Mattoo, and I. C. Neagu. 2000. Trade in international maritime services: how much does policy matter? Mimeo, World Bank.

Fisher, D. 1989. The price revolution: a monetary interpretation. *Journal of Economic History* 49:883–902.

FitzGerald, C. P. 1966. *A Concise History of East Asia.* New York: Praeger.

Flam, H., and M. J. Flanders (eds). 1991. *Heckscher–Ohlin Trade Theory.* Cambridge, MA: MIT Press.

Flandreau, M., and M. Maurel. 2005. Monetary union, trade integration, and business cycles in 19th century Europe. *Open Economies Review* 16:135–52.

Fletcher, M. E. 1958. The Suez Canal and world shipping, 1869–1914. *Journal of Economic History* 18:556–73.

Fletcher, R. 1992. *Moorish Spain.* Berkeley, CA: University of California Press.

Flynn, D. O. 1996. *World Silver and Monetary History in the 16th and 17th Centuries.* Aldershot: Variorum.

Flynn, D. O., and A. Giráldez. 1995. Born with a silver spoon: world trade origins in 1571. *Journal of World History* 6:201–21.

———. 2004. Path dependence, time lags and the birth of globalisation: a critique of O'Rourke and Williamson. *European Review of Economic History* 8:81–108.

Fogel, R. W. and S. L. Engerman. 1974. *Time on the Cross.* Boston, MA: Little, Brown.

Foreman-Peck, J. 1995. *A History of the World Economy: International Economic Relations since 1850,* 2nd edn. New York: Harvester Wheatsheaf.

Foust, C. M. 1961. Russian expansion to the east through the eighteenth century. *Journal of Economic History* 21:469–82.

———. 1969. *Muscovite and Mandarin: Russia's Trade with China and Its Setting, 1727–1805.* Chapel Hill, NC: University of North Carolina Press.

Frank, A. G. 1998. *ReORIENT: Global Economy in the Asian Age.* Berkeley, CA: University of California Press.

Frankel, J. A. 1982. The 1808–1809 embargo against Great Britain. *Journal of Economic History* 42:291–307.

Franklin, S., and J. Shepard. 1996. *The Emergence of Rus 750–1200.* London and New York: Longman.

Frantz-Murphy, G. 1981. A new interpretation of the economic history of Medieval Egypt: the role of the textile industry 254–567/868–1171. *Journal of the Economic and Social History of the Orient* 24:274–97.

Friedman, M. 1953. The case for flexible exchange rates. In *Essays in Positive Economics.* University of Chicago Press.

Friedman, M., and A. J. Schwartz. 1963. *A Monetary History of the United States, 1867–1960.* Princeton University Press.

Friedman, M., and A. J. Schwartz. 1965. *The Great Contraction, 1929–1933.* Princeton University Press.

Furber, H. 1976. *Rival Empires of Trade in the Orient, 1600–1800.* Minneapolis, MN: University of Minnesota Press.

Gaddis, J. L. 2005. *The Cold War: A New History.* London: Penguin.

Galor, O. 2005. From stagnation to growth: unified growth theory. In *Handbook of Economic Growth,* volume 1A (ed. P. Aghion and S. N. Durlauf). Amsterdam: Elsevier.

Galor, O., and D. N. Weil. 2000. Population, technology, and growth: from Malthusian stagnation to the demographic transition and beyond. *American Economic Review* 90:806–28.

Games, A. 2002. Migration. In *The British Atlantic World, 1500–1800* (ed. D. Armitage and M. J. Braddick). London: Palgrave Macmillan.

Garbade, K. D., and W. L. Silber. 1978. Technology, communication and the performance of financial markets: 1840–1975. *Journal of Finance* 33:819–32.

Garcin, J.-C. 1998. The regime of the Circassian Mamluks. In *The Cambridge History of Egypt*, volume 1, *Islamic Egypt 640–1517* (ed. C. F. Petry). Cambridge University Press.

Gardella, R. P. 1990. The Min-Pei tea trade during the Late Chien-lung and Chia-ching Eras: foreign commerce and the Mid-Ching Fukien Highlands. In *Development and Decline of Fukien Province in the 17th and 18th Centuries* (ed. E. B. Vermeer). Leiden: Brill.

Gaspar, J. C. 1979. *Limón: 1880–1940: Un Estudio de la Industria Bananera en Costa Rica.* San José: Editorial Costa Rica.

Gatrell, P. 2005. Poor Russia, poor show: mobilising a backward economy for war, 1914–1917. In *The Economics of World War I* (ed. S. N. Broadberry and M. Harrison). Cambridge University Press.

GATT. 1980. *Les Négotiations Commerciales Multilatérales du Tokyo Round*, volume II, *Rapport Additionnel du Directeur Général du GATT.* Geneva: GATT.

Gernet, J. 1982. *A History of Chinese Civilization.* Cambridge University Press.

Gerschenkron, A. 1962. *Economic Backwardness in Historical Perspective: A Book of Essays.* Cambridge, MA: Harvard University Press.

———. 1970. *Europe in the Russian Mirror: Four Lectures in Economic History.* Cambridge University Press.

Gibb, H. A. R. 1986. *Ibn Battuta: Travels in Asia and Africa 1325–1354.* New Delhi: Oriental Books Reprint Corporation.

Gibbon, E. 1907. *The History of the Decline and Fall of the Roman Empire*, volume 11. New York: Fred de Fau. (Available at http://oll.libertyfund.org/Home3/Book.php?recordID=0214.11.)

Girard, L. 1966. Transport. In *Cambridge Economic History of Europe*, volume VI, *The Industrial Revolution and After: Incomes, Population and Technological Change (I)* (ed. H. J. Habakkuk and M. Postan). Cambridge University Press.

Glahn, R. von. 1996a. Myth and reality of China's seventeenth-century monetary crisis. *Journal of Economic History* 56:429–54.

Glahn, R. von. 1996b. *Fountain of Fortune: Money and Monetary Policy in China, 1000–1700.* Berkeley, CA: University of California Press.

Glamann, K. 1958. *Dutch–Asiatic Trade 1620–1740.* The Hague: Martinus Nijhoff.

———. 1974. European trade 1500–1750. In *The Fontana Economic History of Europe*, volume 2, *The Sixteenth and Seventeenth Centuries* (ed. C. M. Cipolla). London and Glasgow: Collins/Fontana.

Glick, R., and A. M. Taylor. 2006. Collateral damage: trade disruption and the economic impact of war. Revised version of NBER Working Paper 11565.

Glick, T. F. 1994. Hydraulic Technology in al-Andalus. In *The Legacy of Muslim Spain* (ed. S. K. Jayyusi). Leiden: Brill.

Goitein, S. D. 1967. *A Mediterranean Society,* volume 1, *Economic Foundations.* Berkeley, CA: University of California Press.

Gokhale, B. G. 1979. *Surat in the Seventeenth Century.* London and Malmö: Curzon Press.

Goldberg, P. K., and F. Verboven. 2005. Market integration and convergence to the law of one price: evidence from the European car market. *Journal of International Economics* 65:49–73.

Golden, P. B. 1998. *Nomads and Sedentary Societies in Medieval Eurasia.* Washington, DC: American Historical Association.

Goldin, C. D., and F. D. Lewis. 1980. The role of exports in American economic growth during the Napoleonic Wars, 1793 to 1807. *Explorations in Economic History* 17:6–25.

Goldin, I., and D. van der Mensbrugghe. 1993. Trade liberalisation: what's at stake? OECD Development Centre Policy Brief 5.

Goldstone, J. A. 2002. Efflorescences and economic growth in world history: rethinking the "Rise of the West" and the Industrial Revolution. *Journal of World History* 13:323–89.

González de Lara, Y. 2005. The secret of Venetian success: the role of the state in financial markets. IVIE Working Paper AD-2005-28.

Goody, J. 1996. *The East in the West.* Cambridge University Press.

Gordon, M. S. 1941. *Barriers to World Trade: A Study of Recent Commercial Policy.* New York: Macmillan.

Gourevitch, P. 1986. *Politics in Hard Times: Comparative Responses to International Economic Crises.* Ithaca, NY: Cornell University Press.

Grafe, R., and M. A. Irigoin. 2006. The Spanish Empire and its legacy: fiscal re-distribution and political conflict in colonial and post-colonial Spanish America. Working Papers of the Global Economic History Network (GEHN) 23/06.

Gray, J. 1998. *False Dawn: The Delusions of Global Capitalism.* New York: The New Press.

Greif, A. 2006. *Institutions and the Path to the Modern Economy: Lessons from Medieval Trade.* Cambridge University Press.

Grilli, E. R., and M. C. Yang. 1988. Primary commodity prices, manufactured goods prices, and the terms of trade of developing countries: what the long run shows. *World Bank Economic Review* 2:1–47.

Grossman, G. M., and E. Helpman. 1991. *Innovation and Growth in the Global Economy.* Cambridge, MA: MIT Press.

Grover, B. R. 1994. An integrated pattern of commercial life in the rural society of North India in the seventeenth and eighteenth centuries. In *Money and the Market in India 1100–1700* (ed. S. Subrahmanyam). Delhi: Oxford University Press.

Haberler, G. 1943. *Quantitative Trade Controls: Their Causes and Nature.* Geneva: League of Nations.

Habib, I. 1969. Potentialities of capitalistic development in the economy of Mughal India. *Journal of Economic History* 29:32–78.

Habib, I. 1980. The technology and economy of Mughal India. *Indian Economic and Social History Review* 27:1–34.

———. 1982. Monetary system and prices. In *The Cambridge Economic History of India*, volume 1, c. 1200–c. 1750 (ed. T. Raychaudhuri and I. Habib). Cambridge University Press.

———. 1997. *Essays in Indian History: Towards a Marxist Perception*, 1st paperback edn. New Delhi: Tulika.

Haddas, Y. S., and J. G. Williamson. 2003. Terms-of-trade shocks and economic performance, 1870–1940: Prebisch and Singer revisited. *Economic Development and Cultural Change* 51:629–56.

Haider, N. 1996. Precious metal flows and currency circulation in Mughal India. *Journal of the Economic and Social History of the Orient* 39:298–364.

———. 2002. Global networks of exchange, the India trade, and the mercantile economy of Safavid Iran. In *A Shared Heritage: The Growth of Civilization in India and Iran* (ed. I. Habib). New Delhi: Aligarh Historians Society, Tulika Books.

Hajnal, J. 1965. European marriage patterns in perspective. In *Population in History* (ed. D. C. Glass and D. E. C. Eversley). Chicago, IL: Aldine.

Hall, D. G. E. 1968. *A History of Southeast Asia*, 3rd edn. London: Macmillan.

Hall, J. W. 1970. *Japan: From Prehistory to Modern Times*. New York: Delacorte Press.

Hall, K. R., and J. K. Whitmore. 1976. Southeast Asian trade and the Isthmian struggle 1000–1200 AD. In *The Origins of Southeast Asian Statecraft* (ed. K. R. Hall and J. K. Whitmore). Michigan Papers on South and Southeast Asia.

Halperin, C. J. 1987. *Russia and the Golden Horde: The Mongol Impact on Medieval Russian History*. Bloomington, IN: Indiana University Press.

Hambly, G. 1969. *Central Asia*. New York: Delacorte Press.

Hamilton, E. J. 1934. *American Treasure and the Price Revolution in Spain, 1501–1650*. Cambridge, MA: Harvard University Press.

———. 1936. *Money, Prices, and Wages in Valencia, Aragon, and Navarre, 1351–1500*. Cambridge, MA: Harvard University Press.

Hansen, B., and K. Nashashibi. 1975. *Egypt*. New York: NBER.

Hanson, G. H., K. F. Scheve, and M. J. Slaughter. 2005. Public finance and individual preferences over globalization strategies. NBER Working Paper 11028.

Hanson, J. R. 1980. *Trade in Transition: Exports from the Third World, 1840–1900*. New York: Academic Press.

Hara, A. 1998. Japan: guns before rice. In *The Economics of World War II* (ed. M. Harrison). Cambridge University Press.

Hardach, G. 1977. *The First World War 1914–1918*. London: Allen Lane.

Harley, C. K. 1978. Western settlement and the price of wheat, 1872–1913. *Journal of Economic History* 38:865–78.

———. 1980. Transportation, the world wheat trade, and the Kuznets cycle, 1850–1913. *Explorations in Economic History* 17:218–50.

———. 1982. British industrialization before 1841: evidence of slower growth during the Industrial Revolution. *Journal of Economic History* 42:267–89.

Harley, C. K. 1988. Ocean freight rates and productivity, 1740–1913: the primacy of mechanical invention reaffirmed. *Journal of Economic History* 48:851–76.

——. 1989. Coal exports and British shipping, 1850–1913. *Explorations in Economic History* 26:311–38.

——. 1990. North Atlantic shipping in the late nineteenth century: freight rates and the interrelationship of cargoes. In *Shipping and Trade, 1750–1950: Essays in International Maritime History* (ed. L. R. Fischer and H. W. Nordvik). Pontefract: Lofthouse.

——. 1999. Reassessing the Industrial Revolution: a macro view. In *The British Industrial Revolution: An Economic Perspective* (ed. J. Mokyr), 2nd edn. Boulder, CO: Westview Press.

——. 2004. Trade: discovery, mercantilism and technology. In *The Cambridge Economic History of Modern Britain*, volume I, *Industrialisation, 1700–1860* (ed. R. Floud and P. Johnson). Cambridge University Press.

Harley, C. K., and N. F. R. Crafts. 1995. Cotton textiles and industrial output growth during the Industrial Revolution. *Economic History Review* 48:134–44.

——. 2000. Simulating the two views of the British Industrial Revolution. *Journal of Economic History* 60:819–41.

Harrigan, J. 2005. Airplanes and comparative advantage. NBER Working Paper 11688.

Hartwell, R. 1962. A revolution in the Chinese iron and coal industries during the Northern Sung, 960–1126 A.D. *Journal of Asian Studies* 21:153–62.

——. 1966. Markets, technology, and the structure of enterprise in the development of the eleventh-century Chinese iron and steel industry. *Journal of Economic History* 26:29–58.

——. 1967. A cycle of economic change in imperial China: coal and iron in northeast China, 750–1350. *Journal of the Economic and Social History of the Orient* 10:102–59.

——. 1982. Demographic, political and social transformations of China, 750–1550. *Harvard Journal of Asiatic Studies* 42:365–442.

Hartwell, R. M. 1967. The causes of the Industrial Revolution: an essay in methodology. In *The Causes of the Industrial Revolution in England* (ed. R. M. Hartwell). London: Methuen.

Harvey, G. E. 1925. *History of Burma*. London: Longmans, Green and Company.

Hasan, A. 1969. The silver currency output of the Mughal Empire and prices in India during the 16th and 17th centuries. *Indian Economic and Social History Review* 6:85–116.

Hatcher, J. 1977. *Plague, Population and the English Economy 1348–1530*. London: Macmillan.

Hatton, T. J., and J. G. Williamson. 2005. *Global Migration and the World Economy: Two Centuries of Policy and Performance*. Cambridge, MA: MIT Press.

Hautcoeur, P.-C. 2005. Was the Great War a watershed? The economics of World War I in France. In *The Economics of World War I* (ed. S. N. Broadberry and M. Harrison). Cambridge University Press.

Hayek, F. A. von (ed.). 1954. *Capitalism and the Historians*. University of Chicago Press.

Hays, J. C., S. D. Ehrlich, and C. Peinhardt. 2005. Government spending and public support for trade in the OECD: an empirical test of the embedded liberalism thesis. *International Organization* 59:473–94.

Headrick, D. R. 1981. *Tools of Empire: Technology and European Imperialism in the Nineteenth Century*. Oxford University Press.

Heaton, H. 1941. Non-importation, 1806–1812. *Journal of Economic History* 1:178–98.

Heckscher, E. F. 1922. *The Continental System: An Economic Interpretation*. Oxford: Clarendon Press.

Helleiner, G. K. 1973. Manufactured exports from less-developed countries and multinational firms. *Economic Journal* 83:21–47.

Hellie, R. 1986. In search of Ivan the Terrible. In *S. F. Platonov, Ivan the Terrible* (ed. J. L. Wieczynski and R. Hellie). Gulf Breeze, FL: Academic International Press.

Herlihy, D. 1967. *Medieval and Renaissance Pistoia: The Social History of an Italian Town, 1200–1430*. New Haven, CT: Yale University Press.

——. 1997. *The Black Death and the Transformation of the West*. Cambridge, MA: Harvard University Press.

Heston, A., R. Summers, and B. Aten. 2002. *Penn World Table Version 6.1*. Center for International Comparisons at the University of Pennsylvania (CICUP).

Higonnet, P. 1968. Origins of the Seven Years' War. *Journal of Modern History*. 40:57–90.

Hill, P. 1963. *Migrant Cocoa-Farmers of Southern Ghana: A Study in Rural Capitalism*. Cambridge University Press.

Hirth, F., and W. W. Rockhill. 1964. *Chau-Ju Kua: His Work on the Chinese and Arab Trades in the Twelfth and Thirteenth Centuries*. Taipei: Literature House.

Ho, P. T. 1956. Early-ripening rice in Chinese history. *Economic History Review* 9:200–18.

Hobsbawm, E. J. 1954. The general crisis of the European economy in the 17th century. *Past and Present* 5:33–53 and 6:44–65.

Hodges, R., and D. Whitehouse. 1983. *Mohammed, Charlemagne and the Origins of Europe*. Ithaca, NY: Cornell University Press.

Hoetzsch, O. 1966. *The Evolution of Russia*. New York: Harcourt, Brace and World.

Hoffman, P. T., and K. Norberg. 1994. Conclusion. In *Fiscal Crises, Liberty, and Representative Government, 1450–1789* (ed. P. T. Hoffman and K. Norberg). Stanford University Press.

Hoffmann, W. G. 1955. *British Industry, 1700–1950* (trans. W. O. Henderson and W. H. Chaloner). Oxford: Blackwell.

Hofstadter, R. 1967. *The Paranoid Style in American Politics and Other Essays*. New York: Vintage Books.

Holmes, A. B. 1970. The Gold Coast and Nigeria. In *Tropical Development 1880–1913* (ed. W. A. Lewis). Evanston, IL: Northwestern University Press.

Holt, P. M. 1970. The Later Ottoman Empire in Egypt and the Fertile Crescent. In *The Cambridge History of Islam*, volume 1, *The Central Islamic Lands* (ed. P. M. Holt, A. K. S. Lambton, and B. Lewis). Cambridge University Press.

Honohan, P., and B. Walsh. 2002. Catching up with the leaders: the Irish hare. *Brookings Papers on Economic Activity* 1:1–77.

Horn, J. 1998. British diaspora: emigration from Britain 1680–1815. In *The Oxford History of the British Empire*, volume II, *The Eighteenth Century* (ed. P. J. Marshall). Oxford University Press.

Horton, M. 1987. The Swahili corridor. *Scientific American* 257:86–93.

Horton, M., and J. Middleton. 2000. *The Swahili: The Social Landscape of a Mercantile Society*. Oxford: Blackwell.

Hourani, A. 1991. *A History of the Arab Peoples*. Cambridge, MA: Harvard University Press.

Houtte, J. A. van. 1977. *An Economic History of the Low Countries 800–1800*. London: Weidenfeld and Nicholson.

Howard, M. 1989. The legacy of the First World War. In *Paths to War: New Essays on the Origins of the Second World War* (ed. R. Boyce and E. M. Robertson). New York: St. Martin's Press.

Hrbek, I. (ed.). 1992. *Africa from the Seventh to the Eleventh Century*, volume 3, *General History of Africa*, abridged edn. Berkeley, CA: University of California Press.

Htin Aung, M. 1967. *A History of Burma*. New York: Columbia University Press.

Huang, R. 1990. *China: A Macro History*. New York: M. E. Sharpe.

Huber, J. R. 1971. Effect on prices of Japan's entry into world commerce after 1858. *Journal of Political Economy* 79:614–28.

Huberman, M. 2004. Working hours of the world unite? New international evidence of worktime, 1870–1913. *Journal of Economic History* 64:964–1001.

———. Forthcoming. Ticket to trade: Belgian labour and globalization before 1914. *Economic History Review*.

Huberman, M., and W. Lewchuk. 2003. European economic integration and the labour compact, 1850–1913. *European Review of Economic History* 7:3–41.

Hucker, C. O. 1975. *China's Imperial Past*. Stanford University Press.

Hugill, P. J. 1993. *World Trade since 1431*. Baltimore, MD: Johns Hopkins University Press.

Hummels, D. 1999. Have international transportation costs declined? Mimeo, University of Chicago.

———. 2001. Time as a trade barrier. Mimeo, Purdue University.

Hummels, D., J. Ishii, and K.-M. Yi. 2001. The nature and growth of vertical specialization in world trade. *Journal of International Economics* 54:75–96.

Hurd, J. 1975. Railways and the expansion of markets in India, 1861–1921. *Explorations in Economic History* 12:263–88.

Hynes, W., and K. H. O'Rourke. Ongoing. Commodity market disintegration during the interwar period. Trinity College Dublin.

Imlah, A. H. 1958. *Economic Elements in the Pax Britannica*. Cambridge, MA: Harvard University Press.

Inalcik, H. 1994. The Ottoman state: economy and society 1300–1600. In *An Economic and Social History of the Ottoman Empire 1300–1914* (ed. H. Inalcik and D. Quataert). Cambridge University Press.

Inikori, J. E. 2002. *Africans and the Industrial Revolution in England: A Study in International Trade and Economic Development.* Cambridge University Press.

Irwin, D. A. 1991. Mercantilism as strategic trade policy: the Anglo-Dutch rivalry for the East India trade. *Journal of Political Economy* 99:1296–314.

———. 1993a. Free trade and protection in nineteenth-century Britain and France revisited: a comment on Nye. *Journal of Economic History* 51:146–52.

———. 1993b. Multilateral and bilateral trade policies in the world trading system: an historical perspective. In *New Dimensions in Regional Integration* (ed. J. de Melo and A. Panagariya). Cambridge University Press.

———. 1995. The GATT's contribution to economic recovery in post-war Western Europe. In *Europe's Post-War Recovery* (ed. B. Eichengreen). Cambridge University Press.

———. 1998a. Changes in U.S. tariffs: the role of import prices and commercial policies. *American Economic Review* 88:1015–26.

———. 1998b. From Smoot–Hawley to reciprocal trade agreements: changing the course of U.S. trade policy in the 1930s. In *The Defining Moment: The Great Depression and the American Economy in the Twentieth Century* (ed. M. D. Bordo, C. Goldin, and E. N. White). University of Chicago Press.

———. 1998c. The Smoot–Hawley Tariff: a quantitative assessment. *Review of Economics and Statistics* 80:326–34.

———. 2003. Explaining America's surge in manufactured exports, 1880–1913. *Review of Economics and Statistics* 85:364–76.

———. 2005. The welfare cost of autarky: evidence from the Jeffersonian trade embargo, 1807–1809. *Review of International Economics* 13:631–45.

Irwin, D. A., and P. Temin. 2001. The antebellum tariff on cotton textiles revisited. *Journal of Economic History* 61:777–98.

Irwin, R. 1986. *The Middle East in the Middle Ages: The Early Mamluk Sultanate 1250–1382.* Carbondale and Edwardsville, IL: Southern Illinois University Press.

Israel, J. I. 1989. *Dutch Primacy in World Trade 1585–1740.* Oxford: Clarendon Press.

Issawi, C. 1966. *The Economy of the Middle East 1800–1914.* University of Chicago Press.

Isserlis, L. 1938. Tramp shipping cargoes and freights. *Journal of the Royal Statistical Society* 101:53–146.

Jacks, D. S. 2005. Intra- and international commodity market integration in the Atlantic economy, 1800–1913. *Explorations in Economic History* 42:381–413.

James, H. 2001. *The End of Globalization: Lessons from the Great Depression.* Cambridge, MA: Harvard University Press.

Jellema, D. 1955. Frisian trade in the Dark Ages. *Speculum* 30:15–36.

Johnson, H. B. 1984. The Portuguese settlement of Brazil, 1500–1580. In *The Cambridge History of Latin America*, volume 1, *Colonial Latin America* (ed. L. Bethell). Cambridge University Press.

Johnson, H. G. 1965. A theoretical model of economic nationalism in new and developing states. *Political Science Quarterly* 80:169–85.

Jones, C. I. 1995. Time series tests of endogenous growth models. *Quarterly Journal of Economics* 110:495–525.

Jones, E. L. 2003. *The European Miracle: Environments, Economies and Geopolitics in the History of Europe and Asia*, 3rd edn. Cambridge University Press.

Jones, J. M. 1934. *Tariff Retaliation: Repercussions of the Hawley–Smoot Bill.* Philadelphia, PA: University of Pennsylvania Press.

Jones, M. T., and M. Obstfeld. 2001. Saving, investment, and gold: a reassessment of historical current account data. In *Money, Capital Mobility, and Trade: Essays in Honor of Robert A. Mundell* (ed. G. A. Calvo, M. Obstfeld, and R. Dornbusch). Cambridge, MA: MIT Press.

Kahan, A. 1974. Observations on Petrine foreign trade. *Canadian–American Slavic Studies* 8:222–36.

———. 1985. *The Plow, the Hammer and the Knout.* University of Chicago Press.

Kamen, H. 2003. *Empire: How Spain became a World Power 1492–1763.* New York: Harper Collins.

Kathirithamby-Wells, J., and J. Villiers (eds). 1990. *Southeast Asian Port and Polity: Rise and Demise.* Singapore University Press.

Katz, L. F., and D. Autor 1999. Changes in the wage structure and earnings inequality. In *Handbook of Labor Economics*, volume 3A (ed. O. Ashenfelter and D. Card). Amsterdam: Elsevier.

Kedourie, E. 1968. The Middle East 1900–1945. In *The New Cambridge Modern History*, volume XII, *The Shifting Balance of World Forces 1898–1945* (ed. C. L. Mowat). Cambridge University Press.

Kee, H. L., A. Nicita, and M. Olarreaga. 2006. Estimating trade restrictiveness indices. World Bank Policy Research Working Paper 3840.

Keller, W., and C. H. Shiue. Forthcoming. Markets in China and Europe on the eve of the Industrial Revolution. *American Economic Review.*

Kelly, M. 1997. The dynamics of Smithian growth. *Quarterly Journal of Economics* 112:939–64.

Kennan, G. F. 1984. *American Diplomacy*, expanded edn. University of Chicago Press.

Kennedy, H. 1986. *The Prophet and the Age of the Caliphates: The Islamic Near East from the Sixth to the Eleventh Century.* London and New York: Longman.

Kennedy, P. 1987. *The Rise and Fall of the Great Powers.* New York: Random House.

Kenwood, A. G., and A. L. Lougheed 1983. *The Growth of the International Economy 1820–1980: An Introductory Text*, 2nd edn. London: Unwin Hyman.

Kieniewicz, J. 1969. The Portuguese factory and trade in pepper in Malabar during the 16th century. *Indian Economic and Social History Review* 6:61–84.

Kindleberger, C. P. 1951. Group behavior and international trade. *Journal of Political Economy* 59:30–46.

———. 1973. *The World in Depression.* Boston, MA: Little, Brown.

Kindleberger, C. P. 1989. Commercial policy between the wars. In *The Cambridge Economic History of Europe*, volume VIII, *The Industrial Economies: The Development of Economic and Social Policies* (ed. P. Mathias and S. Pollard). Cambridge University Press.

Kirchner, W. 1966. The role of Narva in the sixteenth century: a contribution to the study of Russo-European relations. In *Commercial Relations between Russia and Europe, 1400 to 1800: Collected Essays*. Bloomington, IN: Indiana University Press.

Koebner, R. 1959. Adam Smith and the Industrial Revolution. *Economic History Review* 11:281–91.

Kosambi, D. D. 1969. *Ancient India: A History of Its Culture and Civilization*. New York: Pantheon Books.

Kramers, J. H. 1931. Geography and commerce. In *The Legacy of Islam* (ed. T. Arnold and A. Guillaume). Oxford University Press.

Kravis, I. B. 1970. Trade as a handmaiden of growth: similarities between the nineteenth and twentieth centuries. *Economic Journal* 80:850–72.

Krueger, A. O. 1997. Trade policy and economic development: how we learn. *American Economic Review* 87:1–22.

Krugman, P. 1995. Growing world trade: causes and consequences. *Brookings Papers on Economic Activity* 1:327–77.

Labib, S. 1970. Egyptian commercial policy in the Middle Ages. In *Studies in the Economic History of the Middle East* (ed. M. A. Cook). Oxford University Press.

La Croix, S. J., and C. Grandy. 1997. The political instability of reciprocal trade and the overthrow of the Hawaiian kingdom. *Journal of Economic History* 57:161–89.

Lancaster, K. 1979. *Variety, Equity, and Efficiency: Product Variety in an Industrial Society*. New York: Columbia University Press.

Landes, D. 1969. *The Unbound Prometheus: Technological Change and Industrial Development in Europe from 1750 to the Present*. Cambridge University Press.

——. 1990. Why are we so rich and they so poor? *American Economic Review* 80:1–13.

Landes, D. 1998. *The Wealth and Poverty of Nations: Why Some Are so Rich and Some Are so Poor*. New York: W. W. Norton.

——. 1999. The fable of the dead horse; or, the Industrial Revolution revisited. In *The British Industrial Revolution: An Economic Perspective*, 2nd edn (ed. J. Mokyr). Boulder, CO: Westview Press.

——. 2006. Why Europe and the West? Why not China? *Journal of Economic Perspectives* 20:3–22.

Lane, F. C. 1933. Venetian shipping during the Commercial Revolution. *American Historical Review* 38:219–39.

——. 1940. The Mediterranean spice trade: its revival in the sixteenth century. *American Historical Review* 45:581–90.

——. 1968. Pepper prices before da Gama. *Journal of Economic History* 28:590–97.

Lane, F. C. 1973. *Venice: A Maritime Republic*. Baltimore, MD: Johns Hopkins University Press.

Latham, A. J. H. 1978. *The International Economy and the Undeveloped World 1865–1914*. London: Croom Helm.

——. 1981. *The Depression and the Developing World, 1914–1939*. London: Croom Helm.

Lattimore, O. 1973. Beyond the Wall. In *Half the World: The History and Culture of China and Japan* (ed. A. Toynbee). London: Thames and Hudson.

League of Nations. 1927. *Tariff Level Indices. Economic and Financial Section, 1927.II.34, Documentation for the International Economic Conference*. Geneva: League of Nations.

——. 1939. *Review of World Trade 1938*. Geneva: League of Nations.

——. 1942. *Commercial Policy in the Interwar Period: International Proposals and National Policies*. Geneva: League of Nations.

——. 1944. *International Currency Experience: Lessons of the Interwar Period*. Geneva: League of Nations.

——. 1945a. *Industrialization and Foreign Trade*. Geneva: League of Nations.

——. 1945b. *World Economic Survey 1942/44*. Geneva: League of Nations.

Leff, N. H. 1969. Long-term Brazilian economic development. *Journal of Economic History* 29:473–93.

Leith, J. C. 1974. *Ghana*. New York: NBER.

Lenman, B. P. 1998. Colonial wars and imperial instability, 1688–1793. In *The Oxford History of the British Empire*, volume II, *The Eighteenth Century* (ed. P. J. Marshall). Oxford University Press.

Le Roy Ladurie, E. 1981. A concept: unification of the globe by disease (fourteenth to seventeenth centuries). In *The Mind and Method of the Historian*. University of Chicago Press.

Leur, J. C. van. 1955. *Indonesian Trade and Society*. The Hague: Royal Tropical Institute.

Levanoni, A. 1995. *A Turning Point in Mamluk History: The Third Reign of al-Nasir Muhammad Ibn Qalawun (1310–1341)*. Leiden: Brill.

Levtzion, N. 1968. Ibn-Hawqal, the cheque, and Awdaghost. *Journal of African History* 9:223–33.

Lew, B., and B. Cater. 2006. The telegraph, co-ordination of tramp shipping, and growth in world trade, 1870–1910. *European Review of Economic History* 10:147–73.

Lewis, A. R. 1958a. *The Northern Seas: Shipping and Commerce in Northern Europe AD 300–1100*. Princeton University Press.

——. 1958b. The closing of the medieval frontier 1250–1350. *Speculum* 33:475–83.

——. 1988. *Nomads and Crusaders AD 1000–1368*. Bloomington, IN: Indiana University Press.

Lewis, B. 1993. *The Arabs in History*, new edn. Oxford University Press.

Lewis, M. A., and K. E. Wigen. 1997. *The Myth of Continents: A Critique of Metageography*. Berkeley, CA: University of California Press.

Lewis, W. A. 1949. *Economic Survey 1919–1939.* London: George Allen and Unwin.

———. 1952. World production, prices and trade, 1870–1960. *Manchester School* 20:105–38.

———. 1969. *Aspects of Tropical Trade 1883–1965.* Uppsala: Almqvist and Wiksell.

———. 1970. The export stimulus. In *Tropical Development 1880–1913* (ed. W. A. Lewis). Evanston, IL: Northwestern University Press.

———. 1978a. *Growth and Fluctuations 1870–1913.* London: George Allen and Unwin.

———. 1978b. *The Evolution of the International Economic Order.* Princeton University Press.

———. 1981. The rate of growth of world trade, 1830–1973. In *The World Economic Order: Past and Prospects* (ed. S. Grassman and E. Lundberg). London: Macmillan.

Li, T. 1998. *Nguyen Cochinchina: Southern Vietnam in the Seventeenth and Eighteenth Centuries.* Ithaca, NY: Cornell University Press.

Lidman, R., and R. I. Domrese. 1970. India. In *Tropical Development 1880–1913* (ed. W. A. Lewis). Evanston, IL: Northwestern University Press.

Lieber, A. E. 1968. Eastern business practices and medieval European commerce. *Economic History Review* 21:230–43.

Lieberman, V. 1980. Europeans, trade and the unification of Burma, c. 1540–1620. *Oriens Extremus* 27:203–26.

———. 1991. Secular trends in Burmese economic history, c. 1350–1830, and their implications for state formation. *Modern Asian Studies* 25:1–31.

———. 1993. Was the seventeenth century a watershed in Burmese history? In *Southeast Asia in the Early Modern Era: Trade, Power and Belief* (ed. A. Reid). Ithaca, NY: Cornell University Press.

Liepmann, H. 1938. *Tariff Levels and the Economic Unity of Europe.* London: Allen and Unwin.

Lindert, P. H. 2004. *Growing Public: Social Spending and Economic Growth since the Eighteenth Century,* volume I, *The Story.* Cambridge University Press.

Lindert, P. H., and J. G. Williamson. 2003. Does globalization make the world more unequal? In *Globalization in Historical Perspective* (ed. M. D. Bordo, A. M. Taylor, and J. G. Williamson). University of Chicago Press.

Little, I., T. Scitovsky, and M. Scott. 1970. *Industry and Trade in Some Developing Countries: A Comparative Study.* London: Oxford University Press.

Livi-Bacci, M. 2006. The depopulation of Hispanic America after the conquest. *Population and Development Review* 32:199–232.

Lloyd, C. 1965. Armed forces and the art of war. In *The New Cambridge Modern History,* volume VIII, *The American and French Revolutions 1763–93* (ed. A. Goodwin). Cambridge University Press.

Lloyd, T. O. 1996. *The British Empire 1558–1995,* 2nd edn. Oxford University Press.

Lo, J.-P. 1955. The emergence of China as a sea-power during the Late Sung and Early Yuan Periods. *Far Eastern Quarterly* 14:489–503.

———. 1969. Maritime commerce and its relation to the Sung Navy. *Journal of the Economic and Social History of the Orient* 12:57–101.

Lombard, M. 1975. *The Golden Age of Islam*. Amsterdam: North-Holland.

Longworth, P. 2005. *Russia's Empires, Their Rise and Fall: From Prehistory to Putin*. London: John Murray.

Lopez, R. S. 1943. Mohammed and Charlemagne: a revision. *Speculum* 18:14–38.

———. 1952. The trade of medieval Europe: the South. In *The Cambridge Economic History of Europe*, volume II, *Trade and Industry in the Middle Ages*, 1st edn (ed. M. M. Postan and E. E. Rich). Cambridge University Press.

———. 1967. *The Birth of Europe*. London: Phoenix House.

———. 1971. *The Commercial Revolution of the Middle Ages, 950–1350*. Englewood Cliffs, NJ: Prentice Hall.

———. 1987. The trade of medieval Europe: the South. In *The Cambridge Economic History of Europe*, volume II, *Trade and Industry in the Middle Ages*, 2nd edn (ed. M. M. Postan and E. Miller). Cambridge University Press.

Lopez, R. S., and H. A. Miskimin. 1962. The economic depression of the Renaissance. *Economic History Review* 14:408–26.

Lopez, R. S., H. A. Miskimin, and A. L. Udovitch. 1970. England to Egypt 1350–1500: long-term trends and long-distance trade. In *Studies in the Economic History of the Middle East* (ed. M. A. Cook). Oxford University Press.

López-Córdova, J. E., and C. M. Meissner. 2003. Exchange-rate regimes and international trade: evidence from the classical gold standard era. *American Economic Review* 93:344–53.

Lovejoy, P. E., and D. Richardson. 1995. British abolition and its impact on slave prices along the Atlantic coast of Africa, 1783–1850. *Journal of Economic History* 55:98–119.

Lucas, R. E. 2000. Some macroeconomics for the 21st century. *Journal of Economic Perspectives* 14:159–68.

Luzzatto, G. 1961. *An Economic History of Italy: From the Fall of the Roman Empire to the Beginning of the Sixteenth Century*. London: Routledge and Kegan Paul.

Ma, L. J. C. 1971. *Commercial Development and Urban Change in Sung China (960–1279)*. Ann Arbor, MI: University of Michigan.

Macfarlane, A. 1979. *Origins of English Individualism*. Cambridge University Press.

Mackinder, H. J. 1904. The geographical pivot of history. *Geographical Journal* 23:421–37.

Macleod, M. J. 1984. Spain and America: the Atlantic trade, 1492–1720. In *The Cambridge History of Latin America*, volume 1, *Colonial Latin America* (ed. L. Bethell). Cambridge University Press.

MacMillan, M. 2001. *Peacemakers: The Paris Conference of 1919 and Its Attempt to End War*. London: John Murray.

Madariaga, I. de. 2005. *Ivan the Terrible*. New Haven, CT: Yale University Press.

Maddison, A. 1962. Growth and fluctuation in the world economy, 1870–1960. *Banca Nazionale del Lavoro Quarterly Review* 61:127–95.

———. 1995. *Monitoring the World Economy 1820–1992*. Paris: OECD.

———. 1998. *Chinese Economic Performance in the Long Run*. Paris: OECD.

———. 2001. *The World Economy: A Millennial Perspective*. Paris: OECD.

———. 2003. *The World Economy: Historical Statistics*. Paris: OECD.

Magalhães-Godinho, V. 1953. Le repli Vénitien et Égyptien et la route du Cap, 1496–1533. In *Éventail de l'Histoire Vivante: Hommage à Lucien Febvre, Offert par l'Amitié d'Historiens, Linguistes, Géographes, Économistes, Sociologues, Ethnologues*, volume I. Paris: Librarie Armand Colin. (Reprinted in *Spices in the Indian Ocean World* (ed. M. N. Pearson). Gateshead: Variorum, 1996.)

Malanima, P. 2002. *L'Economia Italiana: Dalla Crescita Medievale alla Crescita Contemporanea*. Bologna: Il Mulino.

Malenbaum, W. 1953. *The World Wheat Economy 1885–1939*. Cambridge, MA: Harvard University Press.

Maloughney, B., and W. Xia. 1989. Silver and the fall of the Ming: a reassessment. *Papers in Far Eastern History* 40:51–78.

Malowist, M. 1958. Poland, Russia and Western trade in the 15th and 16th centuries. *Past and Present* 13:26–41.

———. 1966. The problem of inequality of economic development in Europe in the later Middle Ages. *Economic History Review* 19:15–28.

Mamalakis, M. J. 1971. The role of government in the resource transfer and resource allocation processes: the Chilean nitrate sector 1880–1930. In *Government and Economic Development* (ed. G. Ranis). New Haven, CT: Yale University Press.

Mancall, M. 1964. The Kiakhta trade. In *The Economic Development of China and Japan* (ed. C. D. Cowan). London: George Allen and Unwin.

Mantoux, P. 1962. *The Industrial Revolution in the Eighteenth Century*, revised edn. New York: Harper Torchbooks.

Markovits, C. (ed.). 2004. *A History of Modern India 1480–1950*. London: Anthem Press.

Marks, S. 2002. *The Ebbing of European Ascendancy: An International History of the World 1914–1945*. London: Arnold.

Marshall, P. J. 1987. *Bengal: The British Bridgehead, Eastern India 1740–1828*. Cambridge University Press.

———. 1998. The British in Asia: trade and dominion 1700–1765. In *The Oxford History of the British Empire*, volume II, *The Eighteenth Century* (ed. P. J. Marshall). Oxford University Press.

———. 1999. Private British trade in the Indian Ocean before 1800. In *India and the Indian Ocean 1500–1800* (ed. Ashin Das Gupta and M. N. Pearson). New Delhi: Oxford University Press.

Martin, J. 1995. *Medieval Russia 980–1584*. Cambridge University Press.

Martin, W. 2001. Trade policies, developing countries, and globalization. Mimeo, World Bank.

Mastanduno, M. 1988. Trade as a strategic weapon: American and alliance export control policy in the early postwar period. *International Organization* 42:121–50.

Mathias, P., and P. K. O'Brien. 1976. Taxation in England and France 1715–1810. *Journal of European Economic History* 5:601–50.

Matthee, R. P. 1999. *The Politics of Trade in Safavid Iran: Silk for Silver, 1600–1730.* Cambridge University Press.

Mauro, F. 1961. Towards an "intercontinental model": European overseas expansion between 1500 and 1800. *Economic History Review* 14:1–17.

———. 1984. Portugal and Brazil: political and economic structures of empire, 1580–1750. In *The Cambridge History of Latin America*, volume 1, *Colonial Latin America* (ed. L. Bethell). Cambridge University Press.

Mayda, A. M., and D. Rodrik. 2005. Why are some people (and countries) more protectionist than others? *European Economic Review* 49:1393–430.

Mazumdar, S. 1998. *Sugar and Society in China: Peasants, Technology and the World Market.* Cambridge, MA: Harvard University Press.

McClelland, P. D. 1969. The cost to America of British imperial policy. *American Economic Review* 59:370–81.

McCormick, M. 2001. *Origins of the European Economy: Communications and Commerce, A.D. 300–900.* Cambridge University Press.

McCusker, J. J. 1996. British mercantilist policies and the American colonies. In *The Cambridge Economic History of the United States*, volume I (ed. S. L. Engerman and R. E. Gallman). Cambridge University Press.

McCusker, J. J., and R. R. Menard. 1991. *The Economy of British America 1607–1789.* Chapel Hill, NC: University of North Carolina Press.

McEvedy, C. 1961. *The Penguin Atlas of Medieval History.* Harmondsworth: Penguin Books.

McEvedy, C., and R. Jones. 1978. *Atlas of World Population History.* Harmondsworth: Penguin Books.

McKitterick, R. (ed.). 1995. *The New Cambridge Medieval History*, volume II, *c. 700–c. 900.* Cambridge University Press.

McNeill, W. H. 1998. *Plagues and Peoples.* New York: Anchor.

Meek, D. B. 1937. Some measures of economic activity in India. *Journal of the Royal Statistical Society* 100:363–95.

Meilink-Roelofsz, M. A. P. 1962. *Asian Trade and European Influence in the Indonesian Archipelago between 1500 and About 1630.* The Hague: Martinus Nijhoff.

———. 1980. The structures of trade in the sixteenth and seventeenth centuries: Niels Steengard's "Carracks, caravans and companies," a critical appraisal. *Mare Luso-Indicum* 4:1–43.

Menard, R. R. 1991. Transport costs and long-range trade, 1300–1800: was there a "transport revolution" in the early modern era? In *The Political Economy of Merchant Empires* (ed. J. D. Tracy). Cambridge University Press.

Metzer, J. 1974. Railroad development and market integration: the case of Tsarist Russia. *Journal of Economic History* 34:529–50.

Miller, R. 1981. Latin American manufacturing and the First World War: an exploratory essay. *World Development* 9:707–16.

Milner, H. V., and K. Kubota. 2005. Why the move to free trade? Democracy and trade policy in the developing countries. *International Organization* 59:107–43.

Milton, G. 1999. *Nathaniel's Nutmeg*. London: Penguin Books.

Milward, A. S. 1977. *War, Economy and Society 1939–1945*. Harmondsworth: Penguin.

Miron, J. A., and C. D. Romer. 1990. A new monthly index of industrial production, 1884–1940. *Journal of Economic History* 50:321–37.

Miskimin, H. A. 1975. *The Economy of Early Renaissance Europe, 1300–1460*. Cambridge University Press.

Mitchell, B. R. 1988. *British Historical Statistics*. Cambridge University Press.

———. 1992. *International Historical Statistics: Europe 1750–1988*, 3rd edn. New York: Stockton Press.

———. 1993. *International Historical Statistics: The Americas 1750–1988*, 2nd edn. New York: Stockton Press.

———. 1995. *International Historical Statistics: Africa, Asia & Oceania 1750–1988*, 2nd edn. New York: Stockton Press.

———. 2003a. *International Historical Statistics: The Americas 1750–2000*, 5th edn. New York: Palgrave Macmillan.

———. 2003b. *International Historical Statistics: Africa, Asia & Oceania 1750–2000*, 4th edn. New York: Palgrave Macmillan.

Mitrany, D. 1936. *The Effect of the War in Southeastern Europe*. New Haven, CT: Yale University Press.

Mokyr, J. 1977. Demand vs. supply in the Industrial Revolution. *Journal of Economic History* 37:981–1008.

———. 1990. *The Lever of Riches: Technological Creativity and Economic Progress*. Oxford University Press.

———. 1999. Editor's introduction: the new economic history and the Industrial Revolution. In *The British Industrial Revolution: An Economic Perspective*, 2nd edn (ed. J. Mokyr). Boulder, CO: Westview Press.

———. 2002. *The Gifts of Athena: Historical Origins of the Knowledge Economy*. Princeton University Press.

———. 2004. Accounting for the Industrial Revolution. In *The Cambridge Economic History of Modern Britain*, volume I, *Industrialisation, 1700–1860* (ed. R. Floud and P. Johnson). Cambridge University Press.

———. 2005a. Long-term economic growth and the history of technology. In *Handbook of Economic Growth*, volume 1A (ed. P. Aghion and S. N. Durlauf). Amsterdam: Elsevier.

———. 2005b. The intellectual origins of modern economic growth. *Journal of Economic History* 65:285–351.

———. 2006. The great synergy: the European Enlightenment as a factor in modern economic growth. In *Understanding the Dynamics of a Knowledge Economy* (ed. W. Dolfsma and L. Soete). Cheltenham: Edward Elgar.

Moosvi, S. 1987. The silver influx, prices, money supply and revenue-extraction in Mughal India. *Journal of the Economic and Social History of the Orient* 30:47–94.

Morineau, M. 1985. *Incroyables Gazettes et Fabuleux Métaux: Les Retours des Trésors Americains d'après les Gazettes Hollandaises (XVIe–XVIIIe siècles)*. Cambridge University Press.

Morrison, K. F. 1963. Numismatics and Carolingian trade: a critique of the evidence. *Speculum* 38:403–32.

Munro, J. H. 2003. The monetary origins of the "price revolution": south German silver mining, merchant banking, and Venetian commerce 1470–1540. In *Global Connections and Monetary History, 1470–1800* (ed. D. O. Flynn, A. Giráldez, and R. von Glahn). Aldershot: Ashgate.

———. 2004. Builders' wages in southern England and the southern low countries, 1346–1500: a comparative study of trends in and levels of real wages. In *L'Edilizia Prima della Rivoluzione Industriale, secc. XIII–XVIII* (ed. S. Cavaciocchi). Florence: Le Monnier.

Munson, H., Jr. 1988. *Islam and Revolution in the Middle East.* New Haven, CT: Yale University Press.

Murphey, R. 1970. *An Introduction to Geography*, 3rd edn. Chicago, IL: Rand McNally.

Naquin, S., and E. S. Rawski. 1987. *Chinese Society in the Eighteenth Century.* New Haven, CT: Yale University Press.

Neal, L. 1990. *The Rise of Financial Capitalism: International Capital Markets in the Age of Reason.* Cambridge University Press.

Neary, J. P., and C. Ó Gráda. 1991. Protection, economic war and structural change: the 1930s in Ireland. *Irish Historical Studies* 27:250–66.

Needham, J. 1954. *Science and Civilization in China*, volume I. Cambridge University Press.

Nef, J. U. 1987. Mining and metallurgy in medieval civilization. In *The Cambridge Economic History of Europe*, volume II, *Trade and Industry in the Middle Ages*, 2nd edn (ed. M. M. Postan and E. Miller). Cambridge University Press.

Newitt, M. 1980. Plunder and the rewards of office in the Portuguese Empire. In *The Military Revolution and the State 1500–1800* (ed. M. Duffy). University of Exeter Press.

Newitt, M. 2005. *A History of Portuguese Overseas Expansion, 1400–1668.* London: Routledge.

Noonan, T. S. 1998. *The Islamic World, Russia and the Vikings, 750–900: The Numismatic Evidence.* Aldershot: Variorum Collected Studies Series.

North, D. C. 1958. Ocean freight rates and economic development 1750–1913. *Journal of Economic History* 18:537–55.

———. 1966. *The Economic Growth of the United States 1790–1860.* New York: W. W. Norton.

North, D. C., and R. P. Thomas. 1973. *The Rise of the Western World.* Cambridge University Press.

Northrup, D. 2005. Globalization and the Great Convergence: rethinking world history in the long term. *Journal of World History* 16:249–67.

Nunn, N. 2006. The long-term effects of Africa's slave trades. Mimeo, University of British Columbia.

Nye, J. V. 1991. The myth of free-trade Britain and fortress France: tariffs and trade in the nineteenth century. *Journal of Economic History* 51:23–46.

Obolensky, D. 1957. *The Byzantine Commonwealth: Eastern Europe, 500–1453*. New York: Praeger.

O'Brien, P. K. 1982. European economic development: the contribution of the periphery. *Economic History Review* 35:1–18.

——. 1988. The political economy of British taxation, 1660–1815. *Economic History Review* 41:1–32.

——. 1993. Political preconditions for the Industrial Revolution. In *The Industrial Revolution and British Society* (ed. P. K. O'Brien and R. Quinault). Cambridge University Press.

—— (ed.). 2002. *Philip's Atlas of World History*. London: Philip's.

O'Brien, P. K., and S. L. Engerman. 1991. Exports and the growth of the British economy from the Glorious Revolution to the Peace of Amiens. In *Slavery and the Rise of the Atlantic System* (ed. B. L. Solow). Cambridge University Press.

Obstfeld, M., and A. M. Taylor. 2004. *Global Capital Markets: Integration, Crisis, and Growth*. Cambridge University Press.

Offer, A. 1989. *The First World War: An Agrarian Interpretation*. Oxford: Clarendon Press.

Officer, L. H. 2006. Exchange rates. In *Historical Statistics of the United States: Millennial Edition* (ed. S. Carter, S. Gartner, M. R. Haines, A. Olmstead, R. Sutch, and G. Wright). Cambridge University Press.

Ó Gráda, C. 1999. *Black '47 and Beyond: The Great Irish Famine in History, Economy, and Memory*. Princeton University Press.

Ó Gráda, C., and K. H. O'Rourke. 2000. Living standards and growth. In *The Economy of Ireland: Policy and Performance of a European Region* (ed. J. O'Hagan). Dublin: Gill and Macmillan/St. Martin's Press.

Öhberg, A. 1955. Russia and the world market in the seventeenth century: a discussion of the connection between prices and trade routes. *Scandinavian Economic History Review* 3:123–62.

Oliveira Marques, A. H. de. 1976. *A History of Portugal*, 2nd edn. New York: Columbia University Press.

Oliver, R., and J. D. Fage. 1970. *A Short History of Africa*, 3rd edn. London: Penguin.

Olson, M. 1963. *The Economics of the Wartime Shortage: A History of British Food Supplies in the Napoleonic War and in World Wars I and II*. Durham, NC: Duke University Press.

——. 1993. Dictatorship, democracy, and development. *American Political Science Review* 87:567–76.

Ormrod, D. 1998. Northern Europe and the expanding world-economy: the transformation of commercial organization 1500–1800. In *Prodotti e Tecniche d'Oltremare nelle Economie Europee, secc. XIII–XVIII* (ed. S. Cavacocchi). Prato: Istituto Internazionale di Storia Economica "F. Datini."

——. 2003. *The Rise of Commercial Empires: England and the Netherlands in the Age of Mercantilism 1650–1770*. Cambridge University Press.

O'Rourke, K. H. 1991. Burn everything British but their coal: the Anglo-Irish economic war of the 1930's. *Journal of Economic History* 51:357–66.

O'Rourke, K. H. 1995. The costs of international economic disintegration: Ireland in the 1930's. *Research in Economic History* 15:215–59.

——. 1997. The European grain invasion, 1870–1913. *Journal of Economic History* 57:775–801.

——. 2000. Tariffs and growth in the late 19th century. *Economic Journal* 110:456–83.

——. 2001. Globalization and inequality: historical trends. *Annual World Bank Conference on Development Economics*, pp. 39–67.

——. 2002. Europe and the causes of globalization, 1790–2000. In *From Europeanization of the Globe to the Globalization of Europe* (ed. H. Kierzkowski). Basingstoke: Palgrave Macmillan.

——. 2006. The worldwide economic impact of the French Revolutionary and Napoleonic Wars, 1793–1815. *Journal of Global History* 1:123–49.

——. 2007a. War and welfare: Britain, France and the United States 1807–14. *Oxford Economic Papers* 59 (in press).

——. 2007b. Culture, conflict and cooperation: Irish dairying before the Great War. *Economic Journal* 117 (in press).

O'Rourke, K. H., and R. Sinnott. 2001. What determines attitudes towards protection? Some cross-country evidence. In *Brookings Trade Forum 2001* (ed. S. M. Collins and D. Rodrik). Washington, DC: Brookings Institution Press.

O'Rourke, K. H., and A. M. Taylor. 2007. Democracy and Protectionism. In *The New Comparative Economic History: Essays in Honor of Jeffrey G. Williamson* (ed. T. J. Hatton, K. H. O'Rourke, and A. M. Taylor). Cambridge, MA: MIT Press.

O'Rourke, K. H., A. M. Taylor, and J. G. Williamson. 1996. Factor price convergence in the late nineteenth century. *International Economic Review* 37:499–530.

O'Rourke, K. H., and J. G. Williamson. 1994. Late 19th century Anglo-American factor price convergence: were Heckscher and Ohlin right? *Journal of Economic History* 54:892–916.

——. 1999. *Globalization and History: The Evolution of a Nineteenth Century Atlantic Economy*. Cambridge, MA: MIT Press.

——. 2002a. After Columbus: explaining the global trade boom 1500–1800. *Journal of Economic History* 62:417–56.

——. 2002b. When did globalization begin? *European Review of Economic History* 6:23–50.

——. 2005. From Malthus to Ohlin: trade, industrialisation and distribution since 1500. *Journal of Economic Growth* 10:5–34.

——. Forthcoming. Did Vasco da Gama matter to European markets? Testing Frederick Lane's hypotheses fifty years later. *Economic History Review*.

Özbaran, S. 1994. *The Ottoman Response to European Expansion: Studies on Ottoman–Portuguese Relations in the Indian Ocean and Ottoman Administration in the Arab Lands During the Sixteenth Century.* Istanbul: Isis Press.

Pakenham, T. 1991. *The Scramble for Africa 1876–1912.* London: Weidenfeld & Nicolson.

Pamuk, Ş. 1994. Money in the Ottoman Empire, 1326–1914. In *An Economic and Social History of the Ottoman Empire 1300–1914* (ed. H. Inalcik and D. Quataert). Cambridge University Press.

——. 2000. *A Monetary History of the Ottoman Empire.* Cambridge University Press.

——. 2004. Institutional change and the longevity of the Ottoman Empire, 1500–1800. *Journal of Interdisciplinary History* 35:225–47.

——. 2005. Urban real wages around the Eastern Mediterranean in comparative perspective, 1100–2000. *Research in Economic History* 23:209–28.

——. 2006. The Black Death and the origins of "the Great Divergence" across Europe, 1300–1600. Mimeo, Bogaziçi University.

Panikkar, K. M. 1953. *Asia and Western Dominance: A Survey of the Vasco da Gama Epoch of Asian History, 1498–1945.* London: George Allen and Unwin.

Paolera, G. della, A. M. Taylor, and C. G. Bózzoli. 2003. Historical statistics. In *A New Economic History of Argentina* (ed. G. della Paolera and A. M. Taylor). Cambridge University Press.

Parker, G. 1979. *Spain and the Netherlands 1559–1659: Ten Studies.* Glasgow: Fontana/Collins.

——. 1988. *The Military Revolution: Military Innovation and the Rise of the West 1500–1800.* Cambridge University Press.

Parry, J. H. 1964. *The Age of Reconnaissance: Discovery, Exploration and Settlement 1450–1650.* New York: Mentor Books.

——. 1966. *The Establishment of the European Hegemony 1415–1715: Trade and Exploration in the Age of the Renaissance.* New York: Harper Torchbooks.

——. 1967. Transport and trade routes. In *The Cambridge Economic History of Europe*, volume IV, *The Economy of Expanding Europe in the 16th and 17th centuries* (ed. E. E. Rich and C. H. Wilson). Cambridge University Press.

Parsley, D. C., and S.-J. Wei. 2002. Currency arrangements and goods market integration: a price based approach. Mimeo, Vanderbilt University and IMF.

Pearson, M. N. 1987. *The Portuguese in India.* Cambridge University Press.

—— (ed.). 1996. *Spices in the Indian Ocean World.* Aldershot: Variorum.

——. 2001. Asia and world precious metal flows in the early modern period. In *Evolution of the World Economy, Precious Metals and India* (ed. J. McGuire, P. Bertola, and P. Reeves). New Delhi: Oxford University Press.

Pelzman, J. 1977. Trade creation and trade diversion in the Council of Mutual Economic Assistance 1954–70. *American Economic Review* 67:713–22.

Perdue, P. 2005. *China Marches West: The Qing Conquest of Central Eurasia.* Cambridge, MA: Harvard University Press.

Perkins, E. J. 1988. *The Economy of Colonial America*, 2nd edn. New York: Columbia University Press.

Persson, K. G. 2004. Mind the gap! Transport costs and price convergence in the nineteenth century Atlantic economy. *European Review of Economic History* 8:125–47.

Petry, C. F. 1994. *Protectors or Praetorians? The Last Mamluk Sultans and Egypt's Waning as a Great Power.* Albany, NY: State University of New York Press.

Phelps Brown, H., and S. V. Hopkins. 1981. *A Perspective of Wages and Prices*. London: Methuen.

Phillips, C. R. 1990. The growth and composition of trade in the Iberian empires 1450–1750. In *The Rise of Merchant Empires: Long Distance Trade in the Early Modern World 1350–1750* (ed. J. Tracy). Cambridge University Press.

Phillips, J. R. S. 1998. *The Medieval Expansion of Europe*, 2nd edn. Oxford University Press.

Pirenne, H. 1939. *Mohammed and Charlemagne*. New York: Harper and Row.

Pires, T. 1990. *The* Suma Oriental *of Tome Pires: An Account of the East, from the Red Sea to Japan, Written in Malacca and India in 1512–1515*, volumes 1 and 2. New Delhi: Asian Educational Services.

Planhol, X. de. 1959. *The World of Islam*. Ithaca, NY: Cornell University Press.

Plumb, J. H. 1963. *England in the Eighteenth Century*. London: Penguin.

Pombejra, D. na. 1993. Ayutthaya at the end of the seventeenth century: was there a shift to isolation? In *Southeast Asia in the Early Modern Era: Trade, Power and Belief* (ed. A. Reid). Ithaca, NY: Cornell University Press.

Pomeranz, K. 2000. *The Great Divergence: China, Europe and the Making of the Modern World Economy*. Princeton University Press.

Postan, M. M. 1970. Economic relations between Eastern and Western Europe. In *Eastern and Western Europe in the Middle Ages* (ed. G. Barraclough). New York: Harcourt Brace Jovanovich.

Power, E. 1941. *The Wool Trade in Medieval English History*. Oxford University Press.

Prakash, O. 1998. *European Commercial Enterprise in Pre-Colonial India*. Cambridge University Press.

———. 2004. *Bullion for Goods: European and Indian Merchants in the Indian Ocean Trade 1500–1800*. New Delhi: Manohar.

Prebisch, R. 1950. *The Economic Development of Latin America and Its Principal Problems*. New York: United Nations.

Preeg, E. H. 1970. *Traders and Diplomats: An Analysis of the Kennedy Round of Negotiations Under the General Agreement on Tariffs and Trade*. Washington, DC: Brookings Institution.

Price, J. M. 1998. The imperial economy, 1700–1776. In *The Oxford History of the British Empire*, volume II, *The Eighteenth Century* (ed. P. J. Marshall). Oxford University Press.

Pritchard, J. 2004. *In Search of Empire: The French in the Americas, 1670–1730*. Cambridge University Press.

Pritchett, L. 1997. Divergence, big time. *Journal of Economic Perspectives* 11:3–18.

Pryor, J. H. 1977. The origins of the *commenda* contract. *Speculum* 52:5–37.

Pulleyblank, E. G. 1955. *Chinese History and World History: An Inaugural Lecture*. Cambridge University Press.

Quinn, S. 2001. The Glorious Revolution's effect on English private finance: a microhistory, 1680–1705. *Journal of Economic History* 61:593–615.

Radelet, S., and J. Sachs. 1998. Shipping costs, manufactured exports, and economic growth. Mimeo, Columbia University.

Rapp, R. T. 1975. The unmaking of the Mediterranean trade hegemony. *Journal of Economic History* 35:499–525.

Rauch, J. E., and V. Trindade. 2002. Ethnic Chinese networks in international trade. *Review of Economics and Statistics* 84:116–30.

Ray, R. K. 1998. Indian society and the establishment of British supremacy 1765–1818. In *The Oxford History of the British Empire*, volume II, *The Eighteenth Century* (ed. P. J. Marshall). Oxford University Press.

Raychaudhuri, T. 1962. *Jan Company in Coromandel 1605–1690: A Study in the Interrelations of European Commerce and Traditional Economies*. The Hague: Martinus Nijhoff.

———. 1982. The state and the economy: the Mughal Empire. In *The Cambridge Economic History of India*, volume 1, *c. 1200–c. 1750* (ed. T. Raychaudhuri and I. Habib). Cambridge University Press.

Raymond, A. 1970. North Africa in the pre-colonial period. In *The Cambridge History of Islam*, volume 2, *The Further Islamic Lands, Islamic Society and Civilization* (ed. P. M. Holt, A. K. S. Lambton, and B. Lewis). Cambridge University Press.

Reid, A. 1975. Trade and the problem of royal power in Aceh, c. 1550–1700. In *Pre-Colonial State Systems in Southeast Asia* (ed. A. Reid and L. Castles). Kuala Lumpur: Malaysian Branch of the Royal Asiatic Society.

———. 1988. *Southeast Asia in the Age of Commerce 1450–1680*, volume 1, *The Lands Below the Winds*. New Haven, CT: Yale University Press.

———. 1990. An "Age of Commerce" in Southeast Asian history. *Modern Asian Studies* 24:1–30.

———. 1993a. *Southeast Asia in the Age of Commerce 1450–1680*, volume 2, *Expansion and Crisis*. New Haven, CT: Yale University Press.

Reid, A. (ed.). 1993b. *Southeast Asia in the Early Modern Era: Trade, Power and Belief*. Ithaca, NY: Cornell University Press.

———. 1996. Flows and seepages in the long-term Chinese interaction with Southeast Asia. In *Settlers and Sojourners: Histories of Southeast Asia and the Chinese* (ed. A. Reid). Honolulu, HI: University of Hawaii Press.

———. 1999. *Charting the Shape of Early Modern Southeast Asia*. Chiang Mai: Silkworm Books.

Reilly, B. F. 1993. *The Medieval Spains*. Cambridge University Press.

Reischauer, E. O., and J. K. Fairbank. 1962. *East Asia: The Great Tradition*, modern Asia edn. Tokyo: Charles E. Tuttle.

Reuter, T. 1985. Plunder and tribute in the Carolingian Empire. *Transactions of the Royal Historical Society* 35:75–94.

——— (ed.). 1999. *The New Cambridge Medieval History*, volume III, *c. 980–c. 1024*. Cambridge University Press.

Reynolds, L. G. 1985. *Economic Growth in the Third World, 1850–1980*. New Haven, CT: Yale University Press.

Riche, P. 1993. *The Carolingians: A Family Who Forged Europe*. Philadelphia, PA: University of Pennsylvania Press.

Ricklefs, M. C. 1993. *A History of Modern Indonesia since c. 1300*, 2nd edn. Stanford University Press.

Ritschl, A. 1999. Peter Temin and the onset of the Great Depression in Germany: a reappraisal. Mimeo, University of Zurich.

———. 2005. The pity of peace: Germany's economy at war, 1914–1918 and beyond. In *The Economics of World War I* (ed. S. N. Broadberry and M. Harrison). Cambridge University Press.

Roberts, M. 1967. *Essays in Swedish History*. Minneapolis, MN: University of Minnesota Press.

———. 1979. *The Swedish Imperial Experience 1560–1718*. Cambridge University Press.

Robertson, D. H. 1938. The future of international trade. *Economic Journal* 48:1–14.

Robinson, F. (ed.). 1996. *The Cambridge Illustrated History of the Islamic World*. Cambridge University Press.

Rockoff, H. 2004. Until it's over, over there: the U.S. economy in World War I. NBER Working Paper 10580.

Rodger, N. A. M. 1998. Sea-power and empire 1688–1793. In *The Oxford History of the British Empire*, volume II, *The Eighteenth Century* (ed. P. J. Marshall). Oxford University Press.

Rodríguez, F., and D. Rodrik. 2001. Trade policy and economic growth: a skeptic's guide to the cross-national evidence. In *Macroeconomics Annual 2000* (ed. B. Bernanke and K. S. Rogoff). Cambridge, MA: MIT Press.

Rodrik, D. 1994. The rush to free trade in the developing world: why so late? why now? will it last? In *Voting for Reform: Democracy, Political Liberalization, and Economic Adjustment* (ed. S. Haggard and S. B. Webb). Oxford University Press.

Rodrik, D. 1995. Getting interventions right: how South Korea and Taiwan grew rich. *Economic Policy* 20:53–107.

———. 1996. Understanding economic policy reform. *Journal of Economic Literature* 34:9–41.

———. 1998. Why do more open economies have bigger governments? *Journal of Political Economy* 106:997–1032.

———. 1999. *The New Global Economy and Developing Countries: Making Openness Work*. Washington, DC: ODC.

Rogers, C. J. (ed.). 1995. *The Military Revolution Debate: Readings in the Military Transformation of Early Modern Europe*. Boulder, CO: Westview Press.

Rogowski, R. 1989. *Commerce and Coalitions: How Trade Affects Domestic Political Alignments*. Princeton University Press.

Ropp, P. S. (ed.). 1990. *Heritage of China: Contemporary Perspectives on Chinese Civilization*. Berkeley, CA: University of California Press.

Rose, A. K. 2000. One money, one market: the effect of common currencies on trade. *Economic Policy* 30:7–46.

Rose, J. H. 1902. Our food supply in the Napoleonic War. *Monthly Review* 6:63–76.

Rosenberg, N., and L. E. Birdzell. 1986. *How the West Grew Rich: The Economic Transformation of the Industrial World*. London: I. B. Tauris.

Rosenbloom, J. L. 2004. Path dependence and the origins of cotton textile manufacturing in New England. In *The Fibre that Changed the World: The Cotton Industry in International Perspective, 1600–1990s* (ed. D. A. Farnie and D. J. Jeremy). Oxford University Press.

Rosenthal, J.-L. 1990. The development of irrigation in Provence, 1700–1860: the French Revolution and economic growth. *Journal of Economic History* 50:615–38.

Rossabi, M. 1990. The "decline" of the Central Asian caravan trade. In *The Rise of the Merchant Empires: Long-Distance Trade in the Early Modern World 1350–1750* (ed. J. D. Tracy). Cambridge University Press.

Rostow, W. W. 1960. *The Stages of Economic Growth: A Non-Communist Manifesto.* Cambridge University Press.

——— (ed.). 1963. *The Economics of Take-off into Sustained Growth.* London: Macmillan.

Rothermund, D. 1996. *The Global Impact of the Great Depression, 1929–1939.* Abingdon: Routledge.

Roy, T. 2000. *The Economic History of India 1857–1947.* Delhi: Oxford University Press.

Ruggie, J. G. 1982. International regimes, transactions, and change: embedded liberalism in the postwar economic order. *International Organization* 36:379–415.

Russell, P. 2001. *Prince Henry "the Navigator": A Life.* New Haven, CT: Yale University Press.

Sachs, J. D., J. W. McArthur, G. Schmidt-Traub, M. Kruk, C. Bahadur, M. Faye, and G. McCord. 2004. Ending Africa's poverty trap. *Brookings Papers on Economic Activity* 1:117–240.

Sachs, J. D., and A. M. Warner. 1995. Economic reform and the process of global integration. *Brookings Papers on Economic Activity* 1:1–118.

———. 2001. The curse of natural resources. *European Economic Review* 45:827–38.

Sakamaki, S. 1964. Ryukyu and Southeast Asia. *Journal of Asian Studies* 23:383–89.

Sansom, G. 1963. *A History of Japan 1615–1867.* Stanford University Press.

———. 1973. *The Western World and Japan: A Study in the Interaction of European and Asiatic Cultures.* New York: Vintage Books.

Saul, S. B. 1960. *Studies in British Overseas Trade 1870–1914.* Liverpool University Press.

Savory, R. 1980. *Iran under the Safavids.* Cambridge University Press.

Sawyer, P. H. 1994. *Kings and Vikings: Scandinavia and Europe AD 700–1100.* New York: Barnes and Noble.

Schlote, W. 1952. *British Overseas Trade from 1700 to the 1930s.* Oxford: Basil Blackwell.

Schmidt, K. J. 1999. *Atlas and Survey of South Asian History: India, Pakistan, Bangladesh, Sri Lanka, Nepal, Bhutan.* New Delhi: Vision Books.

Schön, L. 1984. Svensk Utrikeshandel 1800–1871. Mimeo, Lund.

Schonhardt-Bailey, C. 1991. Specific factors, capital markets, portfolio diversification, and free trade: domestic determinants of the repeal of the Corn Laws. *World Politics* 43:545–69.

——. 2006. *From the Corn Laws to Free Trade: Interests, Ideas, and Institutions in Historical Perspective.* Cambridge, MA: MIT Press.

Schroeder, P. W. 1992. Did the Vienna settlement rest on a balance of power? *American Historical Review* 97:683–706.

——. 1994. *The Transformation of European Politics 1763–1848.* Oxford: Clarendon Press.

Schulze, M.-S. 2005. Austria–Hungary's economy in World War I. In *The Economics of World War I* (ed. S. N. Broadberry and M. Harrison). Cambridge University Press.

Schurz, W. L. 1939. *The Manila Galleon.* New York: Dutton.

Seeley, J. R. 1971. *The Expansion of England.* University of Chicago Press.

Shaban, M. A. 1976. *Islamic History: A New Interpretation,* volume 1, *AD 600–750.* Cambridge University Press.

——. 1978. *Islamic History: A New Interpretation,* volume 2, *AD 750–1055.* Cambridge University Press.

Shah Mohammed, S. I., and J. G. Williamson. 2004. Freight rates and productivity gains in British tramp shipping 1869–1950. *Explorations in Economic History* 41:172–203.

Sheridan, R. B. 1987. Eric Williams and capitalism and slavery: a biographical and historiographical essay. In *British Capitalism and Caribbean Slavery: The Legacy of Eric Williams* (ed. B. L. Solow and S. L. Engerman). Cambridge University Press.

Shiba, Y. 1983. Sung foreign trade: its scope and organization. In *China Among Equals: The Middle Kingdom and Its Neighbors, 10th–14th Centuries* (ed. M. Rossabi). Berkeley, CA: University of California Press.

Shiba, Y. 1992. *Commerce and Society in Sung China.* Ann Arbor, MI: Center for Chinese Studies, University of Michigan.

Simon, R. S., and E. H. Tejirian (eds). 2004. *The Creation of Iraq 1914–1921.* New York: Columbia University Press.

Singer, H. W. 1950. The distribution of gains between investing and borrowing countries. *American Economic Review* 40:473–85.

Sinor, D. (ed.). 1990. *The Cambridge History of Early Inner Asia.* Cambridge University Press.

Siriwardana, A. M. 1991. The impact of tariff protection in the colony of Victoria in the late nineteenth century: a general equilibrium analysis. *Australian Economic History Review* 31:45–65.

Skinner, G. W. 1996. Creolized Chinese societies in Southeast Asia. In *Sojourners and Settlers: Histories of Southeast Asia and the Chinese* (ed. A. Reid). Honolulu, HI: University of Hawaii Press.

Smith, V. A. 1981. *The Oxford History of India,* 4th edn. New Delhi: Oxford University Press.

Solow, B. L. 1985. Caribbean slavery and British growth: the Eric Williams hypothesis. *Journal of Development Economics* 17:99–115.

Solow, B. L. 1987. Capitalism and slavery in the exceedingly long run. *Journal of Interdisciplinary History* 17:711–37.

Solow, R. M. 1956. A contribution to the theory of economic growth. *Quarterly Journal of Economics* 70:65–94.

Spate, O. H. K. 1979. *The Spanish Lake.* Canberra: Australian National University Press.

Spear, P. 1990. *A History of India,* volume 2, *From the 16th to the 20th Century.* London: Penguin.

Spence, J. D. 1990. *The Search for Modern China.* New York: W. W. Norton.

Spencer, G. W. 1976. The politics of plunder: the Cholas in eleventh-century Ceylon. *Journal of Asian Studies* 35:405–19.

Spufford, P. 1988. *Money and Its Use in Medieval Europe.* Cambridge University Press.

Stargardt, J. 1986. Hydraulic works and Southeast Asian polities. In *Southeast Asia in the 9th to 14th Centuries* (ed. D. G. Marr and A. C. Milner). Singapore: Institute of Southeast Asian Studies.

Steensgaard, N. 1974. *The Asian Trade Revolution of the Seventeenth Century: The East India Companies and the Decline of the Caravan Trade.* University of Chicago Press.

———. 1990. Commodities, bullion and services in intercontinental transactions before 1750. In *The European Discovery of the World and Its Economic Effects on Pre-Industrial Society* (ed. H. Pohl). Stuttgart: Franz Steiner.

Stein, B. 1965. Coromandel trade in medieval India. In *Merchants and Scholars* (ed. J. Parker). Minneapolis, MN: University of Minnesota Press.

———. 1998. *A History of India.* Oxford: Blackwell.

Stemmer, J. E. O. 1989. Freight rates in the trade between Europe and South America, 1840–1914. *Journal of Latin American Studies* 21:22–59.

Stögbauer, C. 2001. The radicalisation of the German electorate: swinging to the right and the left in the twilight of the Weimar Republic. *European Review of Economic History* 5:251–80.

Stover, C. C. 1970. Tropical exports. In *Tropical Development 1880–1913* (ed. W. A. Lewis). Evanston, IL: Northwestern University Press.

Stoye, J. 1969. *Europe Unfolding 1648–1688.* New York: Harper Torchbooks.

Subrahmanyam, S. 1997. *The Career and Legend of Vasco da Gama.* Cambridge University Press.

Subrahmanyam, S., and L. F. F. R. Thomaz. 1991. Evolution of empire: the Portuguese in the Indian Ocean during the sixteenth century. In *The Political Economy of Merchant Empires* (ed. J. D. Tracy). Cambridge University Press.

Sussman, N. 1998. The late medieval bullion famine reconsidered. *Journal of Economic History* 58:126–54.

Svennilson, I. 1954. *Growth and Stagnation in the European Economy.* Geneva: United Nations Economic Commission for Europe.

Tan, C. 1974. The Britain–India–China trade triangle (1771–1840). *Indian Economic and Social History Review* 11:411–31.

Tarling, N. (ed.). 1992. *The Cambridge History of Southeast Asia,* volume 1, *From Early Times to c. 1800.* Cambridge University Press.

Taussig, F. W. 1903. The end of sugar bounties. *Quarterly Journal of Economics* 18:130–34.

Taylor, A. M., and J. G. Williamson. 1994. Capital flows to the New World as an intergenerational transfer. *Journal of Political Economy* 102:348–71.

Temin, P. 1971. The beginning of the Depression in Germany. *Economic History Review* 24:240–48.

——. 1988. Product quality and vertical integration in the early cotton textile industry. *Journal of Economic History* 48:891–907.

——. 1989. *Lessons from the Great Depression.* Cambridge, MA: MIT Press.

——. 1993. Transmission of the Great Depression. *Journal of Economic Perspectives* 7:87–102.

——. 1997. Two views of the British Industrial Revolution. *Journal of Economic History* 57:63–82.

TePaske, J. J. 1983. New World silver, Castile and the Philippines 1590–1800. In *Precious Metals in the Later Medieval and Early Modern Worlds* (ed. J. F. Richards). Durham, NC: Carolina Academic Press.

TePaske, J. J., and H. S. Klein. 1981. The seventeenth-century crisis in New Spain: myth or reality. *Past and Present* 90:116–35.

Thapar, R. 2002. *Early India: From the Origins to 1300.* Berkeley, CA: University of California Press.

Thomas, B. 1985. Escaping from constraints: the Industrial Revolution in a Malthusian context. *Journal of Interdisciplinary History* 15:729–53.

Thomas, R. P. 1965. A quantitative approach to the study of the effects of British imperial policy upon colonial welfare: some preliminary findings. *Journal of Economic History* 25:615–38.

Thomas, R. P., and D. N. McCloskey. 1981. Overseas trade and empire, 1700–1860. In *The Economic History of Britain since 1700,* volume I, *1700–1860* (ed. R. Floud and D. N. McCloskey), 1st edn. Cambridge University Press.

Thomaz, L. F. F. R. 1993. The Malay sultanate of Melaka. In *Southeast Asia in the Early Modern Era: Trade, Power and Belief* (ed. A. Reid). Ithaca, NY: Cornell University Press.

Thorp, R. 1992. A reappraisal of the origins of import-substitution industrialization. *Journal of Latin American Studies* 24:181–95.

T'ien, J.-k. 1981. Cheng Ho's voyages and the distribution of pepper in China. *Journal of the Royal Asiatic Society* 2:186–97.

Tilly, C. (ed.). 1975. *Formation of National States in Western Europe.* Princeton University Press.

——. 1996. Citizenship, identity and social history. In *Citizenship, Identity and Social History* (ed. C. Tilly). Cambridge University Press.

Timmer, A., and J. G. Williamson. 1998. Immigration policy prior to the thirties: labor markets, policy interactions and globalization backlash. *Population and Development Review* 24:739–71.

Tomlinson, B. R. 1993. *The Economy of Modern India 1860–1970.* Cambridge University Press.

Tracy, M. 1989. *Government and Agriculture in Western Europe 1880–1988,* 3rd edn. New York: Harvester Wheatsheaf.

Tripp, C. 2000. *A History of Iraq*, 2nd edn. Cambridge University Press.

Turner, S. (ed.). 2000. *The Cambridge Companion to Max Weber.* Cambridge University Press.

Twitchett, D. C. 1973. The "Middle Kingdom": Chinese politics and society from the Bronze Age to the Manchus. In *Half the World: The History and Culture of China and Japan* (ed. A. Toynbee). London: Thames and Hudson.

Udovitch, A. L. 1962. At the origins of the Western Commenda: Islam, Israel, Byzantium? *Speculum* 37:198–207.

——. 1988. Merchants and amirs: government and trade in eleventh-century Egypt. *Asian and African Studies* 22:53–72.

UNCTAD. 1997. *Trade and Development Report, 1997.* Geneva: United Nations Conference on Trade and Development.

——. 2002. *Review of Maritime Transport 2002.* Geneva: United Nations Conference on Trade and Development.

——. 2003. *UNCTAD Trade Development Review 2003.* Geneva: United Nations Conference on Trade and Development.

——. 2004. *UNCTAD Handbook of Statistics 2004.* Geneva: United Nations Conference on Trade and Development.

United Nations. 1962. International trade statistics 1900–1960. Mimeo, MGT(62)12 (May).

U.S. Department of Commerce. 1975. *Historical Statistics of the United States: Colonial Times to 1970*, part 2. Washington, DC: USGPO.

Vamplew, W. (ed.). 1987. *Australian Historical Statistics.* Broadway, NSW: Fairfax, Syme and Weldon.

Vamvakidis, A. 2002. How robust is the growth-openness connection? Historical evidence. *Journal of Economic Growth* 7:57–80.

Verhulst, A. 2002. *The Carolingian Economy.* Cambridge University Press.

Vernadsky, G. 1948. *Kievan Russia.* New Haven, CT: Yale University Press.

Villiers, J. 1990. The cash crop economy and state formation in the Spice Islands in the fifteenth and sixteenth centuries. In *Southeast Asian Port and Polity: Rise and Demise* (ed. J. Kathirithamby-Wells and J. Villiers). Singapore University Press.

Viner, J. 1923. *Dumping: A Problem in International Trade.* University of Chicago Press.

——. 1924. The most-favored-nation clause in American commercial treaties. *Journal of Political Economy* 32:101–29.

——. 1948. Power versus plenty as objectives of foreign policy in the seventeenth and eighteenth centuries. *World Politics* 1:1–29.

——. 1950. *The Customs Union Issue.* New York: Carnegie Endowment for International Peace.

——. 1951. *International Economics.* Glencoe: Free Press.

Viraphol, S. 1977. *Tribute and Profit: Sino-Siamese Trade 1652–1853.* Cambridge, MA: Harvard University Press.

Vives, J. V. 1969. *An Economic History of Spain.* Princeton University Press.

Voth, H.-J. 1998. Time and work in eighteenth-century London. *Journal of Economic History* 58:29–58.

Voth, H.-J. 2003. With a bang, not a whimper: pricking Germany's "stock market bubble" in 1927 and the slide into depression. *Journal of Economic History* 63:65–99.

Vries, J. de. 1993. Between purchasing power and the world of goods: understanding the household economy in early modern Europe. In *Consumption and the World of Goods* (ed. J. Brewer and R. Porter). London: Routledge.

——. 1994. The Industrial Revolution and the industrious revolution. *Journal of Economic History* 54:249–70.

——. 2003. Connecting Europe and Asia: a quantitative analysis of the Cape-route trade, 1497–1795. In *Global Connections and Monetary History, 1470–1800* (ed. D. O. Flynn, A. Giráldez, and R. von Glahn). Aldershot: Ashgate.

Vries, J. de, and A. van der Woude. 1997. *The First Modern Economy: Success, Failure, and Perseverance of the Dutch Economy, 1500–1815.* Cambridge University Press.

Wacziarg, R., and K. H. Welch. 2003. Trade liberalization and growth: new evidence. NBER Working Paper 10152.

Wade, G. 2004. The Zheng He voyages: a reassessment. Asia Research Institute Working Paper Series 31. Asia Research Institute, National University of Singapore.

Wade, R. 1990. *Governing the Market: Economic Theory and the Role of Government in East Asian Industrialization.* Princeton University Press.

Wake, C. H. H. 1979. The changing pattern of Europe's pepper and spice imports, ca. 1400–1700. *Journal of European Economic History* 8:361–403.

——. 1986. The volume of European spice imports at the beginning and end of the fifteenth century. *Journal of European Economic History.* 15:621–35.

Wakeman, F. 1986. China and the seventeenth century crisis. *Late Imperial China* 7:1–26.

Walt, S. M. 1998. International relations: one world, many theories. *Foreign Policy* 110:29–46.

Walton, G. M. 1971. The new economic history and the burden of the navigation acts. *Economic History Review* 24:533–42.

Walton, G. M., and J. F. Shepherd. 1979. *The Economic Rise of Early America.* Cambridge University Press.

Wang, G. 1981. *Community and Nation: Essays on Southeast Asia and the Chinese.* Singapore: Heinemann and Asian Studies Association of Australia.

——. 1998. *The Nanhai Trade: The Early History of Chinese Trade in the South China Sea.* Singapore: Times Academic Press.

——. 2000. *The Chinese Overseas: From Earthbound China to the Quest for Autonomy.* Cambridge, MA: Harvard University Press.

Waters, W. G. 1970. Transport costs, tariffs, and the pattern of industrial protection. *American Economic Review* 60:1013–20.

Watson, A. M. 1983. *Agricultural Innovation in the Early Islamic World: The Diffusion of Crops and Farming Techniques, 700–1100.* Cambridge University Press.

Webb, W. P. 1952. *The Great Frontier.* Boston, MA: Houghton Mifflin.

Webster, A. 1990. The political economy of trade liberalization: the East India Company Charter Act of 1813. *Economic History Review* (New Series) 43:404–19.

Wheatley, P. 1959. Geographical notes on some commodities involved in Sung maritime trade. *Journal of the Malayan Branch of the Royal Asiatic Society* 32:1–140.

———. 1980. *The Golden Khersonese: Studies in the Historical Geography of the Malay Peninsula before AD 1500.* Kuala Lumpur: University of Malaya Press.

Wicker, C. V. 1956. Cortez—not Balboa. *College English* 17:383–87.

Wiet, G. 1964. *Cairo: City of Art and Commerce.* Norman, OK: University of Oklahoma Press.

Williams, E. E. 1966. *Capitalism and Slavery.* New York: Capricorn.

Williamson, J. G. 1974. *Late Nineteenth Century American Development: A General Equilibrium History.* Cambridge University Press.

———. 1984. Why was British growth so slow during the Industrial Revolution? *Journal of Economic History* 44:687–712.

———. 1995. The evolution of global labor markets since 1830: background evidence and hypotheses. *Explorations in Economic History* 32:141–96.

———. 2000. Land, labor and globalization in the pre-industrial Third World. NBER Working Paper 7784.

———. 2002. Land, labor and globalization in the Third World, 1870–1940. *Journal of Economic History* 62:55–85.

———. 2006. *Globalization and the Poor Periphery before 1950.* Cambridge, MA: MIT Press.

Wills, J. E., Jr. 1979. Maritime China from Wang Chih to Shih Lang: themes in peripheral history. In *From Ming to Ch'ing: Conquest, Region and Continuity in Seventeenth-Century China* (ed. J. D. Spence and J. E. Wills Jr). New Haven, CT: Yale University Press.

———. 1993. Maritime Asia, 1500–1800: the interactive emergence of European domination. *American Historical Review* 98:83–105.

———. 1998. Relations with maritime Europeans, 1514–1662. In *The Cambridge History of China,* volume 8, *The Ming Dynasty, 1368–1644,* part 2 (ed. D. C. Twitchett and F. W. Mote). Cambridge University Press.

Wilson, C. 1949. Treasure and trade balances: the mercantilist problem. *Economic History Review* 2:152–61.

———. 1957. *Profit and Power: A Study of England and the Dutch Wars.* London: Longmans.

———. 1960. Cloth production and international competition in the seventeenth century. *Economic History Review* 13:209–21.

Wohlstetter, A. 1959. The delicate balance of terror. *Foreign Affairs* 37:211–34.

Wolcott, S. 1997. Did imperial policies doom the Indian textile industry? *Research in Economic History* 17:135–83.

Wolf, M. 2004. *Why Globalization Works: The Case for the Global Market Economy.* New Haven, CT: Yale University Press.

Wolf, N. 2003. Economic integration in historical perspective: the case of interwar Poland 1918–1939. Ph.D. thesis, Humboldt Universität, Berlin.

Wolters, O. W. 1967. *Early Indonesian Commerce: A Study of the Origins of Srivijaya*. Ithaca, NY: Cornell University Press.

———. 1970. *The Fall of Srivijaya in Malay History*. Kuala Lumpur: Oxford University Press.

———. 1999. *History, Culture, and Region in Southeast Asian Perspectives*, revised edn. Institute of Southeast Asian Studies, Singapore.

Wong, R. B. 1997. *China Transformed: Historical Change and the Limits of European Experience*. Ithaca, NY: Cornell University Press.

Wood, A. 1994. *North–South Trade, Employment and Inequality: Changing Fortunes in a Skill-Driven World*. Oxford: Clarendon Press.

World Bank. 1991. *World Development Report 1991: The Challenge of Development*. Washington, DC: IBRD.

———. 1993. *The East Asian Miracle: Economic Growth and Public Policy*. Washington, DC: IBRD.

———. 2001a. *Global Economic Prospects and the Developing Countries*. Washington, DC: IBRD.

———. 2001b. *World Development Indicators 2001*. Washington, DC: IBRD.

———. 2002. *Global Economic Prospects and the Developing Countries*. Washington, DC: IBRD.

Woytinsky, W. S., and E. S. Woytinsky. 1955. *World Commerce and Governments: Trends and Outlook*. New York: The Twentieth Century Fund.

Wright, G. 1990. The origins of American industrial success, 1879–1940. *American Economic Review* 80:651–68.

Wrigley, E. A. 1988. *Continuity, Chance and Change: The Character of the Industrial Revolution in England*. Cambridge University Press.

———. 2000. The divergence of England: the growth of the English economy in the sixteenth and seventeenth centuries. *Transactions of the Royal Historical Society* (Sixth Series) X:117–42.

———. 2004. British population during the "long" eighteenth century, 1680–1840. In *The Cambridge Economic History of Modern Britain*, volume 1, *Industrialization 1700–1860* (ed. R. Floud and P. Johnson). Cambridge University Press.

Wrigley, E. A., and R. S. Schofield. 1989. *The Population History of England 1541–1871: A Reconstruction*. Cambridge University Press.

Wyatt, D. 1984. *Thailand: A Short History*. New Haven, CT: Yale University Press.

Yamamura, K. 1981. Returns on unification: economic growth in Japan 1550–1650. In *Japan before Tokugawa: Political Consolidation and Economic Growth, 1500–1650* (ed. J. W. Hall, N. Keiji, and K. Yamamura). Princeton University Press.

Yamamura, K., and T. Kamiki. 1983. Silver mines and Sung coins: a monetary history of medieval and modern Japan in international perspective. In *Precious Metals in the Later Medieval and Early Modern Worlds* (ed. J. F. Richards). Durham, NC: Carolina Academic Press.

Yasuba, Y. 1978. Freight rates and productivity in ocean transportation for Japan, 1875–1943. *Explorations in Economic History* 15:11–39.

Yasuba, Y. 1996. Did Japan ever suffer from a shortage of natural resources before World War II? *Journal of Economic History* 56:543–60.

Yates, P. L. 1959. *Forty Years of Foreign Trade*. London: George Allen and Unwin.

Yeats, A. J. 1998. Just how big is global production sharing? Mimeo, World Bank.

Young, A. 1995. The tyranny of numbers: confronting the statistical realities of the East Asian growth experience. *Quarterly Journal of Economics* 110:641–80.

Zahedieh, N. 1986. Trade, plunder, and economic development in early English Jamaica, 1655–89. *Economic History Review* 39:205–22.

Zanden, J. L. van. 2004. Colonial state formation and patterns of economic development in Java, 1800–1913. Mimeo, International Institute of Social History.

———. 2005. What happened to the standard of living before the Industrial Revolution? New evidence from the western part of the Netherlands. In *Living Standards in the Past: New Perspectives on Well-Being in Asia and Europe* (ed. R. C. Allen, T. Bengtsson, and M. Dribe). Oxford University Press. (The underlying database can be found at www.iisg.nl/hpw/brenv.php.)

Zanden, J. L. van, and M. Prak. 2006. Towards an economic interpretation of citizenship: the Dutch Republic between medieval communes and modern nation-states. *European Review of Economic History* 10:111–45.

INDEX

An italic page number indicates a reference to an illustration or a table.

Aachen, 7
Abahai (Hong Taiji): the son of Nurhachi, founder of the Manchu Empire, 285
Abbas I, shah of Persia, 210, 221–23
Abbasid caliphate, 17–21
Abd al-Malik, Hisham ibn, caliph, 16, 48–49
Abd al-Rahman I, 23
Abd al-Rahman III, 23, 60
Abd El-Kader, Amir of Mascara, 390
Abraham, M., 68, 69
Abu-Lughod, J. L., 44, 96, 106, 108, 130
Abulafia, D., 107, 128
Abulfatah Agung, sultan of Bantam, 198–99
Acadia, 251. See also Nova Scotia
Accominotti, O., 396
accounting. See bookkeeping
Acemoglu, D., 308, 347, 363, 524, 533
Acheh, 153, 201
Act of Union (1707), 230
Acton, Lord, 145
Aden, 99
Adshead, S. A. M., 105, 108, 124, 216
Africa: 19th-century trade policies, 401–2; 21st century, 533–34; independence of European colonies, 483; partitioning by European powers, 390–91; per capita income relative to U.S., 520. See also Royal African Company
Age of Reconnaissance, 149
Aghlabid dynasty, 20–21
Agung, sultan of Mataram, 201
Ahmad ibn Majid, 149
Ahmad Shah Durrani, Amir of Afghanistan, 264
Ain Jalut, Battle of, (1260), 92
air transport, 504–5
Akbar, Mughal emperor, 220, 263

Al-Qayrawan, 21
Ala'uddin, sultan of Makassar, 199–200
Alaungpaya, king of Burma, 276–77
Albuquerque, Afonso de, 151
Alcuin of York, 10
Aldcroft, D. H., 435, 437, 438, 439, 440, 441
Alderman Cockayne Plan, 240
Alesina, A., 441, 538
Alexander the Great, 30, 48
Alexandria, 56
Alexis I, tsar of Russia, 193
Alfred, king of Wessex, 10, 83
Algeria, 390, 483
Algonquin tribal federation, 248
Ali, M. A., 271
Allen, D. W., 256
Allen, R. C., 119, 123, 210, 308, 316, 317, 344, 349, 352, 356, 362, 519
Almeida, Francisco de, 155
Almohad dynasty, 89
Almoravid dynasty, 22, 89
Alpine passes, 83
Amalfi, 83
ambergris, 55, 70, 90
Amboyna, 180
Ambrosiani, B., 79
al-Amin, Muhammad ibn Harun, caliph, 18
Amjadi, A., 505
Amsden, A., 521
Amsterdam, 175, 207. See also *Heeren XVII*
An Lu Shan rebellion, 29, 39
Anaukhpetlun, king of Burma, 196
al-Andalus: economic basis, 58–59; exports, 89–91; population, 60; settlement, 23
Andaya, B. W., 280
Andaya, L. D., 280
Andean Pact (1969), 488
Anderson, F., 253, 255
Anderson, J. E., 500, 505
Andrews, K. R., 230, 265